BENCHMARKING

(Text and Cases)

Prof. K. SHRIDHARA BHAT

B.E. (Mech), PG DIM, M.B.A. F.I.I.M.M.

Managing Director

Akshaya Management Consultancy Services

Bangalore - 560 085

Karnataka, India

Himalaya Publishing House

MUMBAI • NEW DELHI • NAGPUR • BENGALURU • HYDERABAD • CHENNAI • PUNE • LUCKNOW • AHMEDABAD • ERNAKULAM • BHUBANESWAR • INDORE • KOLKATA • GUWAHATI

First Edition : 2013

Published by : Mrs. Meena Pandey for **Himalaya Publishing House Pvt. Ltd.**, "Ramdoot", Dr. Bhalerao Marg, Girgaon, **Mumbai - 400 004.** Phone: 022-23860170/23863863, Fax: 022-23877178 **E-mail: himpub@vsnl.com; Website: www.himpub.com**

Branch Offices :

New Delhi : "Pooja Apartments", 4-B, Murari Lal Street, Ansari Road, Darya Ganj, New Delhi - 110 002. Phone: 011-23270392, 23278631; Fax: 011-23256286

Nagpur : Kundanlal Chandak Industrial Estate, Ghat Road, Nagpur - 440 018. Phone: 0712-2738731, 3296733; Telefax: 0712-2721215

Bengaluru : No. 16/1 (Old 12/1), 1st Floor, Next to Hotel Highlands, Madhava Nagar, Race Course Road, Bengaluru - 560 001. Phone: 080-32919385; Telefax: 080-22286611

Hyderabad : No. 3-4-184, Lingampally, Besides Raghavendra Swamy Matham, Kachiguda, Hyderabad - 500 027. Phone: 040-27560041, 27550139; Mobile: 09390905282

Chennai : No. 8/2, Madley 2nd Street, Ground Floor, T. Nagar, Chennai - 600 017. Mobile: 09345345055

Pune : First Floor, "Laksha" Apartment, No. 527, Mehunpura, Shaniwarpeth (Near Prabhat Theatre), Pune - 411 030. Phone: 020-24496323/24496333; Mobile: 09370579333

Lucknow : House No 731, Shekhupura Colony, Near B.D. Convent School, Aliganj, Lucknow - 226 022. Mobile: 09307501549

Ahmedabad : 114, "SHAIL", 1st Floor, Opp. Madhu Sudan House, C.G. Road, Navrang Pura, Ahmedabad - 380 009. Phone: 079-26560126; Mobile: 09377088847

Ernakulam : 39/176 (New No: 60/251) 1st Floor, Karikkamuri Road, Ernakulam, Kochi - 682011, Phone: 0484-2378012, 2378016; Mobile: 09344199799

Bhubaneswar : 5 Station Square, Bhubaneswar - 751 001 (Odisha). Phone: 0674-2532129, Mobile: 09338746007

Indore : Kesardeep Avenue Extension, 73, Narayan Bagh, Flat No. 302, IIIrd Floor, Near Humpty Dumpty School, Indore - 452 007 (M.P.). Mobile: 09301386468

Kolkata : 108/4, Beliaghata Main Road, Near ID Hospital, Opp. SBI Bank, Kolkata - 700 010, Phone: 033-32449649, Mobile: 09883055590, 07439040301

Guwahati : House No. 15, Behind Pragjyotish College, Near Sharma Printing Press, P.O. Bharalumukh, Guwahati - 781009, (Assam). Mobile: 09883055590, 09883055536

DTP by : Page Designers, Bengaluru

Printed at : M/s. Aditya Offset Process (I) Pvt. Ltd., Hyderabad. On behalf of HPH.

Preface

No matter how good an organisation is, how well its products and/or services are, the organisation can not relax and stop improving. It can not stand still. When it does, it really is not standing still, it is slipping backward, because its competition is constantly improving.

One of the best ways for an organisation to keep improving is to benchmark. Benchmarking is a systematic way to identify superior products, services, processes and practices that can be adopted by or adapted to an organisation to reduce costs, decrease cycle time, increase reliability, cut inventories and provide greater satisfaction to its customers.

"High Performance Benchmarking" provides specific information, suggestion, guidelines and check lists to help an organisation start, maintain and wrap up a benchmarking project.

In the 21st century, the organisations that prosper and thrive will be those organisations that have learnt to change – change quickly, change effectively and change for the better. Effective change has always been a requisite for the survival of an organisation but change now need to take place at a faster pace than before.

Over the last 25 years or so, organisations were more and more aware of the need for organisational learning and change for their very survival in the highly competitive environment. They have been through the era of "Total Quality Management" (TQM), "Process Management", "Six-Sigma Quality", "Business Process Management", "Business Process Reengineering" (BPR) and so on.

While TQM was instrumental for continuous improvement of organisations, Business Process Reengineering focussed on revolutionary rather than evolutionary change. The most efficient way to promulgate effective change is by learning from the positive experience of others. That is what learning is all about. Learning takes place when one is exposed to another's knowledge and experience. Most knowledge is gained incrementally. You can learn because another learnt first and was willing and able to share that knowledge with you. And that is what benchmarking is all about. It involves learning, growth and effective change. Benchmarking doesn't substitute for BPR or any other strategy. Benchmarking is the search for those best practices that will lead to the superior performance of a company. Establishing operating targets based on the best possible industry practices is a critical component in the success of every business.

Benchmarking is a positive, proactive, structured process which leads to changing operations and eventually attaining superior performance and a competitive advantage. Benchmarking is simply the most efficient way to assure the success of a business change initiative.

Benchmarking has been growing more popular in the US at least since Xerox began to do it in the late 1970s. A growing number of progressive companies started using benchmarking during the early 1980s. The original framers of the Malcolm Baldrige National Quality Award included benchmarking among the criteria for the award. Today, benchmarking is viewed as a managerial tool that helps organisations to regain their competitive edge.

In Japan, no word for benchmarking exists, and few business people refer to the practices of benchmarking. The Japanese have captured the essence of striving to be the **"best of the best"** in the single word: **"dantotsu".** 'Dantotsu' implies a degree of awareness about the environment, particularly of others who also strive to be the best of the best. Even though the Japanese do not call the practices as "benchmarking", they have become benchmarking masters through generations of practices. Of all the countries in the world, Japan is by far the most advanced in benchmarking.

Benchmarking is much more than mere "industrial tourism" and "competitive analysis". The best organisations today are those that use benchmarking and use it well. These organisations are consistently among the leaders in their industries and they have learnt how to learn.

Knowing very well the importance of benchmarking in improving business, it is necessary for business executives, to have a complete understanding of how to manage the total benchmarking process in any organisation to maximise results.

This book comprising 21 chapters, attempts to provide a basic understanding of the benchmarking approach to the students of management programs as well as to the practicing executives and managers in business organisations. As there are not may books available in this subject, I have made a humble attempt to bring out this book for the benefit of the readers.

I have great pleasure to express my heartful thanks to Sri Niraj Pandey of Himalaya Publishing House whose encouragement was instrumental to motivate me to author this book. I also thank Sri Vijay Pandey of HPH for printing and promoting this book.

I also thank Sri B.S. Madhu and Smt. Divya of M/s Page Designers for their excellent D.T.P. work.

I also thank my wife, daughters, friends and well-wishers for their encouragement which enabled me to complete this book in a short time.

I invite readers to offer their constructive criticism and suggestions to me as their valuable feedback which will facilitate improvement of the quality of this book in its future editions.

K. SHRIDHARA BHAT
No.680, 'Akshaya', 1 'C' Main,
Kempegowda Layout, 3rd Block,
3rd Phase, Banashankari III Stage
Bangalore - 560 085.
Phone : (080) 26694761
Email : sbhat680@yahoo.com

Brief Contents

Contents

CHAPTER 1

The Benchmarking Concept

INTRODUCTION

No matter how good your organisation is , or how well regarded your products and/or services are, you can not stop improving. You can not stand still. When you do, you really are not standing still; you are slipping backward, because your competition is constantly improving.

One of the best ways to keep improving your organisation is to **benchmark. Benchmarking** is a systematic way to identify superior products, services, processes and practices that can be adopted by or adapted to your organisation to reduce costs, decrease cycle times, increase reliability, and inventories and provide greater satisfaction to your emotions.

Benchmarking is a powerful process to improve your competitive position. It looks beyond the prevailing conditions and practices of a particular market segment. Benchmarking helps you identify and study processes, techniques and practices of innovative market leaders often operating in different industries and markets. You can then apply those proven processes, techniques and practices to the problems and opportunities that you face in your markets thereby improving your competitive position. It can be a valuable source or ideas and approaches that have worked well elsewhere but never quite adapted to your business.

THE LANGUAGE OF BENCHMARKING

What is Benchmarking?

Benchmarking is an **improvement process** used to discover and incorporate best practices into your operation. Benchmarking is the **preferred process** used to identify and understand the elements (causes) of superior or world-class performance in a particular **work process.**

What is a Process?

A **process** is a repeatable sequence of steps used to transform an input into an output that has value to an internal or external customer.

Most firms use some combination of the following four elements to describe and analyse process performance: *(i)* **Process**, *(ii)* **Practice**, *(iii)* **Metric** and *(vi)* **Enabler**.

All work is performed using one or more processes. ***Exhibit 1.1* shows the four steps of a simple lawn mowing process:** *(a)* prepare the mower, *(b)* mow the lawn, *(c)* dispose of the grass clippings and *(d)* store the mower.

EXHIBIT 1.1 : LAWN MOWING PROCESS

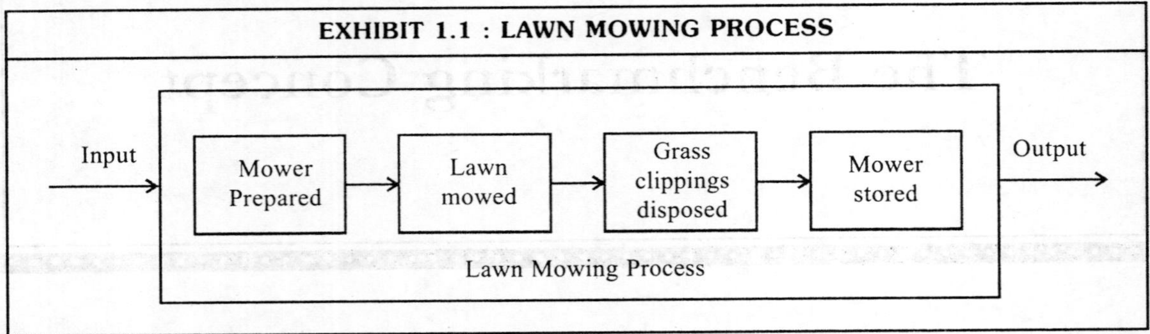

What is Practice?

A practice is a method or technique used to perform a process step. Practices describe **how** we perform a step within a work process.

***Exhibit 1.2* illustrates two practices associated with the process step of mowing the lawn:** a self-propelled gas mower and a rectangular mowing pattern.

EXHIBIT 1.2 : EXAMPLE OF PRACTICE IN THE LAWN MOWING PROCESS

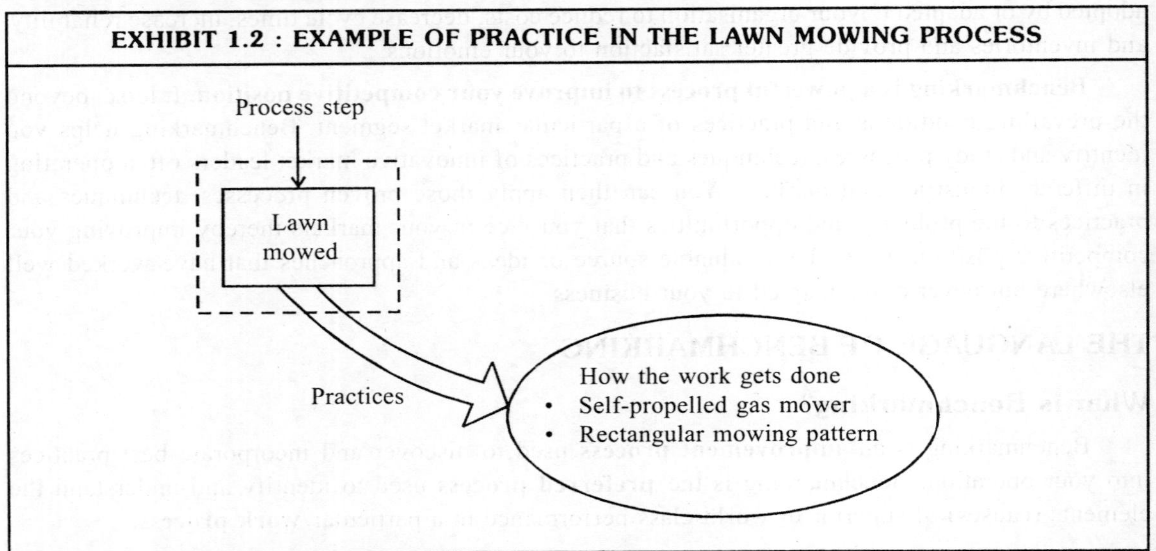

How does a Practice Relate to a Process?

A single process generally contains many practices because every process consists of multiple steps and each step may contain one or more practices.

***Exhibit 1.3* shows the relationship between practice and process.**

EXHIBIT 1.3 : RELATIONSHIP BETWEEN PRACTICE AND PROCESS, LAWN MOWING PROCESS

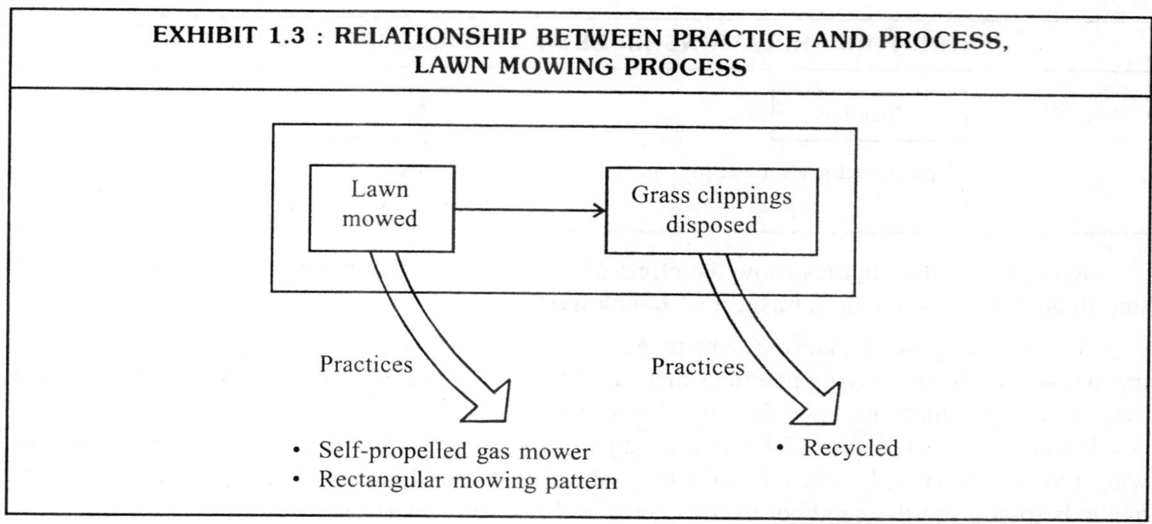

In addition to the practices of a self-propelled gas mower and a rectangular mowing pattern, the process also contains the practice of recycling associated with the step "grass clippings disposed".

What is Metric?

A **metric** is a measure of process performance. One metric we might be **interested** in for the lawn mowing process is "**cycle time**" or the total elapsed time from start to finish of the process. ***Exhibit 1.4* illustrates this example.**

EXHIBIT 1.4 : CYCLE TIME METRIC IN THE LAWN MOWING PROCESS

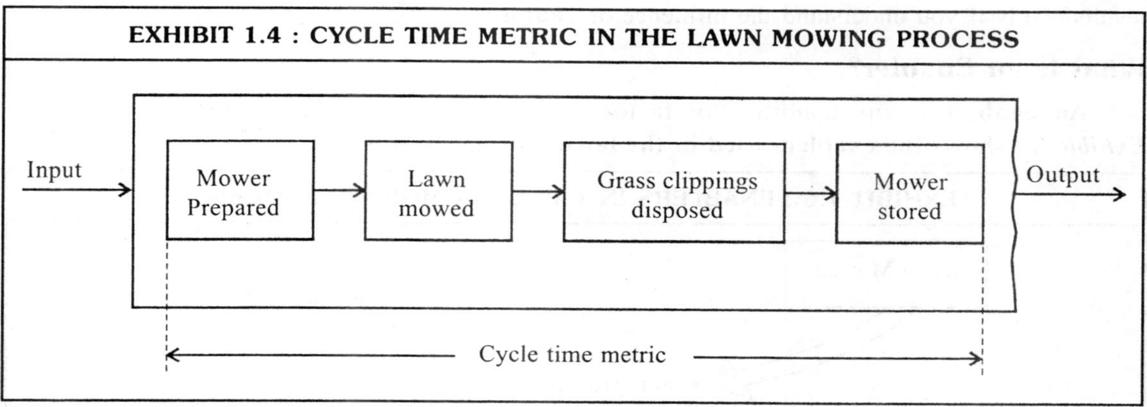

How does practice relate to a metric?

A metric quantifies the effect of installing and using one or more practices. For example, suppose we are concerned with fuel use. In that case two possible metrics for this lawn mowing process might be: *(a)* Cost per liter per lawn and *(b)* Number of tank fills per lawn

Changing the practice of a self-propelled gas mower to an electric or manual push mower would immediately show up in both of these metrics.

***Exhibit 1.5* shows the relationship between practice and metric.**

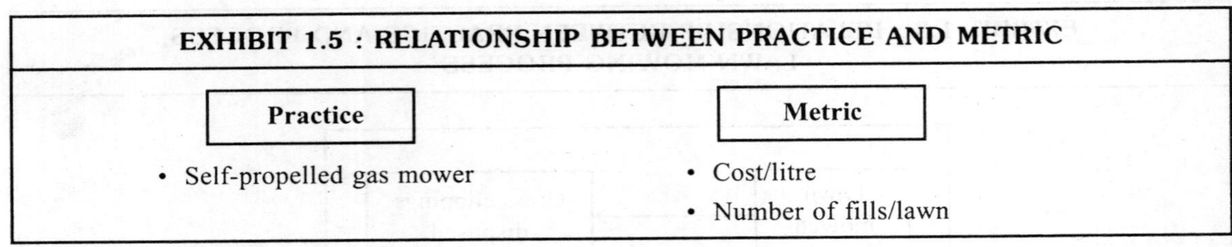

EXHIBIT 1.5 : RELATIONSHIP BETWEEN PRACTICE AND METRIC	
Practice	**Metric**
• Self-propelled gas mower	• Cost/litre • Number of fills/lawn

Recognising that metrics show the effect of using one or more practices to perform a process step in an extremely important aspect of **benchmarking**.

To succeed in benchmarking, whenever you observe a favourable metric, you should always try to discover the underlying practices that cause the metric. Suppose you are concerned with how long it takes to mow the lawn for your lawn mowing process. The metric that measures this is "cycle time", that, let us say is 30 minutes. As part of your data collection, you learn that a neighbor with a similar lawn only takes 15 minutes and still gets good results. You want to discover the methods (practices) the neighbor uses to achieve this level of performance.

Once you understand these practices, you then can determine whether and to what extent they may be adapted and incorporated into your own mowing process. By understanding the effect that each practice has on the cycle time metric, you also can estimate (quantify) how the performance of your mowing process will change. In this case using the same practices will achieve a 50 percent improvement (reduction) in your mowing cycle time.

You talk to the neighbor and learn that he uses a self-propelled gas mower, You use a manual push mower. If you purchase and use the same self-propelled gas mower, will you get similar results? Only if you understand the influence of **enablers**.

What is an Enabler?

An **enabler** is any condition or factor that influences the effectiveness of a practice. ***Exhibit 1.6*** **shows the enablers used in the lawn mowing process.**

EXHIBIT 1.6 : ENABLERS IN THE LAWN MOWING PROCESS

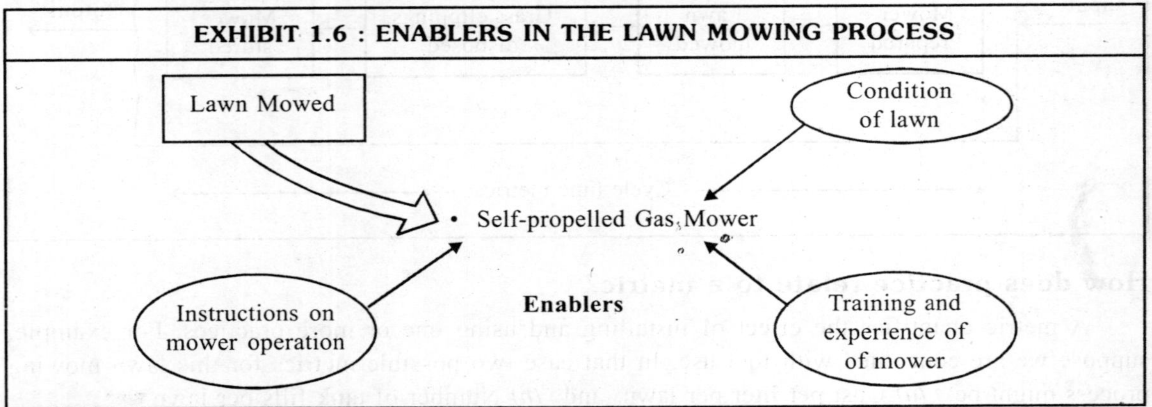

For the practice (self-propelled gas mower), the condition of the lawn (dampness, freedom from debris), the clarity and accessibility of the written instructions to operate the mower, plus the effectiveness of the persons training and experience all directly impact the results you should expect.

Often it is the quality of the enablers present that make a given "best practice" so effective.

BENCHMARKING DEFINED

Benchmarking in simple words, refers to the "outreach activity of comparing yourself against others". **Benchmarking can be defined in many ways:**

(i) A process of rigorously measuring your performance versus the best-in-class companies and for using the analysis to meet and surpass the best-in-class.

(ii) A standard of excellence or achievement against which other similar things must be measured or judged.

(iii) Search for industry best practices that lead to superior performance.

(iv) Benchmarking is the **continuous process of measuring** products, services and practices against the toughest competitors or those companies recognised as industry leaders.

(v) Benchmarking is a **continuous**, **systematic process** for **evaluating** the **products**, **services** and **work processes** of **organisations** that are recognised as representing **best practices** for the purpose of **organisational improvement**.

The nine key elements of this definition are shown in *Exhibit 1.7.*

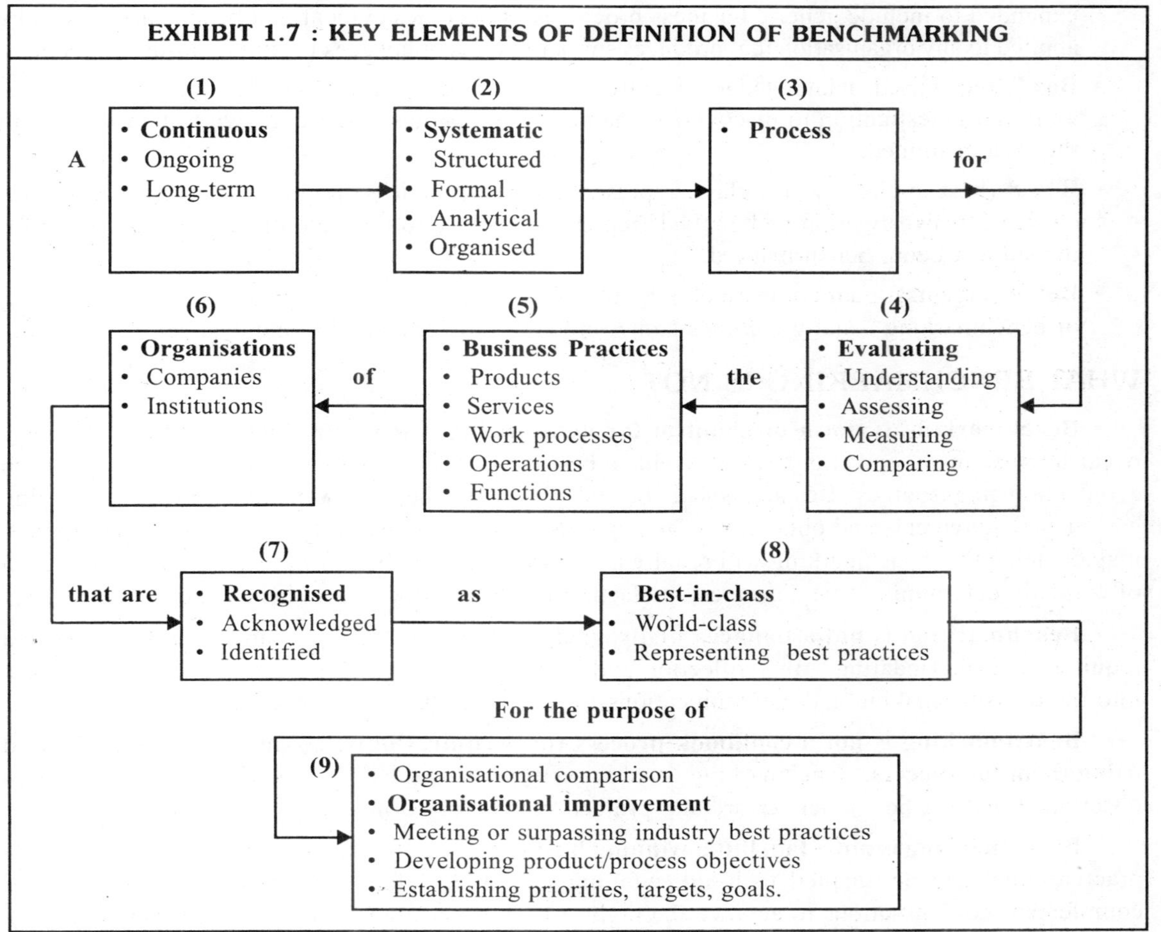

- **Box 1** (continuous, ongoing, long-term) suggests that benchmarking is something that takes place over an **extended period of time**. It is not a short-term or a one-time activity.
- **Box 2** (systematic, structured, formal, analytical, organised) refers to the method of benchmarking.
- **Box 3** (process) – represents the idea that benchmarking is a process. Benchmarking involves a series of actions that define issues, problems or opportunities, measures performance, draws conclusions based on an analysis of the information collected and stimulates organisational change and improvement.
- **Box 4** (evaluating, understanding, assessing, measuring, comparing) denotes action. Benchmarking is an investigative process – a process of inquiry. Benchmarking does not deliver answers. It is through the process of measuring, evaluating, comparing that one produces information that will add to the quality of decision making.
- **Box 5** (business practices, products, services, work processes, operations, functions) implies that benchmarking is not limited to any one facet of an organisation's activities.
- **Box 6** (organisations, companies, situations) implies that the focus of benchmarking is not limited to competitive products, services or practices. As the definition of benchmarking is expanded to include generic business processes, it becomes evident that benchmarking can be applied to any organisation that produces similar outputs or engages in similar business practices.
- **Box 7** (recognised, acknowledged, identified) implies that the process of benchmarking involves an initial investigation to discover the names of companies that are known to be excellent in the area examined.
- **Box 8** (best-in-class, world-class, representing best practices) implies that the organisations chosen for investigation and analysis represent as close to the state-of-the-art as possible for the subject being bench-marked.
- **Box 9** (organisational comparison, organisational improvement etc.) implies that the purpose of benchmarking usually includes some references to comparisons and change.

WHAT BENCHMARKING IS NOT

Benchmarking is not a mechanism for determining resource reductions. While that may occur because many operations do not emulate best industry practices, it does not necessarily mean a reduction in resources. Resources will be redeployed to the most effective way of supporting customer requirements and obtaining customer satisfaction as a result of benchmarking activities. It may be noted that benchmarking will require a resource increase, both people and money, as a result of correctly determining true customer satisfaction levels and needs from benchmarking activities.

Benchmarking is not a panacea or program. It must be ongoing management process that requires constant updating – the collection and sifting of external best practices and performance into the decision making and communications functions at all levels of the business.

Benchmarking is not a cookbook process that requires only looking up ingredients and using them for success. Benchmarking is a discovery process and a learning experience. It requires observing what the best practices are and projecting what performance should be in the future.

Benchmarking is not a fad, but a winning business strategy. It assists managers in identifying practices that can be adapted to build, winning, credible, defensible plans and strategies, and complement new initiations to achieve the highest performance goals (*i.e.,* superior performance).

DISTINCTION BETWEEN BENCHMARKING AND BENCHMARKS

Benchmarking is the on-going search for best practices that produce superior performance when adapted and implemented in one's organisation.

Benchmarks in contrast to benchmarking , are measurements to gauge the performance of a function, operation or business relative to others.

In the electronics industry for instance, a benchmark has long referred to an **operating statistic** that allows you to compare your own performance to that of another or to an industry standard.

Operating statistics employed as benchmarks provide incomplete comparisons. In a sense, they are superficial, for they draw attention to performance gaps without offering any evidence or explanation for why those gaps exist. At times, the performance gaps surfaced through benchmark comparison may reflect significant differences in operating systems and procedures; on other occasions, benchmark variances may reflect differences in the way different organisations track and measure the performance of their systems.

The root causes of operating differences usually can not be discerned from bench marks alone. In this respect, the benchmarks are like divining rods that lead the organisation to hidden opportunities to innovate and improve performance.

Benchmarking is the actual process of investigation and discovery that emphasizes the operating procedures as the things of greatest interest and value. Consequently, **best practices benchmarking** can be described as the process of seeking out and studying the best internal and external practices that produce superior performance. One measures this performance through various financial and non financial performance indicators. ***Exhibit 1.8* illustrates the relationship between benchmarks and benchmarking**.

EXHIBIT 1.8 : BENCHMARKING FOR BEST PRACTICES

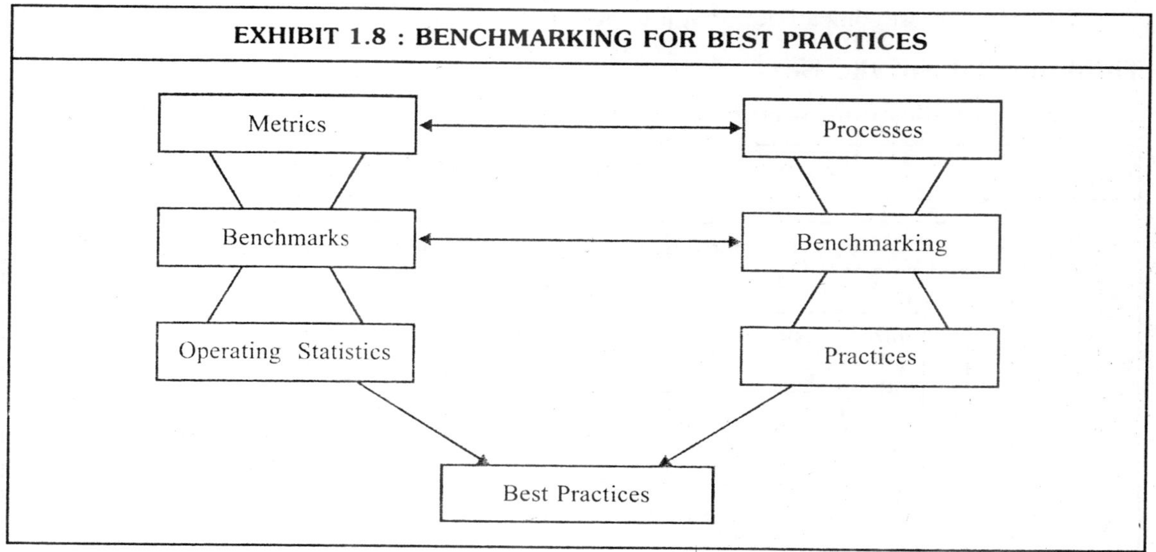

The benefits of benchmarking have been well recognised in certain industries and operating areas. For instance, many benchmarking projects have targeted critical technical functions such as distribution and logistics, billing order entry and fulfillment and training. However, benchmarking is also an advanced business concept with general management applications for high-level functions such as strategic planning, restructuring, financial management, succession planning and supplier and joint venture management.

BENCHMARKING AS LEARNING

Benchmarking involves "learning from others". Behind all of the planning and organising and analysis activities that define the benchmarking experience lie the fundamental objectives of learning something new and bringing new ideas into an organisation. A term that has gained importance in the past few years is **the learning organisation**. One of the implications of this concept is that organisations need to step outside of themselves and scrutinise their internal view of the world. This is done when one "exposes" one's own thinking and makes that thinking open to the influences of others. Within this concept, benchmarking becomes a fundamental tool that guides people-through the process of looking to the outside for ideas and inspiration – in essence, a tool for the learning organisation.

WHY USE BENCHMARKING?

Organisations use benchmarking for a variety of purposes. Some organisations position benchmarking as part of an overall problem-solving process with a clear mantle for organisational improvement. Others position benchmarking more as a proactive mechanism to keep themselves aware of state-of-the-art business practices.

By benchmarking you will find out:

- Who performs the business very well and has process practices that are adaptable to your own organisations?
- Who is the most compatible for you to benchmark with?

Thinking "Out of the Box"

***Exhibit 1.9* illustrates what is meant by – Thinking "out of the box".**

EXHIBIT 1.9 : THINKING "OUT OF THE BOX"

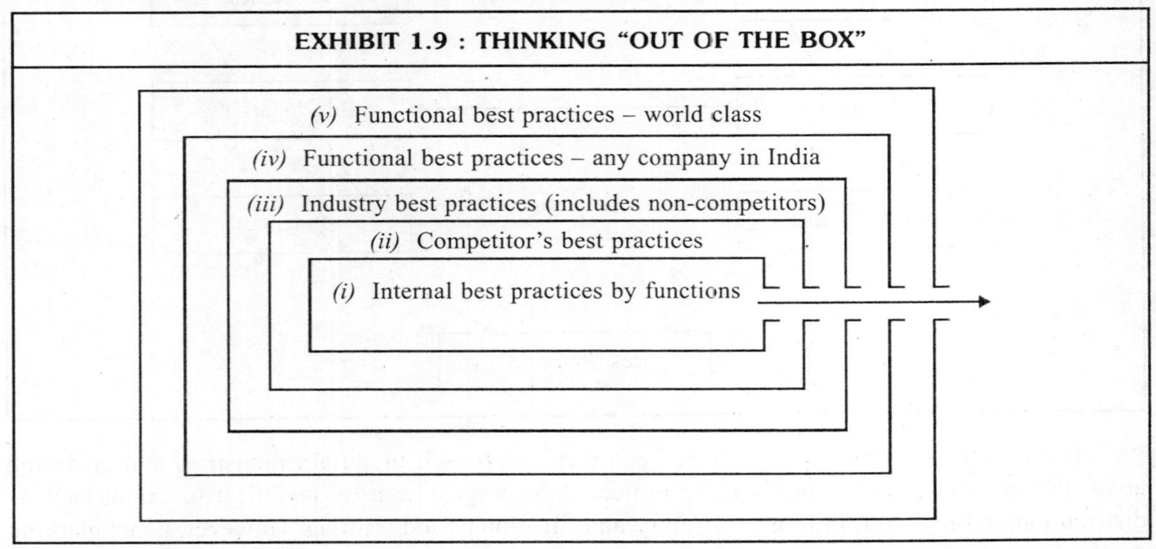

(i) The inner most box is that we are in. It is defined by our management, our personal histories and our experiences. We have learnt what it takes to be successful in our own box, and we have become very good at managing each other to get what we want. We have carved a comfortable space for ourselves, and we could exist quite comfortably by staying smug in our own little spaces.

(ii) On occasion we take a look outside of our box and see what the competitor is upto. If our market share is holding and our sales are ok, then we don't bother looking at our competitors for too long. However if we are in a downturn and there is some pressure on the bottom line, we look outside the box a little longer and analyse the competition. We make some adjustments and hope for the best. We used to call that **"competitive analysis"**.

(iii) Now with benchmarking , we not only take a more systematic look at our competitors, but we also take a hard look at other companies in our industry that are not necessarily our competitors. We do this because they do a lot of the same things we do and many of those companies are a lot like us in terms of the technologies and equipments they use, the people they hire, the customers they serve, and the suppliers they do business with. We seem to be able to learn something new each time we look.

(iv) We benchmark other companies in the country which do not belong to the industry which we are in. We compare our processes with that of best-in-class companies outside our industry but within our country. For example, we investigated the subject of design changes and identify about ten companies that had a reputation for minimising design changes and had greatly reduced their cycle times and then select the best among them. Then we redesign our entire process using the model of the best-in-class company.

(v) We learn that the best-in-class company we benchmarked had patterned their process after a world-class company.

Organisations that begin the benchmarking process with a clear purpose or objective have greater success than those that undertake a benchmarking effort without a sense of purpose or direction. Companies that have strongly integrated benchmarking into their cultures have spent a good deal of effort defining and positioning benchmarking in the minds of their employees.

***Box 1.1* lists some of the reasons organisations use the benchmarking process.**

BOX 1.1 : WHY USE BENCHMARKING?

(i)	Strategic planning	–	Developing short and long-term plans
(ii)	Forecasting	–	Predicting trends in relevant business areas
(iii)	New ideas	–	Functional learning, thinking "out of the box"
(iv)	Product/process comparisons	–	Comparing competitors or best-practices organisation
(v)	Goal setting	–	Establishing performance goals in relation to the state-of-the-art practices.

The reasons for benchmarking listed in the *Box 1.1* are briefly discussed in the following paragraphs:

(i) Strategic Planning

Strategic planning requires a thorough knowledge of the market place, the likely activities of the competition, the state-of-the-art regarding products or services being produced, financial requirements for doing business in a market, and the customer base. Benchmarking is a useful tool for gathering information in these areas during the process of strategic planning. This type of information can be useful in shaping a business strategy in a more realistic direction or at best be helpful to identify the risks of doing business in certain markets.

(ii) Forecasting

Bench marking information is often used to gauge the state of the market place and to forecast market potentials. Benchmarking also provides a source of information regarding the business directions of key players in the market place; trends in product/service development, patterns of consumers behaviour, and so on.

In many industries, the business direction of a few major companies can shape the direction of an entire market place (*e.g.,* Tata Steel, Titan Industries, Tata Consultancy Services, Maruti Udyog etc.). Forecasting the activities of these types of organisations often provides their competitors and support services companies with significant information about future implications for their businesses. Industry analysts often gauge the direction of entire markets based on the business activities of just a few companies who are the key players in the market.

(iii) New Ideas

Benchmarking is an excellent source of business ideas. One of the primary benefits of benchmarking is that it exposes individuals to new products, work processes and ways of managing company resources.

Benchmarking requires that individuals establish formal contacts outside their organisations. In many cases the process of benchmarking involves personal visits outside the organisational facilities. The reward for many employees who participate in the process is exposure to different ideas and approaches to conducting business. IBM originally considered the benchmarking process as an effective means of identifying and closing gaps between its performance and what it considered to be best practices. The same thinking shaped the development of benchmarking at Xerox. Over the years, both companies have recognised the benefits of benchmarking purely as a learning experience and its potential as a tool to stimulate the transfer of new ideas into their business. The stimulation of new ideas and the exposure to new ways of doing business have become sufficient reasons for initiating the benchmarking process.

Benchmarking causes people to think about potential ways of conducting business. It also provides an opportunity for employees to **think "out of box"** – to consider alternative paradigms and to engage in **"what if" thinking**.

(iv) Product/Process Comparisons

A common type of benchmarking activity involves the collection of information about the products or processes of competitors or excellent companies. This information is often collected and used as a standard of comparison for similar products or services of the benchmarking organisation. This type of benchmarking conforms most closely with traditional competitive intelligence activities. In these situations, a competitor's product or services is compared feature by feature with the product or service of the company performing the analysis. In addition, a product or service produced by a non-competitor (including producers from other industries) may be analysed to gain insight into factors such as design, product quality, services support, or production processes. The business products or processes of excellent companies are often analysed by noncompetitors attempting to incorporate elements of the business practices of these companies into their own work environments.

(iv) Goal Setting

'Benchmarking is used as a means of identifying best practices. Although many organisations do not realistically aim to achieve best-in-class levels of results, they do use this information to establish specific product or process objectives. The standards set by excellent companies in many cases define what is possible on a state-of-the-art performance scale. These goals can help organisations accelerate their performance curves as they strive for continual improvement. For example, many small to medium size companies cannot hope to achieve the levels of performance of excellent companies that have far greater access to technologies, capital and other resources. However, these companies can benefit considerably by benchmarking specific work processes that are not dependent on organisational resources. Organisations that are entering new markets also find that benchmarking the best practices of established organisations helps them establish goals that accelerate their learning curves and improve their performance.

BOX 1.2 : REASONS FOR USING BENCHMARKING

Organisations undertake benchmarking initiative for a number of reasons. Among them are:

(i) To set challenging but realistic goals
(ii) To define how goals can be accomplished
(iii) To define gaps between the organisation's performance and its competitor's performance
(iv) Because a breakthrough improvement is required to stay competitive
(v) Because the organisation is losing market share and needs to be turned around
(vi) Because overhead costs are running too high
(vii) Because the competitors quality is much better
(viii) Because the competition is bringing product to market much faster
(ix) Because the management feels there is a need to break down the "not invented here" syndrome
(x) To test the soundness of the organisation's strategy
(xi) To define competitor's future strategies and resource investment plans
(xii) Because there is a need to supplement the organisation's ideas with fresh thoughts
(xiii) To overcome management's complacency by exposing inaccurate perceptions
(xiv) To find out how the organisation measures up against the world's best
(xv) To identify more stringent improvement targets
(xvi) To identify organisational strengths and weakness
(xvii) To help management direct the improvement effort
(xviii) To uncover emerging technologies or practices
(xix) To improve stakeholder's satisfaction level
(xx) To learn from the experience of world-class organisations
(xxi) To provide early warning when the organisation is falling behind.

Organisations have also encouraged their suppliers to use benchmarking practices in order to help them meet quality or production goals. Motorola, for example, has been very active in encouraging its supplier's networks to benchmark Motorola and other suppliers as a means of helping the suppliers meet strict quality objectives. ***Box 1.2* lists the reasons for using benchmarking**.

OBJECTIVES OF BENCHMARKING

Benchmarking should have objectives that are clearly understood and agreed to by a functional management team before there is a commitment to supporting benchmarking activities.

Benchmarking is first a goal-setting process. It is a means by which the practices needed to reach new goals are discovered and understood.

Beyond the basic goal-setting objective of benchmarking the motivational worth of benchmarking also is significant. When fully integrated into the responsibilities, work processes, and reward system of the organisation, it empowers and encourages the organisation to move forward to realistic goals and change existing work practices which otherwise would have to be dictated.

Benchmarking legitimises the goals and targets by basing them on an external orientation. Ownership of and commitment to the benchmark is assured through agreement of the practices on which they are based. Agreement on the practices ensures attainment of the benchmarks.

BENEFITS OF BENCHMARKING

The major benefit to be had from the successful implementation of benchmarking practices is enhanced process performance, resulting in fewer errors, less waste, knowledge of the process and its present and potential capabilities.

Benchmarking results in a rational method to set performance goals and to gain market leadership and a broader, more accurate organisational management perspective.

The benefits of benchmarking include:

(i) The provisions of numeric goals and indicators of relative performance

(ii) The development of insights into innovative approaches by other organisations (departments) that affect process performance positively

(iii) Generating a vision that is outward looking, while focusing internally in critical managerial issues and processes

(iv) Top management know how their organisations fare against comparable organisations

(v) Assisting in the development of effective strategic management plans, organisational reengineering, redesign and / or restructuring initiatives.

(vi) Supporting a learning culture that values continuous improvement

(vii) Focusing resources on developed performance targets that relate to demonstrated superior external performances.

(viii) Sharing information between process partners

***Box 1.3* lists the benefits of benchmarking.**

BOX 1.3 : BENEFITS OF BENCHMARKING

(i) Defines the gap between the organisation's performance and other organisation's performance, creating a desire to change

(ii) Bases goals on external consideration and known performance standards

(iii) Integrates the best practices into the organisation

(iv) Creates goals that are more aggressive and more credible

(v) Leads to faster implementation of new approaches, with less risk

(vi) Provides a better focus on external customers and consumers

(vii) Develops effective measurement systems

(viii) Improves individual and team creativity

(ix) Provides many options to solve an individual problem

(x) Results in break-through improvements

(xi) Brings together strategic plan and the organisation's improvement efforts

(xii) Breaks down old road block attitudes ("we have done that before")

(xiii) Identifies strengths that the organisation can build upon as well as weaknesses that need to be improved (*i.e.*, reduced)

(xiv) Has a positive impact on employee pride and morale

(xv) Provides a high return-on-investment

(xvi) Helps the organisation to become the best it can be

(xvii) Develops valuable professional contacts

(xviii) Provides more realistic implementation plans

(xix) It is an important enabler that helps the organisation compete for national and international awards

(xx) Builds a high degree of cooperation among different functions and individuals within the organisations.

LIMITATIONS OF BENCHMARKING

1. Although the basis for benchmarking is continuous improvement of a recipient process, the time, effort and value of the benchmarking process must be evaluated. As organisations become more effective, the increased performance achievement reduces and thus further improvement is difficult to obtain.
2. Benchmarking to world-class performance is demonstrably helpful only to top-performing companies.
3. **Fashion:** It is fashionable to implement benchmarking. Implementing benchmarking because it is fashionable raises expectations of staff, without management becoming committed to its outcomes. Consequently benchmarking loses much of its potency.
4. **Legal / ethical issues:** Notions of ethics and legal questions may need to be addressed surrounding the exchange of working information between organisations, especially competitors
5. **Dependence:** Benchmarking relies on partnership dependence. This is the main resister to benchmarking competitor processes effectively, as much of the information is calculated to be confidential.

WHAT TO BENCHMARK?

Just about anything that can be measured can be benchmarked. However, identifying what is to be benchmarked, or the benchmarking outputs, is often the most difficult steps in the process. There is a way to arrive at benchmarking output in a logical, well-thought-out manner.

The key to determining what should be benchmarked is to identify the product of the business function. The product (output) may be tangible goods or intangible services. While benchmarking is primarily based on business processes and practices, many other things can be benchmarked. Among them are a physical product produced or a service provided or the level of customer satisfaction desired. Benchmarking in this sense is used to develop a standard or measure against which to compare. The distinguishing feature of a benchmark is that it is based on best practices found externally. ***Box 1.4*** **lists "What to Benchmark?".**

BOX 1.4 : WHAT TO BENCHMARK?
(i) **Customer requirements:** Products, Services (finished goods, product and service features)
(ii) **Work processes:** How a product or service is produced or supported
(iii) **Support functions:** Indirect labour, e.g. finance, human resources
(iv) **Organisational performance:** Costs, revenues, production indicators, quality indicators
(v) **Strategy:** Short or long term plans, the planning process.

(i) Products and Services

Finished products and services that are offered to the market place to external customers are a common subject for benchmarking. Often these finished goods are observed in their retail state and not in the process of production. These products and services are readily available for analysis although some products and services such as aircraft, supercomputers, weapon systems etc. are not easily procured for analysis.

Often product or service features are the subject of benchmarking instead of, or in addition to, the entire product or service. These features often account for product differentiation in the market place. They may be embedded in the product or service itself or they may be features that accompany the product or service.

Product and service benchmarking is often the subject of competitive analysis. This type of benchmarking is similar to the traditional competitive analysis techniques.

(ii) Work Processes

If product and services define the **what** of benchmarking, work processes define the **how**-that is , how the products or services are produced and / or supported. Work processes are often benchmarked in an effort to establish an understanding of design processes, R&D practices, production processes, work place design, equipment used for manufacturing and testing, work methods, the application of specific technologies, distribution and so on.

The benchmarking of work processes is often the subject of investigation when examining organisations outside your competitive area. Once an organisation has established a reputation for producing world-class-quality goods or services, a lot of interest is generated regarding how this reputation was earned. The belief that drives this interest is that excellent work processes will produce excellent products and services in practically any industry to which they are applied.

(iii) Support Functions

Support functions most often involve benchmarking processes and procedures that are not directly involved with the actual production of products or services offered to external customers. These functions often include the activities of departments such as finance, human resources, marketing and service. The area of investigation in this case usually involve the activities that support employees and internal customers.

An example of this type of benchmarking is the analysis of employee compensation system, this might include levels of pay, variety of compensation choices, the process of adjusting compensation levels, and so on.

(iv) Organisational Performance

Organisational performance includes those outcomes that define an organisation's bottom-line success-costs (expenses) and revenues (income). In addition, specific performance indicators relevant to the process of production may be the subject of benchmarking investigations (*e.g.*, yields, asset turnover, depreciation rates, cost of capital)

Often, organisations begin the process of asking the "how" question of benchmarking after reviewing information regarding performance data. The performance data of competitors or excellent companies may be stimulating enough to encourage a more thorough analysis of products/services, the processes employed to produce those outputs, and the support systems required to maintain excellent levels of products and services quality.

(v) Strategy

Some organisations benchmark organisational or functional strategies in order to understand how certain companies gain competitive advantage. The idea of benchmarking strategies extends well beyond the analysis of competitors and focuses on strategies of almost any organisation that has established a reputation for excellence. The focus of strategic benchmarking today is often on a particular functional area and not on overall corporate or industry strategy. For example, an organisation that is interested in improving its customer-service strategy might bench mark organisations that have established a strong reputation for effective and / or efficient customer-service strategies. Other functions that are commonly benchmarked in the strategy area include distribution, manufacturing operations, marketing, human resources, and finance. In addition to strategies themselves, the strategic planning process is often the subject of benchmarking activity.

BENCHMARKING – WHAT IT IS AND WHAT IT IS NOT?

There should be some understanding of what benchmarking is and is not, and its relationship to target setting. There are many misconceptions of what benchmarking is and these should be clearly understood and reinforced. Also what benchmarking is not should be quickly dispelled. Also since benchmarking involves setting new directions, its relationship to targets should be understood.

***Box 1.5* illustrates what benchmarking is and is not.**

BOX 1.5 : WHAT IT IS AND WHAT IT ISN'T

Benchmarking is	Benchmarking isn't
• A continuous process	• A one-time event
• A process of investigation that provides valuable information	• A process of investigation that provides simple answers.
• A process of learning from others, a pragmatic search for idea	• Copying, imitating
• A time-consuming labour intensive process requiring discipline	• Quick and easy
• A variable tool that provides useful information for improving virtually any business activity.	• A buzz word, a fad

BENCHMARKING MYTHS

1. Benchmarking targets should be established first and practices investigated later.
2. There is only one way to benchmark; against direct product competitors.
3. Benchmarks are only quantitative, financially based statistics.
4. Benchmarking investigations are focused solely on operations showing a performance gap.
5. Benchmarking is something that needs to be done occasionally and can be accomplished quickly.
6. There is a single company, somewhere, most like our firm, only much better, that is "the benchmark"
7. Staff organisations can not be benchmarked.
8. Benchmarking is a target-setting stretch exercise.
9. Benchmarking can most effectively be accomplished through third-party consultants.
10. It is difficult to decide what to benchmark for each business unit.
11. Processes don't need to be benchmarked.
12. Internal benchmarking between departments and divisions has only minimum benefits.
13. There is no benefit in qualitative benchmarking.
14. Benchmarking is comparing our firm to the dominant industry firm and emulating them six months later.
15. Benchmark practices are the same as enablers.

Difference Between Market Research, Competitive Analysis and Benchmarking

***Box 1.6* lists the approaches for Market Research, Competitive Analysis and Benchmarking.**

Box 1.6 : APPROACHES TO MARKET RESEARCH, COMPETITIVE ANALYSIS AND BENCHMARKING

	Market Research	Competitive Analysis	Benchmarking
Approach	Analyse industry segments or customer groups	Analyse competitive strategies and capabilities	Analyse industry leader, their strategies and tactics
Focus	Market requirements and customer needs	Competitors strategies and market position	Business practices that seems to work effectively
Application	Product and services	Competitive offerings and market share	Business practices as well as products and services
Limitations	Past and current market trends	Market activities and current market share	Not limited to past or current conditions, study of innovative trends
Information sources	Customers	Customers, competitors, trade shows, literature	First hand experience with industry leaders with proven success

COMMON CRITICISMS OF BENCHMARKING

Not everyone thinks benchmarking is a good thing. When practiced poorly, it probably does more harm than good. Using benchmarking to set goals without providing those who must meet those goals with an understanding of the underlying processes can cause a great deed of frustration in the ranks. And burning up corporate resources on shoddy benchmarking is a terrible waste. But neither of these scenarios implies that benchmarking is not a powerful tool when used correctly.

There are, however, some common criticisms of benchmarking. Awareness of these criticisms can only help your benchmarking, especially if it helps, you avoid some of the pit-falls that have been identified.

The three common criticisms are:

1. Spying

Competitive benchmarking is nothing but corporate spying or industrial espionage.

In Japan, knowing the competition is part of every manager's job description. An entire industry of benchmarking firms in Japan gathers detailed competitors information for clients but they do not have a catchy name for it like benchmarking.

2. Copycatting

Another common criticism is that benchmarking results in copy catting, which reduces creativity and may be detrimental in the long run. This combined with aiming at targets as if they were fixed points to hit may, in fact, reduce the value of any management insight gleaned from the process. However benchmarking is not supposed to make managers copy cats. It is supposed to make them **learn new ways to think about old problems**. And any well done benchmarking endeavor recognises that competitors are moving targets and requires that managers adjust planned actions accordingly. Benchmarking is not about copying, it is about learning and the differences between the two terms should be considered real.

3. "Not Invented Here"

Also holding benchmarking back in some organisations and to some degree, in entire industries is the **"not invented here"** response some managers have for any learning that originates outside their organisations. This "ostrich like" argument can be detrimental to an organisation's health.

One still sees manifestations of the "not-invented-here" syndrome frequently accompanying the smartest and the youngest firms, especially when they have met with nothing but success during their short lives. And the **"if it isn't broke, don't fix it"** philosophy might apply as long as things are going well, but **continuous improvement** seems to be the new law of the universe. There is a lot of learning that can come from outside one's organisations.

WHAT BENCHMARKING CAN DO TO AN ORGANISATION?

Benchmarking not only defines how certain items measure upto similar items of competitors and non-competitors but also provides the organisation with a future-state solution for the negative gaps. **What benchmarking can do to an organisation are listed in the *Box 1.7*.**

BOX 1.7 : WHAT BENCHMARKING CAN DO TO AN ORGANISATION

- Increases the desire to change for improvements
- Focuses on meeting end-user expectations
- Improves the benchmark item
- Improves key financial indicators
- Focuses on the use of best world-wide practices
- Provides a way to improve customer satisfaction
- Helps eliminate the "not invented here" syndrome
- Includes the use of proven approaches, methods, processes and technologies
- Improves employee morale and pride
- Improves relationships and understanding between benchmarking partners
- Identifies strengths and weaknesses
- Identifies your competitive position
- Increases the effectiveness, efficiency and adaptability of your processes
- Transforms complacency into an urgent desire to improve
- Defines and incorporates best, applicable processes and management practices
- Helps set attainable, but aggressive targets
- Provides breakthrough types of improvement
- Concentrates on the major contributors to the success of the organisation
- Allows you to project future trends in your industry
- Sets new standards of performance
- Prioritises improvement activities
- Provides a faster, lower-risk approach to meeting aggressive targets
- Provides your organisation with a competitive advantage
- Creates a culture of continuous improvement
- Reduces the cost of the improvement process
- Develops a professional interface with other organisations.

When an organisation starts applying the benchmarking process, a significant change in internal attitude takes place.

***Box 1.8* lists the situation before benchmarking and after benchmarking.**

BOX 1.8 : SITUATION BEFORE AND AFTER BENCHMARKING	
Before benchmarking	**After benchmarking**
• Not invented here	Let us use that good idea
• One answer to a problem	Many options
• Internal focus	External focus
• History based targets	Best performance targets
• Low market understanding	High market understanding
• Internal priorities	Customer priorities
• Reactive improvements	Proactive improvements
• Problem focus	Opportunity focus
• Driven by personality	Driven by best industry practices
• Path of least resistance	Best value path
• We are good	We need to be better
• Managed by experience	Managed by facts
• Following the industry	Leading the industry

SUCCESS INDICATORS FOR BENCHMARKING

***Box 1.9* lists the various success indicators for benchmarking**

BOX 1.9 : SUCCESS INDICATORS FOR BENCHMARKING

- An active commitment to benchmarking from management.
- A clear and comprehensive understanding of how one's own work is conducted as a basis for comparison to industry best practices.
- A willingness to change and adapt based on benchmark findings.
- A realisation that competition is constantly changing and there is a need to "shoot ahead of the duck".
- A willingness to share information with benchmark partners.
- A focus on benchmarking first on industry best practices and second on performance metrics.
- The concentration of leading companies in the industry or other functionally best operations that are recognised leaders.
- Adherence to the 10 step benchmarking process.
- An openness to new ideas and creativity and innovativeness in their application to existing processes.
- A continuous benchmarking effort.
- The institutionalisation of benchmarking.

BARRIERS TO SUCCESSFUL BENCHMARKING

Business experts point to several factors that can hinder a company's effort to institute meaningful benchmarking practices. These include:

(i) **Unexamined core business process:** The ultimate quality, price or reliability of the end product or service that is made available to customers is predicted on many aspects of company's operations, and these facts need to be taken into consideration when examining internal processes.

(ii) **Inadequate people or technology resources:** A business should make sure that it has resources (in terms of workforce, technology or funding) to both launch a thorough benchmarking program and implement its findings.

(iii) **Unwillingness or inability to accept the legitimacy of business ideas or practices from outside sources:** Many employees and organisations are resistant to change, because of general contendness, fear of the unknown, perceived challenges to their abilities etc. Resistance can be minimized , however if owners and managers make it clear that benchmarking is not a fault-finding exercise but rather an established program to help the company grow and prosper in a fast changing business world.

(iv) **Speed of in-house benchmarking processes:** Effective benchmarking programs are given mandates to conduct their investigations in a timely manner, so that improvements can be implemented quickly.

(v) **Inadequate follow-up training:** Benchmarking programs can uncover many areas in which companies can improve their performance. But if the company does not provide its workforce with sufficient training to implement needed changes in a timely and effective fashion, then the initiative becomes a waste of time and resources.

(vi) **Effective performance measurement with status, benchmarking.**

BOX 1.10 : BENCHMARKING IN PRACTICE - BIRTH OF BENCHMARKING
In 1912, Henry Ford of the Ford Motor Company watched men cut meet during a tour of a Chicago slaughter house. The carcasses were hanging on hooks mounted on a monorail. After each man performed his job he would push the carcass to the next station. Less than six months later, the world's first assembly line started producing Magnetos in the Ford Highland Park Plant. In other words, the idea that revolutionised modern manufacturing and automotive history was imported from another industry. This is what is known as **"benchmarking"** concept today.

POINTS TO REMEMBER

- One of the best ways to keep improving your organisation is to **benchmark**.
- **Benchmarking** is a powerful process to improve your **competitive position**.
- **Benchmarking** is an **improvement process** used to discover and incorporate **best practices** into your operation.
- A **process** is a repeatable sequence of steps used to **transform** an **input** into an **output** that has **value** to an internal or external customer.
- A single process generally contains many **practices** because every process consists of multiple steps and each step may contain one or more practices.

- A **practice** is a method or technique used to perform a process step.
- A **metric** is a measure of process performance.
- An **enabler** is any condition or factor that influences the effectiveness of a practice.
- **Benchmarking** is defined as a **continuous process** for evaluating the **products, services** and **work processes** of organisations that are recognised as representing **best practices** for the purpose of organisational **improvement**.
- **Benchmarking** is not a mechanism for determining resource reductions.
- Benchmarking is not a panacea or program.
- Benchmarking is not a cook book process that requires only looking up ingredients and using them for success.
- Benchmarking is not a fad, but a winning business strategy.
- **Benchmarks** are measurements to gauge the performance of a function, operation or business relative to others.
- Benchmarking involves **learning from others**.
- Benchmarking is a useful tool for gathering information during the process of **strategic planning**.
- Benchmarking information is often used to **forecast market potentials**.
- Benchmarking is an excellent source of **new business ideas**.
- Benchmarking causes people to think about **potential ways** of conducting business. It also provides an opportunity for employees to think **"out-of-box"**.
- Benchmarking activity involves the collection of **information about the products and processes** of competitors or excellent companies.
- Benchmarking is used as a means of identifying **best practices**.
- Benchmarking is a **goal setting** process. It is a means by which the practices needed to reach new goals are discovered and understood.
- The **major benefit** from the successful implementation of benchmarking practices is enhanced process performance, resulting in fewer errors, less waste, knowledge of the process and its present and potential capabilities.
- While benchmarking has numerous **benefits**, there are some **limitations** also.
- **What to benchmark? The answer is:**

  (i) Customer requirements (products and services), *(ii)* Work processes, *(iii)* Support functions, *(iv)* Organisational performance and *(v)* Strategy.
- There are many **myths** about benchmarking.
- Approaches to market research, competitive analysis and benchmarking are not the same.
- **The three common criticisms of benchmarking are:**
  - *(i)* Competitive benchmarking is nothing but corporate **spying** or industrial espionage.
  - *(ii)* Benchmarking results in **copy catting** which reduces creativity and may be detrimental in the long-run.
  - *(iii)* Benchmarking in some organisations is affected by the **"not invented here"** response some managers have for learning that originates outside their organisations.
- Benchmarking not only defines how certain items measure upto similar items of competitors and non-competitors but also provides the organisation with a **future-state solution** for the negative gaps.

- When an organisation starts applying the benchmarking process, a significant **change in internal altitude** takes place.
- **Barriers to successful benchmarking include:**
  - *(i)* Unexamined core business process
  - *(ii)* Inadequate people or technology resources
  - *(iii)* Unwillingness or inability to accept the legitimacy of business ideas or practices from outside sources
  - *(iv)* Speed of in-house benchmarking processes
  - *(v)* Inadequate follow-up training and
  - *(vi)* Effective performance measurement with status, benchmarking.

REVIEW QUESTIONS

1. Define the terms "Benchmark" and "Benchmarking".
2. Define the terms "Process", "Practice", "Metric" and "Enabler".
3. How does practice relate to a metric?
4. What bench marking is not?
5. "Benchmarking involves learning from others" – Elaborate
6. What is meant by "Thinking out-of-the-box".
7. Why benchmarking is used? Discuss.
8. Discuss the objectives of benchmarking.
9. Discuss the benefits of benchmarking.
10. Discuss the limitations of benchmarking
11. Discuss the benchmarking myths.
12. Distinguish between "Market Research", "Competitive Analysis" and "Benchmarking"
13. Discuss the common criticisms of benchmarking.
14. Explain what benchmarking can do to an organisation.
15. Make a comparative statement of a situation before and after benchmarking.
16. Mention the success indicators for benchmarking.
17. Discuss the barriers to successful benchmarking.

DISCUSSION QUESTIONS

1. "Benchmarking is a powerful process to improve your competitive position" – Discuss
2. "Benchmarking is not a mechanism for determining resource reductions". Do you agree or disagree? Justify your answer.
3. Comment on the following statements:
   - *(a)* Benchmarking is a onetime event
   - *(b)* Benchmarking provides situations to business issues.
   - *(c)* Benchmarking is quick and easy.
   - *(d)* Benchmarking is copying or imitating.
   - *(e)* Benchmarking is a fad.
4. "Benchmarking is basically an objective-setting process" – explain.
5. "Benchmarking is the route to competitive advantage". Do you agree or disagree? Give reasons for your answer.

CHAPTER 2

Introduction to Benchmarking

INTRODUCTION

With the intense competition in industry today, simply meeting or beating past performance will not result in the level of improvement necessary to remain competitive. Organisations must achieve quantum improvements in productivity, quality, reliability, and responsiveness to drive down costs and keep customer/ consumers delighted.

When an organisation realises that it is falling behind its competitors in its performance and market share, it should do one or more of the following: Standardise processes, Reengineer processes, Retrench, Redesign processes, Develop new systems, Set up service centers, Buy new technology, Downsize, Centralise, Train employees, Decentralise, Outsource, Reorganise, Automate, Use more information technology, Change management, Declare bankruptcy and the like.

The most common mistake organisations make is to do nothing. It is a mistake because it harms management's credibility and often impacts future competitiveness. Many managers have burnt their fingers in the past by some of the improvement activities they have implemented and as a result, they are reluctant to implement any unknown, untried concept designed to improve the organisation's performance.

This is where benchmarking steps in, with a proven concept that defines how the organisation can close the gap between its own performance and the performance of its very best competitors.

Many major organisations around the world invested vast sums of money in the 1980s and 1990s to bring about continuous improvement in their performance. The results were good and the typical improvement rate has been between 5 to 20 percent a year. Still many organisations continued to lose their market share and experienced decreased profit margins. **Now management is beginning to ask themselves the following questions:**

1. How much change is really necessary or possible?
2. What is the world-class standard for these processes and products?
3. Is it possible for our processes or products to be better?
4. If so what can we do to make them better?
5. Where do we go from here?

The organisation has used up all ideas and has gone as far as it can go with improvement process. What it needs is a major breakthrough that will decrease costs and error rates by 50 percent.

What the organisation needs to do now is to look outside its own location at other, similar processes and / or products within the organisation and at outside organisations as well. Its purpose is to understand what other organisations are doing and use this combined experience and knowledge to help improve its process even further. ***This art of systematically defining the best systems, processes, procedures and practices is called benchmarking.*** The benchmarking process can improve an item's (product or process) performance by as much as 60 percent in less than 12 months.

Organisations use benchmarking to understand what level of performance is really possible and to understand why the gap exists between their current performance and that optimum performance.

Being the very best in any field is a difficult and lonely road to travel. Once you reach your goals, there is only one direction to go: down. When you are the best, you are envied, undermined, frequently criticized and expected to outperform the competition no matter what the circumstances are.

Many people, teams and organisations want to be recognised as the very best because excellence brings: *(i)* customers, *(ii)* employee and management satisfaction, *(iii)* recognition, *(iv)* higher rewards, *(v)* respect, *(vi)* power and *(vii)* money.

The steps you need to take to become the very best are: *(i)* Know yourself, your strengths and your limitations/weaknesses, *(ii)* Recognise and understand what the leading organisations do in the area in which you hope to excel, *(iii)* Use the best processes available, *(iv)* Build on these processes to create even better ones and *(v)* Never stop improving.

The benchmarking process helps you to know your organisation understands its competition, defines the best processes and integrates them into your business activities.

The key to any organisation's or individual's success is:

- Having meaningful measurements to show how well your organisation is performing
- Understanding how well other organisations can perform similar activities (both competitors and non competitors)
- Understanding why others perform better then your organisation.
- Identifying any negative gap between your organisation and another organisation and taking rapid, effective action to close that gap.

Most organisations are faced with the realisation that they need to improve such indicators (measurements) as return on assets, market share, customer satisfaction and net profits. The problem is usually three fold:

1. Management does not know how well the different parts of the organisation should be performing.
2. Management does not think a major improvement in the organisation can be accomplished.
3. Management does not know how to bring about a major improvement in the organisation.

The answer to this dilemma is benchmarking. Benchmarking is a powerful tool that provides the organisation with measurements of how well products, equipments, people, services and processes can perform. It allows the organisation to realise that it needs to break our of the old mode, and that major improvements not only can be made but must be made if the organisation is to survive. Benchmarking also gives the organisation a clear understanding of how other organisations are able to perform at superior levels. It provides managers not only with aggressive, realistic goals but also with the confidence that they can achieve these goals because they know that other organisations are doing so.

A question arises as to whether benchmarking is ethical. Of course benchmarking is legal and ethical if it is done correctly without resorting to industrial espionage or stealing competitor's information. The human race has evolved by building upon other people's ideas. We can not afford the attitude of "It is no good if it is not invented here". Creativity is great and provides a great deal of self-satisfaction, but it is also time consuming. If some one or some organisation has a good idea and is willing to share it with you, take the free gift. When we look objectively at benchmarking, it is simply a systematic way of collecting information about equipment, product and /or process performance, then analysing why some items out-perform others and applying this knowledge to improve your organisation's performance.

Benchmarking Process

- Benchmarking is a powerful process for improving your competitive position. It looks beyond the prevailing conditions and practices of a particular market segment.
- Benchmarking helps you to identify and study processes, techniques and practices of innovative market leaders often operating in different industries and markets. You can then apply those proven processes, techniques, and practices to the problems and opportunities that you face in your markets, there-by improving your competitive position.
- Benchmarking is the search for best industry practices that lead to superior performance.
- Benchmarking helps a company learn its strengths and weaknesses and those of other industry leaders and incorporate the best practices into its own operations.
- Benchmarking aids the development and realisation of improvement objectives, particularly stretch objectives.
- Benchmarking promotes superior performance by providing an organised framework through which organisations can learn how the "best-in-class" do things, understand how these best practices differ from their own and implement changes to close the gap.
- Benchmarking is a tool for continuous improvement.
- Benchmarking involves constantly seeking and applying new ideas, methods, practices and processes used by industry leaders.

The Essence of Benchmarking

The essence of benchmarking is "the continuous process of comparing a company's strategy, products and processes with those of world leaders and best-in-class organisations in order to learn how they achieved excellence and then setting out to match and even surpass it". In other words, it is **"moving from where we are to where we want to be"**.

Basic Elements of Benchmarking

- Know your organisation and operations.
- Know the industry leaders or top competitors.
- Seek out and incorporate the best, gain superiority.

The Evolution of Benchmarking:

The concept of benchmarking is not new. In the early 1800s, Francis Lowell, a New England industrialist, travelled to England to study manufacturing techniques at the best British factories. Henry Ford created the assembly line after taking tour of a Chicago slaughterhouse and watching carcasses hung on hooks mounted on a monorail move from one workstation to another. Toyota's just-in-time production system was influenced by the replenishment practices of U.S. supermarkets. Modern benchmarking was initiated by Xerox (in the 1980s), an eventual winner of the Malcolm Baldrige National Quality Award. IBM, Motorola and Xerox became the pioneers in instituting the benchmarking process. **Xerox initially studied their direct competitors and discovered that:**

- their unit manufacturing cost equalled the Japanese selling price in the United States.
- the number of production suppliers was nine times that of the best companies.
- assembly line rejects were 10 times higher
- product lead times were twice as long and
- defects per hundred machines were seven times higher.

These results helped them to understand the amount of change that would be required to set realistic targets to guide their planning efforts.

The Xerox Experience : Xerox instituted the benchmarking process in the 1980s because the company's market share shrank to 35 percent in 1981 even though the company invented the photocopier in 1959 and maintained a virtual monopoly for many years thereafter (Xerox name became a generic name for all photocopiers). On introducing benchmarking process, Xerox met with resistance at first by its employees who did not believe that someone else could do it better. When faced with the facts, reaction went from denial to dismay to frustration and finally to action. Once the process began, the company benchmarked virtually every function and task for productivity, cost and quality. Comparisons were made for companies both in and outside the industry.

By the company's own admission, it would probably not be in the copier business if it were not for benchmarking. Results were dramatic:

- Suppliers were reduced from 5000 to 300.
- ***"Concurrent engineering"*** was practiced. Each product development group has input from design, manufacturing and service from the initial stages of the project.
- Commonality of parts increased from about 20 percent to 60-70 percent.
- Hierarchical organisation structure was reduced and the use of cross-functional teams were established.
- Results included :

    (i) Quality problems cut by two-thirds.

(ii) Manufacturing cost cut by 50 percent.

(iii) Development time cut by two-thirds and

(iv) Direct labour cut by 50 percent and corporate staff cut by 35 percent.

However, it should be noted that all of these improvements were not the direct result of benchmarking. What happened in Xerox was that in adopting the process, the climate for change and continuous improvement followed as a natural result. In other words, benchmarking can be a very good intervention technique for positive change.

The Motorola Experience : In the early 1980s, Motorola set a goal of improving a set of basic quality attributes ***tenfold*** in five years. Based on ***internal*** benchmarking, the goal was achieved in three years. The company began to look outside, sending teams to visit competitor plants in Japan. To their chagrin, the team found that Motorola would have to improve its tenfold improvement level another two to three times just to match the competition.

Borrowing process benchmarks from companies as diverse as Walmart, Benetton and Domino's Pizza, the company now routinely fields benchmarking requests from their Japanese competitors.

Reasons for benchmarking : Benchmarking is a tool to achieve business and competitive objectives. It is a powerful and effective tool when used for the right reasons and aligned with organisation strategy. In a competitive market, organisations have to decide which markets to serve and determine the strengths they need to have to gain competitive advantage. Benchmarking helps organisations to develop those strengths and reduce weaknesses.

Traditionally, companies used to set their next year's goals based on previous year's performance. Benchmarking enables goals to be set objectively based on external information rather than internal.

Advantages and Limitations of Benchmarking

Advantages

(i) A primary advantage of benchmarking practice is that it promotes a thorough understanding of the company's ***own*** processes *i.e.,* the company's current profile (***strengths*** and ***weaknesses***) is well understood.

(ii) Benchmarking process involves ***imitation*** and ***adaptation*** of the practices of superior competitors, rather than ***invention,*** thereby saving ***time*** and ***money*** for the company practising benchmarking.

(iii) Intensive studies of existing practices often lead to identification of ***non-value-added activities*** and plans for process improvement.

(iv) Benchmarking enables comparison of ***performance measures*** in different dimensions, each with best practices for that particular measure. It involves comparison with several companies who are best for the chosen measure. (Some common performance measures are return on assets, cycle time, percentage of on-time delivery, proportion of defects, percentage of damaged goods and time spent on administrative functions).

(v) Benchmarking focusses on performance measures and processes and not on products. Thus, it is not restricted to the industry to which the company belongs. It extends beyond these

boundaries and identifies organisations in other industries that are superior with respect to chosen measures.

(vi) Benchmarking allows organisations to set realistic, rigorous ***new performance targets*** and this process helps convince people of the credibility of these targets. This tends to overcome the ***"not invented here"*** syndrome and the ***"we are different"*** justification for the status zero. Benchmarking indicates to a company that there may be people else where who do things better than they do.

(vii) Benchmarking allows organisations to define ***specific gaps in performance*** and to select the processes to improve. It enables the company to redesign its products and services to achieve outcomes that meet or exceed customer expectations.

(viii) Benchmarking provides a basis for ***training human resources***. Employees begin to see the gap between what they are doing and what best-in-class are doing. Closing the gap emphasises the need for personnel to be involved in techniques of ***problem solving*** and ***process improvement***. The synergy between organisational activities is improved through cross-functional cooperation.

Limitations

(i) The primary limitation or weakness of benchmarking is the fact that best-in-class performance is not a static but a moving target. New technology can create quantum leap performance improvement – *for example,* the use of electronic data interchange (EDI).

(ii) Benchmarking is ***not a panacea*** that can replace all other quality efforts or management processes that can improve the competitive advantage of a company.

(iii) Benchmarking is not an ***"instant pudding"***. It will not improve performance if the proper infrastructure of a total quality program is not in place. Unless a corporate culture of quality and the basic components of TQM such as information system, process control and human resource programmes are in place, trying to initiate the best-in-class may very well disrupt operations.

Pitfalls of Benchmarking

The potential pitfalls of benchmarking include the failure to do the following :

(i) Involve the employees who will ultimately use the information and improve the process. (participation can lead to enthusiasm).

(ii) Relate process improvement to strategy and competitive positioning.

(iii) Define the firm's own process before gathering data for the purpose of comparison.

(iv) Perceive benchmarking as an ongoing process and not as an one-time project with a finite start and completion dates.

(v) Expand the scope of the companies studied instead of confining to one's own area, industry or to direct competitors, which is a narrow approach in identifying excellent performances that are appropriate to one's own processes.

(vi) Perceive benchmarking as a means to process improvement, rather than an end itself.

(vii) Set goals for closing the gap between the existing performance (what is) and the benchmark (what can be).

(viii) Empower employees to achieve improvements that they identify and for which they solve problems and develop action plans.

TYPES OF BENCHMARKING

There are at least four types of benchmarking that can be conducted. They are:

1. Benchmarking against internal operations (*e.g.*, Internal Benchmarking)
2. Benchmarking against external direct product competitors (*e.g.*, External Benchmarking, Competitive Benchmarking, Technical/Product Benchmarking)
3. Benchmarking against external best operations or industry leaders (*e.g.*, Functional Benchmarking, Process Benchmarking, Performance Benchmarking, Best Practice Benchmarking)
4. Generic Benchmarking.

In addition to the above, benchmarking can also be categorised as:

(*i*) Formal benchmarking
(*ii*) Informal benchmarking
(*iii*) Co-operative benchmarking
(*iv*) Collaborative benchmarking
(*v*) Strategic benchmarking
(*vi*) Best-in-class benchmarking
(*vii*) International benchmarking
(*viii*) World-class benchmarking
(*ix*) Financial benchmarking
(*x*) Energy benchmarking
(*xi*) Metric benchmarking

The various types of benchmarking are briefly discussed in the following paragraphs:

(*i*) Formal benchmarking versus Informal benchmarking:

Formal benchmarking is a systematic process for identifying and implementing best or better practices. For example, Performance benchmarking and Best-practice benchmarking are categorized as formal benchmarking.

Informal benchmarking is a type of benchmarking that most of us do unconsciously at work and in our home life. We constantly compare and learn from the behaviour and practices of others whether it is how to use a software program, how to cook a better meal or play our favorite sport.

In the context of work, most of the informal benchmarking comes from the following:

(*a*) Talking to work colleagues and learning from their experience (coffee breaks and team meetings are a great place to network and learn from others)

(*b*) Consulting with experts (for example, business consultants who have experience of implementing a particular process or activity in many business environments).

(c) Networking with other people from other organisations at conferences, seminars and Internet forums.

(d) On-line databases/websites and publications that share benchmarking information provide quick and easy ways to learn of best practices and benchmarks.

(ii) Internal benchmarking versus External benchmarking:

Internal benchmarking: Internal benchmarking is done within one's organisation or perhaps in conjunction with another division or branch office. Internal benchmarking is the easiest to conduct since data and information should be readily available and confidentiality concern are minimised.

In most large multidivision or international firms there are similar functions in different operating units. One of the easiest benchmarking investigations is to compare these internal operations. This may involve comparisons of logistics operations for different divisions. The data and information can be as complete and extensive as desired.

This first step in benchmarking investigations is an excellent basis for not only uncovering differences of interest, but also focusing on the critical issues that will be faced or are of interest for understanding practices from external investigations. The internal investigations may also help define the scope of an external study.

It also may in and of itself provide useful information. It may even define an internal operation that is the benchmark.

Internal benchmarking assumes that there are differences in the work processes of an organisation as a result of differences in geographical location of the business units, the nature of managers and employees in different locations and the like. Internal benchmarking assumes that some of the work processes that exist in one part of the organisation may be more effective or efficient than the work processes in other parts of the organisation. The objective of internal benchmarking activity is to identify the internal performance standards of an organisation.

External benchmarking: It is the most common approach to benchmarking wherein an organisation is engaged in benchmarking against external direct product competitors (*e.g.*, competitive benchmarking, best-in-class benchmarking etc.) or benchmarking against functional best operations or industry leaders (*e.g.*, technical/product benchmarking, performance benchmarking, world-class benchmarking etc.)

External competitive benchmarking is an effective approach in industries that are very competitive. External industry (compatible) benchmarking compares the benchmarking item with items produced by the world's best organisations in a general industry category (*e.g.*, banking, insurance, healthcare, electronics etc.) In this case the benchmarking partner's item does not compete directly for the same customers.

External generic (trans-industry) benchmarking extends the benchmarking process outside the specific organisation and its industry, to involve dissimilar industries. Many business processes are generic in application and extend across industries (*e.g.*, warehousing, supplier relations, advertising, order filling, customer relations, hiring, training, service parts logistics etc)

Combined internal and external benchmarking is the most frequently used approach to benchmarking. This combination usually produces the best results.

Internal benchmarking is the starting point and should always be considered before any organisation looks to the outside. If an organisation is just starting its benchmarking program, internal benchmarking is an excellent way to develop the benchmarking process and train people in how to use it.

(iii) Competitive benchmarking versus Non-competitive benchmarking:

Competitive benchmarking involves identification of the products, services and work processes of your organisation's direct competitors. The objective of competitive benchmarking is to identify specific information about your competitor's products, processes, and business results and then make comparisons with those of your own organisation.

Competitive benchmarking is useful in positioning your organisation's products, services and processes relative to the market place. In many cases, the business practices of your competitors do not represent best-in-class performance or best practices, However this information is valuable because your competitors practices affect the perceptions of your customers, suppliers, shareholders, potential customers and "industry watchers"- all of whom have a direct effect on your eventual business success.

Competitive benchmarking compares how well an organisation is doing with respect to the leading competition, especially with respect to critically important attributes, functions or values associated with the organisation's products or services.

Competitive benchmarking involves analysing the performance and practices of best-in-class companies. Their performance becomes a benchmark to which a firm can compare its own performance and their practices are used to improve that firm's practices. However benchmarking the competition could be difficult since it might be difficult or impossible to collect or learn a competitor's secrets. This type of information can often be obtained through a confidential survey of all companies usually conducted by a third party consulting firm.

Advantages of competitive benchmarking are as below:

1. In most cases, the organisations that are being benchmarked use technologies and business practices that are identical or at least to your own. Often your competitors have other things in common with you, such as access to marketing channels, available labour pools or foreign suppliers. The identification of any similarities becomes a possible advantage when benchmarking. In many cases the lessons learnt can be applied to your organisation without a lot of translation.
2. Competitors may have performed their own benchmarking studies and may be willing to trade information.

Non-Competitive benchmarking is learning something about a process a company wants to improve by benchmarking including : *(i)* a related process in the industry with a firm, the company does not directly compete with, *(ii)* a related process in a different industry and *(iii)* an unrelated process in a different industry.

The advantage of this type of benchmarking is that new processes which could easily be adapted to one's organisation might be discovered.

(iv) Co-operative Benchmarking

In co-operative benchmarking, an organisation that desires to improve a particular activity through benchmarking contacts best-in-class firms and ask them if they will be willing to share knowledge with the benchmarking team. The target companies are usually not direct competitors of the benchmarking company, which is a key factor in securing cooperation.

In co-operative benchmarking, the knowledge usually flows in one direction-from the target companies to the benchmarking team.

(v) Collaborative Benchmarking

In collaborative benchmarking, a group of firms (*e.g.*, subsidiaries of a multinational in different countries) share knowledge about a particular activity, all hoping to improve based upon what they learn. Sometimes, a third party often serves as coordinator, collector and distributor of data, although an increasing number of firms are managing their own collaborative studies.

For example, managers from one of the Malcolm Baldrige National Quality Award winners convened an adhoc consortium to study the use of customer satisfaction data at a number of US companies that are considered leaders in this area. Participants in the study included five Baldrige winners – AT&T, IBM- Rochester, Motorola, Solectron and Zytec-Time-Life, and MBNA, the financial services company.

Another example is the UK construction industry which has carried out benchmarking since the late 1990s through its industry association and with financial support from the UK government.

(vi) Technical/ Product Benchmarking

The technique initially used to compare existing corporate strategies with a view to achieving the best possible performance in new situations has recently been extended to the comparison of technical products. This process is usually referred to as **"technical benchmarking"** or **"product benchmarking"**.

Its use is well developed within automotive industry where it is vital to design products that match precise user expectations, at minimal cost by applying the best technologies available worldwide. Data is obtained by fully disassembling existing cars and their systems.

Product benchmarking is the process of designing new products or upgrades to current ones. This process can sometimes involve reverse engineering which is taking apart competitor's products to find strengths and weaknesses of your own products.

(Today, in Japan, benchmarking has fallen out of favour because, the Japanese use benchmarking to identify best practices and adapt them to their own. Most Japanese firms feel that copying another firm's products, processes or procedures ensures falling behind that firm because of the time required to implement the future-state solution.)

Product benchmarking is commonly known as **"reverse engineering"** or **"competitive product analysis"**. It assesses competitor's costs, product concepts, strengths and weaknesses of alternative designs and competitor design trade-offs, by obtaining, stripping down and analysing competitor's products.

(vii) Performance Benchmarking or Operational Benchmarking

Performance benchmarking allows the initiator firm to assess their competitive position by comparing products and services with those of target firms.

It involves comparing the performance levels of organisations for a specific process. This information can be used for identifying opportunities for improvement and / or setting performance targets.

Performance levels of other organisations are normally called benchmarks and the ideal benchmark is one that originates from an organisation recognised as being a leader in the related area. Performance benchmarking may involve comparison of financial measures (such as expenditure, cost of labour, cost of building/equipment, cost of energy, adherence to budget, cash flow, revenue collected etc) or non-financial measures (such as absenteeism, staff turn-over, budget processing time, complaints, environmental impact or call center performance).

Performance benchmarking involves pricing, quality, features and other quality or performance characteristics of products and services. Performance benchmarking is usually performed by direct comparisons or "reverse engineering" in which competitor's products are taken apart and analysed.

Operational benchmarking embraces every thing from staffing and productivity to office flow and analysis of procedures performed.

(viii) Process Benchmarking or Functional Benchmarking:

In **process benchmarking** the initiating firm focuses its observation and investigation of business processes with a goal of identifying and observing the best practices from one or more benchmark firms. Activity analysis will be required where the objective is to benchmark cost and efficiency. It is increasingly applied to back-office processes where outsourcing may be a consideration.

Process benchmarking centres on work processes such as billing, order entry or employee training. This type of benchmarking identifies the most effective practices in companies that perform similar functions, no matter in what industry.

In **functional benchmarking**, a company will focus its benchmarking on a single function to improve the operation of that particular function. Complex functions such as human resources, finance and accounting and information and communication technology are unlikely to be directly comparable in cost and efficiency terms and may need to be disaggregated into processes to make valid comparison.

Companies should not aim benchmarking solely at direct competitors and it would be a mistake if they do so. If a company simply benchmarks within its own industry, it may be competitive and have an edge in those areas in which it is the industry leader. However, if benchmarks are adopted from outside the industry, a company may learn ideas and processes as well as new applications that allow it to surpass the best within its own industry and to achieve distinct superiority.

Functional benchmarking investigates the performance of core business functions. It does not need to focus on direct competitors but, depending on the function to be benchmarked, the benchmark partner may need to be in a similarly characterised industry for useful comparisons to be made.

There are reasons why functional benchmarking is productive. It most often is easier to obtain interest for the investigation and share data. Not only there are fewer problems with confidentiality of information, but there is also a national interest in understanding practices elsewhere.

It has been observed that practices found in dissimilar industries are more readily accepted than those within the same industry. This is because the observation of methods and practices are approached on a more objective basis, not always distracted by the product involved.

(ix) Best-Practices Benchmarking

This is where organisations search for and study organisations that are high performers in particular areas of interest. The processes themselves of these organisations are studied rather than just the associated performance levels, normally through some mutually beneficial agreement that follows a benchmarking code of conduct. Knowledge gained through the study is taken back to the organisation and where feasible and appropriate, these high performing or best practices are adapted and incorporated into the organisation's own processes. Therefore, best-practices benchmarking involves the whole process of identifying, capturing, analysing and implementing best practices. There are a number of best practice benchmarking methodologies.

Best-practices benchmarking applies to business processes. Some business processes are the same regardless of the type of industry.

Best practices benchmarking breaks the function down into discrete areas that are targets for benchmarking and is therefore a more focused study than functional benchmarking.

Best practices benchmarking attempts to benchmark not only the work processes but also the management practice behind them.

(x) Generic Benchmarking

The word generic suggests "without a brand" which is consistent with the idea that this type of benchmarking focuses on excellent work processes rather than on the business practices of a particular organisation or industry.

Some business function or processes are the same regardless of dissimilarities of industries. One such process is order fulfillment process. It can be described as the order entry, customer service, warehouse order handling, invoicing and collection functions.

A wide cross-section of firms must perform these functions to satisfy customers. If such a process were to be benchmarked, the product or industry may not be limiting.

Generic benchmarking holds the potential of revealing the best of best practices. It requires broad conceptualisation but careful understanding of the generic process. It is the most difficult benchmarking concept to gain acceptance and use but probably that with the highest long-term pay off.

(xi) Strategic Benchmarking

Strategic benchmarking is concerned with comparing strategies of different companies and assessing the success of those strategies in the market place. Strategic benchmarking examines how companies compete and seeks the winning strategies that have led to competitive advantage and market success. **One way to determine how well a company is prepared to compete in a segment**

and to help define a best-in-class competitor is to construct a "key success factor matrix" similar to the one shown in *Exhibit 2.1* below.

EXHIBIT 2.1 : KEY SUCCESS FACTOR MATRIX

Key success factor	Compeitive Analysis - Computer Industry ... Segment				
	Performance Rating				
	Weight	Our company	Competitor A	Competitor B	Competitor C
Sales force					
Distribution					
Suppliers					
R & D					
Service					
Cost structure					

- **Strategic benchmarking analyses strategies with particular reference to:**

  (i) Strategic intent, *(ii)* Core competencies, *(iii)* Process capability, *(iv)* Product line, *(v)* Strategic alliances and *(vi)* Technology portfolio.

- Should begin with the needs and expectations of the customer. This can be achieved through surveys to measure customer satisfaction and the gaps between company's performance and its customers' standards.
- Ensures a coordinated strategic direction regarding benchmarking and reduces the possibility that one improvement project will cancel out the effect of another.

The main difficulty is persuading the benchmark partners to discuss their strategy. However there is a great deal of information which can be obtained from customers, common suppliers and public domain information.

(xii) Best-in-class Benchmarking

This involves studying the leading competitor or the company that best carries a specific function.

(xiii) International Benchmarking

Best practioners are identified and analysed elsewhere in the world, perhaps because there are too few benchmarking partners within the same country to produce valid results.

Globalisation and advances in information technology are increasing opportunities for international projects. However these can take more time and resources to set up and implement and the results may need careful analysis due to national differences.

Where the aim is to achieve world-class status or simply because there are insufficient national businesses against which to benchmark, international benchmarking is appropriate.

(xiv) World-class Benchmarking

This approach to benchmarking is the most ambitious. It involves looking towards the recognised leader for the process being benchmarked – an organisation that does it better than any other.

(xv) Financial Benchmarking

This refers to performing a financial analysis and comparing the results in an effort to assess your overall competitiveness and productivity.

(xvi) Energy Benchmarking

A process of collecting, analysing and relating energy performance data of comparable activities with the purpose of evaluating and comparing performance between or within entities. Entities can include processes, buildings or companies. Benchmarking may be internal between entities within a single organisation or subject to confidentiality restrictions – external between competing entities.

(xvii) Metric Benchmarking

It is an approach to making comparison using more aggregative cost or production information to identify strong and weak performing units.

The two most common forms of quantitative analysis used in metric benchmarking are: *(i)* Data Envelope Analysis (DEA) and *(ii)* Regression Analysis.

DEA estimates the cost level an efficient firm should be able to achieve in a particular market. In infrastructure regulation, DEA can be used to reward companies / operators whose costs are near the efficient frontier with additional profits.

Regression analysis estimates what the average firm should be able to achieve.

Areas to Benchmark

Specific areas to benchmark at the operating level might include the following :

(i) Customer service levels
(ii) Inventory management
(iii) Inventory control (extent of automation)
(iv) Purchasing
(v) Billing and collection
(vi) Purchasing practices
(vii) Quality process
(viii) Warehousing and distribution and
(ix) Transportation.

Guidelines to Benchmarking

Companies approach benchmarking in different ways. **IBM has a four step approach. AT & T has a nine step approach and *Xerox* a *ten step approach*. All these approaches have the general guidelines given below :**

(i) **Do not go on a fishing expedition :** When preparing a benchmarking study, pick-up a specific area in the organisation that needs improvement. This may be quality, customer satisfaction, accounts payable or delivery time. Then do your homework, including thoroughly reviewing your own process and procedures before picking a company that excels in the particular area chosen.

(ii) **Use company people :** The people who are going to implement changes need to see and understand for themselves, so it is they who should make the visits to other firms which are benchmarked and have the discussions with the concerned people. Further the visits should be short and the working teams small.

(iii) **Exchange information :** You should be ready to exchange information and provide answers in turn to any questions you might ask another company.

(iv) **Legal concerns :** Avoid legal problems which might arise as a result of discussions that might imply price fixing, market allocation or other illegal activities. This could lead to problems. Do not expect to learn much about new products of competitors by the benchmarking process. Most benchmarking missions focus on existing products, business practices, human resources and customer satisfaction.

(v) **Confidentiality :** Respect the confidentiality of data obtained. Companies that agree to share information with you may strongly object if that information leaks out to a competitor.

Five Phases of Benchmarking

The five phases of benchmarking are :

(i) **Planning :** Identify the product, service or process to be benchmarked and the firm(s) to be used for comparison, determine the measures of performance for analysis and collect the relevant data.

(ii) **Analysis :** Determine the gap between the firm's current performance and that of the firm(s) benchmarked and identify the causes of significant gaps.

(iii) **Integration :** Establish goals and obtain the support of managers who must provide the resources for accomplishing the goals.

(iv) **Action :** Develop cross-functional teams of those most affected by the changes, develop action plans and team assignments, implement the plans, monitor progress and recalibrate benchmark as improvements are made.

(v) **Maturity :** Leadership position attained and practices fully integrated into processes.

Benchmarking Phases Explained

It is important to have a general understanding of the generic phases of benchmarking process and some understanding of their rationale. The benchmarking process consists of five phases viz. 1. Planning phase, 2. Analysis phase, 3. Integration phase, 4. Action phase and 5. Maturity phase.

Exhibit 2.2 **shows the 5 phases, 10-step benchmarking process.**

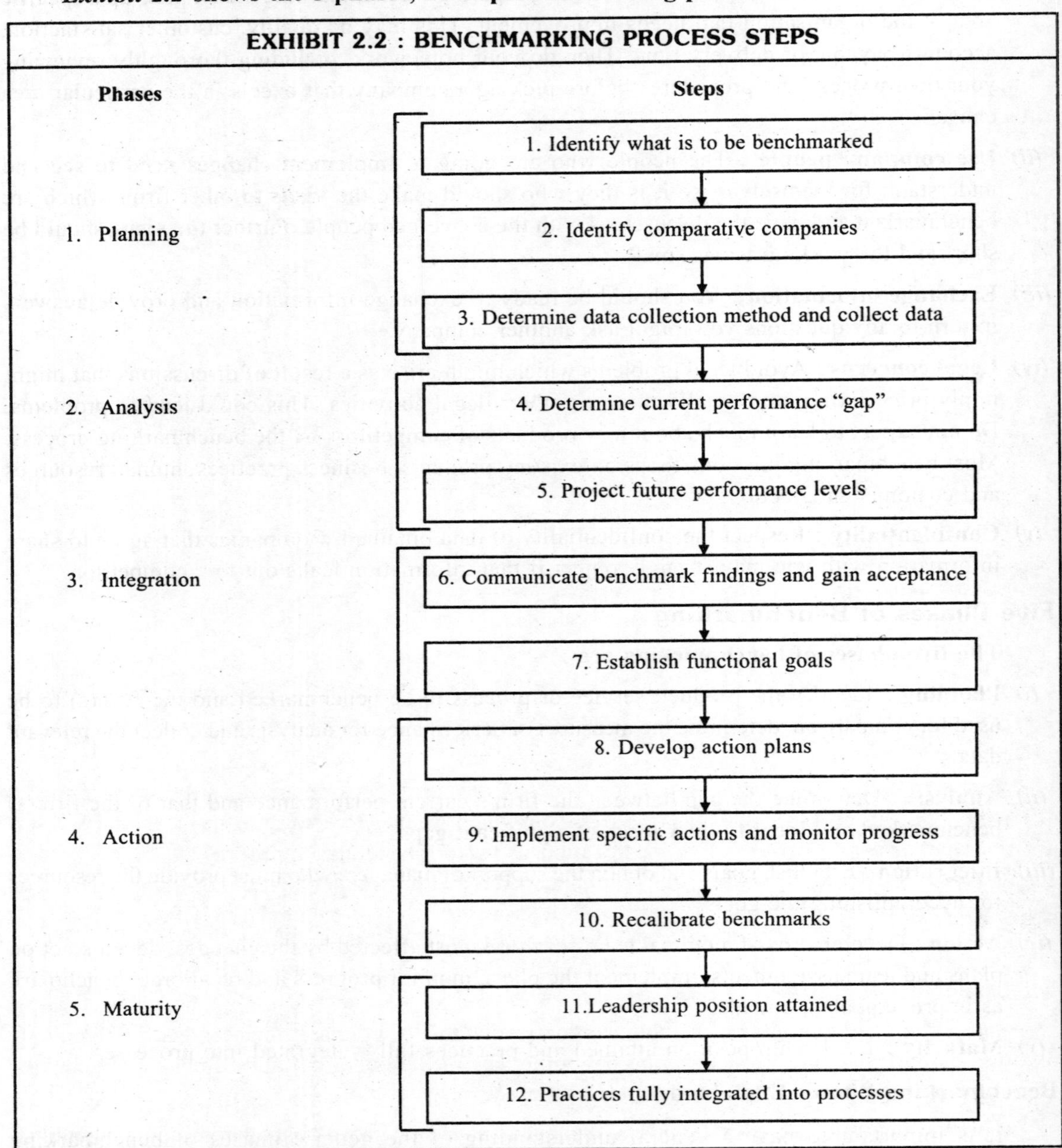

1. Planning Phase

The objective of this phase is to plan for the benchmarking investigations. The essential steps are:

***(i)* What is to be benchmarked?** Every function of a business has or delivers a product. The product is the output of the business process of the function, whether a physical good, an order or a shipment, an invoice, a service or a report. Benchmarking is appropriate for these and all other products. The products therefore must be first determined.

***(ii)* To whom or what will compare?** There are business to business, direct product competitors. These are certainly prime candidates to benchmark. But they are not enough. Benchmarking must be conducted against leadership companies and business functions regardless of where they exist.

***(iii)* How will the data be collected?** There is a process for benchmarking investigation. There are an infinite variety of ways to obtain required data and most data are readily and publicly available.

What will be important is to recognise that benchmarking is a process not only to derive quantifiable metric goals and targets but more importantly to investigate and document those best industry practices which permit achievement of goals and targets.

A benchmarking study should focus on practices and methods.

2. Analysis Phase

After determining what, how and who is to be benchmarked, actual data collection and analysis must be accomplished.

The analysis phase must involve a careful understanding of current process practices as well as those of benchmarking partners. The benchmarking process is a comparative analysis. What is desired is an understanding of internal performance on which to assess strengths and weaknesses. **The questions to be answered are:**

(i) Is the benchmarking partner better? *(ii)* Why are they better? *(iii)* By how much? *(iv)* What best practices are being used now or anticipated? *(v)* How can their practices be incorporated or adapted for implementation?

Answers to these questions will be the dimensions of any performance gap; negative, positive or parity. The gap provides an objective basis on which to act to close the gap or capitalise on a positive one. The gap however is the projection of performance and therefore will be one which changes as industry practices change. What is needed is not only understanding of today's practices but where performance will be in the future. It is important that benchmarking be a continuous process so that performance is constantly recalibrated to ensure superiority.

3. Integration Phase

Integration is the process of using benchmark findings to set operational targets for change. It involves careful planning to incorporate new practices in the operation and to ensure benchmark findings are incorporated in all formal planning processes.

The first step is to gain operational and management acceptance of benchmark findings. Findings must be clearly and convincingly demonstrated as being correct and based on substantive data. Credible data can be supported by deriving data and information from several sources to support the findings. Based on the findings action plans can then be developed.

Benchmarking findings must be communicated to all organisation levels to obtain support, commitment and ownership. The key to the communication approach will be the conversion of benchmark findings into a statement of operational principles to which the organisation can subscribe and by which actions for change will be judged. These principles place the organisation on notice that they are the rules by which the organisation will improve itself to meet customer needs and eventually to attain superiority.

4. Action Phase

Benchmarking findings and operational principles based on them must be converted into action. They must be converted into specific implementation actions and a periodic measurement and assessment of achievement must be put in place. People who actually perform the work tasks are most capable of determining how the findings can be incorporated into the work processes.

In addition, any plan for change should also contain milestones for updating the benchmark findings themselves, since the external practices are constantly changing. Therefore provision should be made for recalibration. Also an ongoing reporting mechanism is needed. Progress toward benchmark findings must be reported to all employees. This feedback is necessary to those who assist with the implementation. They will want to know how they are performing.

5. Maturity Phase

Maturity will be reached when best industry practices are incorporated in all business processes, thus ensuring superiority. Superiority can be tested in several ways. In some instances services are sold to external customers in addition to serving the internal customer. If the now-changed process were to be made available to others would a knowledgeable businessperson prefer it? That becomes a powerful confirmation of a benchmark. Needless to say if other companies benchmark your own internal operations that also would be confirmation.

Maturity also is achieved when it becomes an ongoing, essential and self-initiated facet of the management process. It becomes institutionalised. It is done at all appropriate levels of the organisation and not by specialists. While knowledgeable specialists may exist to consult on the most productive approaches for benchmarking, only when the focus on external practices becomes the responsibility of the entire organisation will benchmarking truly have achieved the objectives of ensuring superiority through incorporation of best industry practices.

How to Get Started in Benchmarking

To get started in the process of benchmarking there are some proven first steps. One must determine **what to benchmark,** assuming there is agreement that the next steps will be directed to gathering available data. This may come from library research and contacting internal personnel and sources. **Those shown in *Box 2.1* Quick Reference Guide are easily initiated approaches and should be done early in benchmarking investigation.** The Quick Reference Guide gives initial target areas to turn to in these starting steps.

The focus of the second area of investigation is more external and on a specific function or area of interest. The information comes from periodicals about functions, service bureaus that offer services surrounding the function and consultants who are knowledgeable about the function. Initial contact with these external sources starts the process of ensuring that all available public information is covered and relevant information is documented.

BOX 2.1 : QUICK REFERENCE GUIDE : HOW TO GET STARTED IN BENCHMARKING

A. Information Sources- Getting started

- Focus on an area / element that needs to be pursued.

  Examples: *(i)* Order entry, *(ii)* Service dispatching, *(iii)* Warehouse storage.
- Contact a Business Library
  - Request a search of information produced in the last three to five years for your topic of interest.
  - Library will identify articles / sources from
    - *(i)* External reports
    - *(ii)* Public magazines
    - *(iii)* Industry journals
    - *(iv)* Annual reports
- Contact Internal experts
  - Market research
  - Competitive analysis
  - Functional experts
- Survey Internal Reports/ Studies
  - Special studies
  - Surveys
  - Market research

B. Information Sources- specific/Functional

- Subscribe / Monitor Trade Periodicals
- Professional Associations
  - Newsletters
  - Seminars
  - Bibliographies
  - Special libraries
- Service Agencies/ Bureaus in the Business Function
  - Ask if they can share anonymous experiences from their client companies
    - *(i)* Industry practices or methods
    - *(ii)* State-of-the-art methods/ practices
- Consulting Firms
  - Functional experts
  - Ask if they are aware of particular breakthroughs/ practices in a special area
- Industry experts
  - Department heads of non-competitors
  - Teachers / professors at schools/ universities
- Systems Software Development and Hardware Vendors
  - Ask about their experiences working in your functional area

Does Benchmarking work for All Organisations?

Studies at Ernst & Young LLP prove that benchmarking works well for organisations classified as "Winners" and "Survivors", but not for those classified as "Losers". ***Exhibit 2.3* shows the distribution of organisations according to performance as "Winners", "Survivors" and "Losers".**

EXHIBIT 2.3 : DISTRIBUTION OF ORGANISATIONS ACCORDING TO PERFORMANCE

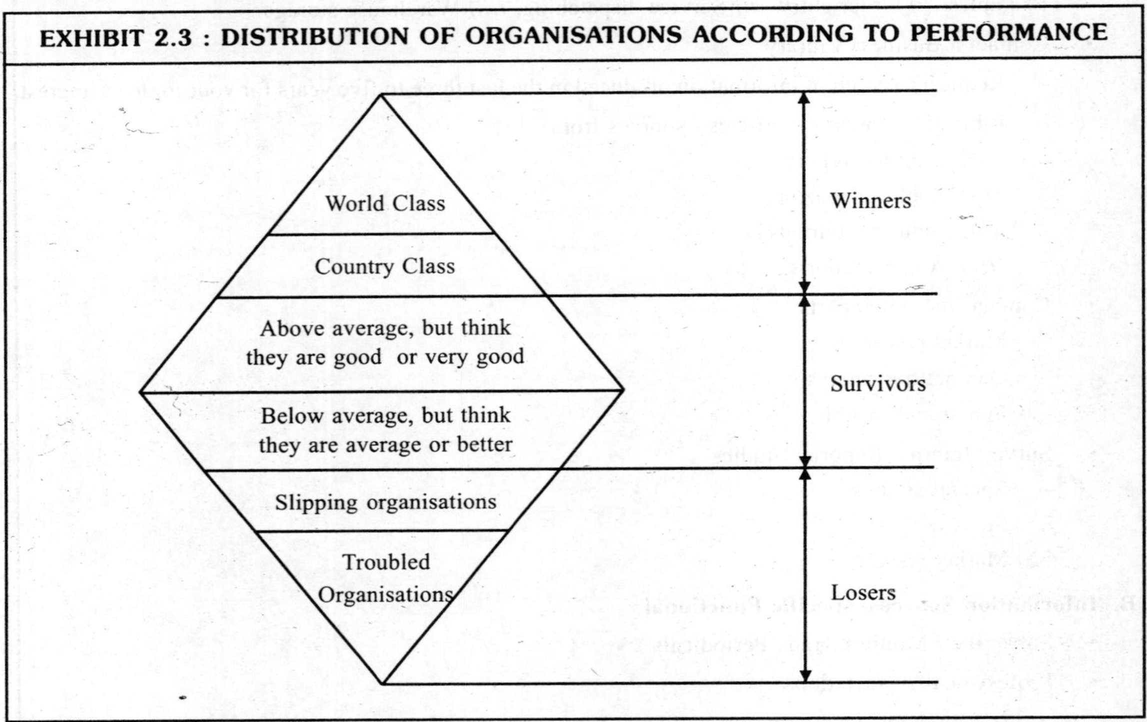

Available data suggest that it can be hazardous for organisations classified as "Losers" to use benchmarking. In fact best-practices process benchmarking can be detrimental to loser organisations, because they need to pay attention to the basics and today's problems rather than focusing on being country class or world class.

Country-class organisations are defined as the top 10 percent in the country in which the benchmarking organisation is located.

World-class organisations are the top 10 percent of the organisations in the world. 50 percent of all organisations are below average. This does not mean that those organisations are not meeting customer requirements. In fact most of them are and some of them are even making a profit doing business at the present time.

***Exhibit 2.4* shows the 10 steps to becoming the "best of the best"** (step 10). There can only be one **"best of the best"** for every benchmark item. Most organisations can consider themselves a success if they reach either step 6 or 7. A few of the very best organisations will reach step 8 or 9 and that one very special organisation will reach step 10. The benchmarking process is designed to help organisations move up this **"stairway to success"**.

EXHIBIT 2.4 : THE STAIRWAY TO SUCCESS

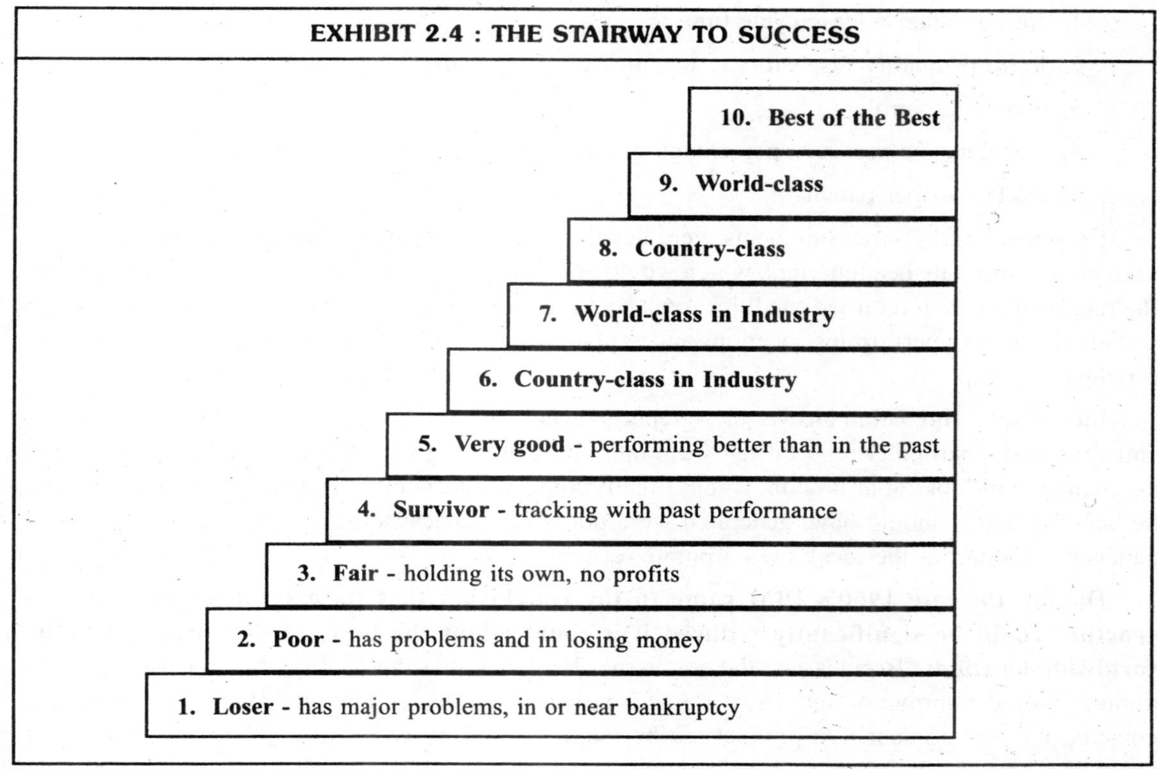

History of the Benchmarking Process

From a product stand point, benchmarking has been used since the early 1900s to understand how the competition was building its products and how well the competitor's product functioned. The Japanese brought the benchmarking concept to new heights after World War II when they toured the world, benchmarking all the best organisations. For the first time the focus was not on product, but on process. The Japanese didn't call it benchmarking, they called it **"industry tours"** - But the process was the same:

1. Research published data to define the best
2. Contact the best and schedule a visit
3. Visit the best and carefully select pertinent data
4. Return home and adopt the lessons learnt in the Japanese organisation to gain competitive advantage.

1. IBM: IBM began its **internal benchmarking activities** in the early 1960s because it saw a great deal of variation in performances among locations. To get the process started, IBM established key indicator measurements for each function (development engineering, product engineering, personnel, quality assurance, accounting, customer engineering etc.).

Once a year, key measurements were reported to corporate head quarters. Typical measurements included:

1. New product release cycle time
2. Ratio of quality inspectors to manufacturing operators
3. Span of control
4. Maintenance cost as a percentage of equipment cost
5. R&D cost per patent

Between 8 and 16 measurements were developed per function and these measurements were turned in to corporate headquarters, which would analyse and plot the data to compare all locations. The reports were then returned to all locations and the locations that had a negative gap were asked to study the better –performing locations and explain to corporate head quarters what could be done to reduce this gap.

Individuals who had to answer these reports faced many challenges. Unfortunately, the people who answered a particular report often spent more time defining why they were different and could not change than looking at how they could really improve. Although the program did some good, the benefits that it should have generated were not realised because of lack of follow-through on management's part at the local and corporate levels.

During the late 1960's IBM came to the conclusion that its overall production cost structure could be significantly reduced if it could adopt the best existing practices at its worldwide locations. Besides just the cost issue, IBM saw that the quality and consistency of its products would improve dramatically. To accomplish this plan, a corporate directive was written requiring all process-sensitive products to be manufactured by compatible processes. The result was a corporate wide effort to have common practices at all IBM plants. If this plan proved impractical, then at the very least, processes had to be compatible among locations, thereby ensuring interchangeability of product at any point within the process. IBM gained a significant international competitive advantage through its ability to determine the best production processes internally and adopt them as the corporate standard.

2. Xerox: In the late 1970s, Xerox decided to follow IBM's example by comparing its US products with those of its Japanese affiliate, Fuji-Xerox. Management was humbled to learn that Fuji-Xerox was selling copiers at a price equivalent to what it cost US-Xerox simply to manufacture the copiers. The initial benchmarking program was so successful that management later incorporated it as a fundamental element in Xerox's worldwide improvement efforts.

This improvement process was so pronounced that **Xerox is often credited as being the forerunner of the benchmarking movement**. In Xerox's program, benchmarking took on new dimensions. As techniques were applied to areas beyond product processes, such as support processes, Xerox discovered that benchmarking could be used in any area of the organisation. The company went beyond benchmarking itself or even its competition, and opened the sphere of potential benchmarking partners to any organisation that performed a similar activity. Benchmarking was a major contributor to stopping Xerox's declining market share and initiating a comeback.

3. Motorola and Beyond: Today many organisations have built upon the works of such early pioneers as IBM and Xerox and have used benchmarking to help drive their continuous improvement efforts. One shining example is Motorola, which cites **benchmarking as one of the major tools**

powering its improvement process. In 1988, Motorola received the prestigious Malcolm Baldrige Award for its quality improvement efforts. Benchmarking played a significant role in the Malcolm Baldrige Award examining committee's decision.

Some of the other organisations that are deeply involved in the benchmarking process are: 1. Alcoa, 2. Allied Signal, 3. AT&T, 4. Bell Atlantic, 5. Boeing, 6. Caterpillar, 7. Digital equipment Corporation, 8. Du Pont, 9. Eastman Kodak, 10. Florida Power & Light, 11. Hewelt-Packard, 12. Hughes Aircraft, 13. John Deere, 14. L.L.Bean, 15. Johnson & Johnson, 16. Milliken, 17. NCR, 18. Procter & Gamble, 19. 3M and 20. Wallace.

BOX 2.2 : BENCHMARKING IN PRACTICE – TOYOTA BENCHMARKS GENERAL MOTORS

In 1959, General Motors was the world leader in the automobile industry and Toyota was just a small supplier to the Japanese domestic car market. At that time, the founder of Toyota sent his son Eliji Toyoda, to the United States on a mission to study American manufacturing processes and practices. During his visit, Eliji Toyoda visited General Motors, Chrysler, Ford and even Studebaker, He took extensive notes describing all that he saw. No detail was too small for his attention. Also during his visit, Toyoda visited American supermarkets where he was impressed by the speed and precision with which glocers restocked their shelves at night so that supplies were replenished in time for customers to shop during day-time hours. The observations and insights from Toyoda's study visits were transported back to Japan, where they were adopted, adapted and improved. As history has recorded, these visits planted the seeds for what would develop into Toyota's now famous just-in-time total quality control program. Toyota launched its U.S. presence on the West Coast and then expanded across the country. During the next three decades, the Japanese car maker flexed its muscles and began challenging the far larger American competitors. By 1983, Toyota captured 23 percent of the US auto market. In the same year, Eliji Toyoda became chairman of Toyota. In 1984, General Motors signed a joint venture agreement with Toyota to manufacture Toyota products in the United States. "I am convinced that GM's main reason for this joint venture is to see how Toyota runs a factory" observed vice president of the Boston Consulting Group at the time. The wheel had turned a full circle. Now General Motors was studying Toyota to learn about its winning strategies.

POINTS TO REMEMBER

- Benchmarking has a **proven concept** that defines how the organisation can **close the gap** between its **own** performance and the performance of its very best **competitors**.
- The **art** of systematically defining the best systems, processes, procedures and practices is called **benchmarking**.
- The benchmarking process can improve an item's (product or process) performance by as much as 60 percent in less than 12 months.
- Being the very best in any field is a difficult and lonely road to travel.
- The benchmarking process helps you to know your organisation understands its competition, defines the best processes and integrates them into your business activities.
- Benchmarking is a powerful tool that provides the organisation with **measurements** of how products, equipments, people, services and processes can perform.

- Is benchmarking **ethical**? Of course, benchmarking is **legal** and **ethical** if it is done correctly without resorting to industrial espionage or studying competitor's information.
- The essence of **benchmarking** is "the continuous process of comparing a company's strategy, products and processes with those of world leaders and best-in-class organisations in order to learn how they achieve excellence and then setting out to match and even surpass it".
- Benchmarking is **"moving from where we are to where we want to be"**.
- Benchmarking promotes a thorough understanding of the company's **own** processes.
- Benchmarking process involves **initiation** and **adaptation** of the practices of superior competitors rather than **invention,** thereby saving **time** and **money** for the company practicing benchmarking.
- Benchmarking enables comparison of **performance measures** in different dimensions, each with best practices for that particular measure.
- Benchmarking focuses on **performance measures** and processes and not on products.
- Benchmarking allows organisations to set realistic, rigorous **new performance targets**.
- Benchamarking allows organisations to define **specific gaps** in performance and select the processes to improve.
- Benchmarking provides a basis for **training human resources**.
- **Limitations of benchmarking are:**
  - *(i)* Best-in-class performance is not a **static** but a **moving target**.
  - *(ii)* Benchmarking is not a **panacea** that can replace all other quality efforts.
  - *(iii)* Benchmarking is not an **"instant pudding"**.
- **Four major types** of benchmarking are:
  - *(i)* Internal benchmarking
  - *(ii)* External benchmarking - competitive benchmarking, technical/product benchmarking.
  - *(iii)* Industry benchmarking - Functional benchmarking, process benchmarking, performance benchmarking, best-practice benchmarking.
  - *(iv)* Generic benchmarking.

  Other types include:

  (i) Formal benchmarking, *(ii)* Informal benchmarking, *(iii)* Co-operative benchmarking, *(iv)* Collaborative benchmarking, *(v)* Strategic benchmarking, *(vi)* Best-in-class benchmarking, *(vii)* International benchmarking, *(viii)* World-class benchmarking, *(ix)* Financial benchmarking, *(x)* Energy benchmarking, *(xi)* Metric benchmarking.
- **Specific areas to benchmark at the operating level include:** *(i)* Customer service levels, *(ii)* Inventory management, *(iii)* Inventory control, *(iv)* Purchasing, *(v)* Billing and collection, *(vi)* Purchasing practices, *(vii)* Quality process, *(viii)* Warehousing and distribution and *(ix)* Transportation.
- **General guidelines to benchmarking include :** *(i)* Do not go on a fishing expedition, *(ii)* Use company people, *(iii)* Exchange information, *(iv)* Legal concerns, *(v)* Confidentiality.
- **Five phases of benchmarking are:** *(i)* Planning, *(ii)* Analysis, *(iii)* Integration, *(iv)* Action and *(v)* Maturity.

- **Planning phase includes the following steps**
  - *(i)* Identify what is to be benchmarked
  - *(ii)* Identify comparative companies
  - *(iii)* Determine data collection method and collect data.
- **Analysis phase includes the following steps**
  - *(i)* Determine current performance gap
  - *(ii)* Project future performance levels
- **Integration phase includes the following steps**
  - *(i)* Communicate benchmark findings and gain acceptance
  - *(ii)* Establish functional goals
- **Action phase includes the following steps**
  - *(i)* Develop action plans
  - *(ii)* Implement specific actions and monitor progress
  - *(iii)* Recalibrate benchmarks
- **Maturity phase includes the following steps**
  - *(i)* Leadership position attained
  - *(ii)* Practices fully integrated into processes
- Studies prove that benchmarking works well for organisations classified as **"winners"** and **"survivors"** but not for those classified as "losers".
- **History of the benchmarking process**
  - Benchmarking has been used since the early 1900s, to understand how the competition was building its products and how well the competitor's product functioned.
  - **IBM** began its internal benchmarking activities in the early 1960s. During the late 1960s, **IBM** came to the conclusion that its overall production cost structure could be significantly reduced if it could adopt the best existing practices at its world-wide locations.
  - In the late 1970s, **Xerox** decided to follow IBM's example by comparing its US products with those of its Japanese affiliate, Fuji Xerox.
  - **Xerox** is often credited as being the fore runner of the benchmarking movement.
  - **Motorola** cites benchmarking as one of the major tools powering its improvement process. Benchmarking played a significant role in Motorola's success in winning the 1988, Malcolm Baldrige National Quality Award.

REVIEW QUESTIONS

1. Is benchmarking legal and ethical? Justify your answer.
2. What is the essence of benchmarking?
3. What are the basic elements of benchmarking?
4. Trace the evolution of benchmarking.

5. Briefly discuss the major categories or types of benchmarking.
6. Distinguish between
   (a) Formal and informal benchmarking
   (b) Co-operative and collaborative benchmarking
   (c) Internal and external benchmarking
   (d) Process and functional benchmarking
7. Write short notes on:
   (a) Competitive benchmarking
   (b) Product benchmarking
   (c) World-class benchmarking
   (d) Performance benchmarking
   (e) Metric benchmarking
   (f) Best-practices benchmarking
   (g) Generic benchmarking
8. Briefly discuss the five phases of benchmarking and the steps involved in each of the five phases.
9. Does benchmarking work for all organisations? – Discuss.
10. Outline the history of the benchmarking process.

DISCUSSION QUESTIONS

1. "Benchmarking is a powerful process for improving your competitive position" Do you agree or disagree? Justify your answer.
2. The essence of benchmarking is "moving from where we are to where we want to be". Explain.
3. "Internal benchmarking is the starting point and would always be considered before any organisation looks to the outside". Why? Elaborate.
4. "Product benchmarking is commonly known as reverse engineering or competitive product analysis" - Discuss
5. "Benchmarking is not a fad, but a winning business strategy. It is a new way of doing business" – Explain.

CHAPTER 3

The Benchmarking Process

INTRODUCTION

Benchmarking itself is a process. You do not use it to prove you are the best at something but *to learn how to become the best.* Benchmarking by itself does not improve performance, it provides information you can use to improve. It is a discovery process aimed at exceeding customer expectations.

Many companies built their quality improvement process on tools, one of which was benchmarking. These companies made benchmarking a primary tool because they believed benchmarking could help them progress further, faster and more efficiently toward their goals.

In the US, benchmarking has been driven substantially by the Malcolm Baldrige National Quality Award, in which the need for benchmarking is a stated requirement in the application criteria. The Baldrige criteria ask how your quality and operational performance results compare to those of competitive and world-class companies, and how you use benchmarking to encourage break-through approaches. The need for benchmarking is evident throughout the award criteria. Directly or indirectly, benchmarking affects upto 50 percent of the award's scoring and therefore is seen as a critical quality tool. Several large firms which applied for the Baldrige award, expecting to be successful and were not, received feed back indicating that their applications showed little evidence of benchmarking. The result has been a substantial increase in interest about benchmarking. But the basic reason for exploring and pursuing benchmarking has always been the drive to be competitive.

In typical internal assessments conducted against the Baldrige award criteria, companies are often concerned about several categories including, outstanding efforts and results, effective integration and sustained results, and national and world-class leadership. It is obvious that without effective benchmarking of both products and processes, as well as the resulting performance goals, units or organisations would not know whether they had achieved those levels of performance.

Many credit the Baldrige Award program with bringing benchmarking to people's attention. The Baldrige criteria ask how your quality and operational performance results compare to those of competitors and world-class companies, and how you use benchmarking to encourage breakthrough approaches. Early Baldrige Award winners (Motorola, Milliken and Xerox) showed how companies could borrow from world-class benchmarks to meet ambitious stretch goals.

Focus on the Business Process

Until recently benchmarking has been pursued to address concerns that may have resulted from customer feedback, the cost base, a desire to reduce error rates, high asset levels, the need to improve cycle times or the like. In benchmarking circles, this approach has been referred to as ***problem-based benchmarking***. It means reacting to some problem and finding effective solutions through benchmarking. Generally, this was the right approach for the earliest applications of benchmarking. A business had problems and benchmarking was used to find innovative solutions to those problems. This was the primary basis for learning benchmarking.

During the past several years, through some extensive benchmarking efforts, leading - edge firms have come to realise that there is a better way to focus benchmarking activities for greater pay back. Firms that have a defined mission, set of objectives, and in particular, focused priorities have found that they need a vehicle to ensure that there will be continuous improvement toward these goals. The most effective vehicle is the concentration on and improvement of, the ***business processes*** that contribute to the goals, that is the ***basic processes*** on which the businesses run. These processes may include ***order taking, order processing, product servicing, billing*** and ***collection***. It is the concentration on the improvement of the business processes that will deliver the outputs that will achieve the results - the firm's objectives, priorities and mission. This is a new, important, and revolutionary perspective for benchmarking. Now benchmarking has a specific, defined role that directly supports and markedly contributes to the goals of the firm. If best practices are found and implemented in the ***basic business processes***, then there is a direct contribution to the firm's priorities and its results from benchmarking. Insightful firms recognise that results will only be obtained by changing the processes. That is, it is only by improving ***key business processes*** by incorporating best practices in them that will achieve results. Thus ***process-based benchmarking*** is ***result-based benchmarking.***

Business processes and ***work-processes*** are not the same. Work processes are those that are entirely within the control of a single function and can be changed as such. Business processes are those cross-functional processes critical to the organisation's success. Benchmarking the work or subprocesses will only lead to sub-optimization and failure to achieve the major improvements envisioned by the culmination of re-engineering and benchmarking.

It is the focus of benchmarking on the business process that had come to be accepted as the correct approach for benchmarking. Then it is the process benchmarking, not problem-based benchmarking, that is needed.

What is Benchmarking Process?

Benchmarking can be described as a ***structural process***. The structure of the benchmarking process is often provided by the development of a step-by-step process model. **Very simply, the benchmarking process involves:**

- Deciding ***what*** will be benchmarked.
- Deciding the items to ***compare.***
- Developing ***measurements*** to compare.
- Defining ***internal sites*** and ***external organisations*** to benchmark.
- ***Collecting*** and ***analysing*** data.

- Determining the ***gap*** between your item and the best item.
- Developing ***action plans***, ***targets*** and ***measurement*** processes.
- Updating the benchmarking effort.

The overall benchmarking task can be broken down into two major processes: *(i)* the ***user process*** and *(ii)* the ***management process***.

The ***user*** process is the 10 or n-step process that is used to complete a benchmarking investigation. Alcoa has a nine-step process, Xerox has a ten-step process, AT & T has a 12-step process, IBM a five-phase, 14 steps process and so on.

Table 3.1 **lists the steps in various benchmarking models.**

TABLE 3.1 : BENCHMARKING PROCESS MODELS

Activity	4 step	6 step	7 step	8 step	10 step
• Planning the study	• Prepare to benchmark	• Plan	• Determine functions or process to benchmark • Identify key performance variables • Identify best-in-class companies	• Determine business issue • Define what to benchmark • Define benchmark measures • Determine who to benchmark	• Identify process • Identify Partner
• Collecting process data	• Research process	• Research • Observe	• Measure Performance	• Acquire data	• Collect data
• Analysing data for results	• Document best practices	• Analyse	• Compare performance and estimate gaps	• Compare performance • Identify actions to close the gap	• Determine gap • Project future performance
• Adapting for improvement	• Report and implement	• Adapt • Improve	• Specify improvement programs and actions • Implement and monitor results	• Implement improvements and monitor results	• Gain support • Set goals • Develop plans • Implement plans • Recalibrate benchmarks

The management process is everything else that has to be done to ensure that benchmarking is effectively pursued. There are before, during and after activities that enhance the user process and infact, ensure its success, whereas the user process by itself may be seen to be necessary but not sufficient. There are specific activities for establishing a benchmarking program prior to the pursuit of the user process, there are supporting activities that take place during the exercise of 'n' steps and there are sustaining activities that are concurrent with and follow the completion of the user process. **These are shown in *Exhibit 3.1*.** These activities add to the overall effectiveness of benchmarking.

The user process is the process followed by the benchmarking team to complete its project. The management process includes those actions that management does to ensure that the team's operation is successful and that benchmarking has some performance. It includes creating the environment so that new ideas are pursued to improve business processes, providing training and support, prioritizing the direction of and encouraging the implementation of, the benchmarking findings.

EXHIBIT 3.1 : BENCHMARKING PROCESSES AND PHASES

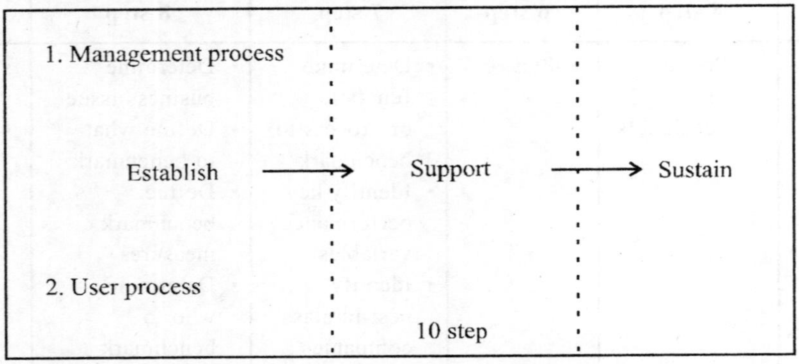

1. Management process

Establish ⟶ Support ⟶ Sustain

2. User process

10 step

Managing the Benchmarking Process

The purpose of benchmarking is to break the paradigm of not being able to learn from others.

The purpose of benchmarking is to:

(i) **Analyse the operation:** Benchmarking firms must asses the strengths and weaknesses of their current work processes, analyse critical cost components, consider customer complaints, spot areas for improvement and cycle time reduction, and find ways to reduce errors and defects or to increase asset turns.

(ii) **Know the competition and industry leaders:** Benchmarking firms must find out who is the ***"best of the best"***.

(iii) **Incorporate the "best of the best":** Benchmarking firms must learn from leaders, uncover ***"where they are"*** and ***"where they are going"***, learn the leaders', superior practices and why they work, and emulate the best practices.

(iv) **Gain superiority:** Benchmarking firms must try to become the new benchmark for other firms:

Benchmarking is an integral part of the planning and ongoing review process to ensure a focus on the external environment and to strengthen the use of factual information in developing plans.

Benchmarking is used to improve performance by understanding the methods and practices required to achieve worldclass performance levels.

Benchmarking's primary objective is to understand those practices that will provide a competitive advantage, target setting is secondary.

Scope of Benchmarking

Benchmarking is the search for and implementation of *best practices.*

Best practices are those methods or techniques that result in increased customer satisfaction when incorporated into your operation. There are no lists or databases of universally accepted best practices for a given industry, function or process. Some practices are clearly better than others, otherwise there would be no reason to benchmark. But what makes a given practice better than another depends on the criteria used to evaluate the practice. *For example,* some practices will be better than others based on impact on cycle time, others may standout if evaluated on cost, reliability, ease of use or simplicity.

A practice only has worth to a company when it measurably contributes to customer satisfaction for the process that the company is benchmarking. Therefore, the criteria a company should use in choosing a practice is the impact on customer satisfaction that the practice will have.

The adoption or adaptation of the best practices allows an organisation to raise the performance of its products, services and business processes to leadership levels.

Benchmarking performance measurements are useful means to identify organisations whose performance is significantly better and who, therefore, may have best practices. The real benefits of benchmarking however, comes from understanding the practices that permit the performance and the reasoned transfer to the organisation.

Therefore benchmarking should be conducted on the following:

1. **Products and services:** This would establish those features and functions desired by customers that are used in product planning, design and development normally expressed as product goals and technology design practices.
2. **Business processes:** These would become the basis for ***business process improvement*** and ***reëngineering***. These should be an integral part of an overall continuous quality improvement initiative that supports achievements of organisational goals and objectives.
3. **Performance measures:** The result of benchmarking products, services and processes is to establish and validate objectives for the vital few performance measures that guide the organisation. Therefore all planning and operational reviews should require presentation of benchmarks and should discuss progress toward the benchmarks as a standard agenda item.

Types of Benchmarking

There are five types of benchmarking. They are:

(i) **Internal benchmarking:** This is a comparison among similar operations within one's own organisation.

(ii) **External competitive benchmarking:** This is the comparison to the best of the direct competitors.

(iii) **External industry (compatible) benchmarking or functional benchmarking:** This is the comparison of methods to compare with similar processes in the same function outside one's industry.

(iv) **External generic (transindustry) benchmarking:** This is a comparison of work processes to others who have innovative, exemplar work processes.

(v) **Combined internal and external benchmarking:** This is the most frequently used approach which usually produces the best results.

***Table 3.2* shows a comparison of the different benchmarking types:**

TABLE 3.2 : A COMPARISON OF DIFFERENT BENCHMARKING TYPES

Benchmarking Type	Cycle time for future-state solution	Benchmarking Partners	Results
Internal	3-4 months	Within the organisation	Major improvements
External-competitive	6-12 months	None	Better than the competition
External-industry	10-14 months	Same industry	Creative break through
External-generic	12-24 months	All industries worldwide	Changes the rules
Combined internal and external	12-24 months	All industries world wide	Best-in-class

Setting Benchmarking Partner Limits

Setting some limitations on the organisations to be benchmarked will provide meaningful results at lower cost, however. Some restrictions that may be considered are:

(i) ***Customer requirements:*** High quality and reliability, or low quality, one time usage.

(ii) ***Product characteristics:*** Size, shape, weight, environment etc.

(iii) ***Output usage:*** Broad industrial categories, not specific products, grocery industry, office products industry, electronics industry, transportation industry and so on.

The benchmarking process can be applied to a product, a process, a subprocess, or even an industrial activity. Xerox has actively applied the benchmarking process at all levels.

Focus Levels in Benchmarking

1. **Strategic focus:** In a strategic focus, benchmarking is concentrated on strategic competitive strengths and weaknesses. It is used to understand and develop competitive product and service strategies, to establish goals for product performance, service, customer support levels, asset usage and financial ratios and to develop key practices that will achieve the strategic goals. Strategically focused benchmarking is typified by technology direction, industry trends, investment selection, and basic competitive product and service offerings.

2. **Operational focus:** In an operational focus, benchmarking is used to understand specific customer requirements, to understand the best practices to achieve customer satisfaction by improving internal work processes, and to determine operational performance levels required

to become the vendor of choice in the eyes of the customer. Operationally focused benchmarking concentrates on the workprocesses through which continuous improvement is delivered by incorporating best practices in the work steps.

Approaches in Benchmarking

Two approaches are: *(i)* Problem-based approach and *(ii)* Process-based approach.

In a ***problem-based approach***, if there is no specific plan for benchmarking, then the activity is characterised as uncontrolled. Thus, it is often pursued on a problem-by-problem basis, as troubles occur.

In a ***process-based approach*** to benchmarking, as organisations mature in their pursuit of quality and continuous improvement they often realise that the benchmarking activity must be managed. The most successful approach is to apply benchmarking activities to the vital few business processes.

Understand the Difference between Benchmarking and Benchmarks

- Benchmarking is a process or activity whereas a benchmark is an industry standard.
- Benchmarking is a continuous process of measuring a company's products, services and practices against its toughest competitors or those companies known as industry leaders.
- Benchmarking is a standard process used to evaluate success in meeting customer requirements.
- Benchmarks may be descriptive, as the description of a best industry practice. They may be converted to a performance measurement that shows the effect of incorporating or adopting the practice.
- Benchmarks may be quantitative or performance measurements. There can be benchmarks for all goals or objectives such as customer satisfaction, employee motivation and satisfaction, quality and cycle time and business results.

Benchmarking Process Model

The structure of the benchmarking process is often provided by the development of a step-by-step process model.

Process models have two basic attributes that make them useful when used appropriately. They provide **structure** and a **common language**.

Structure: Like the frame of a house, a process model provides the basic framework for action. Within that framework all types of variations are possible and the process can be tailored to fit the specific requirements of the individuals, groups and organisations that use it. Any type of benchmarking process model should provide an adequate framework for the successful planning and execution of a benchmarking investigation. In addition, it should be flexible enough to encourage people to modify the process to suit their needs and project requirements.

A Common Language

Ideally, models provide maps of action and behaviour that can be understood by anyone in an organisation. These maps specify logical sequences of activity that, when followed, produce the desired result - in this case a successful benchmarking investigation. The model can help interpret any terminology that is required to use the process.

The various process steps or stages of a model also help to establish a common language among users. Process steps help define clusters of related activities or tasks. *For example,* the IBM benchmarking model consists of five phases and total of fourteen steps. If an IBM employee from the corporate office in New York is talking to another IBM employee in a division in Minnesota and states that he is in phase two of the benchmarking process, the Minnesota employee knows exactly what kinds of activities have already taken place and what specific activities are currently under way and what specific activities still need to be done. The benchmarking model has provided a special language that enables these employees to communicate effectively about a process that may be relatively new to them.

Benchmarking Process Model of Alcoa USA

The number of steps in the benchmarking process model tends to vary from company to company. **A team at Alcoa spent several months studying the Xerox process and developed its six-step process:**

1. Decide what to benchmark
2. Plan the benchmark project
3. Understand your own performance
4. Study others
5. Learn from the data
6. Use the findings

Ameritech's benchmarking process has four phases and eight steps.

Phase 1: Project conception and planning

Step 1: Project conception

Step 2: Project planning

Phase 2: Internal and external data gathering and partner selection

Step 3: Defining internal processes and performance

Step 4: Selecting benchmarking partners

Step 5: Collecting benchmarking partners' data

Phase 3: Analysis and assessment

Step 6: Comparing internal processes with partners' processes

Phase 4: Recommendations and action

Step 7: Recommendations and implementation

Step 8: Recalibration

The Formal 10-step Benchmarking Process

Exhibit 3.2 **shows the formal 10-step benchmarking process and a descriptions of each of the five phases of the process are illustrated in** ***Box 3.1.***

EXHIBIT 3.2 : 10 STEP - 5 PHASE BENCHMARKING PROCESS

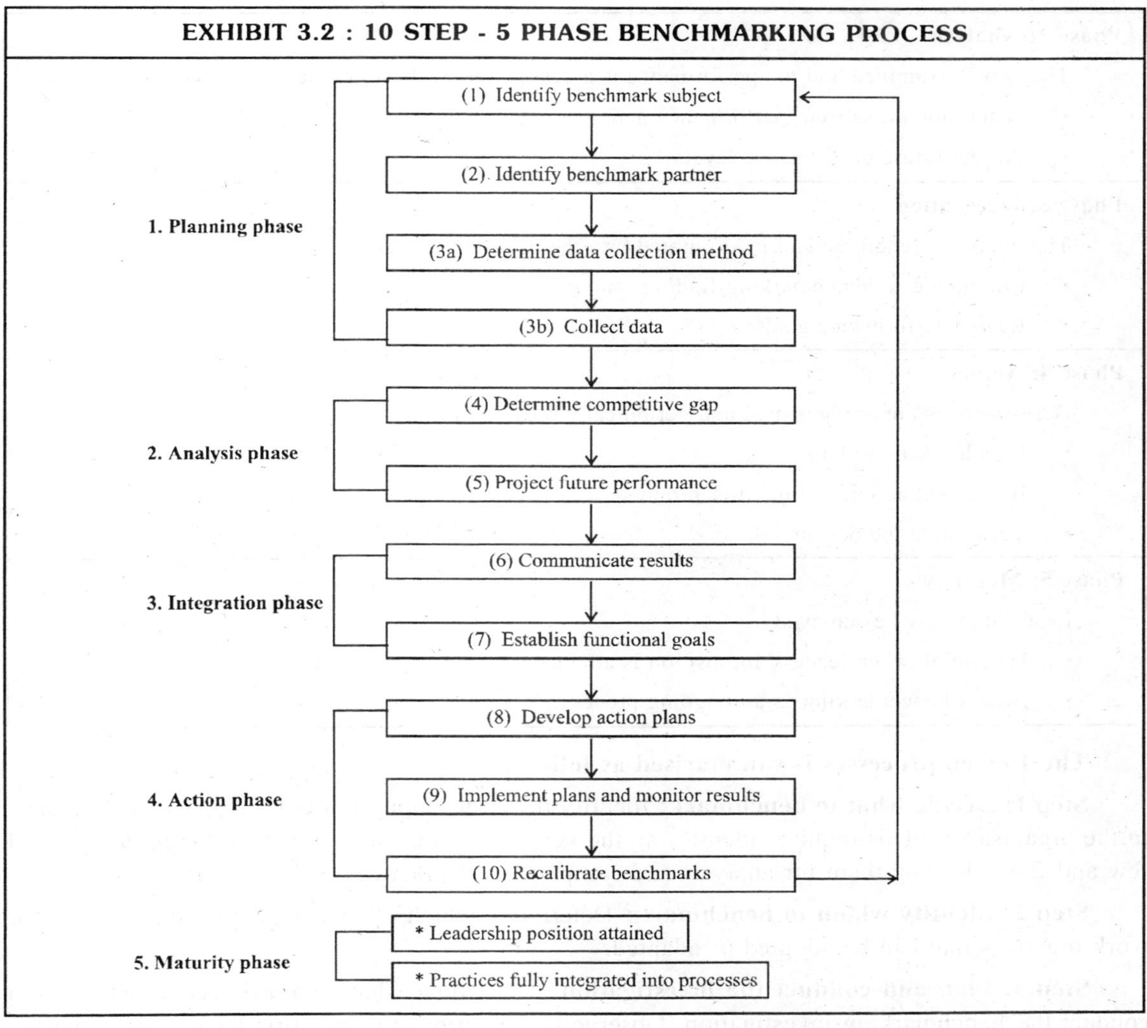

BOX 3.1 : THE FIVE PHASES OF THE BENCHMARKING PROCESS

1. **Planning:** Identify what to benchmark, identify whom to benchmark and gather data.
2. **Analysis:** Examine the performance gap and project future performance.
3. **Integration:** Communicate the findings and develop new goals.
4. **Action:** Take actions, monitor progress, and recalibrate measures as needed.
5. **Maturity:** Achieve the desired result.

Phase 1: Planning : A plan for benchmarking is prepared:

- Decide what to benchmark
- Identify whom to benchmark
- Plan the investigation and conduct it
  - Gather necessary information and data
  - Observe the best practices

Phase 2: Analysis
The gap is examined and the performance is assessed against best practices. • Determine the current performance gap • Project future performance levels
Phase 3: Integration
The goals are redefined and incorporated into the planning process. • Communicate benchmarking findings and gain acceptance • Revise performance goals
Phase 4: Action
Best practices are implemented and periodically recalibrated as needed. • Develop action plans • Implement action and monitor progress • Recalibrate the benchmarks
Phase 5: Maturity
Leadership may be achieved • Determine when leadership position is attained • Assess benchmarking as an ongoing process

The 10 step processes is summarised as follows:

Step 1: Decide what to benchmark: Identify the largest opportunity to improve performance in the organisation. This requires identifying the key work processes, prioritising them to the vital few and flow-charting them for analysis and comparison of practices.

Step 2. Identify whom to benchmark: Determine, which other companies employ superior work practices that can be adopted or adapted.

Step 3. Plan and conduct the investigation: Determine what data are needed and how to conduct the benchmarking investigation. Observe the superior practices first hand. Document the best practices found.

Step 4. Determine the current performance gap: After completing the benchmarking investigation and observation, decide how much better the best practices are than the current work methods.

Step 5. Project future performance levels: Decide how much the performance gap will narrow or widen in the near future and what repercussions this has for the organisation.

Step 6. Communicate benchmarking findings and gain acceptance: Communicate the findings to all those who have a need to know in order to gain acceptance and commitment.

Step 7. Revise performance goals: Convert findings into operational statements that describe what is to be improved based on implementation of the best practices in the business process.

Step 8. Develop action plans: Create specific implementation plans, measurements, assignments and timetables for taking action on the best practices.

Step 9. Implement specific actions and monitor progress: Implement the plan and report progress to key process owners and management.

Step 10. Recalibrate the benchmarks: Continue to benchmark and update work practices to stay current with ongoing industry changes. Determine where the organisation is in its quality pursuit and the implications for benchmarking.

Benchmarking Processes Adopted by Some Typical Companies

Specific steps in benchmarking vary from company to company but the fundamental or basic approach is the same. One company's benchmarking may not work at another organisation because of differences in their operating concerns. Successful benchmarking reflects the culture of the organisation, works within the existing infrastructure and is harmonious with the leadership philosophy.

Motorola Inc., winner of the Malcolm Baldrige Award for 1988, uses a *five step* benchmarking process :

(i) ***decide*** what to benchmark

(ii) ***select*** companies to benchmark

(iii) ***obtain*** data and collect information

(iv) ***analyse*** data and form action plans and

(v) ***recalibrate*** and start the process again.

AT&T, which has two Baldrige winners among its operating units uses a *nine step* process:

(i) Project conception : Identify the need and decide what to benchmark.

(ii) Planning *:* Determine the scope and objectives and develop a benchmarking plan.

(iii) Preliminary data collection : Collect data on industry, companies and similar processes as well as detailed data on your own processes.

(iv) Best-in-class selection : Select companies with best-in-class processes.

(v) Best-in-class collection : Collect detailed data from companies with best-in-class processes.

(vi) Assessment : Compare your own and best-in-class processes and develop recommendations.

(vii) Implementation planning : Develop operational improvement plans to attain superior performance.

(viii) Implementation : Enact operational plans and monitor process improvements.

(ix) Recommendations : Update benchmark findings and assess improvements in processes.

Xerox divided its initial benchmarking procedure into ***ten steps*** but other experts have noted successful programs based on as few as four defined stages. What matters is not the number of steps but that all necessary actions are completed in the benchmarking process. ***Exhibit 3.3* shows one common format for this process.**

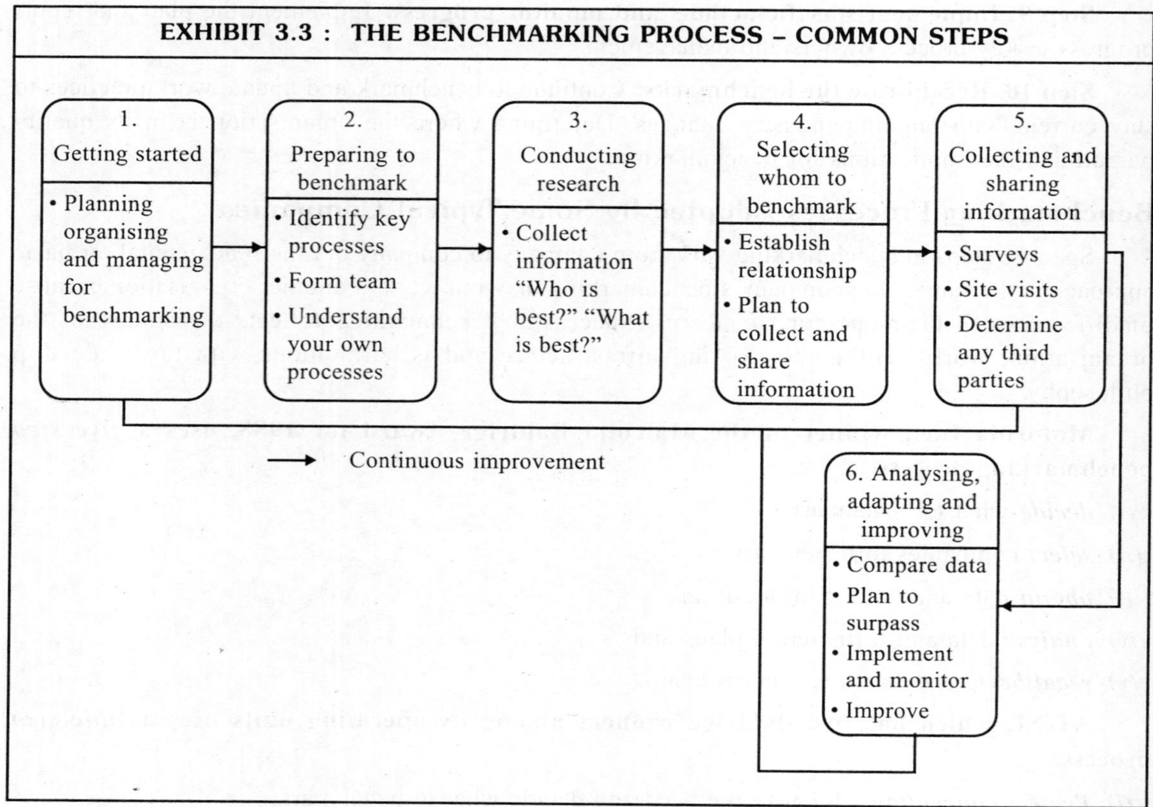

The Seven Step Benchmarking Model

Benchmarking is an ongoing process that requires data gathering, goal setting and analysis. These are accomplished by a seven step model. The seven steps are :

Step 1 : Identify what to benchmark

Step 2 : Determine what to measure

Step 3 : Identify who to benchmark

Step 4 : Collect the data

Step 5 : Analyse data and determine the gap

Step 6 : Set goals and develop action plan and

Step 7 : Monitor the process.

What each step includes is illustrated in *Table 3.3* shown below.

TABLE 3.3 : SEVEN STEP BENCHMARKING		
Step	**Activity**	**What is included**
1.	Identify what to benchmark	*(i)* Clarify the benchmarking objective *(ii)* Decide whom to involve *(iii)* Define the process *(iv)* Consider the scope *(v)* Set the boundaries *(vi)* Agree on what happens in the process *(vii)* Flow-chart the process.
2.	Determine what to measure	*(i)* Examine the flow chart *(ii)* Establish the process measures *(iii)* Verify that measures match objectives
3.	Identify who to benchmark	*(i)* Conduct general research *(ii)* Choose level to benchmark
4.	Collect data	*(i)* Use a questionnaire *(ii)* Conduct a benchmarking site visit
5.	Analyse data and determine the gap	*(i)* Quantitative data *(ii)* Qualitative analysis
6.	Set goals and develop an "Action Plan"	*(i)* Set performance goals *(ii)* Develop an Action Plan
7.	Monitor the process	*(i)* Track the changes *(ii)* Make benchmarking a habit.

The steps listed above are discussed in the following paragraphs:

Step 1 : Identify what to Benchmark?

Benchmarking can be a very powerful vehicle for driving peak process performance. But if the approach to benchmarking is not targeted, well-planned or organised, it can be a very costly investment of resources with minimal return on investment.

The first step which keeps the efforts of the company focussed involves the following sub-steps:

(i) Clarify the benchmarking objective
(ii) Decide whom to involve
(iii) Define the process
(iv) Consider the scope
(v) Set the boundaries
(vi) Agree on the process and
(vii) Flow-chart the process.

These sub-steps are detailed below:

(i) **Clarify the benchmarking objective :** Benchmarking decision may be driven by any one or more of the following factors :

- *An* organisation-wide strategy, setting priorities for improvement.
- The need to address a specific problem that requires immediate attention.
- A new business requirement (a new product line or a modification to the existing one).
- Not meeting goals in previous attempts to improve a process.

(ii) **Decide whom to involve :** After deciding what to benchmark, decide who will be on the team. Even though benchmarking can be done individually, best results typically come from team effort. The team members are selected on the following considerations:

- It is critical for management to be actively involved with the team.
- Include employees involved with the day-to-day flow of the process and
- Include employees who have an interest in and knowledge about what goes on just outside the boundaries of the process.

(iii) **Define the process :** The process should be clearly defined. A process is a series of interrelated tasks that are organised to produce an output. An output might include a product or a service. ***It is important to know as much about your process before you benchmark it against another organisation's process.***

(iv) **Consider the scope :** The scope should not be ***too broad*** or ***too narrow***. If the scope of your focus is too large, you might not be able to tackle it effectively. *For example,* benchmarking the ***"human resources function"*** at another organisation might be too broad in scope. A narrower focus, such as the "recruiting and interviewing process" is more realistic.

If the scope is too narrow, your benchmarking efforts might miss important opportunities. *For example,* benchmarking the "prospective employee interview scheduling process" might miss critical information and opportunities not related to this narrow focus.

(v) **Set the boundaries :** Every system is made up of separate and distinct processes. Boundaries of each process can be defined by identifying its inputs and outputs. Boundaries exist at the point where inputs are received from internal suppliers and outputs go to internal customers. Defining the boundaries more specifically will make you more successful in improving the process. You will be better able to stay focussed, make plans and stay on track as you benchmark.

(vi) **Agree on the process :** Once your team has defined the process, you must agree on the tasks involved. It is a good idea to brainstorm the tasks first and put them in the right order later. The objective is to include all the major tasks in the process from start to finish.

(vii) **Flow chart the process :** A flow chart is a step-by-step picture of the tasks in your process. Use it as a ***"working document"*** to help define the process. Later, it can be used as the tool to continuously improve the process. The following symbols are used to draw the flow chart.

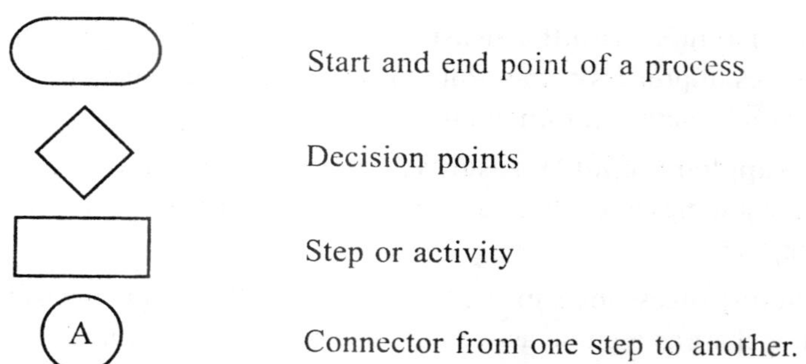

Step 2 : Determine what to measure

Once the process to be benchmarked has been defined, you are almost ready to look at similar processes in other organisations. Comparison of your processes with those in other organisations should be meaningful. This requires clear and accurate *measures* before looking at processes in other organisations.

There are three sub-steps included in determining the process measures. They are:

(i) Examine the flow chart

(ii) Establish the process measures and

(iii) Verify that measures match objectives.

These sub-steps are detailed below:

(i) **Examine the flow chart : Some of the measurable items might include:**

- Overall time to complete the process.
- Completion time at each individual task.
- Time spent at each decision point.
- Number of repeats.
- Variation of task time.
- Number of defects showing up.
- Costs and
- Scrap.

(ii) **Establish process measures**

(a) **Consider measures outside the process** – When deciding which measures to address in benchmarking a process, look outside the process itself. Consider measures of your external customer's requirements and measures of internal suppliers and customer's requirements. You can determine which measures should be benchmarked by identifying who your internal customers and suppliers are and determining which measures are important to them.

(b) **Comparing and selecting your benchmarking measures :** The effective approach to ensure that the measures you decide to benchmark are aligned with measures that are critical to your internal suppliers and customers has the following steps :

(a) **Determine customer "result" measures :** Interview your internal customer to create a list of measures of process output from the customer's perspective – use customer surveys and interviews to gather information.

(b) **Determine supplier "input" measures :** Create a list of measures to assess your supplier's inputs. These are measures that : are in use by you, should be in use by you or are in use by your supplier.

(c) **Brainstorm in-process measures :** Make a list of all possible measures for your process. Use the flow chart as a guide as well as reports and charts currently used in the process.

(d) **Link supplier and customer measures with in-process measures :** Match up the supplier and customer measures that relate directly to-process measures. Select measures to be benchmarked based on what is critical to the process and important for suppliers and customers.

(iii) **Verify that measures match objectives :** When deciding which measures to use, refer back and examine your original objectives. If you improve each benchmarked measure, then you should achieve your overall goals.

Step 3 : Identify who to Benchmark

The steps to be followed are:

(a) **Conduct general research :** Once you have identified "what to benchmark", find organisations to research. **Some sources of benchmarking information are :**

(i) Trade magazines

(ii) Industry publications

(iii) Professional journals

(iv) Market research

(v) Government studies

(vi) Computer databases

(vii) Telephone or mail surveys and

(viii) Benchmarking consultants.

At this point, search for benchmarking targets such as organisations that are recognised as the ***"industry best"*** in process, similar to yours. Since benchmarking has proven to be a very effective quality improvement tool, many large organisations have separate departments or teams setup specifically for benchmarking studies.

(b) **Choose the level to benchmark :** Out of the few organisations that have sparked your interest, narrow the list to most suitable choices for your process. Consider more than one organisation for benchmarking, keeping in mind the four levels *viz.* - internal, competitive, non-competitive and world-class.

Step 4 : Collect the data

Once you have identified the levels and organisations to benchmark, gather information on the performance level of your benchmarking targets and how they manage their processes to achieve these levels. **Three main sources of data are:**

(a) **Internal :** Data from past research available within the organisation (product studies, R & D research, market surveys, customer surveys or in-house surveys) are collected before moving on to information available from external sources such as public access resources and other companies.

(b) **Public Information :** Useful information can be found in public-access resources. Specific information may be collected from each source of information.

(c) **Other Companies :** It is exciting to actually go out and discover new ideas and make careful observations. However, it should be kept in mind that issues such as confidentiality and time constraints need to be carefully considered.

The benchmarking information from other organisations may be obtained by using questionnaires or by conducting a benchmarking site visit.

Step 5 : Analyse data and determine gap

(a) **Quantitative data :** Quantitative data collected can be analysed and plotted on graphs to identify the performance gap between your organisation and other organisations selected for benchmarking. **Some of the performance measures that are calculated are :** *(i)* average process time *(ii)* average down time per unit and *(iii)* average percent of reworks and the like.

Gap analysis is a step in benchmarking which is still growing and evolving advanced statistical techniques to get into the root of a process. However, the basic idea of benchmarking is to make comparisons between a process used in your organisation and in an organisation with a higher level of performance. This comparison or gap is measured to help you set and attain new standards for yourself.

(b) **Qualitative analysis : Some of the qualitative factors you should look for are:**

(i) ***System policies and practices – philosophy or approach used :*** employment level – level and experience of the staff.

Management – cooperative or distant, incentives used.

(ii) ***Procedural policies and practices :***

- Technology
- Task function and
- Method or process

(iii) ***Structural policies and practices***

- Budgeting
- Purchasing and inventory practices and
- Organisational structure.

Step 6 : Set goals and develop an action plan :

(a) **Set performance goals :** After carefully analysing the information and clarifying both the quantitative and qualitative gaps, you will need to set goals for your process. A goal is really a ***"desired state"***. It provides direction and a focus point. The following should be kept in mind while setting the goals :

- goals should be achievable in increments
- goals should be realistic
- goals must be measureable
- goals should be finite and
- goals should be supported.

The goal should be divided into steps. *For example,* if the goal is to decrease ***"turn around time"*** by 15 hours, this goal might be best achieved by decreases of three hours each month for five months.

Realistic goals should be set considering all the resources needed and available, *for example,* consider the issues such as time needed, resources, abilities, skills and budget.

Goals must be measurable in order to be attainable, that is measure the goal before, during and after implementation of the changes.

Goals should be finite, *i.e.* should have a set starting and ending point.

Goals should be supported by both the management and the people who are directly involved with the process.

(b) **Develop an action plan :** After establishing the goals to be accomplished and determining the time periods for completing them, an ***'action plan'*** has to be developed. **Two steps involved in creating an *'action plan'* are:**

(i) **Determine tasks, timeliness and responsibilities by:**

- dividing the goals into separate and measurable tasks and putting them in order.
- determining who is responsible for each task and setting target dates for the start and completion of each task.

(ii) ***Develop a contingency plan :*** This step is actually a ***"What if?"*** step – a contingency plan. Contingency plan is prepared to handle any unexpected problems or occurrences.

Step 7 : Monitor the Process

Once the action plan is in place and everyone is adjusting to all the new changes, it is necessary to monitor the process to keep the benchmarking effort alive. For this, it is important to :

- track the changes and
- make benchmarking a habit.

Track the changes

Tracking the changes requires that the following steps are implemented :

(i) Evaluate measures in increments.

(ii) Publish periodic benchmarking progress reports.

(iii) Hold regular progress meetings.

(iv) Monitor customers (internal and external).

(v) Monitor suppliers (internal and external) and

(vi) Implement benchmarking as an ongoing process.

Make benchmarking a habit

To understand the benefit from benchmarking, it has to be periodic and regular course in action. It should eventually become part of the total quality management system in your organisation.

To summarise, it may be stated that benchmarking is a process of discovering and adapting new and innovative practices to improve overall organisational effectiveness. It is also a ***"learning process"*** – learning and adapting new practices by establishing new goals and introducing new ideas. The seven steps discussed earlier not only guide you through the benchmarking process, but is the roadmap to your success.

Factors to be kept in mind to ensure success with benchmarking

(i) Benchmarking must have the ***full support of senior management***. Management should also be actively involved.

(ii) ***Training*** is critical for the benchmarking team and process.

(iii) Benchmarking should be a ***team activity***. The teams should include management, experts, consultants and especially those people directly involved in the process.

(iv) Benchmarking is an ***ongoing process***. It must be part of an organisation's strategy and development. If well monitored, it serves as an important segment of a total quality management system.

(v) Benchmarking efforts must be organised, planned and carefully managed. It is a ***structured approach*** and requires planning and monitoring just like any other management tool.

Ultimately, benchmarking can be your best weapon against complacency. Used correctly, benchmarking can lead you to the competitive edge in today's business market place.

BOX 3.2 : XEROX'S 10 STEP PROCESS IN BENCHMARKING

1. Identify what is to be benchmarked.
2. Identify comparative organisations.
3. Determine data collection method and collect data.
4. Determine current performance gap.
5. Project future performance levels.
6. Communicate benchmark findings and gain acceptance.
7. Establish functional goals.
8. Develop action plans.
9. Implement specific actions and monitor progress.
10. Recalibrate benchmarks.

BOX 3.3 : 21 STEPS IN BENCHMARKING PROCESS DEVELOPED BY IBM'S ROCHESTER, MINNESOTA FACILITY

1. Determine what to benchmark.
2. Identify key performance variables to measure.
3. Estimate the cost of benchmarking study and obtain management approval.
4. Select benchmarking team and provide training in the technique.
5. Complete a detailed analysis of the firm's own process or business practice.
6. Decide on methods such as phone surveys, mailed questionnaire, personnel visits or some combination.
7. Develop questions to ask through these methods.
8. Identify companies against which to benchmark.
9. Identify contacts within the companies.
10. Collect internal and public domain data on the appropriate companies, processes or business practices.
11. Analyse existing information to determine additional data needs.
12. Plan the specific methods for the benchmarking study.
13. Collect data by performing phone, mail or personal interviews as planned.
14. Analyse the data, projecting future performance levels of the benchmarked companies.
15. Develop recommendations from the study's conclusions.
16. Prepare an implementation plan and budgets for the recommendations.
17. Identify appropriate performance standards for supporting departments or functions in the new process.
18. Present the plan to management for approval.
19. Upon approval, communicate the plan and performance requirements to the supporting departments.
20. Implement the plan, monitor progress and conduct periodic management reviews.
21. Periodically, review market conditions to assure that goals and objectives remain valid.

Development of a Generic Benchmarking Process

During the early stages of development of benchmarking process for continuous improvement, many companies developed their own benchmarking process models, *for example,* the Xerox ten-step process, the Alcoa six-step process, the Florida power and light seven-step process and the AT&T nine-step process and so on. People interested in benchmarking interpreted the variety of models as a sign that the process was not yet well documented or understood.

A few people had attempted to isolate the common generic elements that typified the benchmarking processes that existed at the time. Unfortunately even these generic process models varied in the number of phases or steps they contained. Also, although these generic models summarised the types of activities that occurred at each phase, they often did not give the benchmarking professionals a hands-on process that they could take back to their organisations and implement. So there was a need to develop a generic model that would serve as a framework for action for people who wanted to implement benchmarking in their own organisations. It was necessary that a summary of lessons learnt from the premier benchmarking companies be used to develop a model that could provide a new benchmarker with a basic process map and a set of benchmarking do's and don'ts.

Requirements for a Successful Benchmarking Model

Four general guidelines emerged from the study involving interviewing two benchmarking experts in each of the twenty-four companies. They are:

1. **Follow a simple, logical sequence of activity:** Keep the process model as basic as possible. Do not add process steps for the sake of "numerical superiority". Fourteen steps are not necessarily better than six steps. The basic message is not about the terms ***steps*** or ***phases*** or the number of steps or phases, but about clarity. Clarity mans people should be able to describe the model to others and explain why each part of the process is important to the process user. Another aspect of clarity is the user's ability to understand the process and translate it into action.
2. **Put a heavy emphasis on planning and organisation:** The second requirement is a heavy emphasis on the planning and organising activities that occur before any actual contact is made with a benchmark partner. The type of activities included in this part of the process involve developing a clear understanding of the benchmarking "customer" requirements, procuring adequate resources (*i.e.,* people, time, funding), to enable the benchmarking team to fulfill its mission, selecting and briefing members of benchmarking teams, using effective project planning tools and techniques, developing specific information - gathering tools prior to actual data collection and establishing appropriate benchmarking protocols that define expected behaviour toward benchmark partners.
3. **Use customer-focused benchmarking:** Benchmarking is a process that produces information as a product. Successful organisations treat the benchmarking information product just as they would any other type of product. The product must meet customer requirements if it is to be accepted and used. In this sense, every benchmarking product has a customer or a set of customers. In some cases the customer is the person or team that actually performs the benchmarking analysis. In other cases it may be a manager who commissions a team to conduct a benchmarking analysis. There may be multiple customers for benchmarking information. Each customer, however has a set of requirements or expectations regarding the benchmarking information needed.

   A customer-focused benchmarking process places a heavy emphasis on establishing contact with benchmarking customers and using some type of formal process, protocol and information itself. This contact needs to be established very early in the benchmarking process. One of the key advantages of a customer-focused process is that it provides direction and creates a set of expectations regarding how the information is to be gathered, reported and used. This direction helps benchmarkers avoid wasting their efforts (and the efforts of their benchmark partners) during the course of their benchmarking investigation.
4. **Make it a generic process:** This means that the benchmarking process should be consistent within an organisation. Although there should be some flexibility in any process to accommodate some level of variation, there is no need for a unique benchmarking process model for every department, division or location in an organisation. Many organisations complain of internal

model wars. When different segments of the organisation try to develop their own "improved" versions of the process, they are often unwittingly creating barriers between one another. The result is a movement away from a common organisational benchmarking language.

The problems of multiple models within an organisation affects other aspects of benchmarking as well. Different models and approaches to benchmarking usually indicate the existence of different communications and training programs that must be developed and maintained by different segments of the company. The result is an inefficient use of organisational resources, redundancy of effort and confusion among employees who are confronted with a variety of different models within their own organisation. Another problem is confusion among the organisation's benchmark partners. When approached by different divisions or functions of the same company, benchmark partners should rightfully expect some level of consistency among the approaches used by the various subgroups.

The Five-stage Benchmarking Process Model

Exhibit 3.4 illustrates the five-stage benchmarking process.

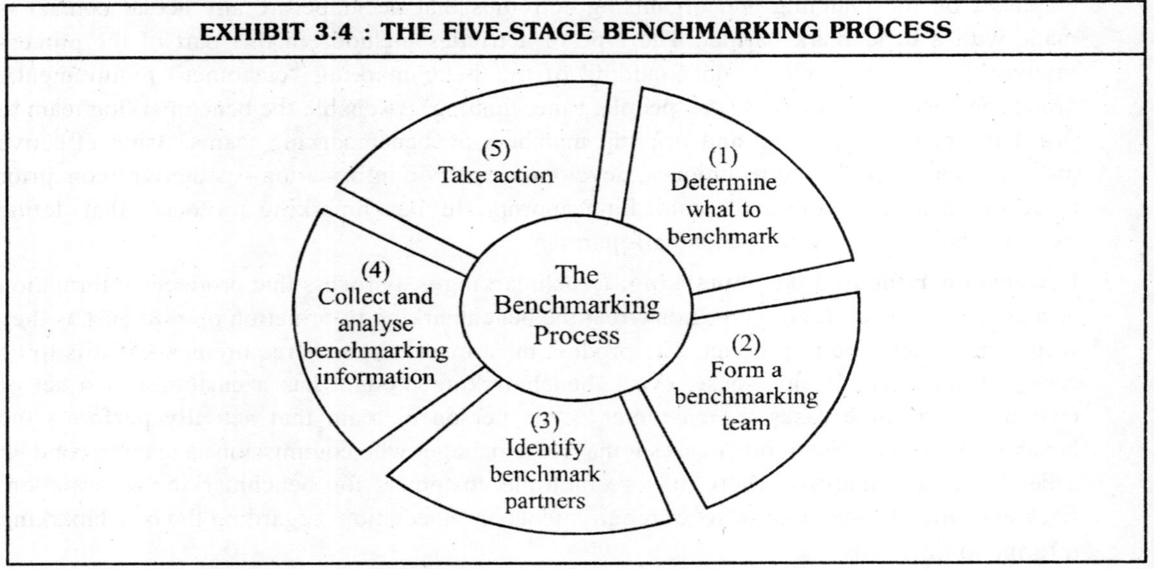

The five processes stages are:

1. **Determine what to benchmark:** The first stage of the process is to identify the customers for the benchmarking information and their requirements and define the specific subjects to be benchmarked. Once the subjects to be benchmarked and the customer requirements are known, the resources required (*e.g.,* time, funds, people) to conduct a successful benchmarking investigation can be identified and secured.

2. **Form a benchmarking team:** Although benchmarking can be conducted by individuals, most bench-marking efforts are team activities. The process of selecting, orienting and managing a benchmarking team is the second major stage of the benchmarking process. Specific roles and responsibilities are assigned to team members. Project management tools are introduced to

ensure that benchmarking assignments are clear to everyone involved and that key project milestones are identified.

3. **Identify benchmark partners:** The third stage of the process involves the identification of information sources that will be used to collect benchmark information. These sources include employees of bench-marked organisations, consultants, analysts, government sources, business and trade literature, industry reports and computerised data bases, to name just a few. Also included in this stage is the process of identifying industry and organisational best practices.
4. **Collect and analyse benchmarking information:** During this stage of the process, specific information - collection methods are selected. It is important that the people responsible for collecting information be proficient in these methods. Benchmark partners are contacted, and information is collected according to an established protocol and then summarised for analysis. Benchmarking information is analysed in accordance with the original customer requirements, and recommendations for action are produced.
5. **Take action:** This stage of the process is influenced by the original customer requirements and uses for the benchmarking information. The action taken may range from the production of a report or presentation to the production of a set of recommendations to the actual implementation of change - based, at least in part, on the information collected in the benchmarking investigation. Any next steps or appropriate follow-up activities are identified, including the continuation of the benchmarking process.

Why a Circular Model?

Most of the benchmarking process models are drawn as a flow chart. The use of flow chart makes sense, considering that it is a reasonable tool to use to illustrate a sequence of events. However most of the models include some form of directive in their final step or phase to **"recycle"** or **"recalibrate"**.

The implication is that benchmarking information needs to be reassessed periodically, in recognition of the fact that the products or processes being benchmarked are dynamic and will change over time. The basic message is to continue the benchmarking process as a way of doing business, constantly striving for improvement. However, flow charts project a process that has a beginning and an end. The only way to illustrate recycling on a flowchart is to draw a long line connecting the final box with one of the previous boxes in the model.

The message inherent in a model that advocates continuous improvement and recycling brings to mind a circular image. Although the five stages of the benchmarking process do not gain any special meaning by being drawn in a circle, the shape suggests continuity. The implication is that the process is active, it is moving, it is continuous.

SOME ISSUES RELATED TO BENCHMARKING PROCESS

1. **Focus of benchmarking :** A benchmarking exercise generally does not cover the entire range of another company's processes. ***Table 3.4*** **details some narrower focuses for typical benchmarking efforts.**

TABLE 3.4 : FOCUSES OF BENCHMARKING

Type of Benchmark	Focus	Teams	Guidelines
Product	Dissecting products	Designers, operations managers and manufacturing engineers	Requires no site visits and provides hard, historical and short-lived design information. Any process information only implicated.
Process	Manufacturing processes	Manufacturing engineers, specialists and operations managers	Requires site visits, focusses on specific functions and requires some humility
Best practices	Management processes	Staff and middle management	Combine visits and industry observations to look beyond an industry to combine process and management practices.
Strategic	Management directions	Top management	Long term and seldom based on site visits or sharing, but on personnel information and is very uncertain and subjective to other benchmarking efforts.

Other types

Tactical	–	Strategic focus not particularly industry specific
Industry	–	Focussed on general characteristics of an industry
Generic	–	Focussed on general, not industry specific, business practices
Competitive	–	Focussed only on head-to-head competitors
Functional	–	Isolates specific business or management functions
Performance	–	Focusses on numerical characteristics of specific products or processes.

2. **Gap analysis :** Benchmarking promotes a thorough understanding of the company's own processes. Intensive studies of existing practices may lead to identification of non value added activities and plans for process improvement. Benchmarking enables comparisons of performance measures in different dimensions each with the best practices for that measure. The comparison is not with one selected company, but with several companies who are best for the chosen measure. **The *"spider chart"* shown in *Exhibit 3.5* is used to compare multiple performance measures and gaps between the host company and industry benchmark practices.**

   Eight Performance Measures (PM) are being considered. The scales are standardised – between zero to 1, zero being the centre and 1 at the outer circumference of the circle which represents the most desired value. Best practices for each performance measure are indicated along with the companies that achieve them. The current performance of the company performing benchmarking (*i.e.* company A) is also indicated in the Exhibit. The difference between company A's level and that of the best practice for that performance is identified as the gap. The analysis that focusses on methods and processes to reduce this gap and thereby improve the company's competitive position is known as ***gap analysis***.

EXHIBIT 3.5 : SPIDER CHART FOR GAP ANALYSIS

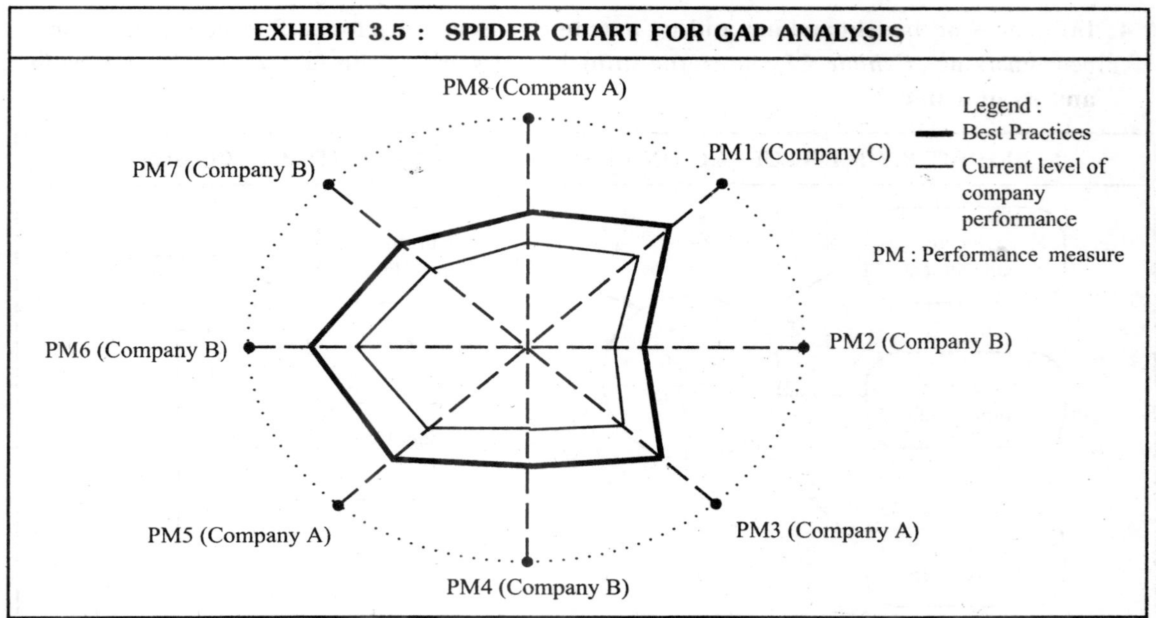

3. **'Hard' and 'Soft' systems in benchmarking process : *Exhibit 3.6* demonstrates how benchmarking brings the *'soft'* and *'hard'* systems together.** Benchmarking not only identifies best practices, but also seeks to determine how such practices can be adapted to the organisation. The real value of benchmarking is accomplished only when the company has successfully integrated the identified best practices into its operations. Meshing the 'soft' and 'hard' systems will complete this task successfully. The emerging organisational culture should empower employees to make decisions based on the new practice.

EXHIBIT 3.6 : ROLE OF BENCHMARKING IN IMPLEMENTING BEST PRACTICES

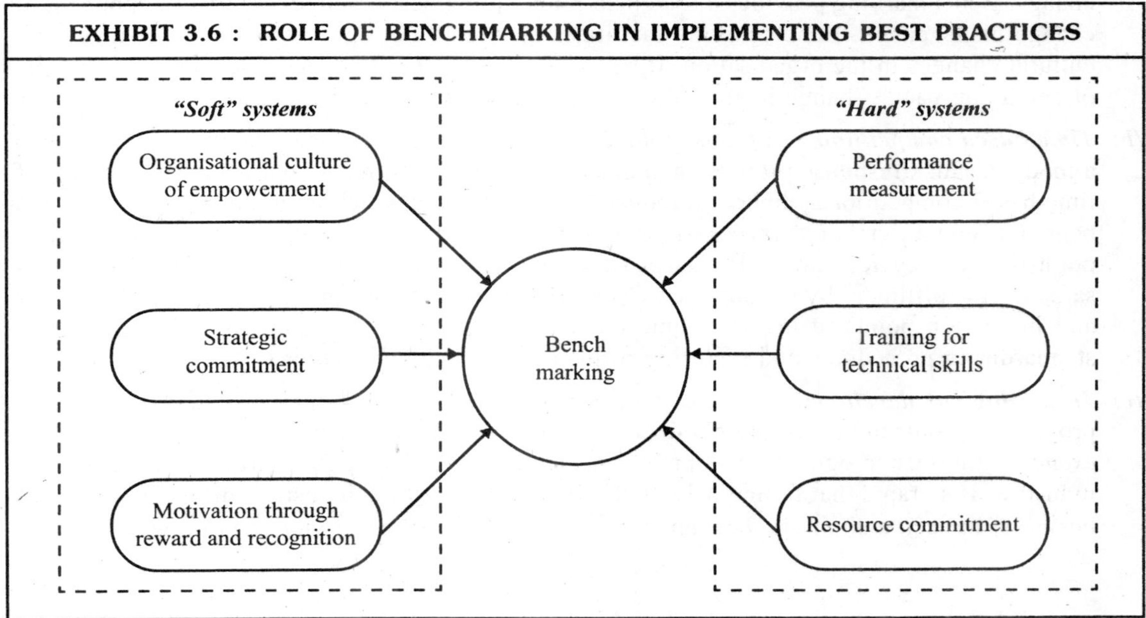

4. **Influences on benchmarking and its outcomes :** Several factors influence the adoption of benchmarking. ***Exhibit 3.7*** **shows the influence of some of the factors on benchmarking and its outcomes.**

EXHIBIT 3.7 : INFLUENCE ON BENCHMARKING AND ITS OUTCOMES

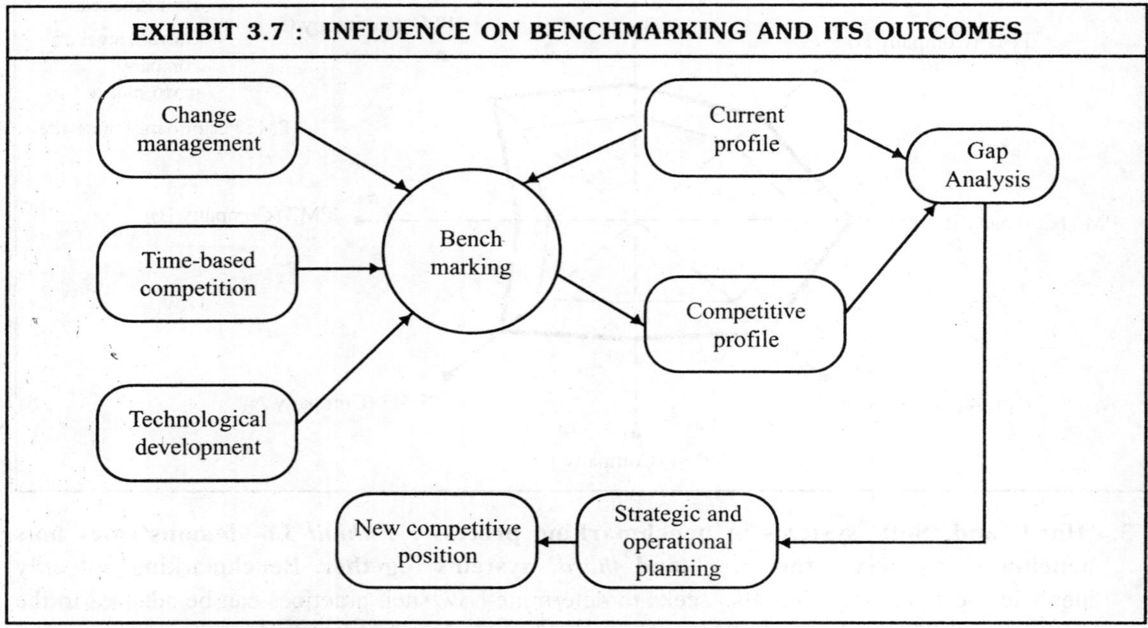

Some of these factors are detailed below:

(a) ***Change management :*** In the current environment of global competition, change is inevitable. Rather than reacting haphazardly to change, benchmarking helps in effectively managing the change. Benchmarking provides a road map for adopting best practices, a major component of change management. Benchmarking facilitates managing both process-oriented changes and cultural changes in the organisation. It helps in overcoming resistance to change by a people oriented approach. Change is not viewed as a threat but an opportunity.

(b) ***Time-based competition :*** In global competition, the ability to reduce process time and create a mode of quick response provides a distinct competitive advantage to a firm. The concept of time based competition is linked to reduction in ***cycle time*** which is the interval between the beginning and the end of a process which may involve a series of activities. From the customer's point of view, cycle time is the elasped time between placing an order by him/her and its satisfactory fulfilment by the supplier. Cycle time can be reduced by reducing decision points and inspection points, using electronic media for communication and flow of information, standardising procedures and reporting forms and consolidating purchases.

(c) ***Technological development :*** The rapid technological development nowadays leaves the progressive companies with no choice other than benchmarking the technology leaders. *For example,* the technological development in electronic and computer hardware and software industries is so rapid that falling behind the competition in these industries means going out of business. In such a situation, benchmarking is critical both for survival and growth.

BOX 3.4 : "BENCHMARKING QUALITY" – IN A NUTSHELL

Benchmarking means measuring one's performance against that of one's competitors.

Two definitions of benchmarking are:

(i) Benchmarking is the continuous process of measuring products and services against the toughest competitors or those companies recognised as industry leaders

(ii) Benchmarking is the search for industry best practices that lead to superior performance.

Competitive benchmarking is gaining importance in the light of increasing global competition. Setting one's priorities and being certain that those priorities are consistent with the needs of the market place are essential. The top five competitive priorities in Europe, Japan and the United States, in 1992 were as below:

Priority	Europe	Japan	United States
1	Conformance quality	Product reliability	Conformance quality
2	On-time delivery	On-time delivery	On-time delivery
3	Product reliability	Fast-design change	Product reliability
4	Performance quality	Conformance quality	Performance quality
5	Delivery speed	Product customisation	Price

The four types of benchmarking are:

(i) Product benchmarking
(ii) Functional or Process benchmarking
(iii) Best practices benchmarking and
(iv) Strategic benchmarking.

Product benchmarking refers to the practice of tearing down a competitor's product to see what can be learnt from its design and construction (also known as reverse engineering).

Functional benchmarking focusses on the process rather than on the product. Typical processes might be order entry, assembly, test, product development and shipping.

Best practice benchmarking is similar to functional benchmarking except that it focusses on management practices rather than on specific processes. Best practices might consider factors such as the work environment and salary incentives for employees in firms with exceptional performance.

Strategic benchmarking has a goal of considering the result of other benchmarking comparisons in the light of the strategic focus of the firm.

What is the purpose of benchmarking? : It is to ensure *continuous improvement* and is only one of the means of achieving this. Competitive benchmarking provides a means of learning from one's competitors.

Phases in benchmarking

(i) **Planning phase :**
- *(a)* Identify what is to be benchmarked.
- *(b)* Identify comparable companies
- *(c)* Determine data collection methods
- *(d)* Collect data.

(ii) **Analysis phase :**
- *(a)* Determine the current performance "gap"
- *(b)* Project future performance levels.

(iii) **Integration phase :**
- *(a)* Communicate benchmark findings and gain acceptance.
- *(b)* Establish functional goals

(iv) **Action phase :**
- *(a)* Develop action plans
- *(b)* Implement specific actions
- *(c)* Monitor progress
- *(d)* Recalibrate benchmarks.

(v) **Maturity phase :**
- *(a)* Determine when leadership position is attained
- *(b)* Assess benchmarking as an ongoing process

To evaluate, we may remember that ***benchmarking*** is a process of discovering and adapting new and innovative practices to improve overall organisation effectiveness. It is also a process of learning and adapting new practices by establishing new goals and introducing new ideas. It is to be kept in mind that the seven steps in the benchmarking process discussed earlier in this chapter are followed metriculously as a road map to success. This will enable a firm not only to match but to exceed competition and achieve total customer satisfaction.

BOX 3.5 : BENCHMARKING IN PRACTICE – THE AT&T UNIVERSAL CARD SERVICES STORY

AT&T Universal Card Services, the Visa and Master Card - issuing subsidiary was one of the world's best known companies and winner of a 1992 Malcolm Baldrige National Quality Award.

During Oscar night in 1990, AT&T introduced the Universal Card to the United States by kicking off a well-published advertising campaign : No annual fees for life, lower interest rates, a discount on AT&T long-distance calls and world-class service were just a few of the features offered to attract customers to the card. And attract customers they did. Within 78 days AT&T Universal Card Services had broken an industry record by signing up their one millionth account. By January 1992, they reached fifth place in the *Nelson Report's* ranking of top general - purpose credit cards by charge volume and by number of cards outstanding, which exceeded 12 million.

These were impressive results and not at all due to luck. The Universal Card Services Organisation was built through benchmarking in a methodical and strategically sound way. Many of the best minds in the business were hired from industry competitors, and with them came, collectively, a very clear picture of what it would take, both strategically and operationally, to be world-class competitor in the credit card industry. No annual fee, lower interest rates, long-distance discounts, and world-class customer service are just a few of the visible results of the benchmarking that built Universal Card Services. Supporting it all are world-class credit procedures, statementing, remittance processing, work station design and quality monitoring, to name of few of the areas in which Universal Card Services is world-class thanks to the knowledge of the industry's best that built the company. This was an extremely different set of circumstances from that which faced Xerox, but the end result was remarkably similar – a world class competitor in its industry.

POINTS TO REMEMBER

- Benchmarking itself is a **process**.
- Benchmarking by itself does not improver **performance,** it provides information you can use to improve.
- In the US, benchmarking has been driven substantially by the **MBNQ Award**, in which the need for benchmarking is a stated requirement in the application criteria.
- Many credit the Baldrige Award program with bringing benchmarking to people's attention.
- **Problem-based benchmarking** involves reacting to some problem and finding effective solutions through benchmarking.
- **Continuous improvement** can be achieved by improving the **key business processes** by incorporating **best practices** in them to achieve the results - firm's objectives/goals.
- **Process-based benchmarking** is **result-based benchmarking**.

- Business processes and work processes are not the same.
- **Business processes** are those cross-functional processes critical to the organisation's success.
- **Work processes** are those that are entirely within the control of a single function and can be changed as such.
- It is the **focus of benchmarking** on the business process that had come to be accepted as the correct approach for benchmarking.
- Benchmarking is a **structural process** – the structure of benchmarking process is often provided by a **step-by-step process model**.
- **Overall benchmarking task can be broken down into:**
  (i) The **user process** and *(ii)* The **managerial process**
- The **user process** is a 10 or 'n' step process that is used to complete a benchmarking investigation.
- **Benchmarking process** models may be a 4 step, 6 step, 7 step, 8 step or 10 step process models.
- The **management process** is everything else that has to be done to ensure that benchmarking is effectively pursued.
- The **user process** is the process followed by the benchmarking team to complete its project.
- The purpose of benchmarking is to break the paradigm of not being able to learn from others.
- **The purpose of benchmarking is to:**
  (i) Analyse the operation *(ii)* Know the competition and industry leaders
  (iii) Incorporate the "best-of-the-best" *(iv)* Gain superiority
- Benchmarking is the **search** and **implementation** of **best practices**.
- **Best practices** are those methods or techniques that result in increased customer satisfaction when incorporated into your operation.
- A **practice** has worth to a company when it measurably contributes to customer satisfaction for the process that the company is benchmarking.
- **Benchmarking performance measurements** are useful means to identify organisations whose performance is significantly better and who, therefore may have best practices.
- **Benchmarking should be conducted on:** *(i)* Products and services, *(ii)* Business processes and *(iii)* Performance measures.
- **Five major types of benchmarking are:**
  (i) Internal benchmarking
  (ii) External competitive benchmarking
  (iii) External industry (compatible) benchmarking or functional benchmarking
  (iv) External generic (trans industry) benchmarking
  (v) Combined internal and external benchmarking
- **Focus levels of benchmarking are:** *(i)* Strategic focus and *(ii)* Operational focus.
- **Two approaches to benchmarking are:** *(i)* Problem-based approach and *(ii)* Process-based approach.
- **Two basic attributes of process models are:** *(i)* Structure and *(ii)* A common language.
- **Structure** of a process model provides the basic framework for action.
- A **common language** among the users is provided by the maps of action and behaviour and the process steps or stages of the process model.

- Benchmarking process model for Alcoa, USA has a **six step** process whereas Ameritech's benchmarking process has **four phases** and **eight steps :**
- A formal benchmarking process has **five phases** and **ten steps.**
- Motorola Inc. uses a **five step** benchmarking process whereas AT & T uses a **nine step** process.
- **The seven step benchmarking model has the following steps:**

  Step 1 : Identify what to benchmark
  Step 2 : Determine what to measure
  Step 3 : Identify who to benchmark
  Step 4 : Collect the data
  Step 5 : Analyse data and determine the gap
  Step 6 : Set goals and develop action plan
  Step 7 : Monitor the process
- Benchmarking has to be periodic and regular course in action. It should eventually become **part of the total quality management** system in your organisation.
- Benchmarking is also a **learning process**, learning and adapting new practices by establishing **new goals** and introducing **new ideas.**
- **The five stage benchmarking process model has the following process stages:**

  (i) Determine what to benchmark
  (ii) Form a benchmarking team
  (iii) Identify benchmark partners
  (iv) Collect and analyse benchmarking information
  (v) Take action
- **Some issues related to benchmarking process include:**

  (i) Focus of benchmarking
  (ii) Gap analysis (spider chart)
  (iii) Hard and soft systems in benchmarking process
  (iv) Influences on benchmarking and its outcome.

  The factors that influence the adoption of benchmarking are:

  (a) Change management
  (b) Time-based competition
  (c) Technological development

REVIEW QUESTIONS

1. Distinguish between problem-based benchmarking and process-based benchmarking.
2. Discuss the purposes of benchmarking.
3. Discuss the scope of benchmarking.
4. What are the various types of benchmarking?
5. Make a comparison of different benchmarking types.
6. Discuss the focus levels in benchmarking.
7. Distinguish between benchmarking and benchmarks.
8. What is a benchmarking process model?
9. Describe the benchmarking process model of Alcoa.
10. Discuss the formal 10 step benchmarking process.
11. Describe the generic benchmarking process.
12. What are the five phases of benchmarking? Discuss.

13. Explain the seven step benchmarking model.
14. Discuss some of the important issues related to benchmarking process.

DISCUSSION QUESTIONS

1. "Process benchmarking is result-based benchmarking" - Discuss.
2. "The overall benchmarking task can be broken down into two major processes: *(i)* the *user* process and *(ii)* the *management* process. – Elaborate.
3. "The purpose of benchmarking is to break the paradigm of not being able to learn from others" – Explain.
4. "Benchmarking is the search for and implementation of best practices" – Critically examine this statement.
5. "Companies should not aim benchmarking solely at direct competitors and it would be a mistake if they do so" – Do you agree or disagree? Give reasons for your answer.

CHAPTER 4

Planning for Benchmarking

INTRODUCTION

Each of the three phases of benchmarking – planning, execution and implementation of benchmarking-based improvement – requires different skills to be done successfully. *Exhibit 4.1* illustrates the 8 step benchmarking process.

EXHIBIT 4.1 : BENCHMARKING - THE 8 STEP PROCESS

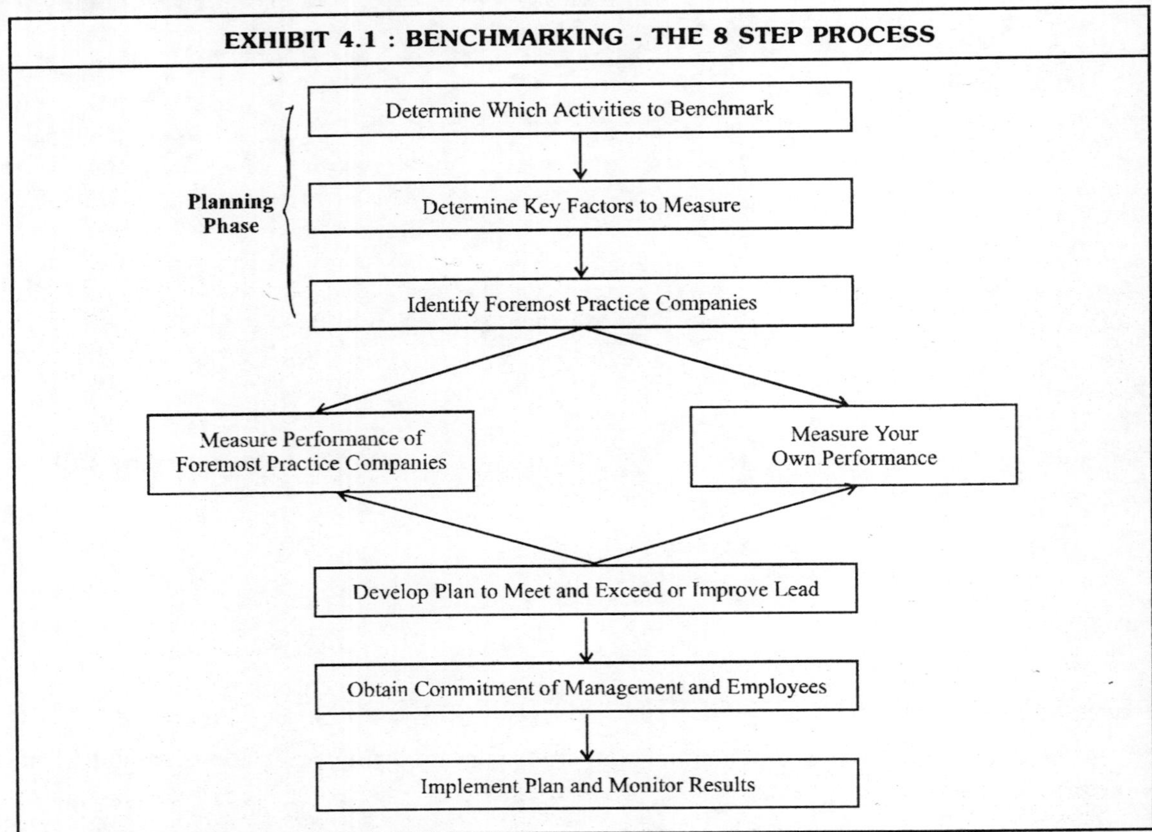

The planning phase requires skill in analysing the issues one chooses to address through benchmarking and then requires great organisational skills to ensure that the study is planned to be executed smoothly and successfully. Poor planning can make your benchmarking project a waste of time and resources but many neophyte benchmarkers underestimate the importance of planning because of the relatively minor amount of time it represents as a component of the whole process. But the time spent in planning the benchmarking study is important and valuable and we should not dive into data collection and analysis without planning.

There are many opportunities for things to go wrong during a benchmarking study. Good planning is helpful in obviating many of them, but one can make mistakes in planning, too.

The three most common mistakes in planning a benchmarking study are:

1. Planning to Benchmark the Wrong Activities

This is fundamental. Understanding precisely the goal of your study *i.e.,* what you and your colleagues want benchmarking to do for you is critical to the success of the project. You need a ***vision***. It is of no use to dive into a benchmarking study and spend much time and money in collecting and analysing data before developing this ***vision***, if your analysis written report, when presented to your board of directors do not create any enthusiasm in them.

You should benchmark activities where improvement is going to contribute significantly to the competitiveness of your organisation.

2. Measuring Something other than Key Factors

Managers at a wholesale building materials chain benchmarked some of the best-in-class retailers to develop an understanding of some of the key metrics in retailing that would allow them to improve customer satisfaction. They measured such factors as customer/salesperson ratios, on-time delivery, and product availability. They developed plans to meet or exceed the leaders in each of these measures. They met or exceeded these measures but subsequent customer - satisfaction surveys surprised them. These surveys were conducted by the contractors' wives, who typically handle the administrative duties for their husbands. Many of their opinions were developed when paying the bills from suppliers such as the building materials chain. Unfortunately the bills from the building materials chain were full of errors and the contractor's wives spent many hours in most months resolving these billing errors. When the management came to know about this, they used benchmarking to improve their customer billing operation. This effort from the managers enabled them to improve customer satisfaction to a high level.

3. Underestimating Timing Issues

Plan for cushion in timing-related issues, especially those dependent on people outside your own organisation because you may not be in a position to exert any influence to speed things along at the target plants or organisations which you have selected for benchmarking visits.

PLANNING YOUR STUDY - SEVEN "TO DO" ITEMS

When you are planning a benchmarking study, the following seven items should be on your "to do" list:

1. Determine which activities to benchmark.
2. Identify the benchmarking team.

3. Schedule the study.
4. Determine the key factors to measure.
5. Identify target organisations.
6. Frame your report.
7. Identify your "prisoners".

These seven items are briefly discussed in the following paragraphs:

1. Determine which Activities to Benchmark

Identifying what is to be benchmarked or the benchmarking outputs is one of the most difficult steps in the benchmarking process. The key to determining what should be benchmarked is to identify the product of the business function which may be a physical, visible, quantifiable product or an intangible service (*e.g.,* logistics or billing and collection of invoices).

Identifying areas for improvement is not difficult for most organisations, but prioritising them may be difficult. When all else fails, listen to your customers to know the areas which need improvement. Assuming that your organisation has limited resources to devote to benchmarking, the main criterion in selecting activities for benchmarking studies is to get the most for your money. If you have resources to do three benchmarking studies per year, benchmark areas where improvements will help your organisation's performance.

Identify activities that increase explicitly your organisation's value. *For example,* the greater percentage of your total costs that an activity or purchased input represents, the greater can be the impact of any savings generated by benchmarking that particular activity or input. If materials cost represent 60 percent of your total cost chain, a small percentage savings in materials cost will make significant savings to your bottom line.

Not all benchmarking studies are cost studies because not all companies compete on cost. Infact, most don't compete on cost. While it is very important to keep costs in line, most companies try to differentiate themselves somehow because they realise there can be only one lowest-cost competitor in an industry. The greater the value perceived by your customers in one of your organisation's activities, the greater the impact of any performance improvements generated by benchmarking.

Benchmarking is sometimes done for less tangible reasons too. The hungrier an organisation's people are for improvements, the more likely bench-marking-driven improvements will be successful. Some organisations benchmark because they realise the climate for change is right and that benchmarking can help.

Some companies determine the activities they plan to benchmark in a particular period based on the results of internal polling of employees. This approach does two things at once:

(i) It ensures that areas in need of improvement are considered.

(ii) It is a good indicator that those who will be responsible for making any benchmarking-driven improvements will buy into the improvement program.

The ultimate goal of any for-profit business is to enchance shareholder value. Given limited resources to devote to benchmarking, benchmarking projects may be evaluated like capital-budgeting alternatives, where those that appear able to add the most value are chosen.

Some organsiations conduct internal surveys to determine activities to benchmark. Assuming you do not have unlimited time or money to benchmark everything on the list, one of the best techniques to use is often the ***"forced-choice survey"*** where potential choices for benchmarking are required to weight each choices.

Another framework used to analyse potential areas for benchmarking is the ***competence gap matrix***. **Activities at which the organisation must excel to be competitive are mapped along two dimensions:**

(i) the organisation's level compared to its competitor's and

(ii) the level required for competitive advantage.

***Exhibit 4.2* illustrate a competence gap matrix for a software firm.**

EXHIBIT 4.2 : COMPETENCE GAP MATRIX FOR A SOFTWARE COMPANY

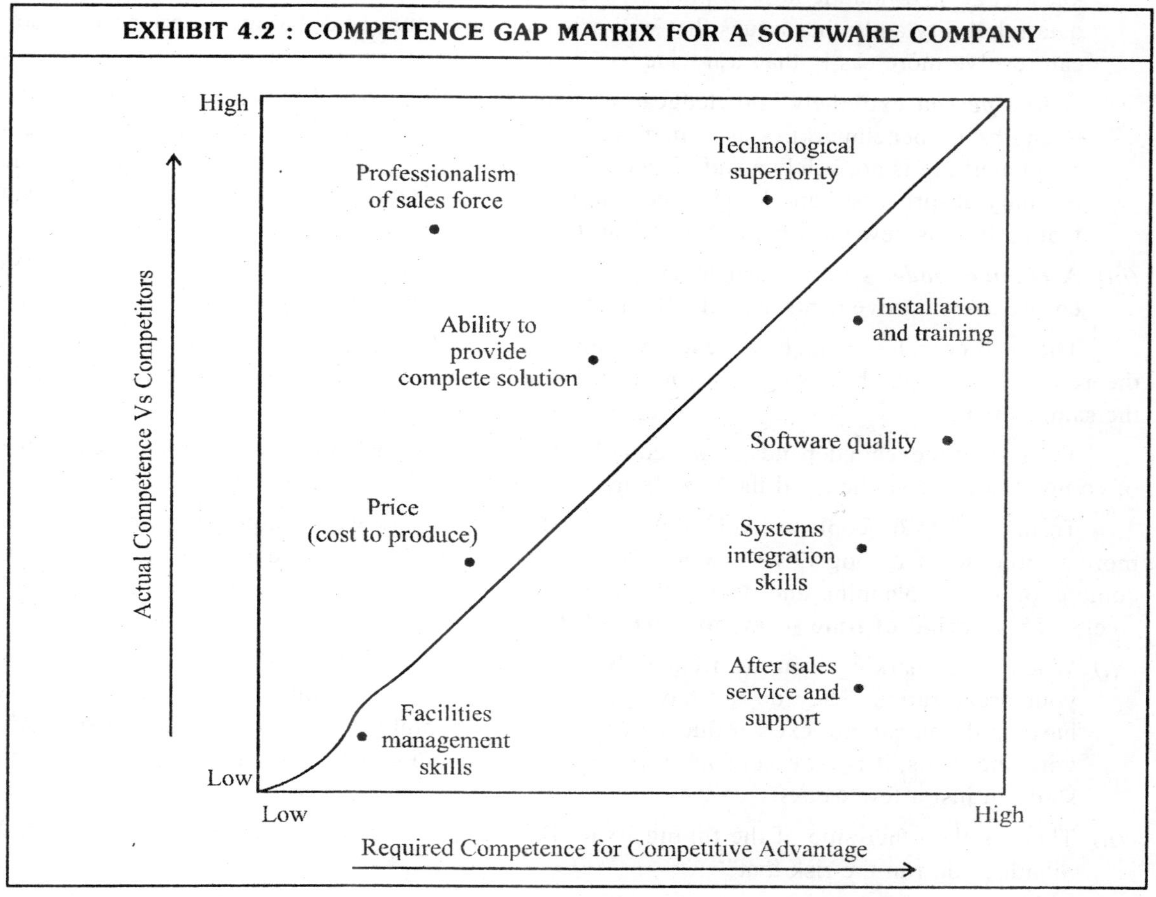

Management used the matrix to communicate to the organisation the urgency of making improvements in various key processes. The "actual" level of the company's competence compared to its competitors and the required level were determined by surveying customers, competitor's customers, managers and employees. The lower right-hand corner is the "hot corner" *i.e.,* it contains the areas where management should focus benchmarking efforts.

2. Identify the Benchmarking Team

Appropriate people must be included on the benchmarking team in order to increase the likelihood of the ultimate success of the benchmarking project. **There are no inviolable rules in team formation, but experience shows the following guidelines to be generally helpful:**

A ***core group*** of benchmarking experts may be a good use of resources if the organisation plans to do six or more studies per year. This group can efficiently build their skills in data collection and analysis if they undertake approximately six studies annually.

The team, whether a core group or ad-hoc for a particular study, should include *at least one* of each of the following:

(i) A ***benchmarking expert*** who brings knowledge of benchmarking process to the table. This knowledge will include how to plan the study, how and where to obtain data, how to ensure data reliability and other issues that will arise during a study and that an experienced person can resolve more easily than a novice.

(ii) A ***line person*** extremely knowledgeable about the activity being benchmarked. One of the strengths of benchmarking as a management tool is that it is practiced by line people - benchmarking is not solely a staff function. By participating in the study, people from the line not only absorb first hand knowledge learnt through the study but also overcome skepticism that ambitious new performance level can be achieved.

(iii) A ***change leader*** who has whatever qualities or authority necessary in your organisation to ensure that improvements are actually made based on the results of your benchmarking study.

These three roles, namely a benchmarking expert, a line person and a change leader can theoretically be played by a single person. Infact, the line person and change leader are frequently the same person.

The size of the team depends on the complexity of the activity being benchmarked, the number of companies to be studied and the time frame within which the study should be completed.

Teams of 3 to 6 people are very common and seem to work well. Large teams, say of 10 or more people seem to bog down. Generally, the team should have enough members to permit completion of the planning and data collection and analysis phases of the study within 10 to 12 weeks. **This period of time seems to workwell because:**

(i) When benchmarking, you are frequently at the mercy of others' schedules - people outside your organisation. They do not have the same motivation to complete your study that you have, and you can not exert influence on them as you might if they were insiders. Especially with site visits, it is unreasonable to believe that you can complete a vigorous benchmarking study in just a few weeks.

(ii) There is the other side of the timing issue. By dragging a study out for much larger than 3 months, you run the risk that

(a) Team members will not be around to complete it.

(b) People will lose interest in the study and it will wither on the vine.

(c) Data collected early will be out of date by the end of the study.

(d) Team members will be very inefficient in execution due to a lack of focus.

It is often a good idea to have a cross-functional team composition. This ensures that improvements in one area are not wasted because of status-quo in other complementary areas.

3. Schedule the Study

Once the benchmarking team has been established, a well-thoughout and well-documented plan of action will ensure you have covered all the steps and designated responsibility to get them accomplished (A Gantt chart that includes all steps in the benchmarking process and the discrete activities within each step is a valuable tool to use to ensure the ultimate success of the study). The benchmarking team leader should take responsibility for holding all members of the team to completion of their tasks by the dates set. Letting dates slip by without completion of various tasks is usually detrimental to the project's entire likelihood of success.

4. Determine Key Factors to Measure

A few truly comparable numbers are worth much more than volumes of poorly understood unverifiable data. Cost, quality and timeliness are the three variables to be measured. Cost, quality and timeliness are, in a different sequence another way to say better, faster and cheaper. The key is to focus on those measures that are going to tell you the most about the process you are studying.

The following are some key guidelines to follow when you are determining the key factors to measure *i.e.,* metrics.

(i) ***Keep focused:*** It is easy to measure every input that could contribute to success in a particular function, process or activity. Not only this is costly but also it could lead to data overload, the benchmarker's nemesis: Too many data to analyse. Try to focus your measurement efforts on the smallest number of measures that will enable you to make the improvements you require.

(ii) ***Keep an open mind:*** Imagine the learning that comes from going into a benchmarking study thinking you wanted to measure X and discovering that the best-in-class measure 'Y' instead.

(iii) ***Most importantly, remember the underlying reasons for superior performance are usually more important than the performance numbers themselves.*** Benchmarking is not a numbers exercise.

5. Identify Target Organisations

Your company may target its strongest competitor, or all its competitors, or a large number of companies that have been labelled best-in-class or world-class in some activity. The possibilities seem endless.

There are generally four groups of companies that a benchmarking firm might consider in selecting benchmarking candidates:

(i) Current direct industry competitors.

(ii) Latent competitors, including those in its industry but not currently in its market or those not in its industry at all who could enter.

(iii) Best-in-class groups from within its own organisation.

(iv) Best-in-class companies from other industries.

Which organisation you study depends in large part on what you are trying to improve. If you believe your production costs are too high, you will likely study your direct competitors' costs in a cost benchmarking study to determine their costs and perhaps some latent competitors if comparisons can be made on point-to-point basis.

But if you want to improve in an area where none of your competitors is particularly strong in an absolute sense and you want to leapfrog them all with some new practices, it is likely that your learning will come from outside your industry, from companies that are world-class in particular activities that are also performed in their industries.

***Box 4.1* shows the list developed by an airline seeking to improve its customer service.**

BOX 4.1 : POTENTIAL COMPANIES TO BE STUDIED BY A REGIONAL US AIRLINE (OBJECTIVE : IMPROVE KEY FACETS OF CUSTOMER SERVICE)

1. Direct competitors

- United
- American
- Delta
- Alaska

} Studied to establish absolute minimum service standards to be competitive in the region

2. "Latent" competitors

- Scandinavian
- Singapore
- JAL
- ANA

} Studied to understand best air-line practices, despite the fact that these airlines did not currently fly the regional airline's routes

3. Other Best-in-class

- AT&T universal card services
- Nord strom

} Studied to understand world-class customer service standards by acknowledged leaders

Following are some general guidelines that will help you select the right companies to benchmark.

(i) Direct and Latent Competitors

- **Always consider your direct competitors:** It is not wise for the manager not to study direct competitors because they are not among what he or she considers best-in-class benchmarking candidates. If you are benchmarking firms outside your industry, your competitors may be doing so as well. So you should at least perform competitor analysis of the benchmarking variety.
- **Ask your customers:** Ask them who in your industry is best at the activity you wish to improve. Customers will know. But better than asking your customers may be asking people or companies that don't buy from you. This type of inquiry has to be made discreetly to avoid tipping off the competition to the fact that you are on the improvement trail, but you probably can learn a lot from your competitor's customers.
- **Ask your employees:** Ask your employees, especially your sales people, delivery people, and service representatives. They are in the field, going head to head with the competition every day. They usually have good ideas about who is best and who is not in a wide variety of areas.

(ii) Benchmarking within your Own Organisation

Benchmarking within your organisation, also known as ***internal benchmarking***, is often done by large organisations with widespread operations. These organisations; which may have many thousands of employees spread all over the world, frequently contain pockets of excellence in various processes that are hidden away in remote locations just waiting to be discovered.

Internal benchmarking is typically the first phase in a larger, outward - looking benchmarking study, but can uncover some valuable process improvement with a minimum of resources spent and little or no difficultly in obtaining co-operation from the best-in-class.

(iii) Other Best-in-class Companies

- ***Select companies with obvious strengths in the activity you want to benchmark.*** This is getting easier to do as the practice of benchmarking expands. As more and more companies catch on the power of benchmarking, the identity of best-in-class companies become more widely known.
- ***Look at Melcolm Baldrige National Quality Award winners***. Baldrige award winners are, by and large, quality zealots who are usually extraordinarily gracious in sharing information.
- ***Look for companies with comparable products, services or processes in some important characteristics***. When a big accounting firm wanted to improve its purchasing function, managers identified several firms that purchased, large volumes of comparable items (travel, office supplies, office furniture etc.) and benchmarked them.
- ***Looking at industry practices***. Many industry publications include annual lists of top companies in a particular industry or function. Such publications can be good sources for identifying potential targets.

When you are benchmarking companies outside the industry, the possibility exists for significant gains over current practices in a given activity. If learning from a non-industry company, whether best-in-class or not, is going to allow you to dramatically improve performance and perhaps leapfrog past competitors, you have nothing to lose by doing it. Xerox learnt a tremendous amount about warehousing and distribution by benchmarking L.L. Bean in this area.

Remember, do not limit your benchmarking to direct competitors. What you can learn from competitors in many areas is less than what you can learn from companies outside the industry. And do not limit your search to companies in your immediate geographic area.

Also, when you are benchmarking companies other than your competitors, it is usually a good idea to identify initially more target companies than you think you will eventually study. **A weeding-out process is often done, during which a number of potential benchmarking targets are reviewed preliminarily to identify those that appear to be:**

(a) Most comparable to the team's company in terms of the process to be studied.

(b) Most different from the team's company in terms of the process to be studied, as long as the end product or service is the same. This may open your eyes to a totally new way of doing things.

(c) Best of the initial candidates following some preliminary data collection and analysis.

(d) Most willing to co-operate in the study, which is becoming a real issue as benchmarking becomes more popular. If you really want to benchmark a particular company that you suspect

is a popular target for benchmarking, you may find that managers there just can not give you the time you want. Most of the Baldrige winners are swamped with requests and simply do not have time to provide one or two-day visits to everyone who requests them. **In view of these problems, you should remember**

(i) To make it crystal-clear from the outset that you are doing real, rigorous benchmarking and not wasting everyone's time with industrial tourism and

(ii) Have something to offer the people you want to learn from, in the form of some special expertise of your own.

A few final words on target selection are warranted:

(i) Your first real data collection and analysis efforts begin during the selection process.

(ii) You cannot honestly identify benchmarking targets until you have satisfied yourself that your targets are the "right" organisations, based on whichever combination of the above criteria makes sense for your study.

(iii) The most important criterion in selecting targets is to choose those from which you will be able to learn, learn and learn.

(iv) Try to avoid encumbering the initial target identification process with too many rules. Many benchmarking teams begin with a large list of potential targets and narrow it by a significant factor before ultimately deciding whom to study.

6. Frame Your Report

Framing your report means writing a detailed outline after you have identified the targets but before you have begun in-depth external data collection and analysis. You should view framing the report as an important step in the planning process. At this point you have determined the activities to benchmark and the key factors to measure and you have selected target companies.

Framing the report is a valuable exercise that can be done on almost all benchmarking studies. In essence, it entails writing the report without the data. This exercise is valuable because it forces you to think through in great detail all the data you will need to complete the study, how the data will flow together, and where you have to go to find the data.

Framing the report may seem inefficient because the report will change - sometimes organically before you have finished it. Some unexpected discoveries during the data collection and analysis phase may make part of your data collection moot or may send you down an entirely new path. But the benefits from having thought through the study in great detail almost always outweigh inefficiencies.

One word of caution is not to draw a conclusions when you are framing the report. Framing the report is a planning exercise, but planning conclusions before you have even begun data collection and analysis is neither honest nor wise.

7. Identify your Prisoners

An ***exchange of prisoners*** means that you have something of value to share with those you hope will cooperate or collaborate in a study you are performing. Identifying prisoners is reality for those who wish to perform cooperative benchmarking in the 1990s. Many of the better-known best-in-class companies have been inundated with requests to share by benchmarking teams interested in learning about their best practices.

Having prisoners to exchange may simply mean having one or more best practices of your own practices that others can learn from. *For example,* one of the large credit card issuers offered data about its billing and collections process as an inducement to other organisations to get them share data about customer service, telephony and innovation.

There are three components to identifying your prisoners:

(i) Identify those areas in which your organisation excels.

(ii) Determine which you are willing to share with others and at what level of detail.

(iii) Determine with whom you are willing to share them.

Do not have the misconception that every organisation that has a best practice is willing to share it with the rest of the world. Even the Baldrige winners are not obliged to cooperate in benchmarking studies. Flattery is working with less frequency. But if you bring something to the table, you will enhance your chances of learning what you want to learn.

Of course, not all organisations have something to bring to the table. Lacking any truly superior practices to offer up in trade to potential benchmarking partners, some organisations bring the fact that they are organising and running a collaborative study. Organising and running a study is a great deal of work and many organisations realise that doing this work and delivering value to all the organisations that participate in the study is often enough to get some world-class organisations to play.

The seven "to do" items covered apply on almost any benchmarking study. If you address each one every time you benchmark, your studies will go much more smoothly than if you overlook one or more items.

PLANNING A COMPETITIVE COST – BENCHMARKING STUDY

A thorough **cost – benchmarking study** of your competitors will not only enable you to find ways to become more cost competitive under your present system, but also should enable you to identify strategic alternatives in the form of different business systems *i.e.,* different ways of delivering value to customers in the industry.

Benchmarking competitors' costs is the most challenging application of benchmarking you can undertake. Obtaining direct information is usually difficult at best and seemingly impossible at worst. Competitors seldom mirror precisely your own company in the use of technology and markets served (which makes meaningful comparisons more difficult to derive) and reconstructing cost chains from various cost drivers means combining a good amount of judgement and best guesstimates with incomplete and often inconsistent data from many sources. Multiply all these challenges by a large number of competitors and potential competitors and the task can seem insurmountable. A well-planned methodology will remove many obstacles.

A good way to start a cost benchmarking study is with an analysis of the different ways that value can be delivered to customers in the industry. **This analysis is not actually benchmarking but is a precursor stage that will help you:**

(i) High-light and analyse the different ways companies compete in your industry.

(ii) Identify different ways to approach the issue of satisfying your customers.

(iii) Focus on the high-average-value activities in your value chain.

(iv) Identify and narrow your study to those competitors that will give you the greatest return through benchmarking.

The first step in this analysis is to construct the organisation's value chain and analyse the costs of each link in the chain, typically on a per-unit basis.

Next, identify the various options that exist or could exist for each link in the chain. Different companies deliver value in different ways. It is important to understand how each link in the chain could be delivered in your industry and how changes in one link affect the performance or cost of other links.

Once you have identified the alternatives to delivering value in your-industry, estimate how the various alternatives affect the total cost of a value chain comprising different permutations. Be certain to consider the impact of changes in one area on the other areas in the firm.

This step in the analysis should reflect the best judgement of managers of each area included in the value chain. Actual benchmarking will help you to further refine your understandings of the various costs later. Right now, you want reliable estimates to use in understanding generally how different value chain configurations accumulate their costs.

The final step in the benchmarking analysis is to determine which competitors had value chains that included the alternatives considered to have major cost impacts, based on the preceeding analysis. The company should study with greater accuracy the advantages of differently configured competitors and also learn how the company might better its cost position within its existing value chain configuration before finally selecting the competitor to benchmark before going ahead with actual cost benchmarking.

PLANNING A BROAD BENCHMARKING STUDY

The essence of benchmarking process – learning from others - can be applied in many ways. Benchmarks are getting more ambitious in defining the scope of benchmarking studies which usually adds to the complexity of the process being studied. Benchmarking is a broad process, as opposed to just a piece of the process, can be done but the process itself is frequently easier to understand and study if it is broken down into its various components. Breaking down of a broad process into its components makes the study of the process more understandable and manageable.

For example, if a company wants to use benchmarking process to improve its training function, then it should set out to "benchmark training" with some of the leading training organisations found in the industry or the country. Benchmarking the entire training process is a much broader endeavour than just benchmarking a piece of it, say, benchmarking the techniques used by the leading companies in the area of developing computer-based training programs.

Because the entire training process is so broad, to facilitate its study, the benchmarking team should breakdown the training process into various components of training. **The training process can be broken down logically into each of the components shown in the *Exhibit 4.3* which makes studying the training process much more manageable.** Within each area a specific set of questions can be developed and addressed with target organisations.

EXHIBIT 4.3 : THE TRAINING BUSINESS SYSTEM

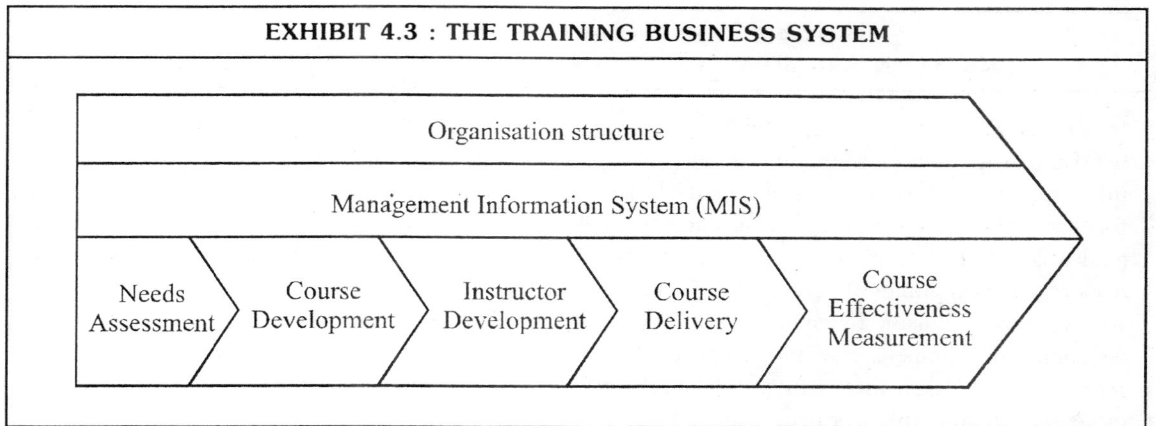

The various components of the training process are briefly discussed below:

(i) ***Organisational structure*** encompasses all the areas of the training process. Information relevant to organisational structure covers where in the overall structure of the organisation the training is situated, the number and experience of training professionals and support staff, the number of people trained, annual training goals/requirements, training budget etc.

(ii) ***Management information system (MIS)*** like organisational structure, spans all the areas of the training process. MIS includes information relevant to measuring and reporting on financial, efficiency and related measures in each of the primary training activities.

(iii) ***Needs assessment*** addresses the organisation's methodology for determining the need for training for all employees in areas relevant to their positions.

(iv) ***Course development*** addresses the organisation's methodology for developing and updating training materials.

(v) ***Instructor development*** addresses the organisation's methodology for identifying, developing and evaluating members of the training staff, including instructors.

(vi) ***Course delivery*** addresses the organisations techniques and logistics for delivering training.

(vii) ***Course effectiveness measurement*** covers the organisation's methodology for evaluating training courses delivered and their impact on employee's performance in the workplace.

You should attempt such a disaggregation of any broad process that you decide to study. Note that activities are linked in the sequence that they normally occur. A chronological flow of events is typically the easiest and most understandable way to disaggregate the broad process.

BOX 4.2 : BENCHMARKING IN PRACTICE – JOHNSON AND JOHNSON FOCUSES ON BENCHMARKING TEAMS

In January 1991, less than 5 per cent of the operating companies at Johnson and Johnson employed benchmarking - and those that did relied on consultants. Realising that employees know more about the corporation's businesses than outside consultants, Johnson and Johnson management shifted its focus to create benchmarking teams staffed by Johnson and Johnson employees. The new corporate goal was for J & J teams to perform 70 percent of all benchmarking projects and for consultants to perform the remaining 30 percent. By September 1992, over 60 teams were actively benchmarking. Johnson and Johnson reached its goal by using training and experience sharing to establish benchmarking competency within the corporation. By establishing internal benchmarking capabilities Johnson and Johnson successfully reduced the cost and cycle time of its benchmarking studies while increasing the quality of project results.

POINTS TO REMEMBER

- **The planning phase of the benchmarking process involves the following three steps:**
  (i) Determine which activities to benchmark
  (ii) Determine key factors to measure and
  (iii) Identify foremost practice companies
- **The three most common mistakes in planning a benchmarking study are:**
  (i) Planning to benchmark the wrong activities
  (ii) Measuring something other than key factors
  (iii) Underestimating timing issues
- **Seven "to-do" items in planning your study are:**
  (i) Determine which activities to benchmark
  (ii) Identify the benchmarking team
  (iii) Schedule the study
  (iv) Determine the key factors to measure
  (v) Identify target organisations
  (vi) Frame your report
  (vii) Identify your "prisoners"
- The key to determining what should be benchmarked is to identify the product of the business function which may be a physical, visible, quantifiable product or an intangible service.
- Identify activities that increase explicitly your organisation's value.
- **Forced field survey** is the technique used to determine activities to benchmark.
- **Competence gap matrix** is used to analyse potential areas for benchmarking.
- **The benchmarking team should include at least one of each of the following :** *(a)* A benchmarking expert, *(b)* A line person, *(c)* A change leader.

  Teams of 3 to 6 people are very common.
- The benchmarking study should be scheduled using a Gantt Chart that includes all steps in the benchmarking process and the discrete activities within each step.

- **Cost, quality and time are** the three variables to be measured.
- Your company may target its strongest competitor or all competitors, or a large number of companies that have been labelled best-in-class or world-class in some activities.
- **Four groups of companies that a benchmarking firm might consider in selecting benchmarking candidates are:**
  - *(i)* Current direct industry competitors
  - *(ii)* Latent competitors
  - *(iii)* Best-in-class groups from within its own organisation
  - *(iv)* Best-in-class companies from other industries
- Framing the report entails writing the report without the data, *i.e.,* before you have begun in-depth data collection and analysis.
- Having prisoners to exchange may mean having one or more best practices of your own practices that others (benchmark partners) can learn from.
- A thorough **cost-benchmarking study** of your competitors will not only enable you to find ways to become more cost competitive under your present system, but also should enable you to identify strategic alternatives in the form of different business systems.
- Benchmarking competitors' costs is the most challenging application of benchmarking you can undertake.
- A good way to start a cost-benchmarking study is with an analysis of the different ways that value can be delivered to customers in the industry.
- The essence of benchmarking process is **"learning from others"**.

REVIEW QUESTIONS

1. Discuss the activities involved in the planning phase of the benchmarking process.
2. Discuss the three most common mistakes in planning a benchmarking study.
3. Discuss the seven items that should be on your "to do list" while planning a benchmarking study.
4. Explain how do you determine which activities to benchmark.
5. Discuss the concept of "competence gap matrix" with a diagram taking an example for a software company.
6. Explain how you identify the benchmarking team.
7. Why scheduling of the benchmarking study is important?
8. Explain how would you determine the key factors to measure in a benchmarking study.
9. Explain how would you identify target organisations for benchmarking.
10. How would you perform competitor analysis in the prebenchmarking study?
11. What is internal benchmarking? How it is carried out?
12. How would you select other best-in-class companies to benchmark?
13. What is meant by "framing your report" in planning the benchmarking study?
14. What is meant by "identifying your prisoners"? How would you identify your prisoners while planning for benchmarking study?

15. Explain the planning process involved in

    (a) planning a competitive cost benchmarking study

    (b) planning a broad benchmarking study.

DISCUSSION QUESTIONS

1. "There are many opportunities for things to go wrong during a benchmarking study, Good planning can obviate many of them, but you can make mistakes in planning too" - Explain.
2. "Another framework used to analyse potential areas for benchmarking is the competence gap matrix" - Elaborate.
3. "There are no inviolable rules in the formation of benchmarking team, but experience shows that certain guidelines to be generally helpful" - Discuss.
4. "There are some key guidelines to follow when you are determining the key factors to measure in the benchmarking study". What are they? Discuss.
5. Discuss the general guidelines that will help you select the right companies to benchmark.
6. "Internal benchmarking is typically just the first phase in a larger, outward-looking benchmarking study". Do you agree or disagree? Justify your answer.
7. "Your first real data collection and analysis efforts begin during the selection process" - Elaborate.
8. "Benchmarking competitor's costs is the most challenging application of benchmarking you can undertake". Critically examine the statement.

CHAPTER 5

Organising for Benchmarking

INTRODUCTION

While benchmarking, you benchmark only one item at a time and no more. Once an organisation starts to benchmark, the process quickly becomes habit forming. If you benchmark one item and obtain information from 10 other organisations, your organisation is morally obligated to reciprocate with the 10 benchmarking partners when they want to benchmark one of their items. This could easily mean that you would be engaged in accumulating benchmarking data on 10 other items within a year.

This is not all bad, because benchmarking should be a key input into the organisation's strategic plan and each year's business plan. ***Exhibit 5.1* shows the relationships among the elements of a strategic plan. (The strategic planning pyramid). The planning pyramid contains six interrelated levels which are briefly discussed below:**

EXHIBIT 5.1 : THE STRATEGIC PLANNING PYRAMID

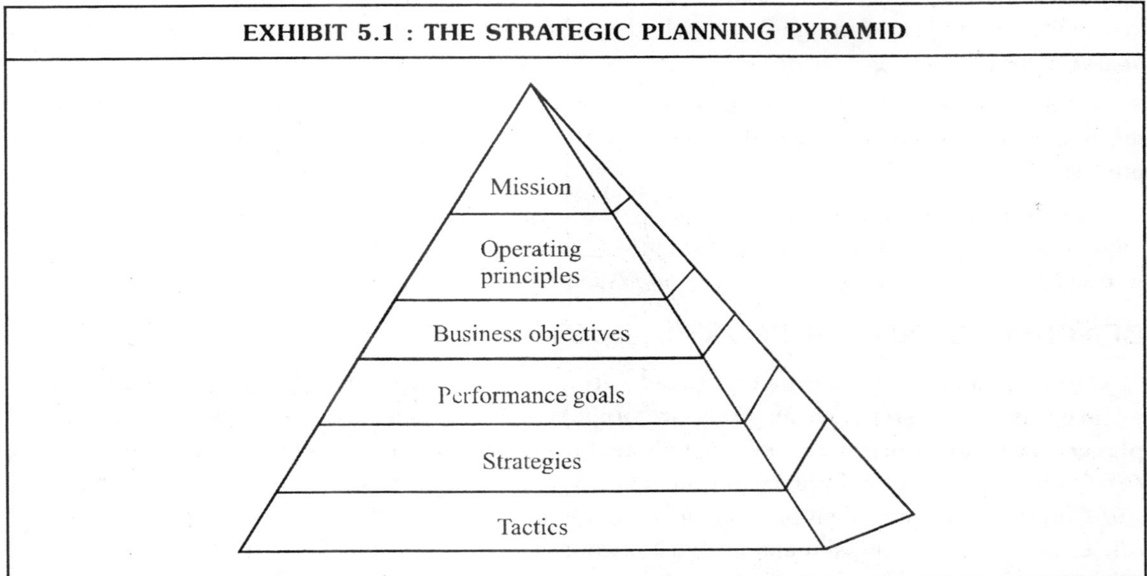

1. **Mission:** Mission is the stated reason for the existence of the organisation. The mission does not change frequently. It changes only when the organisation decides to pursue a completely new market.
2. **Operating principle:** These are the basic beliefs that make up the culture of the organisation. These principles rarely change.
3. **Business objectives:** Business objectives set the direction that the organisation will follow for the future time period (both intermediate and long-term). Business objectives support the organisation's mission.
4. **Performance goals:** These are normally quantified, measurable results that the organisation wants to accomplish in a set period of time to support its business objectives. Performance goals directly relate to business objectives.
5. **Strategies:** The strategies define the way the organisation's performance goals will be accomplished.
6. **Tactics:** The tactical plan defines the way organisation's strategy will be accomplished. Tactics are specific tasks that will be undertaken in the short term to move the organisation towards the performance goals.

It is easy to understand how best practices and future-trend information, gathered through benchmarking, has a major impact on the organisation's mission, operating principles, business objectives and performance goals. The results of the benchmarking projects are reflected in the future state solutions that will also impact the organisation's strategies and tactics.

The annual business plan must also reflect the implementation plans for future-state solutions, as well as the resources to do benchmarking projects for the coming year. Because of the major emphasis that most organisations are placing on breakthrough methodologies, it is very important that benchmarking projects be included in today's business plans. Benchmarking is one of the three key tools used in breakthrough methodologies. The other two are ***business process redesign*** and ***business process reengineering.***

With the potential impact that benchmarking can have on the organisation, it is imperative that the benchmarking process be understood and aggressively supported by top management if the process is to succeed.

Progressive organisations are changing the way in which they work - no longer settling for incremental change when real breakthrough is required. They are pursuing benchmarking approach in order to achieve ***continuous breakthrough improvements.***

BENCHMARKING'S SUPPORT STRUCTURE

Benchmarking can not be embraced within a large or average-size organisation without an organisational structure in place to support this key activity. The following are major players in a large organisation's benchmarking structure. *(i)* Executive improvement team, *(ii)* Corporate benchmarking initiation team or corporate benchmarking steering committee, *(iii)* Corporate vice president or director of corporate benchmarking, *(iv)* Corporate benchmarking office, *(v)* Benchmarking site and/or division coordinators, *(vi)* Site and/or division benchmarking initiation team or benchmarking steering committee, *(vii)* Benchmarking item team, *(viii)* Benchmarking item team facilitator, *(ix)* Benchmarking item team sponsor, *(x)* Internal benchmarking item committee or network.

***Exhibit 5.2* presents a typical benchmarking structure for a large corporation.**

EXHIBIT 5.2 : TYPICAL BENCHMARKING ORGANISATIONAL STRUCTURE FOR A LARGE ORGANISATION

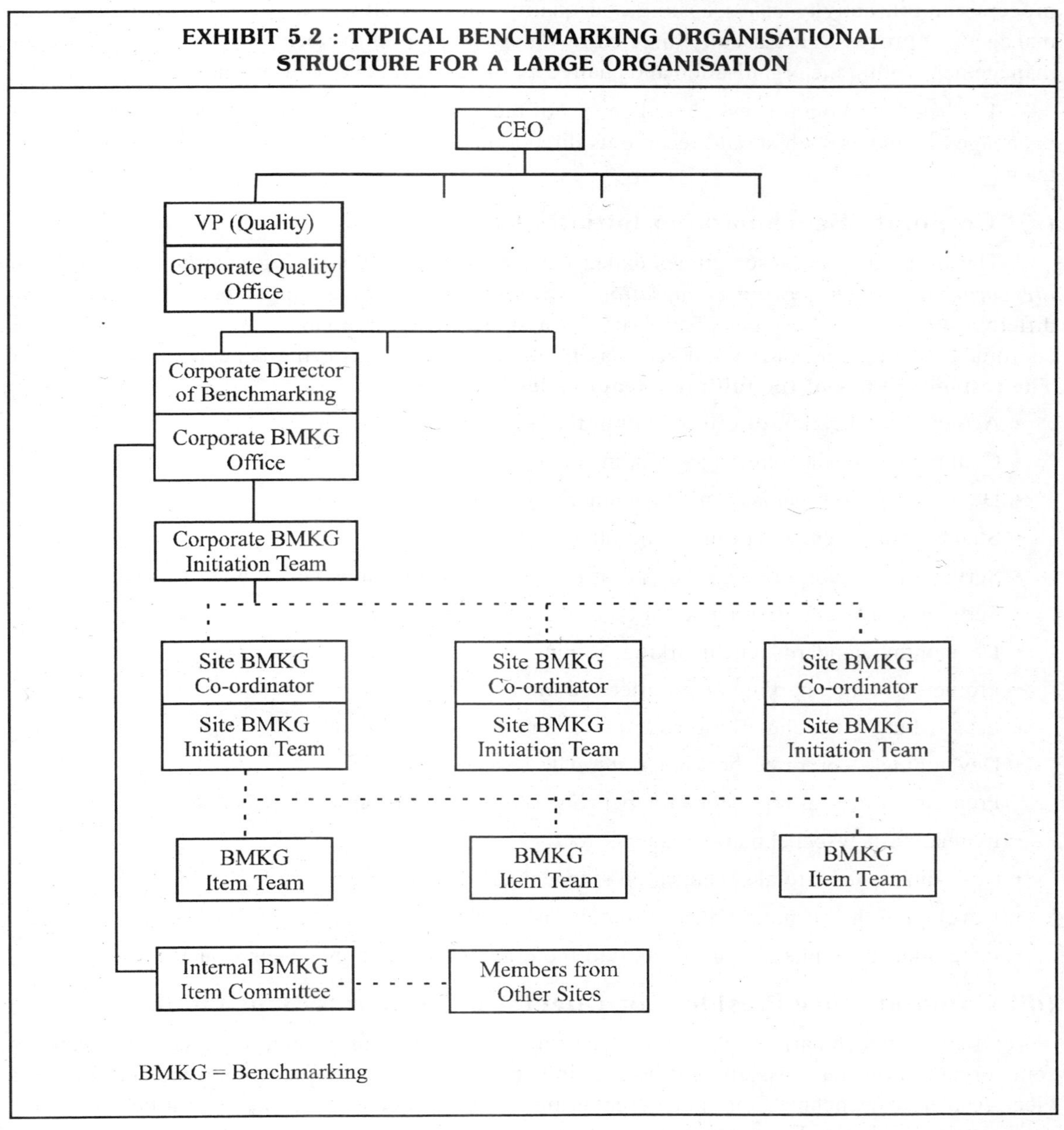

The major players in a large organisation's benchmarking structure are briefly discussed in the following paragraphs:

(i) Executive Improvement Team (Top Management)

Most successful benchmarking programs are part of a ***total improvement management or total quality management strategy***. These strategies include such activities as team building, statistical process control, activity based costing and quality policy deployment. These total improvement management processes are usually directed by an executive improvement team made up of the top management within the organisation and chaired by the chief executive or president of the company.

The benchmarking process should be part of the total improvement effort that the organisation is engaged in and as such should receive its direction and control from the executive improvement team.

(ii) Corporate Benchmarking Initiation Team

The initiation team - sometimes called the ***corporate benchmarking steering committee*** **or** ***the corporate benchmarking cooperation committee*** is a small group of people, usually from different divisions and/or sites. This group is assigned to get the benchmarking process started, coordinate its implementation and serve as in-house consultants for the benchmarking activities. **The responsibilities of the initiative team includes:**

- Avoiding duplication of efforts within the organisation.
- Communicating benchmarking findings and results.
- Developing the organisation's benchmarking process.
- Standardising benchmarking terminology.
- Serving as the corporate contact point to outside organisations which want to benchmark.
- Serving as a benchmarking resource to the entire organisation.
- Developing standard benchmarking training packages.
- Promoting benchmarking as an effective improvement tool.
- Establishing a benchmarking code of conduct (code of ethics).
- Developing a corporate benchmarking data base.
- Preparing a central repository for benchmarking information and results.
- Evaluating new benchmarking tools.
- Co-ordinating the total organisation's benchmarking activities.
- Developing the corporate documentation that supports the benchmarking process.
- Integrating benchmarking projects into the organisation's strategies and business plan.

(iii) Corporate Vice-President or Director of Corporate Benchmarking

Often the benchmarking champion is part of the quality-improvement organisation. Although some organisations have assigned responsibilities for co-ordination of benchmarking activities to a vice president of benchmarking, most organisations have avoided confusion and put benchmarking activities under the quality organisation.

The director of corporate benchmarking is responsible for:

- Serving as champion of the corporate benchmarking process.
- Managing the corporate benchmarking office.

- Being the prime benchmarking contact for outside organisations.
- Ensuring that a standard benchmarking strategy is used throughout the organisation.
- Minimising duplication of benchmarking activities.
- Co-ordinating site and/or divisional benchmarking activities.

(iv) Corporate Benchmarking Office

The corporate benchmarking office is a small team managed by the director of corporate benchmarking. **The corporate benchmarking office is responsible for:**

- Increasing the level of sharing and communication on benchmarking activities.
- Providing a contact point for outside organisations.
- Registering benchmarking item teams.
- Reducing redundancies.
- Establishing and coordinating the corporate benchmarking database.
- Helping to define internal and external benchmarking partners.
- Establishing the benchmarking computer networks.
- Helping to identify high-potential opportunities.
- Maintaining the benchmarking training program.
- Benchmarking the benchmarking process.
- Preparing and maintaining the corporate benchmarking guide.

(v) Benchmarking Site and/or Division Co-ordinators

Each site and/or division should have an individual assigned as its benchmarking champion. The individual plays a key role, serving as the site and/or division mentor for benchmarking process. Site coordinators need to be experienced in the benchmarking process and have a high degree of motivation to make the process a success at the related site and/or division.

All lines of the business and geographic location where the benchmarking process will be deployed should assign an individual to serve as benchmarking coordinator. The site benchmarking coordinators also usually serve as members of the corporate benchmarking initiation team. They function together, providing an internal network that coordinates the benchmarking activities throughout the organisation.

The responsibilities of the site and/or division benchmarking coordinators include:

- Serving on the corporate benchmarking initiation team.
- Chairing the site and/or division benchmarking initiation team.
- Co-ordinating the site and/or division benchmarking activities.
- Serving as benchmarking consultants for the site and/or division.
- Ensuring that benchmarking is done in a professional manner.
- Ensuring that benchmarking rules are followed.
- Serving as a benchmarking facilitator.

- Providing the interface for the site and/or division to the corporate benchmarking office.
- Ensuring that appropriate customer interface personnel are advised of pending benchmarking activities.
- Evaluating incoming and outgoing benchmarking requests for applicability.
- Being the site and/or division benchmarking centre of competence.
- Providing on-site consulting services.
- Establishing an interface with local literature research firms.
- Breaking down road blocks encountered by benchmarking item teams.
- Reviewing the make up of benchmarking item teams.
- Ensuring that all ethical, protocol, and legal guidelines are followed.
- Maintaining outside connections to help with the benchmarking process.

(vi) Site and/or Division Benchmarking Initiation Team (Steering Committee)

Typically, a small group of people, usually from different functions, are assigned to get the benchmarking process started, co-ordinate its implementation and serve as consultants for the benchmarking activities within an individual decision or at an individual site. This team is normally chaired by the benchmarking site and/or division co-ordinator. The team is made up of middle-level managers representing each of the functions within the organisation. **The site and/or division benchmarking initiation team is responsible for:**

- Conducting a business analysis and prioritising benchmarking opportunities.
- Ensuring that the benchmarking activities are reflected in the strategic plans and the yearly operating plan for the site and/or division.
- Registering benchmarking item teams.
- Standardising the implementation of the benchmarking process within the organisation.
- Communicating benchmarking accomplishments.
- Conducting postmortems of benchmarking projects to improve future projects.
- Co-ordinating activities within the site and/or division to eliminate or reduce duplication.
- Promoting benchmarking within each function.
- Ensuring that benchmarking becomes part of each middle manager's performance evaluation.
- Ensuring that all individuals participating in the benchmarking process have been trained appropriately.

(vii) Benchmarking Item Team (BIT)

The benchmarking item team (sometimes called the benchmarking team) usually consists of 5 to 10 people who are assigned to benchmark a specific business process, piece of equipment, product or manufacturing process. A great deal of care should be taken in selecting the members of the benchmarking item team, because the success of the benchmarking study will depend upon the skills and creativity of the individuals who make up the team. **Benchmarking item team members should have the following characteristics and/or knowledge:**

- Good interpersonal skills - first impressions are very important in benchmarking.
- Good understanding of the benchmarking process.
- Good communication skills.
- Excellent technical knowledge of the item being benchmarked.
- The respect of the people in the area where the change will occur.
- Knowledge of organisational change management methodologies.
- Skill in dealing with consultants and/or outside organisations.
- The ability to influence others.
- A high degree of top management credibility.
- The ability to embrace change as a way of life.
- The ability to sell and implement the benchmarking findings.
- High interest in the project.
- A high degree of creativity, innovativeness and flexibility.
- Enough time to take on the assignment.

In addition, a BIT member could be the process owner, the best representative from his or her department and/or a customer of the item. It is sometimes beneficial to have a customer on the benchmarking item team.

The benchmarking item team will operate for 6 to 18 months, depending on what is being benchmarked and the type of benchmarking approach that is used. **A typical team is made up of:**

- A team leader
- A number of content and/or process experts
- A person (not part of the present process) who can give an objective view of the benchmark item's performance.
- A data analyst.
- Key people who will be needed to help implement the future-state solutions developed by the benchmarking item team.
- A facilitator who helps the team leader and the team stay on track and use the proper tools.

The benchmarking item team has seven key responsibilities:

(i) Develop the benchmark item's project plan.

(ii) Define the benchmark item's critical measurements.

(iii) Collect and analyse data about and from the benchmarking partners.

(iv) Develop a future-state solution.

(v) Sell management on the advantages of implementing the future-state solution.

(vi) Assist with implementation of the future state solution.

(vii) Perform periodic reviews of the benchmark item's database after the future-state solution is implemented.

Typically members of the benchmarking item team will spend 15 to 30 percent of their time on the benchmarking project - from project initiation to the point in the process where the future-state solution is accepted by upper management. The team leader will devote 25 to 40 percent of his or her time to the benchmarking project during this same period.

(viii) Benchmarking Item Team Facilitator

A trained, experienced facilitator who is not involved with the item under study should be assigned to each benchmarking item team until the benchmarking process becomes internalised into the organisation.

The BIT facilitator plays a key role in the way the benchmarking item team functions. A facilitator must have an excellent understanding of the benchmarking and team processes, although he or she needs little of any knowledge of the benchmark item. **The BIT facilitator is responsible for working with the team leader to:**

- Establish team agendas.
- Define team roles.
- Obtain agreements.
- Define leader and team weaknesses and how to correct them.
- Develop the organisational change management plan.
- Obtain team ownership of the future-state solution.
- Enforce agreements.
- Keep meetings on track, following the agenda and focusing on outcomes.
- Create a win-win outcome when disagreements arise.

The BIT facilitator is often called upon to provide the benchmarking item team with just-in-time training related to the benchmarking processes. **This individual possesses the following key characteristics:**

- Stays neutral.
- Behaves in a positive way.
- Is a good listener.
- Is not defensive.
- Encourages the team when things are not going well.
- Reacts quickly to body language.
- Talks only when necessary.
- Is not afraid to interrupt the team when it is going off course.
- Can criticise without hurting feelings.

(ix) Benchmarking Item Team Sponsor

A benchmarking item team sponsor is frequently assigned to a BIT that is working on improving a critical business item. The sponsor is usually a very high-level person (typically a director or vice president) who can not commit the required time to be the chairperson of or participate in the specific BIT, but is very interested in seeing that the project meets its goals. Often the BIT chair person will report directly to the benchmarking item team sponsor through the established structure. **The BIT sponsor will:**

- Regularly review the BIT's progress.
- Breakdown road blocks that can not be handled by the BIT.
- Serve as adviser to the BIT on the item being benchmarked.
- Help keep the BIT's resources intact.

(x) Internal Benchmarking Item Committee or Network

The internal benchmarking item committee is made up of representatives from different sites and/or divisions who have a common interest in benchmarking a specific item. By combining their resources, they can accomplish the benchmarking project using fewer individual resources that would be required if independent studies were made. In addition, internal benchmarking item committees usually develop future-state solutions that have a better fit between sites and/or divisions than would be developed if the individual future-state solutions were developed independently. The responsibilities of the internal benchmarking item committee parallel those of the benchmarking item team.

BENCHMARKING SYSTEMS

A ***benchmarking system*** is the infrastructure and organisational linkages necessary to deploy, reinforce and institutionalise a benchmarking process.

***Exhibit 5.3* illustrates the benchmarking system.**

EXHIBIT 5.3 : BENCHMARKING SYSTEM

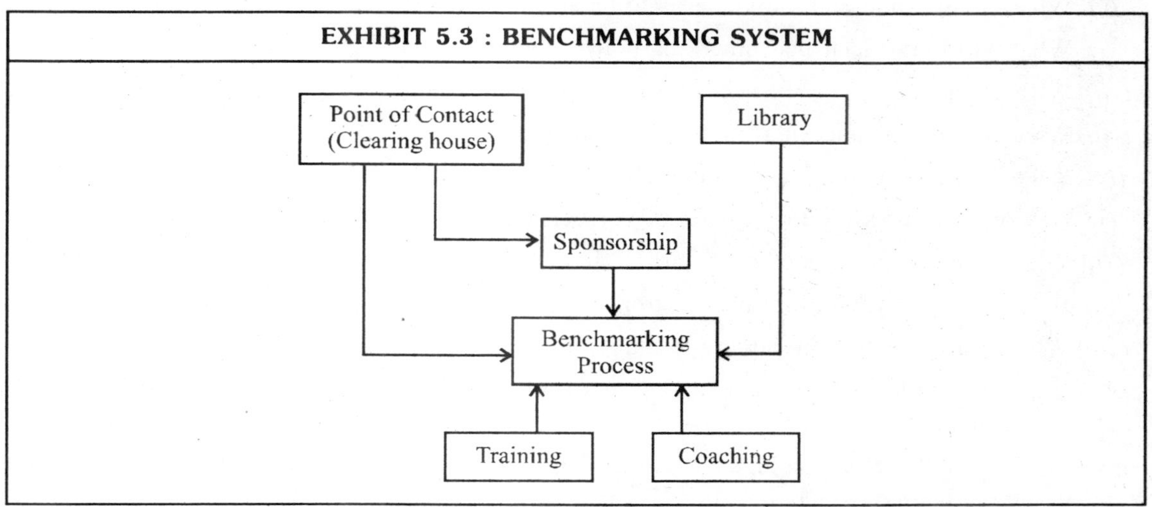

A benchmarking process is the set of steps used to discover and incorporate best practices into day-to-day operations.

The challenge is to add value to successfully weave a benchmarking process into the fabric of the organisation.

In order to effectively integrate a benchmarking process into your organisation, you should consciously address the following questions:

(i) **What do we want from benchmarking?**

- To achieve a sustainable competitive advantage.
- To strengthen core competencies.
- To improve business processes.
- To achieve incremental performance gains or make quantum leaps (breakthroughs).

(ii) **What level of commitment to benchmarking will we make?**

- Companywide implementation.
- Pilot project status.

(iii) **How will the benchmarking process relate to the following existing processes?**

- Quality improvement.
- Strategic planning.
- Competitor analysis.
- Customer satisfaction determination.
- Performance measurement.
- Reward and recognition.

(iv) What are the boundaries of our benchmarking process?

(v) What organisation and individual is to be accountable for benchmarking?

(vi) What will the official benchmarking policy contain?

(vii) What infrastructure do we need to support benchmarking?

(viii) What is our benchmarking implementation strategy?

(ix) What is our benchmarking training strategy?

(x) How will we measure the success of our benchmarking efforts?

(xi) What is the scope of our benchmarking implementation strategy?

(xii) What will we do with information from benchmarking projects?

(xiii) What is our approach to adding to our "corporate memory bank"?

(xiv) What can we learn from the experiences of others to help us accelerate the rate at which we gain from this?

(xv) What pitfalls can we avoid, such as planning effective site visits versus industrial tourism or assigning team members to full-time versus fitting benchmarking in with other duties?

What Capabilities Should the Organisation Have?

The answer depends on the role benchmarking will play in your organisation. Is benchmarking a fundamental part of your business strategy or is it a tactical tool that you simply want to have at your disposal should the need arise?

The minimum capabilities would be:

- A means to access existing information sources such as corporate or external libraries.
- Team members with process analysis, problem solving, research and change management skills.

How Long Does a Typical Benchmarking Project Take and How Much Does it Cost?

To firms that are new to benchmarking the answer to this question is the benchmarking project generally takes too long a time and costs too much.

Xerox reportedly completed its famous L.L. Bean study with one person working half time for six months.

More experienced firms ask a different set of questions first, such as:

(i) What do our customers expect from us?

(ii) What value do we provide?

(iii) What processes are the sources of that value?

(iv) If we increase the value that our customers perceive they get from us by providing world-class levels of performance, what will that mean to their customer satisfaction and our revenues?

BENCHMARKING CONSORTIUM

A benchmarking consortium is made up of organisations that have joined together to help each other perform some part of the benchmarking process. Often supported by electronic networks, the members share contacts for benchmarking studies, assist in data collection, arrange for site visits and share information regarding best benchmarking practices.

A question arises: "Should I join a consortium?" The answer is: "If benchmarking is a well-integrated part of your corporate strategy, you will probably join several consortia". The best advice is to talk to the members of the consortia you are considering, especially former members. Have some specific reasons and objectives for membership, such as to obtain a list of designated contacts in potential partner firms, or a desire to form closer relationships with your suppliers or customers or to share the cost of benchmarking studies.

Keep in mind that there is no such thing as a universal best-practices data base and that metrics represent the tip of the benchmarking iceberg. Perform due diligence, find out how much of your fees go to marketing, promotion, public seminars, and administration versus your specific objectives.

What Happens to the Information Obtained During a Benchmarking Project?

The information obtained during a benchmarking project either gets used or stored in a shelf. If used, the knowledge you gain helps you specify and make operational changes to your current work process so that the new process achieves a world-class level of performance.

Project information gets stored on a shelf when the degree of sponsorship for the project is low, the magnitude of change necessary exceeds the risk profile or resource level available, the study focuses on a comparison of metrics rather than the underlying factors that cause process performance, or when key stakeholders are not involved during the project or feel threatened by the level of performance discovered during the project.

If you have a ***benchmarking system***, you should deposit the project information into the corporate memory bank and send copies to your internal benchmarking clearing house. Your benchmarking system should also feed process performance and customer satisfaction data to the portion of your quality management system associated with process quality assurance or improvement, quality results data and customer feed back. Finally project data should also feed into your business planning process.

If your firm is performing one or more individual benchmarking projects and does not have a benchmarking system in place, the information you gather should go to sponsors, stakeholders, process owners or those charged with the successful operation, health and maintenance of the process that you are benchmarking.

BENCHMARKING CODE OF CONDUCT

The code of conduct is a set of principles and guidelines which have become the defacto standard for firms that successfully perform benchmarking projects.

The Code of Conduct

Benchmarking - the process of identifying and learning from best practices any where in the world - is a powerful tool in the quest for continuous improvement.

To contribute to efficient, effective and ethical benchmarking, individuals agree for themselves and their organisation to abide by the following ***principles*** for benchmarking with other organisations: *(i)* Keep it legal, *(ii)* Be willing to give what you get, *(iii)* Respect confidentiality, *(iv)* Keep information internal, *(v)* Use benchmarking contacts, *(vi)* Don't refer without permission, *(vii)* Be prepared at initial contact.

1. Principle of Legality

Avoid discussions or action that might lead to or imply an interest in restraint of trade: market or customer allocation schemes, price fixing, dealing arrangements, bid rigging, bribery, or misappropriation. Do not discuss costs with competitors if costs are an element of pricing.

2. Principle of Exchange

Be willing to provide the same level of information that you request, in any benchmarking exchange.

3. Principle of Confidentiality

Treat benchmarking interchange as something confidential to the individuals and organisations involved. Information obtained must not be communicated outside the partnering organisations without the prior consent of the participating benchmarking parties. An organisation's participation in a study should not be communicated without their permission.

4. Principle of Use

Use information obtained through benchmarking partnering only for the purpose of improvement of operations within the partnering companies themselves. External use or communication of a benchmarking partner's name with their data or observed practices requires permission of that partner. Do not, as a consultant or client, extend one company's benchmarking study findings to another without the first company's permission.

5. Principle of First Party Contact

Initiate the process, whenever possible, through a benchmarking contact designated by the partner company. Obtain mutual agreement with the contact on any handoff communication or responsibility to other parties.

6. Principle of Third Party Contact

Obtain an individual's permission before providing their name in response to a contact request.

7. Principle of Preparation

Demonstrate commitment to the efficiency and effectiveness of the benchmarking process with adequate preparation at each process step; particularly, at initial partnering contact.

ETIQUETTE AND ETHICS

In actions between benchmarking partners, the emphasis is on openness and trust. **The following guidelines apply to both partners in a benchmarking encounter:**

1. In benchmarking with competitors, establish specific ground rules upfront (*e.g.*, "we don't want to talk about those things that will give either of us a competitive advantage, rather, we want to see where we both can mutually improve or gain benefit").
2. Do not ask competitors for sensitive data or cause the benchmarking partner to feel that sensitive data must be provided to keep the process going.
3. Use an ethical third party to assemble and blend competitive data, with inputs from legal counsel, for direct competitor comparisons.
4. Consult with legal counsel if any information gathering procedure is in doubt (*e.g.*, before contacting a direct competitor).
5. Any information obtained from a benchmarking partner should be treated as internal privileged information.
6. Do not disparage a competitor's business or operations to a third party.
7. Do not attempt to limit competition or gain business through the benchmarking relationship.

Benchmarking Exchange Protocol

As the benchmarking process proceeds to the exchange of information, benchmarkers are expected to:

(i) Know and abide by the benchmarking code of conduct.

(ii) Have a basic knowledge of benchmarking and follow a benchmarking process.

(iii) Have determined what to benchmark, identified key performance variables, recognised superior performing companies and completed rigorous self-assessment.

(iv) Have the authority to share information.

(v) Work through a specified host and mutually agree on scheduling and meeting arrangements.

Follow these Guidelines in Face-to-face Site Visits

(i) Provide a meeting agenda in advance.

(ii) Be professional, honest, courteous and prompt.

(iii) Introduce all attendees and explain why they are present.

(iv) Adhere to the agenda, maintain focus on benchmarking issues.

(v) Use language that is universal, not one's own jargon.

(vi) Do not share proprietary information without prior approval, from the proper authority, of both parties.

(vii) Share information about your process, if asked, and consider sharing study results.

(viii) Offer to set up a reciprocal visit.

(ix) Conclude meetings and visits on schedule.

(x) Thank the benchmarking partner for the time and for sharing the information.

BOX 5.1 : BENCHMARKING IN PRACTICE – ORGANISING BENCHMARKING

- **Top Management Commitment :** When talking about benchmarking, Kay R. Whitmore - Chairman, president and CEO of the Eastman Kodak Company - stated, "We are changing the way in which we work - no longer settling for incremental change when real breakthrough is required. Whitmore demonstrates his commitment to benchmarking by talking about it at regularly scheduled meetings. He also personally served as a facilitator at the Benchmarking Business Roundtable. Benchmarking has been part of Eastman Kodak's improvement strategy since 1989.
- **Executive Improvement Team :** Total improvement management or total quality management strategy involve benchmarking programs. These total improvement processes are directed by an executive improvement team made up of the top management within the organisation and chaired by the highest-ranking officer. Edward Tracy, vice-president of AT & T's MMS Division said "If AT & T had not been into quality, I am not sure we could have pulled off benchmarking because of the culture that it needs.
- **Benchmarking Champion :** Often the benchmarking champion or czar is part of the quality-improvement organisation. *For example,* at Eastman Kodak, the director of corporate quality, vice president Ronald L. Heidke, reports to the CEO and president, Kay R. Whitmore, A. Turk Enustun, the director of corporate benchmarking, reports to Heidke.

  At IBM, the corporate responsibilities for support of the benchmarking strategy were assigned to the senior vice president of Market-Driven Quality.

  At Digital Equipment Corporation, Co-ordination of benchmarking activities was assigned to Frank McCabe, corporate vice president of quality.
- **Corporate Benchmarking Office :** The corporate benchmarking office is a small team managed by the director of corporate benchmarking. *For example,* at Digital Equipment Corporation the corporate benchmarking office consists of three individuals : the director, a consultant and an assistant.
- **Benchmarking Site and/or Division Coordinators :** Each site and/or division should have an individual assigned as its benchmarking champion.

- **Site and/or Division Benchmarking Initiation Team (Steering Committee) :** A small group of people, usually from different functions, are assigned to get the benchmarking process started, coordinate its implementation and serve as consultants for the benchmarking activities within an individual division or site.
- **Benchmarking Item Team (BIT) :** BIT consists of 5 to 10 people who are assigned to benchmark a specific business process, piece of equipment, product or manufacturing process.
- **Benchmarking Item Team Facilitator :** A trained, experienced facilitator who is not involved with the item understudy should be assigned to each benchmarking item team.
- **Benchmarking Item Team Sponsor :** A benchmarking item team sponsor is usually assigned to a BIT that is working on improving a critical business item. A sponsor is usually a very high-level person (a director or vice president).
- **Internal Benchmarking Item Committee or Network :** This committee is made up of representatives from different sites and/or divisions who have a common interest in benchmarking a specific item.

POINTS TO REMEMBER

- While benchmarking, you benchmark only one item at a time and no more.
- Benchmarking should be a key input into the organisation's strategic plan and each year's business plan.
- **Best practices** and future-trend information gathered through benchmarking has a major impact on the organisation's mission, operating principles, business objectives and performance goals.
- Benchmarking requires an organisational structure in place to support.
- **The major players in a large organisation's benchmarking structure include :**
  - *(i)* External improvement team (Top management)
  - *(ii)* Corporate benchmarking initiation team
  - *(iii)* Corporate vice-president or director of corporate benchmarking.
  - *(iv)* Corporate benchmarking office
  - *(v)* Benchmarking site and/or division coordinators
  - *(vi)* Site and/or division benchmarking initiation team (steering committee)
  - *(vii)* Benchmarking item team (BIT)
  - *(viii)* Benchmarking item team facilitator
  - *(ix)* Benchmarking item team sponsor
  - *(x)* Internal benchmarking item committee or network
- **A benchmarking system** is the infrastructure and organisational linkages necessary to deploy, reinforce and institutionalise a benchmarking process.
- **The minimum capabilities that an organisation should have for benchmarking would be :**
  - *(i)* A means to access existing information sources such as corporate or external libraries.
  - *(ii)* Team members with process analysis, problem-solving research and change management.
- **Benchmarking projects** generally take too long a time and cost too much.
- **A benchmarking consortium** is made up of organisations that have joined together to help each other perform some part of the benchmarking process.

- **Benchmarking code of conduct** is a set of principles and guidelines which have become the defacto standard for firms that successfully perform benchmarking projects.
- **Openness** and **trust** are emphasised in actions between benchmarking partners. Certain guidelines apply to both partners in benchmarking encounter to facilitate **etiquette** and **ethics** in benchmarking practices.
- **Benchmarkers** are expected to follow the **"benchmarking exchange protocol"** and **"guidelines in face-to-face site visits"** for successful implementation of benchmarking.

REVIEW QUESTIONS

1. What is "strategic planning pyramid"? Discuss the elements of a strategic plan as shown in the "strategic planning pyramid".
2. Discuss the significance of benchmarking's support structure.
3. Draw a diagram for a typical benchmarking organisational structure for a large organisation and briefly discuss the functions of its major players.
4. Discuss the responsibilities of corporate benchmarking initiation team.
5. State the responsibilities of corporate vice president or director of corporate benchmarking.
6. State the responsibilities of corporate benchmarking office.
7. Discuss the responsibilities of the site and/or division benchmarking coordinators.
8. Discuss the responsibilities of site and/or division benchmarking initiation team.
9. Discuss the characteristics of benchmarking item team members.
10. Discuss the composition of a typical benchmarking item team.
11. Discuss the responsibilities of the benchmarking item team.
12. Discuss the functions of benchmarking item team facilitator.
13. Discuss the characteristics of the benchmarking item team facilitator.
14. Discuss the functions of the benchmarking item team sponsor.
15. What is a "benchmarking system"?
16. What questions must be addressed in order to effectively integrate a benchmarking process into your organisation? Explain.
17. What capabilities should the organisation have to implement benchmarking process?
18. How long does a typical benchmarking take and how much does it cost?
19. What is "benchmarking consortium"?
20. What happens to the information obtained during a benchmarking project?
21. Discuss the importance of benchmarking code of conduct.
22. Discuss the various principles involved in "benchmarking code of contact".
23. What is etiquette and ethics in benchmarking?
24. Discuss the guidelines which apply to both partners in a benchmarking encounter.
25. What is "benchmarking exchange control"?
26. State the guidelines to be followed in face-to-face site visits in benchmarking.

DISCUSSION QUESTIONS

1. "Benchmarking should be a key input into the organisation's strategic plan and each year's business plan" - Elaborate.
2. "It is foolhardy to believe that benchmarking can be embraced within a large or average size organisation without an organisational structure in place to support this key activity". Do you agree or disagree? Give reasons for your answer.
3. "Most successful benchmarking programs are part of a total improvement management or total quality management strategy" - Discuss.
4. "In order to effectively integrate a benchmarking process into your organisation, you should consciously address certain questions". What are they? Explain.
5. "Benchmarking - the process of identifying and learning from best practices anywhere in the world - is a powerful tool in the quest for continuous improvement". Discuss.
6. "To contribute to efficient, effective and ethical benchmarking, individuals agree for themselves and their organisation to abide by certain principles for benchmarking with other organisations". Explain.

CHAPTER 6

Data Collection and Analysis

INTRODUCTION

Data and information collection and their analysis is one of the most extensive steps in the benchmarking process. It is the essence of benchmarking. In any investigation, the benchmarking team must be interested not only in the data but also the sources of it. The team is also concerned with what sources there are, why they are useful and how to access them.

Before the actual collection and analysis of benchmarking information, it is assumed that you have already identified your benchmarking customers, their requirements, and the specific critical success factors that will constitute the core of your investigation, selected and trained the members of your benchmarking team, and identified an initial list of best-practices (or competitive) benchmarking partners.

Also, it should be noted that if the initial planning and preparation stages of the process have not been completed carefully, the process of collecting and analysing benchmarking information can be unproductive or even counter productive. In fact, while discussing benchmark failures, experienced benchmarkers most often blame their difficulties in poor preparation during the planning stages and on being overanxious to begin the data collection phase.

Two aspects of data collection and analysis are: *(i)* Describing the types of data and information sources and *(ii)* How to access them for benchmarking purposes.

The most knowledgeable people to access the information are trained resource librarians. They are search experts.

The generic process chart can be used to catalog information sources. For example, what sources are inputs to a process? These are process-knowledgeable individuals such as experts in the field. Who would be considered from the process? Those with direct information, such as classification schemes, should be consulted. Who would be considered if the output side of the process was examined? These might be organisations responsible for effective performance. Lastly, what results, performance measures, or information sources should be examined? These would be organisations that collect, analyse and maintain performance statistics.

Data collection and data analysis in the real world are hard work. Data never comes packaged neatly, and different sources often provide widely disparate data about the same topic. You need a very healthy tolerance for ambiguity and a strong sense of perseverance in collecting and analysing data.

Data will be less than perfect and will age quickly, so you need always be willing to estimate and make decisions with the best available data at any point. The alternatives are commonly known as **data addiction** or **analysis paralysis**.

Some data are inherently easier to collect than others. You need to keep the following two general guidelines in mind when planning your data collection.

(i) It is usually easier to collect data from non competitors than from direct competitors.

(ii) It is usually easier to collect data about non core activities than core activities (on many industries it may be easier to collect benchmark data about human resource issues or MIS issues than about manufacturing or production costs)

Create a Data Collection Plan

Some careful thoughts should be given to the data collection approach as it takes **time** and **money**. The team should determine which data sources are likely to be most productive given the limited sources available. One approach is to go from the inexpensive source to that which require extensive resources and time. This approach results in the team first considering all **internal sources** of information, which includes electronic and public data base.

The second set of information sources is **external**. It can be extensive. The sources include the wide range of experts in the field and those organisations who by their focus have special knowledge of products and services. This latter group has secondary information, means it is a **source to the source**. Frequently it is a supplier to a benchmarking partner. The third and final category of information sources is the most difficult. It includes **custom-tailored original research** on the topic, which requires special design, development, execution and analysis. It can be quite time consuming and costly.

The benchmarking team should array the potential sources in each of these three categories. Then it should review each source and decide on its possible value and contribution to the study and any potential draw-backs or problems in using it. These tasks will guide the team's efforts as well as serve as a basis of discussion with the information search professional. This matrix will enable the team to prioritise its search. ***Box 6.1*** **lists the various sources of data/information**

BOX 6.1 : SOURCES OF DATA / INFORMATION		
Sources:		
1. **Internal:**	• Library data bases	• Internal reviews
	• Internal publications	
2. **External:**	• Professional associations	• Industry publications
	• Special industry reports	• Functional trade publications
	• General management	• Functional journals
	• Seminars	• Industry data firms
	• Industry experts	• Software / hardware vendors
	• University sources	• Company watchers
	• Advertisements	• News letters
3. **Original Research:**	• Customer feedback	• Telephone surveys
	• Inquiry service	• Networks
	• Consulting firms	• Personal meetings/site visits

Criteria for Information Gathering

Before starting any data gathering effort some thought should be given to the quality of data desired. **There are several data criteria and characteristics that should be considered. Among them are:**

(i) The amount and accuracy of the data

(ii) The cost of obtaining the data

(iii) The time required for data collection and

(iv) Whether specialists need to be used.

The time to determine the data specifications and administer the data collection effort also should not be overlooked.

The amount of data gathered may be the result of not only of the accuracy desired but how the data will be used. Trend data may require few data points while a single point accurate number may require confirmation from several sources. The accuracy will be a function of the use and importance of the data.

Data and information cost money to obtain, analyse and extrapolate to meaningful comparisons. Care should be taken to assess the best benchmarking method to derive the required data at a reasonable cost. Also benchmarking investigations take time. Benchmarking by its nature of searching for and developing data about best practices requires sifting through extensive material to find the few relevant findings and statistics desired. Also establishing productive benchmarking partners takes time. In many instances it will become necessary to confirm the data from several independent sources to ensure valid results. These steps take time. This is one reason why effective benchmarking is continuous over substantial amount of time to catalog data until enough are obtained on which to base a valid analysis.

Special skills needed in benchmarking also should be analysed. While site visits are desirable, it may be more productive to deal directly with equipment manufacturers and their representatives or with consultants. The time and effort required to administer either special studies or site visits should be carefully assessed. These are not insignificant tasks. Since benchmarking investigations are based on single contacts with others, every effort should be made to create successful first contacts.

One way to assess the requirements for these characteristics is to prepare a matrix analysis of them for the alternative benchmarking methods believed to be the most promising. In this way an informed judgment can be made about the quality of the data and gathering efforts required.

DATA COLLECTION APPROACH

Two major approaches to data collection depending on the sources of data / information are:

1. Internal data collection and
2. External data collection

These approaches are discussed in the following paragraphs.

Internal Data Collection

Because one of the primary objectives of benchmarking is to compare your performance to that of competitors or other best-in-class companies, at some point during the study you will have to collect data about your own performance. This is typically done prior to collection of data pertaining to target companies. Usually your data are more accessible than data from other companies. This forces the benchmarking team members to work through their own process at a level of detail they will need when collecting external data. Study of your company's data confirms exactly what external data are needed.

The process of collecting your own data may need to be repeated after external data are collected. The team may find that target companies measure their processes differently. It is usually easier to go back and measure your own processes in the same manner as target companies measure theirs than to get target companies to measure their own processes using your measurements.

The various sources of internal data or information existing within the organisation are:

***(i)* Process owners:** Using the process focus, it is logical to ask process owners and those who work with it what they already know and what information they believe should be tapped. Organisations obtain information either formally in company-mandated file retention, or informally, squirreled away in individual's desks, bookshelves and file cabinets. The basic principle is that those who are closest to the process are the most knowledgeable and they should be tapped first.

***(ii)* Functional experts:** Functional experts are those individuals who have specialised knowledge by virtue of their position in the organisation. They may be distribution, process or industrial engineers or analysts that have the responsibility to continually improve the operation. Because of this responsibility, the functional experts stay in touch with the developments in their field through periodicals, conferences and professional associations. They may participate in the team's benchmarking activities. These experts should be asked for their insight on information sources to tap. There may be special studies of customer service or industry comparisons of different processes that they may have already participated in or prepared that will give the team new insight.

***(iii)* Networks and historical files:** With the rise in interest in benchmarking there has been a significant increase in the number of databases to archive historical information. Thus new information is available to a wide audience that uses electronics networks.

Frequently, these networks consists of designated individuals to source information into and out of their organisation.

These data bases (or knowledge bases), because they are more populated with information rather than data-have primarily been created to ensure that best practices are documented, shared and saved for future references. These knowledge bases serve as significant repositories of benchmarking information. They are usually unique and developed within organisations with retrieval software.

In addition to the knowledge bases, there are electronic networks and people networks of professional benchmarking individuals. These are both internal and increasingly external. The electronic networks permit broadcast messages to a distribution list of knowledgeable individuals.

Internal networks of designated individuals who represent their organisations for benchmarking purposes are another significant information source. Generally there are two types of internal networks: *(a)* Informational and *(b)* Operational. Many large firms have a semiannual internal benchmarking seminar which is a means of **information exchange**. There is also an **operational network** to update ongoing benchmarking investigations, to co-ordinate company visits and to share contacts so companies will not in-advertently be visited by the same firm several times, perhaps even for the same topic.

External Data Collection

Two main ways to obtain data from external data resources are: *(i)* retrieving published data (completed research) that is in the public domain (books, magazine articles, technical reports) and *(ii)* conducting original research (interviews, testing / disassembling competitive products, site visits, surveys),

You probably will need to use both methods in developing your data base. Each data source should be carefully evaluated for: *(i)* reliability and accuracy, *(ii)* availability, *(iii)* cost, *(iv)* coverage, *(v)* timelines, *(vi)* usability, *(vii)* source and *(viii)* level of backup.

The various external data collection methods used are:

1. Published and electronic data sources
2. Live data sources
   (a) Current employees of your company
   (b) Customers
   (c) Industry Analysts
   (d) Distributors and Agents
   (e) Vendors
   (f) Data sharing Arrangements
   (g) Current and Former employees of Target Companies
   (h) Telephone Interviewing
   (i) Personal meetings / Site Visits
   (j) Surveys

These data collection methods are briefly discussed in the following paragraphs:

1. Published and Electronic Data Sources

Data come from a variety of sources from published sources to personal interviews. Some of the more common published data sources are: *(i)* Annual reports, *(ii)* Prospectuses, *(iii)* Trade journals, *(iv)* General business periodicals, *(v)* Company newsletters, *(vi)* Competitors' sales literature, *(vii)* Government/regulatory filings, *(viii)* Industry directories.

The process of getting data from **published** sources is usually referred to as **literature search**, Published sources must be accessed before the real learning in most benchmarking studies can be done. Prospectuses are a wealth of information on a relatively macro level. You should always review any current ones, if available, for a company you are studying, lots of published data in various trade journals can be found about the big players in the industry.

It is important to stay focused during the collection of published data.

Who should conduct literature searches

There are professional services with access to on-line data bases and published periodicals, directories, and they will conduct a literature search for you for a nominal fee. Using topics, companies and key words, they compile a list of abstracts of articles, you review the abstracts and identify the articles you want and they supply them. The people who work at these services are often trained librarians and they conduct a literature search very efficiently.

Publications / Media: Choosing the publications you will review as part of your information search is sometimes difficult, given the number of resources that may be available. Most of the primary sources of information are readily identifiable and accessible : the well-known business, trade and popular press sources that are commonly reviewed in your industry or functional specaility. The more difficult task is to consider those secondary sources that may be less known or difficult to locate. If your benchmarking team is familiar with any on-line databases for information in your subject area, a database search is often a good place to begin your review of publication and media resources.

Some basic recommendations for using publications and other media as a key information sources are:

***(i)* Avoid overlap:** Make sure that other members of your benchmarking team are not covering the same ground in the process of researching publications and media sources. Ensure that data gathering assignments are clear before beginning the data search.

***(ii)* Avoid rare documents:** Examples of rare documents include unpublished working papers, articles of defunct publications, esoteric academic works, foreign language resources and transcripts of speeches delivered at meetings or conventions. These rare documents are difficult to locate, consuming a considerable amount of your research time to track down.

***(iii)* Take advantage of staff support:** Use librarians, officials, managers and other employees of publications and other media. Request their help in tracking down information and providing leads for locating information.

***(iv)* Set up a document repository:** Develop a filing system for the printed materials you collect. Organise the files so that team members can easily access information collected by others. Attempt to integrate information that is collected with other information in your organisation's files or library system.

***(v)* Develop a list of names of media resources:** Maintain the list of editors, publishers, librarians, and marketers for future use and possible follow-up regarding additional leads.

Advantages and disadvantages of data collection through publications/media are listed in *Box 6.2.*

BOX 6.2 : ADVANTAGES AND DISADVANTAGES OF PUBLICATIONS / MEDIA FOR DATA COLLECTION

Advantages	Disadvantages
(i) Ease of collection / access	*(i)* Over abundance of information in some industries
(ii) Variety of resources	*(ii)* Need to validate sources/statistics
(iii) Assistance available from data sources	*(iii)* Many obscure references
(iv) Inexpensive to collect	*(iv)* May be time-consuming
(v) Public access to information	*(v)* Need to translate foreign material
(vi) Large quantities of information produced for many types of industries	

2. Live Data Sources

The best data-the data with the "answers" – typically from living, breathing sources. Some of the more common "live" sources of data include:

(A) Current employees of your company, (B) Customers, (C) Industry analysts and other industry experts, (D) Distributors, agents and manufacturer's representatives, (E) Suppliers, (F) Data-sharing arrangements, (G) Current and former employees of target companies, (H) Telephone interviews, (I) Personal meetings / Site visits, (J) Surveys.

The order mentioned above from (A) to (J) typically approximates the optimal sequence in which these sources should be approached when you are seeking data, although it is unlikely that all sources will be tapped in any single study. The reverse order (starting at the bottom of the list and moving up) best approximates the value of data or information to be obtained from these sources. The best data are those that usually require a great deal of work to obtain. Literature search- the easiest sources of data about companies you are benchmarking – usually provide only superficial levels of data. Site visits, however can provide the absolute clearest understanding of companies you are studying, but site visits are very difficult to arrange and conduct properly.

***Exhibit 6.1*, the data collection staircase, depicts the normal course of data collection.**

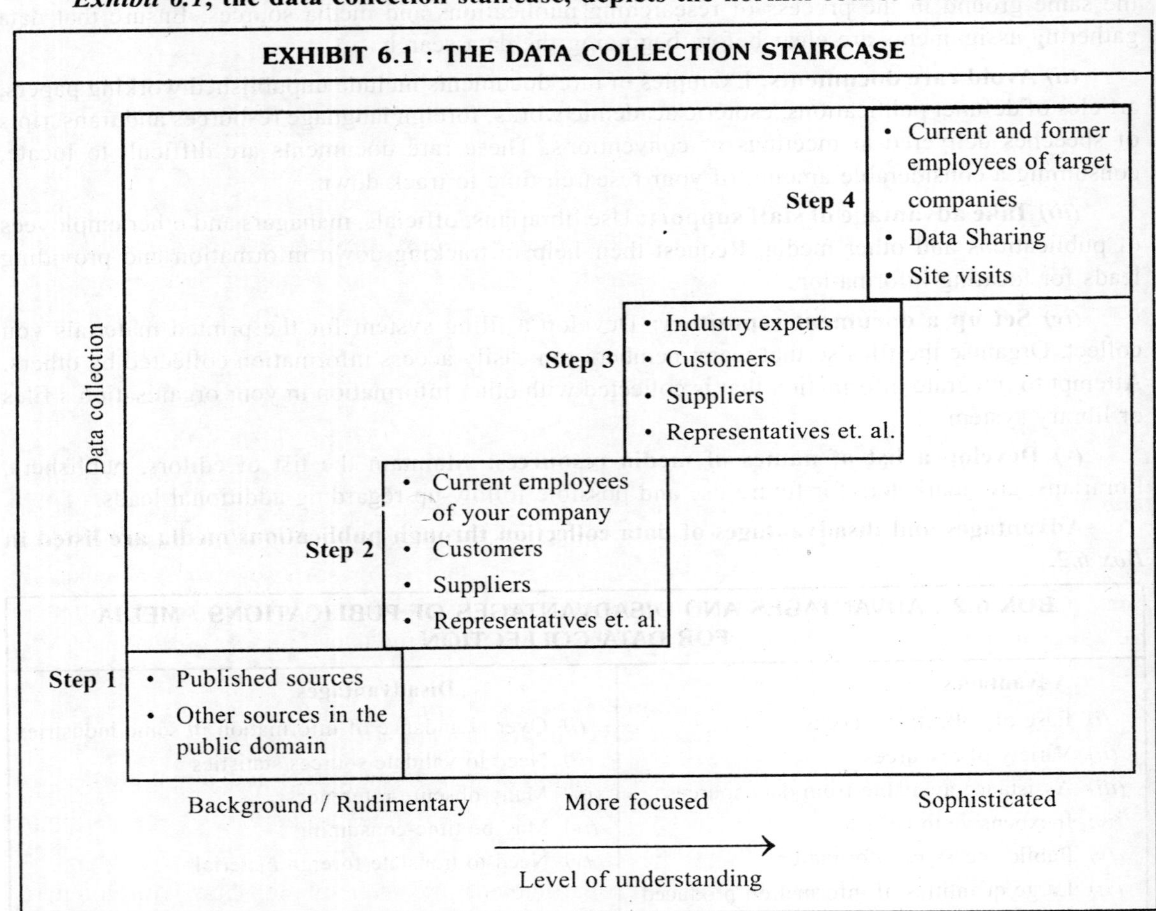

We summarise as below:

Step 1: Literature search, reading, beginning to learn.

Step 2: Early conversations with people who know more than you. Typically interspersed with what you will later consider smart or dumb questions you asked. Of course, you probably will not realise just how smart or dumb you were asking them.

Step 3: Good conversations with people who still know more than you, but you are getting smarter, you are learning a lot, and the inane or useless questions pop up less frequently.

Step 4: You are putting the icing on the cake with your interviewing and are feeling a growing, but not yet reliable sense of expertise about your level of knowledge. If you have arranged site visits or data-sharing exercises, you can easily learn something. Be sure to avoid reverting to the second step in any site visits you have arranged. At this point, your questions should be as incisive as you can make them. The unpublished sources of external data collection are discussed in the following paragraphs:

A. Current employees of your company

It is amazing how much your employees know about your competitors and sometimes about relevant companies outside the industry. A benchmarking team is remiss if internal employees are not among the first to be interviewed. Further, you may return to these people later to verify data you obtain or to fill in the pieces of questions you did not have enough knowledge to ask earlier.

You may be able to locate your employees who used to work for your benchmarking targets, taking help from your human resources department.

Your sales and service people probably encounter your competitors daily and so are a great knowledge base. The sales and service people are often the frontline of your company and they should be able to gather data on competitors on a continuous basis.

B. Customers

Your benchmarking target's customers will be quite knowledgeable about: *(a)* prices, *(b)* distribution channels, *(c)* promotions, *(d)* product and service quality, *(e)* product and/or service comparisons among industry competitors, *(f)* after-sales services and *(g)* sales pitches.

It is usually best to make these interviews appear to be standard operating procedure, unless you do not care whether your competitors learn of your enquiries. Smart customers will tell you all you want to know if they see their "sharing" information to provide them an advantage. These customers may also tell your competitors all they want to know. For purposes of a benchmarking study, it is often advisable to have a third party conduct customer interviews for you, so that customers are not made aware that your company is the one interested in the data.

C. Industry analysts

Industrial analysts generally should have the knowledge of:

(a) Individual company strategies for competing in their industries and the strengths and weaknesses of each.

(b) Strategic groups within industries

(c) Forces affecting industries and their participants and their relationships with company strategies

(*d*) Financial characteristics of industry participants and their relationships with company strategies

(*e*) Future plans of industry participants

This widely diverse group of people can be very helpful and includes those who work for trade associations, academicians and investment analysts (*e.g.*, Wall street analysts).

D. Distributors and agents

Distributors and agents are generally knowledgeable about: *(a)* Channel structure, *(b)* Channel compensation practices, *(c)* Company product and / or service strengths and weaknesses compared to those of competitors, *(e)* Channel conflicts and *(f)* Trends in evolution of channel structure.

Distributors and agents may be able to supply a wealth of information, but they may also be difficult to track down, especially if they travel extensively and if they realise, when they speak with you that you are not buying something from them. These people, like customers may pass the word along to your benchmarking partners that you are studying them. So, you may want to consider enlisting outside help to interview agents and distributors.

E. Vendors

Vendors of target companies in your benchmarking study can provide information about: *(a)* Costs and usage of materials and components, *(b)* Quality and yields of materials and components, *(c)* Substitutes for materials and components and their costs and benefits, *(d)* Trends in costs and quality (e) Inventory levels and composition, *(f)* Payment terms and practices, *(g)* Supply channels and channel characteristics.

Like customers and distributors, vendors can provide in-depth information about target companies. Vendor data should be scrutinised to ensure that what you are hearing is free of sales pitch hyperbole. Because vendors too, tend to talk with your competitors, you may wish to consider having a third party interview vendors also.

F. Data-sharing arrangements

Data can be obtained through some data-sharing arrangements among groups of companies that desire to compare their performance within an industry or across different industries. Within industries, data exchanges are usually administered by an independent third party that gathers, compiles and often analyses and interprets data. The participant's identities may or may not be revealed in an industry data exchange depending on the level of detail exchanged and the competitive sensitivity of the data. Data exchanges however, many of which are presently being conducted by the accounting firms and consulting firms that specialise in various industries, often do not include the qualitative information about where a firm stands in relation to its competitors in a given area. This is how that makes benchmarking so valuable. For this reason data exchanges are seldom at the end of a benchmarking effort.

Across industry lines, data exchanges can be more open as long as participants do not compete with one another in significant makes or as long as the activity being shared is non core in nature. Inter-industry data exchanges may be administered by an independent party or by one of the participants, depending on the various factors that affect confidentiality.

G. Current and former employees of target companies

There is not much you can not learn from current and former employees of target companies if you spread the net wide enough and relentless in your pursuit of data. You must have enough analytical skills to make sense of the many seemingly unrelated pieces of data after the filtering process. When their benchmarking targets are competitors, many companies use outside firms to collect data. **Outsiders are often able to do a better and more efficient job of collecting data from their client's competitors for two reasons:**

(i) They are specialists. They have offices with consultants whose sole job is to call competitors all day long, looking for that one person in a hundred who can give them the data they need for the "industry study" they are conducting.

(ii) If you were working for Coke and someone for Pepsi called to inquire about the production capacity of your main bottling line, you wouldn't be inclined to answer. And you must identify yourself and your organisation, when calling, for ethical, if not legal reasons.

H. Telephone interviewing

Telephone interviewing is one of the most efficient means of gathering data from target companies, it can also be very frustrating, Interviewing people who you do not know over the phone requires perseverance.

The telephone is the bench marker's most valuable tool. In just a few minutes the caller can solicit answers to questions from a wide variety of sources.

With some basic skill training, employees can become effective telephone interviewers and develop a high degree of efficiency in their information collection activities.

There are several advantages to gathering information over the telephone. In general, telephone interviews are easy to plan and conduct. A basic outline and ability to communicate are the primary requisites. Telephone interviews are also economical when a large number of contacts need to be made to collect data/ information. International benchmarking creates additional opportunities to take advantage to time zone differences.

Telephones also provide flexibility regarding place. You can conduct a benchmarking interviews from any telephone located anywhere – a hotel, a car, even an airplane. Another advantage is that you don't have to be dressed in business attire to collect information over the telephone.

Difficulties in collecting information over the telephone often occur when the caller is not sufficiently prepared. There are many instances of "cold callers" who waste people's time talking on generalities, failing to adequately describe their mission and objectives; not properly identifying themselves and intruding on people's schedules. It is also difficult to get people to return telephone calls. You are also more likely to be interrupted when speaking on the telephone, be prepared to be put on hold. Finally, people often limit the amount of time they will spend with you on the telephone at a single time. You may have to call some of your sources several times to complete your information – collection activities.

The following recommendations are made by those who are skilled and experienced using the telephone as a data gathering tool:

(i) **Prepare ahead of time:** Before you even pick up a telephone, you should have a specific set of questions arranged in a logical sequence. You should also have some type of

formal data-gathering outline that identifies the types of information to be recorded and provides space for recording the response of each organisation contacted.

(ii) **Develop a list of preferred contacts:** Organise your resource list in order of preference and contact the organisations in that order. Make "call status" notations next to each resources you call (*e.g.,* conducted interview, will return call, call back later)

(iii) **Co-ordinate your calling with the team members:** Ensure that only one team member is assigned to call each resources. Meet the team members to share information regarding your experiences to date. Check any internal benchmarking data bases that list previous benchmarking efforts that might be used as a reference. Make sure that you are aware of other individuals or teams from your organisation that might be calling the same resources.

(iv) **Contact a specific individual:** By knowing the name and titles of knowledgeable sources, you avoid wasting time with someone who doesn't understand your need. The public relations department of the target company can generally put you in touch with experts in the company as well as direct you to outside sources.

(v) **Explain who you are and why you are calling:** By doing so, you establish credibility and put the contact at ease. Prepare a written statement of your benchmarking activity, your own personal background, and a brief outline of the subjects you want to review. Send this information to your benchmark partner as part of your introduction.

(vi) **Feed information:** Remember that you are calling people without prior notice. To help orient their thoughts and adjust their thinking towards your needs, share some of the information you have found out to date and tell them what you still need.

(vii) **Mention the source of your referral:** Referrals are door openers. Whenever you call some one based on a referral, ensure that the first thing you tell him or her is the name of the person who referred you. Because of previous benchmarking efforts that have involved the source's company and refer by name to individuals who have cooperated with you or your organisation in previous benchmarking situations.

(viii) **Exchange information:** Offer to exchange information or send a brief summary of the results. This is especially an effective technique when soliciting information from service professionals who make their living dispensing advice. Many organisations will not give you information unless you can offer something in return.

(ix) **Give the other party a realistic estimate of the amount of time you require:** Never say that the interview will take a few minutes when an hour is more realistic. Acknowledge the time requirements and suggest multiple interviews as a way of coping with time constraints.

(x) **Follow up:** Prepare a standard "thank – you" note to send to those individuals who have participated in your telephone interviews. A brief summary of project results or progress to data should also be included; if appropriate. Remember, you and your benchmarking team will probably be engaging in benchmarking projects in the future. As you begin to develop your benchmarking network, you should keep a file of contacts who have provided you with useful information. Following up with your benchmark partners is one way to begin to develop your own information network.

In addition to the recommendations cited above, the following ideas work quite well when they are used by consultancies gathering data over the phone and may also make your phone interviewing efforts go more smoothly.

(i) Target the lowest-level person within an organisation who might be able to help you first, and move up from there. It is like climbing the data collection staircase: you are learning so you can have higher-level conversations with higher-level people.

(ii) Always identify yourself and your organisation, and give an overview of your project. Try not to give too many details – your potential interviewers may become confused, or you may lead them to believe that what you want is not something they can help with, even though you believe you can learn from them.

(iii) Ask whether you can take just a moment of their time.

(iv) If your party is too busy to talk, ask when it would be convenient for you to call back. Also ask for the names of others with whom you might talk.

(v) If you get connected to voice mail, don't bother to leave a message. Most people will call you back eventually, but calling you likely is not a high priority for them and it can be more stressful waiting for them to return your call than continuing to try them. Keep trying to reach them yourself.

(vi) Ask open ended questions and let your interviewers discuss what they want. You never know where the conversation might take you.

(vii) Be prepared to offer some information as a stimulus to get them talk.

(viii) Remember, it is the human nature to socialise. Exchanging information is social experience. Skilled interviewers can get answers they need to questions they don't ask simply by engaging in conversation.

I. Personal meetings / Site Visits

One of the most interesting and potentially rewarding experiences of benchmarking is the personal interview or site visits. In these situations, you arrange personal meetings with benchmarking resources and if possible, arrange to conduct the meetings in their facilities. A well-planned site visit can be the single best way to cap a benchmarking study. No other forum provides the efficiency and ability to dig on a particular study that a site visit does.

"Personal interview or site visits" method of data collection has several advantages:

(i) A personal meeting provides you with a better opportunity to gather more detailed information. In-person interviews almost always yield a higher quality of information than telephone interviews or surveys.

(ii) You may have the opportunity to observe the work process in action. Try to arrange a site tour with your benchmark partner and offer a reciprocal tour to your site.

(iii) Personal meetings are more likely to result in the development of a long-term relationship with your benchmark partners than other forms of data gathering. There is really no substitute for a face-to-face meeting when establishing relationships with benchmark partners.

Other opportunities for face-to-face interactions occur at conferences, conventions and trade shows. This type of meetings is useful when a benchmarking project is extended over a long period and there is no immediate need for information.

Personal meetings and site visits have some draw-backs:

They are time-consuming and depending on the travel involved, expensive. One strategy to consider is to reserve personal meetings and site visits for those organisations that truly represent best practices or for direct competitors that have offered an invitation for a personal meeting. Do not initiate a personal visit with every organisation on your data gathering list unless they are all highly select best-practices resources.

There are some basic recommendations to consider when planning personal meetings or interviews:

(i) ***Confirm all appointments in writing:*** This is a normal business courtesy and ensures that you have scheduled adequate time to conduct your interviews. Follow up to confirm your appointment by telephone several days in advance of your meeting.

(ii) ***Travel in pairs:*** For very detailed or technical interviews that require extensive note taking, have another member of your benchmarking team accompany you. This facilitates one individual focusing on the interview and the other recording the information.

(iii) ***Use a structured outline:*** As with telephone interviews, prepare your questions in advance . If possible establish an interview matrix that lists the specific information you want to collect and provide space for entering the source of information. If appropriate, forward a copy of your questions or the data-collection form to the interviewee in advance. This may save a lot of time for both of you.

(iv) ***Arrange for a follow-up:*** Even if you don't follow up in person or by telephone it is recommended that you create an expectation that some level of follow-up may be required. This expectation facilitates any second-phase data gathering you may need to initiate.

(v) ***Send a thank you note:*** Acknowledge the meeting in writing or by telephone. Development of a personal benchmarking network is often affected by the level of professional courtesy and personal attention you show your benchmark partners.

Site Visits: Even though site visits have many advantages, not all studies are best completed with a site visit. Infact, site visits can be a waste of time. In benchmarking a manufacturing process or some other physical activities, a site visit can add considerable value. The flow of product through a plant may be hard to understand without a site visit. But in benchmarking a managerial process such as training, a site visit may add little value.

To be of real value, site visits should be preceded by a great amount of acquisition and analysis of data, preferably acquired directly from the organisation being benchmarked in an agreed upon format that permits ease of analysis and ensures that the data collected are consistent with comparable data from the benchmarking team's organisation. The site visit itself should focus on those few, very detailed issues that are left unanswered by the data alone. The visit should include the line managers of the areas being benchmarked so they can see first hand that improvement is possible.

One of the most difficult and sensitive problems of site visits is obtaining a level of cooperation from host management that will enable the benchmarking team to maximize its learning opportunity. Three issues are critical and must be addressed when you are contemplating a site visit:

(i) ***Timing:*** Host management will need time to prepare for the benchmarking team's unit, which often includes obtaining approval from the home office, arranging the schedules of all those who will be involved in the visit, collecting, packaging, and shipping a previsit data package, and preparing the site presentation. Patience and gentle persuasion are valuable virtues when you are arranging a site visit with a group of managers you have never met. Timing is often a critical issue when a single site is being visited. The complexity of time increases greatly when several sites are being visited. Flexibility and keen logistical skills are keys to smooth success in planning and executing multiple site visits.

(ii) ***Confidentiality:*** *(a)* ***Yours**:* If confidentiality is an issue, an artfully crafted letter from an outside firm that is coordinating the benchmarking process can often be used to gauge a target company's willingness to participate. After positive interest have been expressed by the target organisation, the outside firm may disclose the benchmarking team's affiliation. *(b)* ***Theirs**:* The benchmarking team should be prepared to execute a confidentiality agreement of some sort to ensure that sensitive data from the target organisation are not misused. All members of the team must be well informed of the details of the agreement.

(iii) ***Quid pro quo:*** This is commonly known from the host company's point of view as "What is in it for me?" When several sites from different organisations are being visited, an offer to prepare a compilation of data to be distributed to each participant in the study is often sufficient to obtain participation from target sites.

To avoid later misunderstandings, these issues should be addressed at the outset of any communications with potential benchmarking partners.

J. Surveys

Surveys are often used as a means of collecting information from a large sample of individuals or organisations. They are most useful when collecting information that is easy for the respondent to provide and is not of a sensitive nature. The advantages of surveys are that they are relatively inexpensive to administer and summarise and they allow you to canvas a large audience in a short time. Many experienced benchmarking organisations use surveys as a method of narrowing their lists of potential benchmark partners.

The disadvantages of surveys include their traditional low return rate and the fact that information you can gather is limited. Surveys do not allow for follow-up questions or detailed process information. Also there have been reports of companies refusing to respond to surveys of any type due to lack of survey quality.

There are some basic recommendations to be considered when planning the use of surveys:

(i) ***Keep it short:*** People are willing to dedicate 20 to 30 minutes maximum to a survey questionnaire they receive in the mail.

(ii) ***Call before you send:*** If possible, call the individuals who will be receiving the survey questionnaire. By requesting their cooperation and providing some basic information about your project, you significantly increase your return rate and might establish a rapport that could lead to further contact or site visits.

(iii) ***Avoid lengthy response requirements:*** Avoid questions that require the respondent to write lengthy responses. Avoid open-ended questions.

(iv) ***Provide a self-addressed, stamped return envelope:*** This is a basic requirement.

(v) ***Identify yourself and how you can be reached:*** Endorse a business card or telephone number where the respondents can reach you if they have any questions to ask.

(vi) ***Design your survey for easy data transfer:*** Design your survey so that information can easily be transferred onto data summary sheets. Avoid crowding the document so that data are forced together.

(vii) ***Acknowledge receipt of the survey:*** Send a response card back to the respondents acknowledging your receipt of the survey questionnaire and thanking them for their response.

Table 6.1 **lists the advantages and disadvantages of three major data-collection methods discussed *viz.,* telephone interview, Personal meetings / site visits and Surveys.**

TABLE 6.1: ADVANTAGES AND DISADVANTAGES OF SOME MAJOR DATA COLLECTION METHODS

Methods	Advantages	Disadvantages
1. Telephone interviews	*(i)* Easy to plan and conduct *(ii)* Enables contact with a large number of resources *(iii)* Can be conducted at almost any time *(iv)* Relatively inexpensive	*(i)* "Cold calling" can be time-consuming *(ii)* Difficult to get return calls *(iii)* May be interruptions *(iv)* People are less likely to spend a lot of time on telephone.
2. Personal meetings/site visits	*(i)* Establishes personal and professional relationship *(ii)* Provides more quality time *(iii)* Likely to produce good deal of information	*(i)* Expensive (travel costs) *(ii)* Time-consuming *(iii)* There can be scheduling difficulties
3. Surveys	*(i)* Ability to collect information from a large population *(ii)* Easy to construct *(iii)* Relatively inexpensive *(iv)* Easy transfer of information for analysis	*(i)* Low return rate *(ii)* Impersonal *(iii)* No possibility to ask follow-up questions *(iv)* Questionable validity of some information *(v)* Must be relatively brief *(vi)* Little possibility for detailed response.

Original Research and Investigations

Original research must be conducted where data does not exist in internal or external public sources. A major draw back of original research is that it is expensive. Ensuring that the data / information desired is correctly sourced requires careful thought, attention to detail, and successful planning.

It is best to approach these investigations in a step-by-step fashion to obtain what is desired. The steps should proceed from the difficult to more difficult. The first approach will be questionnaires, then site visits and later more advanced techniques, such as panels of benchmarking partners. Direct site visits are most often associated with benchmarking and thus will receive the greatest focus.

The conduct of original research is the last way to source information and the most difficult to perform. It requires the most resources to define the project, conduct the search, analyse the data and prepare the findings. It also requires the most time to complete.

Making Contact With Potential Target Companies

Contacting a real human being at a potential target company that you would like to have joined a cooperative or collaborative benchmarking study seems to be the toughest task in any benchmarking study.

You can increase the likelihood of getting potential targets to participate in your study by doing a few simple things. There are no guarantees, of course. Some organisations have a policy against sharing information, some managers are too busy and others just do not want to be bothered. On the other hand, some who might be willing participants may be turned off if you send wrong signals. The following are some points to consider regarding making first contact with potential targets.

***(i)* When to contact:** Peer to peer usually has the best results, plant manager to plant manager, vice president of sales to vice president of sales etc. Some companies funnel all benchmarking information through a central benchmarking function, others do not. Your peer ultimately will make the decision, though and may push to participate in a study that some one else in the organisation may not consider as important. Selling the idea to your peer is imperative.

***(ii)* How to make contact:** Best results are usually obtained by using a two-step approach a letter followed by a phone call.

The letter is best sent via overnight delivery so it catches the recipient's attention on arrival and you are sure that it reached there on time.

Then, if you have mentioned in your letter, you would call on a certain day, be sure to do so. Before calling, brainstorm with the benchmarking team to develop a list of potential questions that the recipients may have for you and appropriate response to each. Then make the call.

***(iii)* Anticipate some rejection**: It is unlikely that every organisation you invite to participate in your study will accept. And of those who accept, some may not fulfill their obligations. Don't take it personally. Expect some attrition and you will be able to maintain a positive altitude.

The most important thing you convey to potential target organisation is your sincerity and intention to complete a value-adding study. The best-in-class companies, which are the most frequent recipients of bench marking requests, have learnt to weed out the serious requests from the industrial tours.

Data Collection- Science and Art

Data collection is a mix of science and art. It is science in the sense that you need to know where to look for data. You need also to use great care in planning their acquisition to ensure that all the data needed for bench-marking study are obtained on time. Data will not be useful to the team if they arrive outside the team's specified time frame.

Actually obtaining data, however, can be quite an art, especially when the information you seek is locked in somebody else's mind. These data are usually the most valuable pieces of benchmarking jigsaw puzzle. They may be the most difficult pieces to obtain, especially when the data concern your competitors. You need to know how to ask, once you have identified the appropriate person to address.

In a truly competitive situation, it is likely that an outside consultant will do the data gathering, which will span the gamut of data sources and collection techniques.

DATA ANALYSIS

Data analysis is a critical phase of the bench marking process, because you must organise masses of numbers and statements into coherent, usable information to direct all your future activities. The success or failure of the benchmarking process depends on how well the collected data are translated into usable information.

The **measurement data** provide you with indicators of where the best practices, procedures, and the processes can be found. As you compare the data on benchmarking items against your item, you may find that you are the best (world class), the same or worse, If your comparison is negative or the same, an opportunity exists to improve by studying another organisation's or location's item.

Two types of data collected and used in the benchmarking study include qualitative data (descriptive) and quantitative data (numbers, ratios etc.). Your benchmarking strategy should be designed to collect both types of data as opportunities present themselves.

As data has been collected and summarised, you are ready for the next step in the benchmarking process – data analysis. Consider the following recommendations as you begin the process for determining the meaning of the information you have collected.

(i) Check for Misinformation

Misinformation is information that is incorrect due to such factors as misinterpretation, improper recording or transcription, purposeful misrepresentative of data (from the source) and errors (from the source). Misinformation may be difficult to identify by simply reviewing the data summaries. There are however, clues that can indicate misinformation in your data. One indicator is information that deviates significantly from what was expected or from other data that should be comparable.

Another indicator of possible misinformation is conflicting data from multiple sources-for example, information collected on the same subject by different members of the team or by different means (*e.g.,* interviews, published reports). Some allowances must be made for minor differences in data collected from different sources. However, major discrepancies should be investigated.

If there is any indication of misinformation in your data, consider taking the following actions:

(i) Recheck your sources for accuracy and make any necessary corrections.

(ii) If your sources continue to provide conflicting information, you can attempt to reconcile the differences by informing your sources of the conflict and asking for their help to resolve the issue. You may also identify alternative sources that may be more accurate.

(iii) If rechecking the data is not worth the time or effort required, simply eliminate the data from the data base.

If you discover that misinformation is a common factor in your database, you may have to reexamine your data-collection strategy and consider alternative strategies or methods.

(ii) Identify Patterns

This is one of the most basic forms of analysis you will conduct. General patterns or trends are often noticeable as you examine your data matrices. For example, trends in sales data reported by year for a set of competitors are often noticeable when the data are arranged in a matrix. Cost and revenue data are generally analysed immediately for patterns or trends.

(iii) Identify Omissions or Displacement

What is not present after you have completed your analysis can often be as significant as what is present. Problems in this area usually consist of two major types: The first one of **omission**-missing data that should be available. Although some data are difficult to collect and interpret, other pieces of information should be available – for example, information on employee demographics, such as education level or geographical location. Omission of these kinds of data is worth exploring. The second type of problem is called **displacement** and often involves significant changes in data trends without explanation. For example an organisation may provide information that represents a radical departure from its normal or expected routine (*e.g.,* pricing practices, warranty provisions). This information may even be cross-checked and found to be accurate. The lack of an explanation for this type of puzzling data is considered a displacement.

(iv) Check for Anamalies

An anamaly is defined as "data what do not fit, usually an indication that one's working assumption are wrong or that an unknown factor is affecting the results. Seek out anamalies and figure out why they occurred. Something out of ordinary should not automatically be rejected as an aberration or mistake. If you spot an anamaly, first ensure that it is not a mistake in the way the data were presented or collected. Then look for other indicators that these data could be true. The existence of an anamaly may indicate that your basic assumptions about what is true or what is possible are not current or correct.

(v) Draw Conclusions

The ultimate goal of benchmarking analysis is to better understand relevant activities of other organisations and use that information to improve your own organisational performance. In most benchmarking analyses, you review information that was gathered from a number of organisations. One of the most difficult challenges is to make logical comparisons and draw reasonable conclusions from information that, in some case, may seem contradictory or confusing. At the very least, some of the information you collect from your benchmarking partners will force you to challenge your assumptions or question the practices of your partners.

The data-evaluation process involves collecting facts and eliminating unreliable, inaccurate, false and irrelevant data. You organise and assemble the useful data for patterns that reveal trends and business developments.

Then you draw inferences about the actions, strategies, plans and results of other organisations. Finally you are ready to draw conclusions based on the information you have collected.

The level of analysis and types of conclusions that organisations make as a result of their benchmarking activities generally fall into several categories:

***(i)* Defining competitive advantage:** Most companies attempt to establish their competitive advantage, even if that was not one of their initial requirements- attributes this to human nature. **Before you set out to define your competitive advantage, there are three things to be done:**

(a) View your own organisation impartially and objectively.

(b) Accept information concerning what others think about you.

(c) Accept what you find about your competitors or best-practice companies, even if it does not agree with your perceptions.

Once you have accepted these, you can begin to define your opportunities for improvement.

***(ii)* Establishing the business context:** Most companies use a position of their benchmarking effort to develop a perspective on the business and regulating environment. This usually involves determining the present and future regulatory and financial environments facing your organisation, your industry group, and your comparative others (*i.e.,* your benchmarking partners)

***(iii)* Knowing your strengths and weakness:** A fundamental outcome of most benchmarking investigation is an understanding of your strengths and weaknesses. This information comes from those who know your operations- your employees, customers, suppliers, competitors and competitor's customers. Other perspectives about your organisation may be provided by your benchmark partners.

***(iv)* Understanding the strengths of other organisations:** Having identified your competitors or best-practice organisations, you should focus on how they achieve their level of performance and prominence. Review the benchmarking information you have collected to answer the following questions:

(a) What is that organisation's single greatest competitive asset?

(b) With respect to critical success factors, what is the specific strengths of the other organisation that have the most potential to improve my own organisation's performance.

***(v)* Determine the performance gap:** One of the more traditional objectives of a benchmarking investigation involves a comparison between your organisation's products, services, work processes, or results and those of your competitors or excellent or best-practice organisations. The objective of this analysis is to identify any type of performance gap that exists. For the most part, attention is focused on negative gaps- that is when your performance; products, or services are operating at a level below that of the organisations you have benchmarked.

DATA ANALYSIS METHODS

The type of data collected and used in the benchmarking process may include both qualitative data and quantitative data. A quantitative data matrix should be developed and filled out during the data collection cycle. This matrix should highlight the parts of the process requiring additional data and study. It is best to complete the matrix as thoroughly as possible before doing surveys or visiting organisations.

***Table 6.2* gives the example of a data matrix**

TABLE 6.2 : DATA MATRIX FOR NEW HIRING PROCESS BENCHMARK

Data	Company			
	A	B	C	Ours
(i) Average days to bring new employees on board	45	65	20	45
(ii) Number of approvals required	5	5	2	4
(iii) Percentage of new employees who leave in first 12 months because of unsatisfactory performance	10	8	5	12
(iv) Wages compared with average	1 : 1	0.8 : 1	1.1 : 1	1.1 : 1

Qualitative data also should be collected and analysed. Some effective ways to present and analyse qualitative data are:

1. Word charts (Refer *Table 6.3*)
2. Work word flow charts (Refer *Box 6.3*)
3. Comparable process flow chart (Refer *Exhibit 6.2*)

TABLE 6.3 : WORD CHART FOR THE HIRING PROCESS

	Company			
	A	**B**	**C**	**Ours**
Forms	One form for new hire and budget change	Four forms for budget, internal hire, external hire, and offer.	Computers process all data, different screens used for budget and hiring.	Two forms; One for budget, one for hiring
Budget Change Approval	2nd level 3rd level Controller Accounting manager	2nd level 3rd level Controller Accounting manager Division V.P	2nd level Accounting manager	2nd level 3rd level Accounting manager
New Employee Hiring Approval	2nd level 3rd level Plant manager Division personnel Industrial engineering	2nd level 3rd level Plant manager Corporate personnel Personnel manager	2nd level Personnel manager	2nd level 3rd level Industrial engineering Personnel manager

Do not be misled by the measurement data. Just because a location of an organisation has better overall performance, it does not mean that all the activities within its process are world class. Every item has its strong and weak points. Use all the data you have collected to search out the very best of each part of the item being studied. Frequently, the world's best organisation does not have all the best individual parts of the item being studied and input from organisations that are not quite as good can give your organisation the competitive advantage it is looking for. What the benchmarking organisation needs to do is to select the best parts of each benchmarking partner's item and put them together to design a "future-state solution" that is better than any one of the individual items that were benchmarked.

BOX 6.3 : QUALITATIVE WORK WORD FLOWCHART PROCESS USED BY A MANAGER TO START THE HIRING CYCLE

1. Check to see what the overtime has been for the last 3 months. (Can get approval for a new hire if overtime in the department has been greater than 60 hours / week for the last 3 months).
2. Prepare job description for new employees.
3. Have salary administration evaluate the new job and classify it.
4. Prepare a payback analysis.
5. Fill out a personnel requisition, fill out a budget variation request and get next-level approval.
6. If added budget is required, fill out a budget variation request and get next-level approval.
7. Prepare a letter of justification and send it to the controller for approval.
8. Send approval personnel request, budget variation request and job description to personnel department.

EXHIBIT 6.2 : COMPARABLE PROCESS FLOW CHART OF FOUR DIFFERENT COMPANIES

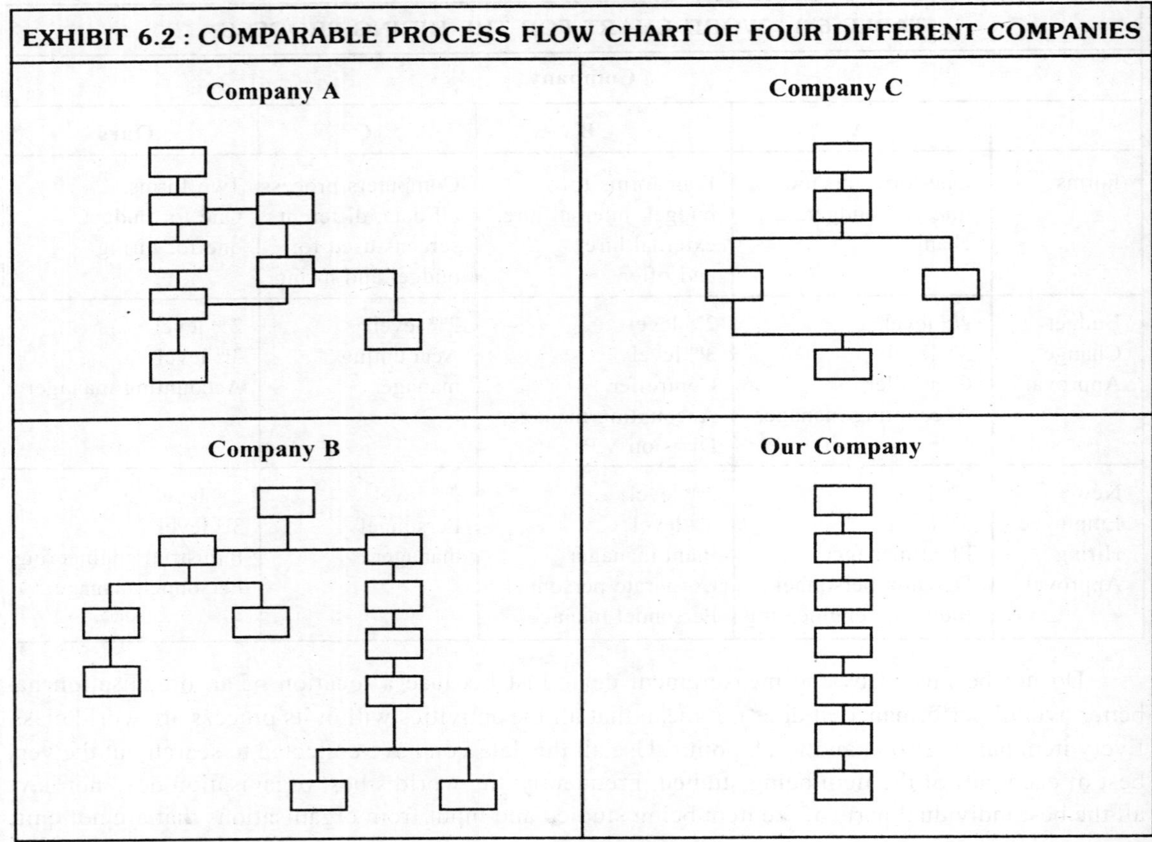

Often, you will find that no one organisation has all the right answers and it will be necessary to combine activities from the organisations studied to establish a new best item. Combining the best elements from different benchmarking partners allows you to develop a new standard of excellence, and to become the benchmark organisation for your item.

It is a good idea to have the measurement chart updated to reflect all the surveys conducted, and all the data collected from other sources, before you visit an organisation. Having this information on hand pinpoints to activities in the process with the greatest potential for a major break through at your organisation. The primary purpose of these visits is to observe activities firsthand and to collect detailed qualitative data about planned-for or projected improvements to the item. The information collected not only should provide you with a picture of the current gap between you and the benchmarking partner, it should also furnish you with some insights into the benchmarking partner's item's past and future performance. It is essential to use this information to project where the world-class standard will be in the future. Change takes time and event the best item must continue to improve. That is how it got to be the best.

Performance Projection Chart

The most dramatic and effective way to illustrate the difference between your item and the benchmarking partner's item is by a "performance projection chart" often called a "gap/trend analysis chart" which is illustrated in *Exhibit 6.3.*

EXHIBIT 6.3 : PERFORMANCE PROJECTION CHART

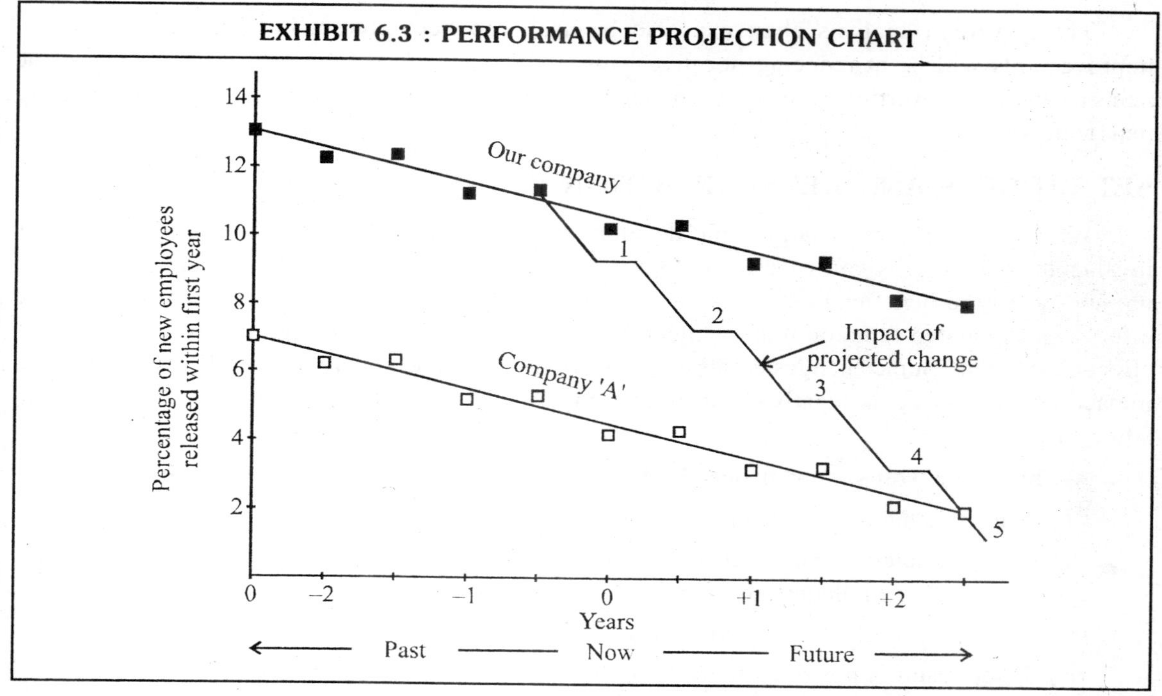

In this chart, the new points are fixed by collected data. You can obtain your organisation's past performance data by consulting its history file. Most organisations have registered some performance improvement over the years as a result of normal goal setting. Improvement in productivity of 2 to 5 percent per year is common. If your organisation is using a continuous improvement process, it should be improving at the rate of 10 to 20 percent a year without benchmarking. Using the established trend, the benchmarking team can project how the item will be performing over the next 3 years.

Additional consideration should be given to any planned-for improvement in the item's performance over the same 3 year period. If no data are available from the benchmarking partner, substitute your organisation's slope for that of the benchmarking organisation.

Normally the best-of-breed organisations got there because their improvement rate was much better than that of other organisations. **Analysing each key measurement will reveal one of the following:**

(i) The gap is in favour of your organisation.

(ii) There is no gap between your organisation and the benchmark organisation.

(iii) The gap is not in favour of your organisation because

(a) The gap is staying the same

(b) The gap is widening when your item is performing worse.

(c) The gap is narrowing when your item is performing better.

When there is no gap or the gap is unfavourable, the performance point is a candidate for an improvement action plan.

The gap/trend analysis chart can also be useful to help predict how effective potential improvements will be at reducing negative gaps. Exhibit 6.4 shows the projected impact on the items performance overtime when five separate improvements are implemented in the benchmarking item team's item.

SET TARGETS AND DEVELOP ACTION PLANS

When you start setting targets and developing action plans, qualitative information becomes invaluable, since it tells you what to do to bring about positive change. Many organisations try to implement all the beneficial activities and process changes they have discovered in one massive effort to make a step-function improvement in their item. This approach frequently has disastrous effect on the item. Some changes do not work, and bring the process to a stand still. Others have no impact, either positive or negative. But all of them cost something to implement and most of them add cost to the item.

At this stage, you should proceed with caution and follow the steps given below:

(i) Prioritise the potential changes

(ii) Use a simulation computer model to prove out the proposed future-state solution before changes are implemented

(iii) Then pilot each change and measure the results.

(iv) If the result is positive, implement the change and measure the effects of the completed implementation.

(v) If the results show a negative impact or no improvement, eliminate the change and proceed with the next change.

EXHIBIT 6.4 : IMPACT OF CHANGE IN THE HIRING PROCESS

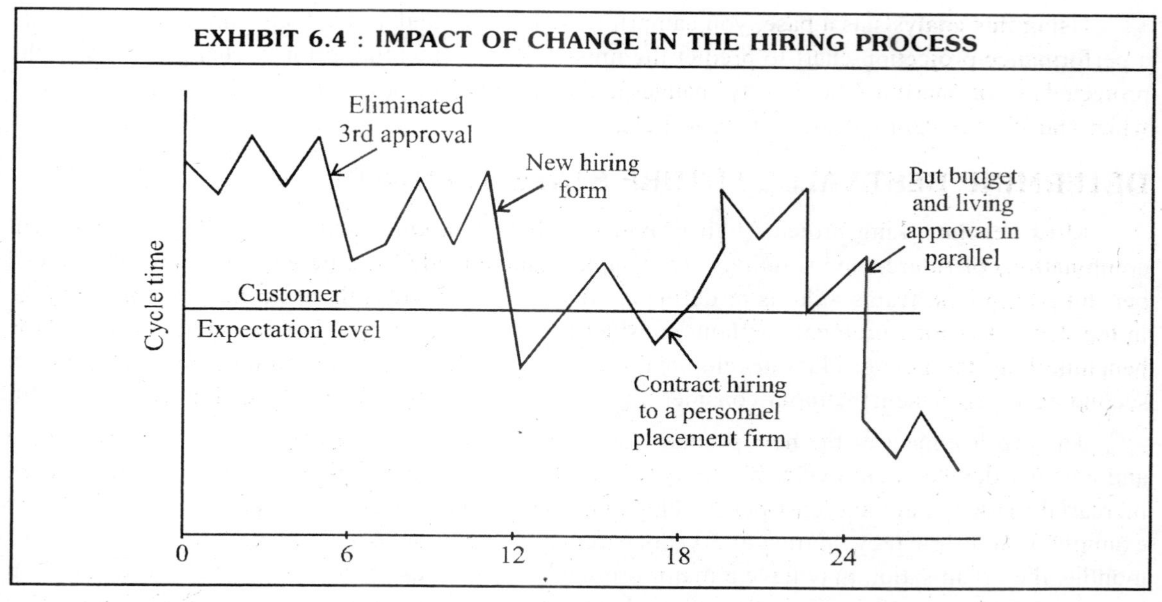

Change Impact Analysis

The best way to prioritise your change activities is to prepare a change impact analysis (Refer *Table 6.4*)

TABLE 6.4 : CHANGE IMPACT ANALYSIS

Change	Measurement					Cost to implement
	A	B	C	D	E	
1	+5	N/A	+2	N/A	N/A	₹ 30,000/-
2	N/A	+6	N/A	–1	N/A	₹ 20,000/-
3	+1	+3	N/A	+5	+1	₹ 500/-
4	–3	+1	N/A	N/A	+6	₹ 1000/-
5	N/A	N/A	+6	N/A	N/A	₹ 1000/-

N/A = Not applicable.

In this analysis, each of the key measurements you hope to improve is listed horizontally and each of the proposed changes is listed vertically. The estimated impact in percentage or actual value that the proposed change will have on the measurement is recorded directly below the measurement.

The change analysis must consider the total impact of the change. Many changes interact to impact more than one measurement. Often, a change may have a positive impact on one measurement but a negative impact on others. Record the estimated cost to implement the change at the far right side of the projected activity line.

Using this analysis as a base, you can prioritise changes and assess their impact. Then prepare a performance projection chart to predict the impact of implementing priority changes. Adding the projected performance for the priority changes to the performance projection chart will help determine when and if your item will become world class.

DETERMINE BEST-VALUE FUTURE STATE SOLUTION

Most benchmarking projects will provide the benchmarking item team with many different combinations of future-state solutions. The major mistake made by experienced and inexperienced benchmarking item teams alike is to define a solution that provides the maximum positive change in the item's key measurements without considering other alternatives. For example, a team that is benchmarking the new product development process usually focuses on minimising cycle time (a secondary measurement) without considering the primary measurement and its impact upon profit.

The profit impact of the new product development cycle is driven by increased market share and cost per development cycle. It is easy to see that there is an optimum operating point between increased market share and cost per development cycle that defines the best-value cycle time. For example, if an original cycle time of 3 years is reduced to 8 months for a product whose cycle is 12 months, the organisation may have a major problem on its hands. As a side effect, the organisation has erected some major peaks and valleys in the people resource requirements for new product development. It may be much better for the organisation to have an 11 month development cycle if it can reduce the cost per cycle, because the shorter cycle is not viewed as value added to the customer.

Generally, at least three different potential future-state solutions should be prepared and evaluated to determine the best-value solution for the item. Often the best value solution is not the one that maximises the items' secondary measurements.

UPDATE THE BENCHMARK ITEM'S DATABASE

Benchmarking is a process of continuous discovery. As soon as you stop adding information to the database, it becomes out of date. Public domain data should be added to the database regularly and some one should be assigned to review these new inputs to identify specific breakthroughs. Every 5 to 8 years, the total benchmarking process should be repeated. This is absolutely necessary, In today's high-technology world, key items are changing very rapidly. A simple technological breakthrough could revitalise an organisation's item and bring a dark horse up into first place overnight.

BOX 6.4 : BENCHMARKING IN PRACTICE – COMPETITIVE SERVICE ANALYSIS/COMPETITIVE SHOPPING

It is just as important to understand the difference between competitive service levels and your service level as it is to understand the difference in product performance. Your competitors will probably be reluctant if not hostile, benchmarking partners. The answer in the service industry is to buy the competitor's service. This is called ***competitive shopping*** and is used throughout the world. **Safeway** markets have a list of products that can price out against other supermarkets to determine cost differentials. Department managers at the **Emporium** price out name brands at **Macy's** to be sure that they are not being undersold and that they are getting the best price from their suppliers.

Hotels, banks and airlines buy competitive services and have their people stay in competitor's hotels, open accounts at competitor's banks and travel or competitor's airlines. These ***competitive shoppers*** measure the competitor's performance against their own organisation's performance.

In Japan, bank employees regularly use competitive bank services to compare their bank's performance against the competitive bank's standards. Typical points to be evaluated include : *(i)* Wait time, *(ii)* Ease of use, *(iii)* Cleanliness, *(iv)* Customer interface process, *(v)* Noise level, *(vi)* Cost, *(vii)* Accuracy, *(viii)* Employee capability and knowledge, *(ix)* Reliability and *(x)* Predictability.

In the service sector, competitive shopping is required to define the level of performance needed to compete in today's fierce market and to determine where improvement opportunities exist.

Although many organisations develop their own staff of competitive benchmarkers, there are organisations that specialise in this activity.

For example, **Evaluation Systems for Personnel (ESP)** is one of these organisations. ESP provides internal and external competitive shopping data to their customers throughout the United States. Its competitive benchmarkers are known as ***mystery shoppers***. Gerry Blumenthal, president of ESP, defines the organisation's activities as follows :

"A mystery shopper is an individual who enters a place of business, posing as a regular customer, whose sole aim is to evaluate the level of service and sales ability.

We at ESP have developed mystery - shopping questionnaires for almost every industry. Each question in our questionnaire is scored and weighted according to its specific importance. This enables us to evaluate, quantitatively, the service rendered by that specific industry or its sales person. Thus we are able to measure performance between departments or individuals comprising a company or between different companies. This provides a tool for companies to determine where they stand in relation to competition. The competition, if they excel in the industry, can then be mystery - shopped to "collect or learn their secrets". In effect, the competition has become a ***benchmark***.

During the past 8 years we have, through the eyes and ears of over 8000 mystery shoppers, established the specific "things" that people in service or sales do or do not do, in their interaction with customers or clients. Naturally, we come into contact with all levels of operators, including the most successful operators.

By examining these successful operators we have established the ***benchmarks*** for each industry. Many companies are now actively shopping the competition, specifically for this reason.

POINTS TO REMEMBER

- **Data and information collection and their analysis** is one of the most extensive steps in the benchmarking process. It is the essence of benchmarking.
- **Two aspects of data collection and analysis are:**
  (i) Describing the types of data and information sources and
  (ii) How to access them for benchmarking purposes.
- Data collection and data analysis in the real world are hardwork.
- Data never comes packaged neatly and different sources often provide widely disparate data about the same topic.

- Data will be less than perfect and will age quickly, so you need always be willing to estimate and make decisions with the best available data at any point of time.
- Some data are inherently easy to collect than others.
- As data collection takes time and money, the benchmarking team should determine which data sources are likely to be most productive, given the limited sources available.
- The benchmarking team should first consider all **internal sources** of information which includes electronic and public data base.
- The **external sources** of information can be extensive. The sources include the wide range of experts in the field and those organisations who by their focus have special knowledge of products and services.
- **The benchmarking team** should array the potential sources in each of the following categories: *(i)* Internal sources, *(ii)* External sources and *(iii)* Original research.
- **There are several data criteria and characteristics that should be considered. Among them are :**
  - *(i)* The amount and accuracy of data
  - *(ii)* The cost of obtaining data
  - *(iii)* The time required for data collection and
  - *(iv)* Whether specialists need to be used
- Data and information **cost** money to obtain, analyse and extrapolate to meaningful comparisons.
- The **time** to determine the data specifications and administer the data collection effort also should not be overlooked.
- Special skills needed in benchmarking also should be analysed.
- **Two major approaches to data collection depending on the sources of data/information are:**
  1. Internal data collection and
  2. External data collection
- The various sources of internal data or information existing within organisations are: *(i)* Process owners, *(ii)* Functional experts, *(iii)* Networks and historical files.
- **Two main ways of obtaining data from external sources are :**
  - *(i)* Retrieving published data that is in the public domain and
  - *(ii)* Conducting original research (interview, testing/disassembling competitive products, site visits, surveys, etc.).

  The various external data collection methods are:
  - *(i)* Published and electronic data sources
  - *(ii)* Live data sources *viz.,* current employees in your company, customers, industry, analysis, distributors and agents, vendors, data sharing arrangements, current and former employees of target companies, telephone interviewing, personal meetings/site visits and surveys.
- **Original research** must be conducted where data does not exist in internal or external public sources.
- Contracting a real human being at a potential target company that you would like to have joined a co-operative or collaborative benchmarking study seems to be the toughest task in any benchmarking study.

- The following points should be considered regarding making first contact with potential targets (human beings) : *(i)* When to contact, *(ii)* How to make contact and *(iii)* Anticipate some rejection.
- **Data collection** is a mix of science and art.
- **Data analysis** is a critical phase of the benchmarking process.
- **The measurement data** provide you with indicators of where the best practices, procedures, and the processes can be found.
- Two types of data collected and used in the benchmarking study include qualitative data (descriptive) and quantitative data (numbers, ratios, etc.).
- **Recommendations** to be considered as you begin the process for determining the meaning of the information you have collected are:
  (i) Check for misinformation *(ii)* Identify patterns
  (iii) Identify omissions or displacement *(iv)* Check for anamalies
  (v) Draw conclusions
- **Data analysis methods include :** *(i)* Data matrix for quantitative data, *(ii)* Work charts, work word flow charts and comparable process flow charts for qualitative data.
- "Performance projection chart" or "gap/trend analysis chart" is used to illustrate the difference between your items and the benchmarking partner's items.
- When you start setting targets and developing action plans, qualitative information becomes invaluable, since it tells you what to do to bring about positive change.
- Most benchmarking projects will provide the benchmarking team with many different combinations of future-state solutions.
- Generally, at least three different potential future-state solutions should be prepared and evaluated to determine the best-value solution for the item

REVIEW QUESTIONS

1. Why data collection and analysis is important in benchmarking?
2. Briefly discuss the various sources of data / information.
3. Distinguish between internal and external sources of data / information.
4. Discuss the criteria for information gathering.
5. What is meant by "creating a data collection plan"? Why is it necessary?
6. Discuss the two major approaches to data collection.
7. Who should conduct literature research?
8. Discuss the recommendations for using publication and other media as a key information source.
9. Discuss the advantages and disadvantages of data collection through publications / media.
10. What are the various "Live data sources" of collection of data / information?
11. Describe the "data collection staircase" with a block diagram.
12. Discuss the telephone interviewing method used for data / information collection.
13. Discuss the recommendations for using the telephone as data gathering tool.
14. Discuss the importance of site visits as data collection method.

15. Why "survey" is recommended as a data collection tool?
16. Discuss the recommendations to be considered when planning the use of surveys for data collection.
17. Discuss advantages and disadvantages of the following data collection methods:
    (a) Telephone interviews, *(b)* Personal meetings/site visits and *(c)* Surveys.
18. Why original research and investigations become necessary for data collection?
19. Discuss the points to be considered regarding making first contact with potential targets in benchmarking study.
20. Why data collection is viewed as both a science and art?
21. What is "data analysis"?
22. Discuss the recommendations as you begin the process of determining the meaning of data / information you have collected.
23. Discuss the data analysis methods used for analysing: *(a)* Qualitative data and *(b)* Quantitative data.
24. What is a "data matrix". Give an example.
25. Write short notes on: *(a)* Word charts, *(b)* Work word flow charts, *(c)* Comparable process flow charts
26. What is "Performance projection chart". Illustrate with an example.
27. Discuss the impact of change in the benchmarking process.
28. What is "change impact analysis"?
29. What is "best-value future-state solution?"
30. Why it is important to update the benchmark item's data base?

DISCUSSION QUESTIONS

1. "Data and information collection and their analysis is one of the most extensive steps in the benchmarking process" - explain
2. "The best data – the data with the "answers" – typically from living, breathing sources" – elaborate.
3. "Telephone interviewing is one of the most efficient means of gathering data from target companies, it can also be very frustrating". Do you agree or disagree? Give reasons for your answer.
4. "One of the most interesting and potentially rewarding experiences of benchmarking is the personal interview or site visit" - Discuss
5. "Contacting a real human being at a potential target company that you would like to have joined a cooperative or collaborative benchmarking study seems to be the toughest task in any benchmarking study". Examine this statement critically.
6. "Data collection is a mix of science and art" – Discuss.
7. "The level of analysis and types of conclusions that organisations make as a result of their benchmarking activities generally fall into several categories" – Explain.

CHAPTER 7

Phases/Stages/Steps involved in the Benchmarking Process

INTRODUCTION

Once people learn about benchmarking in general, they may ask "Is there a world-class benchmarking process?" "Shouldn't we use the best benchmarking practices to help us discover the best practices for our work processes?"

Just as there is no standard definition of benchmarking, there is, of yet, no universally recognised best-in-class benchmarking process. Even the Xerox benchmarking process (which is the most copied and used benchmarking process) should not be considered best-in-class. Why? Although it works well for Xerox and for those other firms that use similar processes, the ten-step benchmarking process pioneered at Xerox is evolving and continuously improving.

Rather than attempting to describe the one best benchmarking process, it is important to focus on the common components that may be used to analyse any benchmarking process, such as phases, questions answered and outputs produced.

Benchmarking has been viewed as consisting of phases, or stages or steps in different ways by different companies. *For example,* a typical benchmarking process consists of **three phases** namely: *(i)* **Analysis phase**, *(ii)* **Discovery phase** and *(iii)* **Implementation phase**. As teams progress through each phase, they seek to answer specific questions and produce certain outputs.

During the analysis phase, for instance, you define the benchmarking project, create a team and focus team's energy on understanding the root causes of performance for the process to be benchmarked. We will discuss the three phase benchmarking process in more detail later in this chapter.

In some other companies, benchmarking process has been viewed as consisting of **four phases** namely: *(i)* **Planning phase**, *(ii)* **Analysis phase**, *(iii)* **Integration phase** and *(iv)* **Action or implementation phase**.

Motorola, uses a five step benchmarking process :

Step 1 : Decide what to benchmark.

Step 2 : Select companies to benchmark.

Step 3 : Obtain data and collect information.

Step 4 : Analyse data and form action plans.

Step 5 : Recalibrate and start the process again.

Alcoa spent several months studying the Xerox benchmarking process (10 step process) before developing its six step process:

Step 1 : Decide what to benchmark.

Step 2 : Plan the benchmarking project.

Step 3 : Understand your own performance.

Step 4 : Study others.

Step 5 : Learn from the data.

Step 6 : Use the findings.

Ameritech, has a benchmarking process consisting of four phases and **eight steps:**

Phase 1. Project Conception and Planning

Step 1 : Project conception

Step 2 : Project planning

Phase 2. Internal and External Data Gathering and Partner Selection

Step 3 : Determining internal processes and performance.

Step 4 : Selecting benchmarking partners.

Step 5 : Collecting benchmarking partner's data

Phase 3. Analysis and Assessment

Step 6 : Comparing internal processes with partner's processes.

Phase 4.

Step 7 : Recommendations and implementation.

Step 8 : Recalibration.

AT&T uses a nine step process for benchmarking:

Step 1 : Project conception: Identify the need and decide what to benchmark.

Step 2 : Planning: Determine the scope and objectives and develop a benchmarking plan.

Step 3 : Preliminary data collection: Collect data on industry, companies and similar processes as well as detailed data on your own processes.

Step 4 : Best-in-class selection: Select companies with best-in-class processes.

Step 5 : Best-in-class collection: Collect detailed data from companies with best-in-class processes.

Step 6 : Assessment: Compare your own and best-in-class processes and develop recommendations.

Step 7 : Implementation planning: Develop operational improvement plans to attain superior performance.

Step 8 : Implementation: Enact operational plans and monitor process improvements.

Step 9 : Recommendations: Update benchmark findings and assess improvements in processes.

Xerox uses a 10 step process in benchmarking.

Step 1 : Identify what is to be benchmarked.

Step 2 : Identify comparative organisations.

Step 3 : Determine data collection method and collect data.

Step 4 : Determine current performance gap.

Step 5 : Project future performance levels.

Step 6 : Communicate benchmark findings and gain acceptance.

Step 7 : Establish functional goals.

Step 8 : Develop action plans.

Step 9 : Implement specific actions and monitor progress.

Step 10 : Recalibrate benchmarks.

Seitz Corporation, USA, presents its benchmarking process as a flow chart consisting of **14 steps** and **IBM's Rochester, Minnesta facility** in the US has developed **21 step** benchmarking process.

While the number of phases or stages or steps in the benchmarking processes developed by various companies to meet their individual needs vary widely, what matters is not the number of phases or steps, but that all necessary actions are completed in the benchmarking process irrespective of the number of phases/stages/steps involved. **Consequently, we will discuss the following models:** 1. The three phases of benchmarking, 2. The five phases of benchmarking process, 3. The five stage benchmarking process and 4. The seven step benchmarking process.

1. THE THREE PHASES OF BENCHMARKING PROCESS

The three phases of a typical benchmarking process are:

(i) Analysis phase

(ii) Discovery phase and

(iii) Implementation phase.

***Box 7.1* illustrates the analysis phase.**

During the analysis phase, you define the benchmarking project, create a team and focus the team's energy on understanding the root cause of performance for the (internal) process to be benchmarked.

During the discovery phase, the team concentrates its attention on learning what the best-of-the-best do and how and why they do it. Once the knowledge is acquired, the team recommends the desired process changes in order to achieve world-class performance.

BOX 7.1 : PHASE 1 : ANALYSIS PHASE

Questions answered during the analysis phase	Outputs produced during the analysis phase
• What do we want to benchmark? • How are we going to organise and allocate resources to achieve the project objective?	• Project plan
• Who will be involved on the project? • What are the roles and responsibilities of each team member?	• Team
• How well is the process operating currently?	• Internal process analysis results

Box 7.2 **illustrates the discovery phase.**

BOX 7.2 : PHASE 2 : DISCOVERY PHASE

Questions answered during the discovery phase	Outputs produced during the discovery phase
• Based on current performance, what do we want to know more about? • How will we gather this knowledge?	• Data collection plan
• From whom? • What did we learn? • How do we compare to the best	• Partners • Findings • Gap analysis
• What should we do to apply what we have learnt?	• Recommendations

During the implementation phase, the team makes the changes and takes the actions needed to improve the process. They also periodically monitor their partners' progress to determine how best-in-class performance levels evolve over time. ***Box 7.3*** **illustrates the implementation phase.**

BOX 7.3 : PHASE 3 : IMPLEMENTATION PHASE

Questions answered during the implementation phase	Outputs produced during implementation phase
• How do we become world class?	• Implementation plan
• How do we know we are still the best?	• Recalibrate plan

Analysis Phase Outputs

During the analysis phase, you should produce the following outputs: *(i)* Project plan, *(ii)* Benchmarking team and *(iii)* Analysis results of your internal work process.

- **Project plan:** The project plan is the document that describes the **what, who, how, why** and **when** for the benchmarking project.
- **Benchmarking team:** The benchmarking team is the group of people responsible for performing the benchmarking project.
- **Internal process analysis results:** Internal process analysis results consist primarily of a description of the performance elements (practices, metrics and enablers) for the **work process** within your own firm that you wish to benchmark.

Discovery Phase Outputs

During this phase, you will create the following outputs:

(i) Data collection plan

(ii) Partners (list of)

(iii) Findings (data collection)

(iv) Gap analysis (performance)

(v) Final report

(vi) Recommendations

- **Data collection plan:** It is a document that describes the existing and original data you plan to collect, plus how and when you plan to collect it.
- **Partners:** Benchmarking partners are the individuals within firms that have agreed to share data with you or a third party.
- **Findings (Data collection):** Findings are the results (the raw data documented) of your research and data collection activities.
- **Gap analysis:** Gap analysis is the comparison of findings data to internal operations data (us versus them).
- **Final report:** A final report is an executive summary of the project describing what you learnt and how you learnt it.
- **Recommendations:** Recommendations are the specific changes you wish to make to the work process to achieve world-class levels of performance.

Implementation Phase Outputs

As a result of your work during the analysis and discovery phases of your benchmarking project, you know what the elements of best-in-class performance are and what the impact would be once you incorporate those elements into your own operations. To achieve the anticipated benefits and to make sure you stay out front, there are two key outputs you should produce during the implementation phase. **They are: *(i)* implementation plan and *(ii)* a recalibration plan.**

- **Implementation plan:** The implementation plan is the document that describes how the knowledge gained from the project will be successfully applied to your own work process.
- **Recalibration plan:** A recalibration plan is the document that describes the steps you will use to determine whether the best-in-class levels of performance for the benchmarked process have changed over time.

2. THE FIVE PHASES OF THE BENCHMARKING PROCESS

The five phases of the benchmarking process are:

Phase 1 : Planning the benchmarking process and characterisation of the item(s).

Phase 2 : Internal data collection and analysis.

Phase 3 : External data collection and analysis.

Phase 4 : Improvement of the item's performance.

Phase 5 : Continuous improvement.

***Exhibit 7.1* illustrates the five phases of the benchmarking process.**

EXHIBIT 7.1 : THE FIVE PHASES OF THE BENCHMARKING PROCESS (BECOME A STAR USING BENCHMARKING)

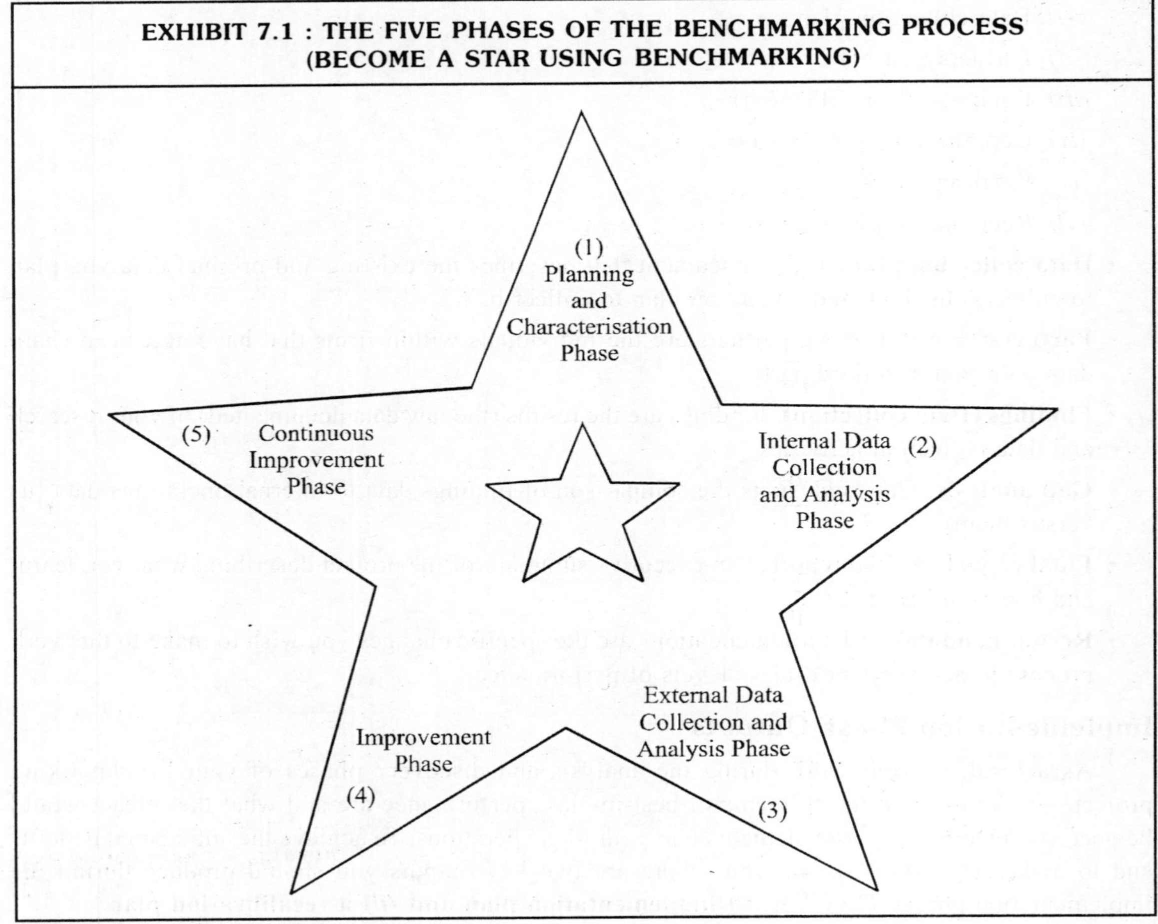

These five benchmarking phases comprise a total of 20 activities (Ref. *Table 7.1*). Each activity is subdivided into a number of specific tasks (See *Exhibit 7.2*).

PHASE 1. PLANNING THE BENCHMARKING PROCESS AND CHARACTERISATION OF THE ITEM(S)

The planning phase entails defining important issues that are necessary for directing the benchmarking activities into the most desirable and profitable areas for the individual and/or organisation. Detailed, specific measurement approaches are then developed to formulate the plans necessary to carryout the benchmarking process.

TABLE 7.1 : THE 5 PHASES AND 20 ACTIVITIES OF THE BENCHMARKING PROCESS

Benchmarking phase	Related activities
Phase 1 Planning the benchmarking process and characterisation of the item(s)	1. Identify what to benchmark 2. Obtain top management support 3. Develop the measurement plan 4. Develop the data collection plan 5. Review the plans with location experts 6. Characterise the benchmark item
Phase 2 Internal data collection and analysis	7. Collect and analyse internal published information 8. Select potential internal benchmarking sites 9. Collect internal original research information 10. Conduct interviews and surveys 11. Form an internal benchmarking committee 12. Conduct internal site visits
Phase 3 External data collection and analysis	13. Collect external published information 14. Collect external original research information
Phase 4 Improvement of the item's performance	15. Identify corrective actions 16. Develop an implementation plan 17. Gain top management approval of the future-state solution 18. Implement the future-state solution and measure its impact
Phase 5 Continuous improvement	19. Maintain the benchmarking data base 20. Implement continuous performance improvement

EXHIBIT 7.2 : HIERARCHY FOR THE TOTAL BENCHMARKING MANAGEMENT PROCESS

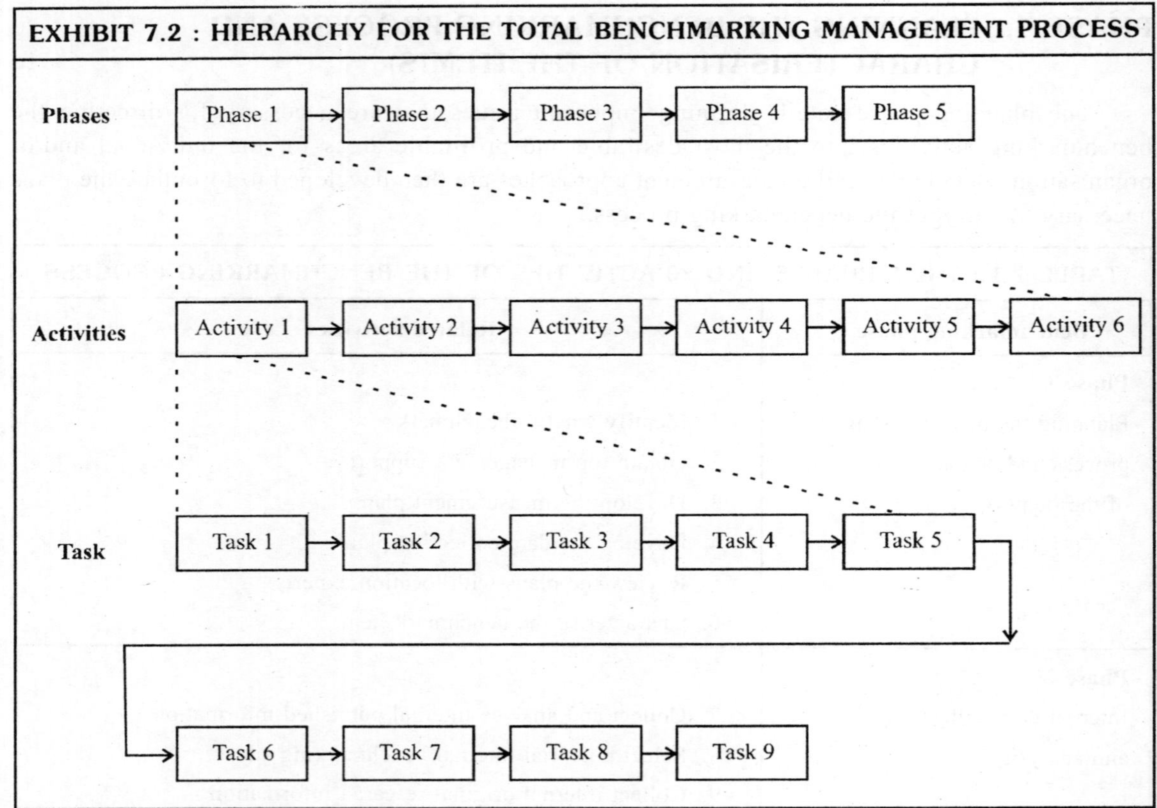

Activity 1. Identify What to Benchmark

To first step in the benchmarking process is the formation of the benchmarking team. This team comprises individuals who accept the responsibility to start and manage the entire benchmarking process.

Once the benchmarking team is formed, it must clearly identify exactly what needs to be benchmarked. This seems to be an obvious and logical starting point for the benchmarking initiation team, since all other decisions will stem from it. None the less, many organisations fail to nail down exactly what they are trying to do before they actually do it.

In identifying what to benchmark, the benchmarking team (BT) will be choosing among four categories:

(i) Business processes

(ii) Equipment

(iii) Manufacturing (production) processes

(iv) Products and services

The benchmarking team members will need to conduct a complete business analysis that requires them to thoroughly understand the organisation's business plan, yearly performance results, critical success factors, and core assets (core capabilities and core competencies). Then they will need to perform a competitive analysis related to the key products and core assets. Once the analysis is complete, the benchmarking initiation team must analyse the data to determine how the benchmarking resources should be deployed to support the organisation's performance measurements and planned for activities (*For example,* part of the 3 year plan might be to install a new, computerised order-entry process. If so, equipment benchmarking would be a priority to support this project). Once the appropriate category has been selected, the BT must learn how to select the specific item to be benchmarked. **The list of the tasks completed during Activity 1 are:**

(i) A benchmarking initiation team was formed.

(ii) A list of critical success factors for the organisation was reviewed or prepared.

(iii) A competitive analysis was completed.

(iv) Core assets (core capabilities and competencies) were reviewed or defined.

(v) The organisation's business plan was reviewed to define its impact on the benchmarking processes.

(vi) The benchmarking categories of importance to the organisation were defined and prioritised.

(vii) Specific items to be benchmarked were defined and prioritised.

(viii) The items were defined and characterised for benchmarking internally and/or externally.

Activity 2. Obtain Top Management (Executive Team) Support

After defining what it is you wish to benchmark, you need to obtain management's support of the items to be benchmarked and a formal benchmarking structure. Benchmarking, done properly, needs the commitment of the organisation's top management, so that adequate time and resources will be made available for the project. Support of top management is required for implementation of the changes that will be required as a result of benchmarking. In order to receive this support, you need to build understanding not only about what benchmarking is but also about how it can help an organisation. In the end, you will create and present a benchmarking proposal to top management. **The proposal will include :**

(i) The detailed benchmarking process that will be used.

(ii) The formal organisational structure required to support the benchmarking activities.

(iii) A code of conduct (ethics).

(iv) A 3-year plan of categories and items per category to be benchmarked.

(v) A list of near-term items to be benchmarked.

(vi) A return-on-investment analysis.

Also during this activity, the organisation's executives will be trained in the use of the benchmarking process. If top management approves the benchmarking project and funds it, benchmarking item teams (BITs) will be formed to conduct the required evaluations. **The list of tasks completed in activity 2 are :**

(i) The benchmarking item team was formed.

(ii) A benchmarking process and strategy were prepared and approved by top management.

(iii) A 3-year benchmarking project plan was prepared and approved.

(iv) A benchmarking organisational structure was defined and approved.

(v) A standard list of terms and definitions was developed.

(vi) A benchmarking training program was established and implemented.

(vii) A list of benchmarking support tools was defined and training programs were developed for each tool.

(viii) A benchmarking code of ethics was developed.

(ix) The proposed benchmark items were reviewed to define how improving them would affect the organisation's primary performance measurements. This analysis was used to prioritise the benchmark items.

(x) Proposals were prepared and approved to support the benchmarking of individual items.

(xi) The pros and cons of outside consultants were discussed and a decision was made on using them. If the organisation decided to go ahead, the consultants were selected.

(xii) The item's benchmarking plan and project file were established.

Activity 3. Develop the Measurement Plan

In this activity the following questions were asked:

(i) What are the characteristics of the benchmark items?

(ii) Which characteristics are candidates for improvement?

(iii) What am I going to measure and how am I going to measure it?

By establishing measurements, you are preparing to compare your benchmark item with a similar item. The accuracy and consistency of your benchmarking study are highly dependent on how well this activity is performed.

The list of tasks completed during activity 3:

(i) The BIT was trained on different types of measurement approaches.

(ii) A cause-and-effect diagram (fishbone diagram) was prepared for each primary measurement

(iii) The benchmark item's measurement characteristics were defined.

(iv) Measurement charts were developed.

(v) The item's measurement procedures were completed.

Activity 4. Develop the Data Collection Plan

In some benchmark studies, it is imperative to collect information from both internal and external sources. There are four sources from which data can be collected for the benchmark item. **The data collection plan will include:**

(i) Information about how the item is performing at other locations and/or sites within your organisation (internal benchmarking).

- Look for published information about internal organisations.
- Collect non-published information (original research).

(ii) Information about how the item is performing at locations and/or sites external to the total organisation (external benchmarking).

- Look for published information about external organisations.
- Collect non-published information (original research).

In this activity, you will determine how to prepare the right data collection plan for a particular benchmark item. You will also develop an initial list of potential benchmarking partners - internal and/or external organisations with items that are the same as or similar to your item and that may be performing better than your item. This list will be the start of your benchmarking plan. **Following is a list of the tasks completed during activity 4:**

(i) The data analysis methods were defined.

(ii) A measurement procedure was developed.

(iii) An item characterisation plan was completed.

(iv) A plan to collect internal information was developed.

(v) A plan to collect external information was developed.

(vi) A list of potential benchmarking partners was developed.

(vii) The item's benchmarking time-line chart was prepared.

(viii) The item's benchmarking plan was expanded and detailed.

(ix) The organisational change management plan was created.

Activity 5. Review the Plans with Location Experts

Location experts are individuals who understand the benchmark item, and can help you find sources of information related to it. In this activity, you will review the plans that you formulated in activities 3 and 4 with location experts to gain their insight on the benchmarking process and identify further potential contacts. After this review, plans will be updated and revised to include the recommendations of the location experts.

Following is the list of tasks completed during activity 5:

(i) The benchmark item's location experts were identified.

(ii) Meetings were held with location experts to discuss the data collection and benchmarking plans.

(iii) The data collection and benchmarking plans were updated on the basis of input from the location experts.

(iv) The organisational change management plan was updated.

Activity 6. Characterise the Benchmark Item

In this activity you will set up measurement systems and collect the data required to completely characterise your benchmark item. The collected information will be used to start your benchmark item data base.

Following is a list of tasks completed during activity 6:

(i) A characterisation work plan was established.

(ii) Employees were trained to collect the required data.

(iii) The forms used to collect and analyse the data were designed.

(iv) The benchmark item was characterised.

(v) A benchmark item's database was established.

(vi) A measurement matrix was created.

(vii) The early phase of the organisational change management plan was implemented and appropriate organisational change management surveys were conducted.

PHASE 2. INTERNAL DATA COLLECTION AND ANALYSIS

It is good practice to look within your organisation to see how departments, functions, divisions and/or locations are using the benchmark item before you start contacting "external organisations". During phase 2, only internal information are collected. The term ***"internal"*** as used in benchmarking refers to all organisations (corporations, conglomerates, governments, companies, etc.) within the same management structure.

Activity 7. Collect and Analyse Internal Published Information

Internal published information most often takes the form of technical reports and studies published within the organisation. **Following is a list of tasks completed during activity 7 :**

(i) A work plan to collect internal published information was developed.

(ii) Publication sources that could contain information about the item's internal performance were identified.

(iii) Copies of important published documents were collected and analysed.

(iv) The benchmarking database was updated to include summaries of the analysed publications.

(v) The benchmarking plan and the internal potential benchmarking partner's list were updated.

Activity 8. Select Potential Internal Benchmarking Sites

During this activity, you will select the internal benchmarking sites or partners that the BIT would like to exchange information with. The benchmarking item's (BIT's) list of potential internal benchmarking partners has already been updated by the location experts (activity 5) and revised as a result of collecting internal information (activity 7). In large organisations this list of potential internal benchmarking partners can be very long, and the BIT may like to limit its contact to the very best sites. A useful approach is to divide the BIT's list into an 'A' list and a 'B' list. The 'A' list defines the sites that the BIT wants to collect data from. The sites on this priority list should be given special incentives to become internal benchmarking partners. The sites on the 'B' list should also be invited to participate in the benchmarking process.

Following is a list of activities completed during activity 8 :

(i) The potential internal benchmarking partner list was prioritised.

(ii) A list of site contacts was prepared.

Activity 9. Collect Internal Original Research Information

Internal original research is any type of research that has not been previously published. In order to get the internal original research activities started, the BIT should send copies of its measurement plan and its characterisation data to each of the internal benchmarking partner's coordinators. The benchmarking partners should collect compatible data and input it into a central data base. The BIT will analyse the information and compare it with the BIT's item's data to identify negative gaps. For each negative gap, a gap/trend analysis chart will be prepared. Since each negative gap represents a potential improvement opportunity, a root cause/corrective action form is prepared for it as well. The BIT will also develop a clarification list for each internal benchmarking partner that defines what additional information is required.

Following is a list of tasks completed during activity 9 :

(i) All potential internal benchmarking partners were contacted and asked to become internal item benchmarking partners.

(ii) A list of internal item benchmarking partners was completed.

(iii) All internal item benchmarking partners assigned a site representative to work with the BIT.

(iv) The benchmarking and measurement plans were updated on the basis of inputs from the internal item benchmarking partners.

(v) All internal benchmarking partner's items were characterised.

(vi) A central database was established for the benchmark item.

(vii) Gap/trend analysis charts were prepared by all sites.

(viii) Each site established a root cause/corrective action list.

Activity 10. Conduct Internal Interviews and Surveys

At this point in the benchmarking process, the BIT begins to identify root causes and the appropriate corrective actions for the benchmarking measurements. A ***root cause*** is a specific reason that some other organisation's benchmark item's performance is better than your benchmark item's performance. A ***corrective action*** is a strategy that details how you can use root cause information to improve your benchmark item. As additional information is obtained, the database is updated.

Following is a list of tasks completed during activity 10 :

(i) All internal benchmarking patterns whose items were out-performing the BIT's item were contacted to understand why their items are performing better.

(ii) Critical indication in the measurement matrix were verified to ensure that they were correct.

(iii) Root causes were defined for all improvement opportunities.

(iv) All root cause/corrective action combinations were classified.

(v) The benchmarking database was updated.

Activity 11. Form an Internal Benchmarking Committee

For some benchmarking items, it may be advisable to form an ***internal benchmarking committee*** made up of the person from each benchmarking site plus additional technical experts are needed. The committee members will work together, sharing information so that each organisation can benefit from the benchmarking process. An internal benchmarking committee is usually formed whenever external benchmarking is used to maximise the benefits from external contact. **Following activities were completed during activity 11 :**

(i) The BIT determined if there was sufficient interest in forming an internal benchmarking committee, made up of the benchmarking partners, for the item under study.

(ii) If sufficient interest was defined, an internal benchmarking committee was formed.

(iii) The internal benchmarking committee was trained in the benchmarking process.

(iv) A set of responsibilities for the internal benchmarking committee was defined and a program plan was prepared.

(v) The internal benchmarking committee's plan was integrated into the total benchmarking plan.

Activity 12. Conduct Internal Site Visits

Among the internal benchmarking sites that were chosen, there will be certain sites that you will need to visit. The site visit is conducted not to collect measurement data, but to define corrective actions. By this point in the process, most of the corrective actions related to each defined root cause probably have also been identified.

The site visit should be well orchestrated. Agreed-to-agendas must be prepared well in advance. Arrangements must be made so that the visitation team will meet with people who can answer questions with factual information. **Following task is were completed during activity 12 :**

(i) The benchmarking partner sites that need to be visited were identified.

(ii) Agendas and lists of questions were customised for each site to be visited.

(iii) Visitation team(s) were identified and trained and made location visits.

(iv) The root cause portion of the root cause/corrective action database was completed.

(v) The implementation part of the database was initiated.

(vi) Trip reports were prepared for each site visit.

PHASE 3. EXTERNAL DATA COLLECTION AND ANALYSIS

This phase is designed to help the BIT collect and analyse data from potential and actual external benchmarking partners.

Activity 13. Collect External Published Information

Once the sources of externally published information relevant to benchmark item have been identified, it is relatively easy to collect the data. Since the information is part of the public domain, and is therefore not proprietary, there is usually no difficulty in acquiring it.

The activities completed during activity 13 are listed below :

(i) The BIT developed a detailed external data collection plan.

(ii) A work plan was developed to acquire relevant external published information.

(iii) Appropriate databases were searched to develop a list of relevant articles, reports and books.

(iv) Copies of relevant publications were obtained, read, analysed and summarised.

(v) The benchmarking plan and the database were updated.

Activity 14. Collect External Original Research Information

During this activity, the BIT's creativity takes on great prominence, because even though unpublished, non-confidential external original research is available to the public, it can be very difficult to actually accumulate this information. The clues are all available, but the BIT has to be very creative in finding them and combining them so that it can identify the right organisations to contact to become benchmarking partners. Activity 14 is the most complex and at the same time, one of the most rewarding activities in the benchmarking process. **It is divided into *seven subactivities* as shown in *Box 7.4* lists the sub activities.**

BOX 7.4 : SUB ACTIVITIES

Activity		Description of subactivities
14A	→	Update the external original research part of the benchmarking plan
14B	→	Collect data from external experts
14C	→	Exchange information with external benchmarking partners
14D	→	Survey external customers and potential customers
14E	→	Conduct competitive shopping
14F	→	Reverse engineer competitive product
14G	→	Update the benchmarking database and root cause/corrective action list

EXHIBIT 7.3 : OVERVIEW FLOW DIAGRAM OF ACTIVITY 14 - COLLECT EXTERNAL ORIGINAL RESEARCH INFORMATION

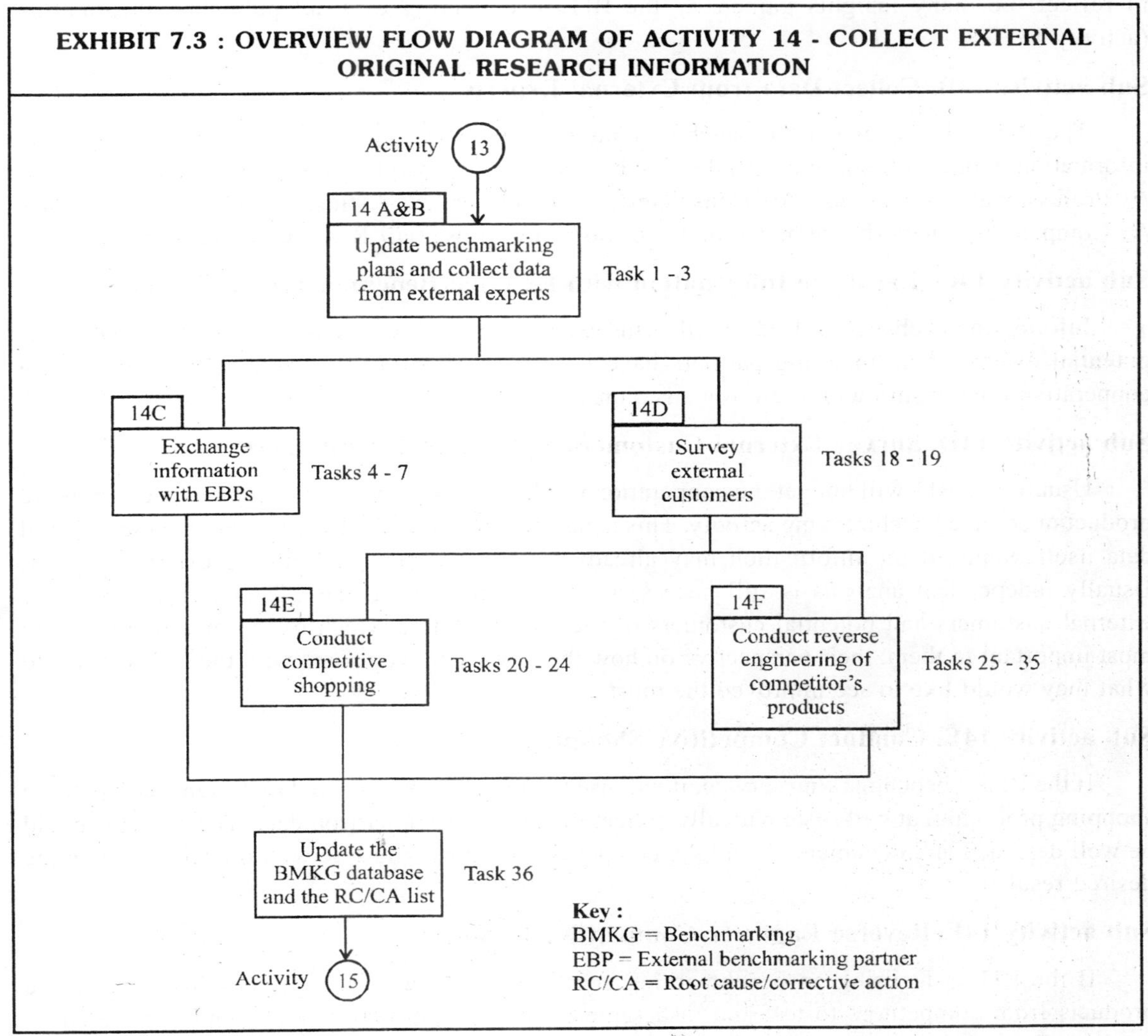

This one activity – Activity 14 accounts for 36 of the 144 tasks that make up the benchmarking process.

The benchmarking item will progress through a very different series of tasks depending on the benchmarking category it falls into. All benchmarking categories will be processed through subactivities 14A and 14B. At that point, manufacturing processes, business processes and equipment will continue through subactivity 14C. Competitive services will be processed through subactivities 14D and 14E. Competitive products will be processed through subactivities 14D and 14F. All products will go through subactivity 14G, at which point the results of the BIT's activities are used to update the benchmarking database and the root cause/corrective action list.

Sub activity 14A. Update the External Original Research part of the Benchmarking Plan

Activity 14 starts by updating the external original research part of the benchmarking plan to reflect the many insights gained by the BIT in collecting external published information (activity 13)

Sub activity 14B. Collect Data from External Experts

The BIT will implement the benchmarking plan by contacting external experts to gain more information about the item under study. Typical external experts that might be contacted include: *(i)* Professional associations, *(ii)* Consultants, *(iii)* Independent testing firms, *(iv)* Universities, *(v)* Company watchers (brokerage firms), *(vi)* Software firms, *(vii)* Research organisations.

Sub activity 14C. Exchange Information with External Benchmarking Partners

Information exchange is used for all items except competitive services and products. Once the potential external benchmarking partners have been identified, the BIT will begin to develop a cooperative relationship with these organisations.

Sub activity 14D. Survey External Customers and Potential Customers

Usually the BIT will not get the cooperation needed from competitors to conduct a competitive product or service benchmarking activity. This means that the BIT will have to generate the required data itself. Some of the information may already have been obtained from the external experts. Usually independent analysis is still necessary. To start this effort, the BIT will need to survey external customers and potential customers of the item to define which of the measurements are most important to them, their perspective on how their own item compares with the BIT's item and what they would like to see improved the most.

Sub activity 14E. Conduct Competitive Shopping

If the BIT is benchmarking service, it will use the information obtained to design a competitive shopping program that will systematically collect the required comparison data. The process should be well designed and documented, and the competitive shoppers must be well trained to obtain the desired results.

Sub activity 14F. Reverse Engineer Competitive Products

If the BIT is focusing on benchmarking competitive products, it will periodically purchase products from competitors to test and disassemble along with a correlation sample of the BIT's product. Typical points to be analysed include: *(i)* Order cycle time, *(ii)* Packaging protection, *(iii)* Installation instruction, *(iv)* Product characteristics, *(v)* Initial performance, *(vi)* Safety factors, *(vii)* Environmental performance, *(viii)* Suppliers, *(ix)* Ease of repair, *(x)* Assembly methods, *(xi)* Workmanship, *(xii)* Cost to produce.

Sub activity 14G. Update the Benchmarking Data base and the Root cause/corrective Action List

The information collected in sub activities 14B-14F is now analysed and added to the benchmarking database. As this point in the benchmarking process, all negative gaps should be understood, their root causes determined and at least one potential corrective action defined for each root cause. In addition, a great deal of information has been collected about the amount of resources required to implement many of the potential corrective actions.

The Purpose of Activity 14

Activity 14 is designed to provide the BIT with the information necessary to define the root cause(s) of negative gap in its item and to identify corrective actions that can eliminate these negative gaps.

The tasks completed during activity 14 are listed below :

(i) The external original research plan was updated.

(ii) Data were collected from external experts.

(iii) The list of external benchmarking patterns was completed.

(iv) A list of organisations that agreed to become benchmarking partners was prepared.

(v) A list of measurements that will be shared with the external benchmarking partners was developed.

(vi) Focus groups meetings were held with the external benchmarking partners.

(vii) Surveys of the performance of external benchmarking partner's items were completed.

(viii) Gap/trend analysis charts were prepared.

(ix) A survey clarification list was prepared and discussed with the external benchmarking partners.

(x) A root cause/corrective action data base was generated for each identified negative gap.

(xi) Visits were made to the external partners' sites.

(xii) Root cause for all improvement opportunities were identified and potential corrective actions were defined for some of them.

(xiii) External customer and potential customer surveys and focus group meetings were conducted.

(xiv) Competitive shopping evaluation procedures were developed.

(xv) Competitive shoppers were trained.

(xvi) Competitive shopping evaluations were conducted.

(xvii) A list of competitor's competitive advantages was developed.

(xviii) Competitor's packaging and documentation were analysed.

(xix) The competitive item's performance reliability was compared with that of the BIT's item.

(xx) The competitive products were reverse engineered.

(xxi) The benchmarking database was updated.

PHASE 4. IMPROVEMENT OF THE ITEM'S PERFORMANCE

With benchmarking data on a particular item on hand, the BIT is now ready to enter the improvement phase. This phase defines not only how an item should be improved but also the steps necessary to implement these changes and to measure their effectiveness.

Activity 15. Identify Corrective Actions

Once you have established a measurement database and understand why gaps exist between your company and your benchmarking partners, you can evaluate different alternatives to identify best-value future-state solutions. In this activity, you will identify the appropriate corrective actions defined during the benchmarking process. Part of this activity will be a benefits/cost/risk analysis.

In most cases, the benchmarking team will define a number of potential future-state solutions. Each of these potential solutions should be evaluated to determine the best-value, future-state solution. To make this determination, the BIT needs to consider three questions:

(i) How much will the item's performance improve?

(ii) How much will it cost and how long will it take to implement the future-state solutions?

(iii) What impact will the change have on each of the item's stakeholders?

The following tasks are completed during activity 15 :

(i) Completion of the list of potential corrective actions by the BIT.

(ii) Updating the gap/trend analysis charts to reflect the potential corrective actions.

(iii) Creation of a measurement interaction chart.

(iv) Prioritising the corrective actions.

(v) Crating and flow-charting a group of potential future-state solution models.

(vi) Creating the simulation models and exercising for the high-potential future-state solutions.

(vii) Making a benefit/cost/risk analysis of high potential future-state solutions.

(viii) Defining the best-value future-state solution.

(ix) Updating the benchmarking plan and database.

Activity 16. Develop an Implementation Plan

Having identified the best-value future-state solution, the BIT must set its sights on developing an implementation plan. Part of the implementation activity will involve designing an "organisational change management" plan that will minimise resistance to change and prepare the organisation to embrace the future-state solution.

The following tasks are completed during activity 16 :

(i) Reviewing the preferred future-state solution and its supporting data with the experts.

(ii) Defining the proposed implementation team.

(iii) Preparation of the implementation plan.

(iv) Developing the "organisational change management" plan.

(v) Preparation of the implementation budget.

Activity 17. Gain Top Management approval of the Future-state Solution

Most benchmarking projects have impact on the organisation and therefore, top management must be committed to the plan. They must support the plan morally and financially. In this activity, the BIT will present its project report and preferred future-state solution to the appropriate upper-management levels for approval.

When the future-state solution is accepted by the top management, a benchmarking implementation team (IT) will be assigned to complete the project. **The following activities are completed during activity 17 :**

(i) Preparation of an item benchmarking project report.

(ii) Reviewing the item benchmarking project report individually with each of the executives.

(iii) Changing the key executive's organisational change management status from a target to a sustaining sponsor or advocate.

(iv) Approving the future-state solution and its supporting budget.

(v) Establishing a budget structure to support the implementation of the future-state solution.

(vi) Sending a customised final report on the project to each benchmarking partner.

Activity 18. Implement the Future-state Solution and Measure its Impact

If it has followed the benchmarking process carefully, the benchmarking implementation team, supported by technologists, will be in the best position to implement the changes to your business. It is necessary to pilot complex changes before they are implemented. Changes should be implemented sequentially, so that each individual change can be measured independently. Care should be taken to ensure that changes to the benchmark items do not have a negative impact on other areas of the organisation.

The following tasks are completed during activity 18 :

(i) Forming an implementation plan.

(ii) Updating the implementation plan.

(iii) Implementing the organisational change management plan.

(iv) Holding regular project reports and reviews.

(v) Making all major changes.

(vi) Measuring the impact of all changes.

(vii) Training the employees to operate in the new process.

(viii) Releasing all supporting documentation including training plans and curriculum.

(ix) Completing the final report defining the return on investment and the impact of the future-state solution on the measurements.

(x) Rewarding the members of the BIT and the implementation teams appropriately.

(xi) Updating the organisational change management plan to support the new process.

(xii) Updating the benchmarking database to reflect the implemented future-state solution.

PHASE 5. CONTINUOUS IMPROVEMENT

Benchmarking needs to be a continuous effort to be effective. To get the most out of all the hard work that you have done in benchmarking an item, you need to ensure that you have a process that will identify when there is a negative shift in the performance gap of the benchmark item. The database of the benchmark item must be continuously updated, and effort must be expended to continuously improve the item's performance.

Activity 19. Maintain the Benchmarking Database

Because of the major investment made in developing an extensive database on the benchmark item, it is necessary to assign some one to research and update the database on a continuous basis. Update should include searches of the information available in public domain literature, internal evaluations, benchmarking partner results and focus group activities.

As other organisations improve the performance of their benchmark item, the BIT should evaluate the potential impact on the relative performance of its benchmark item and repeat activities 16, 17 and 18 if required. At least once a year, the BIT should meet to review the status of the item.

The folowing tasks are completed during activity 19 :

(i) A data analyst maintains the database.

(ii) Regularly scheduled searches of public domain data are conducted and the results are analysed.

(iii) The database is kept current so that it reflects the present item's performance at each internal benchmarking partner's site.

(iv) Yearly benchmark item review meetings are conducted to identify additional action that needs to be taken to maintain the item's positive gap.

Activity 20. Implement Continuous Performance Improvement

Once the future-state solution is implemented and operating effectively, the benchmarking implementation team can be dissolved and the continuous performance improvement of the item turned over to the function that are responsible for portions or all of it. Through the use of ***department improvement teams*** **(DITs)** sometimes called natural work teams (NWTs), the organisation should be able to improve the benchmark team's performance at an annual rate of 5 to 20%.

The tasks completed during activity 20 are :

(i) Department improvement teams (DIT) were formed.

(ii) Each DIT developed a set of effectiveness and efficiency measurements related to its part of the item.

(iii) Establishing improvement requirements and targets.

(iv) Developing and implementing a series of improvement plans by each DIT.

(v) Training the DITs in team and problem solving skills.

(vi) Improvement of the item's performance at a rate of 5 to 20 percent.

3. THE FIVE-STAGE BENCHMARKING PROCESS MODEL

Individual organisations, over a period of time have developed unique benchmarking process models having certain number of phases and steps. *For example,* Xerox has a 10-step process,

AT&T has a nine-step process, the Floride Power and Light has a seven-step process. Therefore it is necessary to develop a generic model that would serve as a framework for action for people who want to implement benchmarking in their own organisations. This could be done by summarising the lessons learnt from the premier benchmarking companies and using this information to develop a model that could provide a new benchmarker with a basic process map and a set of benchmarking guidelines (do's and don'ts).

The challenge was to construct a generic benchmarking model that could be applied to any benchmarking project by any type of organisation. The objective was to consider the common elements of the various benchmarking models that were working out in the real world and to distill the various process phases and steps into a simple model that incorporated the essential elements of the benchmarking process. What emerged from this exercise (identifying the common elements of the twenty-four benchmarking process models) were **five stages of benchmarking** activity, each defining a unique set of activities and ordered in a logical sequence. This model was concise and understandable and seemed to capture the intent of each of the models used by the twenty-four companies. The resulting benchmarking model - **"The five stage benchmarking process" is illustrated in *Exhibit 7.4*.**

EXHIBIT 7.4 : THE FIVE-STAGE BENCHMARKING PROCESS

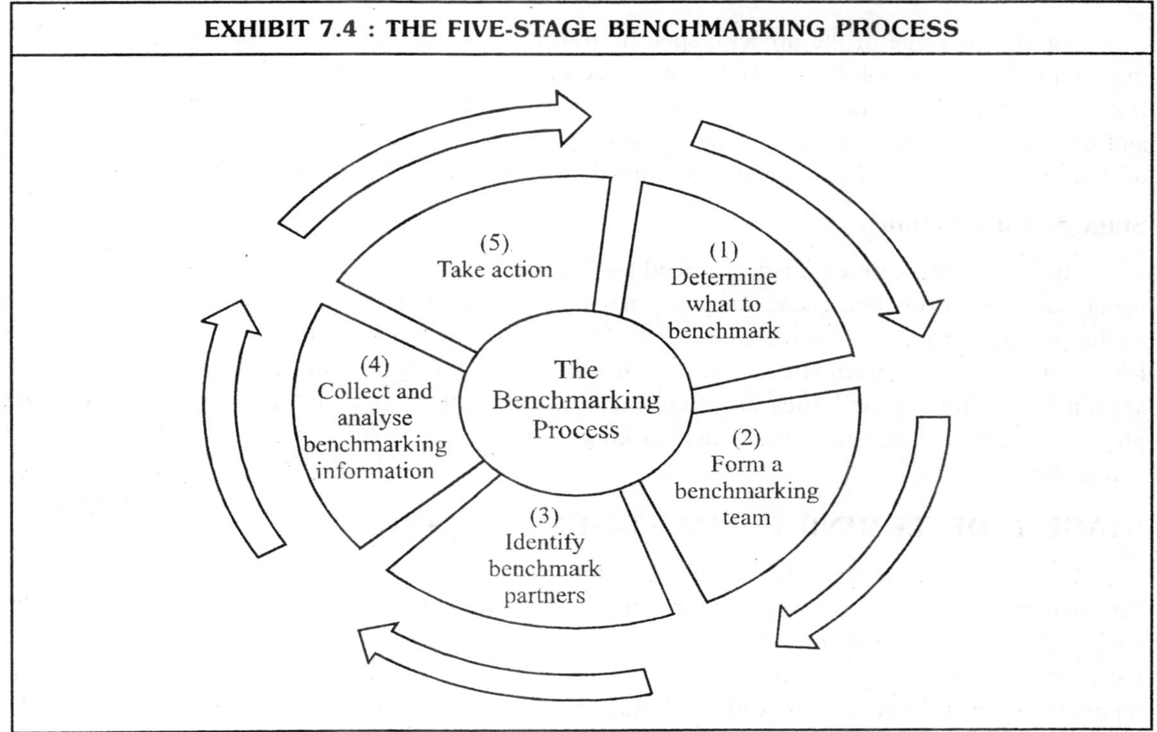

The five process stages are:

Stage 1. Determine What to Benchmark

The first stage of the process is to identify the customers for the benchmarking information and their requirements and define the specific subjects to be benchmarked. Once the subjects to be benchmarked and the customer requirements are known, the resources required (*e.g.*, time, funds, people) to conduct a successful benchmarking investigation can be identified and secured.

Stage 2. Form a Benchmarking Team

Although benchmarking can be conducted by individuals, most benchmarking efforts are team activities. The process of selecting, orienting and managing a benchmarking team is the second major stage of the benchmarking process. Specific roles and responsibilities are assigned to team members. Project management tools are introduced to ensure that benchmarking assignments are clear to everyone involved and that key project milestones are identified.

Stage 3. Identify Benchmark Partners

The third stage of the process involves the identification of information sources that will be used to collect benchmark information. These source include employees of benchmarked organisations, consultants, analysts, government sources, business and trade literature, industry reports and computerised databases to name just a few. Also included in this stage is the process of identifying industry and organisational best practices.

Stage 4. Collect and Analyse Benchmarking Information

During this stage of the process, specific information - collection methods are selected. It is important that the people responsible for collecting information be proficient in these methods. Benchmark partners are contacted and information is collected according to an established protocol and then summarised for analysis. Benchmarking information is analysed in accordance with the original customer requirements and recommendations for action are produced.

Stage 5. Take Action

This stage of the process is influenced by the original customer requirements and uses for the benchmarking information. The action taken may range from the production of a report or presentation to the production of a set of recommendations to the actual implementation of change, based, at least in part, on the information collected in the benchmarking investigation. Any next steps or appropriate follow-up activities are identified, including the continuation of the benchmarking process. These five stages of the benchmarking processes are briefly discussed in the following paragraphs.

STAGE 1. DETERMINING WHAT TO BENCHMARK

The process of determining what to benchmark begins with a fundamental question: Who is the ***customer*** of the benchmarking information? ***Customer*** in this context means ***user***. Once the basic requirements of the information users are understood, the process of developing specific measures can begin. Why this focus on the customer? Because, one of the most common problems reported concerns the ***resources*** needed to conduct a thorough benchmarking investigation. Resources include money to be expended and the time required to conduct the benchmarking investigation or study. **Two common problems noticed are :**

(i) Organisations are anxious to use the benchmarking process. After receiving some basic instruction or direction to benchmark, many organisations rush forward with data collection, taking a wide path through all sorts of subject areas, tackling broad subjects and asking open-

ended questions. In their rush to use this new process, organisations fail in several key areas of benchmarking. They fail to establish a clear mission or purpose for their efforts, they fail to ensure that their own processes are sufficiently understood and documented, they do not thoroughly investigate the companies that legitimately represent best practices, they do not prepare adequately for their meetings with benchmark partners. The result is a poorly planned and executed benchmarking effort.

(ii) The target is too big. The benchmarking study report will be so voluminous that no one will even read the entire report. **To overcome this problem, the following guidelines should be adhered to:**

(a) Identify subjects for benchmarking based on some type of ***critical need***.

(b) Do not attempt to analyse the entire process or product simply because you can.

(c) Create measures that are as specific as possible.

(A) Defining the Customers for Benchmarking Information

The first step in developing a benchmarking plan and deciding ***what to benchmark*** is the identification of the customer for the benchmarking information. Who is requesting the information and who will use it? **This step is important because of the following reasons:**

(i) The customer identifies specific information requirements.

(ii) The customer establishes a time frame for completion of the benchmarking investigation.

(iii) The customer often provides the necessary funding/support for the benchmarking activity.

Another way to define benchmarking customers is to ask: Who will use the benchmarking information? or, whose requirements need to be understood before launching a benchmarking investigation? **There are several key customer types that should be considered when defining the benchmarking customer base.**

In many organisations, the stimulus to engage in benchmarking is generated by a manager or a group of managers who, after determining a need for benchmarking information, commission an individual or a team to conduct a benchmarking investigation. This commissioning may take the form of a task force or task team assignment for a cross-functional or interdivisional group. In some cases, the commissioning manager is part of the benchmarking team, acting as either team leader or a regular member. In many situations, however, the commissioning manager does not participate on the team.

In the vast majority of benchmarking situations, individuals and more typically, teams of employees engage in a benchmarking project using their own initiative. In many cases benchmarking has been positioned as part of a total quality management tool box and thus become integrated with other quality processes and tools such as structured problem solving. In these situations, employees are empowered to take action and initiate benchmarking projects as part of their continuous improvement efforts.

(B) Determining Customer Requirements for Benchmarking Information

The information needs of benchmarking customers should be explicitly defined before launching a benchmarking activity. The customer requirements affect the benchmarking schedule, the scope of the effort, the format for reporting, and the allocation of resources.

In order to establish the information requirements of your benchmarking customers, you absolutely must spend some quality time with them, discussing and documenting their specific benchmarking needs. This process is referred to as ***customer diagnosis***.

The following issues should be discussed as part of the preliminary diagnostic process. **A summary of the contents of the benchmarking diagnosis is presented in *Exhibit 7.5*.**

EXHIBIT 7.5 : CUSTOMER REQUIREMENTS FOR BENCHMARKING

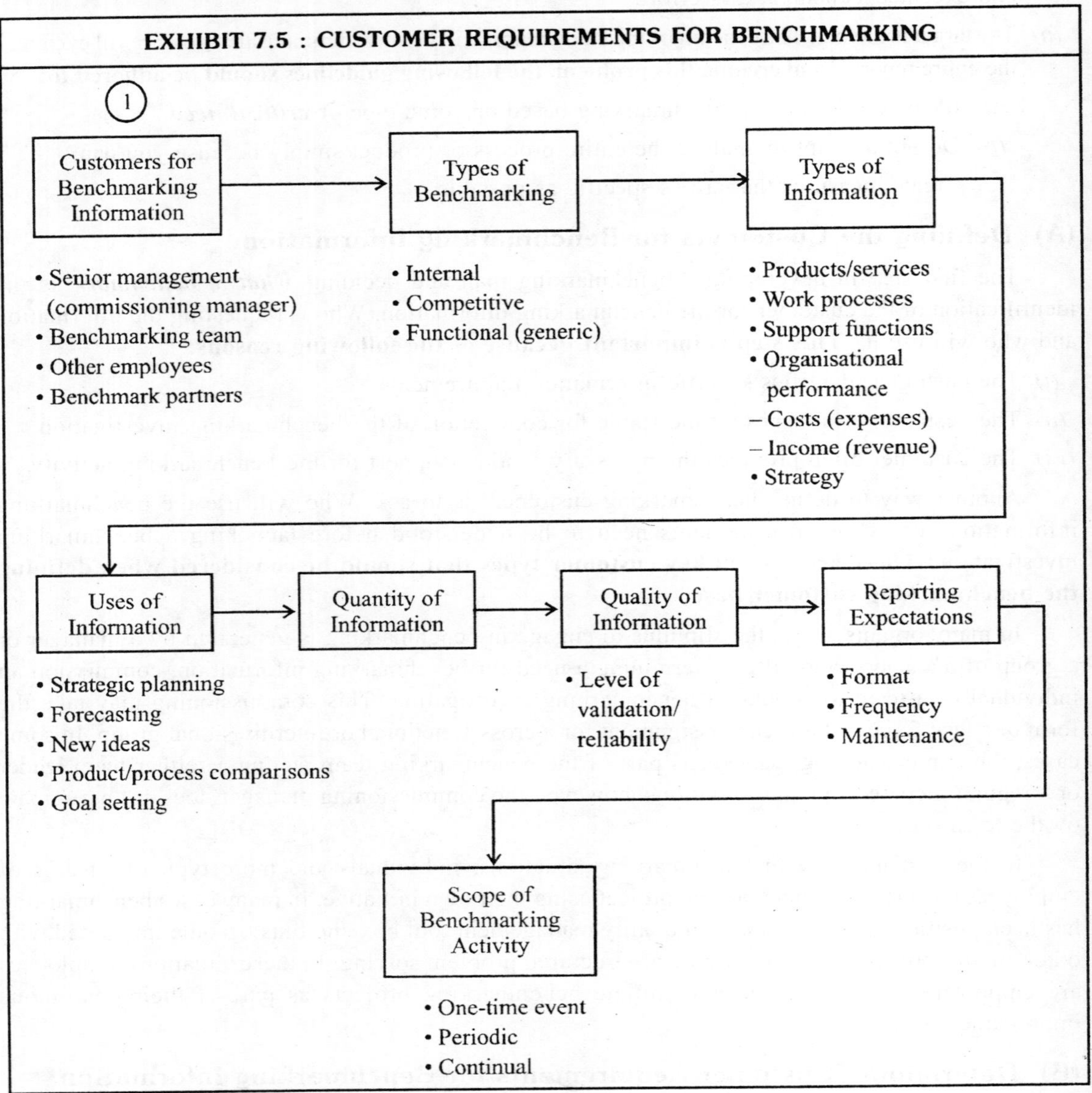

(i) Identifying Customers

This includes the identification of specific individuals and groups that will use the benchmarking information. These customers may include the commissioning manager (the sponsor), the actual members of the benchmarking team and other internal users or potential users of the benchmarking information.

An effort should be made the determine how many of the actual customers of benchmarking should be consulted before embarking on the benchmarking investigation.

(ii) Types of Benchmarking

The basic emphasis of the benchmarking customer is defined by the desired target of the benchmarking activity. The intent and the direction of benchmarking customer can be diagnosed by establishing the types of benchmarking desired. *For example,* a focus on internal and competitive benchmarking indicates an emphasis on competitive positioning.

(iii) Types of Information

What is the focus of the benchmarking investigation as defined by the established need? Is the focus on products or services, work processes, organisational performance indicators, or some other aspect of the organisation? The implications for benchmarking activities are strongly affected by the breadth of the benchmarking focus. The magnitude of the benchmarking effort is increased tremendously when benchmarking work processes. Process benchmarking is a complex activity that involves an intense and lengthy effort. If work processes are included as a focus for benchmarking, it is advisable to work with the benchmarking customer to develop a specific process measurement objective.

(iv) Uses of Information

How will the benchmarking information be used? Specifically is the information needed to make product or process comparisons, to develop strategic plans, as a source of stimulation and new ideas, to set goals? The intended use of the benchmarking information affects the amount of effort required to identify and collect that information. Also, the users significantly affect your choice of the benchmark partners and the types of questions you ask them. If the benchmarking data are to be used for specific product or process comparisons, the level of specificity of benchmarking subjects can be focused and objective.

(v) Quantity of Information

The amount of information desired is an important aspect of customer requirement. *For example,* an exhaustive investigation of best-in-class products or best-in-class processes could involve hundred or even thousands of hours of investigation. Limiting a benchmarking activity to a smaller population of potential organisations greatly reduces the quantity of information generated.

Another aspect of information quantity involves the extent of documentation collected from benchmark partners. The level of detail of benchmarking analyses can vary significantly by organisation and by project. The level of detail expected by the customer affects the amount of time required to collect, analyse, catalog and summarise the benchmark information.

(vi) Quality of Information

We assume that all the information collected in a benchmarking investigation is of high quality. However, distinctions such as the level of validation or reliability can be made.

Validation involves the use of multiple sources of informations multiple interviews per location, cross-checking of archival data with the original source, multiple measures of information over time from the same source. Assuring information validity and reliability increases the amount of time and resources required to generate a benchmarking information base.

(vii) Reporting Expectations

Customers requirements for the reporting of benchmarking results vary significantly by project, by customer, and by organisation. Some benchmarking report formats require extended narratives to describe the benchmarking process and results, some are tabular with very little narrative.

In some cases, benchmarking activity is reported in a formal presentation. The frequency of reporting also has implications for those responsible for benchmarking activity. In some cases, reporting is a one-time activity. In others, benchmarking is a periodic or continuous process that requires repeated report generation. The frequency of reporting also affects the resources required for benchmarking.

Information maintenance must also be considered as benchmarking data are collected and organised. The amount of time and resources dedicated to the development, delivery and maintenance of benchmarking reports varies greatly among benchmarking organisations. There is a definite trend, however, away from the practice of generating extensive reports.

(viii) Scope of the Benchmarking Activity

The scope of benchmarking refers to the amount of benchmarking activity anticipated over time. **The customer requirements on this dimension vary, but they generally fall into one of three categories:**

(a) ***One-time event:*** The benchmarking activity is defined as a singular event with a start date and a completion date. It is often a stand-alone project that is not intended to be repeated. These events are often referred to as benchmarking projects rather than processes. In this type of benchmarking, the information requirements are specific and focus on a limited range of information.

(b) ***Periodic activity:*** Some organisations conduct benchmarking analyses as a standard business practice and plan their benchmarking activities according to a regular calender-for instance, annually or quarterly.

(c) ***Continuous activity:*** Continuous benchmarking activity is ongoing and is not generally limited to a one-time or periodic event. This type of benchmarking is typical of an organisation that has adopted a broad perspective of benchmarking and has incorporated that activity into the goal of continuous improvement of large number of managers and employees.

(C) Identifying Critical Success Factors

Perhaps the must important question that can be answered when selecting the subject of benchmarking investigation is, what factors will have the greatest impact on the performance of the organisation? Most companies dedicate a good portion of their benchmarking orientation and training to the issue of criticality.

Many benchmarking organisations have begun to use a term to refer to subjects that are significant enough to warrant the use of the benchmarking process. The term is ***"critical success factor"*** **(or CSF)**.

Examples of CSFs: ***Box 7.5*** **presents a list of actual CSFs that were identified as the subjects of completed benchmarking investigations by twenty companies experienced in benchmarking.**

BOX 7.5 : CRITICAL SUCCESS FACTORS

1. Market Share:
- ☐ By units
- ☐ By rupees

2. Profitability:
- ☐ Return on sales (margin)
- ☐ Return on equity
- ☐ Return on assets

3. Competitor growth rates
- ☐ Market share by segment

4. Raw materials
- ☐ Cost as a percent of sales
- ☐ Purchase price/unit
- ☐ Yearly purchase volume
- ☐ Exchange rates
- ☐ Freight costs
- ☐ Quality (*e.g.*, defect rates)
- ☐ Yield (unit output per unit input)

5. Direct labour
- ☐ Cost as a percent of sales
- ☐ Head count by department
- ☐ Hourly wage rates
- ☐ Benefit rates
- ☐ Average weekly hour/worker
- ☐ Overtime hours
- ☐ Overtime rates
- ☐ Unit productivity (units produced per man-hour)
- ☐ Revenue productivity (product revenue per man-hour)
- ☐ Worker demographies (age, education level)

6. Indirect labour
- ☐ Overall cost as a percent of sales
- ☐ Benefit rates
- ☐ Head count by function
- ☐ Exchange rates
- ☐ Management to direct labour
- ☐ Unit productivity
- ☐ Salary levels
- ☐ Worker demographics

7. Research and Development
- ☐ Basic R & D costs
- ☐ Refinements of existing products
- ☐ New product development cycle time
- ☐ Cost reduction engineering

8. Sales, administrative, general cost
- ☐ Cost as a percent of sales
- ☐ Worker demographics
- ☐ Head count by organisation
- ☐ Training costs as a percent of sales
- ☐ Salary levels
- ☐ Bad debt expense as a percent of sales
- ☐ Bonus plans
- ☐ Benefit plans

9. Capital costs

- ☐ Overall asset turnover
- ☐ Fixed asset turnover
- ☐ Capital expenditure as a percent of depreciation
- ☐ Depreciation rates
- ☐ Yearly lease costs
- ☐ Maintenance costs
- ☐ Inventory turn over
- ☐ Days receivable
- ☐ Days payable
- ☐ Cost of capital

10. Product features

- ☐ Size, shape (design)
- ☐ Styles
- ☐ Colours
- ☐ Price/pricing strategy
- ☐ Accessories (options)
- ☐ Warranties
- ☐ Guarantees

11. Service

- ☐ Customer complaint volume and type
- ☐ Availability of assistance
- ☐ Response time
- ☐ Mean time to repair
- ☐ Speed of delivery
- ☐ Quality of customer contact personnel
- ☐ Order entry processes
- ☐ Availability of customer "education"

12. Product quality

- ☐ Production yields
- ☐ Amount of rework
- ☐ Repair expense (to company and customer)
- ☐ Mean time to product failure (reliability)
- ☐ Quality methodology (QC processes, worker involvement, statistical process control)

13. Images

- ☐ Customer awareness
- ☐ Levels of advertising
- ☐ Media usage
- ☐ Advertising expense
- ☐ Public perception
- ☐ Lobbyling efforts
- ☐ Promotion activity
- ☐ Customer reaction to image/advertising

14. Manufacturing

- ☐ Make or buy decisions
- ☐ Levels of plant "specialisation"
- ☐ Hardware used for production
- ☐ Workforce skill levels
- ☐ Workplace structure (design, layout)
- ☐ Automation levels

15. Distribution

- ☐ Channels (single/multiple)
- ☐ Territory configuration
- ☐ Sole distributionships or other

16. Sales force

- ☐ Size
- ☐ Experience level
- ☐ Performance level

17. Data processing/MIS

- ☐ Investment in systems
- ☐ Applications
- ☐ Technology (hardware/software)

18. Human resources

- ☐ Sourcing/recruiting activity
- ☐ Compensation practices
- ☐ Benefit plans
- ☐ Training activities/budgets
- ☐ Reward/recognition systems
- ☐ Affirmative action activities
- ☐ Community service activities
- ☐ Communication practices/budgets
- ☐ Health and safety (employee) services

19. Finance

- ☐ Financial policies
- ☐ Tax-related policies and strategies
- ☐ Debt policies
- ☐ Dividend policies

STAGE 2. FORMING A BENCHMARKING TEAM

As soon as the customer requirements for benchmarking are known, the actual process of benchmarking can begin. The planning, organisation and deployment of a well-designed benchmarking investigation involves a considerable amount of time and energy. Engaging reinforcements to share the work load and developing an equitable division of labour are not only practical considerations, in most cases they are required. Also by identifying a qualified and motivated team of benchmarkers early in the process, you can take advantage of the group's diverse experiences, professional affiliations and individual interests.

Benchmarking as a Team Activity

Eventhough benchmarking can be done by individuals, benchmarking teams have to be necessarily formed because of the work load involved in the benchmarking investigations. However there are other reasons why benchmarking is an appropriate team activity. In many benchmarking investigations, a group of employees can designate itself as the primary customer (or user) of benchmarking information. These employees are the primary beneficiaries of the benchmarking process, and they are responsible for implementing changes based in part, on the results of their benchmarking. Another good reason for the use of teams is the level of functional expertise and work experience team represents. Different perspectives, special skills, variety of business connections, physical loaction – these are the dimensions that individual ***team*** members bring to the benchmarking process.

We use the word *team* instead of ***group*** becasue the word ***'team'*** introduces quite a few expections regarding the behaviourof the group, such as a common purpose or goal, co-ordination, co-operation, communication and motivation.

Types of Benchmarking

Generally, there are three basic types of benchmarking teams as defined by their structure and reporting relationships.

1. Intact Work Group

This group is usually in a single location with all members of the group reporting to a common manager. In these groups, the manager may or may not assume the role of the benchmarking team member.

Intact work groups are often the customers for their own benchmarking investigations. This is due to the integration of benchmarking with other tools and techniques such as structured problem solving. One benefit of this situation is that the team does not need to get outside approvals in order to proceed with the process.

2. Cross-functional, Inter Departmental and Interorganisation Teams

These teams are often structured as ***task teams*** or ***task forces*** with specific charters and defined sets of customers who are usually commissioning managers. The individuals selected for these teams are chosen for their specific knowledge or skill levels, but they also act as representatives of their respective departments, locations or divisions. The leader or project manager of these types of teams is usually not the everyday manager of most team members.

In many cases, these types of teams are brought together to work on one specific issue or problem. Once their benchmarking investigation is complete, the team disbands. These types of teams often produce recommendations or reports and present those findings to their sponsors or to upper management.

3. Adhoc Teams

This types of team represents the ultimate in team flexibility. An adhoc team can consist of any numbers of employees who share common interests or responsibilities and decide that a benchmarking investigation on some subject is warranted. Usually an adhoc team can be called together by an individual, or it can be formed as the result of a team decision. Usually the adhoc team defines a specific subject for benchmarking and continues to function until the benchmarking investigation is complete. This type of team may be made up of managers or non managers - any employee or group of employees that has identified a need for benchmarking information.

Who is Involved in the Benchmarking Process?

When you contact another organisation with a benchmarking request, you are likely to come into contact with people who participate in the benchmarking process and are responsible for maintaining benchmarking from an overall organisational stand point. If you are just beginning to introduce benchmarking in your organisation, these are the people you might need to help you start up, maintain and expand your benchmarking activities. Three categories of people involved in the benchmarking process are: *(i)* Internal benchmarking specialists, *(ii)* External benchmarking specialists and *(iii)* Employees.

(i) Internal Benchmarking Specialists

These are employees of the organisation who have been trained in the process of benchmarking and whose normal work responsibilities include benchmarking related tasks. These employees may be staff employees (*e.g.,* quality specialists) or may be from the line organisation (*e.g.,* manufacturing or engineering managers). The amount of time they dedicate to benchmarking activities may vary from 25 percent to 100 percent.

Benchmarking specialists are often assigned by functional area. *For example,* in large organisations, there may be benchmarking specialists for manufacturing, engineering, finance, human resources, marketing etc. In most cases, the benchmarking assignment is a part-time job for these functional specialists.

Benchmarking specialists can also be found in individual divisions or geographical locations of organisations. These people are usually responsible for the benchmarking activities at a particular site.

In general, the responsibilities of benchmarking specialists focus in three major areas:

(i) Organising and managing the benchmarking process (finding benchmarking process resources).

(ii) Training employees on managing and conducting the benchmarking process.

(iii) Benchmarking process - working with benchmarking customers, planning benchmarking activities, gathering and analysing data etc.

(ii) External Benchmarking Specialists

Benchmarking specialists from outside the organisation are typically consultants who specialise in various aspects of the benchmarking process. External benchmarking specialists can perform a variety of services and they often can develop areas of specialisation or competence. There are several types of specialists who can help organisations manage their benchmarking processes.

(i) Consultants who specialise in planning benchmarking projects, training employees in basic benchmarking processes, directing benchmarking projects, and producing reports.

(ii) Consultants who provide specialised support services such as training or facilitation support.

(iii) Consultants who manage entire benchmarking projects from start to finish.

A relatively new service being provided by consultants is helpful in locating best-practices companies.

(iii) Employees

Most benchmarking projects use employees to help plan, conduct, analyse and present benchmarking efforts. The level of involvement of employees may vary from basic data-collection and analysis tasks to project planning and management assignments.

The Benchmarking Team - Roles and Responsibilities

In most benchmarking organisations, there is a fairly common ***core team*** structure. These are the employees who perform the majority of the benchmarking tasks. In addition to this core, there are a variety of other employees or external specialists who can provide specific services to the team on an as needed basis.

***Exhibit 7.6* shows a typical benchmarking team structure.** The basic structure is depicted as a set of intersecting circles that demonstrates the flexibility of the team structure and conveys the idea that these team structures do not necessarily conform to traditional structures and reporting relationships.

(i) **Project manager:** The project manager is responsible for planning and organising the benchmarking activities for the team. This individual is the primary contact with the benchmarking customer or sponsor.

EXHIBIT 7.6 : A TYPICAL BENCHMARKING TEAM STRUCTURE

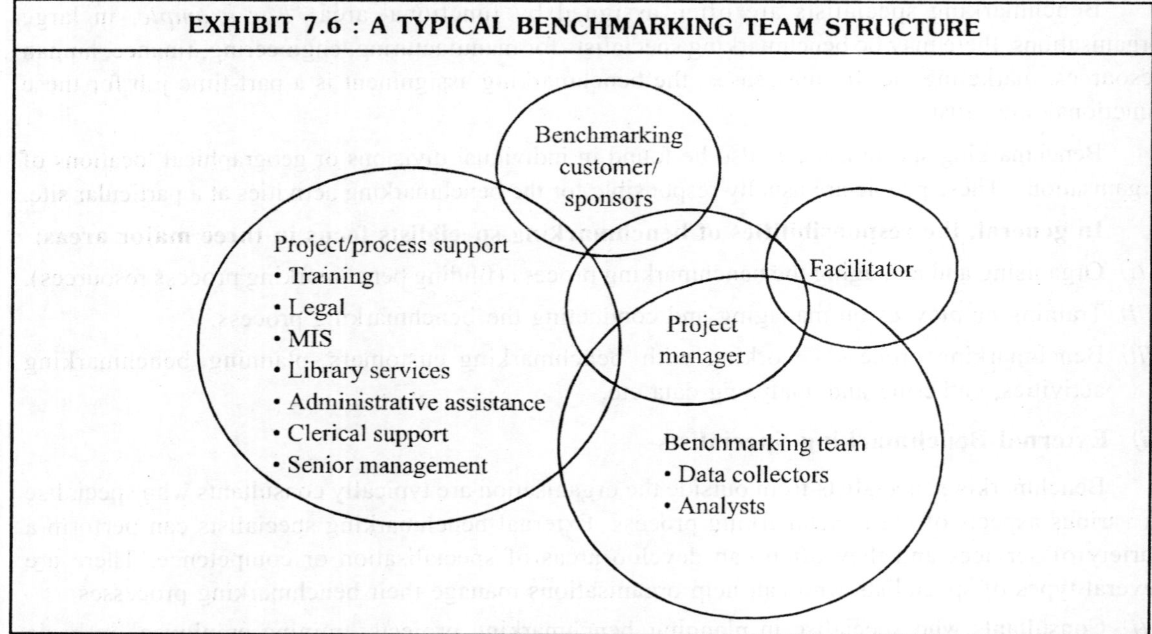

The project manager is also responsible for maintaining basic benchmarking discipline. The project manager also serves as a link between the team and other benchmarking resources or teams throughout the organisation.

(ii) **Data collector/analyst:** The data collectors and analysts are the true core of the benchmarking team. These are the people who assist in the development of the benchmarking plan, identify, contact and interview benchmark partners, analyse and summarise the benchmarking data and produce benchmarking reports.

(iii) **Benchmarking project support: The most frequently needed project support resources are:**

- *(i)* ***Facilitation*** – process facilitation support is required for new teams.
- *(ii)* ***Training*** – training support may be required for new teams or teams that have added new members.
- *(iii)* ***Legal*** – legal support is needed if a benchmarking team is dealing with a sensitive issue that may involve proprietary or sensitive information.
- *(iv)* ***Management information system*** – the MIS function can help a team when benchmarking information calls for a spread sheet analysis or summary.
- *(v)* ***Library services*** – internal library services provide invaluable support to benchmarking teams that are investigating printed information.
- *(vi)* ***Administrative assistance and clerical support*** – required for a variety of tasks, including word processing, forms creation, filing and telephone assistance (for setting appointments, receiving calls from benchmark partners).
- *(vii)* ***Senior management*** – Support is needed when additional resources support in the form of time, funding or people is required.

Table 7.2 **lists the responsibilities of and skills required for various benchmarking role profiles.**

TABLE 7.2 : BENCHMARKING ROLE PROFILES

Role	Responsibilities	Skills
Project manager • Plan, organise, staff, direct and control the benchmarking project. Link the results with other organisational units	• Identify customers and their requirements • Select members of benchmarking team • Develop and monitor budget • Select outside suppliers/consultants • Consider legal, ethical project issues • Provide project briefings • Monitor project progress • Negotiate commitments from internal and external resources • Communicate/present results of project to necessary target audience • Manage group discussions and group processes • Provide benchmarking training	• Communication • Writing • Negotiating • Planning • Organising • Delegating • Presentation • Political • Leadership • Group dynamics
Data collector/analyst • Develop and use benchmarking techniques to collect, analyse and present data	• Assist in development of project plan • Design and produce data-collection instruments • Schedule appointments with data sources • Gather data • Summarise data • Identify performance gaps • Present results • Produce summary reports	• Planning • Organising • Communication • Writing • Interpersonal
Benchmarking project support • Provide support to benchmarking team as required	• Facilitation • Training • Document processing • Graphics support • Legal counsel • Computer support • Database management • Library services	• Communication • Interpersonal • Professional

STAGE 3. IDENTIFYING BENCHMARK PARTNERS

This stage involves the identification of benchmark partners. A ***benchmark partner*** is any person or organisation that supplies you with information related to your benchmarking investigation. Organisations that have taken this ***partnering approach*** report high levels of cooperation and positive results with the organisations they have contacted. A direct, person to person approach when dealing with functional counterparts has yielded dividends in the form of improved levels of information quantity and quality.

Information is a resource which you can use as a tool to improve your decision making process. The sources of information are - employees (internal and external) experts, analyst, researchers, consultants and organisations such as your organisation, other organisations, the government, research groups, universities, trade and professional associations etc. All of these resources are potential benchmark partners.

Information consists of facts, numbers, trendliness, process descriptions and even observations. You can obtain information from a person who offers expertise and experience by asking specific questions over the telephone.

The reference documents and the individuals you use to collect benchmarking information should be considered potential long term resources. Those resources that have produced useful and reliable information overtime can become part of your benchmarking ***information network***.

There are several advantages of forming your own *benchmarking information network*:

(i) You can narrow your list of contacts down to those that have established a history of providing reliable information.

(ii) The amount of time spent tracking information leads can be greatly decreased.

(iii) As your information needs change based on the subject or scope of your benchmarking project, you won't have to begin your information search from scratch - your information network is the automatic starting point for any benchmarking activity.

Identifying Information Resources

Before you begin your benchmarking investigation, ask yourself the following three basic questions:

1. Who produces the information I want?
2. Who else uses the information I want?
3. Who accumulates the data I want?

You will discover that there are many more sources of information than you had imagined. The challenge is to identify benchmark partners that will provide you with useful information to your quest for best practices and continuous improvement.

The Search for Best Practices

The basic premise of benchmarking is to learn something of value from someone or some place else, something that helps you perform more effectively or efficiently. The goal of most benchmarking activities is to learn from the best.

How does one go about discovering what best practices or best-in-class really is? There are companies and associations that offer lists of best-practices companies by functional area and industry. They have conducted their own investigations and identified the best-practices companies for you. You can buy the information you want from those companies for a price. The important point to remember is that these companies represent only a single-source of best-practices information. Their recommendations and referrals should be combined with other sources of information to define best practices for your area of interest.

Best-in-class, World-class or Best Practices?

Some of the common terminology used in benchmarking has to do with the selection of benchmark partners that represent the desired state of organisational performance. The terms used to describe partner companies include ***best-in-class, world-class and best practices***. What companies expect in terms of comparative information when they conduct a benchmarking investigation? The answer is everything from an improvement over their current practices to true world leadership. ***Exhibit 7.7*** **is a pyramid shaped diagram that can be used to demonstrate the relative amounts of information that are available for consideration, depending on how the organisation defines its benchmarking and improvement objectives.** At the very top of the pyramid are the best-in-class and world-class practices, followed by a larger area representing best practices and even larger area representing improvement over current practices. The opportunities for simple improvement are much greater than opportunities defined by the best practices or best-in-class category. As an organisation attempts to identify and analyse business practices at the top of the pyramid, the amount of resources required (*e.g.*, time, funds, people) to pinpoint specific organisations and their activities also increases. Therefore, after gaining some exposure to true "best practices" information, many organisations rethink their benchmarking objectives and quickly shift their direction lower down the pyramid to a more realistic or comfortable position.

EXHIBIT 7.7 : THE SEARCH FOR BEST PRACTICES

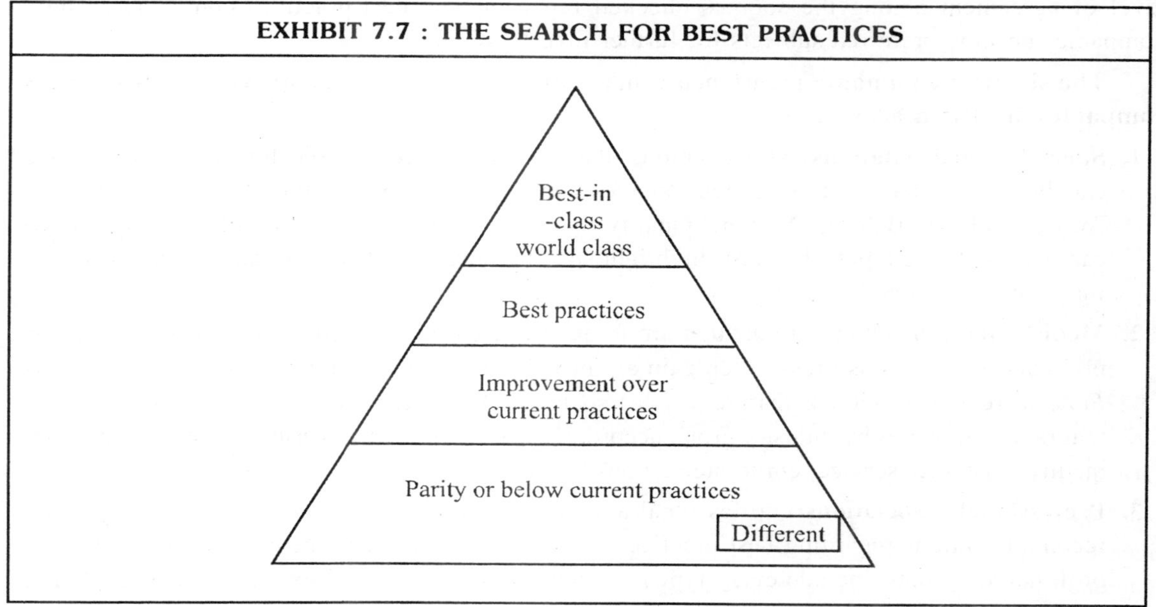

Companies that are simply trying to identify improvement opportunities generally limit their searches to companies from which they can learn something new that can be of benefits. At the other extreme, companies seeking true world-class benchmarks often make extensive use of databases, international networks and association and international consulting firms to locate true world-class performers.

Every organisation that decides to embark on the benchmarking path should consider the fundamental issue of its goals and objectives. For most organisations, the goal of continuous improvement in a learning environment is challenging enough. Certainly benchmarking provides sufficient stimulation and information to help any organisation to achieve this objective. However to become best-in-class or world-class represents a tremendous leap in ambition and implies a much more sophisticated view of information gathering and analysis if not in content, at least in scope. Somewhere in between these extremes is the search for best practices. It requires a dedication to search beyond the new and improved to identify outputs and processes that really set the standard.

Reliable Sources of Best Practices

What are the most reliable sources for identifying best practices? Experience benchmarkers all mention certain general categories of references that should be checked as sources of best-practices information.

The process of identifying best-practices companies is usually as follows:

The benchmarking team identifies the specific ***"critical success factors"*** or functional areas to be benchmarked. A set of resources is identified for investigation. The members of the benchmarking team engage in a basic search of these information sources and meet to compare notes on the organisations identified in their search. As the team examines the companies that emerge from this round of investigation, they are looking for convergence in the names that are mentioned - some level of agreement among the sources checked regarding the best-practices companies. These companies become preferred subjects for further investigation.

The six most commonly mentioned sources of information for identifying best-practices companies are listed below :

1. **Special awards/citations:** Organisations that are formally recognised for product or service excellence by credible independent sources such as CII - Exim Bank Business Excellence Award, Malcolm Baldrige National Quality Award, Deming Prize etc., are likely best-practice candidates. These types of awards highlight specific areas of excellence that provide leads for functional best-practices.

2. **Media attention:** Organisations that are frequently cited in the media, especially the popular press and the business press, often gain a reputation for being exemplary. Magazines such as *Fortune* regularly publish feature articles such as "America's Most Admired Corporations" that rank companies by industry group according to a set of fairly generic criteria (*e.g.*, product quality, customer service, corporate responsibility).

3. **Professional associations:** Professional associations and societies are often able to provide recommendations regarding best practices by functional area. The membership lists of these professional groups include every type of organisations - large and small, public and private, foreign and domestic. Larger associations maintain extensive functional databases and reference

libraries. Professional associations also sponsor national and regional conferences, symposia and conventions. These meetings and their recorded minutes and proceedings provide valuable information regarding state-of-the-art developments.

4. **Independent reports:** Special reports prepared by trade and professional organisations, consumer organisations, analyst, government agencies, specialised institutes or universities all tend to draw attention to organisations that are identified as being special or exemplary. Independent reports are often viewed as reliable, unbiased sources of information.
5. **Word of mouth:** In many cases organisational reputations are enhanced by professionals who speak positively about an organisation to other professionals. Positive comments from a respected and trusted professional tend to be repeated to others.
6. **Consultants:** Consultants often specialise in providing state-of-the-art information regarding specific functional areas. Reputed consulting companies both large and small are beginning to specialise in benchmarking services that include the identification of best-practices companies and the ability to introduce companies to one another as members of benchmarking consortia.

Beware of the "Halo Effect": When selecting benchmark partners, exercise caution not to fall victim to the halo effect. ***Halo effect*** is a psychological term that describes a characteristic defect in rating scales to rate individuals either too high or too low on the basis of one outstanding trait. Two types of halo effects that are typical among benchmarking teams, even among experienced benchmarkers are: *(i)* ***halo positive*** and *(ii)* ***halo negative***. Avoid both types of effects as you conduct your search for benchmark partners.

Halo positive effect occurs when an organisation establishes a reputation for doing one thing particularly well. As a result, many assume that the company does other things or most things well.

Halo negative effect is evident when considering companies whose overall performance or recent market history indicates a significant organisational depression or downturn. Because the organisation is in a slump, it is often overlooked as a resource for any type of benchmarking, eventhough some functional activities may represent best-practices.

Seeking Co-operative Benchmarking Partners

Perhaps the biggest hurdle people have to contend with as they become familiar with the process of benchmarking is the psychological barrier against calling on individuals in other organisations - particularly competitors. People may attempt to find excuses for not benchmarking, such as claiming that all data are sensitive or proprietary. Some may project their own fears into the benchmark partners and assume that other organisations would not cooperate in a benchmarking investigation.

Employees feel uncomfortable about direct contact with employees from other organisations because of three reasons :

(i) ***Tradition:*** The stereotype of the competitor as the bad guy and the enemy dies hard.

(ii) ***Collusion:*** Many people fear that making direct contact with competitors' employees and possibly sharing information with them is a form of collusion.

(iii) ***Awkwardness:*** Quite simply, many people feel awkward calling on employees from other organisations - particularly competitors.

Once the initial reluctance is overcome and actual attempt is made to greater benchmarking information through direct contact with people in other organisations, benchmarkers are surprised at the relative ease of collecting information in this manner. Why people from other companies - especially competitors – co-operate in the data-collection effort at all? The answers are: *(i)* Professional affiliation, *(ii)* Curiosity, *(iii)* The opportunity to learn something, *(iv)* Reciprocity and *(v)* Courtesy.

Benchmarking Networks : A Core Group of Benchmark Partners

One of the most recent phenomena in the practice of benchmarking involves the formation of formal **benchmarking networks** or **consortia**. These groups band together for the explicit purpose of opening benchmarking channels among the participating members. As members of these networks beginning the benchmarking process, their fellow network members represent an automatic starting point for identifying potential benchmark partners. Even if the network members are not included as benchmark partners for a particular investigation, they do not represent another valuable resource that can be checked to find potential candidates for benchmarking. Also, members of these networks may agree to share information from benchmarking reports that have already been completed.

Some of these benchmarking networks are formed by organisations that are members of a particular industry group. *For example,* a group of companies in the telecom industry banded together to form the "Telecommunication Benchmarking Consortium". Other benchmarking networks have been formed in areas such as manufacturing, engineering, finance and human resources.

These kinds of benchmarking networks have proved to be an effective means of initiating benchmarking investigations and taking advantage of the benchmarking resources of a large number of cooperative organisations.

Other Sources of Benchmarking Information

Benchmark partners including organisations or their employees are the direct sources of benchmarking information that provide you with best-practices examples and other comparative data. However, there are other kinds of resources that benchmarking companies have found useful as they begin a benchmarking analysis. These resources can be used by any benchmarking company, regardless of industry, location, size or ownership.

Although the process of benchmarking is just beginning to reach maturity of benchmarking is the process of collecting business information has relatively long history in most companies. Many of the sources of reliable benchmarking information are identical to the sources that have been used to research new technologies, analyse market conditions and investigate competitive practices.

Organisations that collect benchmarking information generally focus their data-collection activities around a common core of information sources. Most companies use the following sources of information for their data collection activities: *(i)* Own salesforce, *(ii)* Customers, *(iii)* Industry periodicals, *(iv)* Promotional materials of other companies, *(v)* Own marketing research staff, *(vi)* Analysis of the products/services of other companies, *(vi)* Annual reports, *(viii)* Meetings, trade shows and *(ix)* Distributors. These sources are almost identical to those that are considered reliable by experienced benchmarking companies.

The following categories are proposed as a basic list of resource areas to consider during the course of your benchmarking investigation :

1. ***Government sources*** – predominantly federal agencies.
2. ***Special interest sources*** – including academic institutions, consumer advocacy groups, consultants, and trade associations.
3. ***Private-sector sources*** – including business information services and market research studies.
4. ***Internal sources*** – including your own organisation and the target organisation for benchmarking.
5. ***The media*** – including the general and business press and databases.
6. ***Foreign data sources*** – including banks, foreign consulates, multinational corporate offices and international databases.
7. ***Miscellaneous sources*** – including customers, manufacturers, suppliers, retailers and distributors.

Selecting Benchmark Partners

The benchmarking process presents an excellent opportunity to learn from best-practices companies. In most cases, those companies will co-operate with your benchmarking efforts, particularly if you approach them in an organised and professional manner.

One of the deficiencies of many benchmarking efforts is a failure to take advantage of the opportunities that are presented by excellent companies. The fact is that even seasoned benchmarkers lose some momentum after a period of time and become lax in the process of investigating potential entries in the best-practices ranks.

Perhaps the most obvious indicator of a potential draw-back in your search for best practices partners is the **"brain storm syndrome"**. This is the process of a benchmarking team brainstorming best-practices companies, reducing the list of companies to a manageable number and beginning the process of data collection. There is little or no effort to investigate other potential candidates for benchmarking and no formal search is made of the traditional sources of information to validate and expand the choices the team has already proposed. Although the organisations identified may represent excellent practices, there is no attempt made to determine whether these organisations truly represent best practices.

STAGE 4. COLLECTING AND ANALYSING BENCHMARKING INFORMATION

This stage involves the actual collection and analysis of benchmarking information. It is assumed that you have already identified your benchmarking customers, their requirements, and the specific **"critical success factors"** (CSFs) that will constitute the core of your investigation, selected and trained the members of your benchmarking team and identified an initial list of best-practices or competitive benchmark partners.

If the initial planning and preparation of the benchmarking process have not been completed carefully, the process of collecting and analysing benchmarking information can be unproductive or even counter productive.

Know Thyself

One of the fundamental rules of benchmarking is to know your own processes, products and services before you attempt to understand the processes, products or services of another organisation. Before you attempt to collect information about another organisation, it is wise to collect and analyse information about your own internal operations. In many cases, this implies an **internal benchmarking effort**. In others, it may require only a simple measurement to document one's own activities.

Why is this so Important?

(i) Without a thorough investigation of your own internal products and services, you may not realise the extent of your improvement opportunities. You may end up over or underestimating your overall organisational position based on a limited awareness of the extent of your own internal activities.

(ii) Without a thorough internal analysis, you may be bypassing some important internal benchmarking opportunities, you may never discover the possible sources of information and assistance available within your own organisation.

(iii) When you begin investigating the activities of other organisations, they often ask you about your activities in the same area. If you are not prepared to respond with assurance regarding your own internal practices, you might give the impression that you are not fully prepared to investigate others or you may appear to be collecting information out of sequence.

Always ensure that your own organisational performance is well documented and understood before engaging in any external benchmarking activities.

Information Collection

Once you have determined the types of benchmarking information you need to collect and the information sources and organisations you will investigate, the next issue to consider is the data-collection methods you will use. The various methods of collecting benchmarking information were already discussed in detail in chapter 6 "Data Collection and Analysis".

What factors determine the methods you use to gather benchmarking data? One key factor is driven by your consumer requirements: *(i)* the type of information needed, *(ii)* the proposed uses of the information, *(iii)* the level of detail required and *(iv)* the quantity and quality requirements. Other factors involve levels of experience with certain information - gathering methods and personal or organisational preferences for using certain techniques. The following factors were cited most frequently by experienced benchmarking companies:

(i) **Time constraints:** The amount of time available to collect information affects the number of sources that can be investigated and the methods used. *For example,* scheduling and conducting personal meetings is more time-consuming than interviewing over the telephone.

(ii) **Resource constraints:** The number and types of people and the amount of funding available to support the data collection activities affect the methods used.

(iii) **Experience:** People have a tendency to use data collection methods which are familiar to them. *For example,* if members of a benchmarking team have extensive experience in telephone interviewing, that technique will most likely be their primary method of gathering information, as opposed to any other method with which the group has little or no experience.

(iv) **Information-collection philosophy:** Based on information collection experiences and the personal preferences of key internal benchmarking experts, most organisations develop an information-collection philosophy that is communicated in benchmarking orientation and process training sessions. This philosophy affects the methods used by benchmarking employees.

STAGE 5. TAKING ACTION

The primary objective of benchmarking is to take action. Although benchmarking is a process of investigation, the motivation for initiating an investigation is to stimulate and support change for improvement. The process of benchmarking is driven by a desire to take action, a rigorous set of customer requirements and an identification of specific critical success factors that serve as the focus of investigation. Infact, in many organisations, benchmarking is encouraged only after the decision has been made to take action.

There are several basic kinds of activities that can take place at the action stage of the benchmarking process. They are :

1. Produce a benchmarking report/summary.
2. Present findings to benchmarking customers.
3. Communicate findings to *(i)* internal - other functional groups and *(ii)* benchmark partners.
4. Look for opportunities: *(i)* product/process improvement, *(ii)* learning-bring new ideas and concepts into your organisation and *(iii)* forming functional networks.
5. Encourage recycling efforts - *(i)* modify/improve your use of the process and *(ii)* introduce new/related subjects for benchmarking.

The activities listed above are briefly discussed in the following section:

1. Producing a Benchmarking Report

Producing benchmarking reports is a typical activity when the customer of the benchmarking information is a commissioning manager. From the outset, these types of benchmarking teams have as an objective the production and delivery of a project report. In some cases, this is a one time activity similar to a task force or task team assignment. In other situations, the benchmarking team prepares a report in order to fulfill an obligation to the various benchmark partners who agreed to participate in the investigation partly because they expected to receive a summary of the findings at the end of the project cycle.

After the basic analysis has been completed, the final major task of the benchmarking team is to generate a report. **This report is intended to serve the following purposes :**

(i) As a report to be delivered to the benchmarking customers.

(ii) As a summary of the data that were collected and analysed.

(iii) As a record of the organisations benchmarked and key project contacts.

(iv) As a communications product for other internal employees and functions.

(v) As the foundation for communications to external parties and

(vi) As a record for the organisation's benchmarking data base and files.

Contents of the Report

The following is a comprehensive table of contents for a benchmarking report:

(i) ***Statement of need/purpose:*** This is a statement of the motivation for conducting the benchmarking analysis. This section should present any data or incidents that have been instrumental in stimulating the benchmarking effort.

(ii) ***Project customers:*** Identify the project customers by job title, name is optional. Identify any information partners that may be co-operating in joint analysis.

(iii) ***Customer requirements:*** List the customer information requirements, including project scope, benchmarking subjects identified, requirements for information quantity and quality, delivery dates and formal requirements.

(iv) ***Project team:*** Identify project team members by name, organisation, job title and work address. As an option, explain the selection process for team members, identify significant project support personnel.

(v) ***Team process:*** Describe the process of team orientation and training. Describe the amount of time each member dedicated to the task. Identify specific roles and responsibilities taken on by team members. Identify key decisions made by the team regarding the team process.

(vi) ***Project calendar:*** Display the project calendar, noting key dates for key meetings, reporting activities, report completion and other events worth noting.

(vii) ***Subjects benchmarked:*** Present a data outline that lists general categories of information and specific measures used to gather information.

(viii) ***Information sources:*** List information sources by type. Identify specific references for printed material. List names of individuals contacted, organisations and job title.

(ix) ***Methodology:*** Describe the methods used for collecting data - interviews, surveys, printed materials search, and so on. Include copies of surveys or questionnaires as an appendix to the report.

(x) ***Results/summary:*** Include a data summary in the form of narratives, summary matrices or both. Include a description of the summary matrices design.

(xi) ***Narrative:*** Provide any additional narrative that may be required to describe miscellaneous topics regarding the benchmarking investigation, such as additional data gathered in the process, difficulties encountered or outstanding events that might be of interest to readers of the report.

(xii) ***Analysis:*** Present charts and narratives that describe the analysis of the data. Include any graphs or charts that help illustrate the results. Avoid technical details regarding quantitative analysis, or include this type of information as an appendix.

(xiii) ***Results:*** Present the results in summary fashion and provide an accompanying narrative if required. Refer to the original customer requirement when presenting the results, summary. Keep the results section factual.

(xiv) ***Next steps:*** Provide any information regarding the next steps of the benchmarking process. *For example,* note any follow-up data collection that is planned and provide a calendar of expected activities and completion dates. Discuss any implications for further benchmarking analysis that were identified during the course of the project.

2. Presenting Findings to Benchmarking Customers

In some situations, the benchmarking team is required to deliver a presentation to its customers. These customers may include groups of managers, other teams within the organisation, or a single commissioning manager. Such a presentation is an oral version of the benchmarking report, in many cases, both a verbal and a written report are required. These presentations also provide the customers with an opportunity to ask questions.

Benchmarking reports and presentations offer an opportunity to expand the audience for the benchmarking findings and stimulate action to initiate change. In some organisations, these presentations are also used as opportunities to acknowledge or reward the efforts of the benchmarking team members.

The benchmarking team may also communicate its findings to other members of the organisation, either directly through written memos to select groups of employees or indirectly by means of other communications vehicles such as news letters, or on-line systems created especially for that purpose.

The value of any benchmarking activity can be increased by sharing the results of the benchmarking effort with others who can benefit from the findings and recommendations. Most organisations that have established a stable benchmarking process record benchmarking summaries onto an on-line system that can be accessed by any employee. New teams are encouraged to check the system for benchmarking results that may affect their projects and to look for leads and benchmarking contacts as they prepare to launch their team activities.

3. Identifying Possible Product and Process Improvements

One of the key activities of a benchmarking team is to find opportunities for product and process improvement. During the course of benchmarking projects, teams will be exposed to all kinds of new ideas, and the temptation to take immediate action based on early findings is strong.

Benchmarking teams have to decide what action they will take as a result of their benchmarking activity. Often, they close the loop and go back to their original customer requirements and reassess any implementation and improvement plans based on the following factors:

(i) ***Customer requirements revisited:*** Have the customer requirements remained stable or has a new set of requirements been added to the original plan?

(ii) ***Funding:*** What level of financial (or human resources) support is available to support the team's recommendations?

(iii) ***Time:*** How much time does the team have available to incorporate change into the environment? What pressures is the organisation putting on the team in terms of other work priorities, new assignments or other benchmarking initiatives?

(iv) ***Interest/energy level:*** Has the team sustained its energy level during the process cycle? Are team members capable of carrying out the total assignment, or are they burned-out after the investigation phase?

(v) ***Original product/process improvement assumptions:*** Has anything changed in the organisational environment since the team started the benchmarking activity? Has the original need decreased or increased dramatically? Have any of the primary customers for the

benchmarking information changed? Has the organisation been faced with another challenge or opportunity that places the team's efforts on the back burner?

Based on these factors, the team either continues with its original plan or adjusts it accordingly. Teams always feel the pressure of time, they are always trying to move the process along as quickly as possible, sometimes to the detriment of the process itself.

4. Improvement Outcomes

The majority of product and process improvements made by benchmarking teams generally involve one or more of the following improvement outcomes :

(i) ***Product/process improvements:*** At this stage, benchmarkers use the benchmarking information to alter their actual products or processes. These alterations may be subtle or dramatic. Teams must also face reality regarding the amount of time and resources it will take to implement the changes.

For most teams, the results of their process improvements are not quite as dramatic. In some cases, the improvements may be so subtle that they are difficult to measure. The key indicator of success is whether the process improvements meet the original customer requirements.

(ii) ***Learning:*** For many teams, the outcome of benchmarking is simply the opportunity to learn something new and bring new ideas into the organisation.

(iii) ***Forming functional networks:*** As individuals participate in benchmarking activities on a continuous basis, they form a variety of professional contacts within their own organisation, within their industry group, and possibly throughout the world. One individual benchmarker can have hundreds of benchmarking contacts. Once these networks are formed, the opportunities for "informal" benchmarking through one's network increase and information can be canvassed, accumulated and summarised in fairly short order.

The trend toward the formation of functional and industry group networks is increasing. As these networks grow in popularity, there will be greater opportunities for joint benchmarking projects cosponsored by large groups of organisations or by whole clusters of network members.

5. Encourage Recycling Efforts

Many of the formal benchmarking models in existence today include a basic direction to recycle or recalibrate. **There are two implications to this directive :**

(i) To make adjustments in the benchmarking process itself - to examine the process during and after each benchmarking cycle in order to improve the fit between the benchmarking team and the process requirements. As individuals and teams gain experience and become proficient in their use of the process, they are able to diagnose their individual process strengths and weaknesses and adjust their benchmarking behaviours accordingly.

(ii) The second focus of recycling has to do with the continuous improvement of the work process itself. Given the basic assumption that functional best practices are a moving target, the search for emerging best-practices organisations and sources of new information and ideas is never-ending. Benchmarking is a continuous activity for those who want to maintain a state-of-the-art perspective. Most benchmarking teams emerge from the investigation process with many ideas and recycling possibilities. But benchmarking begins with a focus on specific critical

success factors. The idea is to start with this specific information and work toward the broader concepts. As one explores these broader concepts, the exposure to new ideas and methods grows. Teams returning from site visits and interviews always have new ideas for improving their business and new ideas for benchmarking.

Seeing the Project Through

One of the problems with the benchmarking process (particularly when one is new to it) is that it is often time-consuming and requires a significant amount of project planning, team coordination and in some cases, travel time. The process often wears people out. After participation in a benchmarking project, there may be a project completion "high" followed by a post-project "low". Many people are too exhausted to spend quality time on the actual implementation of organisational improvements. This problem decreases as people gain more experience with the process and became more efficient at completing their assignments. As you begin to implement benchmarking in your organisation, be careful that you don't fall into the trap of underestimating the amount of time and effort it will take to complete your first few cycles of the process.

As you complete your initial benchmarking cycle, it may be necessary to rally the members of the benchmarking team around to call to take action. Whether you are producing a benchmarking report, communicating findings to others, implementing product or process improvements, or simply applying what you have learnt to your own work, you have to generate enough energy to apply what you have learnt and to continue to move ahead to identify other benchmarking opportunities.

BOX 7.6 : BENCHMARKING IN PRACTICE – THE BENCHMARKING NETWORK INC.

The Benchmarking Network Inc., is an international resource for business process research and metrics. We lead studies with over 1,40,000 process leaders in over 165 countries. We provide benchmarking training and research to individual companies, professionals and trade associations and industry and process groups. Since 1992, over 300 benchmarking studies have spanned virtually all processes and industries to identify measures and collect data to identify best practices including:

- Leading individuals and groups of organisations in face to face benchmarking efforts.
- Creating benchmarking databases to support benchmarking efforts.
- Forming associations to share benchmarking information and
- Conducting sessions and writing books and papers on benchmarking topics.

Outsourcing your benchmarking

The key reasons that organisations outsource internal services include:

- Outsource specialists have a better competency in delivering the process.
- The work load for the process varies, making it difficult to effectively staff employees year round.
- The process benefits from outside experiences.
- Experienced specialists produce a higher quality result.
- Independence from the politics of the organisation improves the service and
- Experience means that outside providers can actually provide the service at a lower cost than doing it internally.

Outsourcing benchmarking makes sense. Our clients have continuously used our services to manage projects and facilitate the findings. We network over 5000 process owners involved in benchmarking and maintain relationships with key organisations that provide linkage to additional contacts. This allows us to forge out a custom group of benchmark companies to meet very specific client needs.

Benchmarking data bases : Tap into our existing databases of over 300 studies that are available to jump starting your benchmarking efforts. Since no database can cover all needs, we also support more customised research activities. The benchmarking network has conducted over 3000 site visits with companies to collect best-practice information.

Real benchmarking : Benchmarking - how it should be done, not just data but real people in face-to-face process discussions:

Our process includes:

- Enlisting major global corporations
- Gathering data bases of details and comparable measures
- Collecting detailed process information
- Identify best practices and performers
- Face-to-face site visits with "Best practice" companies.

POINTS TO REMEMBER

- Just as there is no standard definition of benchmarking, there is, of yet, no universally recognised best-in-class benchmarking process.
- Benchmarking has been viewed as consisting of phases, or stages or steps in different ways by different companies.
- A typical benchmarking process consists of **three phases** namely : *(i)* Analysis phase, *(ii)* Discovery phase and *(iii)* Implementation phase.
- Some companies use benchmarking process consisting of **four phases** namely : *(i)* Planning phase, *(ii)* Analysis phase, *(iii)* Integration phase and *(iv)* Action or Implementation phase.
- Motorola uses a **five step** benchmarking process.
- Alcoa uses a **six step** benchmarking process.
- Ameritech uses a **four phase, eight steps** benchmarking process.
- Xerox uses a **10 step** benchmarking process.
- Seitz Corporation uses a **14 step** process.
- IBM Rochester uses a **21 step** process for benchmarking.
- The **five phases** of the benchmarking process are :

  (i) Planning the benchmarking process and characterisation of the items.

  (ii) Internal data collection and analysis.

  (iii) External data collection and analysis.

  (iv) Improvement of the item's performance.

  (v) Continuous improvement

- **Activities involved in the above 5 phases are :**
- **Phase 1 :** **Activity 1 :** Identify what to benchmark
  Activity 2 : Obtain top management support
  Activity 3 : Develop the measurement plan
  Activity 4 : Develop the data collection plan
  Activity 5 : Review the plans with location experts
  Activity 6 : Characterise the benchmark item
- **Phase 2 :** **Activity 7 :** Collect and analyse internal published information
  Activity 8 : Select potential internal benchmarking sites
  Activity 9 : Collect internal original research information
  Activity 10 : Conduct interviews and surveys
  Activity 11 : Form an internal benchmarking committee
  Activity 12 : Conduct internal site visits
- **Phase 3 :** **Activity 13 :** Collect external published information
  Activity 14 : Collect external original research information
- **Phase 4 :** **Activity 15 :** Identify corrective actions
  Activity 16 : Develop an implementation plan
  Activity 17 : Gain top management approval of the future-state solution
  Activity 18 : Implement the future-state solution and measure its impact
- **Phase 5 :** **Activity 19 :** Maintain the benchmarking data base
  Activity 20 : Implement continuous performance improvement
- **The five stages benchmarking process model has the following stages :**
  Stage 1 : Determine what to benchmark
  Stage 2 : Form a benchmarking team
  Stage 3 : Identify benchmark partners
  Stage 4 : Collect and analyse benchmarking information
  Stage 5 : Take action
- **The various activities involved in each of the above five stages are listed below :**
  Stage 1 :
  Activity 1 : Defining the customers for benchmarking information
  Activity 2 : Determining customer requirements for benchmarking information
  Activity 3 : Identifying critical success factors
  Stage 2 : Benchmarking is a team activity. **Various types of teams used in benchmarking are :** *(i)* Intact work groups, *(ii)* Cross-functional, interdepartmental and interorganisation teams, *(iii)* Adhoc teams.
- **Three categories of people involved in the benchmarking process are :**
  (i) Internal benchmarking specialists

(ii) External benchmarking specialists and
(iii) Employees

- A typical **benchmarking team structure** comprises : *(i)* **Project manager**, *(ii)* **Benchmarking team** consisting of data collectors and analysts, *(iii)* **Benchmarking project support resources** such as facilitator, training, legal, management information system, library services, administrative assistance, clerical support and senior management.

Stage 3 :

- The challenge is to identify **benchmark partners** that will provide you with useful information to your quest for best practices and continuous improvement.
- The terms used to describe **partner companies** include ***"best-in-class"***, ***world-class*** and ***best practices.***
- **The six most commonly mentioned sources of information for identifying best-practices companies are :**

(i) Special awards/citations
(ii) Media attention
(iii) Professional associations
(iv) Independent reports
(v) Word of mouth
(vi) Consultants

- When selecting benchmark partners, exercise caution not to **fall-victim** to the ***"halo-effect".***
- Two types of halo effects that are typical among benchmarking teams are : *(i)* ***halo positive*** and *(ii)* ***halo negative.***
- Avoid both types of effects as you conduct your search for benchmark partners.
- Employees feel uncomfortable about direct contact with employees from other organisations - particularly competitors. Therefore it is important to seek co-operative benchmarking partners.
- **Benchmarking networks or consortia** are formed for the explicit purpose of opening benchmarking channels among the participating members.

Stage 4 :

- Before you attempt to collect information about another organisation, it is wise to collect and analyse information about your own internal operations (*i.e.,* internal benchmarking effort).
- Once you have determined the types of benchmarking information you need to collect and the information sources and organisations you will investigate, the next issue to consider is the data collection methods you use.

Stage 5 :

- **There are several basic kinds of activities that can take place at the action stage of the benchmarking process. They are :**

(i) Produce a benchmarking report/summary
(ii) Present findings to benchmarking customers
(iii) Communicate findings to internal - other functional groups and benchmark partners
(iv) Look for opportunities : *(a)* Product/process improvement, *(b)* Learning-bring new ideas and concepts into your organisation and *(c)* Forming functional networks, *(v)* Encourage recycling efforts.

REVIEW QUESTIONS

1. Describe the three phases of a benchmarking process *viz.,* analysis phase, discovery phase and implementation phase.
2. Discuss the 4 phase, 8 step benchmarking process followed by Ameritech, USA.
3. Discuss the 10 step process of benchmarking used by Xerox corporation.
4. Discuss the 5 phases and 20 activities of the benchmarking process generally used by most companies.
5. Describe the five-stage benchmarking process with a diagram.
6. What is "customer diagnosis"? Discuss the issues related with determination of customer requirements for benchmarking information.
7. What is meant by "scope of benchmarking activity"? Explain.
8. What is meant by "critical success factors"? List the major types of "critical success factors" identified by benchmarking investigation.
9. Why benchmarking is a team activity? Discuss the three basic types of benchmarking teams.
10. Discuss the role of internal benchmarking specialists, external benchmarking specialists and employees of the organisation in the benchmarking process.
11. Describe the typical benchmarking team structure and the roles and responsibilities of various benchmarking team members.
12. Who is a "benchmark-partner"? Discuss the advantages of forming your own benchmarking information network.
13. What is meant by the terms: "Best-in-class", "World-class" and "Best-practices"? What are the most reliable sources for identifying best-practices? Discuss.
14. What is "Halo effect"? Discuss the two types of halo effects.
15. What is meant by "brain storm syndrome"?
16. Discuss the several basic kinds of activities that can take place at the action stage of the benchmarking process.
17. Discuss the contents of a benchmarking reports.
18. Discuss the various improvement outcomes resulting from product and process improvements made by benchmarking teams.

DISCUSSION QUESTIONS

1. "While individual organisations have developed unique benchmarking process models having certain number of phases and steps, the challenge is to construct a generic benchmarking model that can be applied to any benchmarking project by any type of organisation" - Discuss.
2. "The basic premise of benchmarking is to learn something of value from some one or some place else, something that helps you perform more effectively or efficiently". Explain.
3. "One of the most recent phenomena in the practice of benchmarking involves the formation of formal benchmarking networks or consortia". Elaborate.

4. "Many of the formal benchmarking models in existence today include a basic directive to recycle or recalibrate". Discuss the implications of this directive.
5. "One of the fundamental roles of benchmarking is to know your own processes, products and services before you attempt to understand the processes, products and services of other organisations". Do you agree or disagree? Give reasons for your answer.

CHAPTER 8

Benchmarking and Performance Measurement

INTRODUCTION

In the past, a company only had to achieve financial targets and how the company accomplished its financial goals was not important. However, in modern management, the emphasis is on not only to manage processes, but also to mind performance measurements.

Now, managers understand that a myopic focus on short-term financial results-without consideration for the overall health of the operating systems producing those results-can bankrupt the organisation over the long term. Consequently, companies are learning to manage systems and processes that reach across traditional departmental or functional boundaries. In the new world of process management, organisations employ broad-reaching **performance indicators** including financial and non-financial measures, to guide them in managing their businesses. The new generation of process managers create a balanced score-card of operating metrics that enables them to carefully monitor, maintain and improve the health of systems and workflows. **Benchmarking** represents a versatile **process management tool** that helps organisations identify and understand what contributes best operating practices, **benchmarks** are the **operating statistics** or **measures** that define the achievement level of any given practice or system. Together these related concepts lie at the heart of the revolution in performance measurement.

THE WHYS AND HOWS OF BENCHMARKS

Many managers do not have the correct picture over the difference between benchmarks and benchmarking. Identifying benchmarks takes a team only part-way to its ultimate goal of enhancing performance. In turn, an improvement team will also lose its bearings if it navigates by just studying practices or process differences. Without accompanying benchmarks that contrast the relative performance levels produced by different operating approaches, the team can not easily evaluate the merits of different practices and systems.

Successful best practices improvement strategies marry the study of **metrics** and **processes**; they unite benchmarks and benchmarking. Consequently, a successful benchmarking team will very early determine the benchmarks- the operating statistics or metrics-by which to evaluate two or more systems or operating approaches. One hall mark of a well-designed set of project benchmarks is that they enable measurement and comparisons across systems. Trouble quickly ensures for benchmarking teams that choose esoteric or one-dimensional operating statistics that do not translate well across different organisations and systems. A flexible set of benchmarks reflects full process or system capabilities. **Performance indicators may include dimensions such as cost, productivity, cycle time, yields, error rates, waste and turnover**.

Table 8.1 **illustrates how performance may be organized into several different levels of comparison.** Each level represents a different type of comparison. The comparisons progress from a first-reference point or base line (level 1) to best-in-company (level 2), to industry leader, (level 5), to best-in-country (level 6), to best-in-world (level 7) .

TABLE 8.1 : RANGE OF BENCHMARKS

Focus	Benchmark Levels	Type	Improvement Benefit
Strategic Best-in-world	7	Generic processes	30%
• Product/Services			
• Business processes			
• Business function		Functional areas	
Best-in-country	6	and processes	30% - 40%
Performance Industry			
• Customer satisfaction	Leader 5	Direct competitor	15% - 20%
Output	Norm - 4		
• Products	Standard - 3		
• Services			
Process Best-in-company	2	Internal	15%
• Practices			
• Capability			
Baseline	1		
Inputs			
• Material			
• Supplier			

Some important lessons emerge from the experiences of active bench markers :

1. **Do not strive to benchmark everything at best-in-country or best-in-world levels :** No company can be best in every function. Companies that set out to be best in every function-without regard for the function's strategic importance- dilute their resources and their focus.
2. **Seek best-in-class benchmarks for core processes and functions of the highest strategic importance :** Benchmarks for less strategically important areas may come from comparison levels 2 through 5. World and country leadership benchmarks require more time, resources and efforts to develop. Apply them to core processes of business that compete daily in national or global markets.

3. **Seek internal, regional, or industry benchmarks for secondary and support processes :** For some processes and business activities that are not critical to the organisation's strategic advantage, internal, regional or competitive benchmarks may be most appropriate. Such benchmarks produce internal improvements that are substantial- even if not radical or "break-through" in terms of the size of the expected improvement benefits.

Consider the following example of a health insurance provider that undertakes a benchmarking study of billing processes and practices. First, it establishes a measurement or benchmark-**billing inquiries per 100 customer**-by which to evaluate **billing performance**. In this instances, **billing inquiries** are those instances when a customer calls to clarify or dispute a bill, it constitutes a variable numerator and **"100 customers"** is the constant denominator.

The organisation then gathers comparative performance statistics from other companies. If necessary, the health insurance provider recalculates the statistics to achieve a common denominator that allows the statistics to be compared across all participating companies. **The following comparison matrix (Refer *Table 8.2*) illustrates what such a gathering of benchmarks might look like.**

Next the company must interpret the benchmarks in order to choose a select few companies for site visits. In this instance, the insurance company eliminates company 'G". Even though it has the best performance in this measurement, investigations show that company 'G' bills only for kilowatts used at a flat rate, there is no counterpart to the multiple billing variables used in health insurance business. Therefore the utility company's billing practices are not helpful. The other potential best practices companies are comparable in that both bill at least five services and their ratio of billing inquiries per 100 customers is among the lowest. Indeed they are 15 to 30% better than the insurer. Consequently the insurer chooses the credit card company (Company F) and local telephone company (Company E) for further study and site visits.

TABLE 8.2

Benchmark (Inquiries/ 100 customers)	**Company**
16.0	Company 'A' (Local phone company)
13.5	Company 'B' (Long distance telephone company)
12.0	Company 'C' (Local telephone company)
10.0	Company 'D' (Health insurance provider)
8.5	Company 'E' (Local telephone company)
7.0	Company 'F' (Credit card company)
6.5	Company 'G' (Electric utility company)

THE PERFORMANCE MEASUREMENT REVOLUTION

The revolution in performance measurement is creating a new paradigm for how organisations measure and manage performance. Historically four important shifts in perspective have helped to evaluate the importance of benchmarks in this performance measurement revolution:

1. Organisations now more than ever recognize the importance of performance measures or benchmarks in managing complex systems and processes. **"What gets measured is what gets managed and improved."** The growing interest in total quality management and the national quality awards has highlighted the importance of performance indicators used to monitor, control, manage and improve the organisation's processes. "Quality measures present the most positive steps taken to date in broadening the basis of business performance measurement.

2. Customer satisfaction has emerged as a strategic goal for many organisations world-wide. What quality was for the 1980's, customer satisfaction was for the 1990s. Many organisations are developing a broad menu of measurements to gauge satisfaction levels among customers. Some leading indicators of satisfaction include:*(i)* customer retention rates *(ii)* referral rates *(iii)* re-purchase rates *(iv)* market share trends *(v)* complaint rates *(vi)* satisfaction survey trends and *(vii)* litigation rates.

3. Leading-edge managers recognize that many other non-financial benchmarks are useful in achieving total quality excellence within complex systems and processes. Financial measures usually represent outcomes of processes, although they do not always provide the best information about what actually occurs behind the scenes of these processes- or how these processes are related to one another in the big picture. Typical among the growing scorecard of other **nonfinancial benchmarks are measures of work process speed, quality, first-pass yields, employee turnover, reliability, productivity, innovation, training, employee involvement and learning.**

4. The revolution in information technology places powerful computer hardware and software within the reach of virtually every organisation. This technology enables organisations to inexpensively create, distribute, analyse and store more data about their businesses than ever before. All these data represent potential benchmarks and performance measurement indicators. Any measurement that is systematically collected can be trended overtime. By trending information, managers can transform mute data points into performance indicators that reflect the health and progress of individual processes or systems.

***Exhibit 8.1* and *8.2* illustrate the evolution in performance measurement by showing both old and new "dash boards" of performance measures by which managers navigate their organisations.**

EXHIBIT 8.1 : THE DASHBOARD OF OLD PERFORMANCE MEASURES

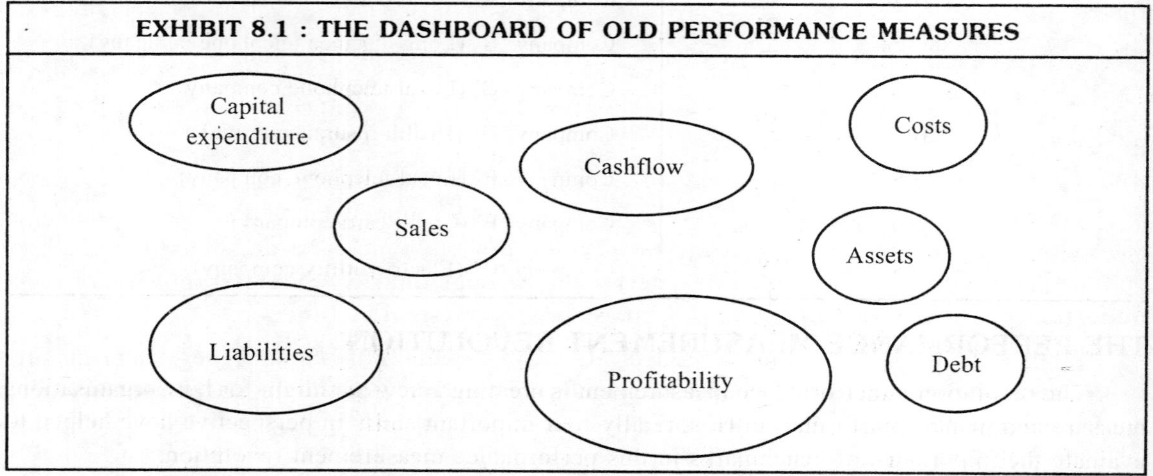

EXHIBIT 8.2 : THE DASHBOARD OF NEW PERFORMANCE MEASURES

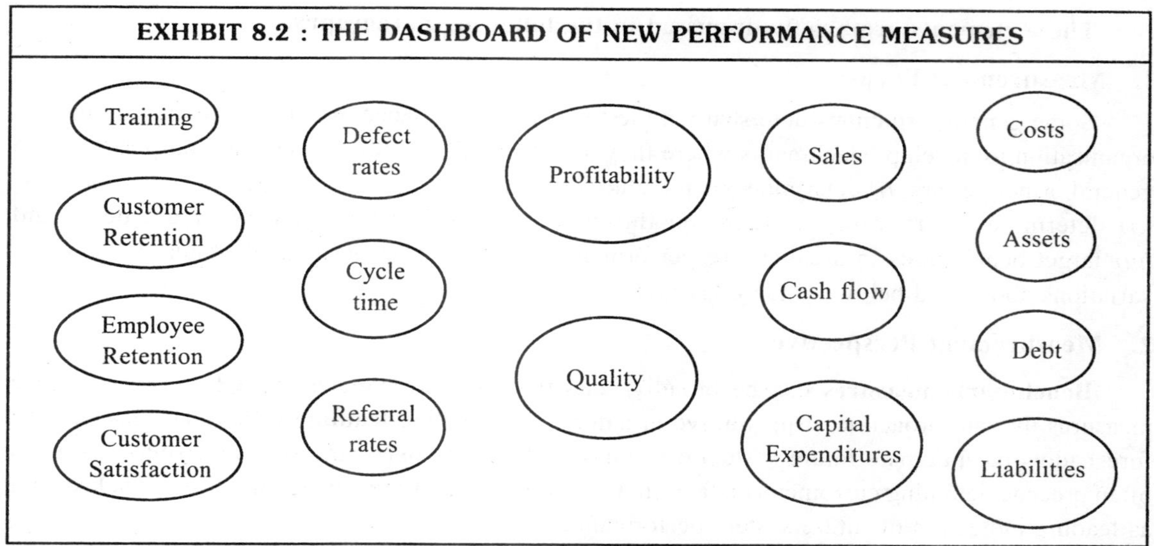

PERFORMANCE MEASUREMENT SYSTEM AT FEDEX

Federal Express (FedEx) in the US, has developed a corporate-wide performance measurement system called the **Service Quality Indicator** (SQI). Fed Ex's SQI illustrates the use of non-financial, customer-service oriented indicators to empower an organisation's performance improvement efforts. The SQI consists of 12 key service and operations measurements or bench marks: *(i)* the number of damaged packages *(ii)* lost packages *(iii)* missed pickups *(iv)* aircraft delays *(v)* reopened complaints that were not resolved on first response *(vi)* wrong day late deliveries *(vii)* over goods *(viii)* abandoned calls *(ix)* invoice adjustment requests, *(x)* missing proofs of delivery, *(xi)* right day late deliveries, *(xii)* traces. After extensive customer research about what customers perceive as failures, Fed Ex chose and weighted the customer importance accorded to each of these 12 measures. The Fed Ex management team looks at the measures every day and computes an average daily failure point score based on actual failures and their weighted value. They post weekly company wide scores. Fed Ex's well deserved reputation for focusing on customer satisfaction is reflected in the non financial performance measurement they use everyday to manage and improve their operations.

Designing Successful Benchmarks

"Successful performance measurements describe factors critical to successful business operations"

At Federal Express, managers recognize that missed pickups and damaged packages are two operating failures that destroy customer satisfaction. If Fed Ex routinely misses pick ups and damages packages, its business will fail. Consequently Fed Ex diligently measures and monitors these two performance characteristics. **"Effective performance benchmarks therefore reflect the most important operating dimensions of a business process, system or function."**

When designing benchmarks, four elements prove especially important. These elements are: ***(i)* the measurement focus, *(ii)* the measurement perspective, *(iii)* the degree of measurement control and *(iv)* the ability to collect data**.

These elements are briefly discussed in the following paragraphs.

1. Measurement Focus

Some general principles help sharpen the focus of performance measurements by guiding the organisation to develop benchmarks where they are most suitable for management purposes. Three general principles are: *(i)* determine where value for the customer is created in work area or process. *(ii)* determine where value is detracted through high costs, errors, rework or accidents and *(iii)* target benchmarks in areas where performance diverges from designated standards or where variations above and below standards is great.

2. Measurement Perspective

Benchmark measures can be broadly classified as **reactive** and **proactive**. Performance measures that are proactive or preventive in nature can be called **leading indicators** because they foreshadow or anticipate future system outcomes. Rating employee turnover and rising error rates often precede declining customer satisfaction. Consequently, these two benchmarks can be classified as leading indicators of future system performance.

In contrast, other performance measures are more reactive or descriptive of the actual results of a system or process in a given time period. These measures can also be called **lagging indicators** because they provide perspective on the completed performance of a system. Traditional financial measures such as sales, profits, return on assets, or cost of sales are descriptive of a system's final performance in a given period (quarter or year). Senior managers, shareholders and government agencies rely greatly on lagging indicators because these indicators assess the impact of real outcome versus target outcomes.

Traditional organisations employ lagging indicators, such as quarterly financial results, as the primary tools to manage system performance. High performing contemporary companies also embrace the use of leading indicators to help them better manage performance improvement. Leading indicators are consistent with the preventive focus endorsed by total quality management. They provide valuable information to help an organisation intervene upstream, in the early stages of project or process. Consequently, many non-financial measures, such as customer retention, cycle time, innovation and quality, are proving to be more useful than traditional financial indicators in predicting and managing future performance. **"Comprehensive performance benchmarks include both leading and lagging indicators".**

3. Measurement Control

Performance benchmarks can be applied at company, unit and individual levels, but people are always the major factor affecting the degree of measurement control. Generally, performance reviews evaluate managers and employees based on the performance measurements that they personally control or that they affect as part of a team with a shared objective. Managers fail at performance improvement when they evaluate individual or system performance using benchmark measures that are uncontrollable by the people overseeing the process. Therefore benchmarks that are designed for performance improvement must be crafted to reflect the individual level of authority, responsibility and skills of those people expected to work with the benchmarks.

4. Data Collection

After defining performance measures, managers must be able to readily collect the data from which performance benchmarks are constructed. Many organisations develop interesting performance measures only to discover that they currently do not collect the required information. They are stymied when they discover that the collection costs for some performance benchmarks can exceed the managerial benefit of the information. Consequently, the best performance benchmarks can be collected without excessive investment of time, systems, staff or capital.

A Benchmark Design Architecture

Step1: This first step in designing a **performance benchmark system** is to create measures that will enable management to achieve the organisation's strategic objectives. When creating benchmarks to evaluate your organisation's performance, plumb those management categories that are critical to your organisation's success. Frequently these categories include: *(i)* customer service and customer satisfaction, *(ii)* product and services distribution, *(iii)* innovation and product development capabilities *(iv)* quality *(v)* people development capabilities and *(vi)* various aspects of time-based competition or the speed with which core processes are performed.

Step2: The second step in designing a benchmark architecture requires managers to create an agreed upon **vocabulary** describing performance measurement in your organisation. Without a **common language** to communicate about performance improvement, employees will find it impossible to agree on the organisation's current status and impossible to build strategies to drive improvements. **"Every company has its own language system by which performance is defined and every manager uses rhetoric to build its meaning and coherence".** How **effective** the rhetoric and how **useful** the language system – these are the issues that separate companies like Motorola from the rest. Motorola invented the concept of Six-Sigma Quality or the goal of creating 99.99966 percent defect-free products. Every Motorola employee, work team, function and business unit is galvanized by the six-sigma concept, consequently, across all Motorola units there is clear, consistent and highly focused communication about improvement efforts, goals, strategies and progress. **Performance measurement vocabulary vary from company to company and from industry to industry.** Moreover corporate values, vision, strategy and culture greatly influence the individual language of performance measurement.

Step3: The third step is to develop plans to collect, process and analyse the performance measures. Start by evaluating how your organisation currently generates needed performance data. Methods are probably established to generate a full menu of financial measures. By building on this information management foundation, you can expand your system to include a full set of non-financial performance benchmarks. These additional measures will describe capabilities and performance levels among your organisation's core processes-human resources, technology and physical and intellectual assets. Many managers now place these non-financial measurements on equal footing with the financial data. A well-designed performance benchmark architecture provides managers with information that is accurate, easy to obtain, easy to read, statistically valid and quickly accessible.

A comprehensive benchmark architecture includes many measurement categories, each of which includes time and quality dimensions such as error or defect rates and process cycle times.

***Box 8.1* lists the ten generic bench mark categories in a benchmark design architecture.**

BOX 8.1 : DESIGNING YOUR BENCHMARK ARCHITECTURE	
A benchmark design architecture : Ten generic benchmark categories	
(i)	Customer-service performance
(ii)	Product / service performance
(iii)	Core business process performance
(iv)	Support processes and services performance
(v)	Employee performance
(vi)	Supplier performance
(vii)	Technology performance
(viii)	New product / service development and innovation performance
(ix)	Cost performance
(x)	Financial performance

These ten generic benchmark categories are briefly discussed in the following section:

1. Customer-Service Performance Measures:

The best customer-related measures come from objective and valid data collected directly from customer. Consequently, many customer-related benchmarks spring from statistical samples that probe a representative customer group randomly selected from among all customers.

Customer – related benchmarks must meet or exceed commonly accepted standards governing statistical factors such as population definition, sample selection rules, sample size, data collection quality, interviewer bias controls and non-response error. Customer-service performance measures include – but are not limited to – satisfaction and dissatisfaction metrics, and customer retention and defection benchmarks.

Many customer-satisfaction measurements represent, statistical probabilities reflecting customer's altitudes and likely behaviour. For instance, retention and deflection metrics reflect the likelihood that customers will continue to act as they have in the past in terms of repurchasing an organisation's services or products. Customer-satisfaction benchmarks frequently employ measurements on a scale which weighs the positive or negative dimensions of their responses. Five factor scales with responses such as "excellent", "good", "average", "below average" and "poor" usually work well and provide survey respondents enough choices to accurately record their opinions.

Customer-service performance measures probe organizational performance in the following areas:

(i) Overall customer satisfaction with products and services.

(ii) Customer evaluation of sales and services representatives

(iii) Customer assessments of your organisation's understanding of customer needs.

(iv) Customer ratings of how clearly your organisation communicates cost information and how well the organisation suggests customer solutions.

(v) Customer appraisals of delivery timeliness

(vi) Customer impressions about the usefulness of your organisation's product and services documentation.

(vii) Customer feelings concerning how easy it is to conduct business with your organisation.

(viii) The value customers place on your organisation's products and services.

Customer dissatisfaction measures can be as revealing as satisfaction measures. Dissatisfaction benchmarks can be formal or informal, formal dissatisfaction indicators include variables such as written customer complaints, defective product returns, cancellation or terminations of service and sales contracts, and payments sought by customers through guarantees, warranties, refunds or litigation. Informal dissatisfaction measures include indicators such as telephone calls from customers complaining about product and service features, timeliness or value, disputing billing accuracy, or reporting service and product failures and problems.

Customer retention rates, repurchase rates, and defection rates are critical benchmarks that serve as leading indicators of future customer behaviour that will directly influence bottom line financial results. Customer feelings about services and products are often complex, at times they are even contradictory. Regardless of what customers **say** about a product or service, their **actions** usually speak most directly about their real feelings and intentions. Consequently, retention, repurchase and defection rates - which reflect customer actions-often represent the most accurate forecasts concerning customers' future market behaviour. Accordingly many companies are expanding their satisfaction measurements to include retention, repurchase, and defection benchmarks.

2. Product / Service Performance Benchmarks:

These benchmarks offer a set of operating statistics, including measures of accuracy, reliability, timeliness, order ease, delivery, packaging, ease of assembly and use, documentation, billing, after-sales service and effective complaint management. These benchmarks may additionally include warranty exchanges and returns, unit productivity and cost, cycle time for key intervals, and market share. Performance measures often vary greatly among industries. For example, automobile manufacturers measure time from order to delivery, fuel efficiency, failure times, and rates for key parts, customer complaints, warranty costs and ease of use for operator manuals. In contrast, overnight package delivery services measures include on-time, error-free deliveries, invoice errors, missed pickups and missing proof of deliveries, deliveries per hour, package damage rates and cost per delivery.

Differences in benchmark measures across industries underscore the need for each organisation to develop a family of benchmark measures that best reflect its processes and operating characteristics. Among many industries, certain types of measures serve as common denominators, such as speed and quality, but the specific applications of these measurement types reflect the organisation's specific services, products and processes.

3. Business Process Performance Measures:

A simple process model can be helpful in identifying your organisation's most important workflows. **This model reveals that all work can be viewed in four sequential stages:**

(i) Inputs (including those from both employees and suppliers)

(ii) Processes (including internal operations and support services)

(iii) Outputs (your organisation's products, services, and documentation) and

(iv) Customer satisfaction.

***Exhibit 8.3* illustrates** the **input-output process model**. The model begins with a series of **inputs** that are delivered to the work process. These inputs include **tangibles** such as supplies, raw materials, and components parts and **intangibles**, such as information. The inputs then enter the work **process** which transforms them into some final **output**, which might be a product or service. The goal of the output is to create **satisfied customer**. Business process performance measures

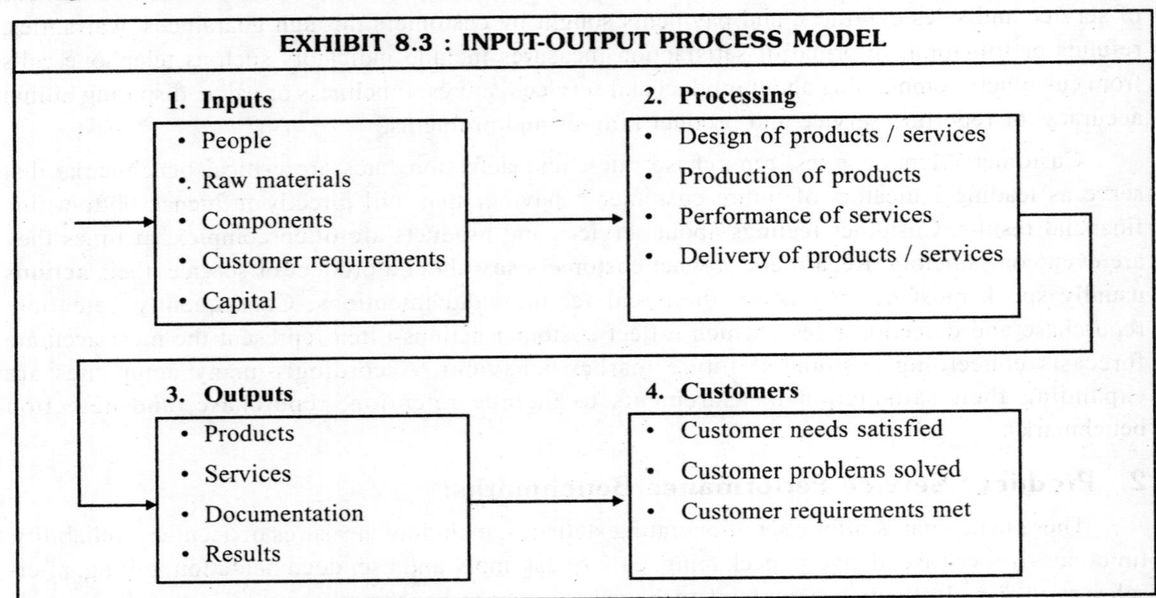

therefore can be viewed in the context of the process analysis model. **Each stage of the input-output model includes performance measures and these measures often include one or all of the following factors:**

(i) Enhanced customer value, often observed through added product features or reduced costs.

(ii) Production costs, frequently described as cost per 100, 1000 or million output units.

(iii) Responsiveness and / or process cycle time

(iv) Defect, error, waste, problem, or failure rates, often formulated as defects per 100 or million output units.

(v) Productivity and resources utilization, often reflected in transactions per person, inventory turn rates or projects operating within budget.

(vi) Public safety and / or legal responsibilities, sometimes observed in accident rates, employee absentee rates, regulatory citations or litigation rates.

4. Support Processes / Services Performance Measures

Support services are activities and operations that enable your organisation's core production and delivery processes. They include functions such as finance, software services, marketing, public relations, information services, purchasing, and facilities management.

Some important support processes / support services performance are:

- **Accounting**
  - *(i)* Percentage of late payments
  - *(ii)* Time to respond to customer requests
  - *(iii)* Number of billing errors
  - *(iv)* Number of incorrect accounting entries
  - *(v)* Number of payroll errors.
- **Information Services**
  - *(i)* Number of errors per line of code
  - *(ii)* Percent of reports received on schedule
  - *(iii)* Number of rewrites
  - *(iv)* Number of errors found after system accepted by customer
  - *(v)* Number of test-case runs for successful completion
- **Marketing**
  - *(i)* Accuracy of forecast assumptions
  - *(ii)* Number of incorrect order entries
  - *(iii)* Overstocked field supplies
  - *(iv)* Contact errors
- **Product Engineering**
  - *(i)* Project completion cycle times
  - *(ii)* Number of engineering changes per document
  - *(iii)* Number of errors found during design review
  - *(iv)* Number of errors found in design evaluation
- **Purchasing**
  - *(i)* Purchase order errors
  - *(ii)* Downtime due to shortage
  - *(iii)* Excess inventory
  - *(iv)* Cycle time (from start of purchase to receipt in-house)
- **Quality Control**
  - *(i)* Percentage of lots rejected in error
  - *(ii)* Number of engineering changes detected after design review
  - *(iii)* Errors in reports
  - *(iv)* Cycle time for corrective action

5. Employee Performance Measures

Employee performance benchmarks cover a wide range of employee activities that may include the following:

(i) **Employee development** such as percentage of employees in mentor programs or percentage of employees with career development plans.

(ii) **Employee education** such as training hours per employee or percentage of employees who have completed course work in statistical process control.

(iii) **Employee empowerment** such as percentage of customer-contact employees authorized to issue up to ₹ 10,000/- in credit to customers.

(iv) **Employee recognition** such as percentage of employees recognised with 5,10,15,20 and 25 years service awards.

(v) **Employee recruitment** such as percentage of employment offers accepted.

(vi) **Employee absenteeism** such as unexcused absences per 100 employees during a given time period.

(vii) **Employee turnover** such as employees terminating employment as a percentage of average annualized work force.

(viii) **Employee grievances** such as disputes or complaints about company labour practices per 100 employees.

(ix) **Employee safety / accidents** such as number of work days lost due to accidents, vehicular accidents per one thousand miles driven, or public liability reports per quarter.

(x) **Employee involvement** such as number of **employees on teams and** number of teams.

(xi) **Employee morale** such as employee opinion survey results.

(xii) **Employee performance appraisal** such as percentage of employees receiving an annual performance appraisal or percentage of appraisals completed on time.

(xiii) **Employee promotion** such as percentage of **positions filled from within the organisation**.

(xiv) **Employee succession planning** such as the increase or decrease in percentage of eligible positions filled through succession planning.

6. Supplier Performance Measures

Supplier performance measures help an organisation qualify or certify the vendors with which it will work. These benchmarks then help the organisation monitor and manage on-going supplier performance. Supplier performance metrics often include measures of cost, quality, speed or responsiveness, agreed-upon service levels, and product specifications. **A representative list of supplier certification performance measures are listed in *Table 8.3.***

TABLE 8.3: SUPPLIER CERTIFICATION PERFORMANCE MEASURES		
Vendor	**Certification indicator**	**Requirements**
Overnight and package delivery service	• delivery on time	• less than 1% late deliveries
	• tracing capability	• 24-hour access to call centre number for status checking
	• monthly discount for volume purchases	• 10,000 or more, 10% discount • 15,000 or more, 12% discount • 20,000 or more, 15% discount
Fiber optic cable supplier	• delivery on time	• less than 5% late deliveries
	• number of defective or damaged 100-foot spans	• less than 0.05 per 10,000
	• after sales service and support	• 24 hour call centre number access to technical assistance and support
Market research service	• adequate data collection	• statistical samples at 95% confidence ± error, controls for interviewer bias and non response errors.
	• valid and reliable analysis	• at least two statistical tests
	• accurate reports	• less than 2% rate per report
	• delivery on time	• less than 2% deliveries

7 & 8. Technology and Innovation - Related Performance Measures

Technology-related measures reflect the productivity, deployment, and effective use of computers and other technology in an organisation. Measures range broadly from processing speeds, deployment percentages, network down-time and error rates. In turn, innovation-related performance indicators reflect issues such as organizational learning and continuous improvement. Measures may include new product development times, employees' suggestion rates, new product sales as a percent of total sales and process improvement rates.

9. Cost-Performance Measures

Cost performance measures are broad and flexible. They include balance sheet liability requirements and information drawn from cost centers through-out the organisation. Companies can develop useful benchmarks by producing cost ratios for specific products, services, organizational units, processing steps, inputs and labour, A mortgage company, for instance, might use such measures as cost per loan application, cost per loan processing, human resources cost per loan, data processing costs per 100 bills and servicing cost per loan.

10. Financial Performance Measures

Financial measures include performance indicators required by stock exchanges, security analysis, public accounting firms, regulatory agencies and other organisations that may oversee reporting standards in your organisation's industry. Many of these measures make up the items on income statements, balance sheets and cash flow statements, including measures such as revenue, gross profit, operating income, net income, earnings per share, long-term debt, book value, cash flow, debt / equity ratio, days / receivables ratio, current ratio etc.

KAPLAN AND NORTON'S BALANCED SCORE CARD

Robert S. Kaplan of the Harvard Business School and David P. Norton of Nolan, Norton and company have designed an approach to managing performance measurements through an integrated system. They conceived of the performance measurement **"balanced score card"**, which combines both financial and operational measures into an integrated system of performance indicators.

The balanced score card approach to performance management assumes that no single measure is adequate for managing all companies at all times. The balanced score card grows out of an organisation's central vision of what it must do to be rated number one by customers in terms of total value delivered. In Kaplan and Norton's view, a balanced performance measurement score card includes at least four perspectives :

1. ***The financial perspective*** which asks "If we succeed, how will we look to our shareholders?"
2. ***The customer view*** which asks "To achieve our vision, how must we look to our customers?"
3. ***The internal operating perspective*** which asks "To delight our customers, what management processes must we excel in?"
4. ***The innovation and learning perspective*** which asks "To achieve our vision, how must the organisation continuously learn and create value?"

These four perspectives are briefly discussed below.

1. The Financial Perspective

The financial portion of a balance performance measurement score card includes three fundamental dimensions: *(i)* **profitability** *(ii)* **growth and** *(iii)* **share holder value**. Each dimensions may include many different types of financial measures. The profitability dimension, for instance, measures both cash flow and real profits versus targeted profits. The growth dimension includes overall sales growth and divisional operating income growth. The share holder-value dimension employs measures such as market share increases, return on equity, stock value appreciation, price-to-earnings performance and dividend yield performance.

2. The Customer Perspective

The customer perspective includes four important dimensions: ***(i)* time *(ii)* quality *(iii)* performance and service** and ***(iv)* cost of ownership**.

The time dimension measures cycle time for meeting customer needs. For existing products this dimension expresses the time it takes from receiving an order through delivery. For new products, it measures the time-to-market or time from product definition to first customer shipment. The quality dimension records defects, errors or problems as perceived by the customer. Defects or errors can be broadly interpreted, ranging from physical product defects, typographical errors and incorrect information to late deliveries, inaccurate forecasts or missing information. The performance and service dimension measures how products and services help create value for the customer. The cost-of-ownership includes measures such as invoice costs, repair costs, downtime and inconvenience. Together, all four dimensions-time, quality, performance and service, and ownership costs- reflect the customer's perception of total value.

3. The Internal Operations Perspective

The balance scorecard's internal perspective examines those business processes and operations that most directly influence customer satisfaction. The internal perspective often includes three dimensions: **cycle time**, **quality** and **productivity**. Internal cycle time measures may track specific process steps, such as time to order and receive materials from suppliers, time to move products and materials between plants, time to produce and assemble products, time to deliver products to customer and time to process customer orders. The quality dimension may include simple defect measures or it may pick up more sophisticated metrics such as first-pass yield rates, which record the number of items passing through a process without any rework or errors. The productivity dimension reflects employee skills, effectiveness, and motivation, especially as they are evidenced in employee's output per person.

4. Organisational Learning

Innovation and learning include three primary dimensions: *(i)* market innovation *(ii)* continuous operational learning and *(iii)* intellectual assets. Market innovation records new product and service introduction rates. Product-rich companies monitor and set goals around the percent of total sales generated by products less than four years old. Other companies track the number of patents they record or the number of major research papers published by employees. In order to meet their goals in these repetitive areas, these companies manage the processes that produce the new products, services, patents or research.

Continuous operational learning and improvement measurement records the rate at which individuals and organisations learn.

Intellectual assets are among the most valuable and most intangible resources of any organisation. Companies are beginning to ask how they can better manage and more fully leverage these intangible assets. To this end, managers are developing measures that evaluate skills deployment, training effectiveness, employee involvement levels, employee suggestion rates, cross-functional activity levels and experience sharing.

***Exhibit 8.4* illustrates the perspective of a balanced performance measurement score card:**

EXHIBIT 8.4 : THE PERSPECTIVES OF A BALANCED PERFORMANCE MEASUREMENT SCORE CARD

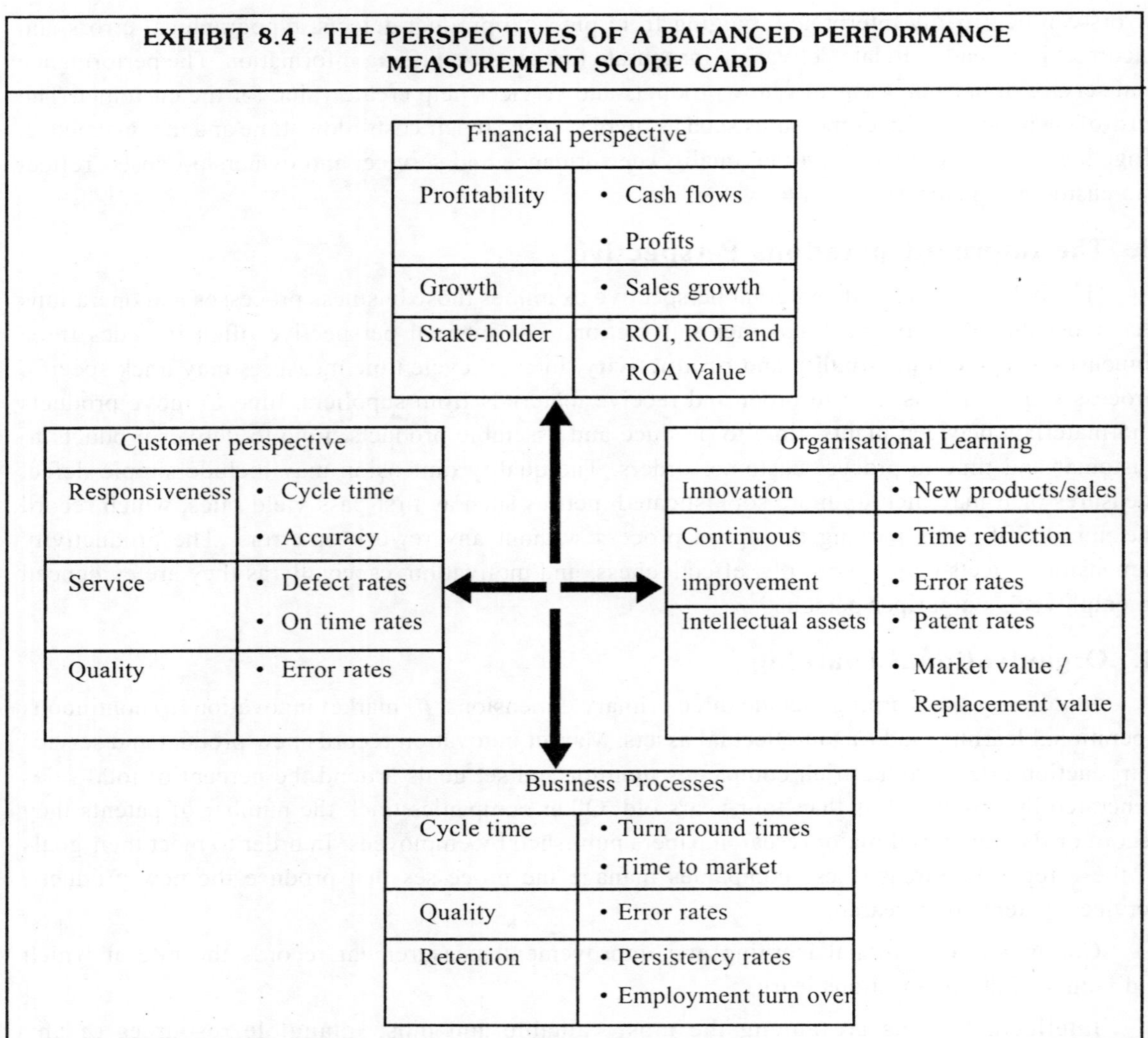

BOX 8.2 : BENCHMARKING IN PRACTICE – PERFORMANCE MEASUREMENT AT EASTMAN KODAK

Eastman Kodak is a company with broad interests in consumer and commercial imaging systems, photographic products, chemicals and diagnostic health equipment. Kodak has developed a comprehensive view of benchmarking and performance measurement. Kodak has refined a performance measurement graphical display tool that enables the company to integrate many related measures into a single view point, in this way the company has created a holistic approach to understanding its own operations and comparing them with others. This approach of kodak is referred to as **"Measures Matrix Chart"** or **M^2 (M-squared) chart.** Other organisations, such as business units of IBM and Chevron use similar tools but call them **"Spider Charts"** or **"Radar Charts"**. All these charts are circular in shape and consolidate various performance measures by arraying different benchmarks along the radii or spokes of a circle graph. Traditional **"gap analysis"** allowed for a single measure tracking over time but did not anticipate how changing that measure would affect other measures of operations. ***Exhibit 8.5* represents an example of the M² chart.**

EXHIBIT 8.2 : KODAK'S BENCHMARKING M² CHART

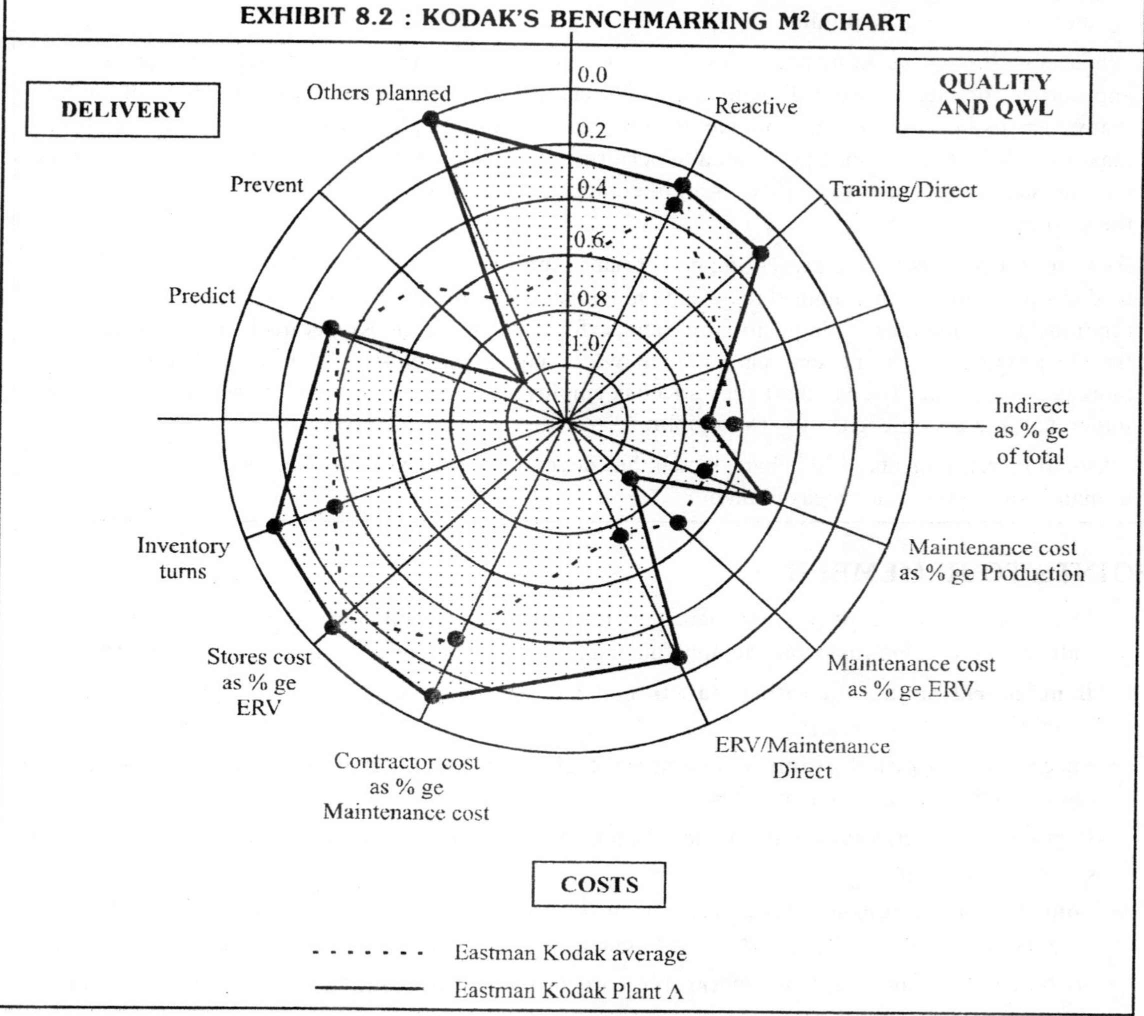

Five features of the refined M² Chart make for easy interpretation :

1. Each radical line or spoke represents a measure
2. Concentric circles range from 1.0 (of the centre) to 0.0 (at the outermost circle)
3. Data is normalised, so all values fall within the range of 1 to 0
4. The benchmark for each measure is placed on the centre of the arc on its respective line. Consequently, the better an operation's performance, the closer its performance measure moves toward the centre of the circular M² chart.
5. Greatest opportunities for improvement are the points that fall farthest from the centre.

The M^2 chart employs three value types :

- Largest value benchmarks where the highest measure is optimal, such as productivity.
- Smallest value benchmarks where the lowest measure is optimal, such as cost.
- Target value benchmarks, where values greater or less than that of the target value are equally undesirable, such as training.

When constructing performance measures, it is important to identify what value or data type is appropriate for each measure. Frequently, an M^2 chart for a single operation or process will include many various benchmarks and include all three value types - high, low and target. This flexibility makes the M^2 chart an especially valuable performance management tool; it portrays the benchmark measures of an operation or process as an integrated system - not as isolated pieces or dimensions of the whole.

As a tool for organising and presenting performance information, the M^2 chart offers a single view of Kodak's operations with graphical representation of benchmark ranking, company ranking and Kodak's relationships to the leadership position in each performance measure. Kodak tracks performance over time by producing a chart every year and then overlaying the current-year chart on charts from one or more previous years. The M^2 chart allows Kodak employees to visualise an entire operation's measures integrated into a single, easy-to-read graphic.

Through its refinements of M^2 chart, Kodak has developed an easy-to-use, unintimidating approach to managing performance measurement.

POINTS TO REMEMBER

- In the present world of process management, organisations employ broad-reaching performance indicators including financial and non-financial measures to guide them in managing their business.
- **Benchmarks** are the **operating statistics** or measures that define the achievement level of any given practice or system.
- Successful **best practices improvement strategies** marry the study of **metrics** and **processes,** they unite benchmarks and benchmarking.
- **Performance indicators** may include dimensions such as cost, productivity, cycle time, yields, error rates and turnover.
- **Some important lessons that emerge from the experiences of active benchmarkers are :**
  (i) Do not strive to benchmark every thing at best-in-country or best-in-world levels.
  (ii) Seek best-in-class benchmarks for core processes and functions of the highest strategic importance.
  (iii) Seek internal, regional or industry benchmarks for secondary and support process.
- Organisations now are more than ever recognise the importance of performance measures or benchmarks in managing complex systems and processes.
- Customer satisfaction has emerged as a strategic goal for many organisations world-wide.
- Many other non-financial benchmarks are useful in achieving total quality excellence within complex systems and processes.
- The revolution in information technology enables organisations to create, distribute, analyse and store more data about their businesses than ever before.

- Successful performance measurements describe factors critical to successful business operations.
- When designing benchmarks, four elements prove especially important. **These elements are :**
  (i) the measurement focus
  (ii) the measurement perspective
  (iii) the degree of measurement control and
  (iv) the ability to collect data
- The focus of performance measurement guides the organisation to develop benchmarks where they are most suitable for management purposes.
- Benchmark measures can be broadly classified as **reactive** and **proactive**.
- Proactive performance measures are called **leading indicators** whereas reactive performance measures are called **lagging indicators**.
- Comprehensive performance benchmarks include both leading and lagging indicators.
- Performance benchmarks can be applied at company, unit and individual levels, but people are always the major factor affecting the degree of measurement control.
- After defining performance measures, managers must be able to readily collect the data from which performance benchmarks are constructed.
- **The steps involved in designing a performance benchmark system are :**
  (i) Create measures that will enable management to achieve the organisation's strategic objectives.
  (ii) Create an agreed upon vocabulary describing performance measurement in your organisation.
  (iii) Develop plans to collect, process and analyse the performance measures.
- **The ten generic benchmark categories in a benchmark design architecture are :**
  (i) Customer-service performance
  (ii) Product/service performance
  (iii) Core business process performance
  (iv) Support processes and services performance
  (v) Employee performance
  (vi) Supplier performance
  (vii) Technology performance
  (viii) New product/service development and innovation performance
  (ix) Cost performance
  (x) Financial performance
- Robert S. Kaplan and David P. Norton conceived of the performance measurement **"balanced score card"** which combines both financial and operational measures into an integrated system of performance indicators.
- **The balanced performanced measurement score and includes four perspectives :**
  (i) The financial perspective
  (ii) The customer view
  (iii) The internal operating perspective and
  (iv) The innovation and learning perspective.

REVIEW QUESTIONS

1. Define the terms *(a)* Metrics, *(b)* Performance measures, *(c)* Performance indicators and *(d)* Performance measurement.
2. Discuss the various levels of benchmark.
3. Discuss some important lessons which emerge from the experience of active bench markers.
4. Describe the performance measurement revolution.
5. Discuss the performance measurement system at Fed EX (USA)

6. Discuss the four elements which prove important when designing benchmarks.
7. Discuss the various steps involved in a benchmark design architecture.
8. List the ten generic benchmark categories in a benchmark design architecture and discuss any three of them.
9. Describe the "input-output process" model with a schematic diagram.
10. Discuss the range of employee activities involved in employee performance measures.
11. Discuss the various supplier certification performance measures.
12. Discuss the financial perspective of performance measurement.

DISCUSSION QUESTIONS

1. "Many managers do not have the correct picture over the difference between benchmarks and benchmarking". Do you agree or disagree? Give reasons for your answer.
2. "The revolution of performance measurement is creating a new paradigm for how organisations measure and manage performance" – Discuss.
3. "Successful performance measurements describe factors critical to successful business operations" – Elaborate.
4. "Effective performance benchmarks reflect the most important operating dimensions of a business process, system or function" – Explain.

CHAPTER 9

The Secrets of Successful Benchmarking

INTRODUCTION

In October 1990, Procter and Gamble conducted a benchmarking project to learn about best practices for product packaging. The P & G team selected eight key measures to study and made four site visits to companies the team had identified as "best-in-class". After nine months, the team realised that "something was not working". Their efforts were not yielding operating insights and no significant improvements had been achieved. The team gathered to conduct a post-morten analysis concerning what was amiss with its project. The team identified the following miss-steps in its initial benchmarking project work:

(i) The topic was too broad.

(ii) The project was not clearly focused because the team was studying too many major measures (eight) and their corresponding operations.

(iii) The ***best-in-class*** companies, chosen because of reputation rather than because of demonstrated performance, provide no true best practices or exemplary operating procedures.

During the second phase of its benchmarking project, the P & G benchmarking team focused only on reliable and dependable operations - that is, operations with the lowest percentage of time to produce a quality product on demand and according to the design specifications or standards. The team also limited its site visits to six and two of them were internal at Procter and Gamble Aircraft Operations. The other site visits took the team outside its industry.

The second phase results were more promising than the results of the first phase of the benchmarking project. The P & G benchmarking team learnt four valuable lessons that apply to all companies conducting benchmarking projects.

Lessons Learnt

(i) ***Clearly focus the project*** : A common pitfall is for the teams to set out on projects that are too large or poorly articulated to allow them to succeed. Teams that set out benchmark expansive topics such as empowerment or customer satisfaction were facing an almost impossible task. For benchmarking projects to be successful, it is essential to start with well-focused project

missions that target manageable topic areas. *Table 9.1* **provides examples of projects that are focused too broadly, too narrowly and just right.**

(ii) To look outside its own industry for important operating lessons. Best business practices don't observe industry, regional or national borders.

(iii) To focus finally on observable systems, practices, and procedures that proved highly effective in the benchmark organisation. Don't obsess over operating statistics and don't become hypnotised by the result of any single subprocess. Superior performance is almost always the cumulative result of many effective actions, procedures, practices, and organisational design factors.

TABLE 9.1 : PROJECT FOCUS - LEVELS AND DETAILS

Process or functional area	Too broad to enable success	Too narrow to enable success	Appropriate level and detail
1. Customer support services	Best customer satisfaction process	Best phone greeting	Best call centre management practices
2. Human resource management	Best empowerment process	Best refund policy below ₹ 200/-	Best values communication system
3. Distribution and logistics	Best distribution process	Best materials receipt stamp	Best warehouse management practices
4. Training	Best training process	Best class room configuration	Best needs assessment process
5. Employee development	Best development process	Best job transfer request form	Best orientation practices

Benchmarking Critical Success Factors (CSFs)

Successful benchmarking projects bear a **"Triple-A" brand - Adopt, Adapt and Advance.** After searching out and examining highly-effective operating practices, experienced benchmarkers ***adopt*** the best, ***adapt*** them to their own work environments and ***advance*** performance through careful implementation and continuous refinement of the practices. Several critical success factors enable Triple-A benchmarking processes.

A well designed performance measurement and benchmark system is essential of course. Other critical success factors include:

(i) Senior management support.

(ii) Benchmarking training for the project team.

(iii) Useful information technology systems.

(iv) Cultural practices that encourage learning.

(v) Resources, especially in the form of time, funding and useful equipment.

Exhibit 9.1 **- 'Benchmarking, its requisities and benefits' describes factors that are critical to successful benchmarking.**

EXHIBIT 9.1 : BENCHMARKING, ITS REQUISITES AND BENEFITS

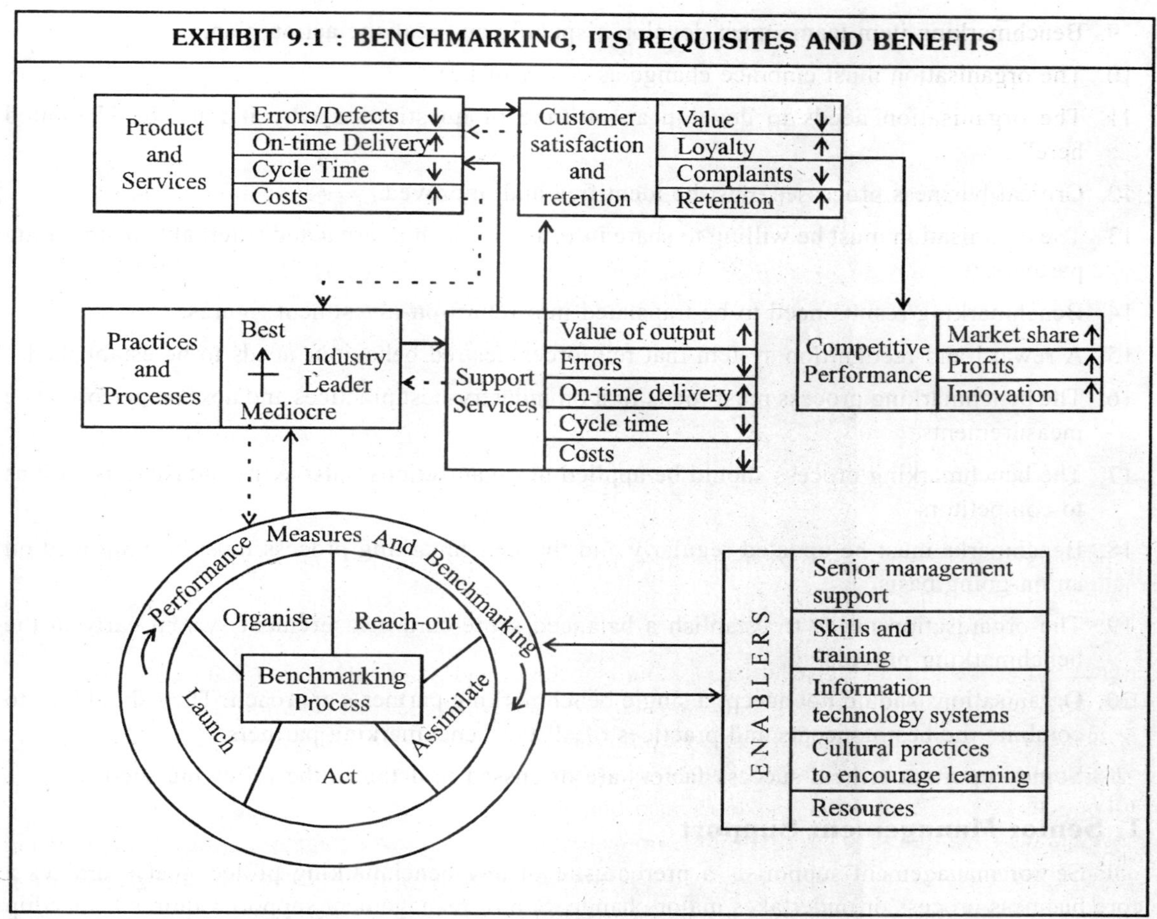

The benchmarking process has produced outstanding results in some organisations, good results in most, fair results in many and little or no results in others. **The following critical success factors must be addressed if an organisation is to have a productive benchmarking process.**

1. Top management/senior management must actively lead and support the benchmarking process.
2. Benchmarking must be defined correctly. It is not just comparative analysis.
3. Resources must be set aside for benchmarking.
4. Projects need to be prioritised and competitive areas addressed first.
5. The organisation must have a comprehensive understanding of how its item functions and performs before it approaches benchmarking partners.
6. The benchmarking process must be focused on implementing the future-state solutions, not on collecting and analysing data.
7. There must be a commitment to a continuous, on-going benchmarking effort that makes it part of the management process.
8. Results must be measured in a way that evaluate the benchmarking effort's impact on the bottom-line.

9. Benchmarking item teams must develop a specific and realistic action plan.
10. The organisation must embrace change as a way of life.
11. The organisation needs to develop an attitude of questioning why it must be "invented here".
12. Critical business processes must be identified and improved.
13. The organisation must be willing to share information with internal and external benchmarking partners.
14. Benchmarking results need to be translated into return-on-investment figures.
15. A reward-and-recognition system that reinforces desired behaviour needs to be established.
16. The benchmarking process must focus first on industry-best practices and next on performance measurements.
17. The benchmarking process should be applied to organisations outside the industry, as well as to competitors.
18. Benchmarks must be updated regularly and the benchmarking process must be improved on an on-going basis.
19. The organisation needs to establish a balanced score-card measurement system early in the benchmarking process.
20. Organisations should not accept a single benchmarking partner's approach. They should try to combine the best concepts and practices of all the benchmarking partners.

Some important critical success factors are discussed in detail in the following section:

1. Senior Management Support

Senior management support is a prerequisite of any benchmarking project that examines a core business process or undertakes major change. Senior management support requires leadership actions and behaviour that signal the importance of the project to the organisation.

Five types of leadership commitment are especially helpful in championing benchmarking efforts:

(i) ***Management should visibly promote benchmarking within the organisation:*** Managers who are effective benchmarking champions both "talk the talk" and "walk the talk". Because of their visibility and positional power, managers influence others and set the stage for employee attitudes. By consistently advocating the importance of benchmarking for best practices and by supporting this message with deeds, resources and personal involvement, managers communicate the corporation's need to accelerate performance improvement.

(ii) ***Management should articulate and reinforce the benefits of benchmarking for best practices:*** Continuous performance improvement means an end to "business as usual". Employees therefore need to understand how innovative adaptation strategies benefit them and the organisation by migrating more effective business practices into their performance systems.

(iii) ***Management should translate general support for benchmarking into clear requirements for all managers:*** Senior managers must learn about benchmarking techniques so they can actively support and direct others who will conduct best practices studies. One proven strategy to accomplish managerial competency in best practices benchmarking is to establish benchmarking requirements for managers.

(iv) ***Management should ensure that the organisational culture supports and encourages a "we-can-learn-from-anyone" attitude:*** In today's environment, employees embrace the idea of life-long learning, for continuous learning can help employees update the skills, tools and concepts that will help make them and their organisations successful. Management plays a leading role in creating the corporate culture that views continuous learning - through best practices benchmarking and other techniques - as critical success factor for the organisation and the employee.

(v) ***Management should empower employees who oversee processes and act as the owners of those performance systems to adapt best practices:*** Managers must trust that employees are capable of improving and managing the systems that they operate. Performance improvement occurs most rapidly when it is driven by those who own and operate the process or system being improved. Good ideas are likely to remain on the drawing board of change if he process owners were excluded from identifying those ideas and best practices. When managers empower line employees to act as "general managers" of their own jobs, they set the stage for employees to become motivated benchmarkers who actively identify, adopt and adapt best practices to advance their own performance systems.

2. Benchmarking Training

Benchmarking is not conceptually difficult, but it is extremely rich in detail. Benchmarking training is the tool to enable a team's success. Without training in the process tools, techniques and philosophy of best practices, benchmarking teams are severely handicapped. **Different organisations employ different strategies in deploying benchmarking skills to line employees, but successful benchmarking training shares seven common characteristics which are given below :**

(i) ***Benchmarking training should familiarise employees with a standard benchmarking process to be used throughout the organisation :*** Every organisation should adopt a common benchmarking process to facilitate training, communication, and collaboration among teams, departments, functions and business units.

(ii) ***Benchmarking training should familiarise employees with basic tools by which to analyse, understand, and improve work processes :*** Process benchmarking and improvement require team members to be comfortable with basic process management skills and tools. Flow-charting or process mapping is the principal tool used to help teams articulate, analyse and improve complex work processes.

(iii) ***Benchmarking training should prepare a team in performance measurement :*** Process management and performance measurement are flip sides of the same project. Work processes represent a composite performance system that produce a tangible or intangible output or result. Performance measures are the indicators that reflect the health of the performance system.

(iv) ***Benchmarking training should provide the team with requisite technical skills, techniques and tools to implement the benchmarking process :*** The benchmarking training should prepare team members to successfully execute the tools and techniques including basic research

techniques, survey development, telephone interviews, site visits, team interviews, gap analysis, development of graphical performance charts, action plans, management reports and implementation plans. Often case studies, role playing, scenario - building, and action exercises that require applicants to apply benchmarking skills are helpful training strategies.

(v) ***Benchmarking training should prepare team members to be effective problem solvers and solution creators :*** Benchmarking training should prepare the team to be comfortable in exercising analytic problem-solving skills and synthetic solution - creation skills. To be effective problem solvers, benchmarking teams must be able to perform process analysis. Solution creation often requires break-through thinking or entirely new ways of looking at a problem.

(vi) ***Benchmarking training should present the benchmarking process in the context of existing quality improvement initiation :*** Benchmarking is an enabler of problem solving and continuous improvement. In this respect benchmarking is a means to an end - not an end in itself. Consequently, benchmarking should be presented as an enabling set of skills and tools that support or complement traditional quality improvement techniques in place.

(vii) ***Benchmarking training should convey the philosophy of best practices as a catalyst for performance improvement :*** Benchmarking training should communicate the purpose, power and benefits of best practices as an improvement strategy that complements traditional improvement approaches.

3. Information Technology Systems

Effective information technology systems are key enablers of successful benchmarking. Current IT systems permit teams to quickly and inexpensively generate, disseminate, analyse, and store vast amounts of information. **Some common applications helping teams effectively develop and manage benchmarking information include :**

(i) Spreadsheet and database software programs that help teams store, track, monitor and compare benchmark information and project progress.

(ii) Process mapping and flowcharting programs that enable teams to depict detailed work flows.

(iii) Graphical presentation programs that help teams organise, display and analyse data.

(iv) CD-ROM information libraries and on-line databases that allow teams to perform literature searches in their own offices.

(v) Computer networks equipped with E-mail systems and group communications or meeting software.

4. Cultural Encouragement of Learning

Benchmarking proliferates in corporate cultures that encourage training. Learning organisations evidence some common characteristics that encourage external out reach and innovative adaptation among employees. The corporate culture in learning organisations focuses more on liberating employees than on controlling them. Commonly these learning organisations encourage prudent risk taking, encourage holistic thinking, expect curiosity and creativity, encourage networking and team work, reward meaningful difference and focus on transformational progress in addition to mere developmental change. **The six golden rules of organisations that nurture learning cultures are:**

(i) Liberate employee potential rather than control it.

(ii) Encourage holistic, systematic thinking and learning in addition to narrow problem solving.

(iii) Expect creativity, innovation and continuous learning - rather than conformity - from managers and employees.

(iv) The corporate culture should encourage networking and information sharing.

(v) The corporate culture should nurture integrated, cross-functional team-work.

(vi) The corporate culture should reward meaningful differences or departures from the status-quo.

5. Resources

Without adequate resources, even the most enthusiastic teams may find themselves hand cuffed. For benchmarking teams, resources are of three primary types: *(i)* Time, *(ii)* Funding and *(iii)* Equipment. **These are briefly discussed below:**

- **Time :** Team members must be allowed time for training, research and team meetings. Teams that never have the time to meet are almost always ineffective. On some occasions, fulfilling team duties may require team members to be released from other work commitments. The benchmarking process will succeed only if the team members are given time to do their job well.
- **Funding :** Resource support must translate into adequate funds to provide for project expenses such as research, training, site visits, data acquisition, report production and interviews. Like any division or business unit, benchmarking teams must operate under budgetary restraints, but without adequate funding, benchmarking teams can not fulfill their change.
- **Equipment :** Equipment - often in the form of technology support - is critical to the benchmarking team's success. For instance, teams often must perform research through public databases that typically have limited points of access in an organisation. Teams must also be able to gather, store, retrieve and share best practice information. Effective benchmarking teams are therefore supported with the computer time and applications that will enable their success.

DESIGNING YOUR BENCHMARKING PROCESS

New comers to the field of benchmarking often puzzle over the great variation among benchmarking processes used at different companies. Some organisations use a four-step benchmarking process while others use a six-step process, seven-step process, eight-step process and so on. The differences are cosmetic. Most companies employ a common approach that helps them plan the project, collect and analyse data, develop insights and implement improvement actions. The best approach reflects common sense. Adopt a benchmarking process that suits an organisation's culture and existing quality-improvement initiatives.

Organisations that excel in benchmarking almost always customise their own benchmarking process to reflect the organisation's culture, infrastructure, and leadership philosophy.

The following four benchmarking process designs are in place at some prominent US companies.

1. **5 step benchmarking process** used in Motorola, a Baldrige Award winner :

Step	Description
1	Decide what to benchmark
2	Find companies to benchmark
3	Gather data
4	Analyse data and integrate results into action plans
5	Recalibrate and recycle the process

2. **The seven-step benchmarking process** used by Bristol-Myers, Baxter International and several other corporations :

Step	Description
1	Determine which function(s) to benchmark
2	Identify key performance variables to measure
3	Identify the best-in-class companies
4	Measure performance of best-in-class companies
5	Measure your own performance
6	Specify programs and actions to meet and surpass
7	Implement and monitor results

3. **The AT & T nine-step benchmarking process :**

Step	Description
1	Identify what to benchmark
2	Develop a benchmarking plan
3	Choose a data collection method
4	Collect data
5	Choose best-in-class companies
6	Collect data during a site visit
7	Compare processes, identify gaps and develop recommendations
8	Implement recommendations
9	Recalibrate benchmarks

4. **The Xerox 12 step benchmarking process :**

Step	
Phase 1	**Planning**
Step 1	Identify what to benchmark

Step 2	Identify comparative companies
Step 3	Determine data collection method and collect data
Phase 2	**Analysis**
Step 4	Determine current performance gap
Step 5	Project future performance levels
Phase 3	**Integration**
Step 6	Communicate findings and gain acceptance
Step 7	Establish functional goals
Phase 4	**Action**
Step 8	Develop action plans
Step 9	Implement specific actions and monitor progress
Phase 5	**Maturity**
Step 11	Attain leadership positions
Step 12	Fully integrate practices into processes

Customised Benchmarking Process

While some managers may feel frustrated by the lack of standardisation among benchmarking processes, benchmarking experts, however agree that no common benchmarking process standard is likely to establish itself. Corporate benchmarking managers contend that the benefits of a benchmarking process design that suits one's individual culture are far greater than the benefits of establishing a national process standard. Three motivating factors that throw the weight of benefits onto the side of each organisation designing its own benchmarking process are given below:

1. ***Customised benchmarking processes complement the individual corporate philosophy toward performance improvement :*** The leadership of every organisation must establish benchmarking's role within the organisation's continuous improvement efforts. In some companies, this role is tactical : benchmarking enables problem-solving and process-improvement efforts. In other organisations, benchmarking plays a more strategic role : Benchmarks are viewed as critical performance measures required for all core processes, benchmarking is viewed as a fundamental business process employed by all effective managers and line employees, benchmarking drives continuous improvements and enables managers to evaluate their unit's progress against competitors, the leadership embraces best practices as primary motivators of organisational change, learning and improvement. Whether benchmarking assumes a tactical or strategic role within the organisation, a customised benchmarking design ensures that the process complements the organisation's existing TQM system.
2. ***Customised benchmarking processes support cultural differences among organisations :*** Organsiations, like people, have different personalities. Some organisations are dominated by people having engineering and technical backgrounds who appreciate structure and detailed procedures. Such organisations may successfully promote a benchmarking process that has many steps when fully and meticulously articulated. Organisation dominated by people from sales, marketing, and service backgrounds may prefer less structured management procedures.

These organisations will probably promote a simpler benchmarking process that reflects their preference for flexibility and individual improvisation.

3. ***Customised benchmarking processes accommodate the need for organisations to feel unique :*** Many organisations believe their operating circumstances are unique. Therefore they distrust all "off-the-shelf" solutions because they were "not invented here". These organisations favour customised approaches because they help managers and employees "buy into" and accept the benchmarking process more quickly.

THE SIMPLE CONSENSUS MODEL

Successful implementation frequently favours simplicity (a simple benchmarking process). One such benchmarking process model has been articulated by the members of the Strategic Planning Institute's (SPI) Council on benchmarking. The SPI council is a loosely knit confederation of corporate benchmarking managers in the US who meet quarterly to share benchmarking experiences. **The essentials of the most successful corporation's individual benchmarking processes are summarised in the form of a simply worded five-step process given below :**

Step 1	Lunch
Step 2	Organise
Step 3	Reach out
Step 4	Assimilate
Step 5	Act

The SPI model represents a user friendly template for designing your own benchmarking process. It is deliberately articulated in ***generic terms*** so that virtually any benchmarking process can be mapped into its five phases. **The benchmarking processes of Motorola and Xerox are mapped onto the SPI generic model as illustrated in *Table* 9.2 and *9.3***

TABLE 9.2 : MAPPING MOTOROLA'S BENCHMARKING PROCESS ON TO THE GENERIC PROCESS

Step	Description	Launch	Organise	Reach-out	Assimilate	Act
1	Decide what to benchmark	✓	-	-	-	-
2	Find companies to benchmark	-	✓	-	-	-
3	Gather data	-	-	✓	-	-
4	Analyse data and integrate	-	-	-	✓	-
5	Recalibrate and recycle the process	-	-	-	-	✓

TABLE 9.3 : MAPPING XEROX'S BENCHMARKING PROCESS ONTO THE GENERIC PROCESS						
Step	**Description**	**Launch**	**Organise**	**Reach-out**	**Assimilate**	**Act**
1	Identify what to benchmark	✓	-	-	-	-
2	Identify comparative companies	-	✓	-	-	-
3	Determine data collection methods	-	✓	-	-	-
3b	Collect data	-	-	✓	✓	✓
4	Determine current performance 'gap'	-	-	-	✓	-
5	Project future performance levels	-	-	-	✓	-
6	Communicate findings and gain acceptance	-	-	-	✓	-
7	Establish functional goals	-	-	-	-	✓
8	Develop action plans	-	-	-	-	✓
9	Implement actions	-	-	-	-	✓
10	Recalibrate benchmarks	-	-	-	-	-
11	Attain leadership position	-	-	-	-	✓
12	Fully integrate practices into processes	-	-	-	-	✓

PLANNING AND MANAGING BENCHMARKING PROJECTS - CASE STUDY OF XYZ COMPANY

The case study of XYZ company reveals how the SPI model provides a useful framework for planning and managing projects and how the model can be used by a benchmarking team. In this example, the benchmarking team sets its sights on improving major-account sales.

1. The Launch Phase

At the outset, management must decide what important opportunity areas have the greatest impact or potential for the organisation. This decision where the benchmarking team should set its sights is addressed immediately in the ***launch phase***. ***Exhibit 9.2*** **illustrates the process, purpose and individual steps that compose the benchmarking launch phase.** Frequently benchmarking projects arise when senior executives identify high-level needs during senior management activities. Consider a few examples :

EXHIBIT 9.2 : BENCHMARKING PROCESS

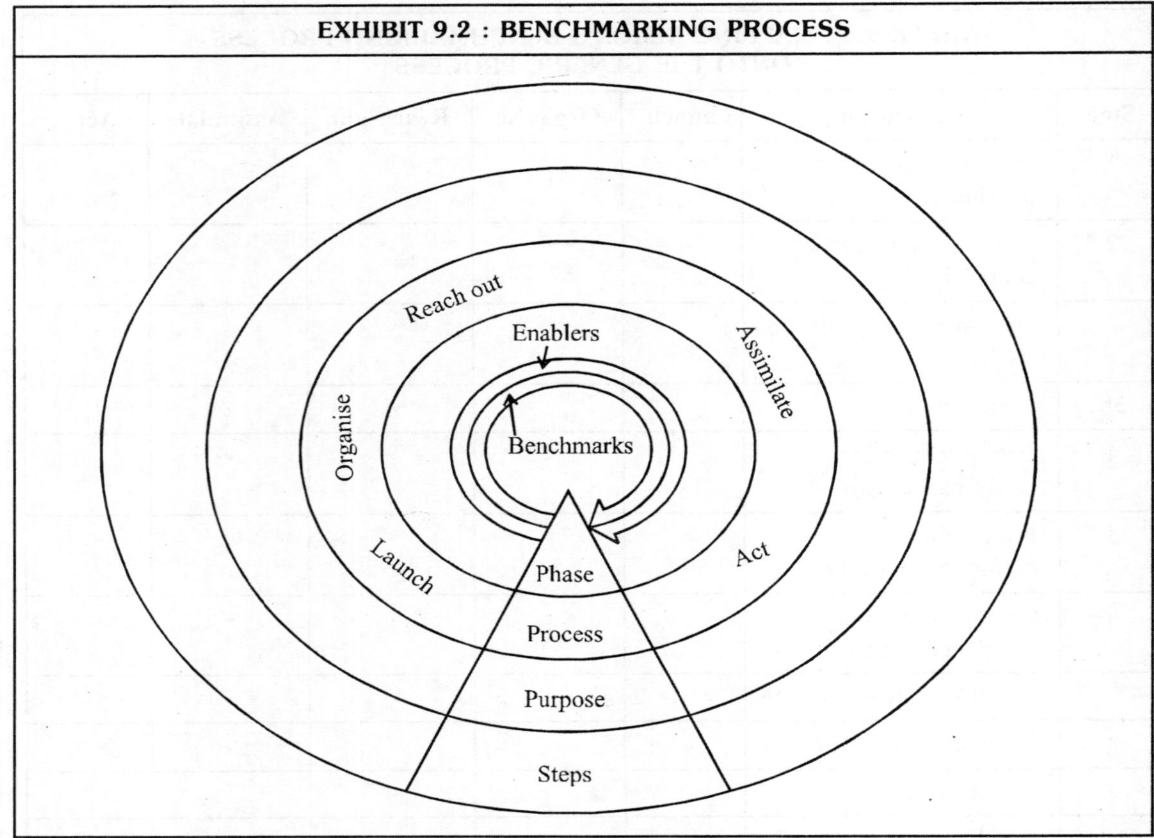

(i) ***During the strategic planning process, management must evaluate business factors critical for the organisation to sustain its competitive advantage :*** Issues surrounding technological competency, core process capabilities, cost competitiveness and fast response capabilities - all issues that could prompt the redesign of core business processes - often command immediate benchmarking. The findings help the leadership evaluate the adequacy of the organisation's current position and ensure the company's future plans will enable it to remain competitive in the market place.

(ii) ***During monthly and yearly operating assessments of core business processes and functions, management identifies opportunities for continuous improvement :*** During quarterly operations performance reviews, management may identify some element of the core business system that appears overloaded, obsolete or inadequate. Benchmarking becomes a tool for achieving three fundamental objectives : *(a)* adapt best practices, get the process back under control, *(b)* identify and adapt current best practices and *(c)* accelerate the journey to improved performance.

(iii) ***Current benchmarking projects trigger awareness of additional opportunities :*** In many instances, one benchmarking project simply gives rise to another as new improvement areas are surfaced.

What XYZ Company Did?

At XYZ company operations, the strategic planning process and company's operations performance reviews were both catalyst that prompted the company to benchmark its major accounts sales. The strategic plan articulated goals for improving capabilities among several professional and technical groups, including the sales force. For sales, one question emerged above all others: ***"What would it like to be the major accounts sales leader in the industry?"*** The company decided to employ benchmarking to identify the most important gaps between its major - accounts sales practices and those of sales leaders.

2. The Organise Phase

During the second benchmarking phase (the organise phase), management organises the project to ensure a clear project focus. At this time, senior managers identify important issues, weaknesses and improvement opportunities. They prioritise the specific functions or processes to be studied, they obtain approval and support from process owners and stake-holders and they assign the project to a benchmarking team that is usually comprised of front-line employees from all functions that help manage the process under study. The team then prepares a benchmarking project plan.

Team Size

The membership size of benchmarking teams should be kept within manageable size. Three to eight members are optional. If it is the team's first benchmarking effort, an experienced benchmarking facilitator should ideally be included on the team to answer questions and guide the group in its efforts. The team's first duty usually is to produce a ***benchmarking project plan*** that serves as the team's road map.

What XYZ Company Did?

XYZ company's operating reviews led its senior management to target four aspects of major -accounts sales management : *(a)* sales-force structure, *(b)* sales-force costs, *(c)* sales-force performance improvement and *(d)* sales-force awards programs. The process owner (the Assistant Vice President of Business Sales) approved the project. Management assembled a benchmarking team and chose a headquarters sales manager to head it. The team soon formulated its project plan, including key priorities, a schedule, expected deliverables, and required resources.

3. The Reach Out Phase

During the third phase of a benchmarking project, the team reaches out to understand its own and other organisation's processes. During this phase, the team performs the following activities :

(i) Documents the process to be studied (based on customer needs).
(ii) Collects secondary data.
(iii) Determines the variables by which to evaluate performance.
(iv) Designs a questionnaire through which to solicit performance information from other organisations.
(v) Conduct telephone interviews and general information gathering.
(vi) Selects benchmarking partners.
(vii) Conduct on-site visits among the best performing partners.

What XYZ Company Did?

During the reach out phase, XYZ company's major accounts sales benchmarking team set its critical performance variables, collected data, selected four benchmarking partners and using a formal questionnaire to guide and focus in-person interviews, completed site visits to the four companies. Among the benchmarking partners, one company was a leader in information technology major-account sales, one company was based in the aluminium industry, another was an electronic corporation, and the fourth was a computer hardware company. By this, XYZ company's project manager had an opportunity to meet and develop relationships with companies that had been identified as the best in the class in his particular areas of interest.

4. The Assimilate Phase

During the fourth phase, the ***assimilate phase***, the benchmarking team assimilates the best practice information it has developed and prepares this information and corresponding improvement recommendations for senior management's review. During this phase, the team normalises any measures that may still be in different reporting formats, studies and highlights performance gaps produced by different operating approaches, targets future performance goals and develops change recommendations. The outcome of the assimilation phase is a best practices report.

What XYZ Company Did?

After completing its fact - finding and site visits, XYZ company assimilated a large body of collected information and focussed on the best practices of the site visit partners. This phase took the most time due to inconsistent measurements among the benchmarking partners.

In the case of XYZ company, the project results supported a host of proposed changes including:

(i) Establishing higher ratios of sales people to sales managers.

(ii) Selecting turnover targets for sales.

(iii) Increasing investment in specific sales training for employees.

(iv) Setting higher requirements for the amount of time spent by each sales employee with customers.

(v) Reducing the amount of time sales people spent on administrative functions.

5. The Act Phase

During the fifth and final benchmarking phase, the ***act phase*** the benchmarking team works with management and the process owners to prioritise recommendations and agree on an implementation strategy. Agreement leads to formalisation of action plans, implementation schedules, measurement and tracking mechanisms and recalibration plans, when the action plans are completed, on-going responsibility for managing the improvement efforts often shifts to an implementation team. The benchmarking team still supports the implementation team, helping place tracking mechanisms, develop process standards, cycle time measures, quality measures and statistical control charting. Overtime, the process or system is continuously fine-tuned and improved. Meanwhile the organisation must eventually recalibrate its benchmarks based on the newly established best practices.

What XYZ Company Did?

At XYZ company, the change recommendations prepared by the major-accounts sales benchmarking team were fully compatible with the parallel findings of a corporate process reengineering team that was evaluating XYZ company's customer contact processes. Consequently, the benchmarking team's improvement recommendations were incorporated into the action plans of the process reengineering implementation team. The implementation plan included monitoring and tracking the impact of the changes, consequently, improved performance benchmarks were put in place. It is critical during this phase to link and integrate action plans coming out of the benchmarking project with action plans coming out of other company initiatives - which in the case of XYZ company involved business process reengineering.

BOX 9.1 : BENCHMARKING IN PRACTICE – JOHNSON & JOHNSON SUCCESSFULLY REDUCED THE COST AND CYCLE TIME OF ITS BENCHMARKING STUDIES

In January 1991, less than five percent of the operating companies at Johnson & Johnson employed benchmarking - and those that did relied heavily on consultants. Realising that employees know more about the corporation's businesses than outside consultants, Johnson & Johnson (J&J) management shifted its focus to create benchmarking teams staffed by J&J employees. The new corporate goal was for J&J teams to perform 70 percent of all benchmarking projects and for consultants to perform the remaining 30 percent. By September, 1992, over 60 teams were actively benchmarking. J&J reached its goal by using training and experience sharing to establish benchmarking competency within the corporation. By establishing internal benchmarking capabilities, Johnson & Johnson successfully reduced the cost and cycle time of its benchmarking studies while increasing the quality of project results.

POINTS TO REMEMBER

- **A benchmarking project may fail because of the following reasons :**
  - *(i)* Topic too broad
  - *(ii)* Project not clearly focused - team studying too many major measures
  - *(iii)* Best-in-class companies chosen as benchmark partners because of their reputation rather than because of their demonstrated performance.
- **The lessons learnt by some benchmarking teams which failed in their benchmarking projects were :**
  - *(i)* Clearly focus the project
  - *(ii)* To look outside its own industry for important operating lessons
  - *(iii)* To focus on observable systems, practices and procedures that proved highly effective in the benchmark organisation
- Successful benchmarking projects bear a "Triple A" - brand – Adopt, Adapt and Advance.
- After searching out and examining highly - effective operating practices experienced benchmarkers **adopt** the best, **adapt** them to their own work environments and **advance** performance through careful implementation and continuous refinement of the practices.
- A successful benchmarking project requires a well designed performance measurement and benchmark system.
- Several critical success factors enable 'Triple A' - benchmarking processes.
- **These critical success factors include :**
  - *(i)* Senior management support
  - *(ii)* Benchmarking training for the project team

(iii) Useful information technology systems *(iv)* Cultural practices that encourage learning

(v) Resources, especially in the form of time, funding and useful equipment

- **Senior management support** – This requires leadership actions and behaviour that signal the importance of the project to the organisation.
- **Five types of leadership commitment necessary for successful benchmarking are :**

  (i) Management should visibly promote benchmarking within the organisation

  (ii) Management should articulate and reinforce the benefit of benchmarking for best practices

  (iii) Management should translate general support for benchmarking into clear requirements for all managers

  (iv) Management should ensure that the organisational culture supports and encourages a **"we-can-learn-from-anyone"** attitude

  (v) Management should empower employees who oversee processes and act as the owners of those performance systems to adapt best practices
- **Benchmarking training** is the tool to enable a benchmarking project team's success. Without training in the process tools, technique and philosophy of best practices, benchmarking teams are severely handicapped.
- Effective **information technology systems** are key enablers of successful benchmarking.
- Benchmarking proliferates in corporate cultures that encourage training.
- For benchmarking teams to be successful, adequate resources, time, funding and equipment must be provided.
- Designing your benchmarking process properly facilitates the success of benchmarking projects.
- Whether the organisations use a four step benchmarking process while others use a six-step, seven-step or eight-step process hardly matters for achieving success.
- The differences are cosmetic.
- Adopt a benchmarking process that suits an organisation's culture and existing quality improvement initiatives.
- Benchmarking experts agree that no common benchmarking process standard is likely to establish itself.
- Customised benchmarking processes complement the individual corporate philosophy toward performance improvement.
- Customised benchmarking processes support cultural differences among organisations.
- Customised benchmarking processes accommodate the need for organisations to feel unique.
- **A simple consensus benchmarking process model has a five-step process.**

  Step 1 : Launch, Step 2 : Organise, Step 3 : Reach-out, Step 4 : Assimilate and Step 5 : Act.

  This model is also known as SPI (Statistical Planning Institute's Council on benchmarking) model.
- In the **launch phase**, management must decide what important opportunity areas have the greatest impact or potential for the organisation.
- During the **"organise" phase,** management organises the project to ensure a clear project focus. Senior managers identify important issues, weaknesses and improvement opportunities. A benchmarking team comprising 3 to 8 members is formed in the "organise" phase.

- During the **"reach-out" phase,** the team reaches out to understand its own and other organisation's processes.
- During the **"assimilate" phase,** the benchmarking team assimilates the best practice information it has developed and prepares this information and corresponding improvement recommendations for senior management's review.
- During the **"act" phase,** the benchmarking team works with management and process owners to prioritise recommendations and agree on implementation strategy.

REVIEW QUESTIONS

1. What are "critical success factors"? - Give examples.
2. List some critical success factors that must be addressed if an organisation is to have a productive benchmarking process.
3. Discuss five major critical success factors which enable a benchmarking project bear a "Triple-A" brand - "Adopt", "Adapt" and "Advance".
4. What is "benchmarking training"? Discuss the seven common characteristics which successful benchmarking training shares.
5. Discuss the six golden rules of organisations that nurture learning cultures.
6. Discuss the various types of resources required for carrying out a benchmarking process.
7. What is "customised benchmarking process"? Discuss the three motivating factors that throw the weight of benefits on to the side of each organisation designing its own benchmarking process.
8. Describe the benchmarking process model articulated by the strategic planning institute's council on benchmarking.
9. List out the steps involved in the following benchmarking processes :
   (a) 5 steps benchmarking process followed by Motorola.
   (b) 7 steps benchmarking process used by Briston-Myers and Baxer International.
   (c) 9 steps benchmarking process used by AT& T.
   (d) 12 steps benchmarking process used by Xerox.
10. Briefly discuss the five step benchmarking process model established by SPI council on benchmarking in the US.

DISCUSSION QUESTIONS

1. "Several critical success factors enable Triple-A benchmarking processes" - Elaborate.
2. "Senior management support is a prerequisite of any benchmarking project that examines a core business process or undertakes major change". Do you agree or disagree? Give reasons for your answer.
3. "Effective information technology systems are key enablers of success benchmarking". Discuss.
4. "Different organisations employ different strategies in deploying benchmarking skills to line employees, but successful benchmarking training shares seven common characteristics". Explain.
5. "Without adequate resources, even the most enthusiastic teams may find themselves hand-cuffed". Critically examine the statement.

CHAPTER 10

Implementing Improvements

INTRODUCTION

You have completed your data acquisition and analysis and put together a nice report detailing how your organisation compares to competitors or other best-in-class companies in the activity you have benchmarked. This is the time for action because till now, you have performed a great intellectual exercise with little or no value added. At this juncture in the benchmarking study, the action or lack of it determines whether the study will be a success or not. If changes are not made, if the benchmarking team does not become a catalyst to make things happen, your benchmarking might turn out to be a waste of time.

DEVELOPING YOUR IMPROVEMENT PLAN : DETERMINING WHAT TO CHANGE

If you have planned your study properly and performed intellectually honest analysis of the data, the changes that your organisation should make to improve the activities studied should be clear.

Developing a plan to meet or exceed the competition to fortify an existing lead begins with an analysis of target companies relative to your company. Your studies are likely to lead you to a point where you will know where and how much you can improve. The challenge is to figure out how to make it happen.

Reality Considerations

One of the biggest dangers for a benchmarking team can be that it tries to do too much at once. Benchmarking can be a very rich learning experience and you may try to improve too many things at the same time, running the risk of making marginal improvements in many different areas but not making substantial improvements in the most key areas. Or a benchmarking team may prescribe actions in the key areas that are simply not feasible, given an organisation's resources. Reality plays a significant role in the implementation of improvements.

Resource limitations, a frequent manifestation of reality, come in may forms. Three of the most common resource limitations are: *(i)* **financial limitations**, *(ii)* **human limitations** and *(iii)* **time limitations. These are briefly discussed below:**

- **Financial limitations :** When improvements suggested by benchmarking studies include significant capital expenditure projects, the analysis of these improvements must include a rigorous financial analysis, preferably, the theoretically correct net present value (NPV) analysis. The company's budget for that year must be adequate to support such large capital expenditures.
- **Human limitations :** Human resources - those who can really influence and promote change, are often as scarce as financial resources. Change leaders who can make things happen are a rare commodity and not every organisation is blessed with a plethora of change leaders. Identifying a change leader is a key task during the planning phase of a benchmarking study.
- **Time limitations :** As with the discrete resources of money and people, time is seldom working for us. Time is often a reality with which the benchmarking team is forced to cope, and a ranking of "to do" items generated by a benchmarking study in their order of relative importance and time requirements is a valuable step in the benchmarking process.

Obtaining Commitment for Change

If you have planned and executed your benchmarking study properly, you have been building consensus for making changes from the outset. Your benchmarking team includes people from the line who realise that improvements in their processes are necessary, have studied best practices to learn how much to improve and have learnt first-hand that improvement is possible and how it could be done. This involvement of line people in the benchmarking processes is one of the most powerful facets of benchmarking.

Figure out who needs to be consulted or considered when making changes as early as you can in any study. Think of all the groups (both inside and outside an organisation) that might be affected by any changes that will result from the improvement program you are planning. Those groups that might be affected could potentially impede the change process. They should be considered carefully in the development of any planned improvement actions. Potential groups include all levels of management within your organisation, and at a minimum the line people involved in the change, customers, suppliers, labour unions etc. Evaluate their support or opposition, both qualitatively and quantitatively.

Competitive Considerations

A large CAD/CAM software vendor benchmarked three large business machines and technology companies that were renowned for their world-class after-sales service and support to gain a sophisticated understanding of what it takes to produce world-class after-sales service and support. As no company stood above the rest in this area in the software industry, to learn what it took to provide superior service and support, management had to study firms outside the industry. However management wisely benchmarked the company's two main competitors to understand precisely their strengths and weaknesses in this area. To ignore competitors would be asking to be caught flat-footed by one or both of them in the event that they were also improving their after-sales service and support operations.

The benchmarking team developed detailed planned action to improve their after-sales service and support in two phases:

Phase 1 : Called for the service and support group to surpass the competition in all important measures within 3 months. These included various response time, staffing and customer satisfaction measures. Competitors were benchmarked because their level of service was considered the absolute floor in level of service the company could offer.

Phase 2 : Called for the service and support group to attain world-class status within 24 months, using processes and metrics from the three world-class companies as starting points.

Through benchmarking their two main competitors, top management had learnt that one company had already begun a serious, but apparently less ambitious, service improvement process of its own. The other company could likely muster the resources to do so quickly if alerted to the fact that the competition was planning organic change within its after-sales service and support function. If either competitor stepped up its after-sales service and support function, it could neutralise any differentiating competitive advantage the company was seeking which was quite dependent on the "first-mover" advantage management hoped to secure.

Managers developed and executed this strategy because they had first developed a comprehensive competitor response profile, which alerted them to the fact that either competitor could follow suit and probably would if it knew that the company was about to change the rules of the game. **A competitor response profile is an important component of any benchmarking study.** It should be developed during data acquisition and analysis and considered carefully when implementation plans are developed. And it should be developed regardless of whether competitors are among the target being benchmarked.

IMPLEMENTING YOUR PLAN AND MONITORING RESULTS

As with any planned action, making benchmarking-driven improvements requires that you include the following in your plan :

(i) ***Detailed actions*** including *(a)* Dead lines and milestones, *(b)* Accountability by identified managers for specific goals and *(c)* Performance targets that are measurable.

(ii) ***Scheduled progress reviews*** in increments large enough to see results but small enough so people do not forget about the task at hand.

(iii) ***Rewards for successful implementation,*** linked to performance targets.

(iv) ***Plans for contingencies*** and corrective actions in the event that things go away.

(v) ***Plans for periodic recalibration***, which are a competitive necessity in today's world as more and more companies turn to benchmarking to improve their competitive positions.

Frequency of recalibration might best be described as a function of two factors :

(i) The rate of industry evolution and the nature of the process being benchmarked. The faster the industry is evolving, the more often you may wish to recalibrate your benchmarks.

(ii) You may wish to recalibrate more frequently those processes that are key to your success, your core functions, and less frequently your support functions.

Benchmarking Process Using "Plan-Do-Check-Act" Diagram

Using Walter Shewhart's "plan-do-check-act" diagram, we might also view the entire benchmarking process as a cycle like that shown in ***Exhibit 10.1.*** The improvement process should be continual, like all improvement processes.

Implementation Planning

Many benchmarking projects have produced excellent reports and recommendations - only to be spoiled by ineffective or failed implementation efforts. The causes for the failures could almost always have been prevented. In many cases failure results from poor implementation planning.

EXHIBIT 10.1 : BENCHMARKING USING SHEWHART'S "PLAN-DO-CHECK-ACT" DIAGRAM

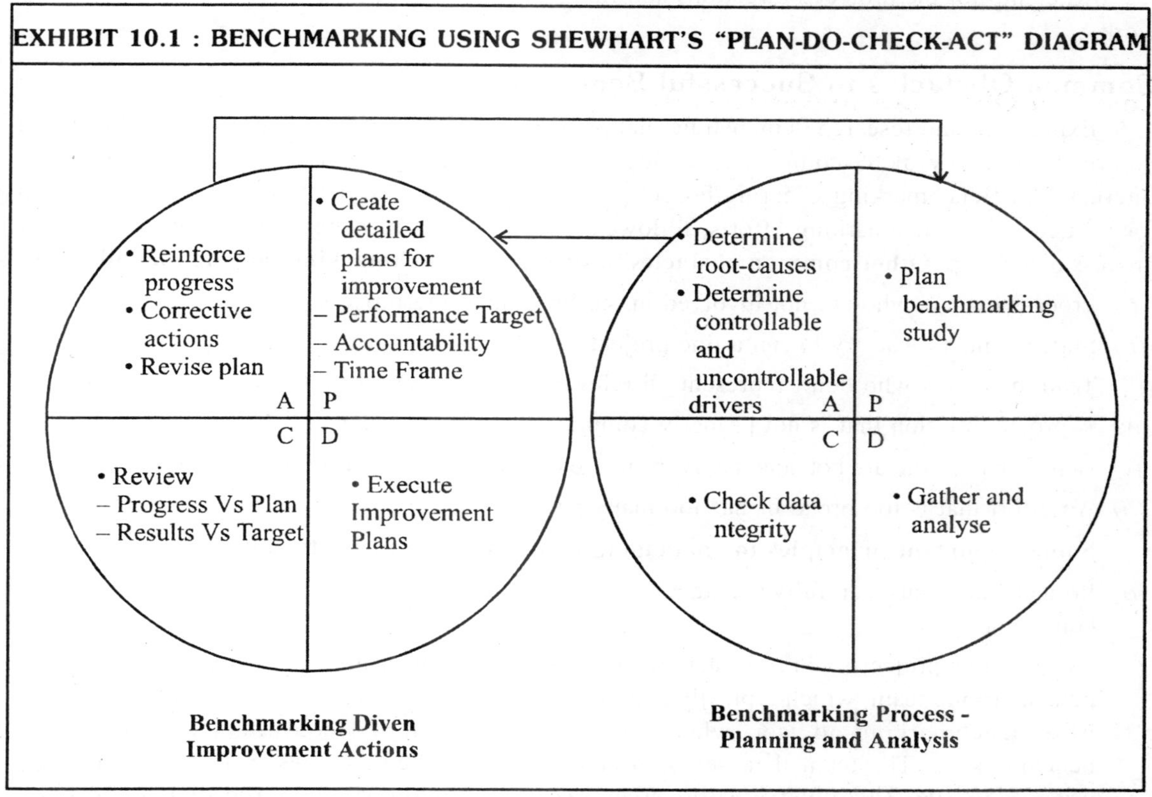

One of the most common pitfalls is failure to plan the research and fact-finding phases of the benchmarking process early so that they reflect implementation realities. Benchmarking and implementation should not be considered as two distinct events. They are separate, but related phases of a common improvement process. Consequently implementation is and should be, regarded as one with the benchmarking process. Benchmarking that results in no improvements is of little value, it wastes time, effort and organisational resources.

DESIGNING FOR IMPLEMENTATION SUCCESS

The principles of integrated communication and prevention - based planning that inspire concurrent engineering can be extended to benchmarking project management. This process of cross-functional teams concurrently planning all aspects of the benchmarking project might be called ***design for implementation*** (or DFI for short). DFI recognises that successful research investigations identifying best practices are of little value if no improvements result through successful implementation. Consequently, benchmark teams must address critical implementation issues even as the benchmarking research and information gathering are being planned. DFI produces better project results by involving representatives from all operating areas that will ultimately implement any improvements. At times, more people may be beneficiaries of a benchmarking project's findings than can effectively work on a single team. In these situations beneficiaries or those who will be influenced directly or indirectly by the project's findings, should still be involved regularly - even if only through communications - in the project's planning and progress. In this way, they can still feel ownership for the project's directions and findings, even if they personally did not execute the work.

Common Obstacles to Successful Benchmarking

Experience and research demonstrate that poor planning is a primary cause for benchmarking failure. In a survey of 88 companies conducted by American Productivity and Quality Centre's International Benchmarking Clearing-house, poor planning was the most frequently cited reason for unsuccessful benchmarking efforts, followed by lack of top-management support and lack of process ownership. **Other common obstacles to successful benchmarking include the following:**

(i) Process owners who are not involved in the benchmarking process.

(ii) Staff members who try to run a line project.

(iii) Team members who don't represent all relevant functions and beneficiaries.

(iv) A project mission that is not properly communicated to the team.

(v) Beneficiaries who are not adequately informed of the project, its purpose, benefits and progress.

(vi) An effort that is too broad or has too many parameters.

Some important principles for managing benchmarking projects include:

(i) Project teams must carefully manage the dynamic relationship that exists among benchmarking constituents.

(ii) Every major project seeking to achieve process change must have a sponsor supporting the benchmarking team, which typically consists of two to ten people and is frequently supported by a benchmarking advisor, who is an internal or external consultant experienced in benchmarking. The team then seeks to actively engage beneficiaries in the benchmarking process. ***Exhibit 10.2* illustrates the structure of a benchmark team and its beneficiaries.**

Project Sponsorship

All ***process owners*** should be involved in the benchmarking project. If possible and feasible, they must be placed on the benchmarking team. In many benchmarking projects, people from different functions and departments will participate. **Some critical questions to be asked at this juncture are:**

(i) What process or function is the benchmarking focus area?

(ii) What subprocesses within the function will be the specific targets for investigation?

(iii) Who are the owner(s) of all processes and subprocesses?

(iv) Are process owners actively sponsoring and/or supporting the benchmarking project?

Selecting the Benchmarking Team

The selection of team members can at times prove difficult because more people may be involved in a function that can effectively serve on a benchmarking team. **The following thumb rules apply when selecting benchmarking team members. Team members should :**

EXHIBIT 10.2 : BENCHMARK TEAM STRUCTURE

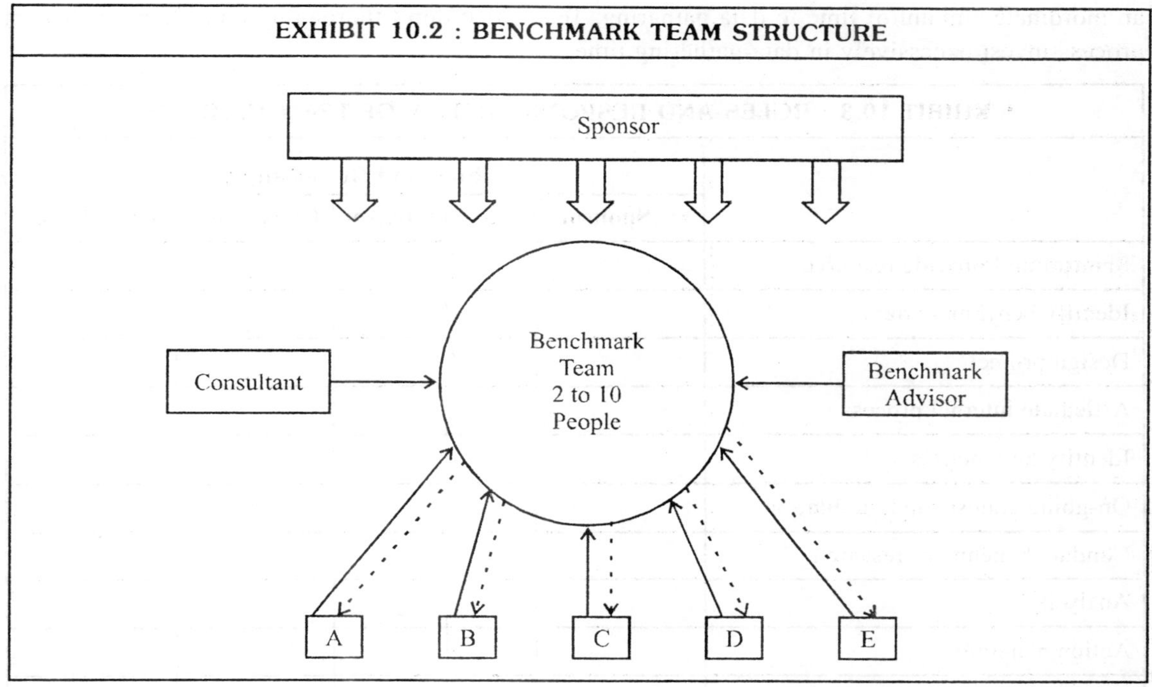

(i) Have line experience in the benchmark area.

(ii) Be credible and competent in the process.

(iii) Represent all primary functions or areas that own or influence the benchmark subject.

(iv) Feel ownership and importance of the process.

(v) Have a designated leader and

(vi) Be team-oriented and team players.

Roles and Responsibilities of Team Members

The roles and responsibilities of benchmarking constituents shift during the benchmarking project. Planning becomes especially challenging because of this dynamic. The benchmarking sponsor, for instance, serves an active and primary role in the early project stages but remains on the sidelines during much of the information gathering and outreach. Other constituents, such as team members, advisors, consultants or beneficiaries, play active and passive roles at different project stages.

***Exhibit 10.3* illustrates the changing roles and responsibilities of benchmarking team members.**

The Benchmarking Learning Curve

Benchmarking, like other management initiatives, is subject to learning curve effects. Benchmarking tends to grow easier, faster and more effective with practice and experience. Consider, the general sequence of a benchmarking project. The project moves from planning and understanding your own process through data gathering, analysis, insights, action planning, communication, implementation and obtaining buy-ins. Inexperienced and undisicplined teams predictably devote an inordinate amount of time to data gathering. Teams that don't thoroughly understand their own process invest excessively in data-gathering time.

EXHIBIT 10.3 : ROLES AND RESPONSIBILITIES OF TEAM MEMBERS

	Roles and Responsibilities				
	Sponsor	**Team**	**Advisor**	**Consultants**	**Beneficiaries**
Sponsor and provide resources	*		□		□
Identify benchmark area	*	*	□		□
Design project	□	*	□	□	*
Articulate internal process	□	*	□	□	□
Identify key metrics		*	□		□
On-going counsel and facilitation	□		*	*	
Conduct benchmark research		*	□	□	
Analysis		*	□	□	
Action planning		*	□		□
Communication	□	*	□	□	
Implementation		*	□		*

Legend : * - active role
□ - passive role

Such investigations usually produce disappointing results. Thorough data gathering can not make up for poor planning and process understanding. Benchmark teams that achieve optimal results also invest adequate time and resources in early planning and in the communication and buy-in process.

Much of the experience curve effect is attained by compressing the time required to perform data gathering. As benchmarking teams grow more proficient, they perform data gathering more quickly.

Designing your benchmarking project for successful implementation is not especially difficult or complex. Careful planning, consideration of all constituencies and attention in detail are all critical success factors. Benchmark teams that embrace the DFI imperative can look forward to significant improvements.

INTEGRATING BENCHMARKING INTO YOUR ORGANISATION

The president of a large chemical producer is of the opinion that it can be counter productive for benchmarking teams to search for world best practices and global benchmarking partners when improvement opportunities abound at home. According to him, his company must keep its competitors under the microscope if it is to stay competitive. He feels that it would be beneficial to understand the best operating practices within his company's many plants and his company managers share experience and ideas more actively.

The search for best practices does not always require an odyssey to distant places. The identification of internal best practices and of industry best practices also hold great value. In the minds of many managers, benchmarking has mistakenly come to mean only the search for best-in-world practices. Essential benchmarking skills can be applied in many situations and at all organisational levels.

Not surprisingly, many managers have the mistaken notion that benchmarking refers only to best-in-class - sometimes called best-in-world benchmarking. Such investigations seek best performers in a given function, without regard to the size, industry, or nationality of benchmark partners. Such investigations may yield significant insights - perhaps even major break through. Still, they often require may resources and consume much time. Best-in-class investigations are certainly not appropriate in all situations, functions and organisations.

Not all companies need to undertake best-in-world benchmarking comparisons. Important factors such as size, quality, maturity, industry and competitor issues may argue against such investigations. The return on investment for such major projects may be low for some organisations. Learning to effectively apply benchmarking means learning to apply it appropriately in different situations.

Benchmarking - Not a Panacea for All

Even the most powerful business tools are counter productive when misapplied. Benchmarking is no exception to this rule. You can hurt yourself and other people with benchmarking. While for the world leading corporations, benchmarking core functions, such as product development and distribution and customer service against the world's best result in higher return on assets and value-added per employee, the benefits are not the same for companies just beginning their quest for quality if they attempt to match the techniques used by world-class companies. There are at least two reasons why lower-performing organisations do not benefit greatly from benchmarking practices. They are: *(i)* they are likely to be looking at inappropriate role models. The common practice in benchmarking is to examine the "best of the best" or world-class organisations. Research studies have found that practices that distinguish higher-performing organisations are often ineffective when adopted by lower-performing organisations. Lower performers probably would find organisations that are on the threshold of medium performance, rather than world-class organisations, to be more helpful models. *(ii)* The lower-performing organisations need to focus their resources on their core infrastructure. They should not diffuse their focus with the sophisticated practice they would see in the best of the best. A better strategy for organisations just getting started or for those honing their skills in quality would be to first emulate worthy competitors and market leaders before trying to match the pace of the best-in-world functional leaders.

A company should carefully select a type of benchmarking based on its organisational maturity and circumstances. Business units that are in the early stages of their quality-improvement process or that lack systems to perform their basic functions - will find it counter productive to go in search of world's best companies as benchmarking partners. Novice and intermediate quality-level companies often reap much greater rewards by studying internal best practices and best practice companies from within their regional markets and industries.

THE SEVEN LEVELS OF BENCHMARKING

Effective benchmarking begins by understanding your position and your needs. Not all benchmarking projects demand the same approach or resource investment. Experienced benchmarkers do not regard every benchmarking opportunity as necessarily a resource-intensive, best-in-world investigation. Instead, they evaluate which tools and skills to apply in the given situation and in what scope and measure to apply them.

As the principal tool to facilitate vicarious learning, benchmarking - or its fundamental investigative and comparative skills - can and should be applied in many ways. For instance, a managers reads about another company's winning strategies and this exposure may lead the company to adapt the other organisation's proven ideas. Such ***informal benchmarking*** may seem indisciplined but it can be highly effective.

Many effective managers also borrow ideas that they glean at conferences or through informal discussion with their peers at other companies.

In appropriate circumstances, visits to excellent companies can also provide excellent opportunities for vicarious learning. The Japanese excel at strategic study visits - searches for business insights rather than process - specific practices. The Japanese business visitors frequently return home with new ideas and insights that drive change and improvement in their organisations. ***Exhibit 10.4* illustrates the seven-level hierarchy for viewing benchmarking applications.**

EXHIBIT 10.4 : LEVELS OF PERFORMANCE BENCHMARKING

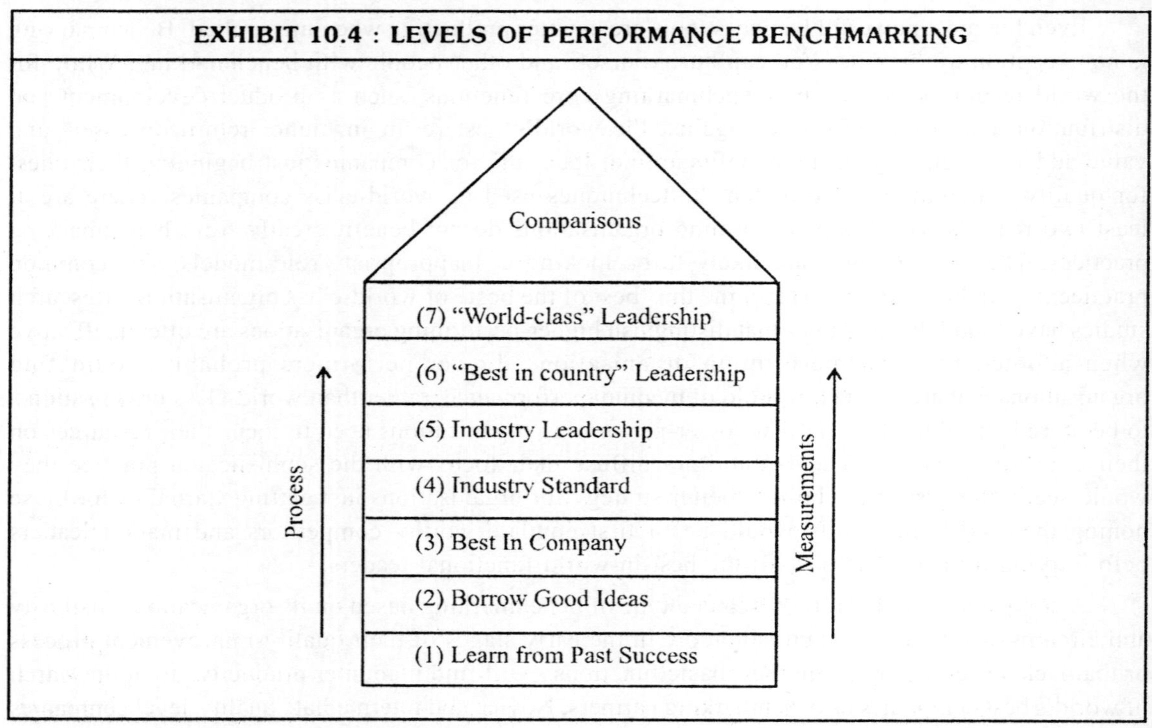

Benchmarking and Vicarious Learning

Benchmarking is viewed as the corner stone concept of ***vicarious learning***. A broad spectrum of benchmarking approaches exists, all of which result in beneficial vicarious learning. Each benchmarking approach brings a different level of rigour to the learning investigation. Less rigorous investigations involve the same essential skills of learning through external comparisons and outreach. They too often result in important insights that lead to significant organisational improvements. Some companies use the knowledge of current employees who had earlier worked in competing companies (targets of benchmarking) to quickly initiate interm improvements. Organisations perform effective outreach, learn vicariously and import external ideas that help jump start their process improvements. This informal benchmarking strategy prove fast and effective.

The model that describes the seven-level hierarchy of benchmarking opportunities helps to remove the confusion and uncertainty that exist in the workplace concerning the different applications. This model organises benchmarking according to approach and resource requirements. This integrated framework enables managers to understand that benchmarking can be formal or informal and highly structured or relatively unstructured. The frame-work recognises that different benchmarking projects require different levels of rigour. It provides a tool by which to evaluate and select the appropriate approach and resource investment. The seven-level hierarchy embraces both informal and formal benchmarking.

The seven benchmarking levels include :

1. Learning from past experiences.
2. Borrowing good ideas without regard to their corporate origin.
3. Developing internal best practices.
4. Matching industry average or standard practices.
5. Establishing leadership through industry best practices.
6. Targeting national best practices without regard to industry.
7. Matching or exceeding world best practices.

These are briefly discussed in the following section:

1. Learning from Past Experience

If managers and groups do not learn from past errors, mishaps, and failures, they will surely repeat them. This truth underlines a core concept of quality improvement. "Lessons learnt" are critical to the improvement process. Effective managers always learn from experience. They evaluate historical and current performance and learn from both. Lessons learnt are reflected in the improvements implemented throughout the organisation.

Identifying successful practices so that they can be understood and commonly related is a philosophically distinct management approach. When coupled with effective problem-solving techniques, success analysis offers rich rewards and returns. First generation benchmarking consists of sharing and studying success stories. In every success story lies the seed of a potential best practice.

2. Borrowing Good Ideas

The road to continuous improvement is paved one good idea at a time. Consequently, basic benchmarking skills embrace creative adaptation of good ideas, no matter how small, and they also support larger scale system and process improvements. Innovative adaptation is a high-yield strategy to surpucharge continuous improvement.

Small companies tend to be especially skillful at idea importation. Starved of resources, small companies naturally develop a beg, borrow and creatively imitate (steel) mentality that enables them to leverage others' experience and learning.

Despite their advanced technology and structured management systems, many large corporations can learn from smaller organisations. Exemplary operating practices can be mined within the fields of many entrepreneurial organisations that operate successfully on market niches.

3. Developing Internal Best Practices

Your biggest asset lies in your organisation. It rests in the internal best practices that reside within your best performing individuals, teams, departments, and operating units. Developing and deploying ***internal best practices*** provides a simple and powerful approach to drive performance improvement.

Why do certain plants consistently out perform others? Product and customer alone can not explain the differences. The differences come down to plant performances. We need to find out what made the best plants perform and translate those practices to all our plants.

To identify its best practices, Johnson Controls Battery Group brought together 42 top managers and supervisors from all 12 plants and all functions and assigned them to five teams. Together they identified and consolidated the division's best practices.

The team found that fundamental management practices, not specific activities or programs, separated the best from other plants. The best plants focused on ***quality, safety, effective delegation, team work, employee involvement*** and ***structured problem solving***. If you build the management team and the basic management process and involve everyone in it, you get tremendous leverage.

Internal best practices prove fruitful for many reasons :

(i) Participants share the same culture and speak the same operations language, making comparisons fast, easy and meaningful.

(ii) In most cases, participants share the same measurement system, again making comparison more meaningful.

(iii) Participants frequently use similar technology, processes and systems. Consequently, small practice differences can have a significant impact on performance.

(iv) Antitrust and competitor barriers do not exist when sharing best practices within an organisation.

(v) It is easier to identify benchmark partners and to establish working partnerships with professional peers within one's own organisation than across companies.

Establishing an internal best practices strategy is akin to conducting external benchmarking. It proceeds in a structured fashion, but usually at a faster pace. Companies can more readily access information and best practitioners can more easily be engaged in these internal projects.

4. Developing External Best Practices

Many organisations discover that their quest for performance excellence through best practices leads them outside their own organisations.

Innovation may occur in the most unlikely places. It is only when you venture outside your own practices that your perspective shifts and your context expands. This journey outside often leads organisations to small incremental improvements, leap frog jumps and-at time-to radical redesign and reengineering of their entire systems.

Competitive benchmarking is the first level above internal best practices. It focuses on the practices of direct and indirect competitors within one's industry. Competitive benchmarking has been refined into an art by companies like Xerox and Motorola. For them, it is a comprehensive skill that begins with competitor intelligence monitoring. It grows to include techniques such as ***reverse engineering*** and then evolves to embrace full-scale benchmarking. ***Advanced benchmarking*** activities may focus on strategy, product and service features, performance levels or core process and technology capabilities.

Classic **reverse engineering** focused on the examination of the competitor's product. Disassembly allows an engineering team to examine issues of design, number of parts, ease of assembly and repair and other engineering oriented issues. Viewed more broadly, reverse engineering also yields important competitor information by scrutinising documentation, warranty and guarantee terms and even after-sales service. When a company reverse engineers its competitor's entire product or service process, it develops an important knowledge about the competitor's general strategy, cost position, and its process, product and service capabilities. All prove critical in assessing one's own strengths and improvement opportunities. This information drives resource investments and strategic planning.

5. Establishing Leadership through Industry Best Practices

Competitive comparisons within the industry can occur at many levels. Frequently, though organisations make the mistake of setting their sights on easily accessible benchmarks such as industry norm, industry average or industry standards. Setting targets on the average, norm or standard condemns the organisation to mediocrity. These measures represent the grouping of all performers into one middle-of-the-road or acceptable point. For benchmarking to have value, you must-in-general-set your sights on the leadership position. For early stage companies, their competitive benchmarks might consist of local market competitors that have excelled. At later stages, leadership may call for targeting the best in your industry, without regard for their location.

6 & 7. Best-in-Class Benchmarking / Best-in-World Benchmarking

Many organisations are ordering up ***best-in-class benchmarking*** studies without regard to cost, need or return. However, it must be remembered that not every improvement project requires a multindustry best-in-class benchmarking study. Not every company is ready to perform a best-in-class investigation. Best-in-class benchmarking seeks the highest performer without regard to industry. Rising above industry comparisons, best-in-class benchmarking first seeks ***best-in-country benchmark*** partners. One rung higher on the benchmarking hierarchy is ***best-in-world benchmark*** partners.

The need must be great to benchmark at this highest level. Before commissioning a best-in-class study, consider whether you truly want and need to search for best-in-class companies.

The company seeking best-in-class benchmarking should ask the following questions before sending its benchmarking team to the field in search of best-in-class benchmark partners:

(i) Are your operations mature enough to emulate a world-class performer?

(ii) Do you compete internationally or globally?

(iii) Are you willing to devote adequate time, resources and capital to undertake a best-in-class search?

(iv) Is your project area strategically important enough to warrant a best-in-class search?

If your answer is "no" to any of these questions carefully consider whether best-in-class benchmarking may exceed your current need. Studying excellent companies from other industries can deliver many results. Stepping outside one's own industry is a useful first step in breaking the cultural mold that confines one's thinking.

Selecting the Appropriate Benchmarking Approach

Best-in-class benchmarking can produce dramatic break-through. Not every company could or should under take an extensive national investigation. Best-in-class benchmarking should be pursued with careful planning and discretion. Managers can learn to integrate benchmarking as a flexible skill into various improvement and outreach approaches. They must evaluate each opportunity to determine the appropriate project scope and investigative rigour required by the benchmarking study. Different projects and situations require different approaches. Each company must work from its own experience and maturity base. Benchmarking, like any important management task, requires judgement, skill and practice. ***Exhibit 10.5* depicts different approaches to benchmarking and reflects the varying resource investments required of each approach.**

EXHIBIT 10.5

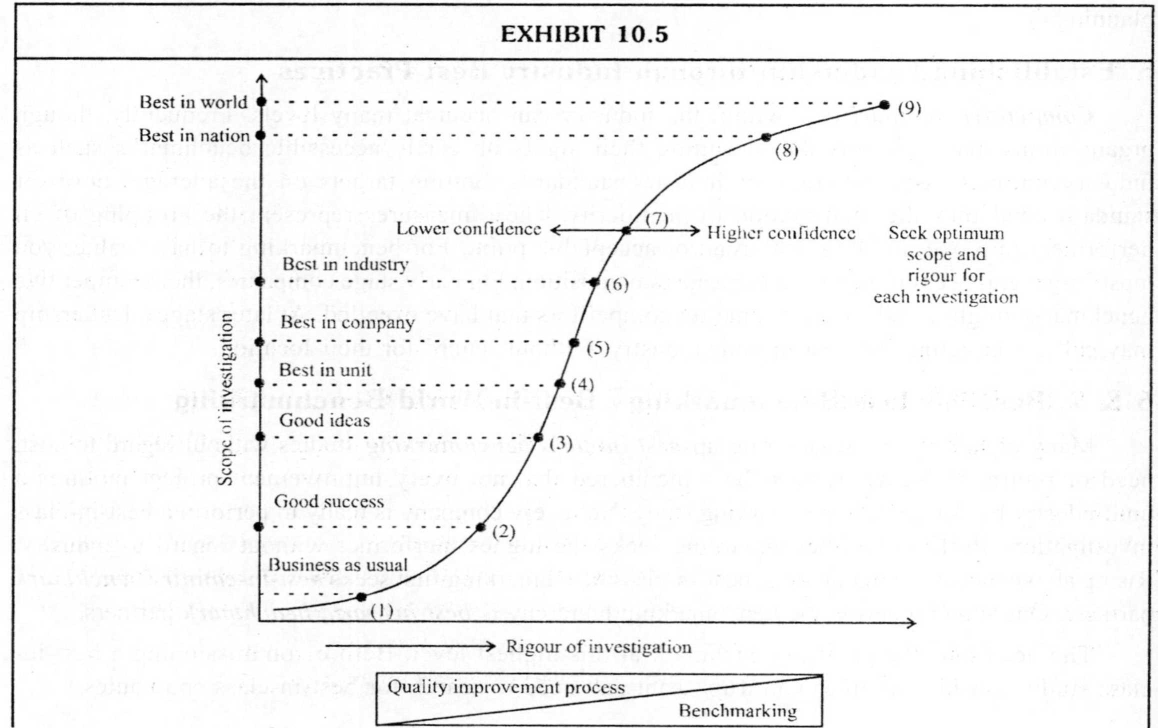

(1) → " Ain't broke, don't fix it"

(2) → Discussion, Performance Assessment

(3) → "Steal this idea", suggestion systems, brainstorming, attend conferences, industry literature, internal expert opinion

(4), (5) → Internal benchmarking : Best unit, best teams, best individuals, internal operating statistics, process analysis

(6) → Competitive benchmarking : Small sample, focus on benchmarks, industry focus

(8), (9) → Comprehensive benchmarking : Large sample, high level involvement, best-in-class view, comprehensive metrics, use of outside expert with benchmarking data base

BOX 10.1 : BENCHMARKING IN PRACTICE – AT&T BENCHMARKS CUSTOMER COMPLAINT HANDLING

What does AT&T have in common with a mail carrier, a hotel chain and an airline? All have customers who at times complain. Dedicating to improving its complaint handling process, AT&T's operator services benchmarked three companies from other industries. All are highly effective at complaint handling. With 15,000 AT&T operators handling six to seven million calls per day, AT&T quickly recognised that complaint handling excellence was important to developing and maintaining customer loyalty. Moreover it understood that the experience of leading companies in other industries might hold valuable lessons for AT&T's operator services.

Until 1984, AT&T had a monopoly on telephone services and did not worry much about losing customers. However, with the rise of competitors such as Sprint and MCI, AT&T elevated customer satisfaction and retention as a major corporate theme. Operator services possessed enough self-awareness to recognise it handled complaints suboptimally.

Consequently, a team of four complaint-handling experts and one benchmarking manager set out to examine AT&T's complaint handling process and to improve it by identifying best practices among leading companies from several industries. The team began by brainstorming problem areas that might help them focus their benchmarking and improvement efforts. *For example,* AT&T did not teach operator services' employees how to project a "friendly, helpful image". Discovering techniques that would enable employees to learn how to project this image would be of great benefit. Establishing high-priority problem areas also helped the team determine the scope and goals of the benchmarking study. These included setting reasonable time frames for handling complaints, developing flexible methods and procedures for complaint handling, providing statistical information for reports to management, tracking complaint status and following up after complaint handling to ensure customer satisfaction.

Ultimately the team identified 11 areas that they used as evaluation criteria for assessing other companies' complaint handling capabilities. These evaluation criteria included elements such as CEO participation in the complaint process, use of statistical reports, use of computers, use of award systems to encourage customer service, a focus on employee empowerment, and the way in which customer calls are received. Profiles of each prospective benchmarking partner and its standing on the evaluation criteria were constructed and summarised in a selection matrix, which enabled the team to make a data-driven decision on benchmarking partners to visit.

During its research, the benchmark team determined that customers complaint about different problems in different industries, but team members observed that the complaint handling process was similar across most industries. Consequently, they decided to seek best complaint handling practices without regard to industry. Ultimately the team selected three companies to be visited - a mail carrier, a hotel chain and an airline. A detailed questionnaire was developed and mailed to the benchmark partner in advance so that they understood the purpose of the visit and could have the right people in the room.

During site visits, the team worked with a carefully constructed agenda that placed the most important topics first on the schedule. One person was selected to open the meeting with a short presentation overview about AT&T, operator services and the complaint handling function. The partners reciprocated with similar presentations.

Each team member was assigned a section of the questionnaire that they were responsible for asking as well as answering if the partner wanted to learn about AT&T program.

Although AT&T was willing to share information during its site visits, the partners did most of the talking.

The AT&T team assessed its findings from the 3 visits and identified as many as 25 critical success factors to improve customer complaint handling in operator services.

With the initial benchmarking study completed, AT&T then launched the difficult process of implementation, which is a multilayer process in view of the scope of benchmarking findings. Already the company has implemented two major improvements :

1. It installed a database to track complaints and
2. It centralised the complaint handling group.

Moving forward, AT&T plans to adapt the other critical success factors it observed among its benchmark partners. The result is a dramatically improved and far more effective complaint handling system than could ever have been internally engineered.

POINTS TO REMEMBER

- After completing data acquisition and analysis, and preparing a nice report detailing how your organisation compares to competitors or other best-in-class companies in the activity you have benchmarked, implementing the improvements identified is important for the success of the benchmarking effort.
- If changes are not made, improvements are not implemented, your benchmarking might turn out to be a waste of time.
- Benchmarking studies are likely to lead you to a point where you will know where and how much you can improve. The challenge is to figure out how to make it happen.
- Implementation of improvements run the risk of making marginal improvements in many different areas but not making substantial improvements in most key areas.
- Reality considerations in the implementation stage include resource limitations - financial limitations, human limitations and time limitations.
- Obtaining commitment for change from the benchmarking team responsible for executing the improvements as well as from the line people in the benchmarking processes that need to be changed for improvement are critical for implementing benchmarking.

- All groups (both inside and outside an organisation) that might be affected by any changes that will result from the improvement program must be consulted or considered when making changes.
- While implementing improvements, the benchmarking firm must consider the competitor's strengths and weaknesses in the area of improvement.
- **Making benchmarking-driven improvements require that you include the following in your plan:**
  (i) Detailed actions including deadlines and milestones, accountability by identified managers for specific goals and performance targets that are measurable.
  (ii) Scheduled progress review.
  (iii) Rewards for successful implementation.
  (iv) Plans for contingencies and corrective actions.
  (v) Plans for periodic calibrations.
- The entire benchmarking process may be viewed as cycle based on **Shewhart's "Plan-Do-Check-Act" diagram.** The improvement process should be continuous.
- Benchmarking projects that have produced excellent reports and recommendations may fail because of ineffective or failed implementation efforts caused by poor implementation planning.
- Implementation should be regarded as one with the benchmarking process.
- Design for implementation (DFI in short) is the process of cross-functional teams concurrently planning all aspects of the benchmarking project.
- Bench mark teams must address critical implementation issues even as the benchmarking research and information gathering are being planned.
- Experience and research demonstrate that poor planning is the primary cause for benchmarking failure followed by lack of top management support and lack of process ownership.
- All process owners should be involved in the benchmarking project. If possible and feasible they must be placed on the benchmarking team.
- **The benchmarking team member should :**
  (i) Have line experience in the benchmark area.
  (ii) Represent all primary functions or areas that own or influence the benchmark subject.
  (iii) Be credible and competent in the process.
  (iv) Feel ownership and importance of the process.
  (v) Have a designated leader and
  (vi) Be team oriented and team player.
- Benchmarking is subject to learning curve effects. Benchmarking tends to grow easier, faster and more effective with practice and experience.
- Much of the experience curve effect is attained by compressing the time required to perform data gathering.
- Effective benchmarking begins by understanding your position and your needs.
- Benchmarking is a principal tool to facilitate **viscarious learning**. Visits to excellent companies can also provide excellent opportunities for viscarious learning.
- **The seven level hierarchy for viewing benchmarking applications is as below :**
  (i) Learn from past success
  (ii) Borrow good ideas
  (iii) Best in company
  (iv) Industry standard

(v) Industry leadership *(vi)* "Best-in-country" leadership

(vii) "World-class" leadership

- Best-in-class benchmarking can produce dramatic break-through. Managers can learn to integrate benchmarking as a flexible skill into various improvement and outreach approaches. Benchmarking requires judgement skill and practice.
- **Different approaches to benchmarking include :**

(i) Business as usual - "Ain't broke, don't fix it"

(ii) Good success - Discussion, performance assessment

(iii) Good ideas - "steal this idea" suggestion systems, brainstorming, attend conferences, industry literature, internal expert opinion

(iv), (v) Best-in-unit, Best-in-company – Internal benchmarking, best unit, best teams, best individuals, internal operating statistics, process analysis

(vi) Best-in-industry – competitive benchmarking : Small sample, focus on benchmarks, industry focus.

(vii) Seek optimum scope and rigour for each investigation

(viii) and (ix) Best in nation, best in world – Comprehensive benchmarking : Large sample, high level involvement, best-in-class view, comprehensive metric, use of outside expert with benchmarking data base.

REVIEW QUESTIONS

1. Discuss the three types of resource limitations.
2. Discuss the elements of the plan for making benchmarking driven improvements.
3. Describe benchmarking using "P-D-C-A" diagram.
4. Explain what is meant by "Designing for implementation success".
5. Discuss the obstacles to successful benchmarking.
6. Discuss how the benchmarking team is selected.
7. Discuss the roles and responsibilities of team members.
8. What is meant by "the benchmarking learning curve"?
9. Discuss the process of integrating benchmarking into your organisation.
10. Discuss the seven levels of benchmarking.

DISCUSSION QUESTIONS

1. "One of the biggest dangers for a benchmarking team can be that it tries to do too much at once". Do you agree or disagree? Give reasons for your answer.
2. "Many benchmarking projects have produced excellent reports and recommendations - only to be spoiled by ineffective or failed implementation efforts". – Discuss.
3. "Experience and research demonstrates that poor planning is a primary cause for benchmarking failure". – Elaborate.
4. "Benchmarking, like other management initiatives is subject to learning curve effects". – Explain.
5. "Benchmarking is viewed as the corner stone concept of viscarious learning". – Discuss.

CHAPTER 11

Benchmarking and Strategic Planning

INTRODUCTION

The benchmarking methodology is arguably the best methodology for analysing process that best-in-class companies use to execute their strategies successfully. But the benchmarking methodology - *identify the best, study them, learn from them* - can also be applied at a higher level to determine the strategies themselves that are most successful within a particular industry. In other words we can use benchmarking to analyse how a firm executes its strategy - how it designs, makes, sells and services its products. We can use benchmarking to back up a step and determine which strategies are most successful or likely to succeed in the first place. Which are the best firms in a particular industry? Why? What strategies make them so successful? Benchmarking methodology can be used to assess the strategies of participants in practically any industry. **You may find this methodology particularly useful when faced with one of the following situations:**

(i) You are considering entry into a new industry.

(ii) An industry in which you currently compete is undergoing rapid change.

(iii) You are contemplating a shift on strategy within your industry.

Strategic planning requires a thorough knowledge of the market place, the likely activities of the competition, the state-of-the-art regarding products or services being produced, financial requirements for doing a business in a market, and the customer base. ***Benchmarking*** is a useful tool for gathering information in these areas during the process of strategic planning. This type of information can literally shape a business strategy in a more realistic direction, or at least help identify the risks of doing business in certain markets.

Strategic benchmarking is concerned with comparing ***strategies*** of different companies and assessing the success of those strategies in the market place. Strategic benchmarking examines how companies compete and seek the winning strategies that have led to competitive advantages and market success.

Organisational strategies are the approaches adopted by organisations to ensure successful performance in the market place. These approaches are typically set forth in a comprehensive document called ***strategic plan***.

To survive and thrive in a globally competitive market place, organisations must adopt a broad strategy that give them sustainable ***competitive advantage***. All such strategies fall into one or more of the following categories :

(i) ***Cost leadership strategies :*** Strategies in this category seek to improve efficiency and control costs throughout an organisation's activity - cost chain.

(ii) ***Differentiation strategies :*** Strategies in this category seek to add value, as defined by customers, to the organisation's product or services. Such strategies typically involve gaining technological superiority over competitors, continually out-performing competitors in the area of quality, providing more and better support services to customers and/or providing customers more value for their money.

(iii) ***Market niche strategy :*** Strategies in this category focus on a narrowly defined segment of the market (market niche) and attempt to make the organisation in question, the market leader in that niche. Leadership can be achieved by adopting cost leadership, or differentiation strategies or both designed to appeal specifically to the target market.

ROLE OF BENCHMARKING IN STRATEGIC PLANNING

Benchmarking has not traditionally been an integral part of strategy setting and strategic planning eventhough it should have been. Without some external reference points by which to evaluate and validate an organisation's strategies, plans and goals, management is flying in the dark. Many companies that tried to fly without looking out for what others were doing and accomplishing, have crashed. If they have gathered benchmarking information in advance, many of these failed efforts might have been avoided.

The Phoenix - like resurrection of Compaq Computer Corp is one of the most dramatic examples of how easily accessible benchmarking information helped a Fortune 500 company redefine its strategy and regain market share that was lost when personal computer market suddenly turned treacherously price sensitive in the early 1990s.

The rapid market shift transformed the personal computer industry from a battle ground where leading-edge technology and quality won significant price premium and market share to a near commodity market place where advanced technology and quality are requirements of doing business and where low prices win sales. This 180 degree shift turned Compaq's originally successful strategy of providing superior technology and engineering and commanding premium prices for it-into a recipe for slow growth and declining market share.

With just this understanding, a growing number of companies have begun to use benchmarking as a critical step in the strategic planning process. By reviewing the products, prices, practices, strategies, structures and services of competition and other companies, managers can evaluate the adequacy of their own goals, plans and strategies. Planning without awareness of what your competitors are doing is like flying a plane over the Himalayas in heavy fog without any instrument controls.

Benchmarking adds a very useful navigational aid to the strategic planning process. By identifying and studying other companies, strategic benchmarking is especially useful in the following areas :

1. Determining where your organisation stands versus the competition and best performers outside your industry.
2. Validating the adequacy of short-term and long-term goals.
3. Setting and refining corporate strategy that has the highest likelyhood of succeeding.
4. Ensuring core processes that are critical to the organisation's success are competitive with the rest of the market.
5. Ensuring the company's use of technology is adequate to help it maintain its position within its chosen markets.
6. Ensuring that critical issues such as structure, price, performance, products and services are adequate to succeed against competition in your chosen markets.
7. Ensuring your supplier capabilities are adequate to enable your company to succeed in its chosen markets.
8. Identifying key factors to attain market leadership.

***Exhibit 11.1* illustrates the role of benchmarking in strategic planning.**

EXHIBIT 11.1

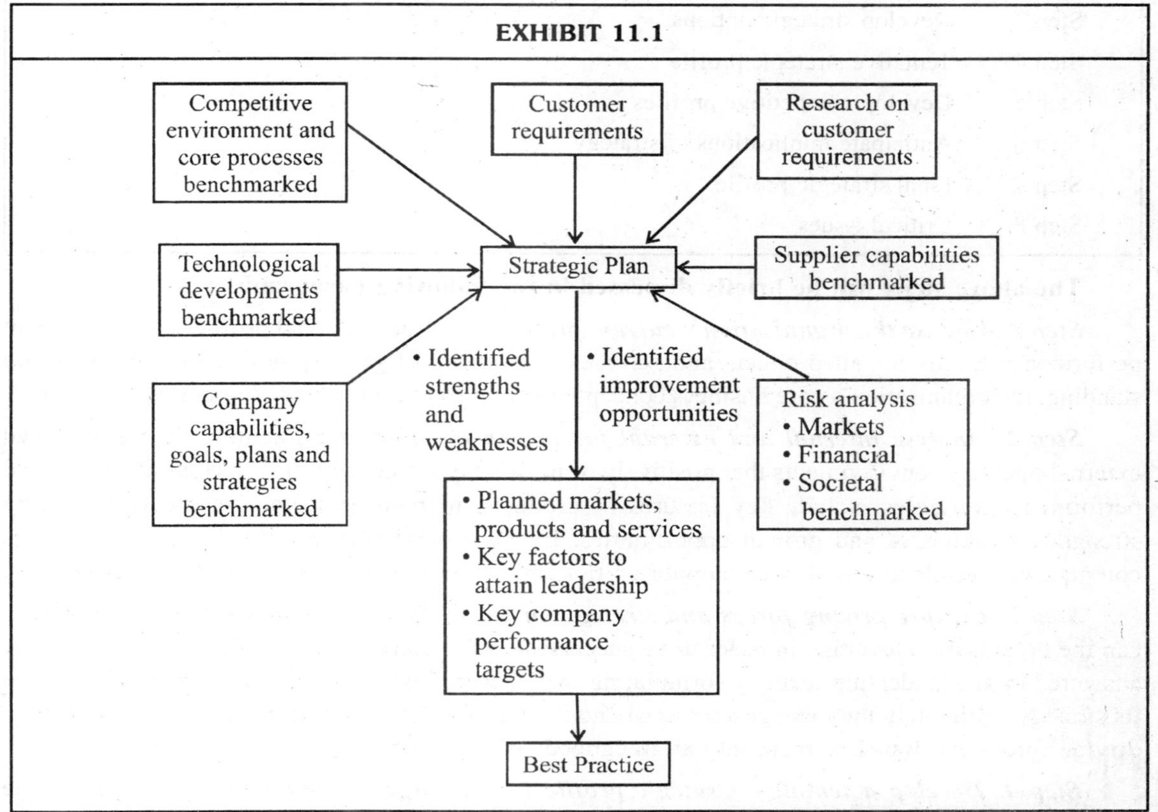

For a growing number of companies, benchmarking has become a critical part of the strategic planning process. Benchmarking is seen as an enterprise and not an operational function by many CEOs worldwide, who would never run their company without using benchmarking for strategic planning.

Strategic benchmarking enables managers to discover that another company has developed a better and more effective approach and such discoveries take place when there is still time to take advantage of the learning. This would avoid prolonged market share shrinkage, profit erosion, plant closings and repeated workforce reductions.

THE STRATEGIC THINKING PROCESS

Business strategy is not merely performing competitive analysis. An organisation must strategise and plan before developing competitive tactics.

An organisation passes through 8 steps during the strategic thinking process and benchmarking can serve as an enabling tool to ensure the success of each step in the strategic planning process. ***Box 11.1* depicts the 8 step strategic thinking process.**

BOX 11.1 : STRATEGIC THINKING PROCESS	
Step 1.	Determine current profile
Step 2.	Internal and external variables
Step 3.	Develop strategic options
Step 4.	Tentative strategic profile
Step 5.	Develop competitive profiles
Step 6.	Anticipate implications of strategy
Step 7.	Final strategic profile
Step 8.	Critical issues

The above steps will be briefly discussed in the following paragraphs :

Step 1. Analyse the organisation's current profile : An organisational profile includes current performance trends for all products and services, growth in all geographical areas, market-share standing, the organisation's core business concept or driving force and areas of operating excellence.

Step 2. Analyse internal and external performance variables : Examine the internal and external operating environments that positively or negatively influence future performance. Internal performance variables include key features of products, markets, customer segments, operating strengths, weaknesses and growth opportunities. External performance variables include various competitive considerations, strategic opportunities and strategic threats or operating vulnerabilities.

Step 3. Explore driving forces and strategic options : What skills, resources or advantages can the organisation leverage in order to be successful in the market place? This question might be answered by the leadership team by formulating two or three high-leverage areas on which to build its strategy. Ultimately the management must choose the best one or two strategic leverage points or driving forces and translate them into an integrated strategic mission, vision or operating plan.

Step 4. Develop a tentative strategic profile for the organisation : The strategic profile articulates the fundamental business concept, including areas of excellence that will exceed competitor's performance. It also delineates key milestones or implementation time frames and it may pinpoint future products to be emphasised and deemphasised. The strategic profile identifies target markets and customer segments, defines corporate beliefs and values, delineates market size, growth rates and expected returns on investment and profit margins.

Step 5. Develop competition profiles : The organisation's management assembles similar profiles for three or four major competitors, scrutinising the competition's products, services, prices and market selections. By examining competitor's profiles over a period of years, management can better anticipate the course each competitor is likely to pursue in the short-term future.

Step 6. Test and evaluate the implications of the organisation's proposed strategic course : By testing the organisation's current profile, management can better assess the extent of change required to fulfil its strategic vision. The leadership wants to be certain that important operating strengths are fully exploited, weaknesses are minimised, key beliefs are not violated, major opportunities are exploited, and major threats are avoided. Management also wants to match its strategic profile against competitor profiles to ensure that the organisation's adopted strategy accurately reflects the competitor's strengths, weaknesses and current and future actions. These strategic profile tests suggest how the organisation's strategy can be modified and strengthened.

Step 7. Finalise the strategic profile : At this step, management reshapes and fine-tunes the strategy by addressing issues that surface during the various tests conducted in step 6.

Step 8. Resolve any remaining critical issues : In this step management resolves any critical issues surfaced through strategic profile analysis. Such ***critical issues*** include but are not limited to considerations of organisational structure, core operating systems, workforce skills and compensation systems.

Strategic thinking is iterative or evolutionary. It typically reflects the contributions of many people including the CEO, president and other members of the senior - management team. **The strongest strategic profiles are anchored on your corner stone decision areas :**

(i) Pinpoint which products and services will be emphasised in the future.

(ii) Identify which customers will receive these products and services.

(iii) Define which market segment will and will not be pursued.

(iv) Outline which geographic markets will and will not be developed.

As a business process, benchmarking consequently adds an all-purpose tool to the strategic planning process.

STRATEGY ASSESSMENT USING BENCHMARKING

Like any benchmarking project, strategy assessment using benchmarking is not an entirely sequential process. **The following steps are presented in an order that roughly approximates the optimal way to approach a strategy assessment study:**

1. Analyse the Overall Industry

This first step is imperative in any type of strategy assessment study. An understanding of the industry structure, its potential for profitability, the state of competition within it and its likely evolutionary path is the foundation for this piece of the study. Michael Porter's five forces (*viz.*, *(i)* Threat of new entrants, *(ii)* Bargaining power of buyers, *(iii)* Threat of substitutes, *(iv)* Bargaining power of suppliers and *(iv)* Intensity of rivalry and other frame works are superb tools for structuring this portion of the study.

2. Identify the Most Successful Firms

Success can be measured in many ways in identifying firms whose strategies you may wish to study. **These measures include :**

(i) ***Superior financial results :*** These include profits, return on sales, return on equity, return on capital employed etc. When identifying firms with superior financial results, it is important to analyse trends with superior financial results into the future. A relatively new measure intended to provide an indication of a company's quality is ***"added value".*** This measure is calculated by subtracting a capital charge from depreciation-adjusted operating profits.

(ii) ***Superior market share :*** Firms with superior market share might not always find their way into the list of firms with superior financial results. This may be the case because the market leader is posturing for the long-run, knowing that higher market share may eventually lead to dominance in the industry. The highest market share and the highest cumulative volume that accompanies it, frequently results in a significant cost advantage in an industry due to the effects of the ***experience curve***.

(iii) ***Growth :*** Fast growing firms might be in neither of the above categories today, but their strategies may be propelling them toward one or both in the future. Another reason a firm contemplating entry into an industry might wish to look at young, fast growing firms is that there may be many parallels between the issues those firms have faced in the industry and those you may face during your entrance period.

3. Analyse the Most Successful Firms Individually

Analysis should encompass, at a minimum, financial results, strategies and processes in the firm's overall business system.

(i) ***Financial results :*** Keeping in mind that accounting differences can skew results and make comparison among firms less meaningful, you should nevertheless be sure to look at some basic financial measures. When possible, look at the following measures at the lowest level possible within the target organisation.

(a) ***Growth :*** Compound annual growth rates in revenues, earning before interest and taxes, net income and assets.

(b) ***Liquidity :*** Current ratio, acid tests etc.

(c) ***Profitability :*** Return on sales, return on assets, return on equity and return on capital employed.

(d) ***Asset utilisation :*** Day's sales outstanding in receivables, day's cost of goods sold, outstanding in inventory and payables, working capital/sales and fixed costs/sales.

(e) ***Leverage :*** Debt to total capital, debt to equity, debt to total assets, interest coverage and fixed-charge coverage.

(ii) ***Strategies :*** Identify each firm's strategy. Is it the overall low-cost producer? If not, how does the firm differentiate its products or services to make buyers perceive higher value and hence pay a higher price?

You should be able to articulate clearly, on macro level, each firm's strategy, using a few sentences. The next step in the analysis - breaking down each firm into its business system -

will shed a lot more light on your preliminary assessment of each firm's strategy and may cause you to rethink it.

(iii) ***Business systems :*** Using Porter's value chain or some variation of it that best fits the firms in the industry you are analysing, break down each firm into its processes. ***Exhibit 11.2* shows a simplified business system for information technology industry.**

EXHIBIT 11.2 : SIMPLIFIED BUSINESS SYSTEM FOR INFORMATION TECHNOLOGY INDUSTRY

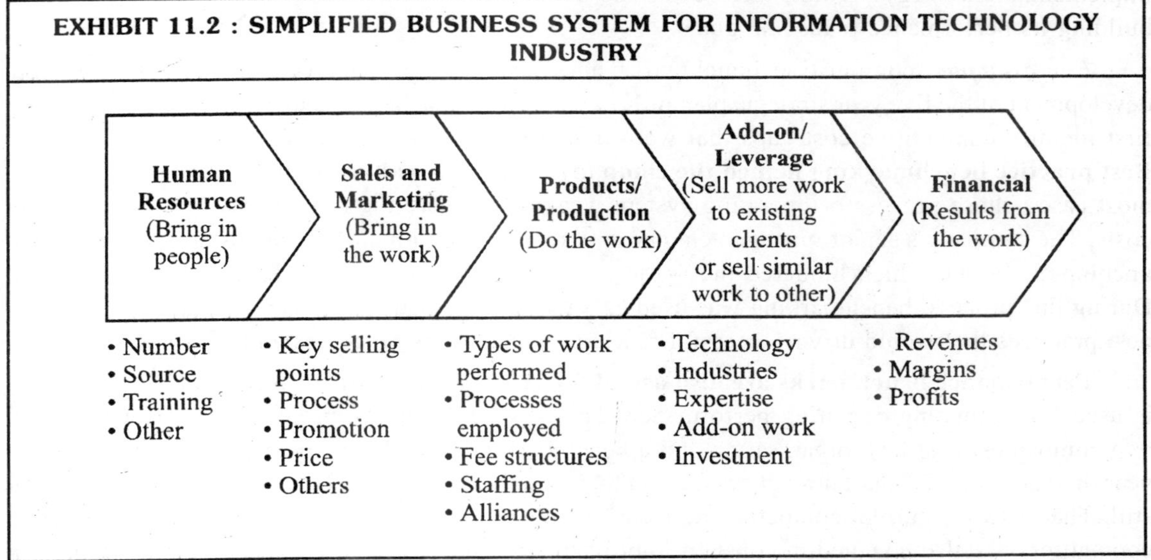

While simplistic, the analysis provided fit the benchmarking team's needs on that particular study. A good rule of thumb is to begin with a comprehensive business system like **"Porter's value chain"** rather than a simplified version of it. Cutting back on the analysis as you go is generally easier than adding it.

When you are looking at each firm's business system, be sure to analyse its upstream and downstream linkages. Careful analysis of relationships with suppliers and customers can reveal keys to strategy that might go unnoticed if the focus is entirely on the internal workings of the firm.

4. Compare the Most Successful Firms

Finally, taking the above analyses, now compare all firms against one another. Look for relationships among the various analyses and ask the two big questions : Why? So what?

Strategic Benchmarks and Competitive Projections

Before setting strategy, the organisation must establish its current position. Managers can do this most effectively by developing base line measures or benchmarks that help define where their organisations stand compared to the competition. Strategic variables, such as market share, customer satisfaction standing, product and service performance (such as defect rates, cycle time, and warranty data), productivity and cost, all help delineate an organisation's competitive position. Other benchmark measures, such as growth rates, profitability, return on assets, or return on equity, may also be useful in evaluating your organisation's relative performance standing.

Analysing strategic performance variables is straight forward. Assemble benchmark profiles for three or four primary competitors. Then compare their benchmark measures with your organisation's to identify your relative strengths and weaknesses and to spot competitive opportunities or threats. Do your organisation's perceived strengths seem consistent and intact after careful comparison with competitor? Under scrutiny, do your strengths remain the basis for a sound, implementable strategy? If not, then revise the strategic foundation on which the organisation is building its performance plans and goals.

For example, competitive benchmarks and best practices played a leading role in the development of the five year strategic plan of XYZ company. Benchmark analysis helped the company first identify competitive cost gaps that were traced to broken, outdated or inefficient processes. **Best practice benchmarking helped the company diagnose weaknesses in its core processes.** In most cases, those process or operating system weaknesses were the root causes of uncompetitive costs. The company's senior management chose to reengineer all major processes that were deemed uncompetitive and which hindered the organisation from achieving its strategic plans and goals. During this process, benchmarking was used as a tool that helped reengineering teams identify the best practices that would drive successful redesign efforts in its processes and systems.

Performance benchmarks are also useful for creating competitive forecasts. The 'Z' chart is used for evaluating operating performance. The 'Z' chart maps or projects the performance of two companies - the host organisation and a benchmark or competitor organisation – over a multi year time horizon. 'Z' chart dramatises the fact that organisations compete in full motion-not standing still. That is to say current competitor performance positions are sure to change because all worthy competitors are also engaged in constant improvement efforts. If your organisation takes a year to match a competitor's current position, expect that the competitor will have advanced by the time your organisation reaches the competitor's original position. Many companies have seen their strategic plans fail because they judged a competitor's capabilities based only on current position, rather than by determining where the competition would move based on its current position and the velocity of historical improvement rate. Therefore, managers must aim ahead of their targets, plotting a performance improvement trajectory that accelerates faster than their opponents' and aims into the future, if they are to do better than their competitors in the market place. (***Exhibit 11.3* demonstrates the creation of a 'Z' chart**).

Benchmarking and Improvement Planning

Benchmarking can inspire incremental improvements (continuous improvement) and major leap-frog advances (break-through improvement). Both applications empower ongoing improvement planning which girds every company's strategic planning process. The current Baldrige criteria speak directly to this linkage among benchmarks, benchmarking, and continuous improvement plans and objectives. The current Baldrige criteria observe the following about the dynamic role performance indicators and benchmarks play in during both incremental and breakthrough improvements.

"Non prescriptive, results-oriented criteria and key measures and indicators focus on ***what*** needs to be improved". This approach helps to ensure that improvements throughout the organisation contribute to the organisation's overall objectives. Results-oriented criteria and key measures and indicators encourage **"breakthrough thinking"** - openness to the possibility of major improvements as well as to incremental improvements. However, if key measures and indicators are tied too directly to existing work methods, processes and organisations, breakthrough changes may be discouraged. For this reason, analysis of operations, processes and progress should focus on the selection of and the value of measures and indicators themselves. This will help to ensure that measure and indicator selection does not stifle creativity and prevent beneficial changes (reengineering) in organisation or work processes.

EXHIBIT 11.3 : THE 'Z'-CHART

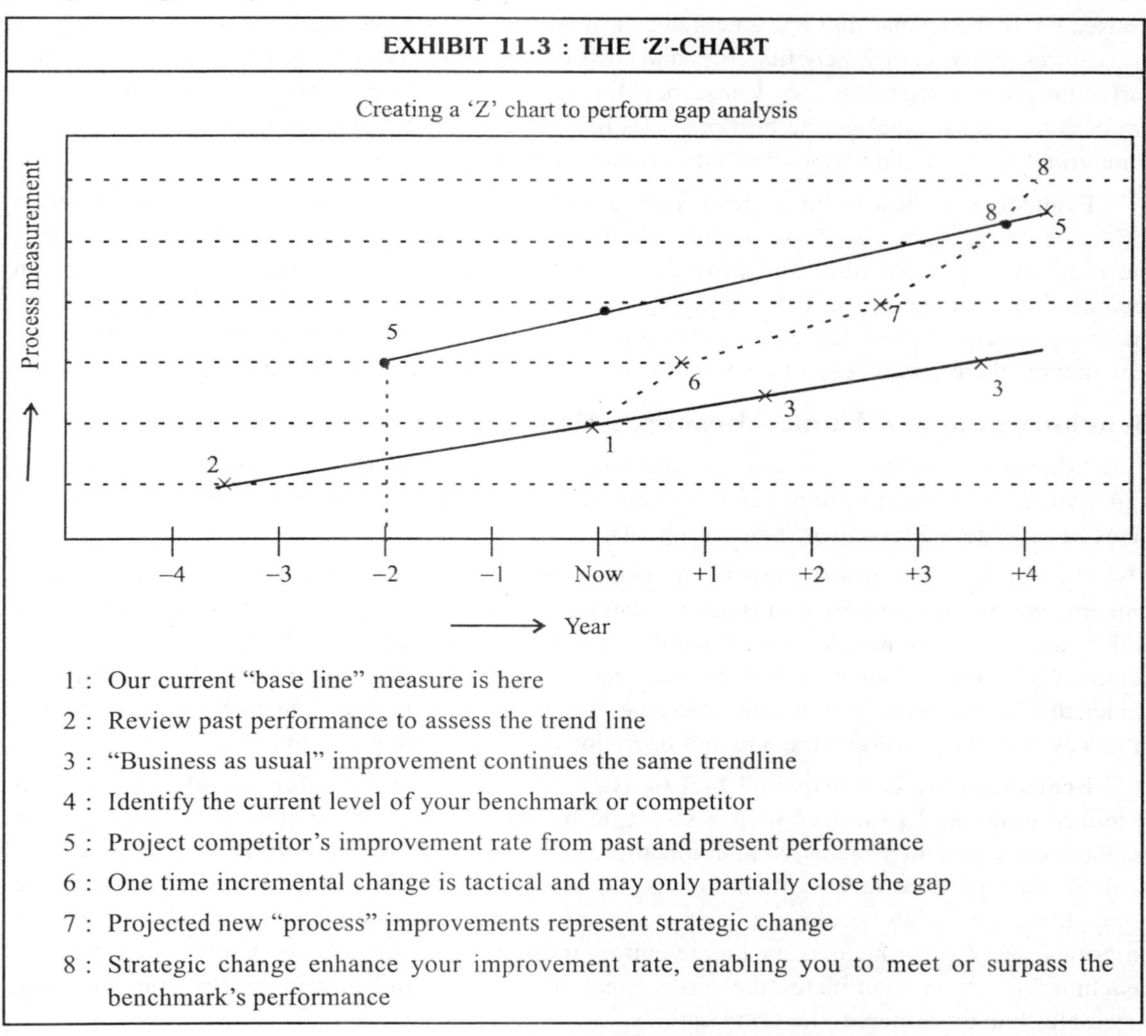

1 : Our current "base line" measure is here

2 : Review past performance to assess the trend line

3 : "Business as usual" improvement continues the same trendline

4 : Identify the current level of your benchmark or competitor

5 : Project competitor's improvement rate from past and present performance

6 : One time incremental change is tactical and may only partially close the gap

7 : Projected new "process" improvements represent strategic change

8 : Strategic change enhance your improvement rate, enabling you to meet or surpass the benchmark's performance

Benchmarks may also serve a useful purpose in stimulating breakthrough thinking. Benchmarks offer the opportunity to achieve significant improvements based on adoption or adaptation of current best practice. As with key measures and indicators, benchmarks selection is critical, and benchmarks should be reviewed periodically for appropriateness.

Benchmarking and the Strategic use of Technology

Many "blue-chip" companies in the US such as American Airlines, Federal Express, Pepsico's Frito-Lay, Wal-Mart etc., have used technology to help them achieve competitive advantages against competitors. When managed well, technology can enhance value to customers, reduce cycle times simplify complex processes and improve costs and productivity - all to the strategic advantage of the corporation. When poorly managed, technology may cause more harm to the organisation. Consequently, benchmarking has emerged as a fundamental tool helping managers better evaluate the features, functionality, benefits, roles and costs of technology. Various benchmarks are a familiar part of the information technology landscape. More over increasing number of information technology professionals are evaluating the best practices of different systems and procedures in the world of computing, telecommunications and other broad-based technologies.

Evaluating the best technologies is only one of benchmarking's many uses in the information technology area. As a management tool, benchmarking provides valuable information concerning the most effective practices and procedures to utilise existing technologies in support of an organisation's strategic plan. Consequently, best practice studies have mushroomed in technology-intensive areas that are strategic corner stones for many organisations. Many organisational processes that support the effective use of technology are linchpins in effective strategy implementation.

Benchmarking and Human Resource Management

"Managing people" - eventhough regarded as the "soft-side" of most business operations, is important because organisations need to integrate the people-side of operations into their strategic plans in order to achieve their long-term goals.

Human resource development and management are so essential to successful strategy implementation that the Malcolm Baldrige National Quality Award assessment criteria dedicate an entire category to the people side of quality. The Baldrige guidelines begin their exploration of a company's human resource system by examing "Human Resources Planning and Management". Under this item, Baldrige applicants describe how they integrate their human resource plans and practices with their overall strategic and operational performance goals and plans.

Benchmarking is a principal tool to assist managers in their effort to integrate human resource plans and practices with a strategic business plan. For companies that view human resource management as a source of competitive advantage, placing the right people with the right skills in the right jobs and then continuously developing and retaining those people are strategic imperatives. Operating benchmarks help managers evaluate their unit's position and performance on critical work force factors, such as retention, training, learning and productivity. Best practice benchmarking then illuminates the most effective practices and procedures for implementing successful human resource plans and actions.

Ritz-Carlton Hotels, a 1992 Baldrige Award winner, has integrated a unique system of benchmarks into the very fabric of its human resource recruitment and selection system. This luxury hotel chain invests significant time, energy, staff and capital to nurture a corporate culture that is passionately devoted to customer service and these human resource benchmarks enable managers to make better hiring decisions. Ritz-Carlton has performed comparative studies to identify and profile the personality traits of the best performing employees in every major job classification within its hotels. Used as a preliminary performance indicator, the Ritz-Carlton personality trait selection system has proven highly effective, enabling Ritz-Carlton hotels to hire better and retain employees longer than other competitors.

Human resource benchmarking is more compelling because many generic processes apply to human resource functions across many industries and organisations; generic processes such as selection and recruiting, orientation, training, development, reward and recognition and performance evaluations, apply to nearly all industries and organisations. This fact makes cross-industry comparisons and learning much easier and more powerful. **Human resource benchmarking has been especially active in the following six operating areas :**

(i) Recruitment and selection

(ii) Employee education and development

(iii) Employee relations

(iv) Reward, recognition, benefits and compensation system

(v) High-performance work teams, self-directed work teams, employee involvement and empowerment

(vi) Work force composition, diversity, scheduling and well being.

Benchmarking and Supplier's Capabilities

World-class organisations increasingly link their operating strategies to the direct capabilities of their suppliers. An organisation can not be world-class if the companies supplying its materials, parts, labour or other components are third rate. If a company is going to be a benchmark supplier of equipment, its suppliers need to be benchmark suppliers of parts.

Xerox, *for example,* regards suppliers as partners or joint venture associates in its business; consequently, Xerox has cut its supplier base from more than 5000 in the early 1980s to 420 in 1993. Xerox works closely with this small cadre of suppliers - awarding them multiyear contracts, sharing business plans and operating information, inviting them into the new product design and development process, providing them with clear quality specifications and with training so they can achieve these aggressive standards.

When viewed in such a light - as operating partners, suppliers assume much greater importance in the strategic planning process. Consequently, developing capable suppliers is of strategic importance for organisations such as xerox and growing number of other leading companies. With capable suppliers, an organisation has a better chance of succeeding in its chosen markets. Benchmarking in turn helps the organisation measure and assess its supplier's relative capabilities in a fast-moving and competitive business environment. Such information is vital for working with suppliers to define, develop, and communicate quality standards and to set meaningful improvement plans. Xerox's supplier management system ensures that suppliers are enablers, not disablers of the companies' strategic plans.

Borrowing Strategies and Projecting Success

All successful companies are captives of their culture, prisoners of the traditional paradigms through which they have previously competed. A survey of winning organisations around the world quickly reveals there are many strategies on which they can successfully compete. Consequently, a growing number of organisations are studying the strategies of other successful enterprises and adapting the best aspects of battle-tested strategies.

Benchmarking enables an organisation to develop, refine or improve its strategy by observing and adapting the competitive approaches of other successful enterprises.

Benchmarking is not an after thought of organisations that are highly skilled at strategic planning. It is not a one-time event to fulfill a reporting requirement of the budget cycle. Quite the contrary, benchmarking is a hall-mark of effective strategy development. It is an on-going enabler of strategic design, strategic planning and strategic thinking.

BOX 11.2 : BENCHMARKING IN PRACTICE – BATH IRON WORKS DEVELOPS A WINNING STRATEGY THROUGH BENCHMARKING

In the 1980s, Bath Iron Works, the fourth largest shipyard in the United States, had allowed itself to become a one-customer company, completely beholden to the U.S. Navy. When the cold war ended abruptly in 1991, the Navy no longer needed to build large combat ships. This reverse trend in customer needs threatened the very existence of Bath Iron Works. Bath CEO Duane D. "Buzz" Fitzerald determined that his company had to devise a new strategic plan. Rather than start from scratch, though, Fitzerald sent a four person team of vice presidents to perform strategic benchmarking at ten shipyards in Holland, which had already undergone a defence conversion. Bath benchmarks found Dutch shipbuilders applying their core competencies or capabilities to design and construct boilers, nuclear containment vessels, and bridges - in addition to shipbuilding. These strategic benchmarking explorations enabled Bath Iron Works to reconceptualise its essential strengths and its future strategic course. Bath CEO Fitzerald eventually concluded. "May be our core competency is not shipbuilding but rather than the design, manufacture, integration, and testing of complex structures. Certainly that would include ships, but it is much broader than just ships".

Rather than develop a strategy from scratch, Bath Iron Works used benchmarking to examine the winning strategies and approaches of companies that were phasing themselves out of or diversifying within the combat shipping business. Benchmarking encourages Bath to abandon its narrowly conceived product orientation and become much more market oriented. Benchmarking helped Bath reconceive its traditional strengths and reinvent its future options. Other companies's success, failures, approaches and lessons learnt - all gleaned through benchmarking - provide valuable evidence by which to formulate and predict the potential success of a strategic plan.

POINTS TO REMEMBER

- Benchmarking can be used to analyse how a firm executes its strategy - how it designs, makes, sells and services its products.
- Benchmarking methodology can be used to assess the strategies of participants in practically any industry.
- **Strategic planning** requires a thorough knowledge of the market place, the likely activities of the competition, the state-of-the-art regarding products or services being produced, financial requirements for doing a business in a market and the customer base. Benchmarking is a useful tool for gathering information in these areas during the process of strategic planning.
- **Strategic benchmarking** is concerned with comparing strategies of different companies and assessing the success of those strategies in the market place.
- A growing number of companies have begun to use benchmarking as a critical step in the strategic planning process.

- Benchmarking adds a very useful navigational aid to the strategic planning process.
- For a growing number of companies, benchmarking has become a critical part of the strategic planning process.
- An organisation passes through **eight** steps during the strategic thinking process and benchmarking can serve as an enabling tool to ensure success of each step in the strategic planning process.
- **The eight steps in strategic planning process are :**
  - *(i)* Determine current profile
  - *(ii)* Analyse internal and external variables
  - *(iii)* Develop strategic options
  - *(iv)* Develop tentative strategic profile
  - *(v)* Develop competitive profiles
  - *(vi)* Anticipate implications of strategy
  - *(vii)* Finalise the strategic profile
  - *(viii)* Resolve any remaining critical issues
- **The steps involved in strategy assessment using benchmarking are :**
  - *(i)* Analyse the overall industry
  - *(ii)* Identify the most successful firms
  - *(iii)* Analyse the most successful firms individually
  - *(iv)* Compare the most successful firms
- Benchmarking can inspire incremental improvements (continuous improvement) and major leap-frog advances (break-through improvement). Both applications empower ongoing improvement planning which girds every company's strategic planning process.
- Benchmarking may also serve a useful purpose in stimulating breakthrough thinking.
- Benchmarking is a principal tool to assist managers in their effort to integrate human resource plans and practices with a strategic business plan.
- Human resource development and management are essential to successful strategy implementation.
- **Human resource benchmarking** is more compelling because many generic processes apply to human resource functions across many industries and organisations, generic processes such as selection and recruiting, orientation, training, development, reward and recognition and performance evaluations, apply to nearly all industries and organisations.
- Developing capable suppliers is of strategic importance for organisations. With capable suppliers, an organisation has a better chance of succeeding in its chosen markets. Benchmarking in turn helps the organisation measure and assess its supplier's relative capabilities in a fast-moving and competitive business environment.
- Benchmarking enables an organisation to develop, refine or improve its strategy by observing and adapting the competitive approaches of other successful enterprises.

REVIEW QUESTIONS

1. Discuss the terms *(a)* strategic planning, *(b)* strategic benchmarking and *(c)* organisational strategies.
2. Discuss the role of benchmarking in strategic planning with a block diagram.
3. Discuss the areas in which strategic benchmarking is useful.
4. What is "strategic thinking process"?
5. Discuss the 8 steps involved in the strategic thinking process.
6. Discuss the steps involved in strategy assessment using benchmarking.

7. Describe how 'Z' chart is used for evaluating operating performance and projecting the performance of the host organisation and a benchmark or competitor organisation.
8. Discuss the role of benchmarking in helping an organisation evaluate it supplier's capabilities and manage its supplier relations to support strategy.

DISCUSSION QUESTIONS

1. "Benchmarking adds a very useful navigational aid to the strategic planning process" – Discuss.
2. "Benchmarking can inspire incremental improvements and major magnitude leap-frog advances" – Elaborate.
3. "Benchmarking stimulates long-term planning to ensure core business process remain competitive" – Explain.
4. "Benchmarking identifies best practices for employing technology to support long-term strategy" – Do you agree or disagree? Give reasons for your answer.
5. "Benchmarking establishes the best human resource practices to fully develop employees and realise workforce potential in support of the organisation's strategy" – Discuss.

CHAPTER 12

Benchmarking Leadership and Management Process

INTRODUCTION

Benchmarking activities can be classified into two distinct processes : *(i) the user process* and *(ii) the management process*. The user process is the exercise of the benchmarking steps (*e.g.,* the 10-step benchmarking process). It is used as a map to be followed up by the benchmarking team. The management process consists of all other activities required to ensure that effective benchmarking investigations are conducted and results are implemented.

There are several ways to examine the benchmarking management process. The ***process perspective*** covers starting, supporting and sustaining the benchmarking process. The user process is also started, supported and sustained like the management process.

Another to examine the benchmarking management process is to categorise the management activities as those that are needed to set-up a benchmarking program and those that are needed to manage the activities over time.

It is also possible to describe the management process in terms of its owners and suppliers, its inputs and outputs, its source and destination processes, its customers, its customer requirements and supplier specifications, and its measurements, inspection methods, and resources. As a part of this documentation a flow chart is created to provide a visual representation of the process.

Of all these ways to examine benchmarking management process, the most useful one is the process perspective. **Thus the benchmarking management process should categorise management activities into establishing, supporting and sustaining a benchmarking program.**

BENCHMARKING AND LEADERSHIP

Actions of leadership is the most powerful communications tools in performance improvement. Accordingly, many corporations are challenging their senior executives to model the behaviours, attitudes, values, skills and actions that they advocate for the organisation. Already a powerful tool of front-line operating managers, professional staff and front-line teams, benchmarking has far-reaching potential for senior executives, CEOs and corporate directors.

Borrowing best practices from market leaders and world-class performers is an effective way to manage change and to supercharge continuous improvement. A clear and steady focus on best practices can provide the impetus for change, can help identify what must change and can provide a clear picture of the end point after change. Benchmarking should, therefore be a common practice among every organisation's leadership team.

Best practices benchmarking has *at least five* critical, high-level applications from which senior executives and board members can benefit. They are as follows :

1. Benchmarking enables executive officer and directors to know where their corporations stand versus the best.
2. Benchmarking is a practical tool for creating a fast-learning organisational culture that is dedicated to continuous improvement.
3. Benchmarking is an essential prerequisite for strategic planning to attain market leadership.
4. Benchmarking is a break through technique to accomplish organisational restructuring, reengineering or redesign.
5. Benchmarking is a valuable tool to assist board members in performing their duties of corporate governance and oversight.

Understanding Where Your Corporation Stands Versus the Best

Benchmarking emerges as a leadership responsibility of first order importance. To be effective leaders, managers must be aware of other corporations' strategies, tactics and operating successes. Senior executives, directors and their corporations need to "know where they stand" relative to competitors and best practice performing organisations. Enlightened leaders recognise that they can learn valuable lessons from outside their corporations and even outside their industries. That is why the search for best practices - inside and outside one's own organisation and industry - is a fundamental part of total quality management. After internal improvement efforts get underway, fast-learning organisations inevitably search outside themselves to other units, companies, and industries, they seek to accelerate their own performance improvements by studying others' best practices. **The goal of all quality and benchmarking initiatives is the same : *"to target and achieve total performance excellence"*.** That means benchmarking serves to continuously improve products, services, sales, profits, cost management, customer satisfaction, employee satisfaction and all other measures of financial and nonfinancial success. As a performance improvement tool, benchmarking is a vital instrument of leadership.

Leaders Set the Culture

Roger Milliken, CEO of Milliken & Company, has created a **"we-can-learn-from-everyone"** corporate culture at the South Carolina textile company in the US. Innovative adaptation or creative imitation is the operative concept encouraging employees of Milliken and Company to look outside their work groups, business units and corporation for ideas that help them continuously improve performance. Roger Milliken supports this active learning culture with personal actions that reinforce the stated values of a fast-learning organisation.

Every senior manager would do well to consider what effect his or her own actions have in developing an operating environment conducive to benchmarking, innovative adaptation, and fast learning. **The Baldrige Criteria for organisational performance excellence systematically probe leadership role in supporting benchmarking as an enabler of continuous improvement.**

While many executives say that they support benchmarking as an activity that fosters quality excellence, however, a gap often exists between managerial intentions and management's supporting actions. In a Best Practices Benchmarking and Consulting Inc. survey of the 80 most senior or executives of a multinational corporation, all operating executives indicated that they frequently attempt to learn about competitors, and most executives said that they "visibly support benchmarking as an activity that fosters quality excellence". However, in many instances, managerial systems and actions did not support or encourage benchmarking and active learning through comparisons and outreach. For instance, benchmarking primarily concerned ***price*** and ***product feature*** comparisons. It did not examine a wider range of operating issues, such as process capability, quality, new product development success, or speed to market. Moreover, managerial systems, such as reward and recognition, performance appraisals, information sharing networks, and the strategic planning process did not support benchmarking in this multinational corporation.

Benchmarking Project Champions

Benchmarking studies are typically most effective when conducted by front-line managers and employees who actually operate the systems and processes under examination, yet benchmarking projects produce suboptimal results if the senior leadership doesn't champion these projects. Clearly senior executives play a leading role in determining the success of benchmarking projects. Senior executives' influence is often disproportionately larger than the actual time and distinct involvement they may indicate to any given project. This is especially true of complex process benchmarking projects.

In the American Productivity and Quality Centre's 1992 survey of 87 companies active in benchmarking, the findings were as below :

(i) 61 percent of respondents stated that ***"no top management support"*** was a "great or very great factor" influencing unsuccessful benchmarking effort. ***Senior management support*** ranked second, behind poor planning as the most frequent reason for failure of a benchmarking study.

(ii) 98 percent of benchmark respondents observed that ***process owner involvement*** was of "great or very great importance" in a successful benchmarking study. This involvement may extend to senior executive team members who are responsible for championing individual processes that are critical to organisation's success.

(iii) 83 percent of benchmark survey respondents indicated that top management commitment was of "great or very great importance" in encouraging benchmarking within the respondent's organisations. In fact, ***"top management commitment"*** was the most frequently cited factor encouraging benchmarking in the surveyed organisations.

From these survey findings, it is evident that senior executives play a critical role - both direct and indirect - in enabling benchmarking investigations and best practice improvement strategies to succeed.

Monitoring the Competition

Benchmarking prompts senior managers to focus systematically on the competition. More over it expands the typical competitive scrutiny beyond price and product feature comparisons.

"Power benchmarking" which embraces process comparisons, performance comparisons and strategic comparisons, embraces the widest range of operating areas. It includes - but not limited to examination of process capability, organisational structure, quality, reliability, warranty costs, cycle times, human resource management, technology management, and many other important competitive factors.

Benchmarking provides senior executives a structured approach by which to develop competitor information. The information may be process-oriented, performance-oriented, or strategic in nature. Moreover, best practices benchmarking provides a systematic process for evaluating the adequacy of one's own position and course relative to competitors. Whether you manage a multinational corporation or a professional sports team, awareness of one's competitors is critical for successful leadership.

Leadership Actions

What can senior executives and board members do to put benchmarking to work in the executive office and board room? How can an organisation's leadership foster creative adaptation throughout the corporation? **Here are some action strategies observed in different companies stretching across diverse industries:**

1. Employ competitive benchmarks to provide an external context for operating reviews.
2. Require benchmarks as part of the strategic planning process.
3. Use benchmarking information to establish aggressive goals and standards.
4. Study the strategies and core processes of other excellent companies.
5. Use benchmarking information to evaluate and improve organisational structure.
6. Review the products, services and practices of other companies and visit their facilities whenever possible.
7. Invest in employee education to bring outside ideas into your organisation.
8. Reward and recognise creative adaptation or the borrowing of good ideas and systems.
9. Invite customers, suppliers and other outside speakers to share their ideas and strategies with your employees.
10. Make best practice information sharing and innovative adaptation a skill evaluated in the performance review and promotion process.
11. Actively promote and publicise the benefits of borrowing from the best.
12. Sponsor regular meetings and discussions where employees and managers exchange ideas and explore best practices.
13. Make benchmarking a responsibility delineated in senior-level job descriptions.
14. Employ best practice information in the problem-solving and continuous improvement process.
15. Link compensation to improvement against benchmarks in core operating functions.
16. Focus organisational resources in identifying and deploying best practices as well as on other quality-improvement strategies, such as defect reduction and error removal.
17. Study what competitors and other leading companies are doing before making major business decisions and capital investments.
18. Lay out work areas to encourage idea sharing and information exchange.

BENCHMARKING MANAGEMENT PROCESS

Earlier in this chapter, we mentioned that the process perspective of benchmarking management process covers three activities namely :

(i) Establishing a benchmarking program.

(ii) Supporting a benchmarking program and

(iii) Sustaining a benchmarking program.

We will discuss these activities in detail in the following section.

1. Establishing a Benchmarking Program

Key components of establishing a benchmarking program include the following activities:

(i) Developing a strategy statement

(ii) Setting expectations

(iii) Providing management awareness

(iv) Establishing a competency centre

(v) Developing guidelines

(vi) Establishing a network

Each of these components is examined in the following section :

(i) Developing a Strategy Statement

At any one point of time, large organisations may have many improvement activities underway, *for example*, total quality management, statistical process control, quality function deployment etc. All these activities are focussed on the reduction of errors and the prevention of defects for overall continuous improvement. Benchmarking is another quality initiative that can be pursued to change and improve an organisation's operation with particular focus on improvement of the business processes.

When benchmarking is introduced, it is important that employees know where it fits in with the existing initiatives. Also employees need to have some rationale for why benchmarking is being pursued. Therefore, a strategy statement which indicates **what** and **why** for benchmarking is desirable. The strategy statement goes a long way toward legitimizing benchmarking. People responsible for benchmarking should be able to state what its strategy is and should gain acceptance from senior management.

One strategy might be the outgrowth of an organisation pursuit of quality and continuous improvement through business process improvement. High-performing business processes allow an organisation to anticipate and react to customer needs more quickly and better than others, and consequently deliver leading-edge customer satisfaction.

If that is the stated perspective of the organisation, then a complementary benchmarking strategy statement could be as follows :

Benchmarking goal : To improve customer satisfaction and business results by continuously searching for and incorporating best practices in work processes.

Benchmarking strategy : To continuously improve work processes to produce better outputs by *(a)* focusing major benchmarking efforts on finding and implementing best practices in key work processes, *(b)* maintaining a critical few benchmark summary output measures as indicators of progress.

This strategy rationale is a direct outgrowth of the organisation's stated objective of improving work processes and benchmarking initiative is specifically linked to the rationale. In effect, it notifies the organisation that superior customer satisfaction and business results are delivered by outputs from high-performing work processes and these processes are based on methods or practices that are the benchmark, namely the best in industry and increasingly world-class.

(ii) Setting Expectations

Next to having a strategy statement is for management to have some stated expectations for benchmarking activities. Two considerations include :

(a) Management wants the benchmarking activity to be continuous and the basis for continuous improvement, not a one-time event.

(b) There are specific management deliverables expected that are requirements for tracking the status of benchmarking activities and for inspecting the benchmarking process. **An example of such a direction - setting statement is shown in *Box 12.1*.**

How benchmarking activities will become continuous must be considered. The key to this need is identifying existing, continuous management activities. There are three activities that are common to most organisations - *(a)* Creation of a business plan, *(b)* Development of an annual or operating plan, and *(c)* On-going operations review. It is logical to have benchmarking a specific requirement in each activity to ensure its permanence and continuity. It is in these documents and activities that benchmarking should be reported. In the business plan, benchmarking supports the focus on priorities and developing objectives to meet customer requirements.

BOX 12.1 : DIRECTION SETTING STATEMENT
(i) Benchmarking is incorporated into the planning process to ensure its continuity and its institutionalisation in the organisation. *(ii)* Benchmarking is part of business process management to ensure that processes are based on incorporation of best practices. *(iii)* Benchmarking is used to provide objective, external comparisons and fact based decisions.

In the annual or operating plan the focus is on specific objectives and on validating the process capability to implement best practices.

Since the focus of operation reviews is on action plans, concentration should be on the vital few practices and inspection.

The specific management deliverables expected in these documents and reviews must be considered next. These deliverables are stated as five requirements: *(a)* a strategy statement, *(b)* identification of key products, services and processes benchmarked, *(c)* reporting of a vital few performance measurements remained as benchmarks, *(d)* a prioritisation of benchmarking activities and *(e)* contribution to business results.

(iii) Providing Management Awareness

Management awareness for benchmarking is required. Managers will need to know what benchmarking is so there is consistent understanding throughout the organisation. This serves as a common basis on which to make decisions about starting benchmarking activities.

The objective of management awareness is to perform a readiness check for establishing and sustaining benchmarking.

(iv) Establishing a Competency Centre

Organisations and benchmarking teams need assistance. They may need facilitators or trainers, consultants and someone to be responsible for the benchmarking program.

Most organisations do not have a benchmarking manager position. Therefore, the position is usually filled from within the organisation through a preferred route. The organisation can grow its own benchmarking manager.

The candidate benchmarking manager should have a background in some, if not all, of the following skills : analysis, library research, quality process, problem solving, process documentation, facilitation, training and project management.

The responsibilities of the benchmarking manager include the following :

(i) Maintain wide outside contacts for benchmarking.

(ii) Pursue a defined benchmarking strategy.

(iii) Lead benchmarking teams.

(iv) Lead the network of individuals representing their organisations for benchmarking.

(v) Provide benchmarking training or see that it is done effectively.

(vi) Act as a resource on the benchmarking process.

(vii) Ensure that benchmarking activities are prioritised to those that will return the greatest benefit and to those that fit with the organisation's objectives, mission and vision.

(viii) Report benchmarking's progress to all appropriate parties.

(v) Developing Guidelines

The organisation needs to develop guidelines for managers and teams conducting benchmarking. The guidelines ensure some semblance of consistency and are the standard procedures for handling benchmarking activities. These guidelines usually involve information sharing, visit protocol, and ethical, legal and non-disclosure considerations. It is extremely beneficial to have these guidelines documented and available to benchmarking teams and their commissioning managers.

(vi) Establishing a Network

Organisation structure is one of the major considerations for managing benchmarking. Most organisations form networks from their functional benchmarking representatives. These networks not only serve the need to source and update benchmarking activities but they also fulfill the need to disseminated benchmarking information and requirements throughout the organisation. There may also be a need to conduct work on the benchmarking program, gain consensus on direction or decisions that affect benchmarking and develop positions and documents to further direct and expand the program. Hence, an international benchmarking network is most worthwhile.

2. Supporting a Benchmarking Program

Key components to support a benchmarking program include the following activities :

(i) Identifying champions for benchmarking

(ii) Commissioning teams

(iii) Providing team skills training

(iv) Documenting the processes

(v) Qualifying partners

(vi) Following the 10-step process

These activities are briefly discussed in the following section :

(i) Identifying Champions

Organisations need champions for major programs that bring about change - and benchmarking is no exception. Benchmarking is an important change process, and selected champions should be designated, so that when change activities are anticipated benchmarking will be considered.

One of the important roles of the champion should be to advocate the pursuit of benchmarking by focusing activities on the business processes. Champions should ensure that business processes are identified, classified in some hierarchical structure, and prioritised for purposes of concentrating on those with the greatest return or leverage of organisational priorities.

(ii) Commissioning Teams

Given that benchmarking activities have been prioritised to the vital few business processes, the teams that will conduct the benchmarking need to be commissioned. Members need to be selected, team size and skills-mix need to be considered, team operation must be agreed to, the scope of the project must be defined and arrangements for removing organisation road blocks should be made known. These are the responsibilities of the person commissioning the benchmarking team.

Teams rarely function effectively if they consist of more than 9 to 12 members. Three to six are preferred for benchmarking. Members of the team should have a good mix of skills. An absolute requirement is that representatives of the process be included in the team, if not given leadership of the team.

The team should have direct operational experience in the process under study. The focus should clearly be on implementing the process improvements that will produce better results. The process operators are most capable of bringing this capacity to the team.

In addition to being knowledgeable of the process, team members should possess analytical research, process documentation and team facilitation skills.

(iii) Providing Team Skills Training

Commissioned team members must have the skills training to conduct benchmarking investigations. Teams should be trained, preferably at the time of need. The primary focus of training should be on identifying what to benchmark and whom to benchmark against, and on reviewing all the data and information sources.

(iv) Documenting the Process

Benchmarking must be started by documenting the work process that is the focus of the investigation. There are many reasons for this important step and they include defining the scope of the project, understanding the appropriate key measurements, and having a clear understanding of the work is conducted.

There are many ways to document the work process. The documentation can vary from a minute detail to the overview but there are some basic requirements. The minimum includes a picture of the process, a word description of the process, and a word description of the step-by-step, procedure **(what is done)** and the practice of each step **(how it is done).**

(v) Qualifying Partners

Benchmarking knowledge varies considerably from that of the naive to the highly experienced. This can be a problem when a company is asked to become a benchmarking partner by an inexperienced newcomer who may be just starting. Under these circumstances some qualification or screening is appropriate. This includes a discussion of the newcomer's level of preparation and the partner's code of conduct.

The minimum requirement of preparation for benchmarking is whether the new comers have thought through the subject adequately to have prepared a questionnaire. If not it is reasonable to ask for the same. This will at least show some thoroughness in preparation to ensure an effective information exchange. A properly documented process is highly desirable and may be essential for complicated processes.

Preparation also includes understanding the basics of partner's business. At a minimum the relevant databases on the company, by name and topical area should be extracted.

(vi) Follow the 10-step Process

To have consistent, replicable results, it is necessary to follow a standard way to conduct benchmarking. There are benchmarking processes which have 9, 10 and 12 steps. But what is important is that there be one process and that it be followed during the initial benchmarking and recalibration.

The accepted process is the road map to ensure credibility in comparisons and consistency in results.

Sustaining a Benchmarking Program

Sustaining a benchmarking program over a period time, say years, includes the following:

(i) Securing external assistance
(ii) Developing a handbook for managers
(iii) Showcasing successes
(iv) Role modeling
(v) Inspecting for use
(vi) Recognising and rewarding benchmarking excellence

These activities will be discussed in the following section :

1. Securing External Assistance

It is often necessary to use external resources to conduct benchmarking study. The various external resources include :

(a) Large recognised management consulting firms that have benchmarking practices.

(b) Firms that have benchmarking as their sole or primary area of expertise and

(c) Individuals who have extensive experience and will act as consultants.

Box 12.2 lists the types of external assistance resources and examples of each.

BOX 12.2 : EXTERNAL ASSISTANCE ALTERNATIVES

***(i)* Quality consulting organisations**

– Company-specific such as Qual Tech and At & T in the US.

***(ii)* Associations and nonprofits**

– Clearing houses and centres such as the American Productivity and Quality Centre (APQC), International Benchmarking Clearing-house (IBC) and the American Management Association (AMA)

***(iii)* Consulting firms**

– General, such as audit and finance

– Specialists, such as management consulting

– Individuals, such as subject experts

***(iv)* Conference organisers**

– Multiorganisation events, such as the one by Industry Week.

In the past, the principal benefit of using outside consultants was to provide confidentiality so that benchmarking partners would participate in the benchmarking studies. However today there is less concern about open sharing of information.

Outside resources usually provide added assistance to accomplish the following :

(a) Reduce the time to conduct benchmarking investigations.

(b) Provide ready contacts as a direct result of their consulting practice.

(c) Provide special skills, such as a specialisation in a high-tech industry.

(ii) Developing a Handbook for Managers

Since benchmarking is not conducted continuously by all managers or process owners, those in a competency capacity must repeatedly answer the same fundamental benchmarking questions. To forestall the questions and to proactively place in the hands of managers some guide to turn to, a manager's benchmarking reference guide is very useful. The guide serves as a reference to available materials with a short abstract on what they contain. It consists of readily accessible job aids and examples of what to do to effectively conduct benchmarking.

The guide should contain the following : *(a)* Reason for the guide, *(b)* The unit's benchmarking strategy, *(c)* Roles and responsibilities of participants, *(d)* Essentials of getting stared, *(e)* Visit guidelines and referral process, *(f)* Conduct of a site visit, *(g)* Information-sharing guidelines and legal considerations, *(h)* Identification and documentation of key processes and measures, *(i)* Use of technical libraries, *(j)* How to archieve benchmarking documents, *(k)* Training and resource materials, *(l)* Operation of benchmarking networks, *(m)* Definitions, *(n)* Appendix with sample forms and letters.

(iii) Showcasing Successes

Showcasing success stories and case histories is an important activity in expanding and intensifying benchmarking throughout the organisation. This is a powerful means to recognition and serves to stimulate the benchmarking activities of others. This includes cataloging benchmarking documents for others' reference, making the results available in some abstract form for consideration and replication by other similar functions, reporting results at internal seminars, and external presentations as appropriate, distributing internal communications from progress reports to formal project reviews and reporting benchmarking results in business plans, operating plans or budgets and at operational reviews.

One way to showcase success is through the internal network of benchmarking representatives and their activities to become the champion of benchmarking within their respective organisations.

(iv) Role Modeling

Managers should take every opportunity to cite best practices derived from benchmarking. This puts the organisation on notice that it is an important and effective way to justify operations. It also sensitises the organisation to the needed external focus to remain competitive. Managers should use benchmarking examples in communications sessions and as a basis for speeches. Senior managers can provide visible evidence of support for benchmarking when they use the term in their internal and external communications. This can vary from incorporating benchmarking activities into monthly program reports, to asking that benchmarking team results be reported at progress reviews, to analysing the benchmarking program in internal assessments.

Benchmarking is a learning experience. It is the accepted way to learn from others to gain innovative insight on how to change the organisation. All senior executives should make use of this opportunity to stress this image.

(v) Inspecting for Use

Like all processes, benchmarking must be inspected at appropriate intervals for effective use. This can be done at two levels : *(a)* inspection of the number and type of benchmarking projects and *(b)* inspection of the effective use of 10-step processes.

What is important is an understanding of the process focus, the companies visited, the best practices found, and what was done to implement them. When inspecting the process, a checklist can be used as an effective tool that serves as a self-assessment by the team or as an evaluation by the project's customer.

(vi) Recognising and Rewarding Benchmarking Excellence

Achieving excellence in benchmarking requires that managers use the array of recognition options and reward that most organisations have. While some organisations may set up a special award for excellence in benchmarking, it is equally effective to use the existing options to recognise superlative performance.

When a benchmarking team has been commissioned to conduct a highly visible and critically important benchmarking study of a key multiprocess project and the team members are relieved from current duties to work on such a cross-functional effort, it may be appropriate to spell out what the rewards will be if the team is successful in accomplishing the objectives during the specified time frame. The astute manger will know how to use the recognition and reward options creatively to continue the benchmarking initiative.

Another way to recognise the organisation of benchmarking is to consider competing for an external award. The International Benchmarking Council (IBC) offers awards to individuals through contributions to research, awards to team in benchmarking study excellence, and awards to organisations for overall excellence in benchmarking activities.

BOX 12.3 : BENCHMARKING IN PRACTICE – BENCHMARKING – AN ESSENTIAL LEADERSHIP SKILL

Reports from corporate workplace demonstrate the growing importance of benchmarking within the executive office. DuPont, for instance has written benchmarking into the job descriptions of all vice-president-level officers. DuPont and other organisations regard benchmarking as an essential skill of all competent managers. Other corporations, such as Ameritech, AT&T, Hewlett-Packard, Pacific Bell, Digital Equipment Corporation, Eastman Kodak, Xerox and IBM, have created executive level benchmarking jobs to oversee and spearhead corporate benchmarking efforts. Texas Instruments Defense Systems and Electronics Group, a 1992 Baldrige Award Winner, understands the broad-reaching relevance of benchmarking as a managerial tool. At TI, benchmarking is one of six "leadership thrusts" employed to help the organisation achieve its fundamental objective of **"customer satisfaction through total quality".**

Universal Card Services (UCS), AT&T's credit card company regards benchmarking as a critical success factor for senior managers. Another 1992 Baldrige Award Winner, UCS classifies benchmarking as one of 12 leadership activities. Senior executives - including the CEO are expected to participate in benchmarking visits to other companies.

In addition to conducting benchmarking visits to other world-class companies, AT&T UCS requires its senior executives to stay tuned to its market by meeting with customers, listening to customers' calls, reviewing daily process measures, meeting quarterly with suppliers, reviewing and using customer feed back, reviewing and using customer feed back, reviewing the program management process monthly, co-chairing monthly customer listening post meetings, hosting team sharing rallies, conducting "meeting the minds" sessions, holding quarterly employee meetings and "owning" Baldrige self-assessment categories. Many of these activities give rise to informal or unstructured benchmarking opportunities.

POINTS TO REMEMBER

- **Benchmarking activities can be classified into two distinct processes :** *(i)* the user process and *(ii)* the management process.
- The user process is the exercise of the benchmarking steps (*e.g.,* the 10 step benchmarking process).
- The management process consists of all other activities required to ensure that effective benchmarking investigations are conducted and results are implemented.

- The benchmarking management process categorises management activities into establishing, supporting and sustaining a benchmarking program.
- Actions of leadership is the most powerful communications tools in performance improvement.
- Best practices benchmarking has five critical, high-level applications from which senior executives and board members can benefit. **They are as follows :**

(i) Enables senior executives and directors to know where their corporations stand versus the best.

(ii) Helps creating a fast-learning organisational culture.

(iii) Acts as a prerequisite for strategic planning to attain market leadership.

(iv) Acts as a break-through technique to accomplish organisational restructuring, reengineering or redesign.

(v) Is a valuable tool to assist board members in performing their duties of corporate governance and oversight.

- Senior executives play a leading role in determining the success of benchmarking projects.
- Benchmarking prompts senior managers to focus systematically on the competition.
- **Power benchmarking** embraces process comparisons, performance comparisons and strategic comparisons. It includes examination of process capability, organisational structure, quality, reliability, warranty costs, cycle time, human resource management, technology management etc.
- **Key components of establishing a benchmarking program include :**

(i) Developing a strategy statement

(ii) Setting expectations

(iii) Providing management awareness

(iv) Establishing a competency centre

(v) Developing guidelines

(vi) Establishing a network

- **Key components to support a benchmarking program include :**

(i) Identifying champions for benchmarking

(ii) Commissioning teams

(iii) Providing team skills training

(iv) Documenting the processes

(v) Qualifying partners

(vi) Following the 10 step process

- **Sustaining a benchmarking program includes :**

(i) Securing external assistance

(ii) Developing a handbook for managers

(iii) Showcasing successes

(iv) Role modeling

(v) Inspecting for use

(vi) Recognising and rewarding benchmarking excellence

REVIEW QUESTIONS

1. Distinguish between "user process" and "management process" in benchmarking.
2. Discuss the relevance of leadership in benchmarking.
3. Discuss how leaders set a learning culture in organisations practicing benchmarking.
4. Discuss the role of benchmarking project champions in benchmarking programs.
5. How benchmarking prompts senior managers to focus systematically on competition.
6. Discuss the actions taken by leadership of organisations to foster creative adaptation through benchmarking.

7. Discuss the key components involved in supporting a benchmarking program in an organisation.
8. Discuss the activities involved in sustaining a benchmarking program in an organisation.
10. Write short notes on :
    (a) Benchmarking strategy
    (b) Power benchmarking
    (c) Benchmarking goals
    (d) Commissioning teams in benchmarking

DISCUSSION QUESTIONS

1. "Actions of leadership is the most powerful communications tool in performance improvement" - Explain.
2. "Benchmarking emerges as a leadership responsibility of the first order importance" - Discuss.
3. "Benchmarking prompts senior managers to focus systematically on the competition" - Do you agree or disagree? Justify your answer.
4. "Showcasing success stories and case histories is an important activity in expanding and intensifying benchmarking throughout the organisation" - Elaborate.
5. "The Baldrige criteria for organisational performance excellence systematically probe leadership role in supporting benchmarking as an enabler of continuous improvement". - Discuss.

CHAPTER 13

Benchmarking and Business Process Reengineering

INTRODUCTION

In modern management practice, we find four fundamental approaches for improving performance. These four cornerstones of improvement are : *(i)* Continuous improvement, *(ii)* Managed reform, *(iii)* Organisation restructuring and *(iv)* Process reengineering.

Benchmarking is noteworthy in this context because it is the single component to all four approaches, it enables both incremental change (for continuous improvement) and major magnitude break-throughs (process reengineering).

Benchmarking turbocharges all forms of performance improvement by leveraging best practice experience both inside and outside the organisation. Its power is greatest when integrated into an enterprise's core processes and infused into all the organisations's performance improvement efforts. By acting as a catalyst for learning benchmarking accelerates the spread of improvement and frequently generates improvement approaches that might otherwise lie outside the thinking, experience or grasp of internal improvement teams.

Continuous improvement can focus on any one or combination of the following performance dimensions :

1. **Value** – enhancing value to customers through the products and services received
2. **Defects** – reducing errors, defects and waste
3. **Fast response** – quickening responsiveness and/or shortening cycle times
4. **Productivity** – more productivity and/or effectively utilising resources

APPROACHES TO PERFORMANCE IMPROVEMENT

The four fundamental approaches to continuous performance improvement efforts can be represented on a simple matrix or conceptual map. The axes of this map relate the ***degree of change*** (*i.e.*, tactical or strategic) with the ***pace and longevity of change* or *velocity of change*** (*i.e.*, immediate or extended). ***Exhibit 13.1* illustrates the four fundamental performance - improvement approaches.** ***Tactical change*** usually represents small-scale improvements such as a process enhancement that reduces ***defect rates*** or improves ***cycle time***. ***Strategic change*** embraces enhancements, modifications and improvements on a much larger scale such as improving product quality by 10 fold or reducing new product development time by 50 percent. Change can occur at different rates or velocities. Immediate change occurs quickly, within one to three month time frame. Extended change unfolds during the course of many months and often plays out for several years. Reengineering projects which are extended change events, may require two, three or more years to completely deploy and embed within the fabric of a large organisation. **These two dimensions of change yield four possibilities for performance improvement :**

1. Immediate tactical change (*i.e.,* continuous improvement)
2. Immediate strategic change (*i.e.,* organisational restructuring)
3. Extended tactical change (*i.e.,* managed reform)
4. Extended strategic change (*i.e.,* process reengineering)

These four performance - improvement approaches an discussed in the following paragraphs:

EXHIBIT 13.1 : FOUR FUNDAMENTAL PERFORMANCE-IMPROVEMENT APPROACHES

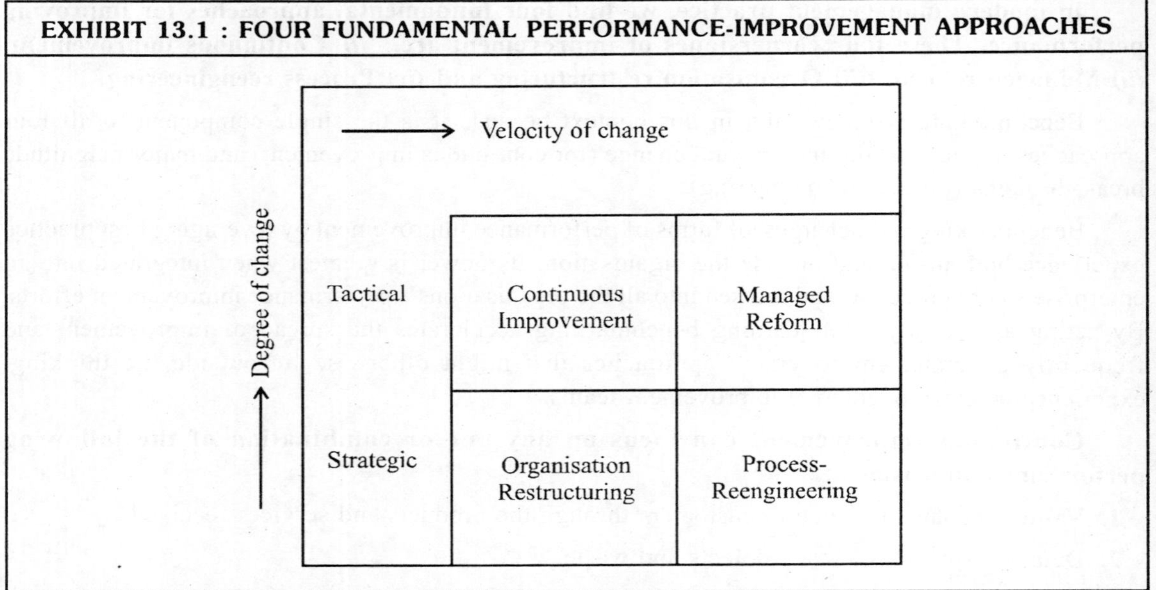

1. Immediate Tactical Change (Continuous Improvement)

Continuous improvement involves daily, weekly or monthly small scale improvements. Managers use performance indicators and regular cycles of planning, implementation and evaluation to drive change. This type of change is evolutionary because it occurs in many small, incremental improvements, none of which may look or feel revolutionary or radical. Over time, these many small improvements powerfully advance the organisation's performance systems.

Benchmarks and best practice benchmarking are invaluable tools of continuous improvement. They point the way to improvement and frequently trigger operating insights that produce operating gains.

2. Immediate Strategic Change (Organisational Restructuring)

Organisational restructuring includes many different approaches to rearranging work within an organisation. Functional transfers, structural reorganisations, dowsizing and realignments - all represent common types of immediate strategic changes. These changes often target the creation of "synergies" where the new structure is intended to be more effective and less costly than the sum of its parts. *For example*, a Fortune 500 corporation had a large headquarters and 10 operating companies, each of which provided various forms of management education. The organisation benchmarked the training practices of five other companies to learn how they managed executive education at half the relative costs. By closing down six of the 11 training groups and transforming the other five (including headquarters) into specialised organisation-wide education centres for financial, marketing, technology, engineering and general management training, the organisation eliminated the redundancy and maintained functional expertise. The organisation accomplished this change within a few months.

3. Extended Tactical Change (Managed Reform)

Managed reform is a catch-all - category embracing a wide array of both reactive and proactive management actions. Such actions are intended over time to remove errors, problems, faults or abuses, to reverse negative trends, or to improve capabilities that will ensure operations meet management objectives. These changes may require several years to roll out, refine, integrate and complete.

Many large companies in the US such as AT&T, Chevron, Caterpillar, Corning, Digital, DuPont, Kodak, Texas Instruments and Xerox have successfully applied benchmarking to enable all four types of improvement. **When it comes to process reengineering, benchmarking is an absolute necessity.**

Benchmarking is the fastest, most resource effective, and most powerful approach to helping an organisation reconceive and redesign the way its core processes operate. Benchmarking and process reengineering have therefore become the focus of tremendous interest and excitement throughout the industry - both private and public sector.

4. Extended Strategic Change (Business Process Reengineering)

Business process reengineering, or process reengineering or simply reengineering is a relatively recent and radical performance improvement approach.

Reengineering is ***extended*** because it can take years to fully implement and it is ***strategic*** because it reinvents the way an organisation conducts its business.

Reengineering starts with a ***clean slate*** and with the underlying assumption that there are no ***sacred cows***. **Reengineering strives to reinvent how work is done**. Consequently it promises dramatic breakthroughs with spectacular performance improvements of 30 to 90 percent. *For example,* Ford Motor Company adopted Mazda's invoiceless accounting system, and as a result reduced its head count for accounts payable by 75 percent from 500 to 125 while also reducing cycle time and the number of errors per transaction.

BENCHMARKING VERSUS REENGINEERING

Best practices benchmarking, the "power tool" for leveraging other leading organisations' experience, learning and innovation, is a principal instrument for achieving breakthroughs that produce such breakthrough results. Benchmarking provides the mechanism for improvement teams to access the larger world outside their organisations. Benchmarking opens the door to the collective treasure of highly-effective practices, approaches, and systems perfected in other industries and operating cultures. These experiences and insights frequently provide the key or inspiration for reengineering teams to completely reinvent their organisation's own core processes and systems. Process reengineering goal is the development of a sustainable competitive advantage - achieved through lower cost, and/or expanded output capabilities, and improved cycle times, quality and productivity. **The defining characteristics of process reengineering are summarised in *Table 13.1.***

TABLE 13.1 : CHARACTERISTICS OF BUSINESS PROCESS REENGINEERING

Factor	Characteristics
1. Time factors	• One-time change frequency • Long-term time requirements • Change measures in years
2. Risks	• Moderate to high
3. People factors	• Top-down participation • Integration of high-level teams • Top-down, bottom-up communication flow
4. Primary enablers	• Senior management support • Process owner concept • Vision of future state • "No sacred cows" • Best practice identification
5. Range	• Clean-slate starting point • Broad, cross-sectional scope • Improvement change through radical break-through
6. Tools	• Data collection techniques • Process mapping techniques • Team work • Break through thinking techniques • Information technology • Best practice benchmarking
7. Benchmarking	• Assess reengineering need • Stimulate breakthrough thinking • Migrate best practices into organisation • Manage culture change • Manage reengineered process refinement and continuous improvement

Benchmarking involves partnering with the owner of a best-in-class process so that you might adopt or adapt that process in your operation without having to spend the time and energy to try to design a duplicate of the superior process. Process-reengineering requires you to do the latter, on your own. Therefore, process reengineering should only be considered when it is impossible to use benchmarking. **That could happen for the following reasons :**

(i) No known process available for benchmarking

(ii) Best-in-class not willing to partner

(iii) Best-in-class inaccessible due to geography or expense.

If your subject process is not satisfactory, and you can not benchmark for any of these reasons, you may have to resort to reengineering. If the process is a wrong process for the job or if the process is out of statistical control, reengineering will not solve the problem. So you must first ensure that the process is appropriate and is in statistical control. If it is still not producing the desired result, suggesting that it is simply not capable, then redesigning it through reengineering is a good approach. One disadvantage with process reengineering is that there is no guarantee that after spending the time and resources, you will have a competitive process. That issue does not arise with benchmarking. With benchmarking you will have observed a competitive process in action.

When we set out to improve our processes, we have two alternative routes :

(i) Flow chart the process to understand how the process really works and give a visual impression of the steps, people and functions involved. Improvement typically comes about by changing or eliminating activity in the process that does not add value or consumes too much time or resources. That is continuous improvement.

(ii) Abandon the current process and replace it with a brand new process that provides the same functionality but better, faster or cheaper. That is process reengineering.

If the organisation could achieve the same results by either one of these two routes, which one would stand the best chance for success in the workplace? The former *i.e.,* continuous improvement route - would be more readily accepted by the workforce and would be, therefore more likely to succeed. People who are most closely related to the process have a major input into any continuous improvement initiative and will not perceive the change as something being forced on them. Process reengineering tends to be radical and sudden, and seldom consideration is given to the human issues. Many times it is seen as a management tool to lay-off workers. That is the way process reengineering is widely perceived today.

If you find process reengineering to be the approach for one of your processes, never let it be a surprise to your employees. It makes sense to involve the process owners and their internal suppliers and customers, along with other appropriate employees, in your process reengineering project. In summary, if you have a very good process to begin with, use continuous improvement techniques to make it better. On the other hand, if the process is clearly inferior to some used by other firms, try benchmarking. When you can not achieve the kind of improvement you need from either of those methods, then process reengineering may be required. But no matter which way you go, be sure to get your people involved. ***Table 13.2* contrasts dimensions of continuous improvement and process reengineering.**

TABLE 13.2 : CONTRASTING CONTINUOUS IMPROVEMENT AND PROCESS REENGINEERING

Defining characteristics	Continuous improvement	Process reengineering
(i) Starting point	Existing process	Clean-slate
(ii) Change frequency	Continuous	One-time
(iii) Typical scope	Narrow, within process	Broad, cross functional
(iv) Improvement change	Incremental with occasional breakthrough	Radical with targeted breakthrough
(v) Time required	Short	Long
(vi) Measures of time	Months	Years
(vii) Participation	Bottom-up	Top-down
(viii) Integration	Front-line employee involvement	High-level team
(ix) Communication flow	Lateral	Top-down, Bottom-up
(x) Risks	Low to moderate	Moderate to high
(xi) Primary enablers	• Systematic process • Process-owner concept • Anticipating future • Continuous improvement of existing systems	• Senior management support • Process-owner concept • Vision of future state • Clean state, "no sacred cows"
(xii) Tools	Problem solving techniques, Process management techniques, Employee involvement, Suggestion mechanism, Statistical process control, Benchmarking, Empowerment of employees, Management of change	Data collection techniques, Process mapping techniques, Team work, Break-through thinking techniques, Information technology, Benchmarking, Project management, Management of culture

SOME COMPLEX CHARACTERISTICS OF PROCESS REENGINEERING

We have earlier listed the characteristics of process reengineering in *Table 13.1.* Of these characteristics we will discuss some which are viewed as complex characteristics. They are :

1. One-Time Change Frequency

Process reengineering is undertaken as a one-time project that focuses on major magnitude performance improvement. Such large-scale change efforts are seldom accomplished quickly or easily. Moreover they create initial discomfort for many people involved, who will be asked to learn to work in new ways. Consequently, constant reengineering is not favoured by most organisations. Yet in a paradoxical sense, reengineering may be complete but it is never done. Reengineered processes must be fine-tuned and steadily advanced; here reengineering eventually crosses the border back into the province of continuous improvement.

Best practice benchmarking moves easily across these borders, saving equally as a tool of leapfrog improvements and incremental change.

2. Moderate to High Risk

Reengineering is revolutionary and revolutions are risky. They embrace change and change is uncomfortable for those who enjoy status-quo. Process reengineering is likely to embrace process redesign, job redefinition, new applications of information technology, employee skill enhancement, and revision of managerial systems such as selection, compensation, performance evaluation and career development. Such radical changes often reshape an organisation's very culture. When an enterprise radically reinvents the way it does business, the organisation requires people to stretch as much as its systems. Fear, anxiety and resistance are no uncommon early reactions.

Indeed not all who undertake reengineering efforts achieve their goals and visions. An estimated 70 percent of organisations undertaking reengineering do not fully achieve their stated goals. Nevertheless, the prospect of creating three-fold to ten-fold performance improvements in a core operating process remains so alluring to many organisations that they embrace reengineering despite its high risks. **Benchmarking then proves an important risk management tool**. By providing reengineering participants with a clear and vivid picture of the end point of their change efforts, the reengineering process becomes less fearful and more manageable.

3. A Clean-slate Starting Point

Unlike continuous improvement teams that build on a foundation already in place, reengineering teams deliberately start with a clean slate. They set out to reinvent the process, they do not intend to manage it toward incremental improvement. Bold breakthroughs often require the reengineering team to step outside customary work approaches and business models. Reengineering teams begin work as if no system preexisted. They work from a clean slate.

4. Senior Management Support

Process reengineering is a radical approach to performance improvement. Senior management's active support and involvement are therefore essential in overcoming the natural resistance to such broad-reaching change. ***Table 13.3* illustrates the role of leadership in lending authority to the four fundamental approaches to performance improvement.** Senior leadership, usually the CEO or COO, play a leading role in process reengineering.

TABLE 13.3 : ROLE OF LEADERSHIP IN PERFORMANCE IMPROVEMENT APPROACHES

Performance improvement mode	Extent of employee resistance	Implementation authority	Authority to overcome resistance
1. Process reengineering	Extreme	COO or CEO	Absolute
2. Focused restructuring	Moderate	Vice president	Specific
3. Focused process improvement	Limited	Director	General
4. Continuous improvement	Somewhat	Process owner	Variable

5. Broad, Cross-functional Scope

Work tends to flow horizontally across departments, consequently, functional boundaries blur when designing a system to perform work quickly, efficiently and with customers requirements in mind. Organisations can be viewed as huge cross-functional processing systems, customer support producers and front-line processes transform materials, information and other "inputs" into products or services that are delivered through front-line processes to customers in the market.

In a model of a huge processing system, the customer sits at the top of the model, front-line processes deliver products and services through distribution channels into customer marketing segments. Front-line processes are sustained by support processes which are in turn supported by administrative processes. This model enables the reengineering team to focus on those primary processes which are most essential to the success of the organisation. By **applying process benchmarking**, the reengineering team can objectively evaluate the adequacy of its current process system and then envision ways to reinvent the system. ***Exhibit 13.2* illustrates the model of a processing system.**

EXHIBIT 13.2 : MODEL OF A HUGE PROCESSING SYSTEM

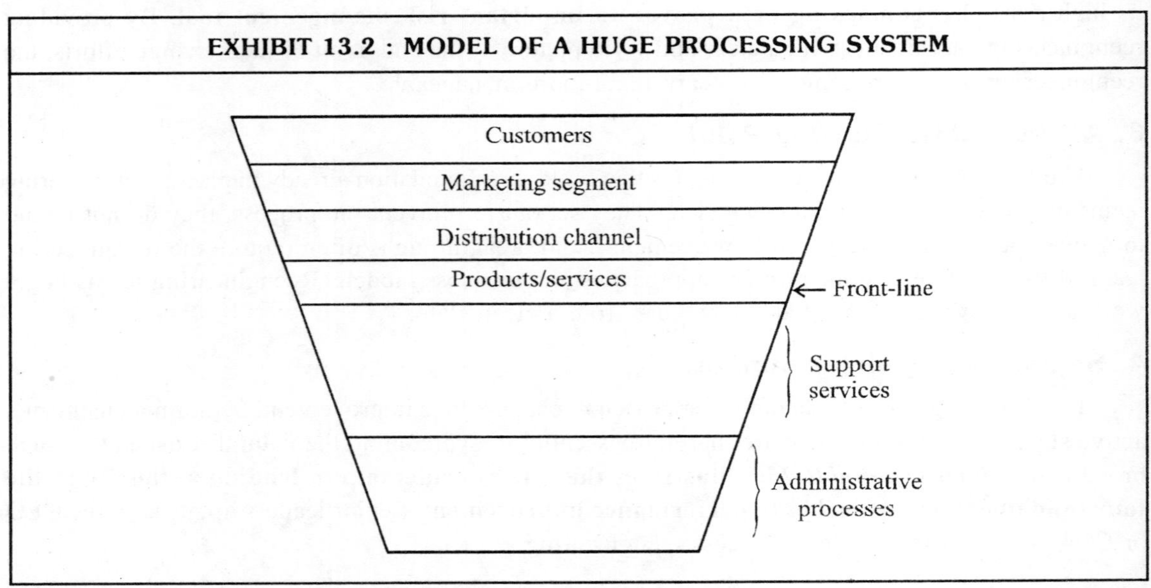

Within every organisation, few processes are ***primary processes***. They are the ones that deliver the greatest value to the customer. During reengineering, organisations must separate primary sequence processes from support service and administrative processes. Support services back up primary sequence processes and produce things needed by the primary sequence. In turn, administrative services plan, regulate and integrate the primary sequence processes and the support service processes.

Reengineering strives to redesign primary sequence processes to create the greatest value for the customer and the organisation. Support and administrative service processes may also be redesigned to provide greater value to the primary sequence.

6. Information Technology

Information technology often acts as a master key allowing companies to open the door to radically new and improved work system designs. The advent of powerful computers and applications software enable companies to simplify once complex processes, to bring information previously available only to diverse specialists into grasp of front-line employees with access to powerful databases and to enable once linear processes to parallel processes. The potential end results are improved economics for the business, improved cycle times for the process and enhanced value for customers. Thomas H. Davenport, author of ***"Process Innovation : Reengineering Work through Information Technology"*** and a noted reengineering expert, identifies nine different ways in which information technology enables innovation in work processes. All nine impact areas can be observed by **benchmarking** innovative applications of information technology to improve work forces in different industries both manufacturing and service.

8. Deciding when to Reengineer

When should a company undertake the risky, long-term strategic commitment of process reengineering? When should an organisation literally reinvent itself? Persistent ***competitive benchmarking*** can help answer this difficult strategic question. Rigorous ***benchmark comparisons*** can provide the early warning system that an organisation's core processes have slipped or completely broken down. If your organisation and competitors are advancing at different rates, how long will it be before one enterprise has a fatal advantage? Do the benchmarks comparisons and future projections demonstrate that only quantum-leap improvement will keep an organisation from brutal quality and cost disadvantages? If the answer is "yes" then process reengineering is probably the process to prescribe.

Reengineer core process that, if competitively weak, are an Achilles heel to the organisation's strategy, market position and future success. Large differences in quality, productivity and cost are the signs that the organisation is vulnerable.

A sampling of business processes that are the grounds on which many industries compete include - but are not limited to :

(i) New product and service development

(ii) Production of products and services

(iii) Delivery of products and services

(iv) Billing, receipt, and processing of customer payments

(v) Management of customer relationships

(vi) Development of innovation and technological capability.

When a strategically important process can not produce the future performance levels that will be required to ensure market place health and success, then the risks of process reengineering seem well justified. The alternative - maintaining the status quo or implementing only continuous improvements may prove fatal in fast moving markets.

THE SEVEN-STEP REENGINEERING PROCESS

Process reengineering can be viewed as a simple seven-step improvement process. These steps are:

Step 1 : Identify the value-added, strategic processes from a customer's perspective.

Step 2 : Map and measure the existing process to develop improvement opportunities.

Step 3 : Act on improvement opportunities that are easy to implement and are of immediate benefit.

Step 4 : ***Benchmark for best practices*** to develop solutions, new approaches, new process designs and innovative alternatives to the existing system.

Step 5 : Adapt breakthrough approaches to fit your organisation, culture and capabilities.

Step 6 : Pilot and test the recommended process redesign.

Step 7 : Implement the reengineered processes and continuously improve.

These steps occur sequentially, although they may at times overlap chronologically and parallel process.

Benchmarking has potential applications in step 1, step 3, step 4 and step 7 of the reengineering process. At times the comparisons may be of simple performance benchmarks that are useful in establishing gaps and evaluating long-term capability, at other junctures, the benchmarking challenge is to determine the best business practices and the most innovative approaches that can be applied in a complex process or work system. Here the best practice focus may be on process design, information systems, technology strategy, organisational structure, employee skill levels, training or other managerial systems.

***Exhibit 13.3* describes the seven steps reengineering process as a simple flow chart and *Table 13.4* describes the role of benchmarking at various steps in the reengineering process.**

Lessons Learnt

A growing body of learning emerges from the successes and failures of recent reengineering efforts. Five reasons that are especially relevant to reengineering and benchmarking stand out:

1. ***Study the best practices of organisations outside your industry***. Benchmarking partners from other fields frequently trigger important insights that inspire the redesign process.
2. ***Study the most highly-effective work-force competencies underlying an organisation's best operating practices***. Recommitment and selection, education and training, employee skill sets, cultural elements, compensation, recognition and performance evaluation systems are often critical success factors enabling the implementation of the most highly-effective operating practices.
3. ***Co-ordinate interviews and site visits among all teams contacting external benchmarking partners***. Such coordination is especially important when two or more reengineering teams identify the same best practice company to benchmark. Lack of coordination can cause damage to an organisation's credibility and discourage potential partners.

4. ***Coordinate benchmarking contact with suppliers*** through the organisation's vendor management group.

5. ***Coordinate benchmarking contact with customers*** through sales account management staff, especially for national or major accounts.

EXHIBIT 13.3 : ROLE OF BENCHMARKING IN THE SEVEN STEP REENGINEERING PROCESS

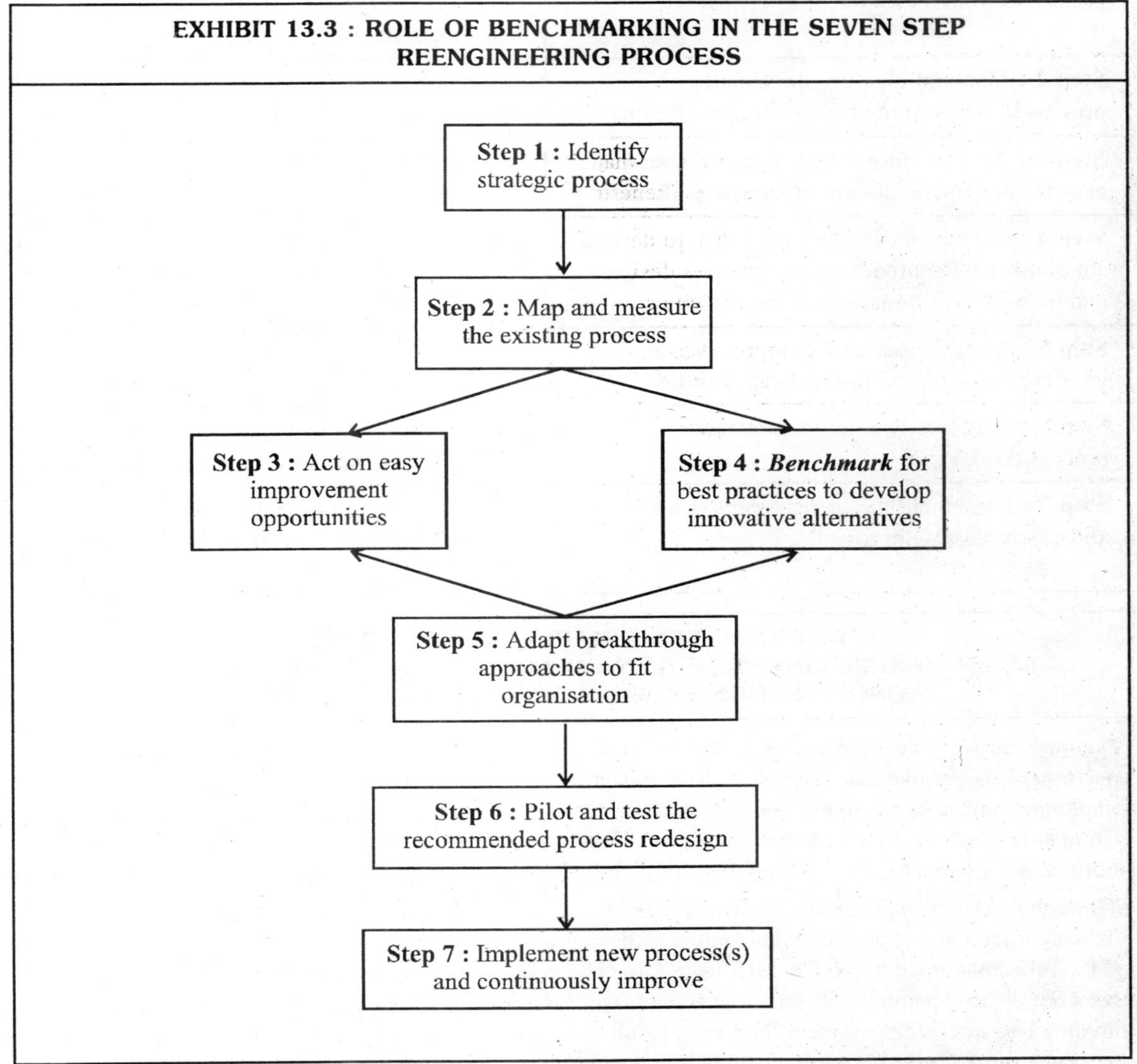

TABLE 13.4 : INTEGRATING BENCHMARKING AND REENGINEERING

Seven step reengineering process	Tools applied
Step 1 : Identify the value added, strategic processes from a customers's perspective	Performance benchmark analysis (cost, quality cycle time etc.) Customer satisfaction benchmark analysis, value analysis
Step 2 : Map and measure the existing process to develop improvement opportunities	Flow charting and process management tools. Performance measurement tools
Step 3 : Act on improvement opportunities that are easy to implement and are of immediate benefit	Informal benchmarking for short-term solutions – implementation planning tools
Step 4 : Benchmark for best practices, to develop solutions, new approaches, new process designs and innovative alternatives to the existing system	Best practices benchmarking among processes and performance systems
Step 5 : Adapt breakthrough approaches to fit your organisation, culture and capabilities	Process redesign tools, implementation planning tools
Step 6 : Pilot and test the recommended process design	Training and pilot test techniques. Apply lessons learnt from past successful pilots
Step 7 : Implement the reengineered process(s) and continuously improve	Train employees, implementation techniques Use benchmarking to maintain continuous improvement process

BOX 13.1 : BENCHMARKING IN PRACTICE
– BENCHMARKING INSPIRES REENGINEERING TEAMS TO REINVENT THEIR ORGANISATION'S OWN PROCESSES AND SYSTEMS

Business process reengineering or extended strategic change is a relatively recent and radical performance improvement approach. Reengineering is ***extended*** because it can take years to fully implement and it is ***strategic*** because it reinvents the way the organisation conducts its business. Companies such as AT&T, Aetna, American Express, Ameritech, Chemical Bank, Deere Company, Ford Motor Company, GTE, Texas Instruments and Westing house are actively reengineering.

Through process reengineering, for instance IBM credit reduced cycle time to a tenth of what it was for its loan processing while producing ten times the number of loan agreements. Thanks to reengineering, GTE Telephone operations increased from 1 to 60 percent, the number of telephone service problems resolved within 5 minutes when their customers call for repairs. Ford Motor Company adopted Mazda's invoice-less accounting system, and as a result reduced its head count for accounts payable by 75 percent from 500 to 125, while also reducing cycle time and the number of errors per transaction.

Best practice benchmarking, the "power tool" for leveraging other leading organisation's experience, learning and innovation, is a principal instrument for achieving breakthroughs that produce such spectacular results. Benchmarking provides the mechanism for improvement teams to access the larger world outside their organisations. Benchmarking springs open the door to the collective treasure of highly-effective practices, approaches and systems perfected in other industries and operating cultures. These experiences and insights frequently provide the key or inspiration for reengineering teams to completely reinvent their organisation's own processes and systems.

POINTS TO REMEMBER

- **Four fundamental approaches for improving performance are :**
  - *(i)* Continuous improvement
  - *(ii)* Managed reform
  - *(iii)* Organisation restructuring
  - *(iv)* Process reengineering
- **Benchmarking** turbocharges all forms of performance improvement by leveraging best practice experience both inside and outside the organisation.
- **Continuous improvement can focus on any one or combination of the following performance dimensions :** *(i)* Value, *(ii)* Defects, *(iii)* Fast response and *(iv)* Productivity.
- **Two dimensions of change *viz.*, degree of change and velocity of change yield four possibilities for performance improvement namely :**
  - *(i)* Immediate tactical change (*i.e.,* continuous improvement).
  - *(ii)* Immediate strategic change (*i.e.,* organisational restructuring).
  - *(iii)* Extended tactical change (*i.e.,* managed reform).
  - *(iv)* Extended strategic change (*i.e.,* process reengineering).
- **Continuous improvement** involves daily, weekly or monthly small scale improvements.
- **Benchmarks and best practice benchmarking point** the way to continuous improvement and frequently trigger operating insights that produce operating gains.
- **Organisational restructuring** includes many different approaches to rearranging work within an organisation.
- **Managed reform** embraces a wide variety of both reactive and proactive management actions. Benchmarking is the fastest, most resource effective, and most powerful approach to helping an organisation reconceive and redesign the way its core processes operate.
- **Process reengineering** starts with a clean slate and strives to reinvent how work is done. It is an **extended strategic change**, extended because it can take years to fully implement and strategic because it reinvents the way an organisation conducts its business.
- **Best practices benchmarking** is the "power tool" for leveraging other leading organisations' experience, learning and innovation.
- If your subject process is not satisfactory and you can not benchmark for any reason, you may have to resort to reengineering.
- **Some of the complex characteristics of process reengineering include :**
  - *(i)* One-time change frequency
  - *(ii)* Moderate to high risk
  - *(iii)* A clean-slate starting point
  - *(iv)* Senior management support
  - *(v)* Broad, cross-functional scope
  - *(vi)* Use of information technology
  - *(vii)* Deciding when to reengineer
- **The seven-step reengineering process involves :**

  Step 1 : Identify the value - added, strategic processes from a customer's perspective.

  Step 2 : Map and measure the existing process to develop improvement opportunities.

  Step 3 : Act on improvement opportunities that are easy to implement and are of immediate benefit.

  Step 4 : Benchmark for best practices to develop solutions, new approaches, new process designs and innovative alternatives to the existing system.

  Step 5 : Adapt break-through approaches to fit your organisation, culture and capabilities.

Step 6 : Pilot and test the recommended process redesign.

Step 7 : Implement the reengineered processes and continuously improve.

- Benchmarking has potential applications in step 1, step 3, step 4 and step 7 of the reengineering process.
- A growing body of **learning** emerges from the successes and failures of recent reengineering efforts.
- **Five reasons relevant to reengineering and benchmarking are :**
  - *(i)* Study the best practices of organisations outside your industry.
  - *(ii)* Study the most highly-effective work force competencies underlying an organisation's best operating practices.
  - *(iii)* Co-ordinate interviews and site visits among all teams contacting external benchmarking partners.
  - *(iv)* Co-ordinate benchmarking contact with suppliers.
  - *(v)* Co-ordinate benchmarking contact with customers.

REVIEW QUESTIONS

1. What is continuous improvement?
2. Name the four performance dimensions of continuous improvement.
3. Discuss the four fundamental approaches to continuous performance improvement.
4. Discuss the following types of change :
   (a) Immediate tactical change *(b)* Immediate strategic change
   (c) Extended tactical change *(d)* Extended strategic change
5. Differentiate between benchmarking and process reengineering.
6. Discuss the characteristics of business process reengineering.
7. Distinguish between the characteristics of continuous improvement and process reengineering.
8. Discuss the following characteristics of process reengineering :
   (a) One-time change frequency *(b)* Modulating to high risk
   (c) Clean-slate starting point *(d)* Senior management support
   (e) Broad, cross-functional scope *(f)* Information technology
9. Describe the seven-step reengineering process.
10. Discuss the role of benchmarking in the seven-step reengineering process with a simple flow chart.
11. Describe how benchmarking and reengineering are integrated.

DISCUSSION QUESTIONS

1. "Benchmarking turbochanges all forms of performance improvement by leveraging best practice experience inside and outside the organisation" - Discuss.
2. "Benchmarking is the fastest, most resource effective and most powerful approach to helping an organisation reconceive and redesign the way its core processes operate" - Explain.
3. "Unlike continuous improvement teams that build on a foundation already in place, reengineering teams deliberately start with a clean state" - Elaborate.
4. "Process reengineering is a radical approach to performance improvement. Senior management's active support and involvement are therefore essential in overcoming the natural resistance to such broad-reaching change" - Do you agree or disagree? Justify your answer.

CHAPTER 14

Benchmarking and Time-Based Competition

INTRODUCTION

Companies must be competitive to sell their goods and services in the market place. Competitiveness is an important factor in determining whether a company prospers, barely gets by or fails. Competitiveness is "how effectively an organisation meets the wants and needs of customers relative to others that offer similar goods or services".

Business organisations compete through some combination of their marketing and operations functions. Marketing influences competitiveness in several ways, including : *(i)* identifying consumer wants and needs, *(ii)* pricing and *(iii)* advertising and sales promotion.

Operations influences competitiveness through product and service design, cost, location, quality, response time, flexibility, inventory and supply chain management and service.

Firms compete with one another in a variety of ways. The dimensions of competitiveness that measure the effectiveness of the production function are : *(i)* Cost or price, *(ii)* Quality, *(iii)* Product or service differentiation, *(iv)* Dependability as a supplier, *(v)* Flexibility/service and *(vi)* Time to perform certain activities.

Time to perform certain activities refer to several aspects of an organisation's operations such as:

(i) How quickly a product or service is delivered to customers (*i.e.,* speed to market or minimum lead time to supply).

(ii) How quickly new products or services are designed, developed and launched to the market (*i.e.,* speed to market of new products or services) and

(iii) The rate at which improvements in products or processes are made.

TIME-BASED COMPETITION

Also known as ***speed to market, fast cycle times or fast response, time-based management or time compression***, it is competition based on time, rapidly developing products and moving them to market. Nowadays, a growing number of organisations are focusing their performance-improvement efforts on the competitive dimension of time to have competitive advantage because, the other factors on which companies compete *viz.,* cost/price, quality, product features etc., are no longer the **core competencies** of firms by which they can gain competitive advantage in the market place. Therefore, much of the current competitive battle field is focused around the speed of product to market.

To reduce the time it takes to perform operations, organisations are being challenged to simplify their processes, eliminate waste, remove redundancy and drive down costs. Cycle time reduction or time-based competition is a powerful improvement focus because it correlates so directly with important performance indicators, such as cost, quality, market share and customer satisfaction.

The concept of time-based competition is based on the wisdom **"time is money"**. Many organisations have set aggressive corporate-wide goals to reduce cycle times by 50 percent or more.

Time-based competition makes business process speed a primary focus of improvement and establishes cycle time as a key measure of performance. It can play a leading role in any of the four fundamental approaches to performance improvement *viz., (i)* Continuous improvement, *(ii)* Organisational restructuring, *(iii)* Managed reform and *(iv)* Process reengineering. Certainly, cycle time reduction is almost always emphasized in process reengineering and continuous improvement efforts in organisations which consider **"being first to market"** is important.

Time-based Strategies

Time-based strategies focus on reducing the time required to accomplish various activities (*e.g.,* develop new products or services and market them, respond to a change in customer demand, or deliver a product or perform a service). By doing so, organisations seek to improve service to the customer and to gain a competitive advantage over rivals who take more time to accomplish the same tasks.

Time-based strategies focus on reducing the time needed to carryout the various activities in a process. By reducing time, costs can be reduced, productivity can be increased, quality tends to be better, product innovations can appear in the market sooner and customer service is improved. **Organisations have achieved time reduction in some of the following :** *(i)* planning time, *(ii)* product/service design time, *(iii)* processing time, *(iv)* change-over time in production set ups, *(v)* delivery time and *(vi)* response time for complaints.

The Benefits of Speed

Time-based competition has emerged as a central concept articulated in the Malcolm Baldrige National Quality Award. In the Baldrige criteria **"fast response"** is identified as a **"core value"** or foundation concept of high-performing, customer-focused organisations.

"Success in competitive markets increasingly demands ever shorter cycle times for new or improved product and service introduction" note the Baldrige guidelines for quality excellence. Also faster and more flexible response to customers is now a more critical requirement to achieve desired level of customer satisfaction. Major improvement in response time often requires simplification of work organisations and work processes. To accomplish such improvement, the time performance of work processes should be measured. Response time improvements often drive simultaneous improvements in organisation, quality and productivity. By reducing the time it takes to bring new product or service to market, an organisation can significantly increase its profits. Increase in process speed will result in business benefits of greater cash flow, greater profitability, higher market share due to greater customer responsiveness and more capacity from cycle time reductions.

Benefits of Fast Response Capabilities

The benefits of fast-response capabilities are borne out in a growing body of business research. Recent finds from a Mckinsey and Company study revealed that a new product six months late to market loses 33 percent of its potential profit over its product life cycle. Mckinsey's study is a wake-up call to service providers and product manufacturers alike. **"Reduce the time it takes to bring a new product or service to market and the organisation significantly increases profits".**

***Table 14.1* summarises the negative profit impact of being late to market.**

TABLE 14.1 : THE COST OF BEING LATE TO MARKET		
If your new product is late to market by	Your gross profit potential over the life of the product is reduced by	A one-month improvement in time-to-market improves the product's life time profit by
6 months	→ 33%	→ 11.9%
5 months	→ 25%	→ 9.3%
4 months	→ 18%	→ 7.3%
3 months	→ 12%	→ 5.7%
2 months	→ 7%	→ 4.3%
1 month	→ 3%	→ 3.1%

Measuring Speed Through Cycle Time

Speed is primarily measured in terms of cycle time in business. 'Cycle time' can be defined as the interval between the start and the finish of a process, which can be described inturn as the sequence of events and activities that occur in order to accomplish a piece of work. From the customers view point, ***"total cycle time"*** is the time that elapses between expressing a need and having the need satisfactorily fulfilled. During that period many events and activities may occur.

Virtually, any enterprise can measure and manage the cycle time of its most critical processes. Cycle time can measure the entire interval from creation through delivery of a product or service, or it can measure the duration of a subprocess which is a component of larger experiences or processes.

Work is represented as a cycle, in turn, the primary work cycle is composed by ***subprocesses*** each of which has its own cycle time contributing to the total elapsed cycle time. This concept that every work process is comprised of many smaller processes or subprocesses - is often referred to as ***nesting***. Within any core process nest many smaller sequences or subprocesses. Consequently, the first-step in understanding a process is to identify its many subprocesses and map them. A detailed process map also allows an improvement team to reach consensus on how it will measure cycle time.

***Exhibit 14.1* illustrates the cycle-time model.** With a detailed process map an improvement team can systematically analyse the obstacle that slow down the cycle, then they can develop solutions to improve processing speed. Frequently teams reduce the overall cycle time by systematically identifying and implementing improvements in the subprocesses.

EXHIBIT 14.1 : WORK IS A PROCESS OR CYCLE MEASURED IN TERMS OF CYCLE TIME

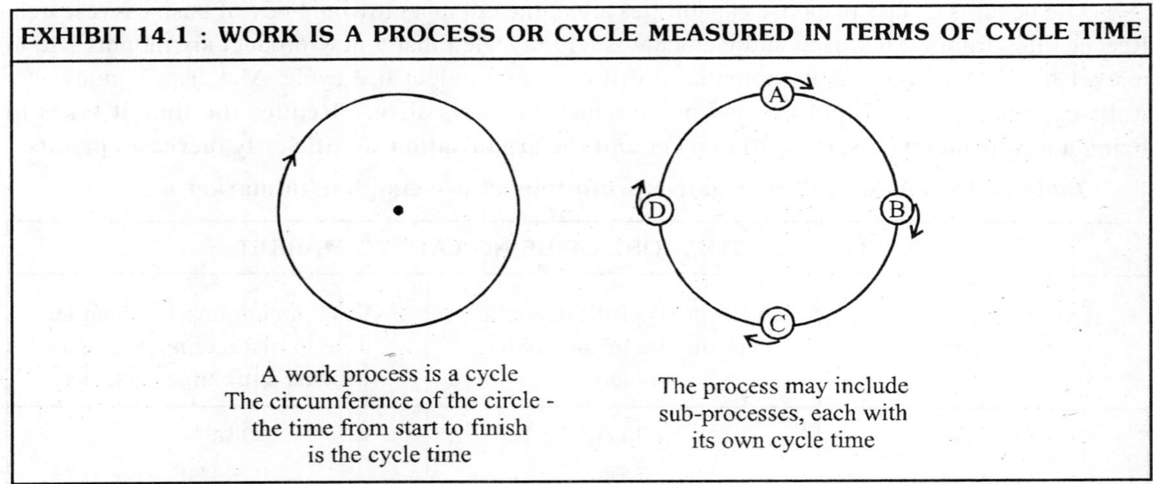

"Cycle-time analysis and benchmarking go hand in hand". *For example,* consider the case in point : A Chevron team set out to improve a complex oil analysis process. The team first examined process quality and found that its process quality was equal to that of competitors. However, when the team next studied cost and time factors, it was surprised to discover that certain competitors achieved superior performance. How? They spent less time in early planning phases which had a disproportionately beneficial impact on total cost. When Chevron benchmarked how the competitors achieved this time advantage, they discovered the best practice companies approached planning very differently than did Chevron. Without the benefit of this benchmarking, which spurred by the cycle-time analysis, the Chevron improvement team would never have discovered this new approach to planning. This is an example where cycle time and benchmarking really create a synergistic effect. Cycle time analysis alone would not have provided the solution. **Cycle time analysis is assisted and made more powerful by benchmarking. Cycle time analysis instructs you where to benchmark.**

Cycle time reduction is a fertile ground for improvement for many organisations. Those corporations that have undertaken broad-reaching time-compression campaigns find that improvement gains of 50 to 80 percent are within grasp. How is it that such major magnitude improvements are possible? Experience shows that 80 to 90 percent of process cycle time is spent waiting. Many cycle-time reduction and reengineering efforts therefore devise ways to improve work processes by reducing or eliminating waiting.

When cycle-time-reduction vigilantes apply ***process benchmarking*** here, they find the results can be especially effective. Waiting occurs when service or product creation proceeds more rapidly than the efforts of those managing or operating the process. To prevent the process from speeding out of control, operators therefore press on the brakes. In organisations, this breaking effect takes the form of waiting for managerial decisions, supplies, repairs, information and the like. If all these forms of waiting can be removed, the process would proceed from start to finish much more rapidly.

Unfortunately, the process operators, who created the many different 'wait' stations in the original process, don't always know how to eliminate these buffers that prevent the process from operating at faster speeds. Benchmarking other enterprises and industries that more effectively manage similar processes often provide the process operators with greater insights. These insights provide the impetus to reshape or reform the process in way that eliminates waiting and thereby increases process speed or reduces the process cycle time.

Rework and redundancy represent another major cycle time reduction opportunity area in most work systems. Rework is often systemic, that is to say the process embeds rework and waste into its design. Process management experts estimate that 25 to 40 percent of work effort is typically re-do effort. Benchmarking inspires process operators by providing them with vivid examples of highly-efficient work systems that have minimised or driven rework from the performance system.

***Table 14.1* identifies some of the examples of waiting and rework.**

TABLE 14.1 : WHERE TO BEGIN WHEN REDUCING CYCLE TIMES

Where waiting occurs	Where rework occurs
(i) Waiting for managerial decisions	*(i)* Retype
(ii) Waiting for maintenance	*(ii)* Redesign
(iii) Waiting for supplies	*(iii)* Respecify
(iv) Waiting for equipment availability	*(iv)* Reorder
(v) Waiting for information	*(v)* Rework
(vi) Waiting for signatures	*(vi)* Repurchase
(vii) Waiting for instructions	*(vii)* Reread
(viii) Waiting for materials	*(viii)* Redocument
(ix) Waiting for next shift	*(ix)* Restate
(x) Waiting for personnel	*(x)* Rebuild
(xi) Waiting for parts	*(xi)* Retool
(xii) Waiting for installation	*(xii)* Reprogram
(xiii) Waiting for priority	*(xiii)* Retest

Other Cycle-time Reduction Methods

Cycle time analysis is rooted in process mapping and process management. The keys to effective cycle time analysis are a ***process map*** and ***time-based performance measure***. Working from a detailed flow chart, cycle time managers can systematically examine the work system with an eye to improving process speed. Some of the tell-tale signs of cycle time improvement opportunities are frequent management review, decision loops, bottlenecks, missing steps, process rework, poorly sequenced steps and steps that do not add value to the customer. Though many of these tell-tale signs would appear to be cost-based or quality considerations, they invariably affect cycle times. **"Cycle time is inseparably linked to cost and quality"**. All three must be considered at the same time.

Table 14.2 **summarises some of the initiatives for cycle time reduction.** It also shows how and where benchmarking empowers the cycle time analysis and improvement process.

TABLE 14.2 : INITIATIVES FOR CYCLE TIME REDUCTION

Opportunity area	Benchmarking opportunities
1. Process flow	Benchmark similar process of excellent companies to identify simpler, faster, less redundant, more error-free practices
2. Resource scheduling	Benchmark resource planning, scheduling, delivery and management practices for similar processes
3. Decision making/ communications	Benchmark decision making, communication and empowerment approaches for similar processes
4. Capacity/flexibility	Benchmark cross-training, pay-for knowledge, planning, scheduling and high performance teams to seek best practice approaches in these areas
5. Organisation	Benchmark plant/office layouts, organisational and team structures, and job designs
6. Consistency	Benchmark process control approaches in similar processes
7. Supply chain management	Benchmark various aspects of supplier management such as communication, standardisation, scheduling, training etc.
8. Product and service design	Benchmark new product development processes, design for manufacturability systems and so on

BENCHMARKING AND CYCLE TIME REDUCTION

"Faster, cheaper, better" was the holy trinity of customers in the 1990s. **"Faster"** is the first concept in this trinity. **"Time"** is money, **faster drives cheape**r. Simplified processes which are faster, inevitably deliver lower cost. In most circumstances, faster is also better. Processes which compress time by simplifying sequences, by reducing rework and redundancy, by error-proofing tasks, also produce higher-quality results than slower predecessor processes. Quality, cycle time and cost are inextricably linked. As fewer defects are produced, less time is spent on rework, so both cycle time and manufacturing costs shrink.

Quality has sometimes been described as the **"race without a finish line"**. However, there is a clearly marked finish line from the customer's point of view. The company that can routinely deliver products and services to market faster than its competitors wins. "The bottom-line is that when customers decide they want to buy, the first supplier who can fill that need with a product or service will flourish. Customers increasingly demand high quality, a good price and timeliness all at once. Consequently the goal is quick response, and the only variants are "fast" and "faster".

As a managerial tool that helps accelerate organisational learning, benchmarking acts as a primary catalyst in the cycle-time reduction process. Once cycle time measurements are put in place and processes are mapped, benchmarks may be developed and improvement opportunities identified.

Cycle-time reduction is achieved through the systematic analysis of complex processes with a clear focus on improving process speed. Those practices that actually compress time and improve speed in one company are almost always eminent targets for innovative adaptation in another organisation.

Generic Practices to Reduce Cycle Time

1. ***Establish dynamic information flows :*** The instantaneous exchange of critical information is often achieved through Electronic Data Interchange (EDI) and other computer-based communications systems.

   Electronic data interchange (EDI) is the direct, computer-to-computer transmission of inter-organisational transactions, including purchase orders, shipping notices, debit or credit memos and more. **Among the reasons companies are increasingly using EDI are :**

   (i) Increased productivity

   (ii) Reduction of paper work

   (iii) Lead time and inventory reduction

   (iv) Facilitation of just-in-time systems

   (v) Electronic transfer of funds

   (vi) Improved control of operations

   (vii) Redution in clerical work

   (viii) Higher accuracy

2. ***Reduce bottlenecks :*** The ***express lane*** concept is frequently used to reduce process bottlenecks. Any time a first-in, first-out system is applied at high-volume processing points, easy-to-process items slow down as they wait in queue behind more difficult-to-process items. Directing easy-to-process items through an express lane keeps traffic moving, just like in the supermarket.

3. ***Reduce the number of inspection items :*** When organisations learn to improve process designs so that errors are prevented, repeated inspections become time-wasting and redundant activities.

4. ***Reduce decision and approval points :*** Every time a process requires management approval or requires supervisory decisions, the process slows and waiting frequently occurs. These non-value added waiting situations can be removed by better training employees, by empowering line workers with decision making authority and by designing processes that don't require regular management approval and decision points.

5. ***Simplify the decision making process.***

6. ***Standardise information, reporting forms and procedures to reduce variation :*** Processes without standards tend to run slowly and out of control. A customer order centre, for instance that receives orders in 100 or more different formats runs more slowly than a centre with a single standardised order format. Consequently, a first-line of standardisation often involves the creation of well-designed forms that facilitate several process steps and establish information standards.

7. ***Avoid frequent process hand offs :*** The use of technology and powerful databases can be helpful to simplify processes by enabling one person to accomplish what previously different departments or specialist individually handled.

8. ***Improved plant or office layouts that separate work groups or disrupt processes.***
9. ***Group lots or work with similar requirements.***
10. ***Organise or "pre-kit" tools, paperwork, gages and the like, to facilitate rapid work flow.***
11. ***Consolidate purchases :*** Frequent material and supply purchases by work groups, departments and operating teams take time and resources. Consolidating purchases can achieve cost and time savings.
12. ***Eliminate unnecessary variation in design :*** Frequent change-overs in products or services generate additional work and process steps, all of which increase cycle time.
13. ***Automate repetitive handling operations :*** Repetitive tasks in both service and manufacturing industries can be automated. Automation may range from the use of robots in an automobile plant to the creation of form files and macro-computer commands in a law firm. By reducing repetitive handling tasks, process speed increases.

These time-compression tactics work because they address the basics of cycle time reduction: process simplification, error proofing (Poka-Yoke), rework elimination, waiting time reduction, bottle-neck removal and redundancy elimination.

As time-based management has become an integral part of many organisation's competitive strategies, cycle time has emerged as a primary benchmark or operating statistic studied by companies. Cycle-time gaps between competitive organisations can be viewed as a red flag that one organisation operates more slowly and probably at higher cost. Savvy process managers carefully scrutinise their organisation's cycle-time gaps, recognising that each gap signals an important process-improvement opportunity. By studying how faster companies achieve their superior cycle times, process managers can adapt those approaches and drive similar improvements in their own organisations.

Benchmarking therefore acts as a time-compression catalyst. It supercharges the cycle-time reduction process in at least three ways :

(i) Cycle-time benchmarks or comparative performance measures provide an early warning system that alerts an organisation if its processes are running slowly or suboptimally relative to other competitors and process leaders.

(ii) Benchmarking then helps identify where the lard has become marbled into an organisation's processes by providing examples of faster, leaner and more effective operating systems.

(iii) Benchmarking helps generate time-compression solutions by identifying the best practices and approaches of faster companies.

In the 21st century, speed is a distinguishing characteristic of market leaders. Consequently, cycle-time reduction is a primary goal of organisations that wish to remain competitive. Benchmarking, in turn, is a primary means to achieve that end of fast response.

BOX 14.1 : BENCHMARKING IN PRACTICE
– CYCLE TIME REDUCTION SUCCESS STORIES

- Cycle time analysis and benchmarking go hand in hand. Cycle time analysis is assisted and made more powerful by benchmarking. Cycle time analysis tells you where to benchmark.

  In the 1990s, fast cycle time was essential to business success in many-if not most-industries and nations. The Japanese especially had chosen cycle time reduction as a competitive strategy. In an international quality survey studying the practicers of more than 400 companies world-wide, 84 percent of the responding Japanese businesses indicated that they usually or always employ cycle time analysis as a primary tool to compress time in business processes.
- IBM Rochester, a 1990 Malcolm Baldrige Award winner in the manufacturing category includes cycle time reduction as one of its six critical success factors for quality improvement. Since 1984, IBM Rochester has reduced product development time for new mid-range computers by more than half, while they have cut their manufacturing cycle time by 60 percent.
- The Cadillac Motor Company, a 1990 Baldrige winner has reduced cycle time in die-changing from 12 hours to 3.5 minutes through a team of plant workers and common sense - all without any capital investment. The team colour-coded the pieces of the die for easy transfer, (previously colour coding experts were required). They also laid some no-slip floor covering, which prevented the equipment from sliding as the die was being changed.
- Focusing on time-compression as a key corporate-wide goal, 1992 Baldrige winner Texas Instruments Defense and Electronics Group reduced production cycle time by 21 percent in 1992 with a 56 percent reduction in stock-to-production time.
- Using process management and time-compression techniques, 1988 Baldrige winner, Motorola has reduced its corporate auditing process over a three-year period from an average of seven weeks to five days from the time a field auditor first pens a report to the time the final version is delivered to management.
- Globe Metallurgical, also 1988 Baldrige winner, replies to customer inquiries, no matter where in the world, within 24 hours. Response time used to range from 7 days to over a week.
- Xerox, a 1989 Baldrige winner, cut the new-product design-to-market cycle by 50 percent through its quality practices.
- Westinghons Nuclear Fuels, another 1988 Baldrige winner, reduced manufacturing cycle time by 40 percent through its quality efforts.

POINTS TO REMEMBER

- **Competitiveness** is "how effectively an organisation meets the needs and wants of customers relative to others that offer similar goods or services".
- **Marketing** influences competitiveness in several ways, including : *(i)* identifying consumer wants and needs, *(ii)* pricing and *(iii)* advertising and sales promotion.
- **Operations** influences competitiveness through product and service design, cost, location, quality, response time, flexibility, inventory and supply chain management and service.
- **Time-based competition** is competition based on time, rapidly developing products and moving them to market. It is also known as **speed to market, fast cycle time or fast-response, time-based management or time compression.**

- **Time-based competition** makes business process speed a primary focus of improvement and establishes cycle time as a key measure of performance.
- **Time-based strategies** focus on reducing time needed to carryout various activities in a process.
- By reducing time, costs can be reduced, productivity can be increased, quality tends to be better, product innovations can appear in the market sooner and customer service is improved.
- **Time reduction** can be achieved in *(a)* planning time, *(b)* product/service time, *(c)* processing time, *(d)* change-over time in production set ups, *(e)* delivery time and *(f)* response time for complaints.
- In the **Baldrige criteria,** "fast-response" is identified as a core value or foundation concept of high-performing, customer-focused organisations.
- **Speed** is primarily measured in terms of cycle time in business.
- **Cycle time** is defined as the interval between the start and the finish of a process.
- **Total cycle time** is the time that elapses between expressing a need and having the need satisfactory fulfilled.
- **Work** is represented as a cycle, in turn, the primary work cycle is composed of subprocesses each of which has its own cycle time contributing to the total elapsed cycle time.
- **Cycle time analysis** and benchmarking go hand in hand.
- **Rework and redundancy** represent another major cycle time reduction opportunity area in most work systems.
- **Cycle time analysis** is rooted in process mapping and process management.
- The keys to effective cycle time analysis are a process map and time-based performance measure.
- **Cycle time** is inseparately linked to cost and quality.
- As a managerial tool that helps accelerate organisational learning, benchmarking acts as a primary catalyst in the cycle time reduction process.
- **Generic practices to reduce cycle time include :**
  - *(i)* Establish dynamic information flows
  - *(ii)* Reduce bottle necks
  - *(iii)* Reduce the number of inspection items
  - *(iv)* Reduce decision and approval points
  - *(v)* Simplify the decision making process
  - *(vi)* Standardise information, reporting forms and procedures to reduce variation
  - *(vii)* Avoid frequent process hand offs
  - *(viii)* Improve plant or office layouts that separate work groups or disrupt processes
  - *(ix)* Group lots or work with similar requirements
  - *(x)* Organise or "pre-kit" tools, paperwork, gages *etc.,* to facilitate rapid work flow
  - *(xi)* Consolidate purchases
  - *(xii)* Eliminate unnecessary variation in design
  - *(xiii)* Automate repetitive handling operations
- Benchmarking acts as a time-compression catalyst.
- In the 21st century, speed is a distinguishing characteristic of market leaders.

REVIEW QUESTIONS

1. What is "competitiveness"? Explain how business organisations compete in the market place.
2. List the dimensions of competitiveness.
3. What is "time-based competition"?
4. Discuss the concept of "time-based competition".
5. Discuss the various "time-based strategies" used for reducing time required to accomplish various activities in manufacturing/service firms.
6. Discuss the benefit of "speed" or "time-to-market".
7. What is "cycle time"? Explain how "speed" can be measured through cycle time.
8. Explain how "process benchmarking" facilitates cycle-time reduction.
9. Discuss the various opportunities available for cycle-time reduction.
10. List the various examples of waiting and rework.
11. Discuss the various initiatives for cycle time reduction through benchmarking.
12. Discuss the role of benchmarking in cycle time reduction and time-based competition.
13. Discuss the various generic practices to reduce cycle time.
14. Discuss how benchmarking acts as a time compression catalyst.

DISCUSSION QUESTIONS

1. "Time-based competition makes business process speed a primary focus of improvement and establishes cycle time as a key measure of performance" - Explain.
2. "Cycle time is the primary measure of speed in business". Do you agree or disagree? Give reasons for your answer.
3. "As a managerial tool that helps accelerate organisational learning, benchmarking acts as a primary catalyst in the cycle-time reduction process" - Elaborate.
4. "Response time improvements often drive simultaneous improvements in organisation, quality and productivity" - Discuss.
5. "Cycle-time analysis and benchmarking go hand in hand". Discuss.

CHAPTER 15

Benchmarking and Change Management

INTRODUCTION

Change is any alternative in the current work environment. The shift may be in the way things are perceived or in how they are organised, processed, created or maintained. Change is experienced by every individual in the organisation.

Change refers to a significant difference in what was before. This could mean doing things in a new way, following a new path, adopting new technology, installing a new system, following new management procedures, merging, reorganising or any other highly significant, disruptive event.

Change is significant, prolonged and often disruptive. It represents a departure in whole or in part of what came before it. It might include venturing into completely new territory, facing something unexpected, making a major course redirection, or getting up to speed in record time with insufficient resources.

To survive in today's market place, a business must constantly examine its performance, strategy, processes and systems to understand what changes need to be made. At the same time, an organisation must also understand the implications of a new business change in its employees, given their culture, values, history and capacity for change. Employees ultimately perform the new day-to-day activities and make the new processes and systems come to life in the business. Change management is about managing people in a changing environment so that business changes are successful and the desired business results are realised.

The Importance of Change

For organisations committed to pursuing total quality, change is a way of life. Organisational change is needed to implement total quality and constantly thereafter. To start with, effort must be put to begin to change the culture of the organisation. Total quality is essentially based on a culture based on customer satisfaction, continuous improvement and teamwork. Once total quality is established in an organisation, continuous improvement efforts will relentlessly create changes in product designs, standard operating procedures and virtually every other aspect of organisations. One important aspect of continuous improvement is reengineering in which the processes by which organisation operates are reexamined and redesigned to provide higher quality at lower cost.

Why are Changes Necessary?

The major reason driving change is that customer expectations continually evolve. Features or services that delight customers today may be taken for granted after sometime, say a year or so and fail to delight them any more. Products that are acceptable to customers today may be perceived as substandard sometimes in the future. Competition continues to raise the standard for quality and organisations must keep up the elevated standards to survive the competition. **"Quality is a race without a finish line"**. Change is also required because processes become unnecessarily complicated over a period of time and advances in technology forces processes to be changed to catch up with technology.

Strategic Change versus Process Change

Organisational changes resulting from strategy development and implementation (*i.e.*, strategic change) and organisational changes resulting from operational assessment activities (*i.e.*, process change) are not the same.

Strategic change stems from strategic objectives which are generally externally focused and relate to significant customer, market, product/service and technological opportunities and challenges. This is what an organisation has to undergo to remain or become competitive in the market place. Strategic change has a broader scope, is driven by environmental forces and is tied closely to the organisation's ability to achieve its goals. Some examples of strategic change are General Electric's implementation of Six-Sigma throughout the corporation, and Hewlett-Packard's decision to merge with Compaq.

In contrast, ***process change*** deals with the operations of an organisation. *For example,* changes in purchasing procedures, accounting systems, inventory control practices, warehousing practices etc. Unlike strategic changes which motivate organisation-wide changes in behaviour, process change is often confined to a particular department, division or unit of an organisation. Although change to a business process tends to have long lasting-effects, the change tends to be narrow in scope. ***Table 15.1* describes the characteristics of strategic change in contrast with process change.** Strategic changes are the ones that impact culture the most.

TABLE 15.1 : STRATEGIC CHANGE VERSUS PROCESS CHANGE

Parameter	Strategic change	Process change
Theme of change	Shift in organisational direction	Adjustment of organisational processes
Driving force	Usually environmental forces-market, rival technological change	Usually internal - "How can we align our process better?"
Typical antecedent	Strategic planning process	Self-assessment of management system
How much of organisation changes?	Typically widespread	Often narrow divisional or functional
Examples	Entering new markets, seeking low-cost position, mergers and acquisitions	Improving information systems, establishing hiring guidelines, developing improved customer satisfaction measures

Cultural Change

A major strategic change that organisations must make in pursuing total quality is a change in culture. ***Culture*** is a set of beliefs and values shared by the people in an organisation. Culture is a powerful influence on people's behaviour. It is what binds the people together and helps them make sense of what happens in their organisation. Cultures vary dramatically between one company and another, and between one country and another.

The organisational culture needed to support total quality is one that values customers, improvement and teamwork.

As environments change, the organisational cultures must adapt (*i.e.,* change). Many firms have recognised the importance of changing corporate culture as they launch new strategies. New strategies based on quality may conflict with old strategies that may have emphasised schedules and productivity.

The cultural elements that are necessary to sustain a total quality environment include the following: *(i)* Visionary leadership, *(ii)* Customer-driven excellence, *(iii)* Organisational and personal learning, *(iv)* Valuing employees and partners, *(v)* Agility, *(vi)* Focus on the future, *(vii)* Managing for innovation, *(viii)* Managing by fact, *(ix)* Social responsibility, *(x)* Focus on results and creating value and *(xi)* System perspective.

What is Change Management?

Change management is about helping people through change. It is the process, tools and techniques for proactively managing the people side of change in order to achieve the desired business results.

Change management is the application of many different ideas from the fields of engineering, business and psychology. As changes in organisations have become more frequent and a necessity for survival, the body of knowledge known as "change management" has also grown to encompass more skills and knowledge from each of these fields of study.

There are two views of change-the top-down executive's view and the bottom-up employee's view, which create two distinct challenges for managing change. These two challenges can be referred to as *(i)* Organisational change management and *(ii)* Individual change management. Both are skills that today's leaders need for success.

Organisational change management is the perspective of business leadership from the top looking down into the organisation. The focus is around broad change management practices and skills that will help the organisation understand, accept and support the needed business change. The emphasis is on communication, training and the overall culture or value system of the organisation.

Individual change management is the management of change from the perspective of the employees. They are the ones who ultimately must implement the change. The focus for individual change management is around the tools and techniques to help employees through the transition. Managers and supervisors must provide the coaching required to help individuals understand their role and the decisions they make in the change process.

ROLE OF BENCHMARKING IN CHANGE MANAGEMENT

Although sometimes difficult to accept, change is inevitable both at the individual level and the organisational level. Organisations do not have the luxury of choosing whether they are for or against change. Change is the most certain of operating realities. The question is whether you want to deal with change systematically to arrive at some place good or whether you want to take what comes willy-nilly. If organisations decide to approach the management of change in a systematic way, benchmarking is the single most powerful tool within their grasp.

As an instrument for managing change in a positive fashion, benchmarking does the following:

(i) Creates motivation for change.

(ii) Provides a vision of what an organisation will look like after the change.

(iii) Instructs employees what to change.

(iv) Provides data, evidence and success stores for inspiring change.

(v) Raises awareness of competitor position and headway that stimulates innovative change.

(vi) Reduces the cycle time required to achieve change.

(vii) Identifies best practices for how to manage change.

(viii) Creates a baseline or yardstick by which to evaluate the impact of earlier changes.

Motivating Change Through Benchmarking

There are two kinds of managers - those who anticipate change and those who wait for a crisis and fail. Benchmarking is a favoured tool of this first sort of leader. By applying benchmarking as an on-going business practice, they create an early warning system alerting the organisation when change is necessary.

Benchmarking provides employees and managers the tool, the rationale and the process to embrace change as constant and inevitable. In today's world, no one organisation can ever hope to corner the market on effective operating practices and good ideas. To be a leader in today's market place, one must by necessity look outward - as well as inward, for constant improvement in the fast changing environment.

The on-going study of best-practices can help an organisation avoid being ambushed by unexpected change. By systematically studying others and comparing one's own operations and performance with the best and most effective practices of highly-innovative and successful companies, an organisation can evaluate when change is a necessity for market leadership - or for survival. The on-going search for best practices quickly draws you outside the confines of your own culture. ***Best practice benchmarking*** is therefore a pragmatic approach to managing change. Benchmarking provides the navigational system that helps employees chart a managed course toward proven and effective operating practices and strategies.

One of the most difficult tasks of management is to convince the employees of successful organisations that change may be necessary. Benchmarking can be a blunt instrument to demonstrate the need for change, even in successful organisations. IBM Rochester, for instance solicited user information from 250 customers, adopted Milliken's teamwork, Toyota's short-cycle product development system and Motorola's Six-Sigma defect-prevention system.

Benchmarking has also inspired dramatic change at Caterpillar, a world leader in the design, manufacturing and marketing of earth-moving equipment. Caterpillar realised the need for change after benchmarking seven companies from the aerospace, computer, electronic, industrial equipment, and automotive industries. This ambitions best practice study convinced Caterpillar to streamline the process by which its customers replace or repair electrical and electronic components. Guided by many superior operating practices identified during its benchmarking activities, Caterpillar reduced the cycle time from customer problem reporting to parts retrieval from an average of 42 days to one day. Next Caterpillar reduced second-phase cycle time for parts retrieval and delivery from an average of 54 days to five days. Caterpillar reduced the average repair of electrical components from 120 days to 7 days. Caterpillar's management was inspired by the organisation's benchmarking studies, which served as a catalyst for change. Driven by the imperative of better satisfying customers, the best practice findings of benchmarking projects have become an inspiration for positive change at Caterpillar .

Benchmarking and Visualising Change

The path to change is meandering and slow. Organisations that compete in highly-competitive industries and markets find the long and winding road to improvement takes too long to traverse and often diverges from the organisation's true estimation. ***Benchmarking provides a clear vision of the end point of positive change***. Such a vision helps mangers chart a course that is more direct and less perilous through the rough waters of change. Best practice profiles provide a vivid picture of what an organisation will look like after it accomplishes a proven regimen of change.

EXHIBIT 15.1 : ANY PROCESS HAS THREE VERSIONS

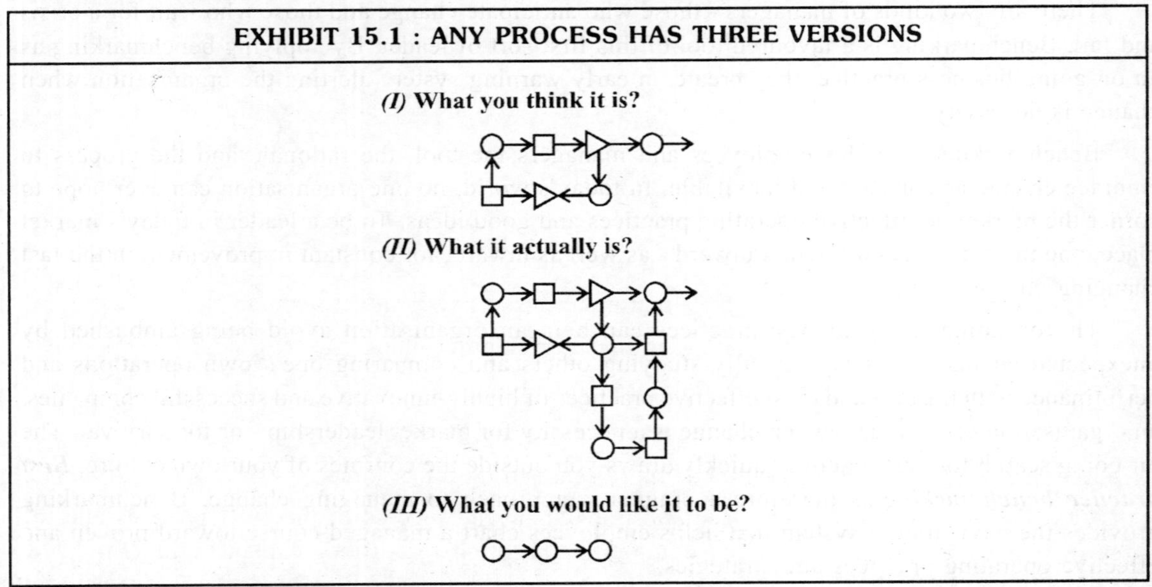

Process mapping techniques illustrate graphically and often dramatically the benefits that accrue when transforming a process from its current state to a best practice state. Every process has three versions: *(i)* ***what the organisation thinks it is,*** *(ii)* ***what it actually is and*** *(iii)* ***what it should be.*** Best practice benchmarking sketches the "future state" portrait of what the process should be. ***Exhibit 15.1*** **illustrates this concept that all unimproved processes have three versions.**

Benchmarking contributes to the creation of the "should be" or best practice state. Using process maps and flowcharts, benchmarking helps people become less resistant to change because they suddenly see the path to the future state.

Ford Motor Company, *for example,* reengineered its accounts payable process in the 1980s. Applying traditional process rationalisation techniques and new technology solutions, Ford projected a 20 percent reduction in head count from 500 to 400 people. Then Ford benchmarked Mazda, which had pioneered a paperless, or invoiceless accounts payables system with its suppliers. After studying Mazda's much superior approach, Ford was able to visualise a paperless or invoiceless accounts payable system. Inspired by the benchmarking, Ford implemented the process change to an invoiceless system and reduced the number of employees required to run the accounts payable system by 75 percent. The changes also helped Ford create simpler material controls, provide more accurate financial information and produce a more efficient accounts payable system.

Deciding What to Change

An organisation can evaluate its position relative to the rest of the market by comparing baseline benchmarks with those of leading competitors or best practice companies. In this context, benchmarking helps assess the need to change and also suggests what to change.

Consider the study of sales-force effectiveness in the pharmaceutical industry. In 1991, a US based health care products manufacturer found that the sales forces of its three major competitors were significantly more productive than its own, moreover, the company's own sales force productivity was declining. What was the reason for this slide?

Research and analysis showed the company's product line was equal to, if not better than its three rivals. But the study also revealed serious problems with its sales force, including poor knowledge of the product line, poor accessibility and responsiveness of salesforce, poor continuity of sales contract, slow price quotation turn around time and poor overall service quality. As a result of benchmarking studies, the company put the following seven actions into place in early 1991 :

(i) A 50 hour sales expectations/effectiveness course for all new hires.

(ii) An ongoing sales effectiveness training program.

(iii) A new sales compensation structure that emphasised new product revenue streams.

(iv) Increasing the power of sales people to make pricing decisions.

(v) A well-defined career path with promotion guidelines.

(vi) A redesigned recruiting process to attract the best people and

(vii) Redefined sales territories that made more sense to the sales force.

By early 1993, management posed questions about the success of the 1991 changes and the potential for keeping the sales force competitive through the strategic plan ending in 1998. Benchmarking created the impetus to ask these questions, it provided the evidence to evaluate the answers and it created a needed sense of urgency to retarget goals through each year of the strategic plan. ***Table 15.2*** **summarises the key benchmarks that signalled the organisation's management that change was necessary.**

TABLE 15.2 : SAMPLE BENCHMARKING DATA FOR SALES EFFECTIVENESS

Pharmaceutical Industry Sales Force Productivity

	Sales per person (millions)					Gap versus	
Year	The host company	Competitor A	Competitor B	Competitor C	Competitor average	Average of A,B and C	Best competitor
1988	$ 2.05	$ 3.10	$ 3.55	$ 3.70	$ 3.45	–$ 1.40	–$ 1.65
1989	$ 1.75	$ 3.25	$ 3.70	$ 3.60	$ 3.52	–$ 1.77	–$ 1.95
1990	$ 1.70	$ 3.40	$ 3.95	$ 3.60	$ 3.65	–$ 1.95	–$ 2.25
1991	$ 2.15	$ 3.50	$ 4.05	$ 3.70	$ 3.75	–$ 1.60	–$ 1.90
1992	$ 2.75	$ 3.55	$ 4.10	$ 3.70	$ 3.78	–$ 1.03	–$ 1.35

Benchmarking study revealed that the seven actions taken in 1991 resulted in considerable improvement. Nevertheless, significant continued improvement in salesforce productivity was critical to competitiveness. The company's benchmark gaps were significant and competitor B was offsetting the company's advances with its own continued improvement. The host company conducted two additional benchmarking studies, one on best sales training practices and the other on best sales compensation practices. In the end, the company implemented a proven approach to its sales training system by creatively adapting both competitor B's sales training program and the training program of the leader outside the health industry. **The organisation adopted the following eight best practices.**

1. Thirteen weeks of class room training for every salesperson to occur within 15 months of hire, five weeks devoted to product line, five weeks devoted to sales techniques and three weeks devoted to customer relationship management.
2. Integration of five case studies into class room learning. The company had commissioned these case studies, on successful and unsuccessful sales contacts from two leading business schools.
3. Extensive video taped role-playing exercises on effective sales techniques with follow-up critique to reinforce learning.
4. Use of award-winning sales people as class room instructors.
5. Regular CEO visits to the class room to articulate the value, importance, and expectations of the sales force for the success of the company.
6. Teaching the sales people to benchmark competitor's prices, quality, services and products in order to enhance their presentations to customers.
7. Assigning senior sales mentors to directly supervise the field exposure of new sales people during their first year.
8. Debriefings to critique every sales contact during the first six month probationary period of all new sales people.

The Two Frontiers of Change

Benchmarking helps organisation find their ways through two frontiers of change :

(i) It provides navigational maps or blue prints describing the most effective practices and approaches for structuring and accomplishing work.

(ii) Benchmarking provides insight and information about how to accomplish cultural change.

These two frontiers circumscribe successful change efforts. Consequently, the work systems or processes and the culture must be considered together. The most perfectly designed work processes still produce suboptimal results if the people and the culture do not accept them. In turn, flawed work systems can affect healthy corporated cultures and most motivated employees.

These two types of change can be envisioned with the help of the metaphor of a fast-running river system. The work process or system is easily visible, just as certain types of life and activity above the water line are visible from the banks of the river. Plant life, and geological activity are all plenty below the water line, but these activities are not visible from the shore. The work processes are essentially above-the-water line activities and organisational culture is below the water line activities. Best practice benchmarking enables change within the process and the culture, both above and below the water line.

At the above the water level of ***how work is done***, benchmarking provides valuable design and operating information that can help employees see ways to improve important work systems such as the sales, order-entry, product delivery, billing or customer service process. For instance, a company may be able to streamline the way accounts are paid by introducing personal computer work stations and a relational data base of purchase orders, vendor invoices and payment records. ***Exhibit 15.2*** **depicts the two levels of managing change above and below the water line.**

EXHIBIT 15.2

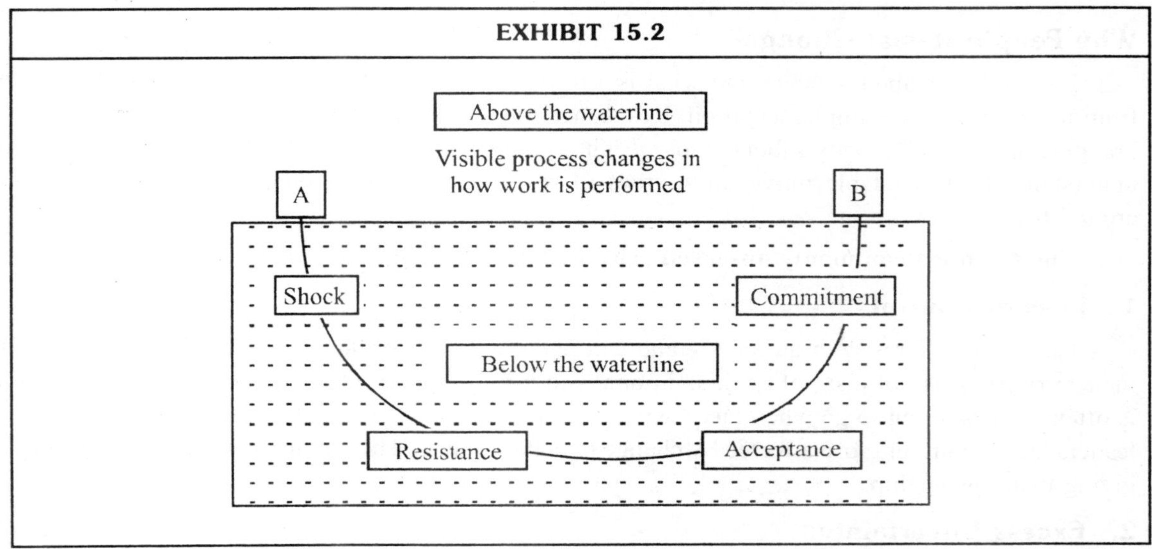

Cultural transformation occurs below the waterline. They embrace softer, less easily charted types of change that link to people's feelings and values, their work related fears and phobias, their acceptance or resistance to new experiences. Change management at this level radically transforms employee behaviour. Generally, people often shrink from change, they assume defensive postures when confronted with unfamiliar or new experiences. Front-line workers resistance is reinforced by traditional "keep-them-in-dark" management behaviours. Unfortunately many organisations have failed to focus dilogently on the cultural level of change management.

Benchmarking reveals that successful cultural change efforts embrace a people-oriented as well as process-oriented-approach to organisational transformation. Successful change managers help employees to understand the vision of change. They communicate the rationale for pursuing that vision, they develop a sense of ownership on the front-line for implementing the change and they provide reward and recognition for those who make the change work. The natural human reaction is to resist change. Managers view change as a splendid opportunity whereas employees view change as a moral threat. For those who see change as threat, their reaction is usually "flight or fight" *i.e.,* avoid or resist change. If they flee both the employee and the organisation lose. If they fight, good ideas suffer when management or employees resort to strong-arm tactics to support their views.

Among organisations that successfully implement cultural change, open communications and managerial honesty emerge as best practices. Open and honest communications about difficult changes such as work force reductions, new skill requirements or job redesign may not inspire cheerfulness among managers and employees, but they enable people to better understand operating circumstances and realities. Understanding the reasons for change is a critical first-step to mastering it.

Benchmarking provides a tool to help managers and employees see that change is necessary. Benchmarking also helps reengineering teams, strategic partners, mid-level managers and front-line employees to craft better solutions than they could have generated alone.

Why People Resist Change?

Leadership is about change, but what is a leader to do when faced with ubiquitous resistance from people to change implementation. Resistance to change manifests in many ways, from foot-dragging and inertia to petty sabotage to outright rebellion. The best tool for leaders of change is to understand the predictable universal sources of resistance in each situation and then strategise around them.

The ten most commonly observed reasons for people to resist change are given below :

1. Loss of Control

Change interferes with autonomy and can make people feel that they have lost control over their territory. It is not just political, as in one who has the power. Our sense of self-determination is often the first thing to go when faced with a potential change coming from some one else. Smart leaders leave room for those affected by change to make choices. They invite others into the planning, giving them ownership.

2. Excess Uncertainty

If change is uncertain, then people will not accept it. People will often prefer to remain mired in misery than to head toward an unknown. To overcome inertia, it requires a sense of safety as well as an inspiring vision. Leaders should create certainty of the change process with clear, simple steps and time schedules for implementation.

3. Surprise

Decisions imposed on people suddenly with no time to get used to the idea or prepare for the consequences are generally resisted. It is always to say "No" than to say "Yes" to any change. Leaders should avoid the temptation to craft changes in secrecy and then announce all at once.

4. Everything Seems Different

Change is meant to bring something different, but how different? Human beings are creatures of habit. Routines becomes automatic, but change jolts us into consciousness, sometimes in uncomfortable ways. Too many differences can be distracting and confusing. Leaders should try to minimise the number of unrelated differences introduced by a central change. Leaders must remain focused on the important things and avoid change for the sake of change.

5. Loss of Face

Change is a departure from the past. Those people associated with the previous version - the one that didn't work or the one that is being superseded - are likely to be defensive about it. When change involves a big shift of strategic direction, the people responsible for the previous direction dread the perception that they must have been wrong. Leaders can help people maintain dignity by celebrating those elements of the past that are worth honouring and making it clear that the world has changed. That makes it easier to let go and move on.

6. Concerns about Competence

Change is resisted when it makes people stupid. They might express skepticism about whether the new software version will work or whether digital journalism is really an improvement, but down deep they are worried that their skills will be obsolete. Leaders should over-invest in structural reassurance, providing abundant information, education, training, mentoring and support systems.

7. More Work

This is a universal challenge. Change indeed means more work. Those closest to the change in terms of designing and testing it are often overloaded, in part because of the inevitable unanticipated glitches in the middle of change. Leaders should acknowledge the hard work of change by allowing some people to focus exclusively on it, or adding extra perquisites for participants. Leaders should reward and recognise participants and their families, too, who often make unseen sacrifies.

8. Ripple Effects

Change creates ripples like tossing a pebble into a pond, reaching distant points in ever-widening circles. The ripples disrupt other departments, important customers, people well outside the venture or neighbourhood, and they start to push back, rebelling against changes they had nothing to do with, that interfere with their own activities. Leaders should enlarge the circle of stakeholders. They must consider all affected parties, however distant and work with them to minimise disruption.

9. Past Resentments

The ghosts of the past are always lying in wait to haunt us. As long as everything is in steady state, they remain out of sight. But the minute you need co-operation for something new or different, the ghosts spring into action. Old wounds reopen, historic resentments are remembered - sometimes going back many generations. Leaders should consider gestures to heal the past before sailing into the future.

10. Sometimes the Threat is Real

Change is resisted because it can hurt. When new technologies displace old ones, jobs can be lost, prices can be cut, investments can be wiped out. The best thing leaders can do when the changes they seek pose significant threat is to be honest, transparent, fast and fair. *For example,* one big lay off with strong transition assistance is better than successive way of job cuts.

Although leaders can't always make people feel comfortable with change, they can minimise discomfort. Diagnosing the sources of resistance is the first step toward good solutions. And feedback from resistors can even be helpful in improving the process of gaining acceptance of change.

MASTERING CHANGE

Cultural or transformational change doesn't take place off and on. It is a cycle or process that unfolds over time. John Schrer, a consultant specialising in change management, conceives of managed change occurring in a seven-step process or cycle that is orderly, if not always neat. ***Table 15.3* depicts this change process and describes the enabling role benchmarking plays in the cycle.**

Transforming corporate culture can be a tough task. It requires enormous effort and support from senior leadership. Benchmarking acts as an instrument for directing and managing change and helps leadership demonstrate to employees the need, urgency, benefits and path to change.

Guidelines for Implementing Change

1. Create an awareness of the need for change.
2. Organise a project with sufficient authority to guide the process.
3. Define the vision and strategies for achieving it.
4. Communicate the vision and demonstrate personal commitment to it.
5. Prevent obstacles that prevent others from acting on the vision.
6. Go for early and visible wins.
7. Build on success by rewarding supporters and involving more people.
8. Institutionalise the new methods by aligning other systems with them.

Common Errors Made in Managing Change

1. Not sufficiently emphasising the urgency and allowing people to be complacent.
2. Those guiding the process do not have sufficient power.
3. Lacking a clear and compelling vision or not communicating it strongly and/or frequently enough.
4. Failing to manage the forces that resist change.
5. Not ensuring some early success that encourage others.
6. Celebrating victory prematurely.
7. Not changing other organisational systems and cultural elements that are required for long-term continuation of the change.

TABLE 15.3 : THE SEVEN-STEP CHANGE MANAGEMENT PROCESS

7 steps to managing change	The enabling role of benchmarking
1. Identify what is working and what is not working in the old culture	Benchmarking provides an objective way to determine what is and what is not working when referenced against the competitive market place
2. Describe the changes needed for the new culture to succeed	Benchmarking other's best practices helps managers visualise what changes will most help usher in the new culture
3. Model the new culture from the top	Benchmarking identifies role model behaviours for leading and supporting the cultural change
4. Train people for the new culture	Benchmarking can help identify what types of skills and behaviours are necessary to support the change and it also provides insight into how to deliver this change
5. Reward people for taking on the new culture	Benchmarking suggests which reward and recognition systems are most effective in supporting the new culture
6. Structure for the new culture	Benchmarking helps identify organisational structures that best support the new culture
7. Assess and maintain the new culture	Benchmarking provides an on-going means of monitoring the market adequacy of the new culture

BOX 15.1 : BENCHMARKING IN PRACTICE – LAUNCHING "POWER OF ONE" CAMPAIGN AT GTE TELEPHONE OPERATIONS

GTE Telephone Operations used customer satisfaction research and cost-related benchmarking data to initially launch its ***"power of one"***, a broad reaching corporate change process.

Power of one emphasised the need to reengineer business processes and concentrate on providing value to four stake holder groups : (1) Customers, (2) Employees, (3) Shareholders and (4) Communities.

GTE's corporate communication then used the benchmarking data as objective market evidence to establish credibility for senior management's mandate for change. Best practice information, generated by GTE employee benchmarking teams that studied 84 high performing organisations, further strengthened employee understanding and acceptance of the required changes. Success stories and empirical evidence brought home from other companies by benchmarking teams inspired employees confidence that the company could successfully transform itself.

During the process, employees began to understand that corporate systems and business processes that generated record earnings in 1992 would not lead to market leadership in the future. Benchmarking provided credibility to the claims, it helped employees understand the reasons why change was necessary and then it enabled the employees to map the course that would lead to the desired change.

"One best way to predict the future is to create it" observed Peter Drucker, one of the most esteemed observers of modern management theory. At GTE and other organisations undertaking major change efforts, the senior leadership-informed by benchmarking-initiates the change. But it is the staff and line employees - enabled by benchmarking who draft and execute the blueprints creating each organisation's future.

POINTS TO REMEMBER

- **Change** refers to a significant difference in what was before.
- **Change** is significant, prolonged and often disruptive.
- To survive in today's market place, a business must constantly examine its performance, strategy, processes and systems to understand what changes needs to be made.
- For organisations pursuing total quality, change is a way of life.
- The major reason driving change is that customer expectations continually evolve.
- **Competition** continues to raise the standard for quality and organisations must keep up the elevated standards to survive the competition.
- **Organisational changes** can be of two types : *(i)* Strategic change and *(ii)* Process change.
- **Strategic change** stems from strategic objectives which are generally externally focused and relate to significant customer, market, product/service and technological opportunities and challenges.
- **Process change** deals with the operations of an organisation.
- A major strategic change that organisations must make in pursuing total quality is a **change in culture**.
- **Culture** is a set of beliefs and values shared by the people in an organisation.
- The **organisational culture** needed to support total quality is one that values customers, improvement and team work.
- **Change management** is about helping people through change.
- **Change management** is the application of many different ideas from the fields of engineering, business and psychology.
- **There are two views of change :**

  (i) Top-down executive's view and *(ii)* Bottom-up employee's view
- **Two distinct challenges for managing change are :**

  (i) Organisational change management and *(ii)* Individual change management
- **Organisational change management** is the perspective of business leadership from the top looking down into the organisation.
- **Individual change management** is the management of change from the perspective of the employees.
- If organisations decide to approach the management of change in a systematic way, benchmarking is the single most powerful tool within their grasp.
- There are two kinds of managers – those who anticipate change and those who wait for a crisis and fail.
- **Benchmarking** provides employees and managers the tool, the rationale and the process to embrace change as constant and inevitable.o
- Best practice benchmarking is a pragmatic approach to managing change.
- One of the most difficult tasks of management is to convince the employees of successful organisations that change may be necessary. Benchmarking can be a blunt instrument to demonstrate the need for change, even in successful organisations.
- Benchmarking provides a clear vision of the end point of positive change.

- **Every process has three versions :**
  (i) What the organisation thinks it is? *(ii)* What is actually is? and
  (iii) What it should be?
- Best practice benchmarking sketches the **"future state"** portrait of what a process should be.
- Benchmarking helps assess the need to change and also suggests what to change.
- Benchmarking reveals that successful cultural change efforts embrace a people-oriented as well as process-oriented approach to organisational transformation.
- Successful change managers help employees to understand the vision of change.
- Among organisations that successfully implement cultural change, open communication and managerial honesty emerge as best practices.
- Understanding the reasons for change is a critical first-step to mastering it.
- Cultural or transformational change doesn't take place off and on. It is a cycle or process that unfolds over time.
- Transforming corporate culture can be a tough task. It requires enormous effort and support from senior leadership.

REVIEW QUESTIONS

1. Define the terms "change" and "change management".
2. Discuss the significance of change in organisations.
3. Distinguish between strategic change and process change.
4. Why are changes necessary?
5. What is "cultural change"?
6. Distinguish between organisational change management and individual change management.
7. Discuss the role of benchmarking in change management.
8. How change is motivated through benchmarking? Explain.
9. Discuss the seven-step change management process and the enabling role of benchmarking in each of these seven steps.
10. Discuss the guidelines for implementing change and the common errors made in managing change.

DISCUSSION QUESTIONS

1. "For organisations committed to total quality, change is a way of life" Discuss.
2. "If organisations decide to approach the management of change in a systematic way, benchmarking is the single most powerful tool within their grasp" - Explain.
3. "Best practice benchmarking is a pragmatic approach to managing change" - Discuss.
4. "Benchmarking helps assess the need to change and also suggests what to change" - Elaborate.
5. "Benchmarking helps organisations find their ways through two frontiers of change" What are they? Discuss.
6. "Benchmarking provides a clear vision of the end point of positive change" - Critically examine the statement.

CHAPTER 16

International Benchmarking

INTRODUCTION

Best practitioners are identified and analysed elsewhere in the world, perhaps because there are too few benchmarking partners within the same country to produce valid results.

Globalisation and advances in information technology are increasing opportunities for international projects. However, these can take more time and resources to set up and implement and the results may need careful analysis due to national differences.

Where the aim is to achieve world-class status or simply because there are insufficient "national" businesses against which to benchmark, international benchmarking is the appropriate approach to improve performance of global organisations.

The objective of international benchmarking is similar to other benchmarking projects. However since international benchmarking involves higher costs and more complexities than other benchmarking projects, it can only be justified by benefits that can not be achieved through other forms of benchmarking.

Why International Benchmarking?

International benchmarking has many benefits that can not be achieved through other forms of benchmarking. Generally, the interest in international benchmarking reflects growing globalisation and international interdependency. The development of the public sector or private sector in one country depends to an increasing extent on developments in other countries.

International benchmarking is particularly useful in the following situations :

1. When an organisation is providing an unique service and there are no organisations within the country that it can be benchmarked against.
2. In macro-benchmarking of whole service delivery systems across countries.
3. To assess the general level of performance of the public sector or private sector industries. Benchmarking across countries may reveal more differences in performance than if the comparison is only done within a country.

4. To try to find innovative and alternative ways of providing a service or responding to a problem. Usually more diverse methods will be found if organisations are compared across a number of countries, for example, benchmarking waste management process in India with that of in Singapore or Japan.

How International Benchmarking Differs from Other Forms of Benchmarking?

International benchmarking involves more complexities than benchmarking within countries. The differences between the countries mean that information that needs to be used in benchmarking is often not directly comparable. These comparability problems are both technical and more fundamental. The technical problems should be solvable but the more fundamental comparability problems are more difficult to tackle. However, some of these differences should not necessarily be seen as a problem. They can just as well be seen as the very substance of international benchmarking.

1. ***Cost information :*** Methods for accounting costs may vary substantially between countries. Some countries report costs on cash basis while other report full accrual costs, including cost of capital. Another problem is that the costs of internal service in the industry may in some cases be allocated to the provider rather than the receiver. Funding practices may also be different, making it difficult to get information about the total cost of a given activity.
2. ***Different prices :*** Prices between countries are variable. Cost information may therefore not be the best indicator of the relevant performance of a given service.
3. ***Differing social systems and differing social roles of the same delivery systems :*** The systems for providing services are different in different countries, services may for example be provided at different levels of government, involvement of private and voluntary organisations may differ and the same or similar services can be provided by different service systems.
4. ***Different needs, conditions and expectations :*** The need for a given service may vary between countries. Comparisons of quantity have to reflect those different needs. Conditions may be different. It is more expensive to provide service in rural areas than in cities. The rural areas on the other side have fewer social problems than large cities. The expectation of customers may vary between countries and this may affect results in relation to many service quality measures.

Approaches to International Benchmarking

International benchmarking can be initiated through a number of approaches :

1. ***Macro benchmarking of major service sectors :*** Experience shows that it takes a lot of efforts to gather and organise information and solve comparability problems.
2. ***Benchmarking of the same type of organisations in a limited number of countries :*** There is a considerable interest for this type of benchmarking and practical difficulties should be solvable. However, the main work would have to be carried out by the organisations themselves.
3. ***Process benchmarking using a standard :*** The use of a process standard may reduce problems in relation to comparability. However, this also means that fewer problems will be exposed and tackled.
4. ***Partial benchmarking focusing on one or few aspects of performance :*** This could for example, involve benchmarking of consumer satisfaction levels between countries. One central problem would be how to take different expectations into account.

International benchmarking projects should aim at exploring general issues and problems. They should be monitored and evaluated to make experience assessable and applicable to other projects. It is important to identify problems, both technical and more fundamental and develop methods to tackle them. This will lead to the development of best practice in relation to international benchmarking.

GLOBAL BENCHMARKING NETWORK (GBN)

The Global Benchmarking Network (GBN) is an alliance of leading benchmarking centres worldwide, which share a common vision and mission. Current membership comprises 20 benchmarking centres in 20 countries, which represent more than 30,000 business and government agencies. The Global Benchmarking Network was founded in November 1994 by representatives from benchmarking centres in Germany, Italy, Sweden, the United Kingdom and the United States.

Structure

The GBN is a non-profit organisation. Funding is raised from affiliates' annual fees and other sources approved at the annual meeting. It has a chairman, vice-chairman and a secretary - general. Services of the GBN was established to promote and support the following core benefits for its affiliates:

(i) To share experience in benchmarking centre operations.

(ii) To promote and to assist with international partnering between individual organisations participating in centre activities.

(iii) To enhance centres with marketing and promotional support for benchmarking.

(iv) To exchange selected publications between affiliates including newsletters and promotional material.

(v) To share advance information on up-coming meetings, activities and events including national and international awards.

Vision-Mission-Values of GBN

(i) **GBN vision :** For the GBN to be recognised as the global hub for benchmarking with active representation in all countries.

(ii) **GBN mission :** The GBN is a global network of organisations and experts focused on promoting and facilitating the use of benchmarking and sharing of best practices by helping each other and working together.

(iii) **GBN values :**

(a) ***Professionalism :*** As evidenced by handling all relations between GBN members in a professional way equally like relations to our members and customers.

(b) ***Working together :*** As evidenced by a willingness to share and assist other members, participation in team or group activities and projects as appropriate and attendance at the annual meeting.

(c) ***Excellence :*** As evidenced by developing expertise in benchmarking, leading or managing benchmarking activities and promoting the role of benchmarking in performance improvements.

(d) ***Ethical behaviour :*** As evidenced by following the benchmarking code of conduct.

(vi) **Services :** The GBN provides the following core services for its members :

(a) ***Meetings :*** The GBN organises an annual general meeting which encourages all members to attend.

(b) ***Projects :*** The GBN supports projects that assist the GBN to achieve its mission and vision.

GLOBAL BENCHMARKING STUDY

Intense pressure to reduce costs, innovate products and expand into new markets has manufacturing worldwide shifting production and spreading out supply chain and other operations well beyond their home geographies. After an indepth benchmarking exercise, Dell computers has created an insightful series of reports that look at the increasingly complex and fragmented supply chain environment, implications for manufacturers, resulting challenges and best practices.

To date, more than 800 companies from Asia Pacific, Central and Eastern Europe, North America and Western Europe participated in the benchmark study. Industries represented include aerospace and defense, automotive, industrial and tele-communications equipment, consumer products, life sciences, process, paper and chemicals and high technology.

Global benchmarking is the process of identifying best practices in organisations anywhere in the world to seek information that can help an organisation to measure and compare its performance against those best practices in order to improve its operations.

A *benchmark* is a reference point for taking measures against.

Best practices are the techniques that have worked reliably in different situations to achieve their desired purpose in the most efficient and effective way. The best practices are demonstrated to repeatedly work in different situations and can be replicated in different situations with more or less the same results. The process of benchmarking is aimed at finding the best practices within and outside the industry to which an organisation belongs.

The purpose of benchmarking is to find the best performers in an area so that one can match them and even surpass them. Thus if Dell is thought to have the best supply chain management practices or Toyota the best manufacturing processes, organisations of any type, anywhere, in the world, can benchmark their own practices and processes against these and make improvements in their own practices and processes. Global benchmarking is a subset of benchmarking, which is a generic term that refers to the systematic and continuous process of measuring and comparing an organisation's practices, products or services against best practices demonstrated to be effective by industry leaders.

Examples of Global Benchmarking

1. At the beginning of 20th century, the German military conducted the first known benchmarking study. The military had realised that moving toops was time-consuming and costly. In a news paper article a soldier had read that American Circus had been managing to break camp, load all goods, animals and persons on a train and move on to the next city - all within just one night. This incredible achievement induced a team of military experts from Germany travel to the United states to have a closer look at this happening. It became clear that the circus not

only employed its own logistics experts, but also that special vehicles had been developed to transport equipments and animals. With this knowledge, the German military achieved considerable improvements in troop movements.

2. The introduction of the first assembly lines in the automotive industry in 1916 is a further example of the early application of benchmarking techniques. Inspired by visits to a large slaughter house in Chicago, in which hog halves were transported from workplace to workplace by a suspension conveyor, Henry Ford introduced assembly lines in the automotive industry.
3. The Kanban system is another concept that was transferred from another branch of industry. Through the study of the organisation of American supermarket chains and especially the process of refilling shelves, Toyota developed the concept of Kanban Cards, an approach that is nowadays applied in many other industries.
4. **The Xerox experience :** Xerox realised that Japanese competitors sold copy machines at a price that was well below Xerox's product costs. As a result, Xerox conducted a market-related benchmarking study (competitive benchmarking) for its production department. The production costs, design and other attributes of all copy machines that are available in the market were studied and analysed. Xerox decided to implement benchmarking to identify ways to improve its performance. It benchmarked against L.L. Bean for distribution procedures, Deere and Company for central computer operations, Procter and Gamble for marketing and Floride Power and Light for total quality management.

BENCHMARKING IN JAPAN

In Japan, no word for benchmarking exists and few business people refer to the practice. The Japanese have captured the essence of striving to be the **"best of the best"** in the single word ***dantotsu***. Dantotsu implies a degree of awareness about the environment, particularly of others who also strive to be the best of the best. Eventhough the Japanese do not call the practice "benchmarking" they have become benchmarking masters through generations of practice. **"Of all the countries in the world, Japan is by far the most advanced at benchmarking"**.

In the late 1800s the house of Mitsui sent a seven-person delegation to the United States to study modern business practices. This effort enabled Mitsui to eventually become one of the largest and most powerful business conglomerates in Japan - in otherwords, "the best of the best".

The general practice of benchmarking, however never really gained momentum until after World War II. Trying to rebuild their war-torn economy and shattered businesses, the Japanese sent teams to the United States to bring back knowledge. One of these early benchmarkers was Taiichi Ohno, the creator of the **Toyota lean production manufacturing system**. On a trip to the United States in 1956, Ohno visited competing automakers. Yet, his greatest inspiration during his US tour came from supermarkets.

Observing how supermarket customers take what they need only in the amounts required and the subsequent replacement of goods by employees in time for the next round of shoppers, Ohno reasoned this same practice could effectively increase the efficiency of the manufacturing process. Building on the ideas of Kichiro Toyoda, the first president of Toyota, and on the fruits of this and other study visits, Ohno created what is known today as the **just-in-time manufacturing process**.

The Japanese have a long and noble tradition of foreign field study and process examination. Almost obsessively they collect and consume information. They devour newspapers and foreign books in record numbers. Government agencies and corporations refuse to entertain new ventures without first acquiring, examining and carefully analysing mountains of information. The Japanese value information as much as any precious natural resource. **"For the Japanese, the statement that knowledge is power is not just a pious truism; it is a basic operating principle"**.

The Japanese Business Culture

This preoccupation with information gathering has made its way into Japan's business culture, where competitor intelligence is almost an obsession. Mitsui, one of Japan's first corporations to embrace benchmarking techniques, has a credo **"Information is the life blood of the company"** Mitsui executives exchange some 80,000 messages each day on the corporation's extensive satellite-enhanced information network. Many of these messages contain intelligence on competitors. The preoccupation with competitor actions, capabilities, tactics, and strategies has helped Japanese businesses achieve many of the competitive advantages they enjoy today.

In other countries, corporations place less emphasis on competitive comparisons. In a survey of over 500 companies from Canada, Germany, Japan and the United States, Japanese businesses emerged as the clear leaders in competitive analysis. About 92 percent of Japanese companies said competitor comparisons are either a major or primary factor in their strategic planning process. This contrasts with a relatively healthy 82 percent in the US and 67 percent in Canada and 61 percent in Germany.

Japanese companies continually monitor their competition to stay one step ahead. For example, Japanese executives may spend time in a large library with 10 years' worth of annual reports from American companies. By reading the annual letters from the CEO, these Japanese executives hope to get a direct impression of how their competitors think.

David Kearns, the former CEO of Xerox, during his flight on a trip to Japan in the early 1980s, was catching up on several weeks of reading and came across an article in a leading business magazine about General Motor's capital investments of several billion dollars in new robotics and technology. GM predicted that this investment would help it achieve significant productivity gains and drive other improvements. However, the magazine article writer was skeptical that the investment would pay off and concluded with a cautionary note, saying only time would tell whether these massive investments would prove to be foolish or far-sighted.

When kearns reached Japan, he visited Toyota. He noted that the article he had just read was posted. The Toyota executives had highlighted the relevant numbers and operating improvements that GM predicted. Toyota presumed that GM would make every one of its targets right on schedule. However Toyota had already reset its schedule and operating goals so that it would be ahead of GM by the time GM reached those targets. The Japanese set their sights unbelievably high and pay close attention to their competitors. **Whether one calls it benchmarking or competitive intelligence the Japanese view careful scrutiny of competitors as a ground rule of effective competition**.

The Japanese are not satisfied with the mere collection of information about their competitors. They endeavour to absorb and adapt that information to their environment. The Japanese constantly compare themselves to other people. They always take ideas to put a Japanese twist on them. They are not satisfied with simple benchmarking, but must improve on it. Sometimes the Japanese can get over-zealous in their thirst for knowledge. In 1982, *for example,* Hitachi tried to pay $ 525,000 to IBM employees for some of Big Blue's trade secrets. In an elaborate sting operation, the FBI foiled the plan. However, it is impossible to know if similar cases of extreme borrowing (*i.e.,* industrial espionage) have gone unchecked.

The philosophy of borrowing runs deep in Japanese culture. Traditionally they have been adapters more notably than innovators. Others do the hard work of discovery and the Japanese exploit those discoveries to create new markets. For instance, Sony was one of the first companies to commercialise the transistor and the charge-coupled device, technologies pioneered by AT&T's Bell Laboratories. The Japanese certainly do not suffer from the **"not-invented here"** syndrome that plagues many American corporations.

The Americans are more open to foreign people and not to foreign ideas. The Japanese on the other hand are open to foreign ideas and not foreign people. Borrowing is prevalent in Japanese culture. Acquiring the information is the first step. The Japanese succeed at borrowing because of their willingness to learn. They view interaction as an opportunity. Japanese companies always accept invitations to participate in activities of the committees whereas the US companies do not show the same interest. **The Japanese view the participation as another opportunity for them to learn.**

The Japanese are perennial students. Even the "best of the best" hope to learn more. They constantly want to know what is going on. Toyota constantly benchmarks against GM, Ford and Chrysler, eventhough many regard Toyota as the industry leader. **Willingness to learn pervades all levels of Japanese organisations**.

Partnership with American corporations have been a particularly fertile learning ground for the Japanese. The Japanese companies are happy with their American partners' approach with the attitude of teachers because the Japanese have the attitude of students and this approach pays off. It is found that in every case in which a Japanese company emerged from an alliance stronger than its Western partner, the Japanese company had made a greater effort to learn. This results from ***dantotsu*** **- the striving to be the "*best of the best*"** - and the Japanese approach to **continuous learning**. Where Western firms see an opportunity to avoid investments and risks, the Japanese see opportunities to improve their skills and subsequently their competitive position. They are not satisfied unless they emerge from collaborative efforts with new abilities or technology.

The Keiretsu

The Japanese share information almost as much as they consume it, particularly among native companies. **Japan is a networked society** - Myriad trade associations, government sponsored conferences, technological societies and the quasi-integrated structure of the **keiretsu** facilitate information exchange. Culturally, the Japanese expect interdependence and the harmony that sharing brings. *For example*, the company that first discovers or imports a new idea becomes the recognised market leader - provided it shares the information.

This willingness to share applies equally to intracorporate relationships. Because of life time employment, a kind of corporate community develops within Japanese businesses. Such an environment closely ties an employee's interest to the company's interests. Employees readily acquire and distribute information throughout the corporation. While facilitating the exchange of information within and into the company, employee loyalty also helps prevent the outflow of sensitive information.

Historical and cultural factors are not the only reasons for Japan's benchmarking adroitness. A number of institutions have also cropped up that facilitate the learning process. Perhaps the most important of these is the ***keiretsu***. These company groups compose a greater community of firms headed by a lead bank. They are designed to promote mutual interest and to deal with a crisis collectively.

But the ***keiretsu*** are neither just a crutch in times of trouble nor merely glorified partnerships. These dynamic alliances allow firms to interact informally on all levels of management as well as among front-line hourly employees. They facilitate sharing and information exchange by providing ready-made introductions. Member executives exchange information at regular meetings. In addition to the usual financial services, the lead banks provide advice and guidance. More importantly, they overcome the constraints of life-time employment by sharing employees. Information resides with the employees. Files belong to the individuals, not to the companies. Consequently, employee-sharing among firms allows the dissemination of this otherwise unavailable information. Invaluable sources of information, the *keiretsu* are veritable benchmarking havens".

Role of the Japanese Government in Benchmarking in Japan

The Japanese government is also in the benchmarking business. Government officials in Japan encourage and even facilitate the sharing of research and other breakthroughs between competing firms. The Japanese government promotes study visits abroad by providing discounts to business people who travel. The ministry of international trade and industry and other related government agencies study cross-company practices and teach about them. For certain strategically important markets and technologies, it also funds industry consortia - an important avenue for learning best practices.

The Japanese government also frequently assumes an active role. Through standards committees, for example, the government endeavors to set up or guide particular industries. By suggesting or requiring certain processes, these committees are virtual clearing houses for benchmarking or best practices information. **Japan is indeed a networked society where the government is an important link in the circuit**.

Role of Industry Associations in Benchmarking in Japan

Industry associations are also important avenues for benchmarking information. Similar in some respects to ***keiretsu***, these organisations enable companies with similar interests to get together to exchange information.

The technological societies that pervade Japan are also warehouses of information. The Union of Japanese Scientists and Engineers (JUSE) is perhaps the most famous of these societies. As the curator of Japan's famous award for quality, the Deming Prize, JUSE plays an important role in the benchmarking efforts of many Japanese companies. This is done foremost through the Deming Prize itself. Applicants for the prize must demonstrate, among other things, how they collect information on quality. This suggests that companies are expected, if not required, to seek out and determine the best quality control practices.

In addition to these more formalised institutions, a strong network of university alumini also get together to exchange information about their companies. These informal dialogues cut across industry lines. Untrammeled by competitive concerns, they provide valuable insights into corporate practices. Furthermore, this network provides important connections within other companies by furnishing the introductions required to truly get an inside look at another company. Whether to facilitate benchmarking itself or as a means to that end, Japanese business people have added incentive to keep in touch with their old university colleagues.

Customer-Supplier Sharing

Corporate relationships - as distinguished from the keiretsu - often provides significant benchmarking opportunities. This is especially true between a large customer dealing with a smaller supplier. In these relationships, the smaller suppliers get benchmarking data through the larger customers, but this is not corporate altruism. It is possibly closer to enlightened self-interest. The large company/consumer has an important stake in the education of its suppliers. In this way, the customer ensures better materials and the suppliers acquire valuable information about how to improve their processes and their products.

Information transfers from the customer - supplier relationships may also take a more circuitous route. Firms often are open to potential customers in an attempt to lure them to their product. In so doing they often reveal important information about their processes and technology.

Eventhough the Japanese language lacks a specific word for benchmarking, these social, cultural and institutional factors make the Japanese among the best natural benchmarkers in the world. Unlike American corporations that emphasise performance benchmarking (product, feature, price comparisons) and process benchmarking, the Japanese excel at performance and strategic benchmarking. Their deep-rooted preoccupation with competitor intelligence continuously tunes them into performance benchmarks. Moreover, they also concentrate broadly on what strategies and general practices make other organisations successful. When performing strategic benchmarking, the Japanese do not limit their focus to a specific process.

The American preference for process benchmarking may be partly explained by the American manager's burden to produce short - term profits. Improvement of a core process can quickly produce a beneficial impact on the bottom line. In contrast, the Japanese have long been focused on process control and improvement. Their process management practices are often among the most sophisticated in the world. The Japanese therefore, focus on questions such as **"what companies** - without regard to industry are world-class performers and what drives their success?". Such **"strategic"** inquiries significantly impact long-term competitive position and direction but have relatively little expected impact on short-term financial results. "The risk of falling behind a competitor is regarded by most Japanese corporations as a far greater risk than the risk that profits will be depressed. To fall behind one's competitor can mean that profits will never materialise. To minimise the risk of falling behind, the Japanese corporations are preoccupied with the activities of their competitors to a degree that is unusual by western standards "This long-term focus and obsession with market share has made the strategic aspects of benchmarking an indispensable tool to the Japanese".

Strategic Benchmarking in Japan

Strategic benchmarking has been effective for the Japanese because they were well equipped to use it. Japanese managers carefully study, understand, control and manage their operational processes. Consequently they seem well able to project the benefits of other strategic approaches to their own systems and processes. Indeed, most top Japanese executives have hands-on experience with their corporation's core processes.

Because the Japanese know more about their own processes, they need only identify those companies which they find excellent in some respect and visit them. Upon looking at a nine-step benchmarking process beginning with (1) Identify benchmarking area, (2) Understand your own process and (3) Select benchmarking partners, it may be noted that Japanese clients always begin with step number three, they want first and foremost to study excellent companies. This coheres with the Japanese traditional benchmarking method : business travel and the study visit. These visits yield considerable insights for many Japanese executives because they already have a precise understanding of what information they require and how they can most effectively implement it.

Benchmarking in Japan, then, is generally a less structured affair than process benchmarking in the United States. The "study visit" itself implies a certain informality. Many Japanese people make study visits on the pretense of fostering good interpersonal relations. But behind the guise of an affable, casual visit the Japanese hope to gain exposure to new business practices. Study visit reporting is equally informal. The reports are generally thin, getting down to the bare bones. Information usually makes its way through corporations by way of seminar - style study groups. The members of the study group then turn the information over to engineers for implementation. Japanese corporations need to distribute information directly to individuals.

Obstacles to Japanese Benchmarking

Despite the Japanese penchant for external learning, there exist some inhibitors to benchmarking. One such obstacle is the cultural converse of ***dantotsu***. Some Japanese corporations are too conscious of rank. The second-tier companies willingly follow the leaders instead of trying to adopt their best practices, innovate on them, and then surpass their competitors. In Japan, many corporations have the attitude of accepting the second-best position rather than putting effort to occupy the top position in their industry. The willingness to accept second-best stifles their ability to adapt creatively. ***"Hubris"*** is another barrier to benchmarking in Japan. Some companies, enamoured of their competitive positions, have apparently forsaken the efforts at continuous learning that helped them achieve their dominant position. Arrogance has led to the blind siding of many successful companies and those in Japan have no special immunity. The reversal of fortunes of companies in the microchip industry are evidence of this. Nevertheless, some Japanese companies believe that they possess superior process and technology and can not learn from any one else. This attitude does not last for long.

BENCHMARKING IN EUROPE IN THE 1990s

Though the Japanese and Americans are the most advanced in their benchmarking applications, other areas of the world are following their course. This is particularly true in Europe where the benchmark concept is growing, paralleling its growth in the US five or six years ago. Having observed foreign affiliates and divisions of US companies effectively apply benchmarking, the Europeans are gradually adapting benchmarking to their own culture and language.

Traditionally, the Europeans have not had to benchmark. High tariffs and other protective efforts kept companies relatively isolated. But the barriers are coming down, and they are afraid of the American and Japanese entering their markets. European companies, therefore, have been forced to evaluate their competitive positions. Benchmarking provides them with the answers. Three primary situations currently are mobilising benchmarking abroad :

(i) Foreign competition threatens a company's traditionally strong domestic market, the goal is to use benchmarking to preempt market intrusion and maintain market share.

(ii) A company desires to enter a new foreign market or new industry segment, the goal is to apply benchmarking so that the company can quickly, effectively and profitably introduce products to the new foreign markets.

(iii) A company is locked in tough competition with several foreign and domestic competitors, the goal is to employ benchmarking to help understand one's strength versus the competition and to generate ideas to surpass the competition.

Unlike Japan, European culture does not encourage sharing. As a result, benchmarking has usually been conducted for them, typically by consultants or third parties to ensure confidentiality. The Europeans have been extremely receptive to benchmarking. Benchmarking gives them knowledge of how to compete globally. The practice is gradually being accepted as a powerful managerial tool in an increasingly competitive environment.

The Europeans have also demonstrated real initiatives in some areas. *For example,* the European Foundation for Quality Management (EFQM) was established by the presidents of Europe's most powerful companies. The EFQM endeavours to establish a European-wide structure to promote quality. Benchmarking is integral to these efforts. The EFQM is not looking to the US or Japan to provide a model. Instead, it is basing itself upon the world's best practice. For member companies eager to begin benchmarking, the EFQM is a storehouse of information on many premier quality practices.

BENCHMARKING IN LATIN AMERICA IN THE 1990s

In Latin America, benchmarking appears to be further out on the horizon. With the North American Free Trade Agreement (NAFTA), Latin American companies - particularly those in Mexico - were waking up to the tools of quality management. Mexican companies were just beginning to understand quality tools and benchmarking has not picked up. Companies have just started defining their strategic quality programs. Benchmarking in Latin America was limited mostly to United States and Japanese affiliates operating there. Countries such as Mexico, Argentina, Brazil, Chile and Columbia have launched National Quality Awards, often modeled directly after the benchmarking rich Malcolm Baldrige National Quality Award of the United States.

BENCHMARKING IN INDIA

Indian companies have done little in the field of organisational innovation to attract global attention. For instance, the editor of "Business world" in one of his recent editorial remarked "I can't remember the last time an Indian company made an organisational innovation and attracted global attention". He then refers to the global management guru, CK Prahlad's comment that "most of us would rather follow **"Best Practices"** from around the world than create **"Next Practices for the world to follow"** as the reason for this lag. It would be rather dismissive of the efforts of Indian industry and many of its respected homegrown companies if their efforts to rewrite the rules of the game are not even cursorily mentioned. It is these companies which really instilled confidence in the domestic economy in general and the other "would-be" entrepreneurs in particular that there was life beyond the MNCs. The success of many of these local (Indian) companies showed that MNC practices were imported lock, stock and barrel from their home, were not always the "best" by any yard-stick, especially when they proved ineffective against competition from local minnows. *For example*, among the old economy companies, Asian Paint's journey from being a tiny Indian outfit in 1942 to an Indian MNC in 2000 is truly remarkable and inspiring.

This was achieved on the back of a constant flow of organisational as well as technical ideas and even some "global first" marketing innovations, which helped the company to acquire market share in global markets earlier held exclusively by established paint goliaths. Among the New Economy enterprises, the birth and growth of companies such as Infosys Technologies, Wipro, TCS and many others involved in software development and other IT services are truly stupendous. And these home grown companies have seemingly effortlessly broken the "sonic barrier" of **"Six-Sigma"** and **"zero-defect"** quality water marks as a matter of routine. Naturally, these companies are now on the threshold of **"Next Practices"** referred to by C.K. Prahlad. What motivated these companies to embark on such onerous expeditions as ISO, SEI-CMM and other certifications in an ever-growing software market? What were the benchmarking tools and techniques adopted by these companies to achieve their business objectives and long-term enterprise goals? How have these exercises helped the companies to change or evolve their own organisational philosophies aligned to their customers' constantly changing needs?

ILLUSTRATION OF GLOBAL BENCHMARKING IN INDIA

Illustration 1 : SBI Lines up Plan for Global Benchmarking (Financial Express dated 26.12.2002)

Aspiring to gain global identity, the country's largest commercial bank, State Bank of India (SBI) which has an asset base of Rs. 3,80,000 crore has embarked upon an ambitious program of achieving global benchmarks on four key parameters. The bank will benchmark itself on the basis of return on assets (ROA), capital adequacy ratio (CAR), administrative expenses and non-performing assets (NPAs) to be on par with the best of international banks by the next 15 months.

With the new mantra of "Quality assets" A.K Purwar, chairman, SBI said in an exclusive interview to Financial Express that he wants ROA of the bank to rise beyond one percent from its present level of below one percent. Administrative expenses of the bank should come down below one percent and NPAs should be within two percent". Mr. Purwar said "SBI's administrative expenses are currently pegged at around three percent, while the NPA ratio is hovering over five percent. The bank which already has a capital adequacy ratio of over 12 percent, wants to continue at that level".

Said Mr. Purwar "Besides completing the ongoing IT framework for the bank, global benchmarking is my immediate agenda and I have already started working on that after taking over as chairman. I have already had rounds of discussions with the bank's top officials on these vital issues and now a modus operandi is being thrashed out meticulously by all of us".

He added "It is time-consuming task, and I can not set an exact deadline for this. I will be happy if I can achieve a few of these parameters like ROA by March 2004".

Sources point out that Mr. Purwar who assumed the chairmanship of the bank in November 2002, is scheduled to be in the post beyond 2006 and is well in a position to achieve his benchmarking targets.

Illustration 2 : Indian Banking Against Global Benchmarks

In an increasingly integrated and complex world market it is necessary that the Indian Banking System should compare its performance against the world benchmarks. **Some important ratios are given below in *Table 16.1* for an understanding as to what is the position of health of Indian schedule banks vis-a-vis global banks.**

TABLE 16.1 : IMPORTANT RATIOS FOR BANKS (IN THE YEAR 2009)

Item	Global average	Indian average	International norm if any	RBI norm if any
CRAR	7.1% - 34.9%	12.3%	8%	9%
ROA	0.2% - 4.3%	0.9%	-	-
NII	1.2% - 6.2%	2.9%	-	-
CIR	0.46% - 0.68%	0.5%		
Gross NPA	0.2% - 24.8%			
RROV to NPA	23.15% - 229.1%	56.1%	-	-
CAP/Asset	4% - 22%	6.30%	-	-
Volatile LIAB/Assets	0.71% - 0.11%	–17%	-	-

Abbreviations used :

CRAR - Capital to Risk Weighted Asset Ratio

ROA - Return on Assets

NII - Net Interest Income

CIR - Cost to Income Ratio

NPA - Non Performing Assets

CAP - Capital

LIAB - Liability

The Indian economy is fairly insulated from the global financial crisis at present since Indian banking system is not directly exposed to sub-prime US mortage market or the failed institutions or their stressed assets in any significant way. The same is not the case with the liquidity since the overseas borrowing market has shrunk. However, looking to the increasing depressed performance of the corporates in general, banks are required to take care of their performance by imbibing more effective risk management tools and taking effective measures.

BOX 16.1 : BENCHMARKING IN PRACTICE – DELOITTE CONSULTING LLP – GLOBAL BENCHMARKING CENTRE – SEEING THROUGH WALLS

A little insight about what yours competitors are doing can dramatically improve your strategy and investment decisions. Among businesses in the same market place, are the most financially successful performers investing heavily on certain functions? Are some businesses vulnerable to attack because they aren't investing enough in a game-changing process? Where are the cost gaps that represent opportunities to improve efficiency? Without industry-specific performance metrics, your company is flying blind.

Take Your Organisation for a Checkup

Benchmarking can help a company in its efforts to understand what its competitors are doing and how its own performance and investments measure up. And it doesn't require industrial espionage.

With blinded, aggregated data from more than 600 organisations in a variety of fields, the Deloitte Global Benchmarking Centre (GBC) can help executives compare their business performance against industry-median and lower-cost performers. Metrics such as cost and staffing can be compared. With a defined set of industry peers to help identify cost gaps that don't just highlight opportunities - they quantify them. In addition, the GBC approach uses highly structured, industry-codified process taxonomies. No matter how you and your competitors name or categorise a process, our analysis can help you develop an "apples-to-apples" comparison.

How we can Help?

Benchmarking can help you better understand how efficiently different parts of your business are operating by comparing your process performance to those of your direct peers. Deloitte's GBC provides customised benchmarking studies that are :

(i) **Relevant :** Each peer set is aligned by industry, such as technology, consumer products, or retail, so the resulting analysis is directly relevant to your business.

(ii) **Process-based :** We collect end-to-end process data (including costs, head count, cycle time and transaction volumes) regardless of where the work is performed within the organisation.

(iii) **Timely :** All of our data is up-to-date, and we encourage annual participation in our studies so companies can compare their performance year after year.

(iv) **Efficient :** Most of our studies have roughly 50 questions, and our online system lets organisations collect their data with minimal effort, usually in less than a week. Yet the resulting customised report details individual performance comparisons and specific area of opportunity.

(v) **Proprietary :** The data that the GBC has collected is available from no other source.

Bottom-Line Benefits

Effective benchmarking can help an organisation in its efforts to :

(i) Identity opportunities to reduce service costs and increase service quality.

(ii) Gain insight into relative strengths and weaknesses compared to other organisations in the same industry.

(iii) Combat organisational complacency and the perception that current performance is acceptable.

(iv) Change the way they view their performance by providing both qualitative and quantitative measures of service operations effectiveness.

(v) Support business imperatives.

Ways to Get More Value Now

Although we do not believe a company acting alone can match the inter-organisation, intra-industry benchmarking enabled by the GBC's proprietary data, a high-level assessment by internal processes can still be valuable. It can also provide a good starting point for external comparisons.

Here are some practiced tips to consider :

(i) **Focus on End-to-End Processes :** *For example,* "Accounts payable" might stand alone, be part of a layer function or reside within a shared services structure. In order to effectively evaluate your "accounts payable" activities, you need to look beyond the organisation chart and analyse the "accounts payable" process from end-to-end.

(ii) **Understand the Limitations :** Evaluating your own processes without knowing how the competition stacks up can yield valuable insights, but it can not determine the critical cost gaps that drive competitive performance. Don't let internal-only metrics lull you into a false sense of security-or spark an unnecessary frenzy.

(iii) **Industry-based Benchmarking in Action :**

- A US based financial institution was spending more in performance management than its peers. Benchmarking of the company's finance operations provided visibility that shed light on its imbalance. They were then able to address it through newly identified opportunities in staffing, technology and reporting.
- A global process and industrial products company was experiencing operating costs that varied by region and were higher than competitors' costs in each location. Benchmarking finance operations in several business regions, helped the company identify staffing and technology solutions to bring costs in line.
- A global technology company had never used external resources to analyse its finance and control operations. When it set out to accomplish a finance transformation initiative, leaders used benchmarking of their finance operations in three countries to verify that their organisation was a leader in overall performance, but still identified opportunities for improvement in shared services and transaction processing.

Deloitte Consulting LLP

POINTS TO REMEMBER

- Globalisation and advances in information technology are increasing opportunities for international benchmarking projects.
- Where the aim is to achieve world-class status or simply because there are insufficient national businesses against which to benchmark, international benchmarking is the appropriate approach to improve performance of global organisations.
- International benchmarking has objectives similar to other benchmarking projects.
- International benchmarking involves higher costs and more complexities than other benchmarking projects.
- International benchmarking has many benefits that can not be achieved through other forms of benchmarking.

- **International benchmarking is more complex than benchmarking within countries because of the following reasons :**
  (i) Methods for accounting costs may vary substantially between countries.
  (ii) Prices between countries are variable.
  (iii) Differing social systems and differing social roles of the same delivery systems.
  (iv) Different needs, conditions and expectations.
- **Approaches to international benchmarking include the following :**
  (i) Macro-benchmarking of major service sectors.
  (ii) Benchmarking of the same type of organisations in a limited number of countries.
  (iii) Process benchmarking using a standard.
  (iv) Partial benchmarking focusing on one or few aspects of performance.
- Global Benchmarking Network (GBN) is an alliance of leading benchmarking centres worldwide, which share a common vision and mission. It is a non-profit organisation.
- The **vision** of GBN is to be recognised as the global hub for benchmarking with active representation in all countries.
- The **mission** of GBN is to become a global network of organisations and experts focused on promoting and facilitating the use of benchmarking and sharing of best practices by helping each other and working together.
- **GBN values** includes : *(i)* professionalism, *(ii)* working together, *(iii)* excellence, *(iv)* ethical behaviour and *(v)* services.
- **Global benchmarking** is the process of identifying best practices in organisations anywhere in the world to seek information that can help an organisation to measure and compare its performance against those best practices in order to improve its operations.
- A **benchmark** is a reference point for taking measures against.
- **Best practices** are the techniques that have worked reliably in different situations to achieve their desired purpose in the most efficient and effective way.
- The **purpose** of benchmarking is to find the best performers in an area so that one can match them and even surpass them.
- In Japan, no word for benchmarking exists and few business people refer to the practice of benchmarking.
- In Japan, the general practice of benchmarking, never really gained momentum until after World War II.
- The Japanese have a long and noble tradition of foreign field study and process examination.
- In Japan's business culture, competitor intelligence is almost an obsession. In other countries, corporations place less emphasis on competitive comparisons.
- Japanese companies continually monitor their competition to stay one step ahead.
- The Japanese are not satisfied with the mere collection of information about their competitors. They endeavour to absorb and adapt that information to their environment.
- The philosophy of borrowing runs deep in Japanese culture. Traditionally they have been adapters more notably than innovators.

- The Americans are more open to foreign people and not to foreign ideas. The Japanese on the other hand are open to foreign ideas and not foreign people.
- The Japanese are perennial students. Even the "best of the best" hope to learn more.
- Willingness to learn pervades all levels of Japanese organisations.
- In partnerships with American Corporations the Japanese companies make greater effort to learn. This results from **"dantotsu"** - the striving to be the "best of the best" - and the Japanese approach to continuous learning.
- Japan is a networked society. In Japan, the quasi-integrated structure of the **"kieretsu"** facilitate information exchange.
- Culturally the Japanese expect interdependence and the harmony that sharing brings.
- The Japanese government is also in the benchmarking business. The Japanese government officials encourage and even facilitate the sharing of research and other breakthroughs between competing firms.
- Industry associations are also important avenues for benchmarking information in Japan.
- Strategic benchmarking has been effective for the Japanese because they were well equipped to use it.
- **Obstacles to Japanese benchmarking include :**
  - *(i)* The second-tier companies willingly follow the leaders instead of trying to adopt their best practices, innovate on them and then surpass their competitors.
  - *(ii)* Some companies, enamoured of their competitive positions, have apparently forsaken the efforts at continuous learning that helped them to achieve their dominant position.
- Europeans are lagging from US and Japan in their benchmarking effort.
- Unlike Japan, European culture does not encourage sharing.
- Indian companies have done little in the field of organisational innovation to attract global attention.

REVIEW QUESTIONS

1. Why international benchmarking becomes necessary?
2. How international benchmarking differs from other forms of benchmarking?
3. What is a "global benchmarking network"? Discuss its structure, vision, mission, values and services provided by it.
4. Define the terms "global benchmarking", "global benchmark" and "best practices".
5. Describe the benchmarking practice in Japan. How it differs from the benchmarking practice in the United States?
6. Discuss the characteristics of Japanese business culture.
7. What is meant by "Keiretsu"?
8. Discuss the role of Japanese government in benchmarking in Japan.
9. Discuss the role of industry associations in benchmarking in Japan.
10. What is meant by "customer-supplier sharing"? Discuss how it affects benchmarking.
11. Discuss strategic benchmarking in Japan.

12. Discuss the obstacles to Japanese benchmarking.
13. Discuss the features of benchmarking in Europe and in Latin America.
14. Discuss the features of benchmarking in India.

DISCUSSION QUESTIONS

1. "In Japan, no word for benchmarking exists and a few business people refer to the practice". Critically examine the statement.
2. "Japanese companies continually monitor their competition to stay one step ahead". Explain.
3. "Even the "best of the best" hope to learn more. The Japanese constantly want to know what is going on" - Elaborate.
4. "Benchmarking in Japan is generally a less structured affair than process benchmarking in the United States". Do you agree or disagree? Justify your answer.
5. "Unlike Japan, European culture does not encourage sharing of information with benchmarking partners". Discuss.

CHAPTER 17

Managing Best Practice Knowledge

INTRODUCTION

One of the most common themes of benchmarking is a search for industry, or functional activities or outputs that can be classified as *best-in-class,* as *world-class* or as representing *best practices.* The basic premise of benchmarking is to learn something of value from some one or some place else, something that helps you to perform more effectively or efficiently. The goal of most benchmarking activities is to learn from the best.

Once, a company finds best practice information, it still must successfully share and deploy that knowledge. Best practice information that is never implemented resembles a national currency racked by hyperinflation. It may look and feel great, but has little value. Those companies that effectively deploy ***best practice information*** reap the compounding dividends of true intellectual leverage. What then are the best ways to share ***best practice knowledge?*** The answer requires both hardware and software solutions.

Companies that successfully leverage best practice information manage both the ***hardware*** or physical systems that enable information exchange and the ***software*** or cultural elements that affect employee's willingness to share and learn from others. Hardware systems range broadly but may include databases, electronic mail, videos, newsletter, articles, newspapers, memos, bulletin boards, competitor reporting forms, demonstration rooms and meetings. The success of any of these options depends largely on the quality of the enabling software systems.

The software solution resides in the managerial systems which develop a culture that supports and encourages best practice information sharing. A public library in which no one comes to read or borrow books is a low-returning community asset. A best practice knowledge-management system is much the same. No matter how expensive or impressive the technology for disseminating information, the system is of little value to the organisation if employees do not regularly use it.

Before discussing the topics of developing effective software solutions and hardware solutions for successfully leveraging best-practice information in benchmarking projects, we will discuss some basic terms such as **"data", "information", "knowledge"** and **"knowledge management"** which are relevant to the topic of managing best practice knowledge.

Data, Information and Knowledge

Data

Data are unorganised and unprocessed facts. Data is a set of discrete facts about events - structural records of transactions. Data are discrete, self-contained and in isolation have no meaning. **All organisations need data and data is a prerequisite for information.** The organisation must decide what data need to be collected, the volume of data and the accuracy of the data because, too much data collected will become problematic as it offers no judgement and basis for action. This means that an organisation must decide on the nature and volume of data needed to create information.

Information

The word ***information*** is derived from the word ***inform*** which means "to give shape to", **information means shaping data to arrive at a meaning in the eyes of the perceiver.**

Information is an aggregation of data that makes decision making easier. It is also facts and figures based on reformatted or processed data.

Unlike data, information is understanding relations. It has meaning, purpose and relevance. It has a shape because it is organised for a purpose. *For example,* a profit and loss account statement or a balance sheet statement provides information. The data may have been reorganised, statistically analysed, or have had errors removed - all performed to add meaning to a message, a report or a document.

Information is accessible to employees and managers through the company's local area networks, intranet, e-mail, Internet, satellite infrastructure, postal service, courier service or hand delivery. Unlike data that emphasises quantity and efficiency of processing, the focus of information is qualitative. Data becomes information when meaning or value is added to improve the quality of decision making.

Knowledge

Knowledge is information in context to produce an actionable understanding. Knowledge is "human understanding of a specialised field of interest that has been acquired through study and experience". It is based on learning, thinking and familiarity with the problem area in a department, a division, or in the company as a whole. The focus is on ***sustainable competitive advantage.*** **Knowledge is not information and information is not data.**

Knowledge is defined as "a fluid mix of framed experience, values, contextual information and expert insight that provides a framework for evaluating and incorporating new experiences and information. **Knowledge is derived from information in the same way information is derived from data**. It may be viewed as an ***understanding*** of information based on its perceived importance or relevance to a problem area. Embracing a wider sphere than information, knowledge includes perception, skills, training, common sense and experience. **It is the sum total of our perceptive processes that helps us to draw meaningful conclusions**. *For example,* an investor requires knowledge to evaluate two companies, profit and loss statements in order to determine which one is the healthier company.

Table 17.1 **summarises the definitions of the terms "data", "information" and "knowledge".**

TABLE 17.1 : SUMMARY OF THE DEFINITIONS OF THE TERMS - "DATA", "INFORMATION" AND "KNOWLEDGE"

Data	Information	Knowledge
• Statement about reality • Unsorted bits of fact	• Organised, systematised data • Data that has been sorted, analysed and displayed	• Human interaction with reality • Meaningful links people make in their minds between information and its application in action in a specific setting
• A representation of a fact, number, word, image, picture or sound	• Data that has been assigned a meaning	• The wholeset of insights, experiences, and procedures that are considered correct and true and that, therefore, guide the thoughts, behaviour, and communication of people
• Measurements	• Data that is meaningful or useful to someone	• Ability to turn information and data into effective action
• A discrete objective fact about events	• Potential for action, resides in the user • A statement of facts about measurements • Descriptive knowledge • Data that makes a difference	• An organisational resource consisting of the sum of what is known • Systematising and structuring information for a specific purpose • Information whose validity has been established through sets of proof

As can be seen, information is all around, but only a fraction of it is useful in problem solving. Knowledge has to be built and requires regular interaction with others in the know in the organisation.

Knowledge, not information can lead to a competitive advantage in business. Information is closer to the decision-making process than data.

Tacit and Explicit Knowledge

Explicit knowledge can be said, written down and transmitted. It is objective, lending itself to rules and definitions. It is easily captured, stored and transmitted electronically. Most of all it is what we know that we can put into words. **Explicit knowledge encompasses the things we know that we can write down, share with others, and put into a database.**

***Tacit knowledge* is what we do not know that we know**. It includes know-how, judgement, experience, insights, rules of thumb and skills and intuition. It exists within context. But it is silent.

Knowledge Measurement

Knowledge measurement (KM) is the systematic processes by which knowledge needed for an organisation to succeed is created, captured, shared and leveraged.

Knowledge management focuses on how an organisation identifies, creates, captures, acquires, shares and leverages knowledge. Systematic processes support these activities, also enabling replication of successes. All these are specific actions organisations take to manage their knowledge.

Implications of Knowledge Measurement

Knowledge awareness benefits entire organisations. With today's emphasis on sustainable competitive advantage, added value, and improved productivity, a firm's management needs to create, innovate, monitor and protect its knowledge inventory. A knowledge management environment means a focus on generating new knowledge, transferring existing knowledge, embedding knowledge in products, services and processes, developing an environment for facilitating knowledge growth and accessing valuable knowledge from inside and outside the firm. When this happens, it is beyond survival. Infact, it is beyond intranets and databases - the technology that supports knowledge management.

It can be said that 20 percent of an information's knowledgeable personnel can operate 80 percent of the informations day-to-day business. ***The human resources manager can play an important role in identifying the knowledge core of the organisation, recommending ways to preserve this critical core, and building a robust long-range plan to ensure top-quality operation and to prevent the potential erosion of corporate talent through brain drain.*** Professionals with expertise must be recognised and rewarded by the organisations that employ them. Otherwise, they are more likely to leave the organisation sooner or later. In many organisations, expertise directly contributes to the firm's productivity and influence the stability and growth of those organisations.

A company needs to do the following in order to perform and create and maintain sustainable competitive advantage :

(i) There should be more emphasis on tapping, sharing, and preserving tacit knowledge and the total knowledge base of the company. A company's knowledge base includes explicit and tacit knowledge and exists internally in the business as well as within the firm's external connections.

(ii) Should focus on innovation and processes that convert innovation into new products and services. Knowledge sharing and an emphasis on the total knowledge base promote innovation.

(iii) Consider a renewed focus on ***organisational learning systems*** and ***systems thinking*** throughout the organisation. Knowledge is closely related and continuous interactive learning. Systems thinking means understanding how the various parts of the company work. This includes learning behavioural patterns in the system and the culture, or system environment in which employees and administrators operate. In otherwords, systemic thinking is expected to support innovation and continuous improvement processes, social competence and interactions, as well as the tacit knowledge base.

Communication and connection make knowledge sharing an ongoing activity. Technology can only create a formal system. Success with knowledge management exists when the culture is ready to communicate and connect. The end result is "community" built around knowledge and based on vision.

BEST PRACTICE SYSTEMS

***Best practice* is something that has been shown to be effective in one place that could be effective in another**. Organisations waste a lot of time and money **"reinventing the wheel"** - or, worse yet, failing at something eventhough someone somewhere has a method that will work. The purpose of the best practice system, then is to make it possible to find and use what is already there.

Best practice systems also add another dimension to finding people by linking people to specific knowledge. The result is targeted. People know what knowledge they want and who can provide the full context for them.

Arthur Anderson defines best practices as **"simply the best way to perform a process"**. The boom in ERP and e-commerce gives rise to the need to institute best practices, to both improve the bottom line and create an air of control over what is to be a new explosion in information. From accounting to marketing data, inventory control to depreciation schedules, it is the art of **data warehousing** that is enabling the small and large business to manage growth in changing economic times. By implementing best practices, from planning to implementation, companies are able to reengineer their business and maximise productivity. A best practice forces a reexamination of the business from all points of view, essentially requiring the corporate entity to redefine itself.

Best practice means finding and using the best ways of working to achieve your business objectives. It involves keeping upto date with the ways that successful business operate in your sector and others - and measuring your ways of working against those used by the market leaders.

Applying best practices means learning from and through experience of others. One way of doing this is through benchmarking, which allows you to compare your business with other successful businesses to highlight areas where your business could improve.

Best Practice Through Standards

Standards are fixed specifications or benchmarks, which are established by independent bodies *for example,* Canadian General Standards Board in Canada. This body develops both technical and management standards. Technical standards are precise specifications against which a business can measure the quality of its product, service or processes. Management standards are models for achieving best business and organisational practice.

Applying the appropriate standards to your business will enable you to apply best practices across the organisation and to work against objective criteria to achieve manufacturing or service quality.

Benefits of Best Practice to Your Business

A best practice strategy can help your business to : *(i)* become more competitive, *(ii)* increase sales and develop new markets, *(iii)* reduce costs and become more efficient, *(iv)* improve the skills of the work force, *(v)* use technology more effectively, *(vi)* reduce waste and improve quality, *(vii)* respond more quickly to innovations in your sector.

Management Best Practice

Management best practice involves : *(i)* the communication of a clear mission and strategy, *(ii)* leadership by example, *(iii)* the setting of demanding but realistic targets, *(iv)* an open and communicative management style, *(v)* clear and careful strategic planning.

There are several business tools that you can use to achieve management best practice. They include : *(i)* **benchmarking,** *(ii)* **forecasting**, *(iii)* **financial planning**, *(iv)* **strategic planning** and *(v)* **performance monitoring**.

A very effective way of monitoring your business is to introduce **key performance indicators** (KPIs). These can be used to measure progress in achieving business objectives across a range of activities and enable you to identify areas that need attention. KPIs can be used to measure activities such as sales volumes, profitability, quality and staff turnover.

Tools such as benchmarking, business planning and performance monitoring will help you to compare the performance of your business with that of your peers and competitors and against your own business objectives. Where necessary you can introduce new ways of working to improve competitiveness and business efficiency. Having accurate and up-to-date information about your business performance will also help future planning and change management.

Communicating your objectives and strategies is an essential part of management best practice. A good communication policy will ensure that everyone in your business knows the direction in which the business is heading and understands their own part in its development.

Improving Business Operations through Best Practice

Most businesses have some operational issues that can be improved through the introduction of best practice methods including : *(i)* quality management, *(ii)* stock control, delivery and supply chain management, *(iii)* purchasing and ordering, *(iv)* information management.

You can identify which operational areas will benefit from best practice methods by : *(i)* benchmarking, *(ii)* internal analysis, *(iii)* reviewing appropriate national and international standards.

Areas for improvement could include the introduction of quality management systems such as total quality management, automated stock control, just-in-time ordering and delivery and "lean" manufacturing and supply.

When you have identified the areas for improvement, you can implement changes. It is important, however to keep your employees, suppliers and customers aware of what you are doing, and to make sure that the changes do not cause unnecessary disruption in your business.

Using Information Technology to Achieve Best Practice

It is possible to give your business a distinct competitive advantage by making good use of Information Technology. High speed telephone networks, along with the Internet, enables you to communicate ever more effectively and to distribute information quickly and accurately.

The Internet has revolutionsied the way businesses communicate with customers and suppliers to market themselves, access information and buy and sell products. In larger organisations intranets and extranets - internal and external communication networks are used to communicate with employees, customers, suppliers and other stakeholders.

Broadband Internet access is much quicker than a dial-up connection and also allows everyone in an organisation to be online all the time. This improves business efficiency and because it is available for a fixed monthly charge, it is easier to control costs. Even in the smallest companies, integrated databases and systems can bring significant cost savings and improvements in efficiency.

IT Security

In addition to improving business efficiency, the wider use of technologies such as the Internet, mobile telephony and wireless networking increases the use of security breaches. It is important, therefore to adopt best practice for IT security. Ensure that you have appropriate safeguards for information access passwords, firewalls and security software and that all of your employees are suitably trained in their use.

Importance of Managing Best Practice Knowledge

We can appreciate the significance of managing best practice knowledge by the following illustration :

A Fortune 100 company performed a comprehensive benchmarking study on best practices in financial management and capital investment. The subjects were relevant to all corporate divisions and operating units. Consequently the study findings were eagerly awaited by the senior executives who commissioned the project. These executives understood that the company could potentially save millions of dollars if it could substantially improve the decision making process for major capital investments.

The benchmarking project proceeded well through its early phases. Team members developed useful insights that promised significant improvements in the company's financial and capital investment processes. But then, despite the benchmarking team's successful investigation and findings, the project fizzled out. The benchmarking research phase was successful and produced excellent information to help the company improve. However, implementation proved to be a disaster. The benchmarking team could not find an effective method for sharing the breakthrough information.

Finally, team members settled on using traditional memos and management presentations to communicate project results. Unfortunately both methods proved disappointing : the best practice recommendations were ignored or soon forgotten by the divisions that could most benefit from them. For this company and many others, ***effectively sharing best practices*** proved a herculean challenge much more difficult than researching and collecting the benchmarking information.

Developing Effective Software Solutions

Companies develop the soft systems that support a best practices culture by focusing on four primary activity areas : *(i)* ***education,*** *(ii)* ***communications,*** *(iii)* ***reward and recognition*** and *(iv)* ***employee development.***

A good strategic point in any organisation is with education and training. Employee education can be a powerful tool to directly and indirectly encourage best practice sharing as an effective operating strategy. By bringing outside speakers, ideas, concepts, tools and practices into the organisation, education can indirectly nurture a culture that encourages best practice sharing. Moreover, some education may be directly targeted at benchmarking, best practices exchange, and the use of technical systems such as data bases that enable employees to share benchmarking information with each other. In addition every manager might ask himself or herself these basic questions.

(i) In what ways can your unit invest in employee education that brings outside ideas and speakers before your employees?

(ii) In what ways can you ensure that all employees are trained and enabled to use existing systems that foster idea exchange and best practice sharing?

The benefits of benchmarking can also be communicated in other ways. To encourage best practice information gathering and innovative adaptation, some organisations make idea exchange and competitor assessment a regular part of meetings. They layout work areas to encourage frequent employee interactions and foster information transfer, the design libraries and bulletin boards to spot light innovations and effective operating procedures of other industries. In business meetings managers and line employees routinely study the successful practices of other business units, other companies and other industries. Even when another company's ideas are not actually adopted or adapted, the routine examination of other industries' innovative practices stretches managers to continually challenge and reconceive their organisation's own business practices.

Reward and recognition systems further encourage innovative adaptation. Managers reinforce acts of creative adaptation with a word of praise and other forms of informal recognition. Some other companies are experimenting with more formal reward programs that recognise creative borrowing through gain-sharing and other rewards. Some companies embedd benchmarking and creative adaptation skills in performance reviews, where they become important factors influencing promotion, incentive pay, job definition and employee development plans.

Best practice knowledge systems must also be well managed to be successful. Usually this means a designated person or group must shoulder the responsibility for maintaining the system.

Some companies may choose not to use a designated reference librarian, nevertheless, some individual or group must be responsible for ensuring that the system runs properly, that information is accessible, and that employees are encouraged and enabled (usually through training) to effectively use the system. Moreover, an organised approach to managing best practices knowledge facilitates learning, estimates redundant work efforts and repetitive research, formalises communications channels and creates a corporate wide network of information contacts and subject experts. ***Table 17.2* summarises the most important lessons learnt by organisations that foster effective best practice information sharing :**

TABLE 17.2 : DEVELOPING THE CULTURE

Education	Meetings
(i) Focus on importance of best practice *(ii)* Encourage bringing in outside ideas *(iii)* Bring in outside speakers *(iv)* Post information	*(i)* Regularly share best practices information *(ii)* Regularly relate success stories *(iii)* Layout work area to encourage information exchange
Reward and Recognition	**Responsibility**
(i) Evaluate best practice information sharing and innovative imitation in performance review *(ii)* Reward great borrowed ideas *(iii)* Link best practices information sharing to compensation	*(i)* Include best practices information collecting/ sharing as part of job descriptions *(ii)* Designate best practice champions *(iii)* Use all systems to broadcast and communicate

Developing Effective Hardware Solutions

After developing an organisational climate or culture that supports best practice information sharing, a company can turn its attention to hardware issues and begin to develop a knowledge management (KM) system appropriate for the culture. There is no single best approach to knowledge management and best practice. Field experience suggests that each organisation must have a tailored system that fits its employees' work habits and cultural preferences. In a study of the best practice knowledge management systems of 11 leading multinational corporations, the **database** emerged as the most popular method of communication, **e-mail** ran a close second. Both systems provide means for communicating best practices information, however, passionate debate brews among users over which is the superior system. Users of each advocate the strengths of their systems and point out the problems of the other. According to Warren Jeffries of Xerox Corporation, databases create persistent maintenance problems in order to keep information current. Jeffries favours the grass roots flexibility of e-mail. In Xerox, many more people are accustomed to using e-mail to informally request to seek information than they are accustomed to probing corporate intelligence or benchmarking data bases.

However, Jim Madigan of Eastman Kodak endorses the benefits of benchmarking databases and describes the capabilities of Kodak's worldwide IBM mainframe database system, which he asserts is both "user friendly" and "well used".

BEST PRACTICE DATABASES

The best practice database presents a fast, centralised method for storing and retrieving information companywide. Consequently, databases are especially popular as a vehicle for managing best practice information. However, more than a few companies have encountered system management snags which have prevented them from effectively leveraging accumulated benchmarking knowledge. **Some of the more frequent problems cited in fully leveraging best practice database include :**

(i) Managers and users fail to update the database frequently enough. This causes information to become aged and discourage frequent use.

(ii) Inflexible database structures discourage frequent use by employees.

(iii) The time and expense of data entry and maintenance become prohibitive.

(iv) The absence of a data screening process, superfluous and redundant information lard the data base.

Best practices databases describe successful efforts, typically from the reengineering of business processes that could be applicable to organisational processes. Best practices differ from lessons learnt in that they capture only successful events, which may not be derived from experience. Best practices are expected to represent business practices that are applicable to multiple organisations in the same sector, and are sometimes used to benchmark organisational processes. *For example,* Microsoft offers a web page that describes best practices for the use of its products which can provide helpful tips, *for example,* to prevent database corruption.

Database Management Systems (DBMS)

A *database management system (DBMS)* is a support software that is used to create, manage and protect organisational data. A database management system works with the operating system to store and modify data and to make data accessible in a variety of meaningful and authorised ways.

A **database** is a shared collection of logically related data, organised to meet the needs of an organisation. A related term is a ***data warehouse,*** a very large database or collection of databases. The DBMS is the software that manages a database.

Data Warehousing

The establishment and maintenance of a large data storage facility containing data on all or at least many aspects of the enterprise, less formally, a popular method for making data accessible to many people in an organisation. To create a data warehouse, a firm pulls data from its operational transaction processing systems and puts the data in a separate **"data warehouse"** so that users may access and analyse the data without endangering the operational systems.

Data Mining

Searching or "mining" for small "nuggets" of information from the vast quantities of data stored in an organisation's data warehouse, employing a variety of technologies such as decision trees and neural networks.

MANAGING BEST PRACTICE DATA BASES

How best practices data bases are managed in large corporations such as IBM, Eastman Kodak, AT&T and Motorola are illustrated in the following paragraphs :

1. **IBM Rochester :** IBM Rochester's database - "Big Blue" has restricted access. IBM Rochester limits access to a relatively few selected people because the database houses confidential information including competitor intelligence and benchmarking reports. Based on a mainframe computer, the "Big Blue" database accommodates benchmarking information in various formats such as text, graphics, tables and matrices. Users can search the database by key word and by a dictionary or index of term. In a large corporation like IBM, where many teams, work groups, and business units are actively conducting benchmarking efforts, a central database can be especially valuable, for it helps the organisation leverage existing work and avoid redundant research. At IBM, benchmarking coordinators for each organisation have the access code for the "Big Blue" system, while a team of top experts decide what information goes into the database.
2. **Eastman Kodak :** At Eastman Kodak, benchmarking efforts are supported through an unrestricted database that is operated through an IBM mainframe computer and that is available to employees throughout Kodak's worldwide operations. The database is menudriven with six categories that offer Kodak's best practices, articles, benchmarking opportunities, research synopses, abstracts, results and references to people who house important benchmarking reports. Users can perform key word searches to retrieve titles and dates of benchmarking studies or they can enter information and add studies by filling out a report. Kodak benchmarkers access the system about 25 times each day.
3. **AT&T :** AT&T employs a database system that can be described as a "sophisticated electronic rolodex. Known as the AAA system, this database contains one-page personnel profiles that can be used to direct benchmarkers to people and information sources that may help them in their benchmarking efforts. These profiles include information about each person's knowledge of companies, products, regions and languages. Each individual supplies information about himself. All the levels of the company can use and be a part of the database, as the database directs users to the appropriate expert. Special features of the system include searches that can be saved and repeated weekly which provide the user with updated information. AT & T employees use the system about 200 times a month and receive information through e-mail.

Three people work on the system full time : a database administrator, a technical advisor and a customer-service manager.

4. **Motorola :** Centralised databases are not right for every company. Motorola abandoned a centralised competitor intelligence database that was designed "to monitor not just the competition, but also the entire business, political and economic environment for the company's worldwide interests". Unfortunately, no one was charged with keeping information current, consequently Motorola employees came to believe information was not updated and few people used the system. Despite the large expense to initiate the system, Motorola eventually abandoned it.

Chastened by this experience, Motorola decided to use a much smaller and less ambitious data base for managing benchmarking information. Its current system tracks benchmarking reports by title and description, providing the report number and geographic location where hand-copy files can be found. Motorola then supports this limited database by regularly informing upper level managers through memos of important benchmarking and competitor intelligence information and by distributing key articles and reports to executives.

ELECTRONIC MAIL

Electronic messages transmitted to specific mail-boxes across computer networks, usually called just ***e-mail***, present another option for communicating best practice information. E-mail provides a method to rapidly transfer information directly to a target group of employees who have mail boxes on the e-mail system. Unlike best practice databases, which actually house subject information under different topical headings, e-mail is a general-purpose broadcast system. Information requests go out to all users on the e-mail system or to some subset of users. If the benchmarker does not know where an internal expert resides, he or she blindly transmits an inquiry and hopes that the appropriate person actually uses the inquiry.

Xerox supports both e-mail and database systems, however most people choose to use e-mail rather than the database. According to Xerox customer services benchmarking manager Warren Jeffries, people want an easy-to-use system and the data base, with a 50 page user manual, is too complex. Xerox's benchmarking database contains some superfluous information and is encumbered by so-called "ancient history" or information that has not been frequently updated.

Xerox therefore communicates information to employees directly at their work stations, which are connected through a worldwide Xerox e-mail network. People from all levels of the company use the system to broadcast information needs, in-turn, they receive information by hard-copy transmittals or e-mail. To facilitate e-mail dispatches to the appropriate employees, special-interest distribution lists are often used. In this way, one inquiry or distribution can be simultaneously directed to many people. However, on specialised benchmarking projects, a Xerox employee must still work hard to identify the appropriate contacts who might provide insight or assistance based on their past work. If a benchmarker does not know who to direct an e-mail inquiry to, response can be poor - even if the organisation has previously performed benchmarking studies in the interest area. "Networking is the lifeblood of benchmarking, both internally and externally" observes Jeffries. If a Xerox employee leaves the company, best practice information or expertise he or she possesses also departs because there is no central archival system such as a best practice database. But Jeffries contends this is not a major problem for Xerox, where benchmarking is viewed as a basic business skill that should be conducted on an ongoing basis. He argues that information or knowledge lost through employee turnover is of little value because the information ages quickly. The broad-reaching networking features of e-mail far outweigh the archival benefits of a centralised database.

Choosing Between Database and e-mail Systems

The experience of "power benchmarkers" such as Xerox, Motorola, AT&T demonstrates the importance of tailoring a benchmarking knowledge management system to the individual organisation's culture. Clearly, one size will not fit all corporations. ***Table 17.1*** **and** ***17.2*** **summarise the advantages and disadvantages of each system for best practice knowledge management.**

TABLE 17.1 : MANAGING BEST PRACTICE KNOWLEDGE THROUGH DATABASE SYSTEMS

Advantages	Disadvantages
(i) Fast retrieval of information	*(i)* Must be updated frequently to be effective
(ii) Centralised location for storing information	*(ii)* May include superfluous information is not succeed
(iii) Companywide access	*(iii)* Time/expense of data entry
(iv) Easy to find information/sources due to search functions	*(iv)* Expense of system, software, upkeep

TABLE 17.2 : MANAGING BEST PRACTICE KNOWLEDGE THROUGH E-MAIL SYSTEMS

Advantages	Disadvantages
(i) Fast method of contacting people	*(i)* Must have access to right user group to find desired contact
(ii) Simple and well-based system for all communication purposes	*(ii)* Does not have centralised location for storing information
(iii) Companywide access	*(iii)* All employees do not actively use the system
(iv) Wide distribution of information	

OTHER KNOWLEDGE MANAGEMENT VEHICLES

Enterprises that lack technology, budget or need for organisation wide databases or e-mail systems, have alternative communication options for leveraging best practice and competitor intelligence information. Moreover, all these alternative communication vehicles can also be had to supplement existing database or e-mail systems. These alternative communication vehicles for knowledge-management are discussed below :

1. Videotapes

Videos present an innovative approach to study work processes in action. However, most best practice videotapes capture internal processes since many companies restrict visitors from filming their core work processes. Hewlett Packard and DuPont have used the medium for knowledge management. Due to the high cost of producing professional quality videos and due to the limited frequency with which they can be easily updated, videotapes are best regarded as supplemental best practice communication form.

2. Internal Publications

Digital Equipment Corp, McDonnel Douglas and Hewlett-Packard all employ newsletters, articles and internal newspapers to communicate best practice information. An inexpensive and ongoing method for reaching large audiences, best practice publications keep readers informed about innovation, continuous improvements and breakthrough findings. However, lead times and circulation cycles can be long.

3. Memos and Miscellany

Memos, bulletin boards, competitor reporting forms, demonstration rooms, reverse engineering labs and benchmarking meetings represent other approaches for sharing best practice and competitor information within an organisation.

The best system is one that fits the size and needs the individual company. A small company with limited budget might not need a formal e-mail or database system. A best practice newsletter or benchmarking meetings can work well when effectively administered. At larger, multisite organisations, an ideal system would likely combine the network advantages of a computer base and an e-mail system. The first generation system would be a database that archives information and provides users with best practice abstracts and contact names. Users would also be able to make contact with internal experts and knowledge sources by e-mail, phone or fax. A more fully evolved, versatile system would integrate database and e-mail systems, as do new groupware applications such as Lotus Notes. These advanced systems would also permit benchmarkers to transfer information and best practice knowledge directly among themselves. To assure its success, the system management would actively promote the benefits of the best practice database and keep information up-to-date, while preserving important historical data to enable on-going trend analysis. A research librarian would be an added benefit, but the system would be simple enough for people to use on their own. Lastly, the organisation's leadership would recognise the organisational benefits of innovative adaptation and would therefore actively support a culture that leverages best practice knowledge.

GUIDELINES FOR KNOWLEDGE MANAGEMENT

The following guidelines emerge from the experience of organisations that actively manage their best practice knowledge :

1. Design a knowledge - management system based on user needs, requirements and usage habits.
2. Choose a system that is consistent with your organisation's culture and user patterns.
3. Set a reasonable budget to develop and maintain the system. Then adhere to the budget.
4. Design a system that adds value to information.
5. Work with existing systems. Do not duplicate existing resources.
6. Organise information simply, complexity discourages usage.
7. Screen information that the company achieves.
8. Frequently update information in the system.

9. Encourage and train people to use the system.
10. Designate an individual to manage and maintain the system.
11. Seek top-management support for the system and ensure a high-level champion actively promotes and encourages use of the system.

BOX 17.1 : BENCHMARKING IN PRACTICE
– MANAGING BEST PRACTICE KNOWLEDGE AT ALCOA

ALCOA uses an e-mail system for all forms of communications, including competitor, intelligence and benchmarking information. All ALCOA employees can access the system and once a week the company transmits a compilation of competitor intelligence and benchmarking summarises to a broad-reaching distribution list. ALCOA business units develop this information, which can be transmitted in many formats, including text files, spread sheets, charts and graphs. ALCOA managers scan externally created documents into its computer system and each week transmit these documents along with internally generated benchmarking summaries. A card catalogue system to identify employees with specialised knowledge and expertise has also been developed but not yet fully deployed. Like other organisations using e-mail for benchmarking communications, ALCOA benchmarkers locate internal experts and information sources by trial and error.

POINTS TO REMEMBER

- Benchmarking involves a search for industry or functional activities or outputs that can be classified as ***best-in-class*** as ***world-class*** or as representing ***best practices.***
- The goal of most benchmarking activities is ***to learn from the best.***
- Once a company finds best practice information, it still must successfully share and deploy that knowledge.
- Companies that successfully leverage best practice information manage both the ***hardware*** or physical systems that enable information exchange and the ***software*** or cultural elements that affect employee's willingness to share and learn from others.
- Hardware systems include data bases, electronic mail, videos, newsletter, articles, newspapers, memos, bulletin boards, competitor reporting forms, demonstration rooms and meetings.
- The software solution resides in the managerial systems which develop a culture that supports and encourages best practice information sharing.
- ***Data*** are unorganised and unprocessed facts. All organisations need data and data is a prerequisite for information.
- ***Information*** is an aggregation of data that makes decision making easier. Unlike data, information is understanding relations. It has meaning, purpose and relevance.
- *Knowledge* is information in context to produce an actionable understanding.
- Knowledge is not information and information is not data.
- Knowledge is derived from information in the same way information is derived from data.
- Knowledge is the sum total of our perceptive processes that helps us to draw meaningful conclusions.
- Knowledge, not information can lead to a competitive advantage in business.
- Information is closer to the decision making process than data.

- Knowledge can be classified as ***explicit knowledge*** and ***tacit knowledge.***
- ***Explicit knowledge*** can be said, written down and transmitted.
- ***Tacit knowledge*** is what we do not know that we know.
- Knowledge management (KM) is the systematic processes by which knowledge needed for an organisation to succeed is created, captured, shared and leveraged.
- **Knowledge awareness** benefits entire organisations. A firm's management needs to create, innovate, monitor and protect its knowledge inventory.
- The human resources manager can play an important role in identifying the knowledge core of the organisation, recommending ways to preserve this critical core and building a robust long-range plan to ensure top-quality operation and to prevent the potential erosion of corporate talent through brain drain.
- ***Communication*** and connection make knowledge sharing an ongoing activity.
- ***Best practice*** is something that has been shown to be effective in one place that could be effective in another.
- ***Best practice systems*** also add another dimension to finding people by linking people to specific knowledge.
- ***Best practice*** means finding and using the best ways of working to achieve your business objectives.
- Applying best practices means learning from and through experience of others.
- Applying the appropriate standards to your business will enable you to apply best practice across the organisation and to work against objective criteria to achieve manufacturing or service quality.
- ***Management best practice*** involves the communication of a clear mission and strategy, leadership by example, the setting of demanding but realist targets, an open and communicative management style and clear and careful strategic planning.
- ***Communicating*** your objectives and strategies is an essential part of management best practice.
- Most businesses have some operational issues that can be improved through the introduction of best practice methods.
- It is possible to give your business a distinct competitive advantage by making good use of ***information technology.***
- Companies develop the soft systems that support a best practices culture by focusing on four primary activity areas : ***(i) education, (ii) communications, (iii) reward and recognition*** **and** ***(iv) employee development.***
- There is no single best approach to knowledge management and best practice.
- Each organisation must have a system that fits its employees' work habits and cultural preferences.
- The best practice database presents a fast, centralised method for storing and retrieving information company-wide.
- ***Best practice databases*** describe successful efforts, typically from the reengineering of business processes that could be applicable to organisational processes.
- **A database management system (DBMS)** is a support software that is used to create, manage and protect organisational data.
- **Data warehousing** and **datamining** are two aspects of DBMS.

- Electronic messages (e-mail) transmitted to specific mail-boxes across computer networks present another option for communicating best practice information.
- **Other knowledge management vehicles include :** *(i)* Videotapes, *(ii)* Internal publications, and *(iii)* Memos.

REVIEW QUESTIONS

1. What is meant by "best practice" and "best practice systems"?
2. Distinguish between the terms "data", "information" and "knowledge".
3. Distinguish between tacit knowledge and explicit knowledge.
4. Define the term "knowledge management" and its significance in benchmarking studies.
5. Discuss the implications of knowledge management.
6. Discuss the importance of managing best practice knowledge.
7. Discuss the benefits of best practices to a business organisation.
8. Discuss how business operations can be improved through best practice.
9. Discuss the role of developing effective software solutions in managing best practice knowledge.
10. Discuss the role of developing effective hardware solutions in managing best practice knowledge.
11. Write short note on:
    (a) Best practice databases
    (b) Database management systems
    (c) Data warehousing
    (d) Data mining
12. Discuss the advantages and disadvantages of using databases versus e-mail in managing best practice knowledge.
13. Describe the following knowledge-management vehicles :
    (a) Videotapes
    (b) Internal publications
    (c) Memos
14. Discuss the guidelines for knowledge management.

DISCUSSION QUESTIONS

1. Discuss the application of hardware and software solutions to successfully leverage best practice information and share best practice knowledge.
2. "Knowledge, not information, can lead to a competitive advantage in business" – Elaborate.
3. "A company needs to do certain functions in order to perform and create and maintain sustainable competitive advantage". What are those functions? Explain.
4. "Companies develop soft systems that support a best practices culture by focusing on four primary activity areas" – Explain.
5. "There is no single best approach to knowledge management and best practice". Do you agree or disagree? Justify your answer.

CHAPTER 18

Benchmarking and 21st Century Organisation

INTRODUCTION

Organisations are constantly looking for new ways and methodologies to improve their performance and gain a competitive advantage. As they seek improvements to their own business processes, many organisations recognise the importance of learning from best practices that have been achieved by other organisations. By removing the need to "reinvent the wheel" and providing the potential to adopt proven practices, benchmarking has become an important methodology for providing a fast-track to achieving business excellence in the 21st century.

EVOLUTION OF BENCHMARKING

During the 20th century after the 2nd World War, the Japanese began to visit the best companies in America and Europe with the intention to gather knowledge and ideas of successful business. The Japanese significantly promoted their business through the application and modification of collected information. The Japanese companies have thus become competitive and leading in the global market. Benchmarking philosophy has roots in Japan where it is called **"Dantotsu"** which means **"striving to be the best"**.

The concept of benchmarking had developed in the United States during the 1960s (*i.e.,* 20th century). Originally, it was developed by companies that function in industrial field. The pioneer in the implementation of benchmarking in the US was Xerox company. Xerox started its overall transformation when Japanese companies appeared in the market for copying machines. The Japanese competitors of Xerox implemented good ideas which were cheap and at the same time profitable without sacrificing quality. In order to be successful in the market and to have competitive advantage, companies started using benchmarking technique as a technique for strategic management at the end of 20th century and the beginning of 21st century.

***Exhibit 18.1* illustrates the evolution of benchmarking.**

EXHIBIT 18.1 : EVOLUTION OF BENCHMARKING

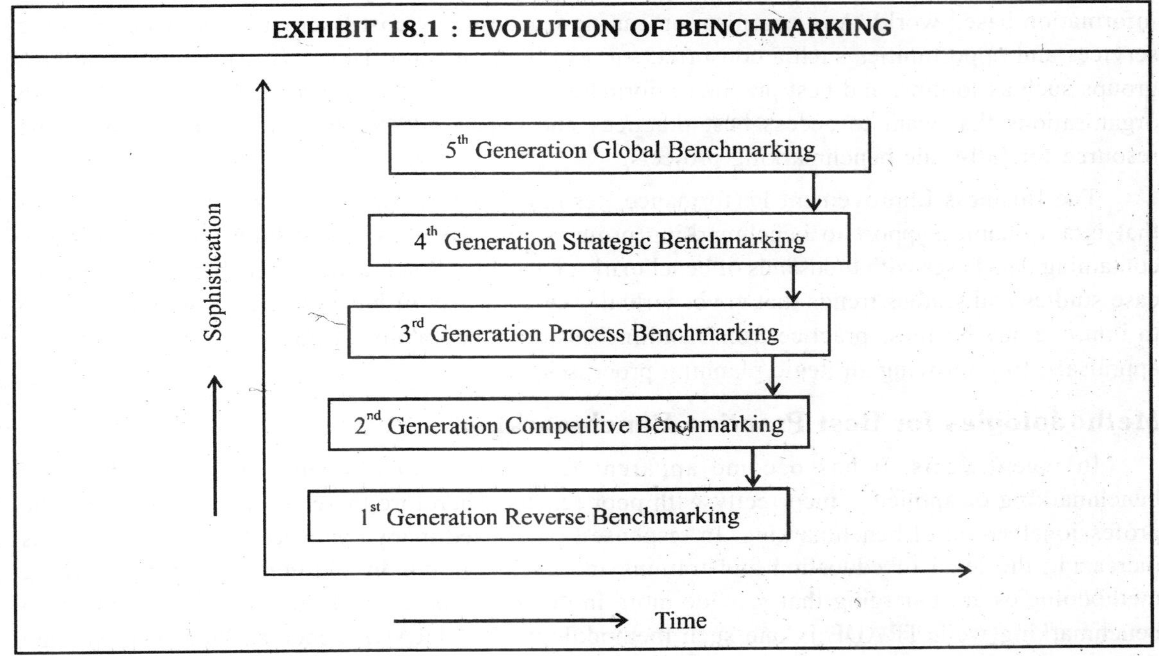

BENCHMARKING IN THE 21ST CENTURY

In order to improve something, you have to change it. In order to change something, you have to understand it. In order to understand something, you have to measure it.

Benchmarking is the process through which a company measures its products, services and practices against its toughest competitors, or those companies recognised as leaders in its industry. Benchmarking is one of a manager's best tools for determining whether the company is performing particular functions and activities efficiently, whether its costs are in line with those of competitors and whether its internal activities and business processes need improvement.

Companies usually undertake benchmarking with a view towards the many improvements that it may offer. These benefits include reducing labour cost, streamlining the workflow through reengineered business processes and common administrative systems, implementing new technology, outsourcing some functions, redesigning the development and support processes and restructuring and reorganising the information technology functions.

As the pace of change accelerates in the 21st century as a result technological opportunities, liberalisation of world markets, demand for innovation, quality and speed, organisations have to readjust and regain their operations to counter all these changes. The pace of change has increasingly forced organisations to be more outward looking, market oriented and knowledge driven. A useful tool that can help businesses build strong capabilities, ensure an inward flow of ideas and establish true competitive gaps in benchmarking.

In the 1980s and 1990s benchmarking was mainly confined to large successful private sector organisations with projects that tended to be extremely costly but gained very high returns. Today's technological advancements have transformed communications and opened up a whole new information based world. Any organisation can now access low-cost Internet based benchmarking services and opportunities such a consortia, surveys-both on and off-line, virtual common interest groups such as forums, and best practice information resources. These resources are a real boon to organisations that want to access best practices and expert advice/opinion but do not have the resource for full-scale benchmarking projects.

The Business Improvement Performance Resource (BIPR. com) is one of the new resources that is a valuable support to benchmarking projects. The BPIR is a vast knowledge respository containing data bases with thousands of benchmarks, measures, best practices, benchmarking partners, case studies and studies/trends that cover virtually every aspect of business. The resource can help to improve any business practice from handling customer complaints, to undertaking performance appraisals, to improving strategic planning processes.

Methodologies for Best Practice Benchmarking

In recent years, it has become apparent that some organisations have misunderstood benchmarking or applied it incorrectly with poor results. Therefore there is a need to increase the professionalisation of benchmarking. In response to this need many countries are moving towards increasing the level of education and training in benchmarking. In addition, new benchmarking methodologies are emerging that provide more in-depth guidelines and instructions on how to do benchmarking well. TRADE is one such methodology. The TRADE benchmarking methodology focuses on the exchange (or trade) of information and best practices to improve the performance of processes, goods and services.

TRADE consists of five stages :

1. ***Terms of reference*** (plan the project - aims, objectives, scope, resources, cost/benefit analysis).
2. ***Research*** (research current state/performance).
3. ***Act*** (undertake data collection and analysis to compare against others).
4. ***Deploy*** (communicate and implement best practices).
5. ***Evaluate*** (evaluate the benchmarking process and outcomes to ensure the project has met its aims).

***Exhibit 18.2* illustrates the TRADE best practice benchmarking methodology.**

EXHIBIT 18.2 : "TRADE" BEST PRACTICE BENCHMARKING METHODOLOGY

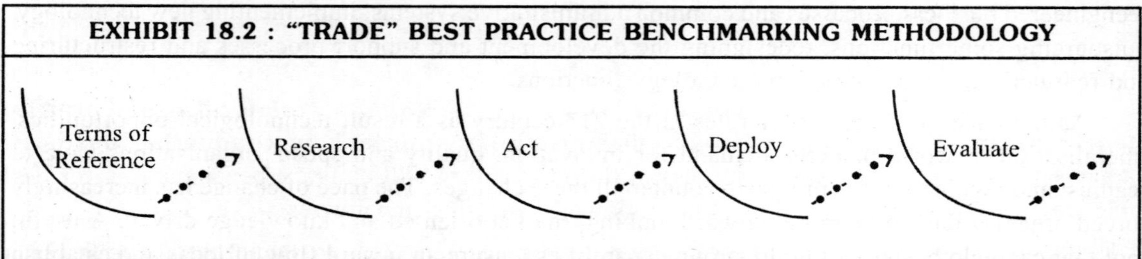

Individuals trained in TRADE can advance their knowledge of benchmarking through its accompanying certification scheme - to ensure that benchmarking is applied professionally. This certification scheme is the best to be offered in benchmarking recognising the need to advance the professionalism in this field.

Benchmarking projects should be targeted at a process area or activity that will deliver the best value to an organisation. The project aim can be broad or specific. The project aim may relate to improving the performance of a process, activity/task, business improvement tool, equipment, strategy or behaviour.

Once a project aim is set the process or activity to be studied should be broken down into its component parts and current performance measured. Benchmarking partners to learn from can then be identified for the component parts and their practices studied through surveys or site visits. An analysis is then conducted to determine which processes or activities should be adapted and implemented.

THE ORGANISATION OF THE FUTURE

An ideal organisation of the 21st century is an investor's favourite, with a history of superlative financial performance. Its operating capabilities and characteristics are also exemplary. It is a winner of **"National Quality Award for Business Excellence"** or an **International Quality Award**. The 21st century organisation worships at the altar of customer satisfaction, ultimately defining its own success through the eyes of its customers. This ideal organisation takes great care in hiring, developing, training and retaining its employees. It involves them intimately in the affairs of the organisation and increasingly empowers them to act on the behalf of the customers as well as the company itself. **The 21st century organisation uses technology as a tool of liberation, not as a way to rationalise jobs. It is lean and habitually focused on productivity, cost management and real growth**.

The high performing 21st century organisation instills or embeds the relentless impulse for continuous improvement into all its processes and systems. It is also a fast company, making speed, quick response and "time to market" the bases for competitive advantage. Fast learning is therefore a defining characteristic and prerequisite for the 21st century enterprise that operates at high velocities without crashing. The organisation makes use of best practice benchmarking as a catalyst that enables the organisation to learn and to improve quickly. Best practice benchmarking drives continuous improvement and is deeply ingrained in every process. It enables the organisation to continuously test its capabilities to uncover improvement opportunities, to spur adoption of the best practices and to press relentlessly toward even greatest performance. **The 21st century organisation embraces a "we can learn from everyone" culture.**

A Call to Action

The call to action for the successful 21st century organisation is a call to make best practice benchmarking a corner-stone of the organisation's approach in conducting business. Organisations that reengineer for success in the 21st century will embrace benchmarking for best practices. In doing so, they will need the following operating imperatives :

1. Employ benchmarking and best practices as management tools to support strategic thinking and planning.
2. Integrate benchmarking into the management of every-day processes.
3. Codify your benchmarking language and approach to leverage learning.
4. Deploy benchmarking as a fundamental business skill with various approaches.

5. Manage benchmarking exchanges and best practice knowledge.
6. Use networking and technology to expedite and optimise benchmarking.
7. Train front-line employees, supervisors and the managers to be receptive learners and skill-ful benchmarkers who actively practice innovative adaptation.
8. Formally evaluate and recognise benchmarking as essential skill.
9. Create a corporate culture supportive of innovative adaptation.

These operating imperatives are discussed in detail in the following paragraphs :

1. Employ Benchmarks and Best Practices as Performance Indicators and Management Tools to Support Strategic Thinking and Planning

Benchmarking empowers the ***strategic thinking*** and ***planning processes***. As critical comparative operating statistics, ***benchmarks*** represent objective reference points that provide the basis for setting and validating the adequacy of performance goals and targets. ***Benchmarking***, in turn, yields best practice information that triggers insights, rapid knowledge acquisition, and operating breakthroughs that lead to superior performance. By integrating the benchmarks or comparative measures with best practice knowledge acquired through the benchmarking outreach process, organisations identify their most important improvement opportunities, set the agenda and priorities for change and map the course by which to attain superior performance.

Benchmarking adds value to the strategic thinking and planning processes in many ways. Benchmarking : *(i)* enables organisations to project competitor's future performance, *(ii)* validates the adequacy of short-term and long-term organisational goals, *(iii)* identifies the critical success factors that can be leveraged to achieve market leadership, *(iv)* stimulates long-term planning to close gaps and make business processes competitive and *(v)* identifies best practices for using technology. The first call for action is an exhortation to make benchmarks and benchmarking essential parts of the strategic thinking and planning processes.

2. Integrate Benchmarking into the Management of Every-day Process

The 21st century organisation will manage a portfolio of short-term and long-term change initiatives and will integrate benchmarking into all four of the fundamental performance improvement approaches namely ***continuous process improvement, organisation restructuring, process reengineering and managed reform***.

Every major process from new product development and sales to billing and after-sales-service will be viewed as a candidate for continuous improvement and benchmarking. Process owners and process teams play key roles to successfully integrate benchmarking and continuous improvement into work processes that flow through different departments and across traditional lines making functional responsibilities. Processes also need clearly defined owners to be responsible for design and execution and for ensuring that customer needs are met. It is difficult to define ownership because the processes seldom follow existing boundaries of organisational power and authority.

21st century organisation concentrates its daily management efforts on those few core processes that create the greatest value and are essential to the organisation's on going success. There are fewer than 20 major processes within any company no matter how large or small. Successful companies of the future will find it desirable to establish process ownership and to designate individual champions or advisors to help integrate benchmarking into daily performance improvement.

3. Codify Your Organisation's Benchmarking Language and Approach to Leverage Learning

Benchmarking language and methods vary superficially from organisation to organisation. The differences between one company's nine-step process and another enterprise's five-step process are inconsequential. It matters little which process model or terminology your organisation adopts. What matters greatly, though, is consistency of language and process within the organisation to ensure easy communication and information sharing among teams, work units, departments or divisions. A systematic benchmarking approach, whether in the form of a multistep process model or a simple checklist, guides the benchmarker from planning to data collection to data analysis to best practice identification, adaptation and implementation.

4. Deploy Benchmarking as a Fundamental Business Skill with Versatile Applications

As a catalyst for learning and performance improvement, benchmarking has both informal and formal applications. Informal benchmarking includes simple idea adaptation and learning from past successes so that they can be repeated. More formal benchmarking is used to examine complex processes and work systems. Process benchmarking may target practices that are best-in-company, best-in-market, best-in-industry or best-in-class. (without regard to country or geographic boundaries). The 21st century organisation will apply benchmarking throughout its portfolio of performance - improvement efforts. Consequently, individual employees and improvement teams will employ all types of benchmarking to their improvement efforts. They will be adept at choosing the most appropriate application for each specific improvement effort. Successful benchmarkers of the future will not be wed to the notion that projects must take three, six, nine or more months. They will blend quick tactical improvements with breakthrough projects that require many months to implement successfully.

5. Manage Benchmarking Exchanges and Best Practice Knowledge

The 21st century organisation will be skilled at knowledge management. Consequently it will develop systems to coordinate benchmarking information exchanges and manage best practices knowledge dissemination within the organisation. Organisations of the future will establish managerial positions to direct best practices development and to act as a central point of contact for inbound and outbound information exchange. The benchmarking champion will help the organisation to focus and concentrate on benchmarking activities. He or she will guide the organisation as it integrates benchmarks and best practice information into the strategic planning and continuous improvement processes. The benchmarking champion will facilitate benchmarking integration into day-to-day business operations. In the 21st century, companies will have to benchmark to survive. The benchmarking champion will facilitate full deployment of benchmarking to ensure survival in the 21st century corporation.

6. Use networking and Technology to Expedite and Optimise Benchmarking

Successful organisations of the future will increasingly draw on associations and networks, common interest groups, consortia, databases and other forms of technology to help them access, share, analyse and absorb benchmark information. In united states, networking groups have been organised by strategic planning institute's council on benchmarking and the American Productivity and Quality Centre's International Benchmarking Clearing house. All these organisations and many other industry associations can help focus, streamline, and optimise the process by which an improvement team determines who and what to benchmark and then explores the practices that enables the best to achieve their superior performance.

Nowadays, information is quickly and easily accessible to large and small organisations because of technology revolution. Computer networks and user friendly databases and e-mail applications make the analysis and sharing of information easier than ever before. Proliferation of these networks, versatile groupware applications and easy-to-use public databases will enable the 21st century organisation to accelerate benchmarking activities and to facilitate best practice knowledge sharing.

7. Train front-line Employees, Supervisors and Managers to be Receptive Learners and Skillful Benchmarkers who Actively Practice Innovative Adaptation

To accelerate the pace of learning and improvement through benchmarking, the 21st century organisation will create benchmarking skill competency among all employees, supervisors and managers. Comprehensive training is the key to creating benchmarking competency throughout the organisation. Training will help employees develop basic benchmarking skills that they can apply in their jobs and to understand the role of best practices in continuous performance improvement, strategic planning, reengineering time-based competition, change management and innovation.

8. Develop Benchmarking as a Skill that is Formally Evaluated and Recognised

Benchmarking training will be buttressed by managerial systems that support ongoing skill competency. Three interlocking managerial systems will be essential in reinforcing benchmarking's importance in the 21st century organisation. First job descriptions will reflect benchmarking as a basic responsibility of competent performance. Second, individual performance appraisals will regard benchmarking and innovative adaptation as basic skills to be reviewed and developed. Third, recognition and compensation systems will view benchmarking and best practice excellence as a cause for praise, promotion, commendation, and incentive pay. Together these three managerial systems will continually highlight benchmarking as a required skill for sustained success in the 21st century.

9. Create a Corporate Culture Supportive of Innovative Adaptation

In many work places, openly borrowing and adapting other people's ideas do not go well with the years of training, education an corporate culture. In the 21st century organisation, the unwritten prohibition against importing other's good ideas will be permanently repealed. The new era will simultaneously celebrate invention of new ideas and creative application of existing excellent ideas.

The 21st century organisation will overcome current cultural barriers to innovative adaptation through a systematic approach to shaping and managing corporate culture. No one managerial system will produce a "we-can-learn-from-everyone" culture. Some previously observed but highly-effective managerial approaches to forge a "we-can-learn-from-everyone" culture include :

(i) Create lending libraries that focus on competitors and other high performer's winning strategies and systems.

(ii) Routinely parade outside speakers and ideas before employees.

(iii) Review the products and practices of other companies and visit their facilities whenever possible.

(iv) Publicise the benefits of borrowing from the best.

(v) Sponsor regular meetings and discussions where employees and managers exchange ideas and explore best practices.

(vi) Layout work areas to encourage impromptu meetings, idea sharing and information exchange.

(vii) Employ best practice information in the problem solving and continuous improvement process.

(viii) Engage high-level executives directly in benchmarking and innovative adaptation.

(ix) Make competitive information-gathering everyone's responsibility, especially including functions such as sales, marketing and personnel.

(x) Regularly identify, study and celebrate internal success stories and best practices with the goal of repeating them.

(xi) Institutionalise learning by making evaluation-and-improvement cycles a required part of performance reviews, focus these reviews on learning from what went right as well as what went wrong.

Conclusion

The call to action for the successful 21st century organisation is a call to make best practice benchmarking a corner stone of the organisation's approach to conducting business. Best practice benchmarking is much more than just a business tool. For the 21st century organisation, it represents a fundamental approach to competing and managing. The best practices strategy complements traditional continuous improvement efforts and sets out to leverage the learning and experiences of the best, rather than merely reforming the practices of the worst which has been the traditional path of performance improvement. The best practices approach concentrates on performance improvement through organisational learning, effective management of intellectual assets and leverage of others' proven experience.

In the 21st century, the effective use of intellectual capital will increasingly become a prerequisite of market place success - perhaps even for survival. Successful organisations will employ best practice benchmarking as a primary catalyst of fast learning. Best practice benchmarking will be regarded as a power tool for leveraging internal and external experience. In the future, return on intellectual assets will be equally as important a performance indicator as return on physical assets. In this new era, best practice benchmarking will be a long-handled lever of the knowledge-age. By creatively adapting the best proven ideas, practices and approaches of others, an organisation can leverage their partners' people, knowledge, resources and experience with very little capital investment. Innovative adaptation creates a compounding effect on the internal rate of improvement, it produces a high-yield knowledge dividend. Consequently best practice benchmarking represents the ultimate competitive weapon: a low-investment, organisation-wide, renewable resource that produces rapid learning and performance improvement by leveraging others' learning and most effective practices. Unleashed in a global market place, this approach to management and continuous improvement promises rich returns.

BOX 18.1 : BENCHMARKING IN PRACTICE – TEXAS INSTRUMENT USES BENCHMARKING CHAMPION

Organisations of the future will establish managerial positions to direct best practices development and to act as a central point of contact for inbound and outbound information exchange. The benchmarking champion will help the organisation focus and concentrate benchmarking activities. He or she will guide the organisation as it integrates benchmarks and best practice information into its strategic planning and continuous-improvement processes. The benchmarking champion will facilitate benchmarking integration into day-to-day business operations. Texas instruments, whose defense systems and electronics division won a 1992 Baldrige Award, has already set out on this path. In the early 1990s, Texas Instruments named Laura Longmire, a veteran manager, to the post of "Benchmarking Champion for world-wide operations". The Texas Instruments benchmarking champion is charged with "co-ordinating, facilitating, training and implementing benchmarking throughout the corporation. A small but distinguished legion of other leading companies has recently created similar positions, and the trend seems sure to continue. When 76 large service and manufacturing organisations - including many of the most admired corporation of the United States were surveyed about their perceptions of benchmarking, 79 percent said "companies will have to benchmark to survive". The benchmarking champion will facilitate full deployment of benchmarking to ensure survival in the 21st century corporation.

POINTS TO REMEMBER

- By removing the need to **"reinvent the wheel"** and providing the potential to adopt proven practices, benchmarking has become an important methodology for providing a fast-track to achieving business excellence in the 21st century.
- Benchmarking had evolved during the 20th century, after World-War II - with the Japanese visiting the best companies in the US and Europe to gather knowledge and ideas of successful business.
- The concept of benchmarking had developed in the US during the 1960s.
- Xerox Corporation was the first company in the US to implement benchmarking to meet the competition from Japanese companies.
- During the end of 20th century (1980s and 1990s) and the beginning of 21st century more and more companies adopted benchmarking technique as a technique for strategic management.
- **The various stages in the evolution of benchmarking over time are :**
  - *(i)* 1st generation Reverse Benchmarking
  - *(ii)* 2nd generation Competitive Benchmarking
  - *(iii)* 3rd generation Process Benchmarking
  - *(iv)* 4th generation Strategic Benchmarking
  - *(v)* 5th generation Global Benchmarking
- The technological advancements in the 21st century have transformed communications and opened a whole new information-based world enabling organisations to access low-cost Internet based benchmarking services and opportunities.
- The **Business Improvement Performance Resource (BPIR.com)** is one of the new resources that is a valuable support to benchmarking projects.

- New benchmarking mythologies are emerging that provide more in-depth guidelines and instructions on how to do benchmarking well - **"TRADE"** is one such methodology.
- **TRADE consists of 5 stages :**
  - *(i)* Terms of reference
  - *(ii)* Research
  - *(iii)* Act
  - *(iv)* Deploy
  - *(v)* Evaluate
- Individuals trained in TRADE can advance their knowledge of benchmarking through its accompanying certification scheme - to ensure that benchmarking is applied professionally.
- An ideal organisation of the 21st century is an investor's favourite, with a history of superlative performance. It is a winner of **"National Quality Award for Business Excellence"** or an **"International Quality Award".**
- The 21st century organisation worships at the altar of customer satisfaction, ultimately defining its own success through the eyes of its customers.
- The 21st century organisation uses technology as a tool of liberation, not as a way to rationalise jobs. It is lean and habitually focused on productivity, cost management and real growth.
- The high performing 21st century organisation instills or embeds the relentless impulse for **continuous improvement** into all its processes and systems. It is also a fast company, making speed, quick response and **"time-to-market"** the bases for competitive advantage.
- The 21st century organisation embraces a **"we can learn from everyone"** culture.
- The call to action for the successful 21st century organisation is a call to make best practice benchmarking a corner-stone of the organisation's approach in conducting business.
- Organisations that reengineer for success in the 21st century will embrace benchmarking for best practices.
- **In embracing benchmarking for best practices, organisations need the following operating imperatives:**
  - *(i)* Employ benchmarking and best practices as management tools to support strategic thinking and planning.
  - *(ii)* Integrate benchmarking into the management of every-day processes.
  - *(iii)* Codify your benchmarking language and approach to leverage learning.
  - *(iv)* Deploy benchmarking as a fundamental business skill with various approaches.
  - *(v)* Manage benchmarking exchanges and best practice knowledge.
  - *(vi)* Use networking and technology to expedite and optimise benchmarking.
  - *(vii)* Train front-line employees, supervisors and the managers to be receptive learners and skill-ful benchmarkers who actively practice innovative adaptation.
  - *(viii)* Formally evaluate and recognise benchmarking as essential skill.
  - *(ix)* Create a corporate culture supportive of innovative adaptation.
- In conclusion we may state that the call to action for the successful 21st century organisation is a call to make best practice benchmarking a corner stone of the organisation's approach to conducting business. **For the 21st century organisations, benchmarking represents a fundamental approach to competing and managing.**

REVIEW QUESTIONS

1. Trace the evolution of benchmarking in Japan.
2. Discuss the growth of benchmarking in the 21st century.
3. Discuss the methodologies used for best practice benchmarking.
4. Describe the characteristics of the organisation of 21st century.
5. Briefly discuss the operating imperatives of the benchmarking for best practices which organisations use for success in the 21st century.
6. Describe how benchmarking can be integrated into the management of every-day processes in the 21st century organisations.
7. Discuss the highly-effective managerial approaches used to forge a "we-can-learn-from-everyone" culture.

DISCUSSION QUESTIONS

1. "The high-performing organisation of the 21st century instills or embeds the relentless impulse for continuous improvement into all its processes and systems" - Explain.
2. "Benchmarking empowers the strategic thinking and planning process" - Discuss.
3. "Benchmarking adds value to the strategic thinking and planning in many ways" - Discuss the most important considerations embraced by 21st century organisation in benchmarking.
4. "As a catalyst for learning and performance improvement, benchmarking has both informal and formal applications" - Elaborate.
5. "Three interlocking managerial systems will be essential in reinforcing benchmarking's importance in the 21st century organisation" - What are they? Discuss.

CHAPTER 19

The Future of Benchmarking

INTRODUCTION

As the pace of change accelerates in the 21st century as a result of technological opportunities, liberalisation of world markets, demands for innovation, quality and speed, organisations have to readjust and realign their operations to counter all these challenges. The pace of change has increasingly forced organisations to be more outward looking, market oriented and knowledge driven. A useful tool that can help businesses build strong capabilities, ensure an inward flow of ideas and establish true competitive gaps is benchmarking.

So where is benchmarking going? How is it going to be applied over the next 5 to 10 years? Benchmarking is being practiced in many different ways, with varying results. As with anything that becomes intellectually fashionable, many people are jumping on the benchmarking bandwagon because it seems like the thing to do. Benchmarking is likely going to help only those who keep the big picture in mind-benchmarking can help improve an organisation's competitiveness only if it is implemented correctly.

When talking about the future one should be cautioned by the words attributed to Mark Twain **"I always hesitate to make predictions, especially when it involves the future"**. In many respects that is what is facing benchmarking. Because of the interest in this business improvement topic and because of the multiplicity of organisations and individuals using benchmarking, it is still in a state of evolution. Since there are many new techniques being developed and used, it is probably more appropriate to talk about benchmarking milestones instead of an end point vision. One way to look at the future of benchmarking is to consider those ***milestones*** as major learning points in benchmarking management. Another is to consider some of the evolving ***challenges*** that will eventually have to be solved to make benchmarking a mature business tool.

The large influx of newcomers to the benchmarking game, often applying their own less rigorous interpretation of the process, has inundated the best-in-class companies with requests to study them. The worst crime against benchmarking - showing up for a site visit without adequate preparation and wasting the host-company's time-has happened frequently enough that many best-in-class firms are making it difficult for the average benchmarker to get an audience. Those that practice poor benchmarking are not doing it intentionally or with malice aforethought. They just don't know better. **Establishing one's organisation as an organisation that practices rigorous, value-adding benchmarking is rapidly becoming one of the prerequisites to learning from the best.**

In the US, winners of the Malcolm Baldrige National Quality Award in particular are overwhelmed with requests for benchmarking visits. Many of these requests come from organisations that are familiar enough with the award to know that one of the requirements of its winners is to share information with other US companies. However **"sharing information on successful quality strategies"** does not necessarily mean honouring every benchmarking request. Managers who are performing real benchmarking and perhaps have some valuable benchmarks of their own to share, will have the best chance of securing cooperation from the potential target companies of their choice.

SOME ISSUES IN THE FUTURE OF BENCHMARKING

1. Inter-Company Communications

It is imperative that benchmarking not be misused to engender co-operation between or among organisations that should be competing. As benchmarking proliferates, companies will form more relationships with other companies that were, prior to benchmarking, their fierce rivals. The sharing of learning and experience that may take place through these interactions is a healthful phenomenon as long as it in no way reduces competition between the companies sharing benchmarking information. **Collaborative benchmarking** among competitors should be adhoc, with a clearly defined purpose from the outset, and should be terminated when that purpose has been fulfilled. Collaboration among industry competitors to increase the overall competitiveness of the industry and move the industry generally forward is the ideal outcome of **collaborative benchmarking.** Anything that reduces overall competition in the industry, however has the potential to do serious long-term harm and should be avoided.

2. Use of Benchmarking Experts as Consultants

As expected from any industry that has substantial profit potential, now scores of consultancies have sprung up in response to the huge demand for benchmarking from corporations. This has resulted in a broad spectrum of "definitions" of benchmarking processes being preferred by the "experts". The free market will determine the approaches that provide the most value to the organisations using outside consultants. Valuable benchmarking will not include completing a series of benchmarking forms, members-only exercises or benchmarking software.

3. Use of Sources of Benchmarking Information

Good benchmarking will not place heavy reliance on benchmarking databases or clearing houses. Databases of benchmarking are worth little to people serious about using benchmarking for making real improvements because the databases alone will not provide a sufficient level of detail about the underlying processes of the best practices. Those databases that purport to do so will likely only serve as one source in a larger data-gathering effort by companies that are performing serious benchmarking. The power in benchmarking comes from sharing ideas - people sharing ideas - and not from some data in a database of benchmarks or from a library of benchmarking best practices. The real-tie live interaction among bright people with good ideas is what makes benchmarking so valuable. Accessing a database or a library is one thing, but it leaves a lot to be desired compared to asking the person who performs the best practice

4. Application of Benchmarking in the Public Sector

Benchmarking should find its way into the public sector too, although the lack of competition within the public sector may not create the same sense of urgency to improve that exists in the private sector. Continued swelling of budget deficits might help promote recognition of the need to do things better, faster and cheaper sometime soon, though, and benchmarking is a natural tool to use for improvement. The opportunities for improvement in the public sector are so vast that benchmarking could have a profound impact on how things are done using tax payers money. The macroeconomic effects of doing things better, faster and cheaper in the public sector are freightening, however. There is so much fat that cutting it off is not the answer to the problem. The challenge is to turn the fat into muscle, to make the fat productive. Looking for ways to increase the services we get for the same, or slightly lower, level of spending is an endeavour that can be helped greatly through benchmarking.

5. Application of Benchmarking in the Area of Public Education

If there is one obvious opportunity to use benchmarking to provide some substantial value to our society, it is in the area of public education. Aside from a radical shift in the entire public school paradigm, benchmarking across school systems can add tremendously to the value of our children's education and to the business and administration practices found in today's public education domain. There are lakhs of schools in India. Some teach science better than others, others English. Some have a lower drop out rate than the others in comparable socio-economic environments. Today these schools are not in direct competition with one another. There is no justifiable reason why they should not be sharing their respective accumulated expertise with one another. Benchmarking can help facilitate that process.

CURRENT POSITION AND FUTURE DEVELOPMENT OF BENCHMARKING

A survey conducted to assess the current position and likely future development of the tool of benchmarking revealed the following findings :

1. The need for mechanisms for transfer of best practice within organisations was clearly expressed and represented the most significant conclusion.
2. The use of computers for various purposes in benchmarking seems to be growing, although first hand contact and observation still seems to be preferred.
3. Formal efforts for benchmarking and benchmarking training were rated highly important, perhaps signalling that benchmarking is about to be increasingly institutionalised and an integral part of business.

Interest in benchmarking has virtually exploded since 1979 when Xerox first introduced it. Today, benchmarking, as a tool is widely used. It has spread geographically to large parts of the world and poliferated in a variety of manufacturing and service businesses including health care, government and education organisations.

Along with the increased use of benchmarking, some changes in its practice have occurred. The focus of benchmarking studies has gradually shifted. In early studies, the focus tended to be on performance measures, often of competitors, and for the purpose of setting more ambitious targets. Recent studies have examined how noncompetitors and industrial outsiders learn how to improve business processes. Comparison of performance measures has developed into learning about best practices (the term benchmarking is also referred to as benchlearning by some authors).

There has also been a trend to use benchmarking in a more coherent fashion and to more closely link it to an organisation's strategy. Some large organisations have established formal benchmarking programs. Benchmarking training is offered by numerous sources. The use of computers has become common and several software packages have been launched that are supposed to lead users through the steps of a benchmarking study.

Assessing the Current Position and Projecting Future Development

To establish the current state of benchmarking and to attempt to project future developments, a survey was conducted among a cross-section of organisations. The survey questions and respondents were specifically structured to gain some insight into emerging benchmarking developments. Among these were the capture, sharing and dissemination of best practices and the influence of technology - including computers, data bases and networks-on benchmarking. A two page questionnaire was designed and mailed to benchmarking managers or persons responsible for benchmarking in a sample of 59 organisations known to be active in benchmarking. The sample was composed to display large differences among the businesses in terms of size and type of industry. Included in the 59 organisations were both large, medium and small companies, ranging from manufacturing and service industries to health care and government institutions.

The survey response rate was 39 percent, which is considered as good for this type of surveys. Survey respondents were asked about the current and future use of benchmarking. Questions covered areas such as the existence of a formal benchmarking program, benchmarking training, mechanisms for transfer of best practices and the use of personal computers, software and on-line services for benchmarking.

Overall Findings

(i) The existence of formal programs for benchmarking was perceived as essential. This issue was given a high priority.

(ii) About 75 percent of the respondents indicated a need for a formal process in the area of mechanisms for transferring best practices found through benchmarking. This issue was given highest priority. Developing a process and mechanisms for transferring best practices is an area of high concern for the respondents.

(iii) The other topics of moderate importance included total quality management, business process management, linking benchmarking to strategy, benchmarking training and the use of networked personal computers for benchmarking.

Summary and Conclusion : The most significant conclusion was that determining the mechanisms for the transfer of best practices within an organisation is truly a high priority issue. Large organisations seem to have experienced major problems in disseminating best practices found in benchmarking studies to other areas of the organisation. Such problems limit the outcome of benchmarking and result in a less-effective use of resources put into benchmarking studies and a loss of opportunity from the adoption of best practices throughout the organisation. This is obviously an area for further work and research.

Formal programs for benchmarking in general and for benchmarking training in particular were also highly important areas likely to be further developed.

The use of computers in benchmarking, both for information sharing internally and externally, and for partnering and searching for best practices seems to be of some growth. On the other hand, direct contact with other companies and first hand observation of best practices still seem to be the preferred methods.

FUTURE TRENDS IN BENCHMARKING FOR COMPETITIVE ADVANTAGE

A global survey was undertaken by the European Centre for Total Quality Management (UK) which was aimed at assessing the trends and future directions of benchmarking and the transfer of best practices. Overall 227 organisations took part in the study. Participant organisations came from 32 different countries, all involved in benchmarking. The survey shed light on current trends in benchmarking and highlighted some issues that will affect its future, mainly the effect of Information Technology and Globalisation. These factors were seen as an opportunity rather than threat by most study participants.

Challenges Ahead

For suppliers of goods and services, there is no longer ***a*** customer but ***the*** customer or even *this* customer. Customers are demanding to be treated individually and they expect products and services to be tailored to meet their needs. With the kind of intense competition in industry today, simply meeting or beating past performance levels will not result in the level of improvement necessary to remain competitive.

While change has become inevitable and forced on us, the factors that caused it have also altered the nature of change itself. Change has become consistent and permanent. It has become the foremost business issue today. On the one hand, change represents growth, opportunity and innovation, on the other hand, it represents threat, disorientiation and upheaval.

Today, in the 21st century, organisations deal with vertical integration, mergers, new technologies, stock-less or just-in-time distribution, captivated contracts, preferred provider organisations, total quality management, business reengineering and so forth. To succeed in the future, organisations need to rethink their structure, products, processes and markets. They must reestablish themselves to be quicker to market, customer focused, innovative, nimble, flexible and be able to handle rapid change. This can only be achieved by continuously benchmarking one's performance with the world's best adapting the new best practice and innovating to become world-class.

Future Issues of Benchmarking

Benchmarking applications are widely spread across geographical and sectorial borders. **It is forecasted that such momentum would grow as benchmarking becomes more and more a "way organisations do business". Future issues of benchmarking include :**

1. The major issue that will affect benchmarking in the future is the advances in Information Technology. It is expected that the Internet and other electronic means will result in more best practice transfer. This spread of IT is accelerated by the fast paced proliferation of knowledge management applications and specialised tools.

2. The other issue is related to the spread of the benchmarking activity itself. More and more companies are adopting this powerful concept. National and international consortia and clubs are actively promoting the use of benchmarking.

3. Lexican and Classification - The Software of Benchmarking

***(a)* Lexicon :** There needs to be a widely accepted lexicon or language of what benchmarking is and is not. There is still confusion about the definition and types of benchmarking and how it can be applied. The most likely place where the standard definition should appear is in some recognised quality institution, which could be an association, institute, clearing house, or centre. The definition could also be embedded as a standard in the many quality awards being implemented. Ultimately, an organisation like the National Institute of Standards and Technology would be the keeper of the benchmarking definition in the United States.

***(b)* Classification :** Just like there is a SIC code for industries there needs to be an accepted classification of the business processes or at least the vital work processes. The classification should be process-oriented, that is, taking the horizontal-not functional or vertical-view of the organisation. **The classification system should :**

(i) take the customer's view point

(ii) be simple to use

(iii) be defined in layperson's language

(iv) show all natural interfaces and relationships

(v) be based on a hierarchic view of the enterprise.

The classification should be used as a diagnostic tool to understand the business of the organisation, namely how the work is done. It should become the plan for improvement. It would become the main basis to reduce duplication of the benchmarking effort. The classification would provide for the identification and improvement of the boundaries and handoffs between processes, which are often the locations of inefficiencies. The classification would become the way to creatively view the business.

4. Template - The Hardware of Benchmarking

In addition to the definition and classification, there needs to be a growing body of knowledge of how to do benchmarking well. This involves understanding the basic processes that organisations run and focusing on the practices in those processes. So a ***template*** also needs to become widely accepted. Without this benchmarking will become any one's approach and that will feed confusion. Eventually without a template, benchmarking will fall into disuse and another management fad. **Thus the template is the hardware of benchmarking.**

Part of the difficulty in developing a benchmarking template is management's impatience with the ability to find best practices quickly enough to feed the rapid pace of change. There is a major disconnection between the need for change and the time to search for best practice. What may evolve is the ability to do quick benchmarking. This could arise either from the technology of computer networks, telephones, fascimils and satellites, or it may evolve from the ability to conduct not only formal benchmarking but also the legitimising of informal benchmarking.

5. Networking - The "Peopleware" of Benchmarking

The use of networks, consortia, clearing houses, common interest groups, exchanges, knowledge bases and other **"people ware"** of benchmarking must constantly evolve to keep this important tool sharp. Fortunately, with the level of interest not only in the various segments of the economy but also in cultures around the globe, there is enough variety, inquisitiveness and innovativeness that benchmarking will be a robust field for some time to come.

Networking may involve an electronic network of external benchmarking professionals or an electronic bulletin board or a distribution list to find partners interested in improving the same process. The bulletin board can also be used to announce items of interest or to disseminate information on services and media for benchmarking. The ultimate goal would be to electronically match one's interest in a given business process with an expert process owner, who would then be willing to share the best practices in exchange for keeping a world-class business process current. The challenge will be to keep in touch with the partner to share the evolving, varied techniques. Thus only through the evolution of software, hardware, and peopleware will benchmarking rise to a higher plane of acceptance and use.

6. Reengineering versus Benchmarking

The difference between benchmarking and process reengineering, or other new initiatives that invariably catch management's attention, needs to be distinguished. The best way to do this is to deal with their definitions. Reengineering has come to mean the ***"radical redesign of business processes"***. The working definition for benchmarking is ***"finding and implementing best practices"***.

Is one approach replacing the other? If reengineering is process redesign to fundamentally alter how organisations deal with their customers and suppliers, then how are the new practices that will become the basis of the new design found? That would seem to be the role of benchmarking. **Thus benchmarking is essential to reengineering. So benchmarking is still a necessary, stand-alone quality tool.**

The radical redesign of business processes is not a necessity. But finding better practices to be the source of continuous improvement is, whether it radically affects business processes or not. That fact needs to be continually reinforced, along with the fact that benchmarking of business processes, used by line managers is the way to get desired results.

7. Rapid Organisational Learning

Xerox undertook its first formal benchmarking study in 1980. That study changed the company dramatically, compared to Japanese competitors, Xerox had nine times as many suppliers, had seven times as many product defects, took twice as long to develop and deliver products, and took five times as long to set up a production line. Organisations can not deal with this magnitude of competitive crisis. There needs to be continuous learning. Organisations need to figure out how to rapidly learn and transfer knowledge in the context of becoming a consistently knowledgeable, learning organisation.

It would be a good-directed activity and would support the achievement of the overall activities of the enterprise. It would be the basis on which the organisation would learn from others to supply insights to drive creative thinking. It would leverage critical success and competency areas. Once best practices from continuous learning were embedded in the work processes, they would achieve organisational goals.

This learning involves internal transfer of best practices. The organisation has to find the mechanisms and foster the motivation for continuous learning. The problem is not with the mechanisms. There will always be ways to document an idea, a practice, or a method that is considered better. The problem is with the motivation. The challenge is how to foster the willingness of every organisation member to : *(i)* want to volunteer a best practice and *(ii)* want to search out, understand and eventually adapt for use the best practice proposed by others.

This is a substantial change and one that is not easily solved. It is however, in the process of being benchmarked to gain understanding and insight to what will make organisation learning successful. **Perhaps some of the answer lies in the key factors for successful change shown in *Box 19.1.***

BOX 19.1: BENCHMARKING CHANGE MANAGEMENT KEY FACTORS FOR SUCCESSFUL CHANGE
• Believing there is a **need** for change • Determining **what** should be changed • Developing a **picture** of how the organisation will look after the change **How benchmarking makes change successful** • The gap between internal and external practices creates the need for change. • Understanding industry best practices identifies **what** must be changed. • Externally benchmarking practices, developed from others, give a **picture** of the end point after change. **Benchmarking desired state** • Effective use of benchmarking is persistent throughout the organisation. • There is a conscious need to find and implement best practices.

8. Attaining Benchmarking Excellence

How is benchmarking excellence attained? How will we recognise it when we see it? At least four factors must be considered :

(i) ***The management process***, that is the things that are done right to establish, support and sustain benchmarking activities.

(ii) ***The rationale taken with benchmarking***, namely, it will be how the business is run.

(iii) Increased recognition of the link between benchmarking and other business process improvements.

(iv) Understanding that benchmarking does not stand alone, but in fact, is looked to other initiatives to continuously improve.

Ultimately, however, attaining benchmarking excellence will come down to how credibly management uses benchmarking to get results. It must continue to be seen as a key quality improvement tool. The direct relationship of benchmarking and operational results will prove its worth. Only then will benchmarking attain the level of excellence along with all the other quality tools. **This means benchmarking has to be seen as a key tool to drive competitiveness, support customers and make organisations and operations effective.**

Conclusion : Benchmarking must come to mean learning from others. Organisations, individuals and leaders need to accept this. We are in the knowledge and learning era, which is rapidly accelerating. Ultimately there may be no other way to learn that will keep pace with change. Organisations can not afford more competitive crises from not keeping active pace with the outside world. That is fatal. **Benchmarking can have no higher purpose than to be known as the effective way to pursue rapid learning and to obtain knowledge to change how we work and how we work differently!**

BOX 19.2 : BENCHMARKING IN PRACTICE – COLLABORATIVE BENCHMARKING

In collaborative benchmarking, a group of firms share knowledge about a particular activity, all hoping to improve based upon what they learn. Sometimes, a third party often serves as co-ordinator, collector and distributor of data, although an increasing number of firms are managing their own collaborative studies. *For example,*

- Managers from the training organisation of a large financial services firm organised an adhoc consortium to study training processes at a number of U.S firms that are considered leaders in training. Participants included American Airlines, AT&T, NCR, Quad Graphics, Solectron and USA A, all of whom openly shared detailed data about their training processes with one another.
- Managers from one of the Malcolm Baldrige National Quality Award winners convened an adhoc consortium to study the use of customer satisfaction data at a number of US companies, that are considered leaders in this area. Participants in the study included five Baldrige winners - AT&T, IBM-Rohester, Motorola, Solectron and Zytec-Timelife and MBNA, the financial services company.

There are many other collaborative efforts that have produced great results. One consortium that includes Arthur Anderson, Eastman-Kodak and Xerox, among others, has been sharing data and knowledge in a number of areas, with many positive gains to show for it. The American Productivity and Quality Centre (APQC) in Houston is compiling a benchmarking cleaning-house database, which they claim will be a database of "best practices in both abstract and full text form".

POINTS TO REMEMBER

- Benchmarking is a useful tool that can help businesses build strong capabilities, ensure an inward flow of ideas and establish true competitive gaps.
- It is difficult to make any prediction about the future of benchmarking because it is still in a state of evolution.
- It is more appropriate to talk about benchmarking milestones instead of an end point vision.
- One way to look at the future of benchmarking is to consider those milestones as major learning points in benchmarking management.
- Establishing one's organisation that practices rigorous value - adding benchmarking is rapidly becoming one of the prerequisites of learning from the best.
- **Some issues in the future of benchmarking include :**
  - *(i)* Inter-company communications
  - *(ii)* Use of benchmarking experts as consultants

(iii) Use of sources of benchmarking information
(iv) Application of benchmarking in the public sector
(v) Application of benchmarking in the area of public education

- **A survey conducted to assess the current position and likely future development of the tool of benchmarking revealed the following findings :**
  (i) The need for mechanisms for transfer of best practice within organisations was clearly expressed.
  (ii) The use of computers for various purposes in benchmarking seems to be growing.
  (iii) Formal efforts for benchmarking and benchmarking training ware rated highly important.
- The focus of benchmarking has gradually shifted. In earlier benchmarking studies, the focus was on performance measures, often of competitors and for setting more ambitious targets. Recent studies have examined how non-competitors and industrial outsiders learn how to improve business processes. Comparison of performance measures has developed into learning about best practices.
- Benchmarking is becoming more and more a **"way organisations do business".**
- **Future issues of benchmarking include :**
  (i) Advances in information technology. *(ii)* Spread of benchmarking activity itself.
- There needs to be a widely accepted lexicon or language of what benchmarking is and is not.
- There is a need for an accepted classification of the business processes.
- There is a need for a growing body of knowledge of how to do benchmarking well.
- The use of networks, consortia, clearing houses, common interest groups, exchanges, knowledge bases and other **"people ware"** of benchmarking must evolve.
- Benchmarking is essential to reengineering.
- There is a need for organisations to adopt continuous learning. Organisations need to figure out how to rapidly learn and transfer knowledge.
- **To achieve benchmarking excellence, we need to consider four factors :**
  (i) The management process
  (ii) The rationale taken with benchmarking
  (iii) Increased recognition of the link between benchmarking and other business process improvements
  (iv) Understanding that benchmarking does not stand alone
- Benchmarking has to be seen as a key tool to drive competitiveness, support customers and make organisations and operations effective.
- Benchmarking can have no higher purpose than to be known as the effective way to pursue rapid learning and then to obtain knowledge to change how we work and how we work differently.

REVIEW QUESTIONS

1. Discuss the following issues related to the future of benchmarking.

   (a) Inter-company communications

   (b) Use of benchmarking consultants

   (c) Use of sources of benchmarking information

   (d) Application of benchmarking in the public sector
   (e) Application of benchmarking in the area of public education
2. Discuss the current position and future development of benchmarking.
3. How do you assess the current position and project future development of benchmarking?
4. Discuss the future trends in benchmarking for competitive advantage.
5. Discuss the following future issues of benchmarking :
   (a) Advances in information technology
   (b) Lexicon and classification - the software of benchmarking
   (c) Template - the hardware of benchmarking
   (d) Networking - the "peopleware" of benchmarking
   (e) Reengineering versus benchmarking
   (f) Rapid organisational learning
   (g) Attaining benchmarking excellence

DISCUSSION QUESTIONS

1. "One way to look at the future of benchmarking is to consider those milestones as major learning points in benchmarking management. Another is to consider some of the evolving challenges that will eventually have to be solved to make benchmarking a mature business tool" - Explain.
2. "As benchmarking proliferates, companies will form more relationships with other companies that were, prior to benchmarking, their fierce rivals". Do you agree or disagree? Justify your answer.
3. "Good benchmarking will not place heavy reliance on benchmarking databases or clearing houses" - Elaborate.
4. "Comparison of performance measures has developed into learning about best practices. Benchmarking is also referred to as benchlearning" - Discuss.

CHAPTER 20

Beyond Benchmarking

INTRODUCTION

Benchmarking is simply defined as going out and finding others in your field-allies or competitors who are doing it better, from a specific process or service to the whole business. You then adapt their solutions in your business. Essentially benchmarking is copying what another business has discovered works for them and then importing it into your business. For instance, you identify the top five critical processes in your business and then benchmark them - compare your current performance levels in those same areas against of another business, **"more ideal levels of performance"** and then strive to **"meet or beat"** that level. This practice has become more popular with many businesses looking for a **"quick fix"** solution to the most pressing issues regarding the quality of the products and/or services they offer.

On the surface, this often sounds like a great idea. Why reinvent the wheel? Why not profit from another organisation's trial and error and take the easy road to improvement? **Indeed, benchmarking has proven to be a valuable catalyst for improvement in many organisations, and can often be a stepping stone to better operations. Yet imitation is not the optimal way to build your bottom line nor assure future growth. There is a better way to greater success, beyond benchmarking : innovation.**

What is Innovation?

Innovation means to come up with your own customised answers to your specific challenges. It means to tap into your own people's innate wisdom and come up with uniquely powerful solutions that custom-fit your business. **Innovation has several advantages over benchmarking. These include :**

1. Innovation fosters breakthrough, **"out-of-the-box"** solutions. Benchmarking merely fosters imitation.
2. Innovation focuses on creating improvements that are customised for your business. Benchmarking only imports solutions customised for some one else's business.
3. Innovation requires that you understand the whole system that leads to best long-term improvements. Benchmarking primarily focuses on getting "quick fix" results, which often compromises long-term performance.

4. Innovation focuses on going as far as you can go and beyond. Benchmarking only focuses on going as far as some one else has gone.

INNOVATION PROCESS

A good place to start any innovation process is to make a list of the most critical processes and customer interaction points in your business. Describe briefly the current less-than-optimal situations and then ask for each one : What would perfect look like?

Write down a short yet detailed description of what perfect would be. Depending on the size of your business, you might simply start by just asking your self this series of questions and brainstorming your answers on paper. You would then want to invite the other key players on your team to contribute their ideas. This greatly increases your "data pool" and also strengthens your team, when it is done in an atmosphere free of fear and internal competition.

Getting Started on Your Innovation Process

The key points are :

1. Define Your Targets

Clarify the best innovation targets as they would apply to you and your business - not whatever levels your competition has reached or what is deemed "successful" in your industry. The key is to start small, single out the top three areas in your business that are obviously ripe for improvement and begin.

Remember your are in business. What is your aim? According to quality guru, Dr. W. Edwards Deming, ***"all businesses are really only in one business - creating loyal customers".*** Merely satisfying customers is no longer enough because four out of five "satisfied" customers will defect, if offered the right opportunity. Building customer, employee and investor royalty is proven to be the best investment strategy any business can make to assure its future. Do you have a clear strategy in place to create and keep loyal customers?

2. Commitment to Innovation

You must commit to continuous innovation in your businesses. This is a vital ingredient in any endeavour to grow and improve.

3. Self-Education

Learn as much as your can about the power of true quality management, systems improvement, and strategic innovation. These critical optimisation methods are very powerful allies, even when applied in small steps. Perhaps best of all, they offer a synergistic, cumulative effect on your whole business. This directly impacts your bottom-line results and future success.

4. Critically Assess your whole Business System

This requires both courage and honesty and should ideally involve every one in your business. Where do you experience the greatest frustrations and waste? Where do your customers experience the most problems doing business with you? The answers to these questions often reveal the biggest opportunities for innovation and improvement.

5. Consider an Innovation Coach

A qualified, objective coach can offer valuable insights and guidance on your innovation journey. It is difficult to work on improving your business systems when you are working in them. A good coach can greatly increase the velocity and value of innovation efforts.

6. Focus on the System

Your business system holds the key to your success. **"Navigating your business by past financial performance is like driving a car by looking at the rear view mirror"**. The key here is to continuously focus on improving your vital few critical systems. According to Deming 85% of the results you will get lie in the 15% of any process. This means that the seeds for success are in the front end, not the back end. Sales are results, not drivers. When we identify and take care of the first 15%, the growth and higher sales naturally will follow.

7. Step Outside Your Box

Regarding any innovation efforts, the key is not to focus exclusively on the desired goals or results. Get focused instead on discovering and applying the best theories and methods and the desired results will follow. Having an ideal target is important, but it is not enough alone to best assure your success. A continuously improving system combined with a clear aim is the key to hitting and exceeding any of your desired targets.

Strategic innovation is a proven "power" tool for success. For optimal results, it is best part of an integrated approach aimed at bringing out the best in your people, processes and performance.

In conclusion, we may say that innovation is the way beyond benchmarking, towards progress. Innovation is the process of discovering the best solutions for your own unique business and customers, implementing those solutions, and then tracking and continuously improving on them with internal (your team) and external (your customers and vendors) feed-back. Innovation, often leads to strategic breakthrough in your business - break-throughs that can be easily missed when we focus on copying the methods developed by others for their unique organisation. Innovation also invariably leads to a greater understanding of your customer, and ultimately, to greater success. So the words to be kept in mind are : **"Innovate - don't imitate"**.

INTELLIGENT BENCHMARKING AND BEYOND

"Measuring is the best way to improve what you are doing. Doing it right is the trick".

Benchmarking is a form of measurement - where you measure something else where you are lagging, identify the areas and take corrective action.

Benchmarking should be a learning process, however, not just a measurement exercise. It is a starting point for continuous improvement. Benchmarking should be a starting point, not an ending point. If you use generic benchmarking results from associations or private organisations, they should simply point you to areas that you will study in more depth. Always take care when you are comparing benchmark results to your business and make suitable adjustments before making any decisions.

Traditional benchmarking simply compares numbers, which can be a good starting point if you are comparing the right things. You need to go beyond traditional benchmarking to look at resources, procedures and systems to find out why you are performing well. More importantly, you should use that information to keep doing the things that are going well and to change the things that are not working. Compare how you operate with processes, people and systems against other high-performing organisations and understand what they do differently. Then assess whether you can emulate what they do to be successful and implement it.

Intelligent benchmarking is not just about comparing benchmark numbers, it is a process to target problem areas, identify solutions and implement changes that will get better results. Benchmarking is a part of the process, including general benchmarking as well as detailed, focused benchmarking, the comparison of processes, resources and systems rather than just numbers. **The following 10 steps will guide you to achieve better results :**

Step 1 : Identify and rank critical success areas.

Step 2 : Select areas to improve.

Step 3 : Compare results using benchmarks.

Step 4 : Choose results that are not superior.

Step 5 : Isolate supporting processes, resources and systems.

Step 6 : Analyse each process, resource and system for impacts.

Step 7 : Focus on problems.

Step 8 : Test your practices against leading practices.

Step 9 : Adopt leading practices and change existing practices.

Step 10 : Repeat for other areas.

Because of the enormous potential for improvement that benchmarking can provide, there is a critical need for senior management's orchestration of this effort. Functional management, left to its own devices, may be highly reluctant to identify productivity opportunities that, they believe could be construed as profits forgone or otherwise be a reflection on their past performance.

Another reason that benchmarking needs to be directed by top management is that the subfunctions performed by an organisation like logistics may vary significantly from firm to firm. Adherence to strict functional comparisons may not yield the optimum outcome because gains from changing the organisational boundaries within the firm might be passed up. Thus top-level oversight is essential for the benchmarking process to succeed. Whether it be internal, competitor or non-competitor, benchmarking should be corporate-wide, comprehensive, controlled, continuous and an integral part of the strategic planning process.

Benchmarking and Business Simplification

What lies beyond benchmarking? If benchmarking uncovers proven industry best practices that meet, but do not exceed customer requirements, then benchmarking provides the standard against which to judge the cost-effectiveness of operations. It becomes the vehicle for business simplification. **A comparison of the characteristics of benchmarking and business simplification is shown in *Table 20.1* below:**

TABLE 20.1 : USES OF BENCHMARKING FOR BUSINESS SIMPLIFICATION

Criterion	Benchmarking	Extended Benchmarking
Objective	Efficiency	Effectiveness
Requirements met	Internally defined	End user defined
Process	Current	Industry standard
Practices and Technology	Best	Best
Cost of non-conformance	Partially reduced	Eliminated
Results	Productivity	Business simplification

Business simplification through benchmarking is an adaptation of the same process where activities necessary to meet customer requirements are identified and those that are not necessary are eliminated.

The characteristics of simplified business processes would include the following : *(i)* meets true customer requirements, *(ii)* is easy to learn and use, *(iii)* makes the firm easy to do business with, *(iv)* is affordable and cost-effective, *(v)* has the fewest steps possible, *(vi)* minimises all possible redundancies with other processes, *(vii)* stresses process control and *(viii)* is sensitive to changing customer requirements.

Achievement of these business simplification benefits derived from industry best practices contributes to improved customer satisfaction and business results.

Benchmarking and Change Initiatives

There was an additional by-product of the L.L. Bean experience. The change of focus from strict comparisons within one's narrow competitive industry to the search for functional best practices often breaksdown the reluctance of managers to actively consider and adapt the ideas of others. When professionals consider competitive comparisons there is a tendency to inspect the differences and put plans in place to achieve parity. The results of this are obvious and potentially disastrous. First, the firm always is playing catch up since competition is also improving productivity. Second, change is gradual since the perception is that all that is needed is to meet competitive practices and the requirements of benchmarking will be satisfied. No strategic view of best practices will be obtained from the approach that would give the firm a technical breakthrough to achieve superiority rather than simply meeting competition.

Key considerations that must receive focus to attain superior performance through benchmarking are shown in *Box 20.1* below :

The 10 step benchmarking process must be brought to bear on business simplification. This means not only practice simplification but also process simplification, that is what can be eliminated and still satisfy end user customers. The focus will still be on industry best practices, and, where possible, reliance on proven technology - one which most likely will be found in another industry.

BOX 20.1 : SCOPE OF BENCHMARKING THAT ENSURES SUPERIOR PERFORMANCE

- Focus on meeting end user customer requirements.
- Focus on best practices.
- Includes proven technology.
- Focus on business simplification - process simplification and business practice simplification.
- Concentrate on major contributors to the cost base.
- Define long-term end point and migration strategy.
- Use of quality improvement tools.

The focus should be on meeting the end users of consumer's requirements. These would be the set that meets but does not exceed those requirements. With these there must be a vision of what the operation will look like once it is converted to emulate industry best practices. That end point definition is easily constructed from the benchmark findings since they incorporate the changes to be made.

While there are many practices that can and should be changed, they should be prioritised by those that concentrate on affecting the cost base, customer satisfaction, or assets to the greatest degree. The quality process tools of cause-and-effect diagramming, force field analysis and weighted prioritization will greatly help in sorting out those practices to concentrate on.

The approach to functional benchmarking as a search for industry-best practices in many instances overcame the **"non-invented here"** syndrome of focussing solely on the competition. If practices could be shown to be superior in diverse industries, there was a more active and ready consideration and acceptance. The weight of evidence outside the industry can be pervasive for getting individuals leave parochial view points behind. Coupled with a personal attraction such as many had with L.L. Bean, the ability for individuals to more openly consider change was substantial.

BOX 20.2 : BENCHMARKING IN PRACTICE – BEYOND BENCHMARKING : THE ROLE OF IT DIAGNOSTICS IN HIGH-PERFORMANCE BUSINESS

When a CEO says to the CIO "I just got back from a conference and we are spending too much on IT", a common response is for the CIO to refer to a benchmark analyst to defend the IT budget.

Accenture believes both the question and the answer will most likely had executives down the wrong path.

Here is why : Senior executives are increasingly concerned with how they can get maximum business value from the money they spend on information technology. The immediate reaction revolves around how best to quickly diagnose issues and deliver results. For many the quickest approach is to turn to benchmarking.

Benchmarking IT spending as a percent of revenue (or by headcount, desktop or other general measures) has long been considered a quick way to get to actionable recommendations to increase the value delivered by information technology. However, Accenture Strategic IT Effectiveness (SITE) professionals maintain that, while benchmarking is sometimes informative, it is seldom actionable because it does not provide a true picture of the effectiveness or value of IT spending and investments.

There are several reasons for this :

(i) The implied question in benchmarking is how much am I spending on information technology? Rather, the critical questions should be: What value am I receiving from IT? What value should I be receiving from IT? How do I get more value from IT?

(ii) Accenture research has shown little correlation between IT spending as a percent of revenue and positive business outcomes.

(iii) Relying on benchmark spending data can, infact, be misleading, as commercially available financial benchmarks do not allow "like for like" company comparisons.

Apart from providing an incomplete picture of how effectively an IT budget is being spent, a significant additional risk of managing information technology as a percentage of revenue is that this often leads to a capability gap. When revenues are down, companies seek rapid cost-cutting initiatives and often at strategic or discretionary spending first, shifting the balance to operational or non-discretionary area - what is sometimes called "keeping the lights on" spending. This approach has the unfortunate consequence of ultimately delaying or eliminating the technology initiatives that would underpin new business value and revenue growth.

Accenture analysis shows one of the key differentiators of the high-performance business is the ability to link IT investments to the creation of business value. Accenture believes high performance business prefer more comprehensive IT capability diagnostics either as an addition or a substitute for benchmarking. Unlike traditional IT benchmarking, an IT capability diagnostics provides are understanding of how to better align discretionary IT investments with business strategy and identifies actionable ways to drive business value for the enterprise.

An IT Investment and Spending Diagnostics

Accenture's SITE research also indicates that high performance businesses allocate IT spending in a ratio of 45 percent discretionary and 55 percent non-discretionary. In a high-performance business, CEOs and CIOś focus on reducing non-discretionary IT spending and redirecting to freed spending to fund powerful new strategically and operationally high-value discretionary investments. High performance business proactively identify and stop investments that will not produce the expected business value.

Accenture has developed a number of unique IT capability diagnostics that focus on the value delivered rather than benchmark how much is spent. The Accenture IT Investment and Spending Diagnostic, *for example,* evaluates current discretionary and non-discretionary spending. More importantly, the diagnostic provides a portfolio view of discretionary spending, showing when spending choices are made and how well aligned and effective those choices are with respect to a company's key business imperatives or objectives. It has been used successfully at a number of companies to help achieve grater business value from their IT budgets.

The diagnostic is a powerful tool to :

(i) Help senior executives balance and redirect spending to projects that create value.

(ii) Stop projects that do not create value and

(iii) Systematically identify where to cut costs in non-discretionary spending.

When properly applied, this diagnostic will culminate in high-value initiatives to help meet business growth targets.

Eye-opening Findings : Experience shows that Accenture IT Investment and Spending Diagnostic can lead to some eye-opening findings. For a health-care services company, *for example,* the diagnostic uncovered that only 16 percent of a company's IT budget was truly discretionary and very little was invested in innovation. The benefits of running the diagnostic for this company included:

(i) Helping senior executives establish the portfolio allocation of discretionary investments to guide investment management overall and to prioritize projects.

(ii) Quantifying why senior executives had been dissatisfied with the company's IT investment.

(iii) Developing a new "portfolio" approach to IT investments by breaking down investments across discretionary categories.

(iv) Providing an on-going mechanism for the business and the IT department to agree on priorities based on discretionary/non-discretionary allotments.

Another part of IT investment and spending diagnostic determines which current or planned discretionary IT projects are related to a company's top three business priorities and then figures out what percentage of the total IT discretionary budget supports those priorities. The results can be startling - a range from 20 percent to 75 percent discretionary spending on the top three priorities.

Taking into account industry sector, company objectives and competitive forces and other factors, there are optimum portfolio allocations of discretionary investments across several categories such as research and development and strategic, enabling and sustaining programs while the allocation strategy will differ by company, over all, experience shows that 60 percent to 70 percent of discretionary IT spending should go towards furthering the top three business priorities to achieve optimal results.

Companies aspiring to achieve high performance should consider going beyond traditional information technology return-on-investment metrics by taking into account the company's specific financial and operating context. Diagonostic tools give senior executives a common language and options with which to assess and create IT-enabled value.

POINTS TO REMEMBER

- Essentially benchmarking is copying what another business has discovered works for them and then importing it into your business.
- There is a better way to greater success, beyond benchmarking. It is **"innovation"**.
- **Innovation** means to come up with your own customised answers to your specific challenges.
- **To get started on your innovation, the key steps are :**
  - *(i)* Define your targets
  - *(ii)* Commitment to innovation
  - *(iii)* Self eduction
  - *(iv)* Critically assess your whole business system
  - *(v)* Consider an innovation coach
  - *(vi)* Focus on the system
  - *(vii)* Step outside your box
- **Innovation** is the way beyond benchmarking, toward progress.
- **Strategic innovation** is a proven **"power"** tool for success.

- **Intelligent benchmarking** is not just about comparing benchmark numbers, it is a process to target problem areas, identify solutions and implement changes that will get better results.
- Benchmarking becomes the vehicle for business simplification.
- **Business simplification** through benchmarking is an adaptation of the same process where activities necessary to meet customer requirements are identified and those that are not necessary are eliminated.
- The change of focus from strict comparisons within one's narrow competitive industry to the search of functional best practices (benchmarking) often breaksdown the reluctance of managers to actively consider and adapt the ideas of others.

REVIEW QUESTIONS

1. What is innovation? Discuss the advantages of innovation over benchmarking.
2. Discuss the key points in the innovation process.
3. What is "intelligent benchmarking"?
4. Discuss the 10 steps in intelligent benchmarking.
5. Discuss the following :

   (a) Management's influence and benchmarking

   (b) Benchmarking and business simplification

   (c) Benchmarking and change initiatives

DISCUSSION QUESTIONS

1. "Innovate - don't imitate" - Comment on the statement.
2. "Benchmarking should be a learning process, however, not just a measurement exercise" - Discuss.
3. "There are implications from benchmarking that transcend the process itself and the benefits to be desired" - Explain.
4. "Intelligent benchmarking in not just about numbers, it is a process to target problem areas, identify solutions and implement changes that will get better results". - Elaborate.

CHAPTER 21

Case Analysis, Caselets and Case Study Exercies

PART - A

Case Analysis

The case study method of teaching and learning has fulfilled a major role in senior level management education for a number of years. The case study approach was pioneered by Harvard Business School in the USA and by Cranfield School of Management in the U.K. It continues to play a major role in business schools.

What is a Case Study?

A case study offers often in great detail, a real-life situation that has been or is currently confronting a senior manager. In this way, a case study is a living scenario within which you are invited to display and demonstrate your ability to apply the theoretical knowledge that you have acquired in the subject to which the case study is linked.

Cases will vary in their layout, style, format, data and background. The case material can comprise one or two pages (about 500 words) or even ten to twelve pages of text with a number of appendices, charts etc. However, in this book only short cases (within 500 words) are discussed taking into consideration the limitation on the length of case study from the examination point of view.

Data in the case will also vary greatly from the copious to the meager. The amount and quality of data presented depends on the data available and considered relevant. The reader must decide what is important and what is not among the given data.

Guidelines for preparing Case Analysis

1. **The need for practicality :** There is no such thing as a complete case and no case gives you all the information you need to conduct analysis and make recommendations. In the business world, managers never have all the information they need to take decisions. All information

may not be available, too costly to obtain or may take too much time to obtain. So, in analysing cases, make reasonable assumptions if necessary, state assumptions clearly, perform analysis and make decisions. Be practical. Avoid saying ***"I don't have enough information".***

2. **The need for justification :** The most important part of analysing cases is not what strategies you recommend, but rather how you propose that they be implemented. ***There is no single best solution or one right answer to a question asked in the case.*** So, give ample justification to your recommendations.
3. **The need for realism :** Avoid recommending a course of action beyond the organisation's means. Be realistic. Make sure your recommendations are feasible. Present the major advantages and disadvantages of several feasible alternatives. Try not to exaggerate, stereotype, prejudge or over dramatise.
4. **The need for specificity :** Do not make broad generalisations while suggesting some strategies. Be specific in telling ***what, why, when, how, where and who.***
5. **The need for originality :** Do not necessarily recommend the course of action that the firm plans to take or actually undertook, if those actions resulted in improved revenues and earnings. The aim of the case analysis is for you to consider all the facts and information relevant to the organisation at the time, generate feasible alternate strategies, choose among the alternatives and defend your recommendations.

Case Analysis Techniques

The checklist to enable the reader to develop a quick approach for case analysis is given below:

1. Quickly glance through the material.
2. Try to get the general ideas by reading the case as a whole.
3. Comprehend the perspective of the case.
4. Make mental notes or marginal notes of important facts and ideas.
5. Arrive at some preliminary information of the problem.
6. Grasp the relevant facts and firm up logically and orderly relationships between them.

One must remember that one is not aiming at perfection in analysing a case, but is developing analytical capability for problem solving. The following practical guide-lines will assist in the case analysis.

1. Suggestions offered for analysis of facts are :
   (a) List of facts should be prepared in a logical manner.
   (b) If any assumption has been made, the same should be stated clearly.
   (c) Quantitative analysis should be done with the help of statements, charts and graphs.
2. Main questions to be answered should be identified and questions which need to be answered to tackle the main questions should be stated.
3. Criteria for the decision should be based on the objectives.
4. Implementation plans should be determined by examining the following aspects.
   (a) Programme orientation – What is to be done?
   (b) Responsibility identification – Who has to do it?

(c) Schedule of events – When exactly is the job to be done?

(d) Budget perspective – How much will it cost?

5. Contingency plans – contingency plans may be kept ready in case of need.

Case Analysis Process

The steps involved in case analysis process are :

1. Analysis of facts

- Prepare list of facts in a logical order.
- Develop quantitative analysis through statements, charts and graphs.
- Identify statements of attitudes or opinions in the case.

2. Identify questions to be answered

- Determine main questions to be answered.
- State questions which need answering to tackle the main questions.

3. Ascertain objectives and criteria for decision

- Comprehend the objectives.
- Determine the criteria for decisions.

4. Suggest alternate solutions

- State advantages and disadvantages of each alternative.
- Give your suggested solutions stating evidence supporting you position.

5. Information plan

- Programs – Details of actual action to be taken to be developed
- Responsibility – Personnel responsibility to be identified.
- Schedule – Implementation strategy in terms of time should be reviewed.
- Budget – Financial implications should be examined.

6. Contingency plan – Due to uncertainties, contingency plan may be needed.

Caselets

1. BROOK FIELD ZOO IMPROVES PERFORMANCE THROUGH BENCHMARKING

The Brookfield Zoo is one of the top zoological institutions in the US. Yet their ability to generate strong customer loyalty had dropped over several decades. In supporting the organisation in moving in a different direction, key leaders from Brookfield came to Orlando for a week long retreat. From there a **"customer loyalty strategy"** was crafted that included a number of strategies. Leaders were trained to lead customer-focused initiative. Zoo facilitators were selected and trained to deliver customer service programming. The trainers facilitated sessions for approximately 1500 crew members and collectively spending over 900 hours on this effort. Leadership tool kits were implemented so that daily conversations could occur with staff around service excellence. Though the program was implemented late in the Spring of 2005, according to summer surveys, non-member ratings for overall zoo visit - those who were "extremely satisfied" increased 18% over 2004. **Some other significant improvements include:**

- Non-member ratings of overall value for cost-those who said the visit was an "excellent value" – increased nearly 12% over 2004.
- Non-member ratings of the helpfulness of zoo staff - those who thought the zoo staff "exceeded expectations" - increased nearly 8% over 2004.
- Non-member ratings of "Definitely will visit the zoo again next year" increased nearly 7% over 2004.
- Nearly 65% of non-members, listened to or interacted with zoo staff or volunteers regarding animals during their visit, compared to only 9% in 2004. This is an enormous behavioural change among staff.

Discussion Questions :

1. Describe the type of benchmarking undertaken by Brookfield zoo in order to improve their performance.
2. Describe the "customer loyalty strategy" crafted by the key leaders from Brookfield zoo.
3. Discuss the improvement in performance achieved by Brookfield zoo after benchmarking.

2. FREIGHT COST REDUCTION CASE STUDY

HOW COST-BENCHMARKING AND FREIGHT RATE NEGOTIATIONS SAVED 22%

Assignment : Business logistics was contracted by a manufacturer to find ways to reduce freight transportation costs. The client was concerned about retaining high service quality and did not want to sacrifice service quality for reduced freight charges.

Strategy of Business Logistics : The first step was to evaluate the client's service objective. In doing so, Business Logistics interviewed the client company' president, it sales managers, and its traffic manger. It was found by Business Logistics that high service quality was critically important due to competitive and customer service considerations.

The second step involved conducting an evaluation of the client's freight management and shipping activities, a process involving developing a database containing recent shipment history including carriers used, shipment origins, destinations, weights and costs. Business Logistics then interviewed the client's carriers to determine whether they shared the same understanding of service requirements and found that they (the carriers) were not at all aware of the client's specific service needs. Business Logistics also conducted a freight cost benchmarking process, a step that involved comparing the client's freight costs to those of other companies using similar transportation sources with similar service requirements. Their findings were that the client had the potential to significantly reduce freight costs by using their carriers and other shipment modes that would still provide the kinds of service quality desired by the client. They received the client's approval to conduct freight rate negotiations with its existing carriers as well as with new carriers that they were able to introduce.

Results Achieved

After extensive freight rate negotiations, Business Logistics renegotiated the client's carrier contracts and achieved a savings of approximately 22% for the client. They also established standard operating procedures with the client's carriers to assure that the client's service quality requirements were fully understood and that the carriers would meet them. These procedures included steps for the carriers to take to initiate remedial action in the event pending service failures were identified in order to maintain high service quality. Total client freight savings exceeded $ 1,000,000 per year.

Discussion Questions :

1. Discuss the strategy developed by Business Logistics to find ways to reduce freight transportation costs of their client.
2. Describe the freight cost benchmarking process conducted by Business Logistics.
3. Discuss the results achieved by Business Logistics for their client by the freight cost benchmarking process implemented by them.

3. GLOBAL BENCHMARKING FOR AUTOMOTIVE OEM UNCOVERS BREAKTHROUGH IDEAS FOR MATERIAL COST REDUCTION

In order to remain competitive, an automotive OEM required aggressive cost reductions to regain profitability. But the company was struggling to generate new savings ideas internally. So AT Kearney was engaged by the COO and CPO of the company to look beyond their internal portfolio for next generation material cost savings.

Challenge : Traditional commercial and technical cost reduction initiatives did not go far enough. The challenge was to develop a rapid approach to help the OEM company achieve world-class material cost structures.

Approach : A.T Kearney developed a structural innovation program to drive breakthrough ideas for material cost savings, while achieving world-class performance. The approach leveraged competitive product tear downs to identify global benchmarks for material cost. Suppliers were engaged throughout the project to drive innovative solutions. The project team including OEM experts and AT Kearney consultants analysed over 100 subsystems throughout the entire vehicle. A structured approach was used to quantify the opportunities for commercial savings, specification improvement, content rationalisation and complexity reduction.

After prioritising the best savings ideas, a cross-functional team developed the business case and presented recommendations for senior leadership approvals.

Results : The initiative drove tangible results - achieving savings targets within the first year, and identifying strategic changes required for the OEM to become globally cost competitive in the long-term. The methodology was successfully integrated into their ongoing cost reduction program.

Discussion Questions :

1. What was the problem faced by the Automotive OEM company? What was the challenge faced by them?
2. Discuss how A.T. Kearney - a benchmarking consultant helped the automotive OEM to overcome their challenge.
3. Discuss the results achieved by the automotive OEM company after implementing global benchmarking process.

4. INNOVATION AT FLORIDE DEPARTMENT OF TRANSPORTATION (FDOT)

In 2002, the Floride Turnpike became the first governmental toll agency to be given the ability to function as a private enterprise. The Florida Turnpike Enterprise's goal was to become an innovative operation built on providing value at every part of the customer experience. As part of the **"We Drive Smiles"** initiative, a series of awareness and skill-building service training sessions were delivered to all 1400 team members across the entire state of Florida.

Within one year, this ground-breaking effort resulted in many impressive operational improvements, including:

- Dramatic improvement of employee morale (up 18%) and customer satisfaction (92% would recommend to family/friends).
- Has expanded and increased revenue, improved efficiency, cost-effectiveness, and timely project delivery.
- Has leveraged resulting additional revenue to make substantial improvements to existing road system, delivered six expansion projects, contracted most in-house functions to the private sector, promoted customer service, maintained financial stability and improved bond rating.
- Expanded responsibility for all operations on every FDOT owned and operated toll road and bridge. This represents about 600 miles of road way and 80 percent of all toll facilities in Florida.

Based on the amazing success of this service transformation. Florida's Turnpike Enterprise was awarded the prestigious international President's Award for Innovation and Excellence in 2003 and later won the JD Power's Seal of Approval for Excellence in 2005.

Discussion Questions :

1. What was the goal of Florida Turnpike Enterprise? What initiatives were taken by Florida Turnpike to achieve their goal?
2. Discuss the operational improvements achieved by Florida Turnpike because of their innovative operation.
3. What benefits were achieved by Florida Turnpike because of their innovative operation?

5. STARWOOD HOTELS AND RESORTS

In 2005, Starwood Hotels and Resorts known for their Sheraton, West-Inn, Four-Points by Sheraton, St-Regio, and W-Hotels, embarked on a global revitalisation of their many properties. The challenge, as with many hotel chains was that explosive growth during the previous decade created a multitude of different cultures, standards and results. For the Starwood Corporation, this complex initiative encompassed more than 1,25,000 employees across more than 1200 hotels around the world.

As a part of long-term strategy that included re-branded marketing and operational updates, world-class benchmarking provided a comprehensive series of transformation training programs, to reflect the newly clarified brands and the related recommitment to world class guest service. As part of this international roll-out, world class benchmarking designed, developed and delivered the training that resulted in less than a year, according to Star wood executives "a staggering success" in participant evaluation results, with "hundreds, perhaps thousands of guest testimonials about significant improvements in the guest experience".

The initial results reflect only the early stages of a fully-realised cultural transformation. Every indicator shows dramatic improvements in the commonly accepted measures that define world-class success: leadership evaluations, employee excellence metrics, guest satisfaction and intent to return and refer, and initial improvements in operational improvements, savings with revenue trending stronger.

Discussion Questions :

1. What was the challenge faced by Starwood Hotel Chain?
2. Discuss the changes undergone by Starwood Hotels after implementing world class benchmarking for improvement.
3. Discuss the benefits achieved by Starwood Hotels because of the cultural transformation resulted due to benchmarking.

6. TOYOTA STRIVES TO RETAIN ITS BENCHMARK STATUS

Sometimes it is not easy being a benchmark. Toyota Motor Corporation which set the industry standard in terms of manufacturing practices, now is fighting to keep at the front of the pack in the face of growing competition from those who long have emulated the innovative lean system of the No 1 Japanese automaker.

Mr. Gary Convis, President of Toyota Motor Auto Plant in the US, says the other automakers, which benchmarked the lean manufacturing system that Toyota for all practical purposes invented, have taken the system and improved upon it.

Now Toyota has to figure out a method of communicating what is known as the **"Toyota Way"** down company lines as the automaker grows and spreads around the globe.

But the "Toyota way" represents a manufacturing culture so complex, and so entrenched, that Mr. Convis admits it is impossible to know it as deeply as its original founders.

There is no way to teach the unique Toyota Culture except through intensive one-on-one coaching on the shop floor, he says, acknowledging that "there needs to be a better way".

For Toyota - a company where change doesn't come easy - what that better way may be is a little murky. He says the automaker has tried to capture the admittably nebulous "Toyota way" in words for internal training manuals, but that is just a first step.

Mr. Convis discussed Toyota's efforts to adapt at his Wednesday speech titled "Toyota : changes and challenges". And change is the biggest challenge for the evolutionary, not revolutionary automaker.

One change, is Mr. Convis, himself. The fact that an American, not an executive from Japan, is running operations here is a new move for the automaker. Likewise a UK native is running Toyota's manufacturing operations in his home land. Bringing in local executives is a "huge challenge". Mr. Convis formerly a NUMMI and General Motor Corp - says to Toyota's culture.

The automotive is also adapting to technology quickly, using virtual engineering practices that facilitated cutting the development on the 02 Camry to 26 months - a full 10 months shorter than for the last generation.

But Mr. Convis says Toyota doesn't plan to get radical now, in its attempt to retain its benchmark status. Rather it will continue to employ the slow-and-steady principles of the **"Toyota Way"** - Kaizen or continuous improvement and **"Genchi genbusto"** which literally means "go and see" in order to stay the course.

Because, while others are able to initiate, no automaker, Mr. Convis says, understands the intricacies of the system it invented like Toyota.

Discussion Questions :

1. Why Toyota strives to retain its benchmark status?
2. What is meant by the "Toyota way" used by Toyota to spread its culture around the globe.
3. "Change is the biggest challenge for the evolutionary not revolutionary automaker" - Comment on this statement with reference to Toyota Motor Corp.
4. Discuss the strategy adopted by Toyota Motor Corp to retain its benchmark status.

7. FORD SETS INDUSTRY BENCHMARK FOR SEX EQUALITY

Ford of Britain's commitment to equality in the workplace has earned an exceptional tribute from equal rights campaign group "opportunity now" for its industry leading position.

The business-led group's 2004 benchmarking survey which measures the progress employers have made in ensuring equal treatment for men and women, has singled Ford out for particular praise.

It is a member of an elite group of 25 businesses awarded platinum status, an honour only bestowed on companies scoring between 95 percent and 100 percent in the survey.

Ford's ability to motivate employees - everything from establishing a vision and setting goals to creating an optimum management structure - could not be bettered, scoring 100 percent against a survey average of 81 percent. Its ability to turn vision into reality was also flawless. Ford scored 100 percent for ensuring equality in recruitment, work design and redeployment and for developing equality behaviour, culture and accountability.

Monitoring of recruitment, training, promotion and pay, learning and the impact of equality action on the organisation also scored top marks.

Women have thrived in this enlightened climate, occupying senior positions in the organisation. High flyers include Monazz Khan, director of legal affairs, Maureen Graham, director of programming and distribution, Pauline Walsh, manufacturing manager at Dagenham Engine Plant, Kathryn Las South East district manager, Linda Carpenter, small car planning manager and Alexandra Walker, manager of power train manufacturing engineering.

European diversity director Surinder Sharma said "We have only been benchmarking for three years now and this shows the impressive progress the company has made in terms of diversity issues generally, especially after receiving gold last year. We are now seen as one of the leaders in the UK, not just in manufacturing, but across the board.

"Opportunity Now" is a "Business In the Community" - led campaign that works with employers to realise the economic potential and business benefits that women at all levels contribute to the workforce.

Norma Jarboe, director of "Opportunity Now" said "Ford demonstrates an outstanding commitment to women in the workplace and has shown an exceptional dedication to ensuring its working culture is inclusive and diverse. I am personally impressed with Ford's work in this area and think that its exceptional platinum mark clearly reflects the quality of its comprehensive efforts.

Ford Motor Company employs around 14,000 people in 10 locations, including Southampton, house of the Ford Transit, Bridgend and Dagenham, which produce petrol and diesel engines and Dunton, the largest automotive design, product development and engineering facility in the UK.

Discussion Questions :

1. Discuss the achievements of Ford Britain, in the area of ensuring equal treatment for men and women employees.
2. What are Ford's achievements in its progress towards workforce diversity issues?
3. Explain how benchmarking could have helped Ford in setting industry benchmark for sex equality in its workforce.

8. TATA STEEL SETS NEW BENCHMARK IN REHABILITATION AND RESETTLEMENT AT KALINGA NAGAR

Tata Steel, which is setting up a six million tonne per annum green field steel plant at Kalinga nagar steel hub in Jaipur District, has set a new benchmark in rehabilitation and Resettlement (R&R) for the families affected by the project.

This model R&R scheme being implemented under the banner of "Tat Steel Parivar", focuses on reassuring communication, customised rehabilitation and resettlement and rechecking of its implementation for each family through self and independent social audits. Each family covered under the scheme is assured of the benefits for a period of ten years.

While government policy has stipulated for provision of employment for one member from each core household, the "Tata Steel Parivar" policy promises employment opportunities for each major member of the core house who are identified as extended families. Besides, the company is providing training facilities for personality and technical skill upgradation.

Further, scholarships are also being provided for displaced families pursuing higher education in professional education like that in Medicine, Engineering and Management. An amount of Rs. 2.21 lakh is also being provided as one time assistance in lieu of employment.

Under the **"Tata Steel Parivar"** policy, each family is given a monthly maintenance allowance of Rs. 2000 - 2300 till they get an employment in the plant whereas the policy stipulates for payment of maintenance allowance for 12 months only.

As per the R&R policy, each extended family is supported to be provided 4356 sq. ft. of homestead land along with a house building assistance of Rs. 1.5 lakh. Apart from this, the "Tata Steel Parivar" scheme has developed modern rehabilitation colonies at Trijanda, Sansailo, and Gobarghati with 20 kilometers of motorable roads, 32 kms of drainage and 300 sodium vapour halogen lamps for street lighting in the colonies. Each homestead plot has piped water connection with access to 50,000 litres of potable water from the running taps. Further, each colony has a dispensary, community centre and education centres.

Trijanga is not only the Rehabilitation Colony created by Tata Steel but it is a milestone of tribal township with all modern amenities with a cultural and green backdrop. Round the clock free health care facility is being provided in the Rehabilitation Colonies through a dispensary and 24 hours standby ambulance services and complicated cases are referred to Hi-Tech hospital in Bubaneshwar. Further a 'Tata Parivar' hospital in Gobarghati Rehabilitation Colony is on the verge of completion.

Whereas Tata Steel provides additional Rs. 1 lakh (over and above the policy value of Rs. 1.5 lakh) per extended family, it has also provided for all steel temporary housing facilities and rented housing facilities to each family before they shift to their permanent housing.

"Building a better life" is always the purpose of Tata Steel. As Kalinga nagar, it has been taken further by not only rehabilitating Tata Steel Parivar but also ensuring that they step into much better lives, by not just employing them but empowering them with skills for a better future too. Better houses, education for the children and health care for the relocated families has brought in joy and happiness in every relocated tribal family and fulfilled Tata Steel's commitment of making steel and building the community.

Discussion Questions :

1. "Rehabilitation and resettlement is one of the major concerns for Tata Steel in Kalinga nagar" - Discuss.
2. Discuss Tata Steels "Tata Steel Parivar" concept and its initiatives in rehabilitating and resettling the families displaced by its green field projects in Kalinga nagar.
3. Explain the features of "Tata Steel Parivar" and the benefits provided to the displaced families which are treated as extended families of "Tata Steel Parivar".

9. TATA STEEL AIMS TO REACH BLUESCOPE SAFETY BENCHMARK

Tata Steel which entered into a memorandum of understanding (MOU) with DuPont safety Resources in October 2004 for implementing world class safety practices at its steel plant was able to bring down its loss time injury frequency rate from 2.54 in 2004 to 1.01 in 2006. At present it is less than 1. Tata steel implements safety standards at its mines and collieries as well. Corus however is doing a better job on the safety front.

Stan Booth, chief of safety of Corus, said Corus has so far only one fatal accident in 2007 with loss time injuries being between 16 to 20 each month. According to him, it is a tremendous improvement in the company's performance over the seven year period.

Corus too follows Blue Scope's benchmark loss time injury frequency rate of 0.4 and appointed DuPont safety resources as a consultant in the field of safety in 2001.

Tata Steel, chief operating officer (steel) HM Nerurkar said the steel major was still not satisfied with its safety achievements and would like to improve upon its records at the earliest.

"Safety and more importantly, our attitude towards it, is what the challenge is for the next century and we can not really wait for the next 99 years" said Nerurkar "The steel major has already started its journey with DuPont and it didn't have much time, as it needed to become a benchmark organisation in safety very quickly" he added.

Discussion Questions :

1. Explain how Tata Steel implemented world class safety practices.
2. Compare Corus and Tata Steel with respect to their safety performance as per Blue Scope safety benchmark.

10. "ENERGY EFFICIENCY BEST PRACTICE" PROGRAM HELPS AUSTRALIAN HOTELS IN HOTEL ENERGY BENCHMARKING

The case studies were produced by the Common-wealth **Energy Efficiency Best Practice (EEBP)** program and the Australian Hotels Association, after studying six major hotels. Each case study includes benchmark and performance comparisons, a cost-benefit analysis, annual energy savings, capital costs, annual energy cost savings and return on investments.

"The hotels energy use benchmarking project" is a partnership between EEBP and the Australian Hotels Association. EEBP supports industry sectors to identify and implement cost-effective solutions for a more substainable and competitive future. The program has a combined focus on innovations, training and benchmarking and offers practical tools, information and assistance.

Testing Hotel Energy Efficiency

Everyday of every year, hundreds of hotels, from boutique operations to large resorts, rely on significant amount of electricity and natural gas to service tens of thousands of customers across Australia.

A series of energy benchmarking case studies conducted show the hotel industry how to maximise profits, minimise energy costs and demonstrate leadership by reducing energy use and green house gas emissions - without negatively impacting on the comfort or satisfaction of guests and customers.

Since energy is a significant component of any hotel's property operating costs, these opportunities can not be ignored - energy savings go straight to the bottom line and are often an easier route than through increased turn over. Electricity accounts for close to 70 percent of hotel energy use and contributes more than 90 percent of greenhouse gas emissions. Alternatively, natural gas typically represents up to 50 percent of energy consumption.

Real and Proven Results : The hotel energy benchmarking case studies demonstrate real and proven results. They report on ways to improve energy efficiency - ranging from simple changes which involve little or no capital investment to longer - term improvements that may require some funding. Many initiatives have quick payback periods. Hotels can save thousands of dollars annually by implementing changes in key service areas, including kitchen catering, pool and spa heating, water heating, air-conditioning and ventilations, and lighting power.

Features of Energy Best Practice Hotels

The energy benchmarking project concluded that best practice hotels : *(a)* have systems in place to monitor, record, analyse and report on hot water, gas and electricity use, *(b)* achieve significant and cost-effective savings by focusing on best practice energy efficiency, *(c)* incorporate ways to increase energy efficiency into improvements and/or renovations and *(d)* continually look for innovative ways to optimise energy performance.

The Bottom Line From Participants

"Over the past five years, we have reduced energy use by 10 percent. We have achieved big savings from educating hotel division managers about good practice".

- Doug Stemp, Hotel Director of Engineering, Hyatt Regency, Perth

"Refurbishments are good time to install efficient equipments. In 1992, we installed a building management system on air-handling units which saves over $ 5000 a year"

- David Craven, Hotel Director of Engineering, Park Royal Surfers Paradise

"I can count on my fingers the number of after - hours' breakdown call outs we have had since we started our maintenance program.

- Tony Fioraso, Assistant Chief Engineer, Sharaton, Perth Hotel

Discussion Questions :

1. What is meant by "Energy Benchmarking"? Explain how hotel energy benchmarking has benefited hotels in Australia.
2. Discuss the contribution of common wealth Energy Efficiency Best Practice (EEBP) program to improve the energy efficiency of Australian hotels.
3. Discuss the features of "Energy Best Practice Hotels" in Australia.

PART - C

Case Study Exercises

1. BAI RETAIL DELIVERY : RETAILUTION CASE STUDY (RADICAL ADVANCES IN RETAIL BANKING)

Abstract : The successful integration of disparate technologies within banks' branch networks following mergers and acquisitions activity is a common challenge that was recently experienced by a large bank following its acquisition of two financial institutions. The bank implemented an account automation software that seamlessly integrate with its existing core system that whenever a customer walked into any of its 160 branches, the account opening would be consistent, providing the highest level of customer service.

The Challenge : One of the 50 largest banks in the U.S recognised the need for a streamlined account opening process to help support the rapid growth it experienced after acquiring two financial institutions, which added 40 branches to its network.

Pre-existing account openings in the newly acquired banks were tedious and time consuming for tellers and customers alike. Tellers were preoccupied with repetitious data entry gathering customer's personal information and producing required documents. This required excessive amounts of time that resulted in lengthy queues and customer waiting times and did not allow for the kind of personal attention and relationship building the bank liked to see between its staff and customers.

According to the bank's senior vice president of Information Systems, "while growth is important to our bank, we are constantly looking for new ways to maintain the highest efficiency ratios in the industry while continuing to provide the excellent customer service we have been known for since 1917".

In order to maintain its reputation for excellent branch efficiency and customer service, the bank began searching for a solution that would provide a consistent customer experience throughout the entire branch network and seamlessly integrate with its existing core system.

Steps to Address the Challenge/Recommendations

The bank implemented Benchmark Technology Group's new account automation software - **"Compass"** - in each of its branches. Compass was seamlessly integrated with the bank's existing core system to improve branch efficiency and provide a streamlined new account opening process that decreased customer wait times and increased interaction between tellers and customers.

Results : Compass accelerated account openings by guiding tellers through pre-defined workflows and potentially cumbersome account maintenance processes, while complying with bank policies and procedures.

When opening a new checking or savings account, data entry was minimised as required forms were automatically completed and printed with customer information pulled from the core system. Any captured information is intelligently applied when multiple accounts are opened to ensure data is only entered once.

The software's ease of use also enabled the bank to create a uniform training program to quickly educate its expanded team of tellers and staff on how to effectively use the software. As a result, branches were better able to manage the sudden influx of flow of new account openings that followed both acquisitions without compromising customer service or efficiency in the process.

"Compass completely improved the way we open accounts" said the bank's Vice President, Deposit Operations Manager. "It prompts tellers through the entire process and prefills necessary forms and documentation; even the most complex business account can be easily opened in approximately 10 minutes. And, it allowed us to implement a consistent training program across our entire branch network".

About Benchmark Technology Group

Since 1985, Benchmark Technology Group has been a leading provider of branch technology and software solutions for institutions of all sizes. The company offers a complete line of branch automation products and services including teller printers, scanners, ATMs and cash handlers. In addition, Benchmark Technology Group provides web-based fulfillment services, device evaluation and consulting, equipment service and maintenance programs, along with check 21 solutions. Benchmark Technology Group's systems design, integration, implementation and support services include customised and expanded offerings that are customer centric and scalable.

Discussion Questions :

1. Discuss the problems faced in the new accounts opening process of the bank after it acquired 40 new branches. How Benchmark Technology Group helped the bank to overcome the problem.
2. How do you categorise the kind of benchmarking undertaken by the bank to implement an account automation software?
3. Explain the features of the new software "Compass".

2. BENCHMARKING INDIA'S BUSINESS PROCESS OUTSOURCERS (BPOs)

India having captured 46 percent of the global business-process-offshoring (BPO) market, is the leading offshore destination and will probably remain so for sometime. But competition is intensifying as more companies compete to supply such services. This crowded field is driving down billing rates, while the rising demand for talent is boosting the labour costs of India's BPO sector by upto 15 percent annually. Both factors are combining to threaten profit margins. At the same time, clients are now more demanding, having captured the benefits of lower labour costs, they want better quality and higher productivity. If offshore service providers - captives as well as third party ones are to remain cost competitive while meeting these rising expectations, they will need to innovate and to measure and improve their performance.

Until recently, there was no methodology to benchmark the performance of remote - delivery centres. To address this needs, in late 2005, Mckinsey and India's National Association of Software and Service Companies (Nasscom) launched a web-based benchmarking survey to research the performance of the BPO providers. The effort which is called **"Process 360-Operational Excellence"**, classifies operational processes into five key categories : *(i)* costs, *(ii)* quality, *(iii)* speed and flexibility, *(iv)* productivity and innovation and *(v)* risk management. The survey gathered input from four groups of stakeholders - clients, operations managers, senior managers and front line delivery agents - to gauge the degree of alignment across these groups about the relative importance of the five operational factors. The benchmarks, which are equally applicable to the captive back-end operations of multinational companies and to independent third-party providers, also examine the maturity level of 12 key operational practices, including recruitment, training and workflow management.

Completed at the end of 2005, the initial survey covered 50 operational processes across 12 delivery centres in India. **It revealed three interesting findings:**

(i) While clients rated their off-shore partners (captives or third-parties) highly on process performance, they want providers to offer more than just labour cost savings. In the first few years of offshoring, clients tend to focus on cost benefits and on the provider's ability to maintain quality levels comparable to those at onshore sites. Given the availability of skilled talent and lower wage rates, most off-shore partners can meet these initial expectations relatively easily and therefore generate high levels of customer satisfaction. Within two to three years, however as clients become accustomed to the cost savings, they begin to look for productivity benefits and service delivery innovations. Unfortunately, too many providers continue to focus on cost benefits while they struggle to accommodate the evolving needs of their clients.

(ii) The research also highlighted the significant spread in performance between leading outsourcing providers and the rest of the pack : the average total cost per full-time equivalent for a leader was 15 to 20 percent lower than that for an average provider. The leaders thus had higher margins. Similarly, while most providers could improve their client's productivity by 2 to 3 percent each year, the industry leader recorded a staggering annual increase of 8 to 10 percent. Interestingly, performance levels for similar processes also differed across locations within the same provider : given the rapid growth in the scale of operations, most delivery centres had created islands of excellence but hadn't replicated their best practices throughout the organisation.

(iii) The survey found a high degree of correlation between the maturity levels of operational practices and process performance. Companies whose senior management devotes substantial time and effort to streamlining and "industrialising" their processes, *for example,* outperform their peers. Also, since reducing attrition rates is the key to keeping costs low and quality high, providers that innovate in the areas of recruitment, training and people management tend to deliver better value as well.

Result : Benchmarking revealed that newer customers focus more on cost and quality while more tenured customers look to innovation and speed. In most cases, the focus of the provider's senior management lags behind.

Discussion Questions :

1. Analyse the BPO scenario in India and the problems faced by the BPOs.
2. Discuss the methodology adopted by Mckinsey and Nasscom to benchmark the performance of remote-delivery centres.
3. Discuss the findings of the initial survey covering 50 operational processes across 12 delivery centres, completed the end of 2005.

3. BOEING SETS A BENCHMARK IN AIRCRAFT MANUFACTURING

Boeing was founded in 1916 by William Boeing and George Westervelt and was initially called the Pacific Aero Products Company. The company's name was changed to Boeing in 1917. Boeing began manufacturing aircraft for the US military during World War I. After World War II, the company shifted its focus from the defence industry to commercial jets.

In 1952, Boeing launched its first commercial jet, the Boeing 707, a short-range plane. In 1960, Boeing began manufacturing its first jumbo jet - the Boeing 747, which went on to become one of the company's most successful aircraft. In 1962, Boeing manufactured Air Force One for the American President's use. In late 1969, Boeing entered the field of space craft manufacturing by contributing to the Apollo programme. Innovative features and approach to manufacturing established a **benchmark** for development of aircraft in future.

The Need for Boeing 777 : It was the first aircraft to be digitally designed by computers and was expected to be the best in efficiency and quality in its class. The Boeing 777 family came to be known as the builders of the most technologically advanced aeroplanes.

The 777 design, innovative features and approach to manufacturing established a benchmark for development of aircraft in future. The management and technical approach used to develop the 777 were applied to a number of projects including the International Space Station - 2.

The design and development process of Boeing 777 was substantially different from the previous Boeing aircrafts. The company actively sought suggestions from major carriers including United Airlines, Nippon Airways, British Airways, Japan Airlines and Cathay Pacific on how 777 should be designed.

Distinguishing Features : The notable design features of 777 included a unique fuselage cross section ; Boeings first application of "fly-by-wire", an advanced technology, glass flight deck with five liquid crystal displays, a comparatively large scale use of composites (10 percent by weight) and extremely powerful engines. The 777 offered optional folding wings where the outer 6m/21 ft. of each would fold upwards for operations at space restricted airports.

The Benefits : Boeing reaped major benefits by automating its aircraft design process. The development time came down by 91 percent and labour costs by 71 percent. While comparing the design process of earlier aircraft including 757 and 767 models, Boeing 777 had the following additional advantages :

(i) Elimination of over 3000 assembly interfaces, without physical prototyping.

(ii) Reduce aircraft development time significantly.

(iii) Meet customer requirements better by involving them in the development process.

(iv) Eliminate costly modification procedures.

Discussion Questions :

1. Outline the development of Boeing company in its journey from being a manufacturer of aircrafts for US defence to the builder of the most technologically advanced civilian aircrafts.
2. Discuss the innovative features and approach to manufacturing of Boeing 777 that established a benchmark for development of aircraft in future.
3. Discuss the benefits reaped by Boeing company by automating its aircraft design process.

4. KNOWLEDGE MANAGEMENT AT TATA STEEL

Tata Steel was early to recognise the significance of Knowledge Management (KM) for the success of the company. It made it compulsory for all its employees to participate actively in its knowledge management program.

The company based its new performance assessment program on the participation of each individual employee in the KM program through the introduction of "KM index 4". The index tallied the points achieved through participation in the KM program, giving the employees a benchmark for their participation.

Tata Steel also encouraged employees to experiment with new ideas for which they were rewarded.

Tata Steel's KM initiatives were successful and the number of hits at KM sites of Tata Steel in 2001-02 was 1100 compared to Shell's 1000 hits, eventhough Tata Steel had only 3000 registered users as compared to Shell's 10,000 registered users. Shell was the second most admired company in Europe at that time. Through Tata Steel's KM initiatives, expert skills became available throughout the organisation and productivity increased. As employees were encouraged to come out with innovative ideas, their job satisfaction increased, and another benefit was a reduction in R&D expenditure.

In 1983, Tata Steel acquired the Indian Tube Company Ltd., a manufacturer of seamless and welded tubes. In 1991, it acquired the ferro-chrome unit of OMC Alloys Ltd.

KM Initiatives of Tata Steel : The KM program at Tata Steel was started in 1999. The aim of the program was to tap the abundant knowledge base in the form of tacit knowledge and explicit knowledge that was lying unused and make it available for use across the company.

Revamped Strategy : Though Tata Steel did make a good beginning in KM, there were some problems which were not addressed. Connectivity was still poor and access technology was not standardised.

Benefits Reaped from KM : Generally, any KM implementation has two sets of benefits :

(i) It reduces the cost of production and consequently increases the revenue and

(ii) it leads to utilisation of existing knowledge and creation of new knowledge.

Future of KM at Tata Steel : In the future, Tata Steel plans to link "e-learning" with the KM repository and KM communities, devise an intellectual capital index, network with retired employees and develop employee skills for better externalisation of knowledge and integration with customer's knowledge.

Discussion Questions :

1. Discuss the knowledge management initiatives implemented successfully at Tata Steel.
2. What benefits were reaped by Tata Steel from knowledge management program?
3. What are the plans of Tata Steel for the future of KM programs in the company?

5. FOSTERING INNOVATION : WIPRO TECHNOLOGIES' INNOVATION FRAMEWORK

Abstract : This case focuses on the innovation initiatives carried out at Wipro Technologies and explains how it let innovation be the driving force for its product development process. Since the launch of innovation initiatives in 2000, the company offered a comprehensive portfolio of products based on innovative solutions. It also ingrained a culture of innovation at the company to encourage employees to come out with innovative ideas and help the company achieve growth and attain a competitive advantage. The case also discusses Wipro's applied innovation framework that helped the company identify new opportunities for business and resolve business challenges through its innovative solutions.

Because of its constant focus on developing innovative solutions and efforts to nurture a corporate culture which fostered innovation, Wipro was able to achieve its target of earning 10 percent revenues from its innovation initiatives by 2008. Analysts felt that Wipro's constant focus on innovation coupled with its deep-set culture of innovation gave Wipro an edge over its competitors. Moreover, it helped the company establish itself as one of the leading players in the Indian IT industry.

Issues : Analyse Wipro's innovation framework :

- Study the processes and systems that the company had put in place to foster innovation.
- Understand how Wipro's applied innovation framework that helped the company identify new opportunities for business and resolve business challenges through its innovative solutions.
- Understand how an IT company uses innovation as a tool for differentiation.
- Understand how the implementation of an innovative working environment benefits the company and the employees.

In the words of Ashok Tripathy, Head, Wipro Personal Computing, in 2008 "Innovation is a key business driver for us. We use Wipro's Applied Innovation framework to create new innovative solutions that focus on resolving our customers' business challenges".

In the words of Azim Premji, Chairman Wipro Ltd., in 2007 "Innovation comes from applying creativity or applying thought innovation is about action versus just ideas, as much about implementation as about design. It is not about mere incremental improvements in our course of daily operations or a one-off new brilliant idea. It is a culture that needs to be created consciously and pursued assiduously by an organisation".

Awards Won : On August 28, 2008, Wipro Technologies, the flagship company of Wipro Ltd., Won the Intel Global Innovation award for "Storage Platform" based on Intel Architecture.

The company received the award for its innovative "Net power storage server solution", a part of Wipro's Applied Innovation Framework and an outcome of the company's ecological sustainability initiatives.

The award came as a major recognition for the company's decision to let innovation be the driving force for its product development process.

Since the launch of innovation initiatives in 2000, Wipro had emerged as one of the strongest players in the information technology industry. The company offered a comprehensive portfolio of products based on innovative solutions.

Innovation was a prerequisite at Wipro since it believed that this was essential to achieve growth and competitive advantage. It was one of the values in Wipro's promise statement that said "with utmost respect to human values, we promise to serve our customers with integrity through innovative, value for money solutions, by applying thought day after day.

By 2008, Wipro was able to achieve 10 percent of its revenues from its innovation initiatives because of its constant focus on developing innovative solutions and efforts to nurture a corporate culture which fostered innovation. The company gave a lot of importance to innovation and creativity and made a conscious effort to create and maintain a culture which focused on a diverse range of innovative solutions and the benefits that occurred from it.

According to analyst, the deep-set culture of innovation in Wipro gave it an edge over others in this knowledge based industry. The innovation management system enabled Wipro to exploit various path - breaking technological innovations, right from the idea generation stage to the commercialisation stage.

Applied Innovation Framework : Wipro's applied innovation was a 360 degree approach to business that focused on four domains : business, process, technology and delivery.

Ingraining Innovation in the Culture : Analysts credited Wipro with creating a culture that regarded the quest for innovation as its norm. The process of innovation development was ingrained in its corporate culture. The company encouraged employees to come up with innovative ideas and rewarded them for their contributions to the company.

The Results : By 2008, Wipro had made innovation an integral part of its product development process. The company had significantly decreased the **"time-to-market"** new products and linked its revenues to the introduction of leading-edge products.

The Road Ahead : As of 2008, Wipro had 60 COEs for the development of domain-specific solutions and frameworks. More than 500 professionals were employed in developing innovative solutions at Wipro. Wipro's existing portfolio consisted of 101 field patents and 38 granted patents. In addition to these, the company filed for 17 more patents in 2007.

Discussion Questions :

1. Discuss the issues involved in the analysis of Wipro's innovation framework.
2. Discuss the various innovation initiatives launched in Wipro since the year 2000.
3. How Wipro ingrained innovation in the corporate culture?

6. ATTRACTING AND RETAINING TALENT IN THE HEALTH-CARE INDUSTRY

Background : Oakwood Healthcare system, a billion dollar healthcare provider in South East Michigan has approximately 9500 employees spread over four hospitals, multiple ambulatory services and post acute services. Oakwood has ranked among the Top 100 Healthcare Networks in the Nation and won the Top 100 Cardiovascular Hospital award three years in a row.

Corporate Strategy

In an effort to control costs in the late 1990s, Oakwood centralised its business processes and functions. After exceeding the goals of centralisation, Oakwood realised in mid 2003 that it no longer was able to grow at the rate it wanted in order to achieve its future business plans. With a newly decentralised corporate structure, Oakwood wanted to empower Division Presidents to make the best decisions based on respective needs of the market.

The overall goals that Oakwood provided to each of its sites were:

- Market growth
- Profitability
- Operational excellence
- Clinical quality

Additionally in the health care industry a major issue is staffing shortages and Oakwood has not been immune from this issue. Staffing shortages would impact the sustainability of Oakwood's goals. The plan for executing the corporate strategy was left to the respective Division Presidents.

HR Strategy

Oakwood's Executive Vice President of HR came to Oakwood with a passion for measurement and a desire for HR to be seen as a partner within the organisation. The Executive Vice President and Oakwood's leadership agreed to include human capital measurement and a set of routine metrics for measuring operating effectiveness. Based on the goals of Oakwood, HR initially decided to focus its efforts on three areas : *(i)* Staffing, *(ii)* Employee satisfaction and *(iii)* Workforce effectiveness.

HR believed that partnering with Finance would be key to gaining acceptance to their efforts. It would provide HR much needed financial inputs for some of their metrics and would add credibility to their reported results.

HR Action : In an effort to become a business partner, Oakwood's HR group established an HR strategic score board. This high level score board is shared monthly with the Division Presidents. The score board consists of Separation Rate, Accession Rate, Vacancy Rate, Agency costs as a percentage of payroll, and overtime costs as a percentage of payroll, along with other several related metrics.

Monthly Oakwood metrics are compared with "target" and to "best-in-class" as depicted by Saratoga and other data sources.

A separate score board was created for each division. The goal of these high level score boards is to show the divisions the interrelationship between each of the metrics and encourage Divisional Presidents to realise that taking action on results outside the desired range could help reduce operating costs. As leaders ask to learn more about a given area in their score card, greater detail is provided.

Based on these results, HR put together a business case to show projected impacts of slowing down the hiring process to get better quality hires and build a framework for understanding when to hire staff versus using agencies.

Additionally HR partnered with the business units from each site to look at trended data and helped them understand when voluntary turnover is most likely to occur. This enables interested business units to be proactive than reactive with their hiring.

Using Saratoga Metrics

The HR group at Oakwood saw the importance of starting out sharing a small number of results with the organisation. Oakwood uses three Saratoga's metrics as part of their score card : *(i)* Separation Rate, *(ii)* Accession Rate and *(iii)* Vacancy Rate. Understanding how well operations compare to others provides Oakwood with opportunity for improvement.

Results : HR was able to significantly streamline its hiring process while simultaneously increasing their quality of hire (as measured by voluntary separation rate). HR has also been able to help business units reduce expenses by building a model showing when it is more cost effective to hire an employee rather than use sporadic agency labour. By measuring the impact of their workforce, sharing these results, and partnering with their business units, Oakwood HR group has been able to greatly increase their credibility and value to the organisation.

Over the last year, Oakwood reduced its separations in the first 90 days of hire by 34% and separations in the first year of hire by 17%. These results correlated to a reduction of approximately 70 vacancies that didn't need to be filled and improved the bottom line by approximately by $ 7,00,000. This not only helped to control expenses but also helped to improve employee morale, physician's morale and patient satisfaction.

Oakwood's President and CEO believes the HR score card should receive the same level of attention from senior management as the monthly financial reports. These metrics are viewed as excellent decision support tools on which management should take advantage.

Discussion Questions :

1. Discuss the corporate strategy of Oakwood. What were their goals?
2. Explain how Oakwood's HR strategy supported its corporate strategy to achieve its goals.
3. Explain how HR score card helped in implementing the HR strategy.
4. How Saratoga metrics helped to improve the effectiveness of HR group of Oakwood healthcare system?

7. BEST PRACTICES AT THE DELL COMPUTER CORPORATION

(Benchmarking a High-speed Management Communication System)

Introduction : The new set of economic forces which dramatically affect organisational performance include : *(i)* quick market saturation, *(ii)* unexpected global competition and *(iii)* rapid technological breakthroughs. These forces taken collectively require a new management theory based on responding to rapid environmental change, shifting customer needs and competitor's adaptation to those needs.

Between 1984 and 1988, those economic forces gave rise to a new **High-speed Management Communication** theory which focused on the use of computers, tele-communication and extremely well-crafted messages to provide a rapid-response system adapted to customer needs and competitor's products.

High-speed Management includes new, well-developed theories of environmental scanning, value-chain performance, continuous improvement programs, leadership marketing and team work programs. High-speed management is a communication theory rooted in two philosophic and empirically verifiable propositions : *(i)* Reducing the cycle time an organisation takes in getting its products or services to market yields increases in productivity, quality, market shares, profits, management, worker motivation and commitment, and customer satisfaction.

Improving an organisation's communication processes is the most significant ingredient for reducing organisational cycle time. Removing communication bottle necks, standardising information transfer, developing rapid - response systems and improving message quality and adaptation to all organisation's stake holders are the central outputs that yield reduced organisational cycle time.

About the Case Study

This case study benchmarks Dell Computer Corporation and its two top competitors in the PC market namely Compaq and IBM in order to discover how Dell achieved dramatic success in cycle time reduction through improved organisational communication processes. This benchmarking case study will proceed in four stages :

(i) Examination of the competition in the personal computer market

(ii) Benchmarking of Dell's rapid-response system

(iii) Examination of the effect of Dell's rapid - response systems on Dell's customers and competitors and

(iv) Drawing of some conclusions regarding the benchmarking of Dell's reduced cycle times and high-speed management theory.

Competition in the Personal Computer Market

The computer market is highly visible, rapidly growing and competitive, with several well-managed dynamic firms seeking increased market shares. In 1998 the $ 14.8 billion computer market had four segments : *(i)* Main frames, *(ii)* Mini computers, *(iii)* Work stations and *(iv)* Personal computers.

PC sales represented 46 percent of total computer sales.

Table 1 tracks the performance of the three top computer firms in market shares in the PC market between 1996 and 2001.

TABLE 1 : PC MARKET SHARES

Company	Q_1(1996)	Q_1(1997)	Q_1(1998)	Q1(1999)	Q_1(2000)	Q_1(2001)
Compaq	10%	11.5%	13%	14%	13.8%	13.3%
IBM	7.2%	7.3%	7.5%	7%	6.5%	6.0%
Dell	3.4%	5.3%	11.8%	14%	19%	24.9%

* Q_1 = 1st Quarter

Between 1996 and 2001, Compaq's sales growth was +30%, IBM's was - 1.2% and Dell's was + 750%. The PC market has three major components : laptops, desktops and servers. By Nov. 2001, Dell's rank and market shares in each component of the US, PC market were number 2 in laptops with 24% of the market, number 1 in desktops with 29% of the market and number 5 in servers with 16% of the market. This gave Dell 24.9% of the total PC market and allowed Dell to overtake Compaq as the number one producer of PCs in the US.

Dell's financial performance over the past six years (*i.e.,* from 1996 to 2001) is shown in Table 2.

TABLE 2 : DELL'S SIX-YEAR FINANCIAL PERFORMANCE RETURNS (IN BILLIONS OF US DOLLARS)

year	2001	2000	1999	1998	1997	1996
Sales	31.1	31.8	26	18.2	12.3	7.7
Profits	1.2	2.1	2	1.4	1.3	0.7

Dell Computer was and is the low cost, high value provider of PCs backed by world = class rapid - response; continuous improvement and service programs.

Benchmarking Dell Computer's Rapid - Response Communication System

Dell Computer Corporation (DCC) is one of the most visible success stories in the computer market. By selling personal computers directly to customers over the Internet, offering a build-to-order sales system, and then linking suppliers, workers, managers, customers and service personnel together on the Internet, Dell has built a series of rapid - response systems that have revolutionised organisational communication. Dell's rapid - response systems have led to fear, admiration and attempts at imitation among its competitors and other e-businesses alike.

Critical Success Factors

Dell employs four rapid - response systems. Each system uses the Internet to provide a real-time communication system for linking key organisational stakeholder together into a functional community. Each rapid - response system employs a backbone profiling system for precisely adapting the content of communication to each of an organisation's stake holders. These profiles are then used to improve future communication and to maintain interpersonal relationships between stake holders. Individually these four rapid - response systems are necessary conditions for rapid and successful organisational communication and collectively they represent sufficient conditions along with their accompanying targets for successful organisational performance.

1. ***Dell has a rapid - response sales link to customers :*** This interactive online communication system allows customers to order and track their purchase through each stage of the manufacturing and distribution process. Employing mail catalogs and Internet home pages, customers interact directly with Dell and can customise their orders to meet their unique needs.

2. ***Dell has a rapid -response system for providing customer service :*** This interactive real - time communication system can be accessed by telephone or computer for personal or automated technical and customer support in dealing with computer problems. Dell monitors these service

interactions in order to construct maintenance profiles on each piece of equipment and the appropriate instructions for its use and to develop appropriate repair sequences for each type of problem for use by its live and automated repair processes.

3. ***Dell has a rapid - response system for linking all suppliers, workers, managers and customers to Dell's value chain :*** This interactive real - time communication system is employed to order parts, manufacture and outsource computer modules and coordinate assembly and distribution of products to customers.

4. ***Dell has a rapid - response system for the continuous improvement of all organisational activities :*** Dell's stakeholders are tied together in a real - time interactive communication system aimed at focusing team work on improving every aspect of Dell's performance.

Dell's four rapid - response systems - sales, services, value chain and continuous improvement are all online real - time communication systems.

Benchmarking Targets

By 1998, Dell's aggressive pricing of products and rapid - response communication systems had begun to cut significantly into Compaq and IBM's market shares and reduced the profit margins of these firms to zero. In an effort to combat these trends, a benchmarking study of all three firms was undertaken.

Table 3 contains the critical success factors and targets benchmarked.

TABLE 3 : BENCHMARKING THE COMPETITIVENESS OF THE TOP 3 PC FIRMS IN THE US MARKET

Critical success factors	Dell	Compaq	IBM
1. Customer sales			
Web sales	43%	10%	20%
Online customisation	yes	no	no
Computer to customer/online	3 days	12 days	15 days
Computer to customer/stores	0	35 days	30 days
Average retailer costs	0	20%	20%
Average sales incentives	0	$ 1000	$ 1000
Convert sales to cash	1 day	30 days	25 days
2. Customer service			
Online tech support	24 hrs	8 hrs	8 hrs
Online service support	24 hrs	8 hrs	8 hrs
Computer network installed	14 days	60-90 days	60 days
Chat rooms	yes	no	no
Interactive lectures	yes	no	no
Customer service costs	free	paid	paid

3. Value chain			
Parts inventory average	15 min	7-10 days	10 days
Computer inventory average	3 days	30 days	25 days
Produce computer average	4 hrs	15 days	12 days
Computer to customer average	3 days	30 days	25 days
4. Continuous improvement			
% upgrade per year	20%	10%	10%
% of stakeholders involved	100%	40%	40%

1. In 1998, 43 percent of Dell's sales were made over the Internet, and 57% by telephone. By 1999, 60% of Dell's sales were made over the Internet and 40% by telephone. In 1998, this amounted to $ 10 million in Internet sales per day and grew to $ 34 million by 1999. 90% of Dell's sales were to institutions, 70% of which involve $ 1 million in orders each year. In addition, 10% or $ 1 billion of Dell's sales were to individuals. In 1998, Dell was the only firm which could customise Internet PC sales. Direct electronic marketing allowed Dell to convert its sales to cash in one day. Marketing primarily through sales outlets, Compaq and IBM took an average of 25 to 35 days from the day of sales at the outlet to receive payment. Compaq and IBM Internet sales were referred to sales outlets to fill orders. In addition these outlets held 35 to 120 day inventories before the sale of products. Compaq and IBM pay retailers a 20% commission on sales. Dell thus achieves significant time, fit and cost advantages from direct electronic sales to customers.
2. Dell requires all component manufacturers for its PC with the exception of those who manufacture monitors, to warehouse their components within 15 minutes of Dell's various production plants. Computer monitors are mailed directly from Sony to customers and coordinated by FedEx so as to arrive at the same time as the computers for assembly. This allows Dell to save $ 30 in shipping costs per monitor. Compaq and IBM hold 7 to 10 day inventories of parts at manufacturing facilities and 25 to 120 day computer inventories at sales outlets, thus significantly increasing their inventory costs.

   Dell manufactures computers in 4 hours, Compaq and IBM in 15 days and 12 days respectively thus increasing their manufacturing costs. Dell supplies a computer to its customers within 3 days, Compaq and IBM in 15 to 30 and 12 to 25 days respectively, thus increasing their distribution costs. Dell installs computer networks in 14 days Compaq and IBM in 60 to 90 days, thus increasing their installation costs. Once again, Dell achieves a quicker, higher quality, lower price advantage over its competitors.

   Dell can produce PCs at an average cost of 20 percent less than its competitors while retaining its 20% operating profit margins. This in turn allowed Dell to sell its PCs at 20% less than its competitors for comparable equipment, placing pricing pressures on its competitors. If Dell's competitors place their equipment price above that of Dell, they lose significant market shares. If they match Dell's lower prices, they lose their profit margins and operate in the red.
3. Dell's free customer service system is open 24 hours a day, seven days a week. It offers both human and automated support as well as free online interactive chat rooms, lectures and

technical and customer support. Its competitors offer limited eight hour telephone support for which they charge. For small firms, Dell outsources service contracts and service centres.

4. Dell's use of such backbone communication content processes as customer, product, value chain, maintenance and continuous improvement profiles along with stake holder report cards on performance allow Dell to communicate with its stakeholders in powerful ways not accessible to its competitors. This in turn led customers to rank Dell number one and as the most admired among PC firms by its competitors.

The Effect of Dell's Rapid - Response System on its Competitors

To remain competitive with Dell in 1997, both Compaq and IBM cut prices dramatically to match Dell. The result was that Compaq's earnings decreased and IBM lost $ 161 million dollars. In 1998, with Dell's sales growing, Compaq and IBM watched their inventories grow to 120 days. Both firms began a price war in an attempt to reduce inventories at outlets to 20 days in order to cut retailer costs. One result of this price war was that Compaq and IBM saw their 1998 PC profits drop dramatically. Compaq's profits dropped from a projected $ 510 million to $ 16 million eventhough sales grew 38%. On April 18, 1999, Compaq's CEO and CFO were forced to resign. In 1998 IBM's PC unit lost market shares and went $ 992 million in the red and the CEO of its PC unit war forced to resign.

Compaq's PC Strategy

Compaq's continuous improvement program had slowed down in 1998-99. New, more competitive targets were introduced by management that aimed at revitalising and improving the program. At the same time Compaq had decided to cut its prices again in order to become more competitive in the price war with IBM. Compaq seeing its competitive disadvantage vis-a-vis IBM, decided to acquire the Digital Equipment Company, which would allow Compaq to move into data storage, work station, mini and mainframe markets where margins were larger than in PCs. By 2002 with Compaq's market shrinking in all categories, its CEO, under pressure from stockholders, proposed a merger with Hewlett - Packard in an attempt to halt its decline.

IBM's PC Strategy

Between 1994 and 1998, IBM's continuous improvement programs had reduced the number of PC models from 3400 to 150. The number of components was cut from 420 to 200. In addition IBM hired Dell's former head of procurement. He set up a new supplier pipe-line where 60% of IBM parts can be delivered within 24 hours. Today 31% of IBM's PC components are assembled by sales outlets. In addition IBM has opened a web sales site. These changes have brought IBM closer to Dell than Compaq costs. In January 1998, IBM's PC inventories were still high at retail outlets. In an attempt to reduce inventories from 120 down to 20 days, IBM began to cut PC prices dramatically, extending its price war with Compaq to a new level. However by April, 2002, IBM's PC unit losses still continued to mount, with losses of $ 500 million in 1999 and $ 1 billion in 2000 and 2001. IBM discontinued to manufacturing and store sales of its desktop PCs.

Dell's PC Strategy

Dell's high-speed management model between 1999 and 2002 had increased its US PC market shares from 11 to 24% and ranked number one in US market shares. Dell's continuous improvement program had reduced its operating costs to 10% of sales while Compaq's costs were 18 percent of sales with IBM withdrawing from the PC desktop market. Dell's CEO set a target of 40% market share by 2005. In addition Dell decided to take its high speed management model into two new areas : Computer storage, and networking. Dell plans to expand its 8% overseas sales in next three years to 20%. Dell is a formidable competitor with high speed management business model which is difficult to imitate and hard to beat.

Conclusions

Dell's best practices does support the first proposition of high - speed management, namely that reducing the cycle time an organisation takes.

Discussion Questions :

1. Discuss the critical success factors of Dell computer's rapid - response communication system.
2. Who are the benchmarking targets of Dell? Compare the performance of Dell with that of its competitors.
3. Discuss the effect of Dell's rapid - response system on its competitors.
4. Discuss the individual strategies of Compaq, IBM and Dell in their PC manufacture and sales.

8. XEROX - THE BENCHMARKING STORY

Introduction

This case examines the benchmarking initiatives taken by Xerox Corporation, USA, one of the world's leading copier companies, as a part of its "Leadership through Quality" program during the early 1980s. The case discusses in detail the benchmarking concept and its implementation in various processes at Xerox. It also explores the positive impact of benchmarking practices on Xerox.

Background

- In 1938, Chester Carlson, a patent attorney and part-time inventor, made the first Xerographic image in the US. Carlson struggled over five years to sell the invention.
- In 1944, the Battelle Memorial Institute in Columbus, Ohio, contracted with Carlson to refine his new process which Carlson called "electro photography".
- Three years later, The Haloid Company, maker of photographic paper, approached Battelle and obtained a licence to develop and market a copying machine based on Carlson's technology.
- Haloid later obtained all rights to Carlson's invention and registered the "Xerox" trademark in 1948. Buoyed by the success of Xerox copiers, Haloid changed its name to "Haloid Xerox Inc" in 1958 and to "The Xerox Corporation" in 1961. Xerox was listed on the New York Stock Exchange in 1961 and on the Chicago Stock Exchange in 1990. It was also traded on the Boston, Cincinnati, Pacific Coast, Philadelphia, London and Switzerland exchanges. The strong demand for Xerox's products led the company from strength to strength and revenues soared from $ 37 million in 1960 to $ 268 million in 1965.
- Throughout the 1960s, Xerox grew by acquiring many companies including University Microfilms, Micro systems, Electro-optical systems, Basic systems and Glinn and company. In 1962, Fuji Xerox Co. Ltd., was launched as a joint venture of Xerox and Fuji Photo Film. Xerox acquired a majority stake (51.2%) in Rank Xerox in 1969. During the late 1960s and

the early 1970s, Xerox diversified into the information technology business by acquiring scientific Data systems, Daconics and Vesetec.

- In 1969, Xerox set up a corporate R&D facility, the Palo Alto Research Centre to develop technology in-house. In the 1970s, Xerox focused on introducing new and more efficient models to retain its share of the reprographic market and cope with competition from the US and Japanese companies. While the company's revenues increased from $ 698 million in 1966 to $ 4.4 billion in 1976, profits increased five fold from $ 83 million in 1966 to $ 407 million in 1977.
- As Xerox grew rapidly, a variety of controls and procedures were instituted and the number of management layers was increased during the 1970s. This however, slowed down decision-making and resulted in major delays in product development.
- In the early 1980s, Xerox found itself increasingly vulnerable to intense competition from both the US and Japanese competitors. According to analysts, Xerox's management failed to give the company strategic direction. It ignored new entrants (Ricoh, Canon and Sevin) who were consolidating their positions in the lower-end market and in niche segments. The company's operating cost (and therefore the prices of products) was high and its products were of relatively inferior quality in comparison to its competitors. Xerox also suffered from its highly centralised decision-making processes. As a result of this, return-on-assets fell to less than 8% and market share in copiers came down sharply from 86% in 1974 to just 17% in 1984. Between 1980 and 1984, Xerox's profits decreased from $ 1.15 billion to $ 290 million.
- In 1982, David T. Kearns took over as the CEO. He discovered that the average manufacturing cost of copiers in Japanese companies was 40-50% of that of Xerox. As a result, Japanese companies were able to undercut Xerox's prices effortlessly. Kearns quickly began emphasizing reduction of manufacturing costs and gave new thrust to quality control by launching a program that was popularly referred to as "Leadership Through Quality". As part of this quality program, Xerox implemented the benchmarking program. These initiatives played a major role in pulling Xerox out of trouble in the years to come. The company even went on to become one of the best examples of the successful implementation of benchmarking.

Benchmarking at Xerox

- The "Leadership Through Quality" program introduced by Kearns revitalised the company. The program encouraged Xerox to find ways to reduce their manufacturing costs. Benchmarking against Japanese competitors, Xerox found out that it took twice as long as its Japanese competitors to bring a product to market, five times the number of engineers, four times the number of design changes, and three times the design costs.
- The company also found that the Japanese could produce, ship and sell units for about the same amount that it cost Xerox just to manufacture them. In addition, Xerox's products had over 30,000 defective parts per million - about 30 times more than its competitors. Benchmarking also revealed that Xerox would need an 18% annual productivity growth rate for five consecutive years to catch up with the Japanese. After an initial period of denial, Xerox managers accepted the reality.

(i) A highly revered award given for excellence in quality in the US to businesses. It is based on seven parameters - leadership, strategic planning, customer and market focus, information and analysis, human resource focus, process management, and business results.

(ii) APQC is a US based non-profit organisation sponsored by nearly 500 companies, government organisations and educational institutions. It provides the tools, information, expertise, and support needed by companies to discover and implement best practices in areas such as benchmarking and knowledge management.

- Following this, Xerox defined benchmarking as "the process of measuring its products, services, and practices against its toughest competitors, identifying the gaps and establishing goals. **"Our goal is always to achieve superiority in quality, product reliability and cost."** Gradually, Xerox developed its own benchmarking model. This model involved ten steps categorised under five stages - planning, analysis, integration, action and maturity.

  Xerox collected data on key processes of best practice companies. These critical processes were then analysed to identify and define improvement opportunities. For instance Xerox identified ten key factors that were related to marketing. These were customer marketing, customer engagement, order fulfillment, product maintenance, billing and collection, financial management, asset management, business management, human resource management and information technology.

- These ten factors were further divided into 67 sub-processes. Each of these sub-processes then became a target for improvement. For the purpose of acquiring data from the related benchmarking companies, Xerox subscribed to the management and technical databases, referred to magazines and trade journals, and also consulted professional associations and consulting firms.

- Having worked out the model it wanted to use, Xerox began by implementing competitive benchmarking. However, the company found this type of benchmarking to be inadequate as the very best practices, in some processes or operations were not being practiced by copier companies. The company then adopted functional benchmarking, which involved a study of the best practices followed by a variety of companies regardless of the industry they belonged to. Xerox initiated functional benchmarking with the study of the warehousing and inventory management system of L.L. Bean, a mail-order supplier of sporting goods and outdoor clothing.

- L.L. Bean had developed a computer program that made order filling very efficient. The program arranged orders in a specific sequence that allowed stock pickers to travel the shortest possible distance in collecting goods at the warehouse. This considerably reduced the inconvenience of filling an individual order that involved gathering relatively less number of goods from the warehouse. The increased speed and accuracy of order filling achieved by L.L. Bean attracted Xerox. The company was convinced it could achieve similar benefits by developing and implementing such a program.

- Similarly Xerox zeroed in on various other best practice companies to benchmark its other processes. These included American Express (for billing and collection) Cummins Engines and Ford (for factory floor layout), Florida Power and Light (for quality improvement), Honda (for supplier development), Toyota (for quality management), Hewlett Packard (for research and product development), Saturn (a division of General Motors) and Fuji Xerox (for manufacturing operation) and DuPont (for manufacturing safety).

- Benchmarking was implemented at Xerox in the following manner :

1. Supplier Management System

Xerox found that all the Japanese copier companies put together has only 1000 suppliers, while Xerox alone had 5000 suppliers. To keep the number of suppliers low, Japanese companies standardised many parts. Often half the components of similar machines were identical. To ensure part standardisation, Japanese companies worked closely with their suppliers. They frequently trained vendor's employees in quality control, manufacturing automation and other key areas. Cooperation between the company and the vendors extended to just-in-time production scheduling, *i.e.,* delivery in small quantities, as per the customer's production schedule.

In line with the best practices, Xerox reduced the number of vendors for the copier business from 5000 to just 400. Xerox also created a vendor certification process in which suppliers were either offered training or explicitly told where they needed to improve in order to continue as a Xerox vendor. Vendors were consulted for ideas on better designs and improved customer service also.

2. Inventory Management

Xerox's efforts to improve inventory management practices drew inspiration from the innovative spare parts management practices of its European operations. Traditionally, technical representatives decided the level of spare parts inventory to be carried, little information was available on the actual usage pattern of the spare parts. Xerox's European operations developed a sophisticated information system to get around this problem. Actual usage, rather than mere withdrawal from the stocking point, was used to determine inventory levels. In the late 1980s, Xerox replicated the system in the US and saved tens of millions of dollars in the process.

The stocking policy followed by Xerox branch managers was to hold fully finished, fully figured products near to the customer. Because of this policy, they carried vast amounts of inventory, some of which was not even sold during a given period. The company changed the above set up by asking branch managers to match the stocking policy to the customer's installation orders, which considerably reduced the inventory holding time. As a result, working capital cycle time was cut by 70% leading to savings of about $ 200 million.

- The process of benchmarking helped Xerox revamp its manufacturing techniques. Each "family unit" (a manager and his direct subordinates) was encouraged to identify its internal as well as external customers and to meet their needs. For instance, the group that built paper trays identified its external customers as the end user who would load the paper. Its internal customers were the assembly - line workers, who would combine the paper tray with hundreds of other components to assemble the copiers. This process significantly improved the operational efficiency of the work groups.

3. Marketing

Xerox introduced a **"Customer Satisfaction Measurement System"** that integrated customer research and benchmarking activities. The company sent out over 55,000 questionnaires monthly to its customers to measure customer satisfaction and record competitor performance. It then benchmarked against these competitors that had scored high marks on specific measures of customer satisfaction. Xerox also used the vast amount of information gathered by the system to develop business plans for improving quality and meeting customer needs.

4. Quality

As a part of its **"Leadership Through Quality"** program. Xerox reformulated its quality policy. The new policy supplemented the company's benchmarking efforts. Xerox's new quality policy stated "Xerox is a quality company. Quality is the basic principle of Xerox. Quality means providing our external and internal customers with innovative products and services that duly satisfy their requirements. Quality improvement is the job of every Xerox employee". Following this, the company embarked on a complete organisational restructuring exercise that focused on research and development, employee involvement and customer orientation.

Xerox also formed a transition team consisting of 24 senior managers and consultants from Mckinsey and company to help make total quality management (TQM) a part of its organisational culture. The transition team took action at two levels. Firstly, it conveyed the message clearly to the world that Xerox was pursuing more widespread use of TQM, and secondly it identified and addressed the obstacles that were likely to slow down the spread of TQM. These ranged from the corporation's function-dominated matrix structure to the need for new training programs. Consequently, the transition team also replaced the existing complex matrix by three strategic business units (SBUs) - Enterprise Service Business, Office Copiers and Home Copiers. Each of the SBUs was given considerable autonomy in engineering, marketing and pricing.

By the late 1980s, benchmarking had become a day-to-day activity in every division of the company. According to company sources, Xerox's guiding principle was "anything anyone can do better, we should aim to do at least equally well". In 1991, Xerox developed Business Excellence Certification (BEC) to integrate benchmarking with the company's overall strategies. This was also done to ensure continuous self-appraisal of the overall quality performance of the company. The key performance factors measured by BEC were management leadership, human resource management, customer focus, quality support and tools, process management and business priorities/ results.

These factors which were further divided into forty sub-factors, had their specific measuring targets. Each unit's self-appraisal was validated by representatives from sister divisions. BEC helped Xerox determine the causes for the success or failure of a specific quality process and identify the key success factors or obstacles for achieving a specific quality goal. It also helped the company establish key functions for removing obstacles that prevented it from reaching the set quality goals.

By the mid 1990s, benchmarking was extended to over 240 key areas of product, service and business performance at Xerox. The initiatives were also adopted, at varying levels, at Xerox units across the world. The benchmarking process encouraged Xerox's employees to learn from every situation. This new philosophy was dubbed **"steal shamelessly"** though the company used only those ideas that the best practicing companies willingly gave away. The salient rule at Xerox for benchmarking was to "ask no question of another firm that you would be unwilling to answer about your own". This change in attitude was just the beginning of the pay-offs of the benchmarking moves.

Reaping the Benefits

The major pay off of Xerox's focus on benchmarking and customer satisfaction was the increase in the number of satisfied customers. Highly satisfied customers for its copier/duplicator and printing systems increased by 38% and 39% respectively. Customer complaints to the president's office declined by more than 60%. Customer satisfaction with Xerox's sales processes improved by 40%, service processes by 18% and administrative processes by 21%. The financial performance of the company also improved considerably through the mid and late 1980s.

Overall customer satisfaction was rated at more than 90% in 1991. **Some of the other benefits Xerox derived were :**

(i) Number of defects reduced by 78 per 100 machines

(ii) Service response time reduced by 27%

(iii) Inspection of incoming components reduced to below 5%

(iv) Defects in incoming parts reduced to 150 ppm

(v) Marketing productivity increased by one-third

(vi) Distribution productivity increased by 8 to 10%

(vii) Increased product reliability on account of 40% reduction in unscheduled maintenance

(viii) Notable decrease in labour costs

(ix) Errors in billing reduced from 8.3% to 3.5%

(x) Became the leader in the high-volume copier-duplicator market segment

(xi) Country units improved sales from 152% to 328%

Xerox went on to become the only company worldwide to win all the three prestigious quality awards : The Deming Award (Japan) in 1980, The Malcolm Baldrige National Quality Award in 1989 and the European Quality Award in 1992. Analysts attributed this success to the "Leadership Through Quality" initiative and more significantly, to the adoption of benchmarking practices.

Discussion Questions :

1. Explain the circumstances that led Kearns to adopt "Leadership Through Quality" program. In the backdrop of his initiatives to retain Xerox's global competitiveness, comment on the rationale behind the decision to implement benchmarking practices at the company.
2. Define benchmarking and discuss the various types of benchmarking. Explain the steps involved in the implementation of a typical benchmarking process.
3. Describe Xerox's benchmarking model. How did Xerox go about implementing benchmarking practices in the company?
4. What benefits did Xerox derive from the implementation of benchmarking practices?
5. Why do you think benchmarking initiatives sometimes fail to give companies the expected benefits? Explain how you would go about ensuring the success of the benchmarking initiatives undertaken by the company.

9. BENCHMARKING THE CUSTOMER SATISFACTION MANAGEMENT PROCESS AT IBM - ROCHESTER

Background

International Business Machines (IBM) had been a leading company in the information technology and office equipment industries for over 70 years : It was organised into 13 manufacturing and development divisions, a world wide marketing and service force divided into four major geographic and several other operating units.

This case deals with the customer satisfaction management (CSM) process at IBM - Rochester, Minnesota. The AS/400 Division at Rochester facility of IBM was responsible for much of the design and manufacture of IBM's midrange business computer systems.

At IBM - Rochester, a strong sense of quality and customer focus was ingrained in the culture. The success of the IBM AS/400 computer family was based in part on an effective CSM process capable of ensuring that customers' requirements and expectations were continually met or exceeded.

One of the noteworthy strengths identified by Malcolm Baldrige National Quality Award examiners in 1990 was a strong CSM process which is the backbone of high customer satisfaction results and world-class levels. As a Baldrige award winner, IBM - Rochester was and continues to be, flooded with requests for information about the CSM process. In addition, numerous requests to benchmark the process were received.

IBM - Rochester had learnt that satisfied customers mean loyal customers that will continue to purchase products and services from IBM. As any small improvement in customer satisfaction would result in substantial increase in revenue, an effective CSM process, predicted on listening to and acting upon customer concerns, was paramount to the future success of both IBM - Rochester and its customers.

Objectives / Purpose

The objectives of IBM - Rochester's CSM process were :

1. To establish a structured strategy to handle all customer requests, concerns and recommendations
2. To continually improve customer satisfaction levels
3. To develop and create partnerships between IBM and its customers and
4. To improve customer relationships

The mission of the CSM process team was to support IBM - Rochester's goal to be the undisputed leader in customer satisfaction.

Focus / Topic (Work Process Selected)

The CSM process was administered by a small team of specialists who solicit, collect and aggregate customer data and information. Pervasive issues were identified through data analysis and then assigned ownership in areas that have direct responsibility for invoking action. The issues owners conducted further root-cause analysis using a formal six-step process approach. Individual customer complaints identified through surveys or complaint channels were resolved and the results were communicated directly back to customers.

Team Operation

A benchmarking checklist was developed that is comprised of a series of comparable questions that are associated with measurements of efficiency and effectiveness for each element in the CSM process.

The CSM process benchmarking team was composed of customer satisfaction specialists from the IBM - Rochester customer satisfaction department as well as key issue owners from functional areas across the Rochester site. A total of seven members analysed the existing CSM process and associated subprocesses to arrive at the benchmarking checklist.

Customer and Requirements

There were two primary customer groups of the CSM process. The first group consisted of external customers or final users and consumers of IBM - Rochester's products and services. The second group was composed of the internal issues owners who must use the external customer information to involve changes.

Information concerning customer satisfaction and dissatisfaction was generated and collected by the CSM team, analysed for issues and root causes and then disseminated to line areas responsible for corrective actions.

Needs / Reasons for Improvement

The CSM team's mission was : *(i)* to continually improve the CSM process for improved efficiency and effectiveness, *(ii)* to find breakthrough concepts and approaches to keep IBM - Rochester in a leadership position and *(iii)* to remain ahead of competitors.

Organisations or Industries Benchmarked

The current process employed by IBM - Rochester consisted of a series of subprocesses including survey design and structure, complaint management, data aggregation, conversion of data into information to invoke action, issue management and review, and customer feed back. One of the existing subprocesses, that of converting customer satisfaction data into action is shown in *Exhibit 21.1*.

Customer satisfaction data were received from complaints or from surveys. The specific reasons for dissatisfaction was determined and expediently resolved. The action taken were than communicated to the customer, however, the root cause or causes that resulted in the original complaint must then be identified and resolved to prevent similar occurrences.

Key Measures and other Facts

The key measurements and parameters used to conduct a process-to-process comparison were identified.

EXHIBIT 21.1 : ISSUE MANAGEMENT PROCESS AT IBM - ROCHESTER

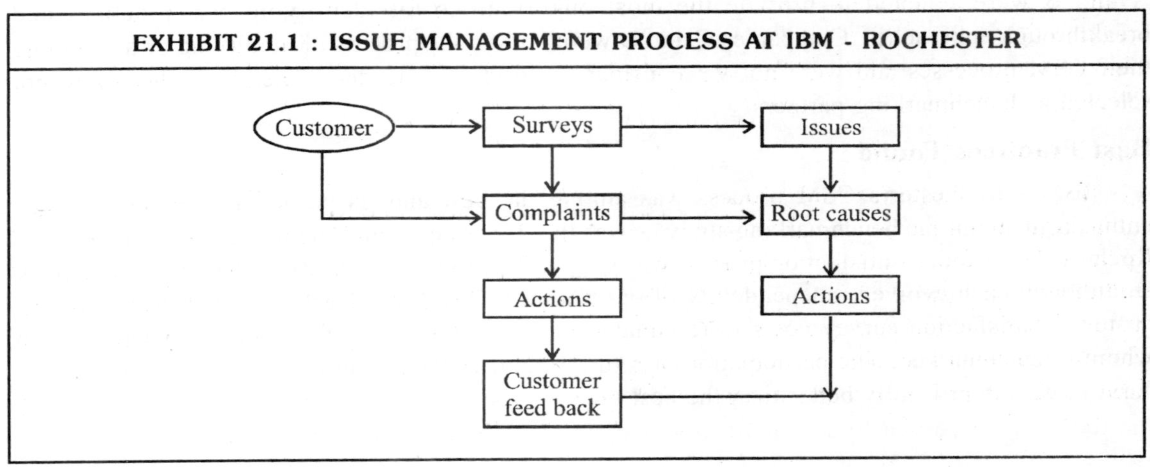

The comprehensive checklist contained all the parameters of the IBM - Rochester's CSM process and associated subprocesses.

Process-to-Process Analysis

Analysis was used to select benchmarking partners who were recognised world-class leaders in customer satisfaction management, particularly those outside the computer industry. **Selection criteria included companies or organisations with the following characteristics :**

1. A formal CSM process that included the administration of surveys and complaint aggregation.
2. Recognised as world class leaders in customer satisfaction management.
3. International sales and managing customer satisfaction on a world wide basis.
4. Similar marketing channels, including direct sales and sales through dealers.
5. Who track customer satisfaction to the end-user customer, regardless of whether sales are made through direct or intermediary channels (dealers).
6. Who monitor and track customer satisfaction of large accounts as well as individual consumers.
7. Who were outside the computer industry in an attempt to discover breakthrough concepts and approaches.

Methods used to identify and select benchmarking partners included :

1. Researching companies and industries using library resources.
2. Accessing the International Benchmarking cleaning house database.
3. Researching international conferences on customer satisfaction.

Benchmarking Partners

Although many benchmarks were done from 1991 to 1991, the IBM - Rochester team focused its attention on two major ones that it initiated. Using the selection criteria, the list was narrowed to four potential partners company 'A' was a large company in the same industry and one of IBM's competitors. Company B was a large company in the automotive industry. Company C was a major division within a large company that specialised in consumer credit and financial transactions. Company D was a large company that specialised in the distribution of packaged goods. Company A and B were selected to provide the most opportunities for identifying best practices and breakthrough approaches. Companies C and D were both in the process of modifying or developing their CSM processes and were not yet considered world-class leaders. Therefore, they were not selected as benchmarking partners.

Best Practices Found

IBM - Rochester's CSM process was among the best and its partner companies were as enthusiastic about the benchmarking study as was the Rochester team. The process flow diagram of Rochester's customer satisfaction process was very similar to the process flow diagram of company B, although each evolved independently of one another. The IBM - Rochester team learnt that its customer satisfaction survey costs were equal to or lower than any of the other companies with whom it benchmarked. The participation or return rate of IBM - Rochester's customer satisfaction surveys was significantly better than the best.

Eventhough IBM - Rochester had been able to develop a formula for quantifying the impact of customer satisfaction on revenue, it was very complex and not easy to update. The formula used to determine a similar impact for company B was simpler and allowed continual updating due to its tracking of loyalty and recommendation factors on all surveys.

Company A had devised a method of comparing worldwide customer satisfaction results into meaningful measurements which allowed the company to derive issues unique by geography. Both companies A and B incorporated importance ratings into their survey process to assist in setting priorities.

Company B incorporated and tracked customer satisfaction results by dealer and thus identified its top dealers using this method company B also focused on buying behaviours and issues unique to geographical areas.

Both company A and B had fewer toll-free telephone numbers to allow customers easy access to customer service specialists company A conducted a consistent customer satisfaction survey on a world wide basis. Company B forwarded customer complaints and customer satisfaction results directly to dealers without going through any intermediary channels.

Company A provided feedback on pervasive issues to its entire customer base on an annual basis.

Actions Taken

As a result of the benchmarks conducted, IBM - Rochester had incorporated the following actions into its CSM process :

(i) Track customer satisfaction results by dealer to identify those needing assistance.

(ii) Track results by geographical area to identify unique issues.

(iii) Incorporate questions on loyalty and recommendation into all surveys and track the relationship of these factors to overall satisfaction to determine revenue opportunities.

Internal customer satisfaction improved nine points since these changes had been made. External customer satisfaction levels had continued to climb, partially because of improved data accuracy ad the availability of actionable data for use in corrective actions.

Implementation

Most of the changes that had been implemented, along with some of the changes yet to be implemented, required enhancement to software used to collect and analyse data. The time required and the availability of programming resources to make the software changes had been the only barriers to implementation. These were overcome by subcontracting for additional programming sources and by scheduling additional time for software changes.

Planned Changes

The following additional changes were planned as a result of the benchmarks conducted :

(i) Reduce the quantity of toll-free numbers to allow customers a single point of contact for inquiries, comments and complaints.

(ii) Devise one consistent customer satisfaction survey and administer it world wide.

(iii) Distribute complaints and customer satisfaction results directly to dealers.

(iv) Determine and implement additional measurements of effectiveness and efficiency commensurate with actions taken and planned.

(v) Implement a feed back program similar to that of company A.

Conclusions

IBM - Rochester has determined that benchmarking needs to be an on-going process aimed at continual improvement and identification of breakthrough concepts. What was once considered a world-class CSM process quickly became status quo as others adapt portions of it and add their own improvements. Ongoing benchmarking is the catalyst to prevent complacency. Constant pressure to reduce costs, eliminate deficiencies and reduce analysis and information transfer cycle time make the concept of benchmarking even more critical. Additionally, a benchmarking strategy, including a structured benchmarking checklist and selection process, is important to control costs associated with benchmarking and to ensure that all key concepts are used effectively.

Discussion Questions :

1. State the mission and objectives of IBM - Rochester and discuss how they were achieved through benchmarking process.
2. Describe the type of benchmarking adopted by IBM - Rochester and discuss its salient features.
3. Discuss the current process employed by IBM - Rochester and the actions incorporated into its CSM process as a result of benchmarks conducted.
4. What additional changes were planned by IBM - Rochester as a result of benchmarks conducted?

10. HOUSEKEEPING SYSTEM CYCLE TIME REDUCTION AT THE RITZ-CARLTON HOTEL COMPANY

Background

The Ritz-Carlton Hotel Company, winner of the 1992 Malcolm Baldrige National Quality Award, operates 30 business and resort hotels throughout the world. It has 13 international sales offices and employs 13,500 people. The hotel company builds its success on the strength of a comprehensive service quality initiative, which is integrated into its marketing and business objectives.

The Ritz-Carlton Hotel Company in Dearborn, Michigan, houses 308 guest rooms and features several dining options over 20,000 square feet of meeting space and a fitness centre.

Focus / Topic

Through focus groups and independent marketing surveys, The Ritz-Carlton Hotel Company (TRCHC) identified several hotel processes that were highly important to customers, but low customer satisfaction ratings.

The company set forth the following tasks :

1. Identify what was important to customers and how they rated those features.
2. Complete a gap analysis.
3. Identify the primary processes and whether the company had existing work areas or processes that were aligned to meet those needs.

The company learnt two things :

1. There were primary processes common to any hotel, such as house-keeping and front office registration and
2. There were vital support processes such as purchasing and human resources for the selection of new employees.

From the research of customers TRCHC identified 19 critical processes as vital to their continuing businesses decision to loyally patronise the company's properties.

One of the 19 processes that customers identified was a clean, fresh, fully stocked guest room. The Ritz-Carlton in Dearborn, Michigan, took on the house keeping system with the goal of creating an error-proof, reliable process that could be standardised within the company to ensure 100 percent customer satisfaction.

Objective / Purpose

Customers indicated that they wanted their hotel services better, faster, cheaper and with greater reliability than before. It was the aim of the Dearborn process team to identify and reduce waste through process analysis by simplifying, eliminating and combining steps within the housing system. This was done to meet the Ritz-Carlton Hotel Company's 1996 quality goals of *(i)* Six-sigma, *(ii)* 50 percent cycle time reduction and *(iii)* 100 percent customer retention.

Team Operation

The team consisted of those individuals active in the housekeeping system and impacted by any changes to it. This included housekeeping and laundry department representatives and engineering and TQM personnel.

Team-building exercises were discussed and practical at weekly meetings. The team used consensus decision making and shared leadership.

Customer Requirements

By listening to the voice of its customers, the Ritz-Carlton Dearborn process team learnt what was wanted, needed and expected in a guest room experience. It included the following characteristics:

1. A clean, fresh, fully stocked room
2. A guest room serviced right the first time
3. Few, if any interruptions
4. Short interruptions when they do occur
5. Consistent service provided for the stay over
6. A room ready when the guest arrives
7. A room cleaned at the guest's convenience
8. Correct and timely honour bar billing
9. The assurance that guest's possessions are safe and secure
10. Reduced housekeeping costs and labour

The last characteristic identified the need to eliminate wase. It was an internal customer requirement.

The process team's goal was to meet these external and internal customer needs with reliability, while reducing the overall housekeeping system cycle time by 50 percent. Reduced internal costs would increase profitability and market competitiveness for the hotel.

Organisation or Industries Benchmarked Current Process

Consecutive, task-by-task work by one room attendant was the time-honoured method of cleaning a guest room. Random sample observations of 30 housekeeping room attendants produced the pie-chart shown below :

EXHIBIT 1 : FIVE STEPS IN CLEANING A ROOM

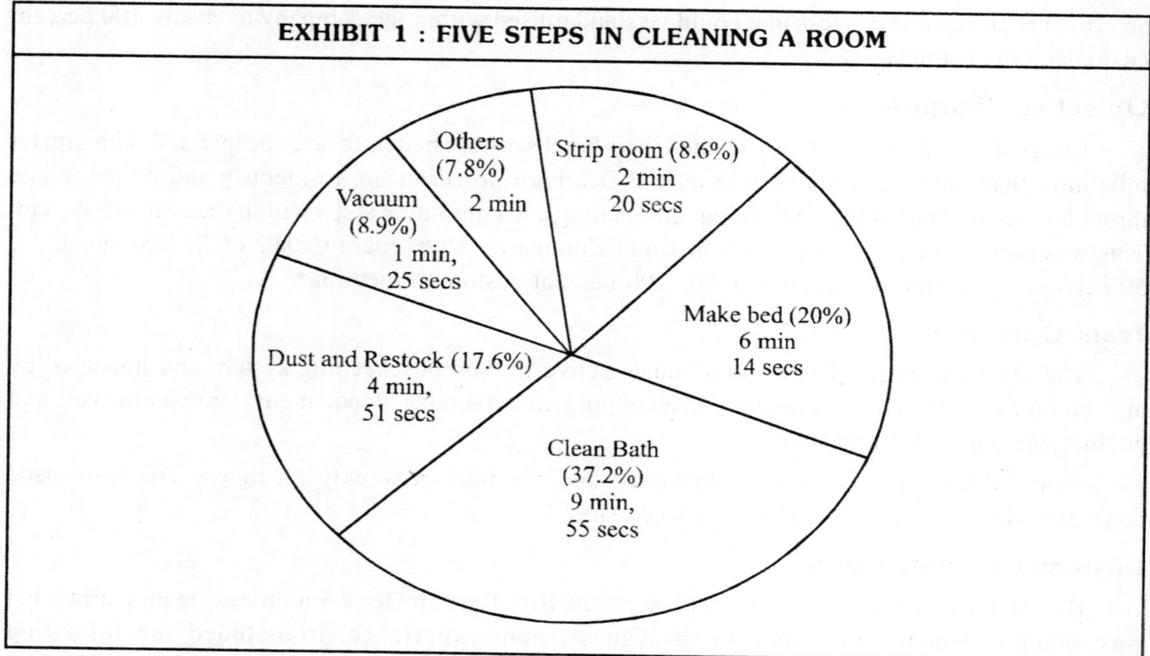

Analysis revealed that the bath-room cleaning work was the most time-consuming of room-cleaning tasks and the obvious limiting factor.

The process team has already brainstormed the concept of simultaneous work, that is multiple task completion by a number of room attendants in one guest room. Thus team-cleaning concept was born. The team-cleaning was observed at a competitor's facility and piloted at the Ritz-Carlton, Dearborn. Initially four-person teams were piloted. After analysis and internal customer feedback, three-person teams were found to have the greatest effectiveness within the house-keeping parameters of the Ritz-Carlton, Dearborn.

Key Measures

Key measures used to collect the base-line data on the reliability of the house-keeping system changes included the following :

1. Defect rate per room
2. Room cycle time
3. Possible interruption rate
4. Honour bar discrepancies and allowances
5. Housekeeping productivity (rooms cleaned per team)
6. Distance traveled

Baseline data collected through random sample techniques and plotted on statistical process control charts proved independent cleaning of a guest room resulted in the following :

1. 7.4 defects
2. A cycle time of 26.45 minutes to clean a room, plus 7 to 10 minutes to service the honour bar
3. Three standard interruptions of maid service, honour bar service and turndown service
4. Chronic honour bar discrepancies
5. Productivity of 13 guest rooms per attendant
6. 525 feet or about one-tenth of a mile travelled to clean a guest room

Benchmarking Partners

Although it was important discovery, finding the team-cleaning process at a domestic competitor's facility was unplanned. The Ritz-Carlton, Dearborn team did adopt some of the competitor's practices. No other external benchmarking partners were sought.

The Dearborn team sought an internal benchmarking partner at the sister property in Naples, Florida. The Naples team provided new practices to reduce the logo finding and matching on the company's towels.

The Dearborn team also examined one of its members hospital laundry experiences and elected to modify part of that process to Ritz-Carlton standards. This new practice reduced the handling of linen and terry items during the transportation and distribution processes.

Best Practices Learnt

Key Findings : Key in the housekeeping study was the customer - supplier relationships vital to productivity. Housekeeping is the primary customer of laundry departments. The entire housekeeping operation can come to a grinding halt if the supply of clean terry and linen is limited or interrupted. A common practice was stocking of supplies and wasting upto 45 minutes daily while collecting materials vital to guest room cleaning.

To overcome these recurring problems, a process change spearheaded by the laundry department to listen to the voice of its internal customer occurred. It was determined that the process from soiled to clean terry and linen was needed within the same day. If distribution centres on each guest floor could be stocked by the turndown attendants before the end of their shift, then supplies would be available for the room attendants at the beginning of their shift. Thus this process would save 30 to 45 minutes per person per day.

Potential Opportunities for Improvement

Team cleaning of guest rooms held both tangible and intangible benefits :

Tangible benefits included the following :

1. Reduction in room cleaning cycle time by 65 percent or 8 minutes
2. Reduction in defects per room by 42 percent to 3.7
3. Reduction of standard guest room interruptions by 33 percent
4. Reduction in time guest would be disturbed if occupying the room at the time cleaning was provided
5. Increase in the property and life safety for guests and staff due to fewer guest room doors being opened at any one time as well as the presence of more than one room attendant within a room
6. Increase in productivity from 13 to 15 rooms per person
7. Reduction in individual travel by 64 percent to 205 feet within a guest room

Intangible benefits of team cleaning included the following :

1. Reduction in lonliness from working independently
2. Increased teamwork through shared tasks and responsibilities
3. Increase in comraderie and morale from team working
4. Job enrichment through the team process, which provided coaching, feedback and stimulation during repetitive housekeeping tasks
5. Increased communication among team members and between guests and team members
6. Increased effect of peer pressure to perform to standards, resulting essentially in self-directed work teams
7. Reduced monotony from switching roles throughout a shift
8. A stronger customer-supplier relationship between the housekeeping and laundry departments

Conclusion

A strong contributor to the success of the team - cleaning concept was involving people directly impacted by the house keeping system and using their expertise to drive change.

Using a total team approach and scientific tools markedly increased the acceptability of all the housekeeping changes implemented.

The reduced process time delighted the hotel's customers in another important way. The front office staff benefited greatly from up-to-the minute room availability. This was accomplished by team self-inspection and status updating directly tied to the hotel's room inventory computer. This practice allowed the front office receptionists to give customers the rooms they wanted. It also reduced the following :

1. Customer queue time at the registration desk
2. Delays at the front office because the right rooms were available when they were needed
3. Defects and errors in out-of-inventory situations

Three important factors contributed to the success of this study :

1. Team meetings were held with the individuals and departments that were impacted by the study and its subsequent changes
2. Daily line ups at the beginning of each shift served as a means of communication
3. Staff members were involved and empowered to make changes and to pilot the same

Two practices that did not work during the study were the following :

1. Small, incremental changes were met with resistance and a "what-next"? attitude. Combined, comprehensive changes were much more welcome by the staff.
2. Managers discussing the team's work and process changes was less effective than peer-to-peer coaching.

Actions Taken

Implementation

The implementation of housekeeping teams to clean guest rooms was a task of great proportion as it was a major change in how work was done. The biggest obstacle was the human response to change or the reengineering of the process. Involving the people impacted by process change was a vital part of the study's overall success. Using a total team approach and scientific tools also markedly increased the acceptability and buy-in of the whole change.

Large-scale change also took place in the laundry department as it is housekeeping's major supplier. Shift changes to accommodate terry and linen productivity, priority of waste loads, and modified handling of sorted, soiled pieces, all contributed to increase productivity to return cleaned supplies to customers. The room attendants contributed to these handling changes by separating linen and terry on the guest room floors. It was discovered that the room attendants were the only ones who combined terry and linen items throughout the entire soiled-to-clean process. Keeping the items separated throughout the cycle saved time-consuming sorting and reduced the possibility of injury in the laundry chute room.

Planned Changes / Net Steps

The final frontiers to tackle for total process reliability in producing a clean, fresh, fully stocked guest room include the following :

1. Linen distribution system
2. Honour bar servicing system
3. Continuous training processes for the housekeeping staff
4. Even use of guest rooms through rotation selling
5. Scheduling of house keeping teams to meet identified customer requirements for room cleaning

Both internal and external customers are affected by these processes. Customer-supplier relationships are crucial to the reliability of the housekeeping system. Error proofing these processes will ensure that the guests are served right the first time and they are served on time. Clearly, the original goal of a 50 percent reduction in cycle time has been achieved and exceeded. For the future the housekeeping system will continue to improve the cycle time and reliability with the participation of the ladies and gentlemen of the Ritz-Carlton, Dearborn.

Discussion Questions :

1. Discuss the objectives / purpose of the Ritz-Carlton Hotel Company. How the same were accomplished?
2. What were the requirements of the customers of the Ritz-Carlton Hotel company?
3. Describe the current process of housekeeping in the Ritz-Carlton Hotel. What were the key measures used to collect the base line data on the reliability of the housekeeping system changes?
4. Discuss the benchmarking process adopted by the Ritz-Carlton Hotel Company.
5. What were the key findings of the housekeeping study?
6. Discuss the tangible and intangible benefits of team-cleaning in house keeping.

Appendices

"APPENDIX - A"

BENCHMARKING BASICS

BENCHMARKING DEFINITIONS

(i) **Formal Definition :** Benchmarking is the continuous process of measuring our products, services and practices against the toughest competitors or those companies recognised as industry leaders.

(ii) **Dictionary Definition :** The process of creating benchmarks. A benchmark is something that can be measured and used as a standard that other things can be compared with. A benchmark is a surveyor's mark of previously determined position and used as a reference point, standard by which something can be measured or judged.

(iii) **Working Definition :** Benchmarking is the search for industry best practices that lead to superior performance.

(iv) **Other Definitions :**

(a) A systematic way to identify, understand, and creatively evolve superior products, services, designs, equipment, processes and practices to improve your organisation's real performance.

(b) Process of continuous improvement without **"reinventing the wheel"**.

(c) Process of identifying, understanding and adapting outstanding practices from any organisation to help your organisation improve its performance and outcomes.

(d) Benchmarking is much more than performance comparisons.

(e) Benchmarking is a powerful method for breakthrough thinking, innovation, improvement and for delivering exceptional bottom-line results.

(f) Benchmarking is a tool to help you improve your business processes. Any business process can be benchmarked.

(g) Benchmarking is the process of identifying, understanding and adapting outstanding practices from organisations anywhere in the world to help your organisation improve its performance.

(h) Benchmarking is a highly respected practice in the business world. It is an activity that looks outward to find best practice and high performance and then measure actual business operations against those goals.

(i) Benchmarking is the continuous search for and adaptation of significantly better practices that leads to superior performance by investigating the performance and practices of other organisations (benchmark partners). In addition, it can create a crisis to facilitate the change process.

(j) Benchmarking is the process of comparing one's business processes and performance metrics to industry bests and/or best practices from other industries.

(k) Benchmarking is a way of helping organisations to compare themselves against others, in order to learn from others. It provides a proven mechanism to help identify and prioritise areas for improvement within a business in an objective manner, as well as providing a simple way to measure progress overtime.

(l) In Europe benchmarking is defined as "a continuous systematic process for comparing performances of organisations, functions or processes against the "best of the world" aiming not only to match those performance levels, but to exceed them".

(m) **Benchmarking is :**

- A continuous process
- A process of investigation that provides valuable information
- A process of learning from others, a pragmatic search for ideas
- A time consuming, labour intensive process requiring discipline
- A viable tool that provides useful information for improving virtually any business process

(n) Benchmarking is emulating the best of continuously implementing change and measuring performance.

(o) Benchmarking is the process of improving performance continuously, identifying, understanding and adapting outstanding practices and processes found inside and outside the organisation and implementing the results.

(p) **Benchmarking is :**

- A systematic and disciplined process of examining your own processes
- Finding who is better or best
- Learning how they do it
- Adapting it to your organisation
- Implementing it
- Doing it continuously

(q) Benchmarking focuses on **"learning from the experience of others"** and is defined as identifying, adapting and implementing the practices that produce the best performance results.

(r) Benchmarking is the process of learning lessons about how best performance is accomplished.

(v) **"Xerox" Definition :** Benchmarking is the continuous process of measuring our products, services and business practices against the toughest competitors or those companies recognised as industry leaders.

(vi) **"Leadership through Quality" Definition :** Benchmarking is a standard process used to evaluate success in meeting customer requirements.

(vii) **A Generic Definition :** Benchmarking is a basis of establishing rational performance goals through the search for industry best performances that will lead to superior performance.

2. What is a Benchmark?

- A benchmark is a program that measures the performance of your product or service.
- A benchmark is the standard of excellence against which to measure and compare
- A benchmark is a measure of performance.
- A benchmark is a reference standard against which other things can be measured.
- **Benchmark : An Industry Standard**
  - Benchmarks may be descriptive, as in the description of a best industry practice. They may be converted to a performance measurement that shows the effect of incorporating or adopting the practice.
- ***Descriptive Benchmarks or Practices :*** Any work process is made up of inputs, a repeatable set of steps based on a set of practices or methods and outputs. If the practices are the best in the industry, they will deliver the outputs that will completely satisfy customers.
- ***Quantitative Benchmarks or Performance Measurements :*** Benchmark measurements are the conversion of benchmark practices to operational measures. There can be benchmarks for all goals and objectives, such as customer satisfaction, employee motivation and satisfaction, quality and cycle time and business results.
- **What to Benchmark?**
  - Products
  - Work processes
  - Support functions
  - Organisational performance
  - Organisational strategy

Benchmarking - What it is and What is it not

Benchmarking is	Benchmarking is not
• A continuous process	• A one-time event
• A process of investigation that provides valuable information	• A process of investigation that provides simple answers
• A process of learning from others	• Copying, imitating
• A time-consuming labour-intensive process	• Quick and easy
• A viable tool that provides information for improving virtually any business activity	• A buzzword, a fad

Objectives/Goals of Benchmarking

1. To identify the weaknesses within an organisation and improve upon them, with the idea of becoming the **"best of the best"**.
2. To help managers to find gaps in performance and turn them into opportunities for improvement.
3. To enable companies to identify the most successful strategies used by other companies of comparable size, type or regional location, and to adopt relevant measures to make their own programs more efficient.

Most companies apply benchmarking as a part of a broad strategic process. **Benchmarking targets roles, process and critical success factors.**

- **Roles** are what define the job or function that a person fulfils.
- **Processes** are what consume a company's resources
- **Critical success factors** are issues company must address for success over the long term to gain a competitive advantage.

Benchmarking focuses on these things in order to point out inefficiencies and potential areas of improvement.

4 'W's and 1 'H' of Benchmarking

A company that decides to undertake a benchmarking initiative should consider the following questions : **When, why, who, what and how**. *i.e.,*

1. **When** to benchmark?
2. **Why** to benchmark?
3. **Who** to benchmark?
4. **What** to benchmark? and
5. **How** to benchmark?

1. When to Benchmark?

Benchmarking can be used at any time, but is usually performed in response to needs that arise within a company. **Some potential "triggers" for the benchmarking process include :**

(i) Quality programs (TQM, Six-Sigma etc.)

(ii) Cost reduction/budget process

(iii) Operations improvement efforts

(iv) Management change

(v) New operations/new ventures

(vi) Rethinkig existing strategies

(vii) Competitive assaults/crises

2. Why to Benchmark?

There are several reasons why companies may embark on benchmarking. They are :

(i) To signal management's willingness to pursue a philosophy that embraces change in a proactive rather than reactive manner.

(ii) To establish meaningful goals and performance measures that reflect an external/customer focus, foster **'quantum leap'** thinking and focus on high pay-off opportunities.

(iii) To create early awareness of **competitive disadvantage** and

(iv) To promote **team work** that is based on competitive need and is driven by concrete data analysis, not intuition or gut feeling.

3. Who to Benchmark?

Companies may decide to benchmark internally, against competitors, against industry performance, or against the **"best of the best"** or **"best-in-class"**.

- **Internal benchmarking** is the analysis of existing practice within various departments or divisions of the organisation, looking for best performance as well as identifying base-line activities and drivers.
- **Competitive benchmarking** looks at a company's direct competitors and evaluates how the company is doing in comparison with competitors.
- **Industry benchmarking** is more trend-based and has a much broader scope. It can help establish performance base lines.
- **The "best-in-class" benchmarking** examines multiple industries in search of new, innovative practices.

4. What to Benchmark?

Benchmarking can focus on roles, processes, or strategic issues. It can be used to establish the function or mission of an organisation. It can also be used to examine existing practices while looking at the organisation as a whole to identify practices that support major processes or critical objectives. When focusing on specific processes or activities, the depth of the analyis is a key issue. The analysis can take the form of vertical or horizontal benchmarking. Vertical benchmarking is where the focus is placed on specific departments or functions, while horizontal benchmarking is where the focus is placed on a specific process or activity. Concerning strategic issues, the objective is to identify factors that are of great importance to competitive advantage, to define measures of excellence that capture these issues, and to isolate companies that appear to be top performers in these areas.

5. How to Benchmark?

Benchmarking uses different sources of information, including published material, trade meetings, and conversations with industry experts, consultants, customers and marketing representatives. The emergence of Internet technology has facilitated the benchmarking process. The Internet offers access to a number of data bases containing performance indicators for thousands of different companies. The Internet also enables companies to conduct electronic surveys to collect benchmarking data. How a company benchmarks may depend on available resources, dead lines and the number of alternative sources of information.

"APPENDIX - B"

TYPES OF BENCHMARKING

Generally one can distinguish among three types of benchmarking, which are found throughtout the world. They are :

1. Benchmarking of companies
2. Benchmarking of industries/sectors
3. Benchmarking of environment

Exhibit below illustrates these three types of benchmarking :

EXHIBIT : TYPES OF BENCHMARKING

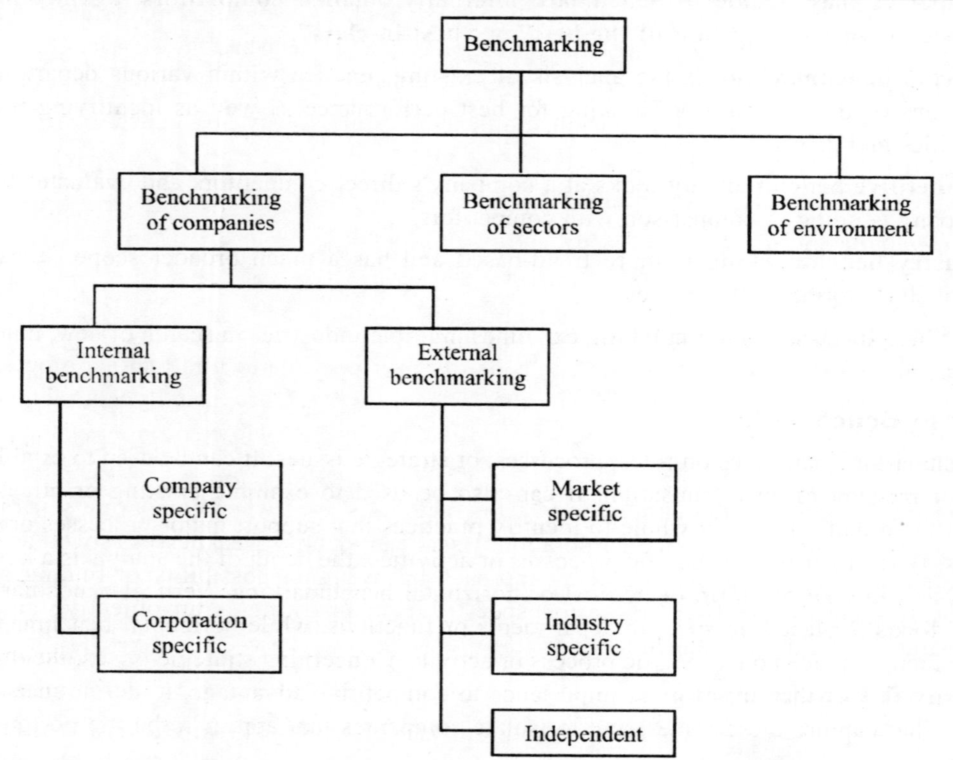

1. **Benchmarking of Companies :** The benchmarking of companies has been spread most widely. Here companies learn from another, they compare index numbers and exchange information about benchmarking objects.
2. **Benchmarking of Sectors :** This type of benchmarking compares the performance of individual sectors. The goal is to learn from other sectors which, according to certain criteria, perform better.
3. **Benchmarking of Environments :** Benchmarking of the environment gains increasing importance nowadays. In the future, countries can compare the political, social or economic environment. Thus will enable them to learn from each other.

Benchmarking of companies can be classified as

(i) Internal benchmarking and

(ii) External benchmarking

These two sub categories of benchmarking of companies are discussed in the following paragraphs :

(i) Internal Benchmarking

Involves benchmarking businesses or operations from within the same organisation (*e.g.*, business units in different countries). The main advantages of internal benchmarking are that access to sensitive data and information is easier, standardised data is often readily available and usually less time and resources are needed.

There may be fewer barriers to implementation as practices may be relatively easy to transfer across the same organisation. However real innovation may be lacking and best-in-class performance is more likely to be found through external benchmarking.

Internal benchmarking is the starting point and should always be considered before any organisation looks to the outside.

Two types of internal benchmarking are :

(a) ***Company specific benchmarking*** and

(b) ***Corporation specific benchmarking***

which are described below :

- **Company specific Benchmarking :** It is hardly ever possible to find internal processes that can really be compared with each other. The processes are usually characterised by technological, organisational and personal influences and are targeted on ancillary plants or departments.
- **Corporation specific Benchmarking :** This method is used when comparing several plants or parts of a company within a corporation. Users can identify weaknesses as well as the best practice within the organisation. This approach has a higher possibility of finding potential areas for improvements. Corporation specific benchmarking is an objective and sound preparation of external benchmarking.

(ii) External Benchmarking

External benchmarking involves analysing outside organisations that are known to be **"best-in-class"**. External benchmarking provides opportunities of learning from those who are at the **"leading edge"**.

External benchmarking is a method to look to the outside. Here the practices of the own company are compared with the practices of outside companies. Comparison implies that there must be basic similarities which must be identified before benchmarking. This type of benchmarking can take up significant time and resource to ensure the comparability of data and information, the credibility of the findings and the development of sound recommendations.

This approach is recommended where examples of good practices can be found in other (outside) organisations and there is lack of good practices within internal business units. **Three sub categories of external benchmarking are :**

(a) ***Market specific benchmarking***

(b) ***Industry specific benchmarking***

(c) ***Independent benchmarking***

These subcategories of external benchmarking are described below :

- **Market specific Benchmarking :** With market specific benchmarking, companies can learn from their competitors, they can introduce improvements and keep an eye on the market objectively. But the prevailing problem is the unwillingness to share information with a competitor.
- **Industry specific Benchmarking :** This goes beyond the simple comparison of two companies. It focuses on trends and studies the efficiency of a certain function industry-wide. It is necessary to study many more companies than in the case of benchmarking with competitors. Industry-specific benchmarking looks for trends instead of competitive positions. Compared with market specific benchmarking, the essential advantage of industry-specific benchmarking is the lack of an immediate competitive situation. The benchmarking partners act on different markets. Usually, the transfer of information in thus easier.
- **Independent Benchmarking :** The key for long-term success of a company is not equality but superiority. Companies want to find out how the **"best"** companies meet their standards and adapt and apply the **lessons learnt** from those approaches and ideas to meet and exceed those standards. This is why benchmarking focuses on the best. Irrespective of the particular industry and regardless of the source, the **"inferior"** company seeks new, innovative practices. To measure success against external criteria implies developing an idea of the best performance. The goal is to raise the company to a new level of performance.

Another approach to classify external benchmarking is :

1. External competitive benchmarking
2. External industry (compatible) benchmarking and
3. External generic benchmarking

These types of external benchmarking are described below :

- **External Competitive Benchmarking** is an effective approach in industries which are very competitive. The **reverse engineering** and **competitive shopping** approaches that are part of this type of benchmarking are very important to organisations whose output is hard or soft goods.

Competitive benchmarking which includes reverse engineering and competitive shopping, requires that the organisation perform a detailed analyis of competitor's products, services and processes. The most common approach is to purchase competitive products and services, then analyse them to identify competitive advantages.

- **External industry (compatible) benchmarking** compares the benchmark item with items produced by the world's best organisations in a general industry category (examples : banking, insurance, healthcare, electronics, etc.). In this case the benchmarking partner's item does not compete directly for the same customers.
- **External generic (trans industry) benchmarking** extends the benchmarking process outside the specific organisation and its industry, to involve dissimilar industries. Many business processes are generic in application and extend across industries (examples : warehousing, supplier relations, service parts logistics, advertising, supplier relations, hiring, etc.). Applying the benchmarking process to these generic items can provide meaningful insights, particularly when information comes from unrelated industries.

Three Primary Benchmarking Types

Three distinct types of benchmarking are : (1) **Process benchmarking,** (2) **Performance benchmarking** and (3) **Strategic benchmarking.**

Exhibit below illustrates these three primary types of benchmarking.

EXHIBIT : THREE PRIMARY TYPES OF BENCHMARKING

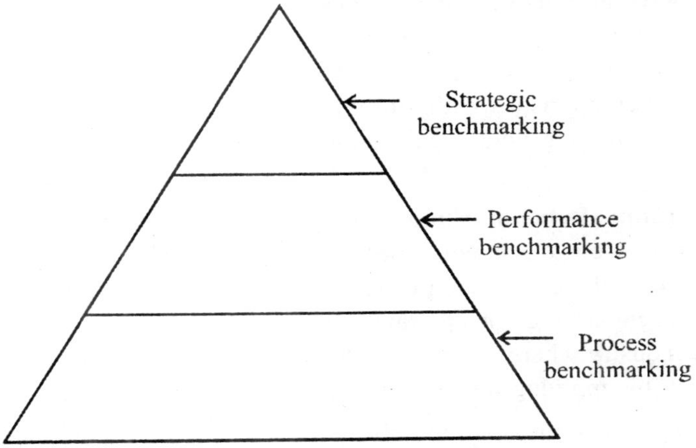

1. Process Benchmarking

Process benchmarking focuses on discrete work processes and operating systems, such as the customer complaint process, the billing process, the order - fulfillment process, the recruitment process or the strategic planning process. This form of benchmarking seeks to identify the most effective operating practices from many companies that perform similar work functions.

Process benchmarking focuses on improving specific critical processes and operations. Benchmarking partners are sought from best practice organisations that perform similar work or deliver similar services. Process benchmarking invariably involves producing process maps to facilitate comparison and analysis. This type of benchmarking often results in short-term benefits *for example,* achieving improvements in key processes to obtain quick results.

- **Functional Benchmarking :** A company will focus its benchmarking on a single function to improve the operation of that particular function. Common functions such as human resources, finance and accounting and information and communication technology are unlikely to be directly comparable in cost and efficiency terms and may need to be disaggregated into processes to make valid comparison. Also known as generic benchmarking.
- **Best Practice Benchmarking :** Applies to business processes. It breaks the function down to discrete areas that are targets for benchmarking and is a more focused study than functional benchmarking. Attempts to benchmark not only work processes, but also the management practices behind them.
- **Operational Benchmarking :** Embraces everything from staffing and productivity to office flow and analyis of procedures performed.

2. Performance Benchmarking

Enables managers to assess their competitive positions through product and service comparisons. Performance benchmarking usually focuses on elements of price, technical quality, ancillary product or service features, speed, reliability and other performance characteristics. Reverse engineering, direct product or service comparisons and analyis of operating statistics are the primary techniques applied during performance benchmarking.

- **Competitive benchmarking** involves identification of products, services and work processes of your organisation's direct competitors. The objective of competitive benchmarking is to identify specific information about your competitor's products, processes, and business results and then make comparisons with those of your own organisation. Competitive benchmarking is useful in positioning your organisation's products, services, and processes relative to the market place.
- **Technical/Product Benchmarking :** The technique initially used to compare existing corporate strategies with a view to achieving the best possible performance in new situations, has recently been extended to the comparison of technical products. The process is usually referred to as "technical benchmarking" or "product benchmarking". Its use is well developed within the automotive industry where it is vital to design products that match precise user expectations at minimal cost, by applying the best technologies available world wide.
- **Product benchmarking** is commonly known as reverse engineering or competitive product analysis. It assesses competitor costs, product concepts, strengths and weaknesses of alternative designs and competitor design trade-offs, by obtaining, stripping down and analysing competitor's products.
- **Best-in-class Benchmarking :** Involves studying the competitor or the company that best carries out a specific function. Embraces everything from staffing and productivity to office flow and analyis of procedures performed.

3. Strategic Benchmarking

In general terms, strategic benchmarking examines how companies compete. Strategic benchmarking is seldom industry - focused. It is concerned with comparing different companies' strategies and assessing the success of those strategies in the market place. It analyses the strategies with particular reference to *(i)* strategic product, *(ii)* core competencies, *(iii)* product line, *(iv)* strategic alliances, and *(v)* technology portfolio.

Strategic benchmarking should begin with the needs and expectations of the customer. This can be achieved through surveys to measure customer satisfaction and the gaps between a company's performance and its customers' standards. Strategic benchmarking ensures a co-ordinated strategic direction regarding benchmarking and reduces the possibility that one improvement project will cancel out the effect of another. Benchmarking candidates are normally direct competitors. The main difficulty is persuading the benchmarking partners to discuss their strategy. However there is a great deal of information which can be obtained from customer, common suppliers and public domain information.

Three Common Types of Benchmarking

(i) Competitive benchmarking

(ii) Co-operative benchmarking

(iii) Collaborative benchmarking

These are briefly discussed below :

- **Competitive benchmarking** is the most difficult form of benchmarking because target companies are not usually interested in helping the benchmarking team. Data gathering which almost always is the most time - consuming task in any benchmarking endeavour, is made much more difficult when your targets are your competitors.

  Competitive benchmarking means measuring your functions, processes, activities, products, or services against those of your competitors and improving yours so that they are ideally best-in-class, but at a minimum, better than those of your competitors.

- **Co-operative Benchmarking :** In cooperative benchmarking, an organisation that desires to improve a particular activity through benchmarking contacts best-in-class firms and asks them if they will be willing to share knowledge with the benchmarking team. The target companies are usually not direct competitors of the benchmarking company, which is a key factor in securing cooperation.

  In cooperative benchmarking, the knowledge usually flows in one direction - from the target companies to the benchmarking team.

- **Collaborative Benchmarking :** In collaborative benchmarking, a group of firms share knowledge about a particular activity, all hoping to improve based upon what they learn. Sometimes, a third party often serves as coordinator, collector, and distributor of data, although an increasing number of firms are managing their own collaborative studies.

Other Types of Benchmarking

1. Formal benchmarking
2. Informal benchmarking

3. International benchmarking
4. Intelligent benchmarking
5. Financial benchmarking
6. Energy benchmarking
7. Metric benchmarking

These are briefly discussed below :

1. **Formal Benchmarking :** Formal benchmarking is a systematic process for identifying and implementing best or better practices. There are two types of formal benchmarking : *(i)* **Performance benchmarking** and *(ii)* **Best practice benchmarking.**

2. **Informal Benchmarking :** Is a type of benchmarking that most of us do unconsciously at work and in our home life. We constantly compare and learn from the behaviour and practices of others. **In the context of work, most learning from informal benchmarking comes from the following :**

   (i) Talking to work colleagues and learning from their experience

   (ii) Consulting with experts

   (iii) Networking with other people from other organisations at conferences, seminars and Internet forums

   (iv) On-line databases/websites such as the Business Performance Improvement Resource (BPIR) and publications that share benchmarking information provide quick and easy ways to learn of best practices and benchmarks.

3. **International Benchmarking :** Best practices are identified and analysed elsewhere in the world, perhaps because there are too few benchmarking partners within the same country to produce valid results.

   Globalisation and advances in information technology are increasing opportunities for international projects. However, these can take more time and resources to set up and implement and the results may need careful analyis due to national differences. Where the aim is to achieve world class or simply because there are insufficient national businesses against which to benchmark, international benchmarking is the answer.

4. **Intelligent Benchmarking :** Many benchmarking results are averages, which can be very misleading driving you to the wrong conclusions and decisions. That is why you need to dig deep and fully understand what you are comparing. Averages can include a wide sampling of comparisons, not all of which will be relevant.

   Not comparing apples to oranges is important, but the bigger risk is the more subtle differences between apples. Accurate comparison is not easy as it seems and using averages provided in published benchmarks can result in wrong decisions. To get proper comparison, assess each component and compare things that are the same, making adjustments as necessary to ensure equal comparison.

   Intelligent benchmarking is not just about company benchmark numbers. It is a process to target problem areas, identify solutions and implement changes that will get better results. Benchmarking is part of the process, including general benchmarking as well as detailed, focused benchmarking of the compared processes, resources and systems rather than just numbers.

5. **Financial Benchmarking :** Performing a financial analysis and comparing the results in an effort to assess your overall competitiveness and productivity. It is a benchmarking from an investor perspective extending the benchmarking universe to also compare to peer companies that can be considered for alternative investment opportunities from the perspective of an investor.
6. **Energy Benchmarking :** Developing an accurate model of a facility's energy consumption with the purpose of measuring reductions in usage.
7. **Metric Benchmarking :** Another approach to making comparisons involves using more aggregative cost or product information to identify strong and weak performing units. The two most common forms of quantitative analysis used in metric benchmarking are **data envelope analysis** and **regression analysis**.

One of the biggest challenges for metric benchmarking is the variety of metric definitions used among different companies and/or divisions. Definitions may also change over time within the same organisation due to changes in leadership and priorities. The most useful comparisons can be made when metrics definitions are common between compared units and do not change over time so improvements can be verified.

"APPENDIX - C"

REASONS FOR BENCHMARKING

1. Benchmarking involves **"learning from others"**. Learning from borrowing from the best and adapting their approaches to fit your own needs is the essence of benchmarking.
2. By exposing organisations and people to new ideas and approaches, the benchmarking experience often spurs extraordinary insights and breakthrough thinking.
3. Some organisations position benchmarking as part of an overall problem-solving process with a clear mantle for organisational improvements.
4. Some other organisations position benchmarking more as a proactive mechanism to keep themselves aware of the state-of-the-art business practices.
5. By benchmarking, you will find out :
   (a) Who performs the business very well and has process practices that are adaptable to your own organisation?
   (b) Who is the most compatible for you to benchmark with?
6. **Thinking "out-of-the-box" :** Benchmarking facilitates thinking **"out of the box"** – that is organisations looking at their own internal best practices by function, looking at competitor's best practices looking at industry best practices (includes non competitors), functional best practices anywhere in the country and finally looking at functional best practices - world class, anywhere in the whole world, with an objective of learning from others and adapting their best practices for continuous improvement.

7. **Strategic planning :** Benchmarking is a useful tool for gathering information in the areas such as *(a)* Knowledge of the market place, *(b)* Likely activities of the competition, *(c)* The state-of-the-art regarding products or services being produced, *(d)* Financial requirements for doing business in a market and *(e)* The customer base.

   The information gathered during the process of strategic planning can literally shape a business strategy in a more realistic direction or at least help identify the risks of doing business in certain markets.

8. **Setting and Refining Strategy :** In today's dynamic markets, important insights can be gleaned by studying the experiences and competitive strategies of others. The strategic lessons learnt by other organisations and industries can help your own company refine its strategy, project the possible outcomes of changing its present course, and forestall potential cataclysmic shifts brought by changing market circumstances.

9. **Forecasting :** Benchmarking information is often used to gauge the state of the market place and to forecast market potentials. Benchmarking also provides a source of information regarding the business directions of key players in the market place, trends in product/service development, patterns of consumer behaviour and so on.

10. **Reengineering Work Processes and Business System :** Benchmarking is essential for companies engaged in reengineering their processes and systems. Benchmarking gives you the ability to see things differently. It enables a company to get outside its conditioned responses or customary structures of thinking. Benchmarking enables true reengineering. Through the study of outside best practices, a company can identify and import new technology, new skills new training and new capabilities.

11. **Continuous Improvement of Work Processes and Business Systems :** Not every benchmarking project or initiative will yield major-magnitude change and system breakthrough. Benchmarking also provides a potential source for incremental changes and improvements. (*i.e.,* continuous improvement of work processes and business systems).

12. **Goal Setting :** Benchmarking is used as a means of identifying best practices. Although many organisations do not realistically aim to achieve best-in-class levels of results, they do use this information to establish specific product or process objectives. Many small to medium size companies can not hope to achieve the levels of performance of excellent companies that have far greater access to technologies, capital or other resources. However these companies can benefit considerably by benchmarking specific work processes that are not dependent on organisational resources. Organisations that are entering new markets also find that benchmarking the best practices of established organisations helps them establish goals that accelerate their learning curves and improve their performance. Benchmarking helps organisations anticipate market changes and validate goals and targets.

    By reviewing the products, prices, practices, strategies, structures and services of competitors and other industry leaders, managers can validate the adequacy of their own goals, plans and strategies. They use benchmarking as an integral part of their strategic planning and goal setting process. Organisations have also encouraged their suppliers to use benchmarking practices in order to help them meet quality or production goals.

13. **Problem Solving :** Benchmarking frequently demonstrates its value in the problem-solving process. Ironically, most corporate problem-solving processes do not methodically look outside the team or organisation for solutions. Standard problem-solving processes provide a structure that make work groups more effective. But most problem-solving processes indirectly encourage teams to reinvent the wheel because they seldom encourage work groups to consider external experience in developing solutions to their problems. As an enabling tool for problem-solving, benchmarking frequently produces elegant answers for thorny operating issues.

14. **Education and Idea Enrichment :** How people, who grow accustomed to operating in certain ways, know there are other approaches - perhaps better ways of performing the same task. Benchmarking is a tool for achieving idea enrichment and general education. By regularly benchmarking critical functions, organisations ensure they remain open to new ideas, changing trends, and evolving technology.

    Benchmarking is an excellent source of business ideas. One of the primary benefits of large-scale benchmarking is that it exposes individuals to new products, work processes and ways of managing company resources.

    Benchmarking requires that individuals establish formal contacts outside their organisations. In many cases, the process of benchmarking involves personal visits outside the organisational facilities. The reward is exposure to different ideas and approaches to conducting business.

    If seeing is believing, then benchmarking is an effective process to ensure that managers and front-line operators see other approaches to accomplishing the activities over which they have control.

    Not all of the ideas or business practices that are uncovered during benchmarking are going to be useful to an organisation. However benchmarking causes people to think about potential ways of conducting business. Benchmarking also provides an opportunity for employees to think **"out-of-the-box"** to consider alternative paradigms and to encourage in **"what if"** thinking.

15. **Market Performance Comparisons and Evaluations :** Organisations and individuals frequently presume that the products and services they provide to customers are of high quality. Yet without carefully comparing them to competitor's offerings, they can not fairly evaluate their relative standing. However fancy gives way to fact when you benchmark your company's products, features and performance against competitors'. This type of performance benchmarking is common in many industries. Industry and professional ratings of performance provide a fact-based market performance test that employs the essential skills of benchmarking. By heading the performance benchmarks, organisations can assess the adequacy of their products, services, features and performance. Such information can help them manage by custom-focused facts.

16. **Product/Process Comparisons :** A common type of benchmarking activity involves the collection of information about the products or processes of competitors or excellent companies. This information is often collected and used as a standard of comparison for similar products or services of the benchmarking organisation.

    This type of benchmarking confirms most closely with traditional competitive intelligence activities. It can also take on a generic flavour. A product or service produced by a noncompetitor may be analysed to gain insight into factors such as design, product quality, service support or production processes.

17. **Catalyst for Change :** Benchmarking is an effective catalyst for change because it involves employees in the personal discovery of more effective operating practices. Benchmarking exposes people to new approaches, systems and procedures. It is first-person experience that helps an employee visualise the final goal of prospective change. In this respect, benchmarking demystifies change, making it more tangible and less threatening. Consequently, benchmarking helps manage organisational change.

Box below lists situations without benchmarking (before benchmarking) and with benchmarking (after benchmarking).

Without benchmarking	With benchmarking
1. Becoming competitive	
• Internally focused	Concrete understanding of competition
• Evolutionary change	New ideas of proven practices and technology
• Low commitment	High commitment
2. Industry best practices	
• Not invented here	Proactive search for change
• Few solutions	Many options
• Average of industry progress	Business practice break through
• Frantic catch up activity	Superior performance
3. Defining customer requirements	
• Based on history or gut feeling	Market reality
• Perception	Objective evaluation
• Low fit	High conformance
4. Establishing effective goals and objectives	
• Lacking external focus	Credible, unarguable
• Reactive	Proactive
• Lagging industry	Industry leading
5. Developing true measures of productivity	
• Pursuing pet projects	Solving real problems
• Strengths and weaknesses not understood	Understanding outputs
• Route of least resistance	Based on best industry practices

"APPENDIX - D"

BENCHMARKING PROCESS

1. Generic Benchmarking Process

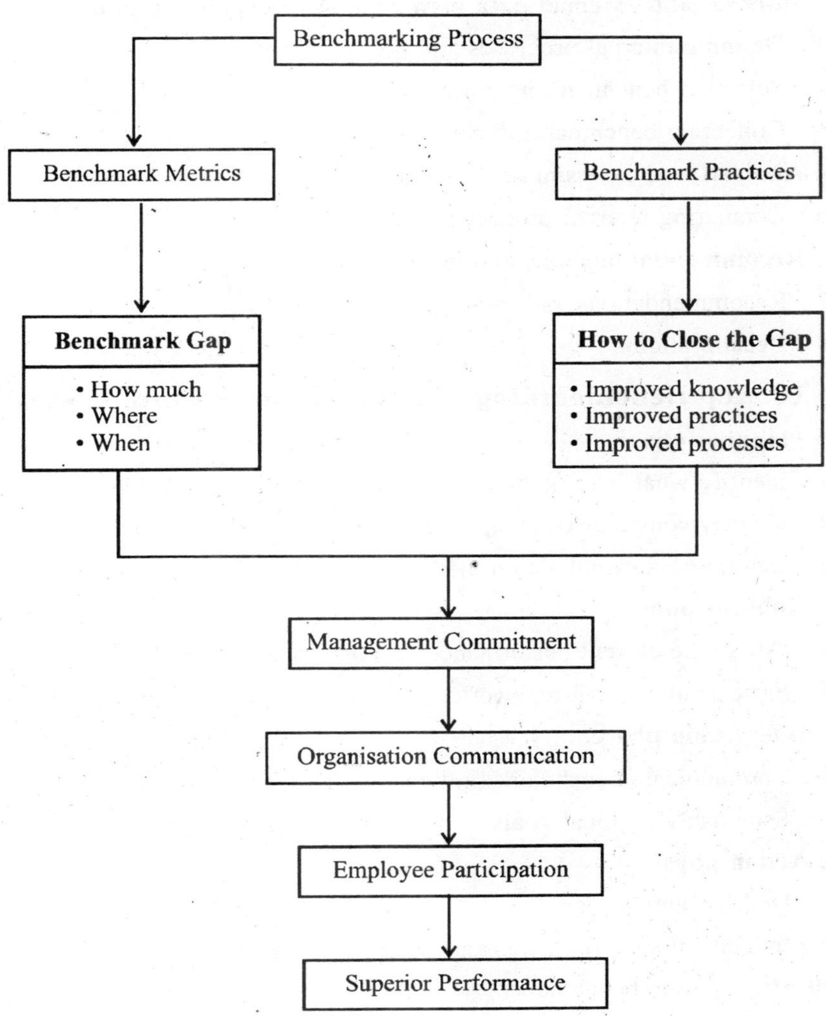

2. Six Step Benchmarking Process of Alcoa USA

Step 1 : Decide what to benchmark

Step 2 : Plan the benchmark project

Step 3 : Understand your own performance

Step 4 : Study performance of others

Step 5 : Learn from the data

Step 6 : Use the findings

3. Four Phases and Eight Steps of Ameritech USA

Phase 1 : Project conception and planning

Step 1 : Project conception

Step 2 : Project planning

Phase 2 : Internal and external data gathering and partner selection

Step 3 : Defining internal processes and performance

Step 4 : Selecting benchmarking partners

Step 5 : Collecting benchmarking partner's data

Phase 3 : Analysis and assessment

Step 6 : Comparing internal processes with partner's processes

Phase 4 : Recommendations and action

Step 7 : Recommendations and implementation

Step 8 : Recalibration

4. 5 Phase, 10 step Benchmarking Process of Xerox Corp. USA

Phase 1 : Planning phase

Step 1 : Identify what is to be benchmarked (*i.e.*, benchmark subject)

Step 2 : Identify comparative companies (*i.e.*, benchmark partners)

Step 3 : Determine data collection method and collect data

Phase 2 : Analysis phase

Step 4 : Determine current performance gap (*i.e.*, competitive gap)

Step 5 : Project future performance levels

Phase 3 : Integration phase

Step 6 : Communicate benchmark findings and gain acceptance

Step 7 : Establish functional goals

Phase 4 : Action phase

Step 8 : Develop action plans

Step 9 : Implement specific actions and monitor progress

Step 10 : Recalibrate benchmarks

Phase 5 : Maturity phase

- Leadership position attained
- Practices fully integrated into processes

5. 9 Step Benchmarking Process of AT&T

Step 1 : Project conception

Step 2 : Planning

Step 3 : Preliminary data collection

Step 4 : Best-in-class selection

Step 5 : Best-in-class collection

Step 6 : Assessment

Step 7 : Implementation planning

Step 8 : Implementation

Step 9 : Recommendations

6. 5 Step Benchmarking Process used by Motorola Inc. USA

Step 1 : Decide what to benchmark

Step 2 : Select companies to benchmark

Step 3 : Obtain data and collect information

Step 4 : Analyse data and form action plans

Step 5 : Recalibrate and start the process again

7. The Seven Step Benchmarking Model

Step 1 : Identify what to benchmark

Step 2 : Determine what to measure

Step 3 : Identify who to benchmark

Step 4 : Collect data

Step 5 : Analyse data and determine the gap

Step 6 : Set goals and develop action plan

Step 7 : Monitor the process

8. Five-stage Benchmarking Process Model (Circular Model)

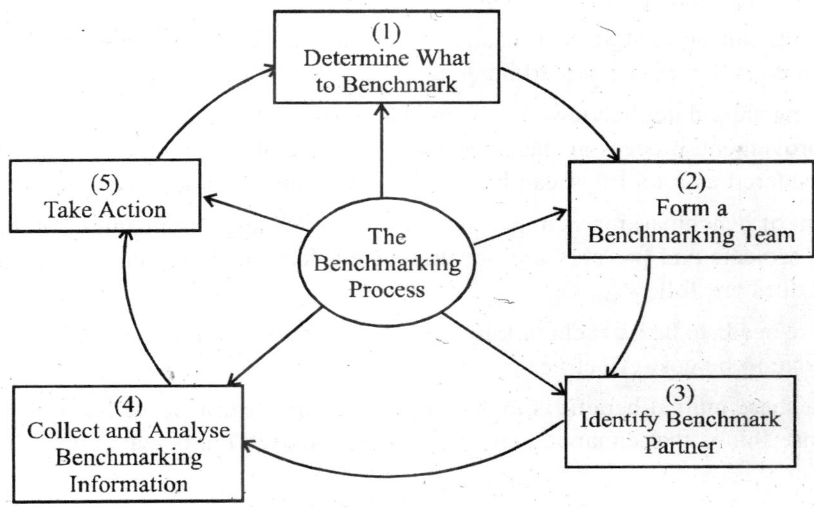

"APPENDIX - E"

Do's and Don'ts of Benchmarking

Introduction

As different companies adapted benchmarking to their own needs, a variety of apparently different processes with different numbers of "steps" began to emerge. Respondents to an International Benchmarking Clearing house survey identified processes between 4 and 33 steps. Examples include ALCOA's 6 step model, AT&T's 9 step model and Xerox's 10 step process. In fact all benchmarking processes are much the same and are built from the same basic model, which was first articulated by Xerox.

The Do's and Don'ts guidelines include activities common to most benchmarking models. These guidelines are organised by generic steps that appear in most benchmarking models. These generic steps to benchmarking include :

Step 1 : Select the process or function to benchmark

Step 2 : Understand the existing process or function

Step 3 : Identify benchmarking partners

Step 4 : Collect data and information

Step 5 : Identify gaps and reasons for them

Step 6 : Develop programs to address findings

Step 7 : Implement changes and monitor results

Preliminary Considerations before Starting Benchmarking

1. Although surveys and competitive assessment studies can be value-added activities, they do need to be distinguished from benchmarking. Surveys and competitive assessment activities can identify gaps, but unlike benchmarking, don't provide information on how to close the gaps or make step change improvements.
2. Benchmarking can be conducted proactively or reactively. There is no reason to wait for a crisis before considering benchmarking.
3. Benchmarking should not be viewed as a stand alone process. It is best integrated into existing quality improvement, process management, and strategic planning models. The objective is to have it considered as a tool that can be routinely applied when appropriate.
4. Management of benchmarking is important, especially for large companies. There is a need to ensure that projects and partners are not duplicated, learnings are shared and that legal and ethical practices are followed.
5. Not everyone needs to be a benchmarking expert. The mass training of the whole organisations may not prove to be cost-effective.

One way to share mutual benefit is to accumulate lessons learnt in the form of two lists : the Dos - that is, those things that enhance benchmarking - and the Don'ts - activities that can create pitfalls.

(A) Selection of the Process to Benchmark

Do's

1. As a general rule, the process or function selected should be one of the most critical to your business strategy. An exception is if this is your first or second project and the team is still developing its skills on how to conduct effective benchmarking projects. In this case, the project may target a less strategic topic, it should still be one of interest, have a good chance of success, be modest in scope, and require less than six months to complete.
2. Projects must be well defined, and generally they should require less than a year to complete the research, analysis, action planning and preliminary implementation.
3. Management must support the project, provide adequate resources and be prepared to champion implementation of best practice findings.
4. The organisation must be willing to change.
5. The team should be comprised of a workable number (4 to 6) of committed cross-functional stakeholders. Ideally a benchmarking expert will help facilitate the benchmarking process, unless the team is already experienced in benchmarking.
6. The team must understand who the customer is for the study. The customer's expectations from the study are established by direct interaction.
7. If the organisation has already developed an existing Quality Improvement (Process Management) model, this model should be used to identify the customer, expectations, measures and so on.
8. It is very useful to have an explicit mission statement which documents the project's deliverables, purpose and metrics.
9. Identify all those that may be affected by the project and secure their ideas, contributions and support.
10. Consider implementation issues early in the planning phase and throughout the project.

Don'ts

1. Don't initially benchmark areas where the organisation already performs well.
2. Don't benchmark topics or processes that aren't important.
3. Don't benchmark processes that are so broad in scope and so poorly defined, that the team can not agree on its mission and can not focus its efforts.
4. Don't undertake benchmarking projects with a team that is too large to be effective (10 or more) or too small to be credible (1 to 2).
5. Don't confuse metric or benchmark with a process, that is, don't make the metric or operating statistic the end of the benchmarking investigation.

(B) Understand the Existing Process

Do's

1. Develop a road map of the benchmarking project.
2. The ideal way to prepare a novice benchmarking team is through just-in-time delivery of training, JIT education provides benchmarking tools, concepts and skills to team members when they are ready to apply them during the project.
3. Develop an understanding of the critical success factors and the process drivers.
4. The use of deployment flowcharting and Ishikawa cause-an-effect diagrams can be extremely useful.
5. Identify the most important performance measures. These often include cost, time, quality, productivity and effectiveness measures.

Don'ts

1. Don't overlook the step of understanding the existing process even if it may be tedious and time-consuming.
2. Don't overlook the power of flow charting.
3. Don't try to use too many measures or inappropriate measures.
4. Don't forget to gather input from customers of the process.
5. Don't forget to check the team's plans with the internal and external customers and the process sponsor.
6. Don't overlook the importance of secondary research.
7. Don't create a flowchart that is too detailed.

(C) Identify Benchmarking Partners

Do's

1. Establish a list of selection criteria for benchmarking partners. Don't be misled by the "Halo Effect".
2. Start with literature searches to help identify partners.
3. Find out who else in your company would have an informed opinion about best practice companies.
4. Ask customers, suppliers, consultants, academics, security analyst, National Award Winners, professional and trade associations for opinions on the best practice companies.
5. Check with benchmarking clearing houses and internal coordinators or consultants.
6. Remember that any company which is significantly better than yours in a given process is a good partner.
7. Always consider companies outside your industry. They are more likely to produce practices that are new, better or never before considered by your company.
8. Be creative in your choice of partner(s).
9. Limit the number of partners to four to eight.

Don'ts

1. Don't limit benchmarking partner selection to the small number of National Award winners. They may not be best in your area of interest.
2. Don't limit your search only for the best practice company, searching for a single best company is an illusive target and only wastes time.
3. Don't limit data collection convenience to be placed ahead of best practices in partner selection.
4. Don't limit selection to companies in your industry.
5. Don't discount selection to companies that are smaller just because of their size.

(D) Collect Data and Information

Do's

1. Use secondary sources to develop background and specific process information about benchmarking partners.
2. Make sure your team understands the benchmarking code of conduct and the appropriate protocols.
3. Do a thorough job of questionnaire development. Test the questionnaire with an internal partner or a friendly external partner before distribution.
4. Limit the questionnaire to a small number of open-ended questions and to no more than two pages of evaluation-by-numbers, multiple choice or yes/no questions.
5. Seriously consider pros and cons of asking questions by written response, telephone interview, or face-to-face interviews.
6. Be specific about the time commitment you are requesting from your benchmarking partner and be prepared to send a written questionnaire or a scoping document ahead of the team's visit.
7. Identify the incentives to your benchmarking partner to participate in the study.
8. Limit the benchmarking site visit team size to about three people and be specific about each person's role.
9. Debrief the visiting team as soon as possible following the site visit.
10. Be prepared to respond to spontaneous questions from the benchmarking host, inturn, ask only questions that your team is willing to answer about your own organisation.
11. Share nonproprietary flowcharts or printed materials that describe the benchmark area before or at the start of a visit.
12. If in doubt, particularly when benchmarking competitors, seek advice from legal counsel.
13. A third-party consultant is often valuable or necessary for gathering and blinding data from competitor.
14. When developing your questionnaire, ask yourself "What is the reason for asking this question?".

Don'ts

1. Don't approach a benchmarking partner without being thoroughly prepared.
2. Avoid making cold calls to benchmarking contacts.
3. Don't design a questionnaire that is large and overwhelming.
4. Don't assemble too large a group for benchmarking visit.
5. Don't permit a site visit team's debriefing to be deferred for even a few days following the visit.
6. Don't get side-tracked by interesting or amusing stories that don't add to the team's knowledge.
7. Don't ignore or reject information that is reported in a different format than that used by your organisation.

(E) Identify Gaps and Reasons for Them

Do's

1. Examine data consistency.
2. Set up data so that direct comparisons are really made.
3. Look for and verify the cause and effect relationships between the measures and the reasons for gaps.
4. Look for trend data.
5. Aim to develop consensus from the team on key issues.

Don'ts

1. Don't aim for too much precision.
2. Don't process or develop too much information.
3. Don't provide only narrative analysis.

(F) Develop Programs to Implement Findings

Do's

1. Agree on key findings and recommendations. Seek informal reviews and obtain feedback from project sponsors and constituents before making recommendations.
2. For each recommendation for change, make sure the owner is identified.
3. Recommend specific tasks and clearly designate which team member has responsibility for accomplishing the task.
4. Identify cost and realistic expected benefits for recommended changes.
5. Agree on how results and recommendations are to be communicated and to whom.
6. Incorporate feedback from customers and process owners into the final report.
7. Obtain commitment and support from management for the implementation plan.
8. Make it as easy as possible to implement recommendations by anticipating any hurdles that will have to be overcome.

9. Make sure that any impact on peripheral groups is considered in the implementation plan.
10. Offer to make personal presentations for every group that will be asked to participate in improvements.

Don'ts

1. Don't rely solely on a final report to communicate your recommendations.
2. Don't underestimate the difficulty of persuading others to buy into the team's plan.
3. Don't make long, dull, or unethusiastic presentations, or long, ponderous reports that provides too much detail.
4. Don't get overly ambitious with your time table for change.
5. Don't forget to identify who is the owner of the change activity and who has the responsibility for specific activities.
6. Don't overestimate the benefits or underestimate the costs of implementation.
7. Don't overlook the impact the implementation may have on peripheral groups.
8. Don't forget to seek input from customers, management and process owners.

(G) Implement Changes and Monitor Results

Do's

1. Make sure all those involved in the process change thoroughly understand the rationale behind the change and what is expected of them.
2. Make sure that management is supportive of the change and takes interest in the process.
3. Consider rolling out the process change with a pilot program.
4. Set up the monitoring activity and process before initiating the change. Focus on key performance measures.
5. Anticipate resistance to change and don't take it personally.
6. Find ways to cascade improvements to other parts of the organisation.
7. Make sure that others peripheral to your process are not adversely impacted by the change recommendations.

Don'ts

1. Don't forget that without implementation, benchmarking and all the team's effort to date are worthless.
2. Don't implement without monitoring.
3. Don't overlook the fact that other factors may impact the result.

Glossary

A

- **Added Value :** The measure, intended to provide an indication of a company's quality.
- **Analysis Phase :** During the analysis phase of benchmarking, you define the benchmarking project, create a team, and focus the team's energy on understanding the root causes of performance for the process to be benchmarked.
- **Analysts :** Watchdog groups that serve as excellent information sources. Often analysts have special knowledge of the firms they follow.
- **Archival Research :** It consists of reviewing archival records in order to establish trends or examine the impact of changes in the business climate, the introduction of new technologies or products and so on.

B

- **Benchmarking :** A continuous, systematic process for evaluating the products, services and work processes of organisations that are recognised as representing best practices for the purpose of organisational improvements.
- **Benchmarking Code of Conduct :** The code of conduct is a set of principles and guidelines which have become the de facto standard for firms that successfully perform benchmarking projects.
- **Benchmarking Consortium :** A benchmarking consortium is made up of organisations that have joined together to help each other perform some part of the benchmarking process.
- **Benchmarking Data Base :** The stored collection of essential data assembled by the individual benchmarking item teams as well as analysed information.
- **Benchmarking Expert:** The person who brings knowledge of benchmarking process to the benchmarking team. This knowledge will include how to plan the benchmarking study, how and where to obtain data, how to ensure data reliability and other issues that will arise during a study and that an experienced person can resolve more easily than a novice.

- **Benchmarking Implementation Team :** A group of people assembled during the improvement phase of the benchmarking process in order to implement the improvements developed by the benchmarking item team.
- **Benchmarking Initiation Team :** A small group of people, usually from different functions who are assigned to get the benchmarking process started, coordinate its implementation and serve as in-house consultants for the benchmarking activities. Sometimes called the benchmarking coordination team.
- **Benchmarking Item :** The focus of the benchmarking project. The benchmarking item may encompass business processes, manufacturing processes, products, services, equipment and/or computer programs.
- **Benchmarking Item Team :** The group assigned with responsibility to benchmark an individual item. Sometimes called benchmarking team.
- **Benchmarking Networks :** These groups band together for the explicit purpose of opening benchmarking channels among the participating members.
- **Benchmarking Partner :** Any internal or external organisation that agrees to cooperate by exchanging data and/or hosting a site visit with the organisation that initiated the benchmarking project.
- **Benchmarking Performance Measurements :** Useful means to identify organisations whose performance is significantly better and who, therefore, may have best practices.
- **Benchmarking Plan :** A document that is used to define the detailed process that the benchmarking item team follows to benchmark a specific item.
- **Benchmarking Process :** A benchmarking process is the set of steps used to discover and incorporate best practices into day-to-day operations.
- **Benchmarking Project Champions :** Senior executives play a leading role in determining the success of benchmarking projects and hence they are referred to as **benchmarking project champions**.
- **Benchmarking Strategy :** An action plan to continuously improve work processes to produce better outputs by
  - *(a)* focusing major benchmarking efforts on finding and implementing best practices in key work areas,
  - *(b)* maintaining a critical few benchmark summary output measures as indicators of progress.
- **Benchmarking System :** A benchmarking system is the infrastructure and organisational linkages necessary to deploy, reinforce and institutionalise a benchmarking process.
- **Benchmarking Team :** The group of people responsible for performing the benchmarking project.
- **Benchmarks :** Performance measurement standards derived from definition or quantification of best practices

- A **benchmark** in land surveying serves as a reference point in determining one's current position or altitude in topographical surveys.
- In the most general terms, **a benchmark** was originally a sighting point from which measurements could be made or a standard against which others could be measured.
- **Benchmarks** are measurements to gauge the performance of a function, operation or business relative to others.
- **Benchmark** is a standard of excellence or achievement against which other similar things must be measured or judged.

• **Best Practices :** The methods used in work processes whose outputs best meet customer requirements.

  - **Best practices** are those methods or techniques that result in increased customer satisfaction when incorporated into your operation.

• **Best Practices :** Those methods or techniques that result in increased customer satisfaction when incorporated into your operation.

• **Best-in-class Benchmarking :** This involves studying the leading competitor or the company that best carriers a specific function.

• **Best-value Future-state Solution :** The solution that results in the most beneficial redesigned item as viewed by the item's stake holders. It is the best combination of desired costs and results. Examples include ROI, customer satisfaction, market share, risk and value-added per employee.

• **Business Objectives :** Business objectives set the direction that the organisation will follow for the future time period. Business objectives support the organisation's mission.

• **Business Process Reengineering :** Also known as business process redesign, business process reengineering is a radical approach to performance improvement adopting the clean-slate approach to reinvent how work is done. Also referred to as **"extended strategic change"**.

• **Business Processes :** Business processes are those cross-functional processes critical to the organisation's success. They are not the same as work processes.

C

• **Change :** Any alternative in the current work environment. Change refers to a significant difference in what was before. This could mean doing things in a new way, following a new path, adopting new technology, installing a new system, following new management procedures, merging, reorganising or any other highly significant disruptive event.

• **Change Leader :** A person who has whatever qualities or authority necessary in your organisation to ensure that improvements are actually made based on the results of your benchmarking study.

• **Change Management :** The application of many different ideas from the fields of engineering, business and psychology. Change management is about helping people through change.

- **Collaborative Benchmarking :** In collaborative benchmarking, a group of firms share knowledge about a particular activity, all hoping to improve based on what they learn. Sometimes, a third party often serves as coordinator, collector and distributor of data, although an increasing number of firms are managing their own collaborative studies.
- **Combined Internal and External Benchmarking :** The most frequently used approach to benchmarking which usually produces the best results.
- **Comparative Analysis :** The first half of a benchmarking project, during which the organisation measures its item's performance and compares it with similar items in other organisations to define the differences in performance.
- **Competence Gap Matrix :** A framework used to analyse potential areas for benchmarking. Activities at which the organisation must excel to be competitive are mapped along the two dimensions : *(i)* the organisation's actual level of competence compared to its competitor's and *(ii)* the level required for competitive advantage.
- **Competitive Benchmarking :** Involves identification of the products, services and work processes of your organisation's direct competitors.

  Competitive benchmarking is useful in positioning your organisation's products, services and processes relative to the market place.
- **Competitive Product Analysis :** Also known as **reverse engineering**, competitive product analysis assesses competitor's costs, product concepts, strengths and weaknesses of alternative designs and competitor design trade-offs, by obtaining, stripping down and analysis of competitor's products.
- **Competitive Shopping :** In competitive benchmarking process, the competitors of the benchmarking company may be reluctant to share information with the benchmarking company. Therefore the alternative is to buy the competitor's product or service. This is called **competitive shopping**.
- **Continuous Improvement :** Involves daily, weekly, or monthly small scale improvements. Continuous improvement involves identifying benchmarks of excellent practice and instilling a sense of employee ownership in the process. It is an inherent part of the total quality management process. Also referred to as **"immediate tactical change"**.
- **Cooperative Benchmarking :** In cooperative benchmarking, an organisation that desires to improve a particular activity through benchmarking contacts best-in-class firms and asks them whether they will be willing to share knowledge with the benchmarking team. The target companies are usually not direct competitors of the benchmarking company, which is a key factor in securing cooperation.
- **Corporate Benchmarking Office :** A small team managed by the director of corporate benchmarking responsible for several benchmarking activities.
- **Cost-Leadership Strategy :** This strategy means low product/service cost and high product quality, usually off-the-shelf. This strategy requires concentration of the operation system on all the elements of system design that make the low cost possible.
- **Country-class Organisations :** Organisations which are defined as the top ten percent in the country in which the benchmarking organisation is located.

- **Critical Success Factor (CSF) :** The term used to refer to subjects that are significant enough to warrant the use of the benchmarking process.
- **Culture :** A set of beliefs and values shared by people in an organisation. Culture is a powerful influence on people's behaviour.
- **Cycle Time :** Cycle time is the primary measure of speed in business. It can be defined as the interval between the start and finish of a process, which can be described in turn as the sequence of events and activities that occur in order to accomplish a piece of work.

D

- **Dantotsu :** The Japanese have captured the essence of striving to be the "best of the best" in the single word **"dantotsu"**. Dantotsu implies a degree of awareness about the environment, particularly of others who also strive to be the best of the best.
- **Data Analysis :** Data analysis involves organising masses of numbers and statements (collected data) into coherent, usable information. It is a critical phase of the benchmarking process.
- **Data Base :** A data base is a collection or pool of information that is recorded, indexed and stored on a computer.
- **Data Collector / Analyst :** The data collectors and analysts are the true core of the benchmarking team. They are the people who assist in the development of the benchmarking plan, identify, contact and interview benchmark partners, analyse and summarise the benchmarking data, and produce benchmarking reports.
- **Data Mining :** Searching on **'mining'** for small **'nuggets'** of information from the vast quantities of data stored in an organisation's data warehouses, employing a variety of technologies such as decision trees and neural networks.
- **Data Warehouse :** A very large data base or collection of data bases.
- **Data Warehousing :** The establishment and maintenance of a large data storage facility containing data on all or at least many aspects of the enterprise. It is a popular method of making data accessible to many people in an organisation.
- **Database Management System (DBMS) :** A support software that is used to create, manage and protect organisational data.
- **Differentiation Strategy :** This form of strategy attempts to differentiate itself from other competitors by offering something that is perceived by the industry and its customers as unique. This strategy does not ignore costs.

E

- **Enabler :** An enabler is any condition or factor that influences the effectiveness of a practice.
- **Energy Benchmarking :** A process of collecting, analysing and relating energy performance data of comparable activities with the purpose of evaluating and comparing performance between or within entities.

- **Exchange of Prisoners :** Means that you have something of value to share with those you hope will cooperate or collaborate in a benchmarking study you are performing.
- **Explicit Knowledge :** Encompasses the things we know that we can write down, share with others and put into a data base.
- **Extended Strategic Change :** Also known as **business process reengineering** it is a relatively recent and radical performance-improvement approach. Reengineering is **extended** because it can take years to fully implement and it is **strategic** because it reinvents the way an organisation conducts its business.
- **Extended Tactical Change :** Also known as **managed reform** it is a catch-all category embracing a wide-array of both reactive and proactive management actions. Such actions are intended over time to remove errors, problems, faults or abuses, to reverse negative trends, or to improve capabilities that will ensure operations meet management objectives.
- **External Benchmarking :** Benchmarking wherein an organisation is engaged in benchmarking against external direct product competitors or benchmarking against functional best operations or industry leaders.
- **External Competitive Benchmarking :** An effective approach in industries that are very competitive, industries whose competitors have very different management philosophies and histories and industries that are driven by emerging technologies and processes. Reverse engineering and competitive shopping approaches are part of this type of benchmarking.
- **External Generic Benchmarking :** This extends the benchmarking process outside the specific organisation and its industry, to involve dissimilar industries.
- **External Industry Benchmarking :** This compares the benchmark item with items produced by the world's best organisations in a general industry category (example, banking, insurance, health care, electronics).

F

- **Financial Benchmarking :** Refers to performing a financial analysis and comparing the results in an effort to assess your overall competitiveness or productivity.
- **Formal Benchmarking :** A systematic process for identifying and implementing best or better practices.
- **Functional Benchmarking :** Involves the identification of products, services and work processes of organisations that may or may not be your organisation's direct competitors. The objective is to identify best practices in any type of organisation that has established a reputation for excellence in the specific area being benchmarked. Also referred to as **generic benchmarking**.
- **Future-State Solution :** A combination of corrective actions and changes that can be applied to the item under study to increase its value to its share holders.

G

- **Gap Analysis :** Gap analysis is the comparison of findings data to internal operations data. It identifies specific elements (practices, metrics and enablers) that cause superior performance and the resultant impact of each if incorporated into your operation.
- **Generic Benchmarking :** This type of benchmarking focuses on excellent work processes rather than on the business practices of a particular organisation or industry.
- **Global Benchmarking :** The process of identifying best practices in organisations anywhere in the world to seek information that can help an organisation to measure and compare its performance against those best practices in order to improve its operations. Also known as **"international benchmarking"**.

H

- **Halo Effect :** Halo effect is a psychological term that describes a characteristic defect in rating scales to rate individuals either too high or too low on the basis of one outstanding trait. Two types of halo effects are *(i)* Halo positive and *(ii)* Halo negative.
- **Halo Negative Effect :** Occurs when considering companies whose overall performance or recent market history indicates a significant organisational depression or downturn.
- **Halo Positive Effect :** Occurs when an organisation establishes a reputation for doing one thing particularly well. As a result, many assume that the company does other things or most things well.
- **Human Resource Benchmarking :** Many generic processes apply to human resource functions across many industries and organisations, generic processes such as selection and recruiting, orientation, training, development, reward and recognition and performance evaluations, apply to nearly all industries and organisations. Human resource benchmarking involves cross-industry comparisons and learning in the area of these generic processes.

I

- **Immediate Strategic Change :** Also known as **organisational restructuring**, it includes many different approaches to rearranging work within an organisation. Functional transfers, structural reorganisations, downsizing, and realignments all represent common types of immediate strategic changes.
- **Immediate Tactical Change :** Also known as **continuous improvement**, it involves daily, weekly or monthly small scale improvements. Benchmarks and best practice benchmarking are invaluable tools of continuous improvement.
- **Implementation Plan :** The document that describes how the knowledge gained from the benchmarking project will be successfully applied to your own work process.
- **Individual Change Management :** The management of change from the perspective of the employees. They are the ones who ultimately must implement the change. The focus of individual change management is around the tools and techniques to help employees through the transition.

- **Informal Benchmarking :** A type of benchmarking that most of us do unconsciously at work and in our home life.
- **Innovation :** Innovation means to come up with your own customised answers to your specific challenges. It means to tap into your own people's innate wisdom and come up with your uniquely powerful solutions that custom-fit your business.
- **Intact Work Group :** This group is usually in a single location with all members of the group reporting to a common manager. Intact work groups are often the customers for their own benchmarking investigations.
- **Integration Phase :** Integration is the process of using benchmark findings to set operational targets for change. It involves careful planning to incorporate new practices in the operation and to ensure that benchmarking findings are incorporated in all formal planning processes.
- **Internal Benchmarking :** A form of collaborative benchmarking that many large organisations use to identify best-in-house practices and disseminate the knowledge about those practices to other groups of the organisation.
- **Internal Benchmarking Item Committee or Network :** The internal benchmarking item committee is made up of representatives from different sites and/or divisions who have a common interest in benchmarking a specific item.
- **International Benchmarking :** Benchmarking used where the aim is to achieve world-class status or simply because there are insufficient national businesses against which to benchmark. Also known as **global benchmarking.**

K

- **Keiretsu :** Tightly-knit communities or operating networks of companies formed around a central bank. In Japan, Keiretsu alliances provide a strong network and a fertile setting for sharing of information and best practices.
- **Knowledge :** Knowledge is information in context to produce an actionable understanding. Knowledge is "human understanding of a specialised field of interest that has been acquired through study and experience".
- **Knowledge Management :** The systematic processes by which knowledge needed for an organisation to succeed is created, captured, shared and leveraged.

L

- **Line Person :** One who is extremely knowledgeable about the activity being benchmarked.

M

- **Managed Reform :** Is a catch-all-category embracing a wide array of both reactive and proactive management actions. Such actions are intended over time to remove errors, problems, faults or abuses, to reverse negative trends or to improve capabilities that will ensure operations meet management objectives. Also referred to as **"Extended tactical change"**.

- **Management Process :** Is everything else that has to be done to ensure that benchmarking is effectively pursued. The management process includes those actions that management does to ensure that the benchmarking team's operation is successful and that benchmarking has some performance. It includes creating the environment so that new ideas are pursued to improve business processes, providing training and support; prioritizing the direction of and encouraging the implementation of the benchmarking findings.
- **Market Niche Strategy :** Strategies in this category focus on a narrowly defined segment of the market (*i.e.,* market niche) and attempt to make the organisation in question, the market leader in that niche.
- **Metric :** A metric is a measure of process performance.
- **Metric Benchmarking :** An approach to making comparisons using more aggregative cost or production information to identify strong and weak performing units.
- **Mission :** The stated reason for the existence of the organisation.

N

- **Non-competitive Benchmarking :** Learning something about a process a company wants to improve by benchmarking including : *(i)* a related process in the industry with a firm, the company does not directly compete with, *(ii)* a related process in a different industry and *(iii)* an unrelated process in a different industry.

O

- **Operating Principles :** Basic beliefs that make up the culture of the organisation.
- **Operational Focus :** In the operational focus, benchmarking is used to understand specific customer requirements, to understand the best practices to achieve customer satisfaction by improving internal work processes and to determine operational performance levels required to become the vendor of choice in the eyes of the customer. Operationally focused benchmarking concentrates on work processes through which continuous improvement is delivered by incorporating best practices in the work steps.
- **Organisational Change Management :** The methodology used to manage the implementation of critical or major changes throughout the organisation to greatly increase the probability of the changes being implemented effectively and efficiently.
- **Organisational Restructuring :** Includes many different approaches to rearranging work within an organisation. Functional transfers, structural reorganisations, downsizing and realignments all represent common types of immediate strategic changes categorised as organisational restructuring. Also referred to as **"immediate strategic change"**.
- **Organisational Strategies :** Approaches adopted by organisations to ensure successful performance in the market place. These approaches are typically set forth in a comprehensive document called strategic plan.

P

- **Performance Benchmarking :** Performance benchmarking enables managers to assess their competitive positions through product and service comparisons. Performance benchmarking usually focuses on elements of price, technical quality, ancillary product or service features, speed, reliability and other performance characteristics. Reverse engineering, direct product or service comparisons, and analysis of operating statistics are the primary techniques applied during performance benchmarking.
- **Performance Goals :** These are normally quantified, measurable results that the organisation wants to accomplish in a set period of time to support its business objectives. Performance goals directly relate to business objectives.
- **Performance Projection Chart :** Also called **"gap/trend analysis chart"** it is graphical representation of the effective way to illustrate the differences between your items and the benchmarking partner's item.
- **Planning Phase :** The objective of this phase is to plan for the benchmarking investigations. The steps involved in this phase are : *(i)* Identify what is to be benchmarked, *(ii)* Identify comparative companies and *(iii)* Determine data collection method and collect data.
- **Power Benchmarking :** Benchmarking which embraces process comparisons, performance comparisons and strategic comparisons, embraces the widest range of operating areas. It includes but not limited to examination of process capability, organisational structure, quality, reliability, warranty costs, cycle time, human resource management, technology management, and many other important competitive factors.
- **Practice :** A method or technique used to perform a process step, practices describe *how* we perform a step within a work process.
- **Problem-based Approach :** In a problem-based approach to benchmarking, if there is no specific plan for benchmarking, the activity is characterised as uncontrolled. Thus it is often pursued on a problem-by-problem basis, as troubles occur.
- **Process :** A repeatable sequence of steps used to transform an input into an output that has value to an internal or external customer.
- **Process Benchmarking :** Process benchmarking focuses on discrete work processes and operating systems, such as the customer complaint process, the billing process, the order-and-fulfillment process, the recruitment process or the strategic planning process. This form of benchmarking seeks to identify the most effective operating practices from many companies that perform similar work functions.
- **Process Change :** Deals with the operations of an organisation. *For example,* changes in purchasing procedures, accounting systems, inventory control practices, warehousing practices etc.
- **Process-based Approach :** In a process-based approach to benchmarking, as organisations mature in their pursuit of quality and continuous improvement, they often realise that the benchmarking activity must be managed. The most successful approach is to apply benchmarking activities to the vital few business processes.

- **Product Benchmarking :** Also called **"technical benchmarking"**, product benchmarking is the process of designing the new products or upgrades to current ones. This process can sometimes involve **"reverse engineering"** which is taking apart competitor's products to find strengths and weaknesses of your own products.
- **Project Manager :** The project manager is the person responsible for planning and organising the benchmarking activities for the team. This individual is the primary contact with the benchmarking customer or sponsor.

R

- **Recalibration Plan :** A recalibration plan is the document that describes the steps you will use to determine whether the best-in-class levels of performance for the benchmarked process have changed over time.
- **Reverse Engineering :** Reversing engineering can embrace the entire sales, order, delivery, billing, use and after sale process. Reverse engineering does not include merely the technical process of disassembling another product, reverse engineering may scrutinise the entire customer path of a competitor.

S

- **Spider Chart :** A chart used to compare multiple performance measures and gaps between the host company and industry benchmark practices.
- **Strategic Benchmarking :** Strategic benchmarking examines how companies compete. It is seldom industry focused. It roves across industries seeking to identify the winning strategies that have enabled high-performing companies to be successful in their market places.
- **Strategic Change :** Strategic change embraces enhancements, modifications and improvements on a much larger scale such as improving product quality ten fold or reducing product development times by fifty percent.
- **Strategic Focus :** In a strategic focus, benchmarking is concentrated on strategic competitive strengths and weaknesses. It is used to understand and develop competitive product and service strategies, to establish goals for product performance, service, customer support levels, asset usage and financial ratio and to develop key practices that will achieve the strategic goals.
- **Strategic Planning :** Strategic planning is the process of thinking through the organisation's current mission and environment and then setting forth a guide for future decisions and results. Strategic plans are usually long range plans done at top management level.
- **Strategies :** The strategies define the way the organisation's performance goals will be accomplished.
- **Surveys :** Surveys are often used as a means of collecting information from a large sample of individuals or organisations.

T

- **Tacit Knowledge :** It is what we do not know that we know.

- **Tactical Change :** Tactical change usually represents small-scale improvements, such as process enhancement that reduces defect rates or improve cycle time.
- **Tactics :** The tactical plan defines the way the organisation's strategy will be accomplished. Tactics are specific tasks that will be undertaken in the short term to move the organisation toward the performance goals.
- **Time Based Strategies :** Strategies which focus on reducing the time required to accomplish various activities, *for example,* develop new products or service and market them, response to a change in customer demand, or deliver a product or perform a service. By doing so, organisations seek to improve service to the customer and to gain a competitive advantage over rivals who take more time to accomplish the same tasks.
- **Time-based Competition :** A growing number of organisations are focusing their performance-improvement efforts on a competitive dimension of time. Cycle time reduction or time-based competition is a powerful improvement focus because it correlates so directly with important performance indicators such as cost, quality, market share and customer satisfaction. Time-based competition is also known as **speed-to-market, time-based management, or time compression or fast cycle time or fast-response**.
- **Total Cycle Time :** The time that elapses between expressing a need and having the need satisfactorily fulfilled. During that period many events and activities may occur.

U

- **User Process :** A part of the overall benchmarking task. It is the process followed by the benchmarking team to complete the benchmarking project.

V

- **Vicarious Learning :** This learning strategy embraces learning through the study and analysis of others' experience. These "others" may include colleagues within one's organisation or people and organisations outside one's own corporation and industry.

W

- **Work Processes :** Work processes are those that are entirely within the control of a single function and can be changed as such.
- **World-class Benchmarking :** Most ambitious benchmarking which involves looking towards the recognised leader for the process being benchmarked - an organisation that does it better than any others.
- **World-class Organisations :** Organisations which comprise the top ten percent of the organisations in the world.

Z

- **Z Chart :** It is a version of the line chart. The 'Z' chart relates a company's performance over time to that of a benchmark partner. The Z chart depicts historical performance and it also projects future improvement rates for all comparison companies.

Index

References

1. Christopher E, Boyan, Michael J. English, *"Benchmarking for Best Practices"*, 1994, McGraw-Hill, Inc.
2. Michael J. Spendalini, *"The Benchmarking Book"*, 1992, American Management Association.
3. Robert J. Boxwell Jr., *"Benchmarking for Competitive Advantage"*, 1994, McGraw-Hill, Inc.
4. Robert C. Camp, *"Business Process Benchmarking"*, 1995, ASQC Quality Press, USA.
5. Robert C. Camp, *"Benchmarking"*, 1985, ASQC Quality Press, USA.
6. H. James Harrington, James S. Harrington, *"High Performance Benchmarking"*, 1996, McGraw-Hill Publications, Newyork.
7. Robert Damelio, *"The Basics of Benchmarking"*, 1995, Quality Resources, USA.
8. K. Shridhara Bhat, *"Total Quality Management"*, 1st Edition, 2002, Himalaya Publishing House, Mumbai.